lonely planet

Slovenia

Neil Wilson
Steve Fallon

LONELY PLANET PUBLICATIONS
Melbourne • Oakland • London • Paris

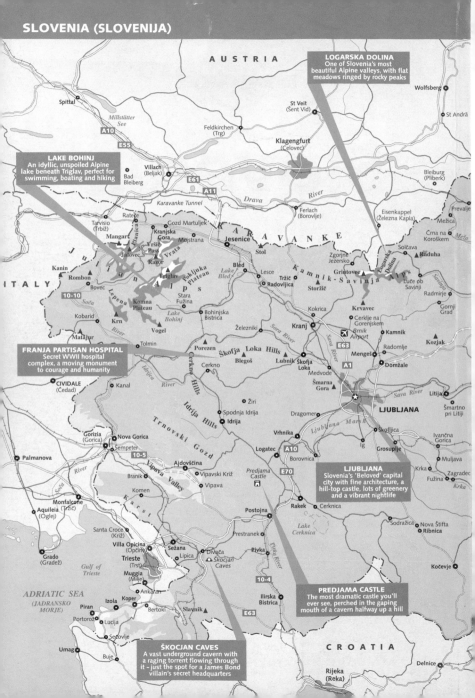

SLOVENIA (SLOVENIJA)

LOGARSKA DOLINA
One of Slovenia's most beautiful Alpine valleys, with flat meadows ringed by rocky peaks

LAKE BOHINJ
An idyllic, unspoiled Alpine lake beneath Triglav, perfect for swimming, boating and hiking

FRANJA PARTISAN HOSPITAL
Secret WWII hospital complex, a moving monument to courage and humanity

LJUBLJANA
Slovenia's 'Beloved' capital city with fine architecture, a hill-top castle, lots of greenery and a vibrant nightlife

PREDJAMA CASTLE
The most dramatic castle you'll ever see, perched in the gaping mouth of a cavern halfway up a hill

ŠKOCJAN CAVES
A vast underground cavern with a raging torrent flowing through it – just the spot for a James Bond villain's secret headquarters

AUSTRIA

ITALY

CROATIA

ADRIATIC SEA
(JADRANSKO MORJE)

HUNGARY

BOGOJINA
A flower-bedecked village with a wonderful church designed by architect extraordinaire Jože Plečnik

Deutschlandberg

Leibnitz (Lipnica)

Goričko Hills

Csesztreg

Mura River

Selnica ob Muri

Moravske Toplice

Murska Sobota

Bogojina

Bad Radkersburg (Radgona)

Gornja Radgona

Bakovci

10-1

Dobrovnik

Lenti

Rédics

KOBANSKO HILLS

Muta

Radlje ob Dravi

Selnica ob Dravi

E57

Lenart

Slovenske

Beltinci

Lendava (Lendva)

Dravograd

Vuzenica

Vuhred

Drava River

Ruše

Žigartov

MARIBOR

Gorice

Ljutomer

Tornyiszentmiklós

Ravne na Koroškem

Slovenj Gradec

Lovrenc na Pohorju

Spodnje Hoče

Bučkovci

10-10

Mislinja

Pohorje Massif

Rogla

Zreče

Slovenska Bistrica

Pragersko

Kidričevo

10

Ptuj

Durnava

Ormož

Središče ob Dravi

Čakovec

Podturen

Šoštanj

Velenje

Slovenske Konjice

Poljčane

Goričak

Cirkulane

Varaždin

Mozirje

Letuš

Nazarje

River

Haloze Hills

PTUJ
A gem of a town crammed with cultural monuments and a nearby spa to while away a warm afternoon

Šempeter

Žalec

Celje

E57

Šentjur

Donačka Gora

Rogatec

Trbovlje

Laško

Podčetrtek

Rogaška Slatina

Kozjansko

Zagorje

Zidani Most

Radeče

Bistrica ob Sotli

Podsreda

Zabok

CROATIA

Boštanj

Sevnica

Senovo

Brestanica

Sava River

Mirna

Mokronog

Krško

Trebnje

Brežice

Vrbovec

Šmarješke Toplice

Šmarjeta

Kostanjevica na Krki

Terme Čatež

Mokrice

Sentjernej

Kostanjevica Cave

Obrežje

Dvor

Soteska

Otočec

Kostanjevica Castle

Samobor

Novo Mesto

Pleterje Monastery

Gorjanci

ZAGREB

Dolenjske Toplice

ELEVATION

Kočevski Rog

Uršna Sela

Rog

Božakovo

Jastrebarsko

PLETERJE MONASTERY
An ancient abbey with a Gothic church, silent monks and pear brandy with a kick like a mule

	2000m
	1500m
	1000m
	200m
	100m
	0

Metlika

Mirna Gora

Podzemelj

Kanižarica

Črnomelj

Dragatuš

Adlešiči

Karlovac

Vinica

Žuniči

ADLEŠIČI
Slovenia's folk 'heart', where you're more likely to hear traditional music than anywhere else in the country

Vrbovsko

Kolpa River

0   10   20km
0   5   10mi

Slovenia
3rd edition – August 2001
First published – October 1995

Published by
Lonely Planet Publications Pty Ltd ABN 36 005 607 983
90 Maribyrnong St, Footscray, Victoria 3011, Australia

Lonely Planet Offices
Australia Locked Bag 1, Footscray, Victoria 3011
USA 150 Linden St, Oakland, CA 94607
UK 10a Spring Place, London NW5 3BH
France 1 rue du Dahomey, 75011 Paris

Photographs
All of the images in this guide are available for licensing from
Lonely Planet Images.
email: lpi@lonelyplanet.com.au

Front cover photograph
Lake Bled, Gorenjska (Ian Shaw, Stone)

ISBN 1 86450 160 X

text & maps © Lonely Planet 2001
photos © photographers as indicated 2001

Printed by Craft Print International Ltd, Singapore

Contents – Text

2 Contents – Text

Contents – Maps

SLOVENIA MAP INDEX

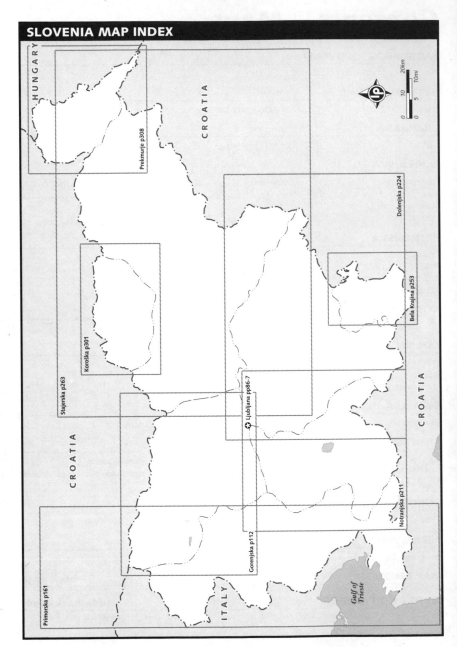

HUNGARY

CROATIA

Prekmurje p308

Štajerska p263

Koroška p301

Dolenjska p224

Bela Krajina p253

Primorska p161

CROATIA

Ljubljana pp86-7

Gorenjska p112

Notranjska p211

CROATIA

ITALY

Gulf of Trieste

The Authors

Neil Wilson

After working as a geologist in Australia and the North Sea and doing geological research at Oxford University, Neil gave up the rock business for the more precarious life of a freelance writer and photographer. Since 1988 he has travelled in five continents and written around 30 travel and walking guides for various publishers. He has worked on Lonely Planet's *Georgia, Armenia & Azerbaijan, Malta, Czech & Slovak Republics, Prague, Slovenia* and *Edinburgh* guides. Although he was born in Glasgow, in the west of Scotland, Neil defected to the east at the age of 18 and still lives in Edinburgh.

Steve Fallon

Born in Boston, Massachusetts, Steve graduated from Georgetown University in 1975 with a Bachelor of Science in modern languages and then taught English at the University of Silesia near Katowice in Poland. After he had worked for several years for a Gannett newspaper, his interest in Asia led him to Hong Kong, where he lived and worked for 13 years for a variety of publications and owned a travel bookshop. Steve lived in Budapest for 2½ years from where he wrote Lonely Planet's *Hungary* and *Slovenia* before moving to London, where he now lives. He has written or contributed to a number of other Lonely Planet titles. Steve regrets not having been able to make it to one of his all-time favourite places on earth for this edition of *Slovenia*, but – to paraphrase the words of General Douglas MacArthur – says: 'I shall return, *moje prijatelji'*.

FROM NEIL WILSON

Many people helped out with the updating of this guide, including – in no particular order – Rok Klančnik, Janja Romih Kulenović, Matej and Mitja Karun, Barbara Jurgec, Jožica Francež, Irena Žlender, Lea Ostrožnik-Stegne, Sergeja Šega, Špela Mavrič, Helena Turk, Tomaž Jukič, Nuša Lisjak, Kristina Stanovič, Sonja Zupan, Malej Tončka, Jasmina Krek and Uroš Sever. Special thanks go to Tatjana Radovič of the Ljubljana Promotion Centre; Miha Rott and Janez Vouk of the Government PR & Media Office; Danilo Sbrizaj of the Alpine Association of Slovenia (PZS); Jana Bolčič at Piran TIC; and Dušan and Eva Podlogar in Bled.

This Book

Steve Fallon wrote the 1st edition of *Slovenia* and updated it for the 2nd edition. Neil Wilson was responsible for updating it for this 3rd edition.

FROM THE PUBLISHER

This edition of *Slovenia* was produced at Lonely Planet's Melbourne office. The editing was coordinated by Shelley Muir, and the mapping, design and layout by Celia Wood. Craig McKenzie assisted with editing and proofing, and Birgit Jordan and Csanád Csutoros helped with mapping. The Language chapter was prepared by Quentin Frayne, climate charts were compiled by Csanád, illustrations were coordinated by Matt King, and Mark Germanchis provided layout support. The cover was designed by Jenny Jones, and photographs were supplied by Lonely Planet Images.

THANKS

Many thanks to the travellers who wrote to us with useful information and suggestions:

Clyde R Appleton, Suzie Bogve, Rev Canon Dr Michael Bourdeaux, Dafydd Bowen, Alex Cessford, Jozef Connolly, David HW Edwards, Nancy Flaherty, Marc B Germain, Helle Ploug Hansen & Carl Vad Jensen, Spencer Harris, Brendan Hickey, Gordon Lake, Peter McCorquodale, Andrew Nash, Ian Parker, Aljoža Rovan, Kate Tomkinson, John Wright & Anna Talbot, Giampiero Torello, Andy Watts.

Foreword

ABOUT LONELY PLANET GUIDEBOOKS

The story begins with a classic travel adventure: Tony and Maureen Wheeler's 1972 journey across Europe and Asia to Australia. Useful information about the overland trail did not exist at that time, so Tony and Maureen published the first Lonely Planet guidebook to meet a growing need.

From a kitchen table, then from a tiny office in Melbourne (Australia), Lonely Planet has become the largest independent travel publisher in the world, an international company with offices in Melbourne, Oakland (USA), London (UK) and Paris (France).

Today Lonely Planet guidebooks cover the globe. There is an ever-growing list of books and there's information in a variety of forms and media. Some things haven't changed. The main aim is still to help make it possible for adventurous travellers to get out there – to explore and better understand the world.

At Lonely Planet we believe travellers can make a positive contribution to the countries they visit – if they respect their host communities and spend their money wisely. Since 1986 a percentage of the income from each book has been donated to aid projects and human rights campaigns.

Updates Lonely Planet thoroughly updates each guidebook as often as possible. This usually means there are around two years between editions, although for more unusual or more stable destinations the gap can be longer. Check the imprint page (following the colour map at the beginning of the book) for publication dates.

Between editions up-to-date information is available in two free newsletters – the paper *Planet Talk* and email *Comet* (to subscribe, contact any Lonely Planet office) – and on our Web site at www.lonelyplanet.com. The *Upgrades* section of the Web site covers a number of important and volatile destinations and is regularly updated by Lonely Planet authors. *Scoop* covers news and current affairs relevant to travellers. And, lastly, the *Thorn Tree* bulletin board and *Postcards* section of the site carry unverified, but fascinating, reports from travellers.

Correspondence The process of creating new editions begins with the letters, postcards and emails received from travellers. This correspondence often includes suggestions, criticisms and comments about the current editions. Interesting excerpts are immediately passed on via newsletters and the Web site, and everything goes to our authors to be verified when they're researching on the road. We're keen to get more feedback from organisations or individuals who represent communities visited by travellers.

Research Authors aim to gather sufficient practical information to enable travellers to make informed choices and to make the mechanics of a journey run smoothly. They also research historical and cultural background to help enrich the travel experience and allow travellers to understand and respond appropriately to cultural and environmental issues.

Authors don't stay in every hotel because that would mean spending a couple of months in each medium-sized city and, no, they don't eat at every restaurant because that would mean stretching belts beyond capacity. They do visit hotels and restaurants to check standards and prices, but feedback based on readers' direct experiences can be very helpful.

Many of our authors work undercover, others aren't so secretive. None of them accept freebies in exchange for positive write-ups. And none of our guidebooks contain any advertising.

Production Authors submit their raw manuscripts and maps to offices in Australia, USA, UK or France. Editors and cartographers – all experienced travellers themselves – then begin the process of assembling the pieces. When the book finally hits the shops, some things are already out of date, we start getting feedback from readers and the process begins again...

WARNING & REQUEST

Things change – prices go up, schedules change, good places go bad and bad places go bankrupt – nothing stays the same. So, if you find things better or worse, recently opened or long since closed, please tell us and help make the next edition even more accurate and useful. We genuinely value all the feedback we receive. A well travelled team reads and acknowledges every letter, postcard and email and ensures that every morsel of information finds its way to the appropriate authors, editors and cartographers for verification.

Everyone who writes to us will find their name in the next edition of the appropriate guidebook. They will also receive the latest issue of *Planet Talk*, our quarterly printed newsletter, or *Comet*, our monthly email newsletter. Subscriptions to both newsletters are free. The very best contributions will be rewarded with a free guidebook.

Excerpts from your correspondence may appear in new editions of Lonely Planet guidebooks, the Lonely Planet Web site, *Planet Talk* or *Comet*, so please let us know if you *don't* want your letter published or your name acknowledged.

Send all correspondence to the Lonely Planet office closest to you:

Australia: Locked Bag 1, Footscray, Victoria 3011
USA: 150 Linden St, Oakland, CA 94607
UK: 10A Spring Place, London NW5 3BH
France: 1 rue du Dahomey, 75011 Paris

Or email us at: talk2us@lonelyplanet.com.au

For news, views and updates see our Web site: www.lonelyplanet.com

HOW TO USE A LONELY PLANET GUIDEBOOK

The best way to use a Lonely Planet guidebook is any way you choose. At Lonely Planet we believe the most memorable travel experiences are often those that are unexpected, and the finest discoveries are those you make yourself. Guidebooks are not intended to be used as if they provide a detailed set of infallible instructions!

Contents All Lonely Planet guidebooks follow roughly the same format. The Facts about the Destination chapters or sections give background information ranging from history to weather. Facts for the Visitor gives practical information on issues like visas and health. Getting There & Away gives a brief starting point for researching travel to and from the destination. Getting Around gives an overview of the transport options when you arrive.

The peculiar demands of each destination determine how subsequent chapters are broken up, but some things remain constant. We always start with background, then proceed to sights, places to stay, places to eat, entertainment, getting there and away, and getting around information – in that order.

Heading Hierarchy Lonely Planet headings are used in a strict hierarchical structure that can be visualised as a set of Russian dolls. Each heading (and its following text) is encompassed by any preceding heading that is higher on the hierarchical ladder.

Entry Points We do not assume guidebooks will be read from beginning to end, but that people will dip into them. The traditional entry points are the list of contents and the index. In addition, however, some books have a complete list of maps and an index map illustrating map coverage.

There may also be a colour map that shows highlights. These highlights are dealt with in greater detail in the Facts for the Visitor chapter, along with planning questions and suggested itineraries. Each chapter covering a geographical region usually begins with a locator map and another list of highlights. Once you find something of interest in a list of highlights, turn to the index.

Maps Maps play a crucial role in Lonely Planet guidebooks and include a huge amount of information. A legend is printed on the back page. We seek to have complete consistency between maps and text, and to have every important place in the text captured on a map. Map key numbers usually start in the top left corner.

Although inclusion in a guidebook usually implies a recommendation we cannot list every good place. Exclusion does not necessarily imply criticism. In fact there are a number of reasons why we might exclude a place – sometimes it is simply inappropriate to encourage an influx of travellers.

Introduction

Every small town in Slovenia has a general store where, as the locals say, you can buy anything *'od šivanke do lokomotive'* (from a needle to a steam locomotive). And Slovenia itself, though undeniably small – it's only half the size of Switzerland – possesses a store of attractions to rival a country many times its size.

From the Venetian harbour towns of the coast to the Hungarian-style farmhouses of Prekmurje; from the subterranean majesty of the Škocjan Caves – a setting fit for the headquarters of a James Bond villain – to the *Sound of Music* scenery of the Julian Alps; from the opera and concert halls of Ljubljana to the WWII Partisan bases hidden in the hills – Slovenia has it all.

First among its many attractions is the great outdoors. Slovenes have a passion for outdoor sports, and this adventure playground on the sunny side of the Alps has nurtured some of the world's best skiers, mountaineers, canoeists and paraglider pilots. Local heroes of recent years have included skier Špela Pretnar, women's slalom World Champion in 1999/2000, and extreme skier Davo Karničar, who became a household name in 2000 when he succeeded in making the first uninterrupted ski descent of Mt Everest.

You too can take advantage of Slovenia's countless opportunities for adventure, from challenging mountain walks and rock climbs among the limestone peaks of Triglav National Park, to underground exploration in the caves of the Notranjska karst, to exhilarating white-water rafting and kayaking on the turquoise rapids of the Soča River. Whatever your passion, be it speleology or snowboarding, music or museums, this book will lead you to the best that Slovenia has to offer.

But let's get a few things straight. First, this is Slovenia – NOT Slovakia. Many people in the West – notably the US president George W Bush – tend to confuse the two. The latter was once half of the state of Czechoslovakia, which split in 1993.

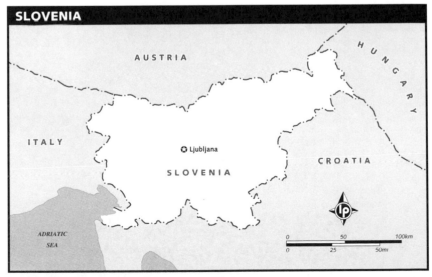

SLOVENIA

AUSTRIA

HUNGARY

ITALY

Ljubljana

SLOVENIA

CROATIA

ADRIATIC
SEA

0   50   100km

0   25   50mi

Slovenia was once a republic in the federation of Yugoslavia, from which it declared independence in 1991.

Second, despite its Yugoslav connections, Slovenia is not, and has never been – geographically, historically or psychologically – part of that volatile region known as the Balkans. Throughout their history, the Slovenian people have had very close cultural and economic ties with Central Europe and have been influenced much more from the west and north than from the east and south.

Third, Slovenia has always been a very safe place to live and to visit. The slump in tourism during and after the war in Kosovo in 1998–99 was based on false perceptions – there was no danger here at all. Except for 10 days in 1991, when rump Yugoslavia tried to prevent its smallest child from leaving its decayed and collapsing House of Usher,

there was no further fighting or terrorism in Slovenia and there is none now. While Croatia and Bosnia-Hercegovina became embroiled in the most bitter conflict in Europe since WWII, Slovenia got on with what it has always done best: working hard, earning money and making progress.

As a part of the former Yugoslavia, Slovenia was always a popular holiday destination – indeed, tourist numbers today have still not returned to pre-1989 levels – and the country retains a robust and rapidly modernising tourism infrastructure. Although not as cheap as Hungary and Slovakia, Slovenia remains a less expensive destination than its Alpine neighbours, Austria and northern Italy. The people are friendly and hospitable, and English is surprisingly widely spoken – among the younger generation it is the second language of choice.

Facts about Slovenia

HISTORY
Early Inhabitants
The area of present-day Slovenia and its immediate borders has been settled since the Palaeolithic Age. Tools made of bone and dating back to between 100,000 and 60,000 BC have been discovered in a cave at Mt Olševa, north of Solčava in the Upper Savinja Valley. In 1995 one of the most important archaeological finds from the Stone Age was made in a cave at Divje Babe near Cerknica in Primorska: a primitive bone flute dating back some 35,000 years. It is now considered to be the world's oldest known musical instrument (see the boxed text 'Stone Age Music' in the Cerkno section of the Primorska chapter).

During the Bronze Age (around 2000 to 900 BC), marsh dwellers farmed and raised cattle in the Ljubljansko Barje area south of present-day Ljubljana and at Lake Cerknica. They lived in round huts set on stilts and traded with other peoples along the so-called Amber Route linking the Balkans with Italy and northern Europe. Finds dating from this period are extensive and include daggers, hatchets, pots and hoes.

Around 700 BC the Ljubljana Marsh people were overwhelmed by Illyrian tribes from the south who brought with them iron tools and weapons. They settled largely in today's province of Dolenjska, built hilltop forts and reached their economic and cultural peak between 650 and 550 BC during what is now called the Hallstatt period. Priceless objects like iron helmets, gold jewellery and embossed pails *(situlae)* have been found in tombs near Stična and at Vače near Litija.

In about 400 BC, Celtic tribes from France, Germany and the Czech lands began pushing southward towards the Balkans. They mixed with the local population and established the first 'state' on Slovenian soil, the Noric kingdom.

The Romans
In 181 BC the Romans established the colony of Aquileia (Oglej in Slovene) on the Gulf of Trieste in order to protect the empire from tribal incursions (see the boxed text 'Patriarchate of Aquileia'). Among its visitors would be Julius Caesar himself, for whom the Julian Alps are named. In the 2nd

Patriarchate of Aquileia

You'd never guess from its present size and population (fewer than 3500 people) but the Italian town of Aquileia (Oglej in Slovene), north of Grado on the Gulf of Trieste, played a pivotal role in Slovenian history and for many centuries its bishops (or 'patriarchs') ruled much of Carniola (Kranjska).

Founded as a Roman colony in the late 2nd century BC, Aquileia fell to a succession of tribes during the Great Migrations and had lost its political and economic importance by the end of the 6th century. But it had been made the metropolitan see for Venice, Istria and Carniola and when the church declared some of Aquileia's teachings heretical, Aquileia broke from Rome. The schism lasted only a century and when it was resolved Aquileia was recognised as a separate patriarchate.

Aquileia's ecclesiastical importance grew during the mission of Paolino II to the Avars and Slovenes in the late 8th century and it acquired feudal estates and extensive political privileges (including the right to coin money) from the Frankish and later the German kings. It remained a feudal principality until 1420 when the Venetian Republic conquered Friuli and Venetians were appointed patriarchs for the first time. Aquileia retained some of its holdings in Slovenia and elsewhere for the next 300 years. But the final blow came in 1751 when Pope Benedict XIV created the archbishoprics of Udine and Gorizia. The once powerful Patriarchate of Aquileia had outlasted its usefulness and was dissolved.

decade AD, the Romans annexed the Celtic Noric kingdom and moved into the rest of Slovenia and Istria.

The Romans divided the area into the provinces of Noricum (today's southern Austria, Koroška and western Štajerska), Upper and Lower Pannonia (eastern Štajerska, Dolenjska and much of Gorenjska) and Histria (Primorska and Croatian Istria) and built roads connecting their new military settlements. From these bases developed the important towns of Emona (Ljubljana), Celeia (Celje), Poetovio (Ptuj) and Virunum (near Klagenfurt in Austria). Each had a forum, sophisticated fortifications, baths, gymnasiums, temples and, later, Christian chapels. Many reminders of the Roman presence can still be seen in Ljubljana, Ptuj, Celje and Šempeter.

The Great Migrations

In the middle of the 5th century AD, the Huns, led by Attila, invaded Italy via Slovenia, attacking Poetovio, Celeia and Emona along the way. Aquileia fell to the Huns in 452, but Attila's empire was short-lived and was soon eclipsed by the Germanic Ostrogoths. In their wake came the Langobards, another Germanic tribe that had also occupied much Slovenian territory. In 568 the Langobards struck out for Italy, taking Aquileia and eventually conquering the Venetian mainland.

The Early Slavs

The ancestors of today's Slovenes arrived from the Carpathian Basin in the 6th century and settled in the Sava, Drava and Mura River valleys and the eastern Alps. Under pressure from the Avars, a powerful Mongol people with whom they had formed a tribal alliance, the early Slavs then migrated farther west to the Friulian plain and the Adriatic Sea, north to the sources of the Drava and Mura Rivers and east as far as Lake Balaton in Hungary. In the end they occupied a total land area of about 70,000 sq km and numbered about 200,000 people.

At that time these people were called Sclavi or Sclaveni, as were most Slavs. Later these 'proto-Slovenes' would be identified by their region: Carniola, Styria, Carinthia. It wasn't until the late 18th century during a period of national consciousness that the name Sloveni or Slovenci (Slovenians) came into common use.

In their original homelands – bordered by the Baltic Sea to the north, the Carpathians to the south, the Oder River to the west and the Dnieper to the east – these Sclavi were a peaceful people, living in forests or along rivers and lakes, breeding cattle and farming by slash-and-burn methods. They were a superstitious people who saw *vile* (both good and bad fairies or sprites) everywhere and paid homage to a pantheon of gods and goddesses: Svarog, the creator of light; Perun, the god of storms, lightning and thunder; Vales, the protector of cattle. As a social group they made no class distinctions, which is why, some historians believe, they never succeeded in establishing a kingdom. But a leader – a *župan* (now 'mayor') or *vojvoda* (duke) – was selected in times of great danger.

The docile nature of these people changed, however, during the migratory periods, and they became more war-like and aggressive.

The Duchy of Carantania

When the Avars failed in their bid to take Byzantium in 626, the Alpine Slavs united under their leader Valuk and joined forces with the Frankish chief Samo to fight them.

The coat of arms of the Duchy of Carantania, the first Slavic state

The Slavic tribal union became the Duchy of Carantania (Karantanija) with its seat at Krn Castle (now Karnburg in Austria). Carantania was the first Slavic state, and its borders extended from the valley of the Sava River as far as Leipzig, including Moravia, Bohemia and Lower Austria.

By the early 8th century, a new class of ennobled commoners *(kosezi)* had emerged, and it was they who publicly elected and crowned the new *knez* (grand duke) on the 'duke's rock' *(knežji kamen)* in the courtyard of Krn Castle. Such a democratic process was unique in the feudal Europe of the early Middle Ages, and it is believed to have influenced Thomas Jefferson in the formation of his contractual theory and the writing of the American Declaration of Independence in 1775–76.

Expansion of the Franks
In 748 the Frankish empire of the Carolingians incorporated Carantania as a vassal state called Carinthia and attempted to convert the population to Christianity. Because of this foreign domination, the new religion was resisted at first. But Irish monks under the auspices of the Diocese of Salzburg in the late 8th century made use of the vernacular and were more successful.

By the early 9th century, religious authority on Slovenian territory was shared between Salzburg and the Patriarchate of Aquileia (the Drava River remained the border until the 18th century) so that no local ecclesiastical centre could develop on its own. At the same time, the weakening Frankish authorities replaced the Slovenian nobles with German counts to help retain what little power they had left. They were absorbed into the new system while the local peasantry was reduced to serfdom. The German nobility was thus at the top of the feudal hierarchy for the first time in Slovenian lands. This would later become one of the key obstacles to Slovenian national and cultural development.

Prince Kocelj & the Carinthian Kingdom
With the total collapse of the Frankish state in the second half of the 9th century, a Carinthian prince named Kocelj established an independent Slovenian 'kingdom' (869–74) in Lower Pannonia, the area stretching south-east from Styria (Štajerska) to the Mura, Drava and Danube Rivers. It was in Lower Pannonia that the Macedonian brothers Cyril and Methodius, the 'apostles of the southern Slavs', had first brought the translations of the Scriptures to the Slovenes (863). And it was here that calls for a Slavic archdiocese were first heard.

Magyar Invasion & German Ascendancy
The Carinthian kingdom was not to last long. In about 900, the fearsome Magyars, expert horsemen and archers, invaded and subjugated the Slovenian regions of Lower Pannonia and along the Sava, cutting them off from Carinthia. They intended to go farther but were defeated by German and Slovenian forces under King Otto I at Augsburg in 955.

The Germans decided to re-establish Carinthia, dividing the area into a half-dozen border counties or marches. By the early 11th century, these would develop into the Slovenian provinces that would remain basically unchanged until 1918: Carniola (Kranjska), Carinthia (Koroška), Styria (Štajerska), Gorica (Goriška) and the White March (Bela Krajina).

A drive for complete Germanisation of the Slovenian lands began in the 10th century. Land was divided between the nobility and various church dioceses (Brixen, Salzburg and Freising), and German gentry were settled on it. But except for the foreign nobles and administrators, the territory remained essentially Slovene. That these people were able to preserve their identity through German and later Austrian rule was due largely to intensive educational work conducted by the clergy.

Most of Slovenia's important castles were built between the 10th and 13th centuries, and many Christian monasteries (eg, Stična and Kostanjevica) were established. Towns also developed as administrative, trade and social centres. Eventually landowners, traders, merchants, artisans and manual workers would find their way to them.

Early Habsburg Rule

The Habsburg dynasty held control over Slovenian territory from the early 14th century until the end of WWI. It dominated the local population in every sense, stifled national aspirations and stunted political and cultural development.

In the early Middle Ages, the Habsburgs were just one of many German aristocratic families struggling for hegemony on Slovenian soil. Others, such as the Andechs, Spanheims and Žoneks (later the Counts of Celje), were equally powerful at various times. But as dynasties intermarried or died out, the Habsburgs consolidated their power.

Between the late 13th and early 16th centuries, almost all the lands inhabited by the Slovenes passed into Habsburg hands except for Istria and the Littoral, which were controlled by Venice until 1797, and Prekmurje, which belonged to the Hungarian crown. Most of Kranjska, Koroška and western Štajerska were united under the Habsburgs by the middle of the 14th century, and the area around Celje, Gorica and parts of Prekmurje followed in the 15th and 16th centuries. Until the 17th century, rule was not directly imposed but administered by diets (parliaments) of 'resident princes', prelates, feudal lords and representatives from the towns, who dealt with matters such as taxation.

By this time Slovenian territory totalled about 24,000 sq km, about 15% larger than its present size. Not only did more towns and boroughs receive charters and rights, but the country began to develop economically with the opening of ironworks (eg, at Kropa) and mines (Idrija). And as economic progress reduced the differences among the repressed peasants, they united against their feudal lords.

Peasant Uprisings & the Reformation

More than 100 peasant uprisings and revolts occurred between 1358 (at Stična) and 1848 (at Ig), but they reached their peak between 1478 and 1573. Together with the Protestant Reformation at the end of the 16th century, they are considered a watershed of the Slovenian national awakening.

Attacks by the Ottoman Turks on southeastern Europe began in 1408 and continued for more than two and a half centuries, almost reaching Vienna on several occasions. By the start of the 16th century, thousands of Slovenes had been killed or taken prisoner. The assaults helped to radicalise the peasants and landless labourers who were required to raise their own defences *and* continue to pay tribute and work for their feudal lords. At the same time, the population was growing and small farms were being divided up even further.

In most of the uprisings, peasant 'unions' demanded a reduction in feudal payments, the democratic election of parish priests and, in at least one case, the formation of a peasant state under direct control of the emperor. The three most violent uprisings took place in 1478 in Koroška; in 1515, encompassing almost the entire Slovenian territory; and in 1573, when Ambrož 'Matija' Gubec led some 12,000 Slovenian and Croatian peasants in revolt. Castles were occupied and pulled down and lords executed. But none of the revolts succeeded.

The Protestant Reformation in Slovenia was closely associated with the nobility from 1540 onward and was generally ignored by the rural population except for those who lived or worked on lands owned by the church (though of Ljubljana's 5000 residents in 1570, two-thirds were Protestant). The effects of this great reform movement cannot be underestimated. Though only 1% of the present population is Protestant, the Reformation gave Slovenia its first books in the vernacular – some 50 in all. Not only did this raise the educational level of Slovenes, but it also lifted the status of the language itself, the first real affirmation of Slovenian culture.

Counter-Reformation & Progress

The wealthy middle class had lost interest in the Reformation by the time it peaked in the 1580s because of the widening economic gap between that class and the nobility. They turned to the Catholic resident princes who quashed Protestantism among the peasants through religious commissions and trials and banished noble families or individuals who persisted in the new belief.

After almost a century of Habsburg decline brought on by the losses of the Counter-Reformation and the Thirty Years' War (1618–48) to gain control of Germany, economic improvements began in the early 18th century and Empress Maria Theresa (1740–80) introduced a series of reforms. These included the establishment of a new state administration with a type of provincial government, the abolition of customs duties between provinces of the empire, the building of new roads, and the introduction of obligatory elementary school in German and state-controlled secondary schools. Her son, Joseph II (1780–90), went several steps further. He abolished serfdom in 1782, paving the way for the formation of a Slovenian bourgeoisie, and allowed complete religious freedom to Calvinists, Lutherans and Jews. He also dissolved the all-powerful (and often corrupt) Catholic religious orders.

Though Joseph II rescinded many of these reforms (including the emancipation of the peasantry) on his death bed, they had a major effect on the economy. Agricultural output improved, manufacturing intensified and shipping from Austria's main port at Trieste increased substantially. The reforms also produced a flowering of the arts and letters in Slovenia, with the playwright and historian Anton Tomaž Linhart and the poet and journalist Valentin Vodnik producing their finest and most influential works at this time. The first newspaper in Slovene – *Lublanske Novize* – was launched by Vodnik in 1797.

Napoleon & the Illyrian Provinces

The French Revolution of 1789 convinced the Austrian rulers that the reform movement should be nipped in the bud, and a period of reaction began that continued until the Revolution of 1848. In the meantime there was a brief interlude – almost a footnote in history – that would have a profound effect on Slovenia and the future of the Slovenian nation.

Following his defeat of the Austrians at Wagram in 1809, Napoleon decided to cut the Habsburg Empire off from the Adriatic.

To do this he created six 'Illyrian Provinces' from Slovenian and Croatian regions, including Koroška, Kranjska, Gorica, Istria and Trieste, and made Ljubljana the capital.

Though the Illyrian Provinces lasted only from 1809 to 1813, France instituted a number of reforms, including equality before the law and the use of Slovene in primary and lower secondary schools and in public offices, and gained the support of certain Slovenian intellectuals, including Vodnik. Most importantly, the Illyrian Provinces and the progressive influence of the French Revolution brought the issue of national awakening to the Slovenian political arena for the first time.

Romantic Nationalism & the 1848 Revolution

Austrian rule, restored in 1814, was now guided by the iron fist of Prince Clemens von Metternich. He immediately reinstituted the Austrian feudal system and attempted to suppress every national movement from the time of the Congress of Vienna (1815) to the Revolution of 1848. But the process of change in the wake of industrial revolution had started in Europe and among the Slovenes too. It could no longer be stopped.

The period of Romantic Nationalism (1814–48) in Slovenia was one of intensive literary and cultural activity and set the stage for the promulgation of the first Slovenian political program. Though many influential writers published at this time (Matija Čop, Bishop Anton Martin Slomšek, Andrej Smole), no-one so dominated the period as the poet France Prešeren (see the boxed text 'France Prešeren: A Poet for the Nation' later in this chapter). His bittersweet verse, progressive ideas, demands for political freedom and longings for the unity of all Slovenes caught the imagination of the nation then, and to an extent have never let it go.

Despite this, the revolution that swept Europe in early 1848 found Slovenia politically weak and relatively unprepared. But it did bring two positive results. First, it did away with absolutism and freed the peasantry from its remaining feudal obligations (though at a price – literally). Second, it provided intellectuals with the opportunity to launch their first national political program, one that came under the banner Zedinjena Slovenija (United Slovenia).

The United Slovenia program, first drawn up by the Slovenija Society in Vienna, basically called for the unification of all historic Slovenian regions within an autonomous unit of the Austrian monarchy. It also called for the use of Slovene in all schools and offices and the establishment of a local university. But the demands were rejected as they would have required the reorganisation of the empire along ethnic lines.

It must be remembered that the Slovenes of the time were not contemplating total independence. Indeed, most looked upon the Habsburg Empire as a protective mantle for small nations against larger ones they considered predators like Italy, Germany and Serbia.

Constitutional Period

The only tangible results for the Slovenes in the resulting 1848 Austrian Constitution were that laws would henceforth be published in Slovene and that the Slovenian flag should be three horizontal stripes of white, blue and red. But the United Slovenia program would remain the basis of all Slovenian political demands up to 1918 and political-cultural clubs and circles began to appear all over the territory.

The rest of the 19th century and the decade before WWI were marked by economic development for the ruling classes – the railway from Vienna to Ljubljana opened in 1849, industrial companies were formed at Kranj and Trbovlje, and a mill began operating at Ajdovščina. However, material conditions declined for the peasantry, whose traditional sources of income were being eroded. Between 1850 and 1910, more than 300,000 Slovenes – 56% of the population – emigrated to other countries.

Some advances were made on the political side. Out of the *čitalnice* (reading clubs) and the *tabori* (camps in which Slovenes of many different beliefs rallied) grew political movements. Parties first appeared toward

the end of the 19th century, with the Clerical Party of newspaper editor Janez Bleiweis representing the conservative side, the Liberal Party on the left, and the Social Democratic Party advocating a new idea: union with the other southern Slavs. The 'Yugoslav' idea was propounded from the 1860s onward by the distinguished Croatian Bishop Josip Strossmayer, whose name still adorns streets in many Slovenian towns and cities. The writer and socialist Ivan Cankar even called for an independent Yugoslav state in the form of a federal republic.

WWI & the Kingdom of Serbs, Croats & Slovenes

Slovenian political parties generally remained faithful to Austria-Hungary (as the empire was known from 1867). With the heavy loss of life and destruction of property during WWI, however, support grew for an autonomous democratic state within the Habsburg monarchy, principles put forward in the May 1917 Declaration of the Yugoslav Club. With the defeat of Austria-Hungary and the dissolution of the Habsburg dynasty in 1918, Slovenes, Croats and Serbs banded together and declared themselves to be an independent state with the capital at Zagreb. Due to a perceived threat from Italy, however, the state joined up with Serbia and Montenegro in December 1918 under the name of the Kingdom of Serbs, Croats and Slovenes. The Serbian statesman Stojan Protić became prime minister while the Slovene leader of the Clerical Party, Anton Korošec, was named vice-premier.

The peace treaties signed at Paris and Rapallo had given large amounts of Slovenian and Croatian territory to Italy (Primorska and Istria), Austria (Koroška) and Hungary (part of Prekmurje) and almost half a million Slovenes now lived in those countries (some, like the Slovenes in Koroška, had voted to do so, however). The loss of more than a quarter of its population and a third of its land would remain the single most important issue facing Slovenia between the wars.

The kingdom, which lasted in one form or another until 1940, was dominated by the notion of 'Yugoslav unity', Serbian control, imperialistic pressure from Italy and political intrigue. Slovenia was reduced to little more than a province in this centralist kingdom – a position supported by both the liberal bourgeoisie and the socialist parties for entirely different reasons. The Slovenes did enjoy cultural and linguistic autonomy, however, and economic progress was rapid.

Following the assassination of the leaders of the most powerful Serbian and Croatian parties, King Alexander seized absolute power, abolished the constitution and proclaimed the Kingdom of Yugoslavia in 1929. But Alexander himself was murdered by a Croatian-backed Macedonian in Marseilles in 1934 during an official visit to France and his cousin, Prince Paul, was named regent until Alexander's son, Peter, came of age.

The political climate changed in Slovenia when the Clerical Party joined the new centralist government of Milan Stojadinović in 1935, proving how hollow that party's calls for Slovenian autonomy had been. As a result, splinter groups from both the Clerical and the Liberal parties began to seek closer contacts with the workers' movements. In 1937 the Communist Party of Slovenia (KPS) was formed under the tutelage of Josip Broz (better known as Tito; 1892–1980) and the Communist Party of Yugoslavia (KPJ).

WWII & the Partisan Struggle

Yugoslavia avoided getting involved in the war until March 1941 when Prince Paul, under pressure from Berlin and Rome, signed a treaty with the Axis powers. He was overthrown in a coup backed by the British, who installed King Peter II. Peter at first attempted neutrality, but German armies invaded Yugoslavia in April, and the Yugoslav army capitulated in less than two weeks.

Slovenia was split up among Germany (Štajerska, Gorenjska and Koroška), Italy (Ljubljana, Primorska, Notranjska, Dolenjska and Bela Krajina) and Hungary (Prekmurje). Repression and deportations were the order of the day in Štajerska and Koroška.

To counter this the Slovenian communists and other left-wing groups formed a

Liberation Front (Osvobodilne Fronte; OF), and Slovenes took up arms for the first time since the peasant uprisings to resist the occupiers. The OF, dedicated to the principles of a united Slovenia in a Yugoslav republic, joined the all-Yugoslav Partisan army of the KPJ and its secretary-general, Tito. Under the Dolomites Proclamation (1943), the KPS was given the leading role in the OF. The Partisans received assistance from the Allies and, given the terrain and long tradition of guerrilla warfare in the Balkans, were the most organised and successful of any resistance movement during WWII.

After Italy capitulated in 1943, the anti-OF Slovenian Domobranci (Home Guards) were active in Primorska and, in a bid to prevent the communists from gaining political control in liberated areas, began supporting the Germans.

Despite this assistance and the support of the fascist Ustaša nationalists in Croatia and later the Četniks in Serbia, the Germans were forced to evacuate Belgrade in 1944. Slovenia was not totally liberated until May 1945.

As many as 12,000 Domobranci and anti-communist civilians were sent back to Slovenia from refugee camps in Austria by the British in June. Most of them were executed by the communists over the next two months, their bodies thrown into caverns at Kočevski Rog in Dolenjska.

Postwar Division

Of immediate concern to Slovenia after the war was the status of liberated areas along the Adriatic, especially Trieste, which the Partisans had occupied for 40 days at the end of the war. A peace treaty signed in Paris in 1947 put Trieste and its surrounds under Anglo-American administration (the so-called Zone A) and the Koper and Buje (Istria) areas under Yugoslav control in Zone B.

In 1954, Zone A (with both its Italian and ethnic Slovenian populations) became the Italian province of Trieste. Koper and a 47km stretch of coast later went to Slovenia, and Istria to Croatia. The Belvedere Treaty (1955) guaranteed Austria its 1938 borders, including most of Koroška.

Tito & Socialist Yugoslavia

Tito had been elected head of the Anti-Fascist Assembly for the National Liberation of Yugoslavia (Avnoj) in November 1943, which provided for a federal republic. Immediately after the war he moved quickly to consolidate his power under the communist banner.

It soon became clear that, despite the efforts of Slovenian communist leader Edvard Kardelj to have them enshrined in the new constitution, Slovenia's rights to self-determination and autonomy within the framework of a federal Yugoslavia would be very limited beyond educational and cultural matters. Serbian domination from Belgrade would continue and in some respects be even more centralist than under the Kingdom of Yugoslavia.

Tito distanced himself from Stalin and domination by the Soviet Union as early as 1948, risking invasion, but efforts to create a communist state, with all the usual arrests, show trials, purges and concentration camps (such as the one on the island of Goli in the Adriatic), continued into the mid-1950s. Industry was nationalised, private ownership of agricultural land limited to 20 hectares, and a planned central economy put in place.

But isolation from the markets of the Soviet bloc soon forced Tito to look to the West. Yugoslavia introduced features of a market economy (including workers' self-management) though what was by then called the League of Communists would retain its decisive political role. Greater economic reforms in the mid-1960s (especially under Stane Kavčič in Slovenia) as well as relaxed police control and border controls for both foreign tourists and Yugoslavs brought greater prosperity and freedom of movement, but the Communist Party saw such democratisation as a threat to its power. A purge against the reformists in government was carried out in 1971–72, and many politicians and directors were pensioned off for their 'liberalism' and 'entrepreneurial thinking'. A new constitution in 1974 gave the Yugoslav republics more independence (and autonomy to the ethnic Albanian province of Kosovo in Serbia), but what were to become known as the 'leaden years' in Yugoslavia lasted throughout the 1970s until Tito's death in 1980. Economically, though, Slovenia was the most advanced republic in Yugoslavia by the end of the decade.

Crisis, Renewal & Change

The economic decline in Yugoslavia in the early 1980s led to inter-ethnic conflict, especially between Serbs and ethnic Albanians in autonomous Kosovo, which persists to this day. Serbia proposed scrapping elements of the 1974 constitution in favour of more uniformity of the state in economic and cultural areas. This, of course, was anathema to Slovenes who saw themselves threatened.

In 1987 the liberal magazine *Nova Revija* in Ljubljana published an article outlining a new Slovenian national program: political pluralism, democracy, a market economy and independence for Slovenia, possibly within a Yugoslav confederation. The new liberal leader of the Slovenian communists, Milan Kučan, did not oppose the demands and opposition parties began emerging. The de facto head of the central government in Belgrade, the Serbian communist leader

Josip Broz Tito dominated post-WWII Yugoslavia until his death in 1980.

Slobodan Milošević, resolved to put pressure on Slovenia.

In June 1988 three Slovenian journalists working for the *Mladina* (Youth) weekly and a junior army officer who had given away 'military secrets' were put on trial by a military court and sentenced to prison. (One of the journalists, Janez Janša, would serve as defence minister for the first 15 months after independence.) Mass demonstrations were held throughout the country in support of the four.

In the autumn, Serbia unilaterally scrapped the autonomy of Kosovo (where 80% of the population is ethnically Albanian). Slovenes were shocked by the move, fearing the same could happen to them. A rally organised jointly by the Slovenian government and the opposition in Ljubljana in February 1989 condemned the move.

In the spring of that year the new opposition parties published the May Declaration demanding a sovereign state for Slovenes based on democracy and respect for human rights. It wasn't all about political altruism, of course. In September the Slovenian parliament amended the constitution to legalise management of its own resources – much more money was still going out of Slovenia than coming in – and peace-time command of the armed forces. Serbia announced plans to hold a 'meeting of truth' in Ljubljana on its intentions. When Slovenia banned it, Serbia and all the other republics except Croatia announced an economic boycott of Slovenia, cutting off 25% of its exports. In January 1990, Slovenian delegates walked out on an extraordinary congress of the League of Communists, thereby sounding the death knell of the party.

Independence

In April 1990, Slovenia became the first Yugoslav republic to hold free elections and shed 45 years of communist rule. Demos, a coalition of seven opposition parties, won 55% of the vote and Kučan, head of what was now called the Party of Democratic Renewal, was elected 'president of the presidency'. The leader of the Christian Democrats, Lojze Peterle, became prime minister.

In the summer, after Serbia had rejected Slovenian and Croatian proposals for a confederation and threatened to declare a state of emergency, the Slovenian parliament adopted a 'declaration on the sovereignty of the state of Slovenia'. Henceforth Slovenia's own constitution would direct its political, economic and judicial systems; federal laws would apply only if they were not in contradiction to it. A referendum on the question of independence was scheduled for just before Christmas.

On 23 December 1990, 88% of the electorate voted for an independent republic – effective within six months. The presidency of the Yugoslav Federation in Belgrade labelled the move secessionist and anti-constitutional. Serbia then proceeded to raid the Yugoslav monetary system and misappropriated almost the entire monetary issue planned for Yugoslavia in 1991 – US$2 billion. Seeing the handwriting on the wall all too clearly, the Slovenian government began stockpiling weapons and on 25 June 1991 Slovenia pulled out of the Yugoslav Federation for good. 'This evening dreams are allowed,' President Kučan told the jubilant crowd in Ljubljana's Kongresni trg the following evening. 'Tomorrow is a new day.'

Indeed it was. On 27 June the Yugoslav army began marching on Slovenia but met great resistance from the Territorial Defence Forces, the police and the general population. Within several days, units of the federal army began disintegrating; Belgrade threatened aerial bombardment and total war, as would soon follow in the Croatian cities of Vukovar and Dubrovnik.

The military action had not come totally unprovoked. To dramatise their bid for independence and to generate support from a less than sympathetic West, which wanted to see Yugoslavia continue to exist in some form or another, Slovenian leaders had baited Belgrade by attempting to take control of the border crossings first. Belgrade apparently never expected Slovenia to resist to the degree that it did, believing that a show of force would be sufficient for it to back down.

As no territorial claims or minority issues were involved, the Yugoslav government agreed on 7 July to a truce brokered by leaders of the European Community (EC). Under the so-called Brioni Declaration, Slovenia would put further moves to assert its independence on hold for three months provided it was granted recognition by the EC after that time. The war had lasted just 10 days and taken the lives of 66 people.

To everyone's surprise, Belgrade announced that it would withdraw the federal army from Slovenian soil within three months, and did so on 25 October. In late December, Slovenia got a new constitution and the EC formally recognised the country on 15 January 1992. Slovenia was admitted to the United Nations on 22 May 1992 as the 176th member-state, and in 1998 it began negotiations for entry into the European Union.

Since independence, Slovenia has remained untouched by the fighting that embroiled Croatia, Serbia and Bosnia-Hercegovina in the mid-1990s, and the war in Kosovo in 1998 and 1999. Instead, it has enjoyed taking its place on the European and world stage, notably in the area of sport – Slovenian athletes won several medals in the Barcelona, Atlanta and Sydney Olympic games, and the national soccer team qualified for the Euro 2000 football championship. The economy is sound, and the people are optimistic about the future – a future that seems certain to include membership of the EU and NATO.

GEOGRAPHY & GEOLOGY

Slovenia is a Central European country with a surface area of only 20,256 sq km – about 0.2% of Europe's total land mass. Compare it with Wales, Israel or half of Switzerland and you'll get the picture. It borders Austria for 324km to the north and Croatia for 546km to the south and south-east. Much shorter frontiers are shared with Italy (235km) to the west and Hungary (102km) to the north-east.

Geographers divide Slovenia into as many as 13 different areas, but there are basically six topographical regions: the Alps, including the Julian Alps, the Kamnik-Savinja Alps, the Karavanke chain and the Pohorje Massif to the north and north-east;

the pre-Alpine hills of Idrija, Cerkno, Škofja Loka and Posavje spreading across the entire southern side of the Alps; the Dinaric karst below the hills and encompassing the 'true' or 'original' Karst plateau (from which all other karst regions around the world take their name) between Ljubljana and the Italian border; the Slovenian littoral, 47km of coastline along the Adriatic Sea; the 'lowlands', comprising about one-fifth of the territory in various parts of the country; and the essentially flat Pannonian plain to the east and north-east.

Much of the interior of Slovenia is drained by the Sava and Drava Rivers, both of which flow south-eastwards and empty into the Danube. Other important rivers are the Soča to the west, which flows into the Adriatic, the Mura in the north-east, the Krka to the south-east and the Kolpa, which forms part of the south-eastern border with Croatia. There are several 'intermittent' rivers (eg, the Unica, Pivka and Reka), which disappear into karst caves, only to resurface elsewhere under different names. Slovenia's largest lakes are Cerknica, which is dry for part of the year, and Bohinj.

Main Regions

These topographical divisions do not accurately reflect Slovenia's cultural and historical differences nor do the 147 *občine* (administrative communes or municipalities) help the traveller much. Instead, Slovenia is best viewed as a country with a capital city (Ljubljana) and eight traditional *regije* (regions or provinces): Gorenjska, Primorska, Notranjska, Dolenjska, Bela Krajina, Štajerska, Prekmurje and Koroška.

Greater Ljubljana, by far the nation's largest city, is pinched between two groups of hills to the west and east, and a non-arable marshland (Ljubljansko Barje) to the south. It is not in the exact centre of the country but close to it.

Gorenjska, to the north and north-west of the capital, is the country's most mountainous province and contains Slovenia's highest peaks, including Triglav (2864m). The provincial centre is Kranj. Primorska, a very diverse region of hills, valleys, karst and a

PROVINCES OF SLOVENIA

short coastline on the northern end of the Istrian peninsula, forms the country's western border. It has two 'capitals', Nova Gorica and Koper, and Slovenia's Italian minority is concentrated here. Notranjska, to the south and south-west of Ljubljana, is an underdeveloped area of forests and karst – Slovenia's 'last frontier'. Its main towns are Cerknica and Postojna.

Dolenjska lies south of the Sava River and has several distinct areas, including the Krka Valley, the hilly Kočevje and the Posavje regions. Novo Mesto is the main city here. Bela Krajina, a land of rolling hills, birch groves and folk culture south of Dolenjska, has its centres at Metlika and Črnomelj.

Štajerska – Slovenia's largest *regija* – stretches to the east and north-east and is a land of mountains, rivers, valleys, vineyards and ancient towns. Maribor and Celje are the centres and Slovenia's second and third largest cities respectively. Prekmurje, 'beyond the Mura River' in Slovenia's extreme north-east, is basically a flat plain though there are hills to the north. The Hungarian minority lives within its borders, and the centre is Murska Sobota. Sitting north of Štajerska, little Koroška, with its centre

at Slovenj Gradec, is all that is left of the once great historical province of Carinthia.

CLIMATE

In general, Slovenia is temperate with four distinct seasons, but the topography creates three individual climates. The north-west has an Alpine climate with strong influences from the Atlantic and abundant precipitation. Temperatures in the Alpine valleys are moderate in summer but cold in winter. The coast and a large part of Primorska as far as the Soča Valley has a Mediterranean climate with warm, sunny weather much of the year and mild winters (though the *burja,* a cold and dry north-easterly wind, can be fierce at times). Most of eastern Slovenia has a Continental climate with hot (and occasionally *very* hot) summers and cold winters.

Slovenia gets most of its rain in the spring (March and April) and autumn (October and November); precipitation amounts vary but average about 800mm in the eastern part of the country, 1400mm in the centre, 1000mm on the coast and 3500mm in the Alps. January is the coldest month with an average annual temperature of -2°C and July is the

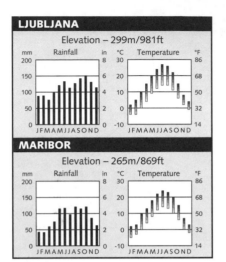

warmest (21°C). The mean average temperature in Ljubljana is 9.5°C. The number of hours of sunshine per year ranges from 1700 to 2300, with Ljubljana at the low end of the scale and Portorož at the top.

ECOLOGY & ENVIRONMENT
Habitation
Slovenia is predominantly hilly or mountainous; about 90% of the surface is more than 300m above sea level. Forest, some of it virgin, covers more than half of the country, making Slovenia the greenest country in Europe outside Finland. Agricultural land (fields, orchards, vineyards, pastures etc) accounts for just under 43% of the total.

The population density is just over 98 people per square kilometre, with the urban-rural ratio split almost exactly in half. The five largest settlements in Slovenia are Ljubljana (330,000), Maribor (103,000), Celje (40,000), Kranj (37,000) and Velenje (27,100).

Cities and towns like Ljubljana, Celje, Ptuj and Koper were built on the foundations of Roman or even pre-Roman settlements while others are essentially new (eg, Nova Gorica). Many cities in Slovenia are ringed by housing estates. Traditional farmhouses are quite different in the Alps, the Karst region, Pannonia and central Slovenia though modern 'European-style' housing appears everywhere nowadays. The hayrack *(kozolec)*, the most distinctly Slovenian of all folk architecture, can be seen everywhere in the country except in Prekmurje and some parts of Primorska.

Pollution
Though Slovenia is a very 'green' country in both senses of the word, pollution is a problem, particularly in the Sava, Mura and lower Savinja Rivers. Rain has washed all sorts of filth dumped in the Karst region underground, and waste carried by the 'disappearing' Unica and Ljubljanica Rivers threatens the Ljubljana Marsh.

Air pollution is also a big worry. Nitrogen oxide emitted by cars on the highway connecting Gorenjska with the coast is hurting the pine forests of Notranjska, and it's also damaging buildings, outdoor sculptures and other artwork in many historical cities. Sulphur dioxide levels are high in cities and towns like Šoštanj, Trbovlje and Ljubljana where coal is burned in thermoelectric power stations and heating plants. The nation's sole nuclear power plant (at Krško in Dolenjska) currently provides 37% of electric power but half is owned by Croatia and Slovenia plans to stop using it altogether in 2023.

Steps have been taken to clean up the mess, with the construction of water-purifying plants, the monitoring of companies discharging waste and the introduction of gas heating. Indeed, over the 10-year period from 1985 to 1995, sulphur dioxide emissions were cut almost in half and nitrogen oxide levels reduced by about 20%. The government adopted a National Environmental Protection Program in 1999, which puts emphasis on tackling the overuse and pollution of surface waters and the increasing problem of refuse disposal.

FLORA & FAUNA
Flora
Slovenia is home to some 2900 plant species and about 70 of them – many in the Alps – are unique to Slovenia or were first classified

here. Triglav National Park is especially rich in endemic flowering plants, including the Triglav 'rose' (actually a pink cinquefoil), the blue Clusi's gentian, yellow hawk's-beard, Julian poppy, Carniola lily and the purple Zois bell flower.

Fauna

Common European animals such as deer, boar, chamois, brown bears, wolves and lynx live in Slovenia in abundance, as well as some rare species like the moor tortoise, cave hedgehog, scarab beetle and various types of dormice. Two species unique to Slovenia are *Proteus anguinus,* a blind salamander that lives in karst cave pools, and the marbled Soča trout *(Salmo trutta marmoratus).*

National Parks

At present, there is only one national park – the 83,807-hectare Triglav National Park encompassing almost all of the Julian Alps – although proposals have been made to set aside four more: in the Kamnik Alps, the Pohorje Massif, the Karst and the Kočevje-Kolpa region. There is one regional park

(the Notranjski Park) and another three dozen zones designated as landscape parks. These range in size from the Sečovlje salt pans (835 hectares) south of Portorož and the Robanov Kot (1423 hectares), a pristine valley in Štajerska, to the Logar Valley (2475 hectares).

GOVERNMENT & POLITICS

Slovenia's constitution provides for a parliamentary system of government. The National Assembly (Državni Zbor), which has exclusive jurisdiction over the passing of laws, consists of 90 deputies elected for four years by proportional representation. The 40 members of the Council of State (Državni Svet), which performs an advisory role, are elected for five-year terms by regions and interest groups. The head of state, the president, is also the supreme commander of the armed forces and is elected directly for a maximum of two five-year terms. Executive power is vested in the prime minister and their 15-member cabinet. The judicial system consists of a supreme court, four high courts which serve

LISA BORG

Slovenia's forests are one of the strongholds of Europe's brown bear *(Ursus arctos).*

as appeals courts, 11 circuit courts, and 44 district courts which are the courts of first instance. Judges exercise full judicial authority and their appointment by the National Assembly is for life. There is no death penalty in Slovenia.

Slovenia counts nine political parties represented in parliament: the Liberal Democrats of Slovenia (LDS), the Slovenian People's Party (SLS), the Slovenian Christian Democrats (SKD), the Social Democratic Party of Slovenia (SDS), the United List of Social Democrats (ZLSD), the Democratic Party of Pensioners of Slovenia (DeSUS), New Slovenia (NSi), the Slovenian Youth Party (SMS) and the Slovenian National Party (SNS). Their political leanings run the spectrum from the far right (SNS) and right (SLS) to the centre (LDS) and the centre-left (ZLSD).

In the first elections held in independent Slovenia (December 1992), a coalition of four parties (Liberal Democrats, Christian Democrats, United List and Social Democrats) won more than 60% of the vote with 63 deputies taking seats. The leader of the Liberal Democrats, Janez Drnovšek, was named prime minister. Milan Kučan was elected president of the republic with 64% of the vote.

Following the November 1996 parliamentary elections Drnovšek was retained as prime minister and in November 1997 President Kučan was returned for his second term after winning nearly 56% of the popular vote. Drnovšek was forced out of power by a vote of no confidence in April 2000, and replaced by the centre-right leader of the New Slovenia party, Andrej Bajuk. However, the October 2000 parliamentary elections saw a chastened Drnovšek returned to power as the Liberal Democrats took 36.3% of the vote. The renewed objective of the government – a coalition of the LDS, ZLSD, SLS/SKD and DeSUS – is to speed up privatisation and complete preparations for joining the EU in 2003.

The Hungarian and Italian ethnic communities are guaranteed certain rights under the constitution including education in their own language and the right to use it in public

President Milan Kučan, head of state since independent Slovenia's first elections in 1992

administration and the courts. They are also guaranteed representation in the National Assembly of one deputy each. The law on foreigners applies to those individuals of other nationalities in Slovenia who did not obtain citizenship by December 1991.

Slovenia is a member of the Alps-Adriatic Association, a regional group bringing together Hungary, Croatia, Bavaria and adjacent regions of Austria and Italy for multilateral cooperation in many fields. It is also a member of Cefta (Central European Free Trade Association), along with Hungary, the Czech Republic, Slovakia, Poland and Romania.

Slovenia's relations with Austria are good, in spite of neo-Nazi attacks on a Slovene-language school and publishing house in Klagenfurt in 1993 and 1994; the rights of ethnic Slovenes there are enshrined in the Austrian constitution. Relations between Slovenia and Hungary are warm though coloured by the 8500 ethnic Magyars living in Prekmurje and the estimated 5000 Slovenes in south-west Hungary. An agreement signed by both countries in 1992 ensures each group's rights.

Difficulties with Slovenia's neighbour to the west stem from the land claims of Italian citizens who either left Slovenia (then Yugoslavia) willingly after WWII (the 'optants') or those who were expelled. Italy even went so far as to grant citizenship to everyone born in Italian-occupied land up to 1943, which included such 'un-Italian' places as Idrija and Postojna.

Slovenia has a long list of disputes with Croatia, including over Slovenian property rights in Croatia and the precise position of state borders, especially those in Piran Bay off Sečovlje, which Slovenia claims entirely.

Slovenia was admitted into the Council of Europe in May 1993. Moves toward membership of the EU were blocked by Italy until March 1995 when Rome dropped its veto. Negotiations for full EU membership began in March 1998, and Slovenia expects to meet the conditions for membership by 2002, in preparation for entry in 2003. Though desire to join the EU is by no means universal in Slovenia, a poll taken at the end of 1999 suggested that over 65% of citizens would vote in favour of it in a referendum, with another 18% undecided. All political parties have signed a declaration in favour of joining NATO.

ECONOMY

After a few tough years following independence, Slovenia has emerged as one of the strongest economies of the former socialist countries of Eastern and Central Europe. Inflation has dropped, employment is on the rise and its per-capita gross domestic product (GDP) – currently 72% of the EU average – is expected to surpass those of Greece and Portugal by 2002. Inflation zoomed up to 200% after independence and has steadily decreased since; it was 8.9% in 2000, predicted to fall to about 5% by 2002. Unemployment continues to hover around 13.5%.

Slovenia has never been a poor country. Prior to independence it was by far the wealthiest republic of Yugoslavia. Although they represented only 8% of the total population, the industrious Slovenes produced up to 20% of the GDP and exported more than a quarter of its goods. A favourite saying in those days was: 'The laws are written in Belgrade, read in Zagreb and carried out in Slovenia.'

The negative effects of the loss of its markets in the former Yugoslavia (once 30% of Slovenia's exports) and the pain caused by reforms needed to modernise the economy have long since faded away. The country has been able to bounce back principally because its highly educated population quickly reoriented itself towards Western Europe. Some 70% of Slovenia's foreign trade is now with the EU, especially Germany, Italy, France and Austria.

With hindsight, Slovenia was fortunate not to have had many large industrial conglomerates that in today's economic climate would prove unviable to maintain. Although Slovenia still has its share of communist-style dinosaur industrial plants, the country's furniture, textile and paper sectors produce high-quality goods that are sold throughout Europe. Skis, for example, are one of the country's niche products.

Anyone searching for smokestacks and mines can find steelworks at Jesenice, textile mills at Kranj and coal mines east of Ljubljana at Trbovlje and Hrastnik. But more typically, the landscape is now dotted with upgraded factories thanks to foreign investment. French Renault cars are assembled at the Revoz plant in Novo Mesto and the Gorenje kitchen appliance manufacturer in Velenje does subcontract manufacturing for Germany's AEG and Quelle and MFI in the UK.

Mass privatisation of unprofitable industries built up by the former regime came about much later than in some other Eastern European countries. A complicated 'transformation of ownership' scheme was put in place in 1994 but got off to a slow start; by 1996 less than a third of the more than 1400 eligible companies had actually been privatised. By the end of 1998, however, the process had been completed. The big sticking point at the start of 2001 was the privatisation of insurance companies and Slovenia's two biggest banks, Nova Ljubljanska Banka and Nova Kreditna Banka Maribor – both still state-owned.

One of the fastest-growing sectors in the Slovenian economy is tourism, though the numbers of tourists have yet to reach pre-1991 levels. In 1997, Slovenia earned US$1.18 billion from tourism, twice the receipts of 1994. This was followed by a slump in visitor numbers caused by the war in Kosovo, but the industry bounced back with good figures for 2000. The majority of visitors come from Italy, Germany and Austria – in that order.

Agriculture plays a remarkably minor role in the economy, considering how rural Slovenia appears at first. It comprises only 5% of GDP, as opposed to industry at 39% (manufacturing accounts for 30% of that figure) and services at 55%.

A little more than one in 10 Slovenes now lives off farming alone – in 1960 nearly half the population was engaged full-time in agriculture. But as Slovenes love the countryside, it is estimated that a quarter of the population farms at some point, growing grapes or keeping bees for honey. The most important farm products are wheat, corn, potatoes, pears, apples and grapes. Štajerska hops for beer are a small but important export crop.

POPULATION & PEOPLE

Slovenia's last census, in 1991 (censuses are conducted every 10 years), counted just under 1,966,000 people; the estimated population in 2000 was 1,987,755. The vast majority (87%) of the population are ethnic Slovenes, descendants of the South Slavs who settled in what is now Slovenia and parts of Italy, Austria and Hungary from the 6th century AD.

There are just over 8500 ethnic Hungarians and some 2300 Roma (Gypsies), largely in Prekmurje, as well as 3000 Italians in Primorska. 'Others', accounting for 11.5% of the population, include Croats, Serbs, ethnic Albanians and those who identify themselves simply as 'Muslims'.

The Italians and Hungarians are considered indigenous minorities with rights protected under the constitution, and they have special deputies looking after their interests in parliament. Though some members of the other groups have lived and worked in Slovenia for many years, most are recent arrivals – refugees and economic immigrants from the fighting in the former Yugoslav republics. Their status as noncitizens in Slovenia remains hazy, and many Slovenes have very racist feelings about them. Several thousand migrants cross over the border from Croatia each day to work in Slovenia.

Ethnic Slovenes living outside the national borders number as many as 400,000, with the vast majority (almost 75%) in the USA and Canada. (Cleveland, Ohio, is the largest 'Slovenian' city outside Slovenia.) In addition, some 50,000 Slovenes or more live in the Italian regions of Gorizia, Udine and Trieste, another 15,000 in Austrian Carinthia (Kärnten) and 5000 in south-west Hungary.

Life expectancy has increased dramatically in Slovenia in recent years and is almost at Western European levels – 70 years for men and almost 78 years for women. Slovenia's birth rate is low – under 10 per 1000 population against 12.5 in the UK and 15.5 in the USA. The age structure is therefore relatively old, with the average age for men about 35 years and for women just over 38.

EDUCATION

Slovenia is a highly educated society with a literacy rate of over 99.6%. Indeed, being able to read and write is ingrained in the culture. 'What is your surname?' in Slovene is *'Kako si pišete?'* or 'How do you write yourself?'

Primary school *(osnovna šola)* is compulsory and free for eight years until the age of 15. Secondary school *(srednja šola)* usually lasts for four years. Some schools are orientated toward a particular profession (eg, nursing); others – like the *gimnazije* (high schools) – prepare pupils for university. Those attending a three-year vocational course go to a *poklicna šola* (technical college). Ethnic Italians and Hungarians can choose to be taught in their mother tongues at 18 elementary schools and 46 secondary-school departments largely in Prekmurje and Primorska.

Slovenia has only two universities – the University of Ljubljana and a smaller one at Maribor – with a total enrolment of just under 50,000 students. Competition for places is stiff, and secondary-school pupils must take exams to be accepted into most faculties. The largest number of students are enrolled at the Faculty of Economics in Ljubljana and at the Technical Faculty of the University of Maribor.

The university course of study usually lasts four years with another year for students to take their degree *(visoka stopnja),* which usually requires writing a thesis. But there are other programs, including a two-year '1st stage' degree *(višja stopnja),* which is equivalent to a college or associate degree abroad and prepares students for administrative work and the like. Study at graduate levels is more individualised and involves independent research. A medical degree takes about seven years to complete.

The academic year for primary and secondary schools lasts from 1 September to 25 June with 10 days holiday around Christmas and the New Year, a week off in early February and another one at Easter. The university year is from 1 October to 30 May, with exams in June and early July.

SCIENCE

Slovenia has a strong tradition in the sciences and has produced many great scientists – from the 17th-century polymath Janez Vajkard Valvasor and Gabriel Gruber, who regulated the Ljubljanica River in the late 18th century, to the patron Žiga Zois and Friderik Pregl, who won the Nobel Prize in 1923 for organic chemistry. The Slovenian Academy of Arts and Sciences has a research centre with 14 institutes studying all aspects of science as well as history and culture.

ARTS
Architecture, Sculpture & Painting

Examples of Romanesque architecture can be found in many parts of Slovenia, including the churches at Stična Abbey, at Muta and Dravograd in Koroška and Podsreda Castle, but fine art from the period is rare, surviving only in illuminated manuscripts.

Gothic painting and sculpture is another matter, with excellent works – some commissioned by burghers and wealthy landowners – at Ptujska Gora (the carved altar in the Church of the Virgin Mary), Bohinj (frescoes in the Church of St John the Baptist) and Hrastovlje (Dance of Death wall painting at the Church of the Holy Trinity). Important painters of this time were Johannes de Laibaco (John of Ljubljana), who decorated the Church of the Assumption in Muljava; Jernej of Loka, who worked mostly around Škofja Loka; and Johannes Aquila of Radgona, who did the frescoes in the magnificent church at Martjanci in Prekmurje. Much Gothic architecture in Slovenia is of the late period; the earthquake of 1511 took care of many buildings erected before then (though Koper's Venetian Gothic Loggia and Praetorian Palace date back a century earlier). Renaissance architecture is mostly limited to civil buildings (eg, the town houses in Škofja Loka and Kranj, and Brdo Castle).

Italian-influenced baroque abounds in Slovenia, and you'll find many great architectural examples, particularly in Ljubljana (Ursuline Church of the Holy Trinity and the cathedral). For sculpture, look at Jožef Straub's plague pillar in Maribor, the golden altar in the Church of the Annunciation at Crngrob or the work of Francesco Robba in Ljubljana (Fountain of the Carniolan Rivers in Mestni trg). Fortunat Bergant, who painted the Stations of the Cross in the church at Stična Abbey, was a master of baroque painting.

Classicism prevailed in Slovenian architecture in the first half of the 19th century (the Kazina building in Kongresni trg in Ljubljana, the Tempel pavilion in Rogaška Slatina) but also in the works of the painter Franc Kavčič and the Romantic portraits and landscapes of Josip Tominc and Matevž Langus. Realism arrived in the second half of the century in the work of artists like Ivana Kobilca, Jurij Šubic and Anton Ažbe, but the most important painters of that time were the impressionists Rihard Jakopič, Matija Jama, Ivan Grohar and Matej Sternen, who exhibited together in Ljubljana in 1900.

The turn of the 20th century was also the time when the Secessionist (or Art Nouveau) architects Maks Fabiani and Ivan Vurnik began changing the face of Ljubljana (Miklošičev Park, Prešeren monument, Cooperative Bank on Miklošičeva cesta) after the devastating 1895 earthquake. But no architect has had a greater impact on their city or nation than Jože Plečnik, a man who defies easy definition (see the boxed text 'Jože Plečnik, Architect Extraordinaire' in the Ljubljana chapter).

In the 20th century, the expressionist school of Božidar Jakac and the brothers France and Tone Kralj gave way to the so-called Club of Independents (the painters Zoran Mušič, Maks Sedej and France Mihelič) and later the sculptors Alojzij Gangl, Franc Berneker, Jakob Savinšek and Lojze Dolinar. The last two would later create 'masterpieces' of socialist realism under Tito without losing their credibility or (sometimes) their artistic sensibilities. Favourite artists of recent years include Janez Bernik, Rudi Španzel (who designed the tolar notes in circulation) and Jože Tisnikar, a painter with a very unique style from Slovenj Gradec.

Postmodernist painting and sculpture has been more or less dominated since the 1980s by the multimedia group Neue Slowenische Kunst (NSK) and the five-member artists' cooperative Irwin.

The apogee of folk painting in Slovenia over the past few centuries has been the traditional beehive panel *(panjska končnica)* illustrated with folk motifs. For more information, see the boxed text 'The Boards and the Bees' in the Radovljica section of the Gorenjska chapter.

Music

The conversion of the Slavs to Christianity from the 8th century brought the development of choral singing – the oldest Slovenian spiritual song dates from 1440 – in churches and monasteries. By the end of the Middle Ages, secular music had developed to the same degree as music elsewhere in Europe. The most important composer in the late 16th century was Jakob Gallus, who wrote madrigals and choral songs as well as 16 Masses. An outstanding composer of Renaissance music was Izak Poš.

Baroque music had gone out of fashion by the time the Filharmonija was founded in Ljubljana in 1701, and classicist forms had become all the rage. *Belin,* the first Slovenian opera, was written by Jakob Francisek Zupan in 1780, and Janez Novak composed classicist music for a comedy written by Slovenia's first playwright, Anton Tomaž Linhart. The 19th-century Romantics like Benjamin Ipavec, Fran Gerbič and Anton Foerster incorporated traditional Slovenian elements into their music as a way of expressing their nationalism. Perhaps Slovenia's most well-known composer was Hugo Wolf (1860–1903), born in Slovenj Gradec.

Slovenian music between the wars is best represented by the expressionist Marij Kogoj and the modernist Slavko Osterc. Contemporary composers whose reputations go well beyond the borders of Slovenia include Primož Ramovš, Marjan Kozina, Lojze Lebič and the ultramodernist Vinko Globokar, who lives in Paris. Opera buffs won't want to miss the chance to hear Marjana Lipovšek, the country's foremost mezzo-soprano.

Popular music runs the gamut from Slovenian *chanson* (best exemplified by Vita Mavrič) and folk to jazz and techno, but it was punk music in the late 1970s and early 1980s that put Slovenia on the world stage. The most celebrated groups were Pankrti, Borghesia and Laibach, and they were imitated throughout Eastern Europe. (Laibach's leader, Tomaž Hostnik, died tragically in 1983 when he hanged himself from a kozolec, the traditional Slovenian hayrack.)

Folk music *(ljudska glasba)* in Slovenia has developed independently from other forms of music over the centuries, and the collection and classification of children's songs, wedding marches and fables set to music began only in the nationalistic Romantic period of the 19th century. Today the Institute of Music and National Manuscripts (Glasbeno Narodopisni Institut) is charged with this task. Traditional folk instruments include the *frajtonarica* (button accordion), cymbalom (a curious stringed instrument played with sticks), zither, *zvegla* (wooden cross flute), *okarina* (a clay flute), *šurle* (Istrian double flute), *trstenke* (reed pipes), Jew's harp, *lončeni bajs* (earthenware bass), and *brač* (eight-string guitar). Folk groups and individuals to watch out for include the Avseniki, Lojzeta Slaka, the Alpski Kvintet led by Oto Pestner and the Romani (Gypsy) band Šukar.

Dance

Much of Slovenian dance finds its origins in folk culture, and folk dance *(ljudski ples)* has a long tradition in Slovenia, including polkas, circle dances and Hungarian-style czardas. The first ballet group was established in 1918 as part of the Ljubljana Opera and a ballet school set up within the National Theatre. The Ljubljana Ballet still performs at the Opera and there's another company in Maribor.

Avant-garde dance is best exemplified by Betontanc, an NSK dance company that mixes live music and theatrical elements (called 'physical theatre' here) with sharp political comment. In the rock ballet *Thieves of Wet Handkerchiefs,* members of the troupe murder one another and then are resurrected. Two contemporary Slovenian choreographers with an international reputation are Matejž Farič and Iztok Kovač.

Literature

Christian monks from Ireland probably introduced the Latin alphabet to the early Slavs living in Slovenia in the 8th century, and St Cyril and St Methodius gave them their first translations of the Scriptures a century later.

The oldest example of written Slovene (or any Slavic language for that matter) is contained in the three *Freising Texts (Brižinski Spomeniki)* dating from around 970. They contain a sermon on sin and penance and instructions for general confession. Oral poetry, such as the seminal tale of *Lepa Vida* (Fair Vida), flourished throughout the Middle Ages, but it was the Reformation that saw the first book in Slovene, a catechism published by Primož

Trubar in 1550. A complete translation of the Bible by Jurij Dalmatin followed in 1584, and Adam Bohorič published a grammar of Slovene in Latin (with the evocative title *Spare Winter Hours*) in the same year. Almost everything else published until the late 18th century was in Latin or German, including Janez Vajkard Valvasor's laudatory account of Slovenia, *The Glory of the Duchy of Carniola* (1689).

The Enlightenment and the reforms of the Habsburg rulers Maria Theresa and Joseph II raised the educational and general cultural level of the Slovenian nation. In large part due to the support and philanthropy of Baron Žiga Zois (1747–1819), Slovenia gained its first dramatist (Anton Tomaž Linhart), poet (Valentin Vodnik) and modern grammarian (Jernej Kopitar) at this time. But it was during the Romantic period when Slovenian literature truly came of age. This period produced the nation's greatest poet France Prešeren (see the boxed text 'France Prešeren: A Poet for the Nation' later in this section). *Kranjska Čebelica* (The Carniolan Bee), an anthology to which Prešeren contributed, was an important literary and nationalist forum in the 1830s and 1840s.

In the latter half of the 19th century, Fran Levstik (1831–87) brought the writing and interpretation of oral folk tales to new heights with his *Martin Krpan* (see the boxed text 'Big Men for Big Times' in the Notranjska chapter), but it was Josip Jurčič (1844–81) who published the first full-length novel in Slovene, *Deseti Brat* (The 10th Brother; 1866). The lyrical poets Simon Jenko (1835–69) and Simon Gregorčič (1844–1906) wrote original and powerful verse.

The period from the turn of the 20th century up to WWII is dominated by two men who single-handedly introduced modernism into Slovenian literature: poet Oton Župančič (1878–1949) and novelist and playwright Ivan Cankar (1876–1918). The latter has been called 'the outstanding master of Slovenian prose' and his works, notably *Hiša Marije Pomočnice* (The Ward of Our Lady of Mercy) and *Hlapec Jernej in Njegova Pravica* (The Bailiff Yerney and His Rights), influenced a generation of young writers.

France Prešeren: A Poet for the Nation

TAMSIN WILSON

Slovenia's most beloved poet was born in Vrba near Bled in 1800 and educated in Ribnica, Ljubljana and Vienna, where he received a law degree in 1828. Most of his working life was spent as an articled clerk in the office of a Ljubljana lawyer. By the time he opened his own practice in Kranj in 1846 he was already a sick and dispirited man. He died in 1849.

Although Prešeren published only one volume of poetry during his lifetime (*Poezije*, 1848), he left behind a legacy of work printed in the literary magazines *Kranjska Čbelica* (Carniolan Bee) and the German-language *Illyrisches Blatt* (Illyrian Sheet). His verse set new standards for Slovenian literature at a time when German was the literary language, and his lyric poems, such as the masterpiece *Sonetni Venec* (A Garland of Sonnets, 1834), are among the most sensitive, original and eloquent works in Slovene. In later poems he expressed a national consciousness that he tried to instil in his compatriots. *Krst pri Savici* (Baptism at the Savica Waterfall, 1836) is such a work.

Prešeren's life was one of sorrow and disappointment, which he met with stoicism and resignation. The sudden death of his close friend and mentor, the literary historian Matija Čop, in 1835 and an unrequited love affair with an heiress called Julija Primic brought him close to suicide. (Julija later married a German, and Slovenes like to point out, with a certain amount of *Schadenfreude*, that she was unhappy with her husband.) But this was when he produced his best poems.

In reality, Prešeren was a drunkard, a philanderer, a social outcast and perhaps even vain. He refused to have his portrait done and any likeness you see of him – including the rather dashing one on the 1000 SIT note – were done from memory after his death.

But Prešeren was the first to demonstrate the full literary potential of the Slovenian language and his body of verse – lyric poems, epics, satire, narrative verse – has inspired Slovenes at home and abroad for generations. And continues to do so.

Slovenian literature immediately before and after WWII was influenced by socialist realism and the Partisan struggle as exemplified in the novels of Voranc Prežihov (1893–1950) and poems by Matej Bor (1913–), but since then Slovenia has tended to follow Western European trends: late expressionism, symbolism (poetry by Edvard Kocbek, 1904–81) and existentialism (novels by Vitomil Zupan, 1914–87, and the drama of Gregor Strniša, 1930–87). Contemporary writers and poets using avante-garde techniques include Drago Jančar (1948–), Tomaž Šalamun (1941–), Kajetan Kovič (1931–), Andrej Hieng (1925–) and Rudi Šeligo (1935–).

Film

Slovenia was never on the cutting edge of film-making as were some of the other republics (eg, Croatia) in the former Yugoslavia, but it still managed to produce about a dozen full-length features annually, some of which – like Jože Gale's *Kekec* (1951) and France Štiglic's *Dolina Miru* (Valley of Peace, 1955) – won international awards. Today that number has dropped to about three per year. Indeed, the panoply of feature films produced in Slovene from the first (*V Kraljestvu Zlatoroga* or In the Realm of the Goldenhorn) in 1931 until 1998 numbers only around 140.

Only two films were produced in Slovenia between the wars, and after WWII and into the 1950s Slovenian film tended to focus on subjects like the Partisan struggle – eg, Štiglic's *Na Svoji Zemlji* (On Our Land, 1948) and *Akcija* (Action, 1960) by Jane Kavčič – and life among the Slovenian bourgeoisie under the Austro-Hungarian Empire (*Jara Gospoda* or Parvenus, 1953) by Bojan Stupica. The 1960s brought a new wave of modernism to Slovenian film best exemplified in the work of Boštjan Hladnik (*Ples v Dežju* or Dance in the Rain, 1961) and Matjaž Klopčič (*Na Papirnatih Avionih* or On Wings of Paper, 1967). Since the 1970s the most popular films in Slovenia like everywhere have been those dealing with crime and suspense and comedies (eg, Franci Slak's *Hudodelci* or The Felons, 1987; Jure Pervanje's *Do Konca in Naprej* or To the Limit and Beyond, 1990; and Vinči Vogue Anžlovar's *Babica Gre na Jug* or Grandma Goes South, 1991). More recent successes have been *Ekspres, Ekspres* (Express, Express) by Igor Šterk, *Herzog* by Mitja Milavec and Andrej Košak's *Outsider,* all released in 1997.

Declining audience figures in the 1990s have led to the closure of more than 35% of cinemas around the country though some 115 remain open. A Festival of Slovenian Film is held in Portorož in March.

RELIGION

Although Protestantism gained a very strong foothold in Slovenia in the 16th century, the majority of Slovenes today – just under 72% – identify themselves as Roman Catholic. An archbishop sits in Ljubljana and there are bishoprics at Maribor and Koper.

Other religious communities in Slovenia include Eastern Orthodox Christians (2.4%), Muslims (1%) and Protestants (1%). Most Protestants belong to the Evangelical (Lutheran) church based in Murska Sobota in Prekmurje.

Jews have played a very minor role in Slovenia since they were first banished from the territory in the 15th century. Although the remains of a synagogue still stand in Maribor and there was one in Ljubljana until WWII, no temple functions in Slovenia today. The rabbi from Zagreb occasionally holds services for the tiny community in Ljubljana.

As in most of Central and Western Europe today, religion doesn't appear to be much of an issue in Slovenia, particularly among the young, and churches are seldom more than half-full outside the most important holy days like Easter, Christmas and the Assumption of Mary (15 August). One Slovenian friend's only memory of ever having been into a church as a child was when his granny brought him to see the *božične jaslice* (crib) one Christmas.

LANGUAGE

The French novelist Charles Nodier (1780–1844), who lived and worked in Ljubljana for a couple of years in the early 19th century, once wrote that Slovenia was like 'an Academy of Arts and Sciences' because of the people's flair for speaking foreign languages. Monsieur Nodier would be happy to know that Slovenci still have that talent almost two centuries down the track.

Virtually everyone in Slovenia speaks at least one other language. In the 1991 census, 88% said they knew Croatian and Serbian, 45% German, 37% were conversant in English and 17% spoke Italian.

Italian is really only useful in Primorska and small parts of Notranjska. German, once the language of education and the elite, is spoken mostly by older people now, especially in Koroška, Štajerska and northern Gorenjska. There may be fewer speakers of English than German overall, but it is definitely the preferred language of the young, with 84% of all students claiming some knowledge of it. Most speak English very well indeed, even if they pepper their speech with 'Slovenglish' slang like 'full cool', meaning 'trendy' or 'fashionable'.

The fact that you will rarely have difficulty in making yourself understood and that you will probably never 'need' Slovene shouldn't stop you from learning a few words and phrases of this rich and wonderful language.

More than anything else, Slovene has kept the Slovenian nation (*narod*) alive and united as a culture over centuries of domination and brutality. And despite all attempts to destroy it from outside, Slovene is very much alive, dynamic and organic. Any effort on your part to speak it will be rewarded one hundred-fold (see the Language chapter at the back of the book).

Facts for the Visitor

HIGHLIGHTS
Natural Wonders
You won't soon forget the Vršič Pass and the Julian Alps in Triglav National Park, the Škocjan Caves, the Vintgar Gorge near Bled, the Logarska Dolina in Štajerska, the Soča River, Lake Cerknica and the Rakov Škocjan Gorge, and the Karst region.

Historic Towns
The most attractive cities and towns – and the ones where you'll get a real feel for the past – are Ljubljana, Ptuj, Škofja Loka, Radovljica, Piran and Kranj.

Museums
The following museums stand out not just for what they contain but for how they display it: the Dolenjska Museum in Novo Mesto, the Posavje Museum in Brežice, the Blacksmith Museum in Kropa, the Municipal Museum in Idrija, the Saltworks Museum in Sečovlje, the Beekeeping Museum in Radovljica, the Kobarid Museum, the Franja Partisan Hospital near Cerkno, the Technical Museum in Bistra Castle and, in Ljubljana, the Museum of Modern History and the Slovenian Ethnographic Museum.

Castles
Slovenia was once known as the 'country of castles' and counted over 1000, but wars and development have taken care of most of them. Of the remaining ones, the most dramatic (open to the public and in varying states of repair) are Bled Castle, Predjama Castle near Postojna, Ljubljana Castle, Snežnik Castle in Notranjska, Bogenšperk Castle in Dolenjska, Podsreda Castle in the Kozjansko region of Štajerska, Celje Castle and Ptuj Castle. For more information, ask for the Castles and Mansions brochure from the Slovenian Tourist Board.

Churches
The following are a half-dozen of Slovenia's most beautiful houses of worship: the Church of St John the Baptist at Bohinj, the Church of the Holy Trinity at Hrastovlje, the Church of the Virgin Mary at Ptujska Gora near Ptuj, the Chapter Church of St Nicholas in Novo Mesto, the Church of the Assumption at Nova Štifta near Ribnica and the Church of the Annunciation at Crngrob near Škofja Loka.

SUGGESTED ITINERARIES
Depending on the length of your stay, you might want to see and do the following in Slovenia:

Two days A day in Ljubljana and a day trip to Postojna or Škocjan Caves

One week Two days in Ljubljana, the rest in Bled and Bohinj, or Škocjan Caves and Piran

Two weeks Two days in Ljubljana, then a circuit north to Bled and Bohinj (five days), over the Vršič Pass to the Soča Valley (three days), Škocjan Caves (one day), Piran and the coast (two or three days); add on a day in Ptuj if you have the time

PLANNING
When to Go
Snow can linger in the mountains until late June and even July, but spring (April and May) is a great time to be in the lowlands and valleys of Slovenia when everything is fresh and in blossom. (April can be a bit wet, though.)

In July and August, hotel rates are increased and there will be lots of tourists, especially on the coast. September is an excellent month to visit as the days are long and the weather warm, the summer crowds will have vanished and it's the best time for hiking and climbing. October and November can be rainy, but the autumn colours in the forests are stunning. Winter (December to March) is for skiers.

Remember, though, that Slovenian school kids have their Christmas holidays during December/January and a week off in early February, so the slopes could be heaving at those times.

Maps

The Geodesic Institute of Slovenia (Geodetski Zavod Slovenije or GZS), the country's principal map-making company, produces national (1:300,000) and regional maps, as well as city plans. Nineteen leisure maps at a scale of 1:50,000 (costing 1350 SIT) cover the whole country, and there are city plans (1250 SIT) for all the major towns. GZS's Ljubljana map (1:20,000; 1350 SIT) is excellent. The Alpine Association of Slovenia (Planinska Zveza Slovenije; PZS) produces some 30 hiking maps with scales as large as 1:25,000.

What to Bring

You don't have to remember any particular items of clothing – a warm sweater (even in summer) for the mountains at night, perhaps, and an umbrella in the spring or autumn – unless you plan to do some serious hiking or other sport. In general, Slovenian society dresses casually (though a bit smarter in Ljubljana than in the provinces) when it goes out on the town.

A swimsuit for the beach, pool or mixed-sex thermal spas (not always required) and a towel and thongs (flip-flops) for mouldy showers in hostels and camping grounds are mandatory. Soap, toothpaste and toilet paper are readily obtainable almost anywhere, as are tampons and condoms, both locally made and imported.

A sleeping sheet with pillow cover (case) is a good idea if you plan to stay in hostels or college dormitories. A padlock is useful to secure your hostel locker. A Swiss Army knife is helpful for all sorts of things. Make sure it includes such essentials as a bottle opener and strong corkscrew!

Other optional items include a compass (to help orient yourself in the mountains and while driving), a torch (flashlight), an adapter plug for electrical appliances, sunglasses, a few clothes pegs (pins) and pre-moistened towelettes or a large cotton handkerchief that you can soak in fountains and use to cool off while touring towns and cities in the hot summer months. And don't forget sunblock, even in the cooler months. Those rays in the mountains can be fierce.

TOURIST OFFICES
Local Tourist Offices

The Slovenian Tourist Board (Slovenska Nacionalna Turistična Organizacija or SNTO; ☎ 01-589 18 40, fax 589 18 41, e info@slovenia-tourism.si), in the World Trade Centre at Dunajska cesta 156 in Ljubljana, is the umbrella organisation for tourist promotion in Slovenia, and can handle requests for information in writing or by email. The SNTO produces about a dozen brochures, pamphlets and booklets in English, all of which can be ordered (and some of them viewed) on its Web site at www.slovenia-tourism.si.

The best office in Slovenia for face-to-face information – bar none – is the Ljubljana Tourist Information Centre (TIC; ☎ 01-306 12 15, fax 306 12 04, e pcl.tic-lj@ljubljana .si) at Stritarjeva ulica 2 in Ljubljana. The staff know *everything* about the capital and a lot about Slovenia. There are also TICs in Bled, Bohinj, Kranjska Gora, Maribor, Portorož and Ptuj and smaller, independent or community-run offices in other cities and towns. If the place you're visiting doesn't have one, seek assistance at a branch of one of the big travel agencies (eg, Kompas or Globtour) or from hotel or museum staff.

Tourist Offices Abroad

The Slovenian Tourist Board maintains tourist offices in the following countries:

Austria (☎ 01-715 4010, fax 713 8177) Hilton Center, Landstrasser Hauptstrasse 2, 1030 Vienna
Croatia (☎ 01-45 72 118, fax 45 77 921) Hotel Esplanade, Mihanovičeva 1, 10000 Zagreb
Germany (☎ 089-2916 1202, fax 2916 1273) Maximilliansplatz 12a, 80333 Munich
Hungary (☎ 1-269 6879, fax 156 2818) Rakoczi utca 14, 1072 Budapest
Italy (☎ 02-29 51 11 87) Galleria Buenos Aires 1, 20124 Milan
Netherlands (☎ 010-465 3003, fax 465 7514) Benthuizerstraat 29, 3036 CB Rotterdam
Switzerland (☎ 01-212 6394, fax 212 5266) Löwenstrasse 54, 8001 Zürich
UK (☎ 020-7287 7133, fax 7287 5476) 49 Conduit Street, London W1R 9FB
USA (☎ 212-358 9686, fax 358 9025) 345 East 12th St, New York, NY 10003

VISAS & DOCUMENTS
Passport
Virtually everyone entering Slovenia must have a valid passport, though citizens of the EU and Switzerland need only produce their national identity card on arrival for stays of up to 30 days. It's a good idea to carry your passport or other identification at all times.

Visas
Citizens of Australia, Canada, Ireland, Israel, Japan, New Zealand, the UK, the USA and most European countries do not require visas for stays of up to 90 days. Those who do require visas (including South African passport holders, at the time of writing) can get them at any Slovenian embassy or consulate (see Embassies & Consulates later in this chapter) for up to 90 days. They cost €25 (or equivalent) for single entry, €50 for double entry, and you may have to show a return or onward ticket. Photographs are not required.

Your hotel, hostel, camping ground or private room arranged through an agency will register your name and address with the municipal government *(občina)* office as required by law – that's why they have to take your passport away, at least for the first night. If you are staying elsewhere (eg, with relatives or friends), your host is supposed to take care of this for you within three days.

If you want to stay in Slovenia longer than three months, the easiest thing to do is simply cross the border into Italy or Austria and return. Otherwise you will have to apply for a temporary residence permit at the Foreigners Office (Urad za Tujce; ☎ 01-431 01 66) in the Kresija building at Adamič-Lundrovo nabrežje 2 in Ljubljana.

Contact any Slovenian embassy, consulate or tourist office abroad for any recent changes in the above regulations, or check the Slovenian Foreign Ministry Web site at www.gov.si/mzz. The staff at any branch of Adria Airways, the Slovenian national carrier, should also be able to help; for its addresses see the Web site www.adria.si (choose 'Reservation').

Travel Insurance
A travel insurance policy to cover theft, loss and medical problems is a good idea. Some policies offer lower and higher medical-expense options; the higher ones are chiefly for countries such as the USA, which have extremely high medical costs. There is a wide variety of policies available, so check the small print.

Some policies specifically exclude 'dangerous activities', which can include mountaineering, paragliding, even trekking. A locally acquired motorcycle licence is not valid under some policies.

You may prefer a policy which pays doctors or hospitals directly rather than you having to pay on the spot and claim later. If you have to claim later, make sure you keep all documentation. Some policies ask you to call back (reverse charges) to a centre in your home country where an immediate assessment of your problem is made.

Check that the policy covers ambulances or an emergency flight home.

Driving Licence & Permits
If you don't hold a European driving licence and plan to drive in Slovenia, obtain an International Driving Permit from your local automobile association before you leave – you'll need a passport photo and a valid licence. They are usually inexpensive and valid for one year only.

Camping Card International
Your local automobile association also issues the Camping Card International (CCI), which is basically a camping ground ID. In the UK, the AA issues them to its members for UK£4.80. These cards are also available from your local camping federation, and sometimes on the spot at camping grounds. They incorporate third-party insurance for damage you may cause, and some camping grounds in Slovenia offer discounts of 5% to 10% if you sign in with one.

Hostel Cards
No hostels in Slovenia require that you be a hostelling association member, but they sometimes offer a discount if you are.

Mladi Turist (☎ 01-425 92 60), at Salendrova ulica 4 in Ljubljana, is the office of the Slovenian Youth Hostel Association and sells hostel cards (1800 to 2200 SIT, depending on age).

Student & Youth Cards

The most useful of these is the International Student Identity Card (ISIC), a plastic ID-style card with your photograph, which provides discounts on some forms of transport and cheap or free admission to museums, sights and even films. If you're aged under 26 but not a student, you can apply for a GO25 card issued by the Federation of International Youth Travel Organisations (FIYTO), which gives much the same discounts and benefits as an ISIC. The Erazem backpacker travel agency (☎ 01-433 10 76) at Trubarjeva cesta 7 in Ljubljana sells both ISIC cards (900 SIT) and GO25 cards (700 SIT).

Copies

All important documents (passport data page and visa page, credit cards, travel insurance policy, air/bus/train tickets, driving licence etc) should be photocopied before you leave home. Leave one copy with someone at home and keep another with you, separate from the originals.

It's also a good idea to store details of your vital travel documents in Lonely Planet's free online Travel Vault in case you lose the photocopies or can't be bothered with them. Your password-protected Travel Vault is accessible online anywhere in the world – create it at www.ekno.lonelyplanet.com.

EMBASSIES & CONSULATES
Slovenian Embassies & Consulates

Here is a selection of Slovenia's foreign diplomatic missions. A full list can be found on the Foreign Ministry Web site at www.gov.si/mzz.

Australia
Embassy: (☎ 02-6243 4830) Advance Bank Centre, Level 6, 60 Marcus Clark St, Canberra ACT 2601
Consulate: (☎ 02-9314 5116) PO Box 188, Coogee, Sydney NSW 2034

Austria
Embassy: (☎ 01-586 1307) Nibelungengasse 13, 1010 Vienna
Canada
Embassy: (☎ 613-565 5781) 150 Metcalfe St, Suite 2101, Ottawa, Ont K2P 1P1
Croatia
Embassy: (☎ 01-631 1000) Savska cesta 41/IX, 10000 Zagreb
France
Embassy: (☎ 01 47 55 65 90) 21 Rue Bouquet de Longchamp, 75016 Paris
Germany
Embassy: (☎ 030-206 1450) Hausvogteiplatz 3–4, D-10117 Berlin
Consulate: (☎ 089-543 9819) PF 150829, Lindwurmstrasse 10, 80045 München
Hungary
Embassy: (☎ 1-438 5600) Cseppkő utca 68, 1025 Budapest
Italy
Embassy: (☎ 06-808 1272) Via Ludovico Pisano 10, 00197 Rome
Netherlands
Embassy: (☎ 070 310 8690) Muzenstraat 89, 2511 WB The Hague
New Zealand
Consulate: (☎ 04-567 0027) PO Box 30247, Eastern Hutt Road, Pomare, Lower Hutt, Wellington
UK
Embassy: (☎ 020-7495 7775) Suite One, Cavendish Court, 11–15 Wigmore St, London W1H 9LA
USA
Embassy: (☎ 202-667 5363) 1525 New Hampshire Ave NW, Washington, DC 20036
Consulate: (☎ 212-370 3006) 600 Third Avenue, 21st Floor, New York, NY 10016
Consulate: (☎ 310-392 4843) 453 Rialto Avenue, Venice, CA 90291

Embassies & Consulates in Slovenia

Selected countries with representation in Ljubljana – either full embassies or consulates – appear below. If telephoning from outside the capital but still within Slovenia, remember to dial ☎ 01 first.

Australia
Consulate: (☎ 425 4252) Trg Republike 3/XII
Austria
Embassy: (☎ 479 0700) Prešernova cesta 23
Canada
Consulate: (☎ 430 3570) Miklošičeva cesta 19

Croatia
  Embassy: (☎ 425 7287) Gruberjevo nabrežje 6
France
  Embassy: (☎ 426 2582) Barjanska cesta 1
Germany
  Embassy: (☎ 479 0300) Prešernova cesta 27
Hungary
  Embassy: (☎ 512 1882) ulica Konrada
  Babnika 5
Italy
  Embassy: (☎ 426 2194) Snežniška ulica 8
Netherlands
  Consulate: (☎ 232 8978) Dunajska cesta 22/I
South Africa
  Consulate: (☎ 433 4180) Pražakova ulica 4
UK
  Embassy: (☎ 200 3910) Trg Republike 3/IV
USA
  Embassy: (☎ 200 5500) Prešernova cesta 31

Your Own Embassy

It's important to realise what your own embassy – the embassy of the country of which you are a citizen – can and can't do to help you if you get into trouble. Generally speaking, it won't be much help in emergencies if the trouble you're in is remotely your own fault. Remember that you are bound by the laws of the country you are in. Your embassy will not be sympathetic if you end up in jail after committing a crime locally, even if such actions are legal in your own country.

In genuine emergencies you might get some assistance, but only if other channels have been exhausted. For example, if you need to get home urgently, a free ticket home is exceedingly unlikely – the embassy would expect you to have insurance. If you have all your money and documents stolen, it might assist with getting a new passport, but a loan for onward travel is out of the question.

CUSTOMS

Travellers can bring in the usual personal effects, two still cameras, one video camera and electronic goods for their own use, 200 cigarettes, a generous 4L of spirits but only 1L of wine (remember, viniculture is big business here). The import or export of more than 500,000 SIT in Slovenian tolars or securities without permission from the Bank of Slovenia is forbidden.

Customs inspections at most border crossings and Brnik airport are cursory or nonexistent and visitors need only make an oral declaration. However, officers are rather strict about enforcing laws regarding pets, and you may have to turn around if Fido's (or Pussy's) papers aren't in order. Basically, a rabies vaccination certificate (in English, German or Italian if you can't manage Slovene) must be at least 30 days old but no older than six months. A veterinarian's certificate of health must be no more than 10 days old.

MONEY
Currency

The Slovenian *tolar*, abbreviated SIT, is a relatively new currency with a distinguished pedigree (see the boxed text 'The Almighty Tolar'). In theory the tolar is divided into 100 *stotinov*, but nowadays you'll rarely come across these worthless aluminium coins. More substantial brassy coins of one, two, five and 10 tolars are in circulation.

Slovenia's colourful paper money, designed by the superb postmodernist artist Rudi Španzel, comes in nine denominations: 10, 20, 50, 100, 200, 500, 1000, 5000 and 10,000 SIT. They bear the likenesses of Slovenian writers, historians, artists, scientists, architects and musicians; gratefully, there's not a general among them.

The 10 SIT note bears the portrait of Primož Trubar (1508–86), the Protestant reformer and translator, while the 20 SIT one portrays the historian and geographer Janez Vajkard Valvasor (1641–93). The 50 SIT note features the mathematician Jurij Vega (1754–1802).

The 100 SIT bill takes us into the 20th century with the stern-faced impressionist painter Rihard Jakopič (1869–1943). Jakob Gallus (1550–91), a composer who worked mostly in Prague, is on the 200 SIT note while the architect Jože Plečnik (1872–1957) is portrayed on the 500 SIT one. The Romantic poet and patriot France Prešeren (1800–49) is on the 1000 SIT and, in a bow to political correctness, a woman – the realist painter Ivana Kobilca (1861–1926) – takes pride of place on the 5000 SIT note.

The 10,000 SIT note features Ivan Cankar (1876–1918), the writer who has been called the 'outstanding master of Slovenian prose'.

Exchange Rates

At the time of printing, approximate conversion rates for the tolar were:

country	unit		SIT
Australia	A$1	=	124 SIT
Canada	C$1	=	157 SIT
Croatia	1KN	=	29 SIT
Czech Republic	1Kč	=	6 SIT
euro	€1	=	217 SIT
Hungary	100Ft	=	81 SIT
Japan	¥100	=	199 SIT
New Zealand	NZ$1	=	99 SIT
South Africa	R1	=	30 SIT
Switzerland	Sfr1	=	142 SIT
UK	UK£1	=	351 SIT
USA	US$1	=	246 SIT

Exchanging Money

Cash & Travellers Cheques It is easy to change cash and travellers cheques at banks, post offices, tourist offices, travel agencies and *menjalnice* (private exchange offices). Look for any of the words *Menjalnica* or *Devizna Blagajna* to guide you.

There's no black market in Slovenia, but exchange rates can vary substantially, so it pays to keep your eyes open. Banks take a commission *(provizija)* of 1% or none at all, but tourist offices, travel agencies, exchange bureaus and hotels charge 3% to 5%.

Banks often give a better rate for travellers cheques than for cash but some private exchange offices (not travel agencies) do the opposite. Post offices are not the best places to change money as some may only accept cash, and when they do take travellers cheques it will be at a relatively poor rate.

You can easily change excess tolars back into US dollars or euros (the exchange office at Ljubljana's train station is a good place); keep your exchange receipts just in case. Slovenia had relatively liberal currency-exchange laws even while part of Yugoslavia, and is also a good place to trade one foreign currency for another – eg, US dollars for euros – without having to convert it into tolars first. You can also receive cash dollars or euros for your travellers cheques at most banks for a flat 3% commission.

Guaranteed Cheques Nova Ljubljanska Banka branches will cash Eurocheques for up to 25,000 SIT (or the equivalent).

Credit Cards & ATMs Visa, MasterCard/Eurocard and American Express credit cards are widely accepted at upmarket restaurants, shops, hotels, car-rental firms and some travel agencies; Diner's Club less so.

Automatic teller machines (ATMs) – known as *bančni avtomat* – have now been

The Almighty Tolar

The Slovenian tolar, the currency that sounds suspiciously like 'dollar', actually shares the same etymology as its more worldly cousin. Both 'tolar' and 'dollar' are modified forms of the German word *thaler*, the name of a silver coin first struck in 1518 under Emperor Charles V of Germany, who was also King of Spain and the Spanish colonies in the New World. The silver was mined at a place called St Joachimsthal (Joachim's Dale) in Bohemia and the coin circulated in Germany from the 16th century onward under various names: *thaler, daler, dalar* and *lallero*. The thaler was replaced by the mark as the German monetary unit only after unification in 1873.

Spanish pesos – the celebrated 'pieces of eight' of sea ditties – circulated in the Spanish and English colonies in 17th-century America and were known as 'dollars' to English speakers. In 1792 the fledgling American government bowed to this familiarity and adopted it as its official currency. Canada adopted the name in 1858, Australia in 1966 and New Zealand a year after that.

In 1991, as the last soldier of the Yugoslav army left Slovenia, the central bank issued its own tolar coupons to replace the Yugoslav dinars in circulation. A year later Slovenia had its own currency.

installed on almost every street corner in the country. If you have a card linked to either the Visa/Electron/Plus or the MasterCard/Maestro/Cirrus network and a PIN (personal identification number) then you can withdraw tolars from almost any ATM in the country. Both A Banka and SKB Banka ATMs are linked to both networks; all banks mentioned in this guide have an ATM unless otherwise indicated.

Visa cardholders can get cash advances in tolars from any A Banka branch, Eurocard/MasterCard holders from a Nova Ljubljanska Banka or SKB Banka, and American Express clients from the Atlas Express representative in Ljubljana.

Though an English-language option is available on the ATM screen, the following are the Slovenian words on the buttons and their English equivalents:

Prekinitev – Cancel
Popravek – Correction
Sprememba – Change/Modification
Potrditev – Enter/Confirm

If you have problems with your Visa card, call the Visa Centre (☎ 01-433 21 32). Eurocard and MasterCard holders should call Nova Ljubljanska Banka (☎ 01-425 01 55).

American Express customers who want to report a lost or stolen card or travellers cheques, or who need an advance, should contact Atlas Express (☎ 01-430 77 20) at Kolodvorska ulica 20 in Ljubljana. It can replace cards (though you must know the account number) and make refunds for lost or stolen American Express travellers cheques. Green Card holders can get up to US$200 in cash tolars and US$300 in US-dollar travellers cheques (US$1000 if you can write a personal cheque). Anyone with a Gold Card can get the tolar cash equivalent of US$500 and US$1500 in dollar cheques. The advance must be approved by the head office in Zagreb, but that usually only takes a few minutes.

International Transfers The Nova Ljubljanska Banka is the agent for Western Union, and you can have money wired to any of its branches throughout the country. Call ☎ 01-540 12 23 for more information.

Costs

Though prices are increasing, with imported items costing as much as they do in Western Europe, Slovenia remains much cheaper than nearby Italy and Austria. But don't expect it to be a bargain basement like Hungary; everything costs about 50% more here.

If you stay in private rooms or guesthouses, eat at medium-priced restaurants and travel 2nd class on the train or by bus, you should get by on under US$40 a day. Those putting up at hostels or college dormitories, eating *burek* (meat- or cheese-filled pastries) for lunch and at self-service restaurants for dinner will cut costs considerably. Travelling in a little more style and comfort – occasional restaurant splurges with bottles of wine, an active nightlife, small hotels/guesthouses with 'character' – will cost about US$65 a day.

Typical costs include:

bed in hostel	1200 SIT
bed in private room	2500 SIT
double room in mid-range hotel	12,000 SIT
cup of coffee	180 SIT
0.5L beer	350 SIT
bottle of wine in supermarket	1100 SIT
street snack (burek)	200 SIT
dinner for two at good restaurant	8000 SIT
100km by bus	1400 SIT
100km by train	1000 SIT
petrol	155 SIT/L
local phone call	4.5 SIT/minute

SIT or Euro?

Prices in shops and restaurants, and train and bus fares, are always quoted in tolars, but some hotels, guesthouses and camping grounds quote in euros – or, prior to the introduction of the euro in January 2002, in Deutschmarks (DM) or Austrian Schillings (AS). For that reason, the rates for some accommodation and a few other items listed in this guide are quoted in euros (€). In these instances you can pay in either euros or tolars.

Tipping & Bargaining

Tipping is not really necessary at Slovenian restaurants, bars or hotels, but no-one is going to complain if you hand them a gratuity. Taxi drivers are almost never tipped, but you can round up if you have been happy with the ride or for the sake of convenience.

As in Eastern Europe, bargaining was not the done thing under communism; everyone paid the same amount by weight and volume. Nowadays people selling folk crafts on the street and especially vendors at flea markets will be very open to haggling. At hotels enjoying less than full occupancy during the off season, you may be able to wangle a *popust* (discount) of up to 25%.

Taxes & Refunds

Value-Added Tax (known as DDV in Slovenia) is applied to the purchase of most goods and services in Slovenia, at a standard rate of 19% (eg, on alcoholic drinks and petrol) and a reduced rate of 8% (eg, on hotel accommodation and food). It is *usually* included in the quoted price of goods, but not of some services, so beware.

Visitors can claim refunds on total purchases of 15,000 SIT or more (not including tobacco products or spirits) through Kompas MTS, which has offices at Brnik airport and some two dozen border crossings; they are marked with an asterisk (*) in the Car & Motorcycle section of the Getting There & Away chapter. There's also an MTS cash-refund office (☎ 01-432 52 85) in Ljubljana north-east of the train station at Neubergerjeva ulica 19. In order to make the claim, you must have a European Tax-Free Shopping (ETS) cheque correctly filled out by the salesperson at the time of purchase and have it stamped by a Slovenian customs officer at the border. You can then collect your refund – minus commission – from the nearby Kompas MTS payment office in cash, and have it sent by bank cheque or deposited into your credit-card account.

Most towns and cities levy a 'tourist tax' on visitors staying overnight (120 to 360 SIT per person per night). This is *not* normally included in hotels' advertised rates, and is not included in the rates quoted in this book.

POST & COMMUNICATIONS
Post

The Slovenian postal system (Pošta Slovenije), recognised by its bright yellow sign, offers a wide variety of services – from selling stamps and telephone cards to sending faxes and changing money. The queues are never very long, but you can avoid a trip to the post office if you just want to mail a few postcards by buying stamps *(znamke)* at certain newsstands and dropping your mail into any of the yellow letterboxes on the street.

Something mailed within Slovenia takes only a day or two. Post to neighbouring countries and ones close by like Germany should take about three days. For the UK, you can count on about five days, and the USA between a week and 10 days. Mail to Asia and Australia takes between 10 days and two weeks.

Postal Rates Look for the sign 'Pisma – Paketi' if you've got a letter *(pismo)* or parcel *(paket)* to post. Domestic mail costs 21 SIT for up to 20g and 40 SIT for up to 100g. Postcards are 20 SIT. For international mail, the base rate is 90 SIT for 20g or less, 186 SIT for up to 100g and 100 SIT for a postcard. Then you have to add on the airmail charge for every 10g: 20 SIT for Europe, 25 SIT for North America and Asia and 30 SIT for Australasia. An aerogram is 120 SIT.

Receiving Mail Poste restante is kept at the main post office in a city or town. In the capital, address it to Glavni Pošta, Slovenska cesta 32, 1101 Ljubljana, where it will be held for 30 days. American Express card members can have their mail addressed c/o Atlas Express, Kolodvorska ulica, 1000 Ljubljana.

Telephone

The easiest – and most private – place to make international calls, as well as send faxes and telegrams, is from a post office or telephone centre; the one at Trg OF near the train and bus stations in Ljubljana is open 24 hours a day. Simply go into one of the

Addresses & Place Names

Streets in Slovenian towns and cities are well signposted, though the numbering system can be a bit confusing with odd and even numbers sometimes running on the same sides of streets and squares.

In very small towns and villages, streets are not named and houses are just given numbers. Thus Ribčev Laz 13 is house No 13 in the village of Ribčev Laz on Lake Bohinj. As Slovenian villages are frequently made up of one road with houses clustered on or just off it, this is seldom confusing.

Places with double-barrelled names like Novo Mesto (New Town) and Črna Gora (Black Hill) start the second word in lower case (Novo mesto, Črna gora), almost as if the names were Newtown and Blackhill. This is the correct Slovene orthography, but we have opted to go with the English-language way of doing it to avoid confusion.

Slovene frequently uses the possessive case in street names. Thus a road named after the poet Ivan Cankar is Cankarjeva ulica while a square honouring France Prešeren is Prešernov trg. Also, when nouns are turned into adjectives they often become unrecognisable to a foreigner. The town is 'Bled', for example, but 'Lake Bled' is Blejsko Jezero. A street leading to a castle *(grad)* is usually called Grajska ulica. The words 'pri', 'pod' and 'na' in place names mean 'at the', 'below the' and 'on the' respectively.

There are a lot of different words for 'street' in Slovene, and the following list will at least help you distinguish between the boulevards, roads and alleys used in addresses. A more extensive list of words, useful for reading maps, appears in the Glossary at the back of this book.

avtocesta – motorway	*obvoznica* – ring road, bypass
breg – river bank	*podhod* – pedestrian underpass
cesta (abbreviated *c*) – road	*pot* – trail
drevored – avenue	*prehod* – passage, crossing
dvorišče – courtyard	*sprehajališče* – walkway, alley
gaj – grove, park	*steza* – path
nabrežje – embankment	*trg* – square
naselje – colony, hamlet, estate	*ulica* (abbreviated *ul*) – street

booths (sometimes you have to take a number first), make your call and then pay the cashier. Some booths have electronic meters telling you exactly how much you're spending in tolars as you chat away.

Public telephones don't accept coins; they require a telephone card *(telefonska kartica)*, available at all post offices and some newsstands. Phonecards cost 700/1000/1700/3500 SIT for 25/50/100/300 *impulzu* (impulses, or units). A three-minute local call will cost 13 SIT during peak rate (7 am to 7 pm weekdays), half that at off-peak times.

A three-minute call from Slovenia to Croatia, Yugoslavia and Eastern European countries will cost about 277 SIT; to Hungary, most of Western Europe (including the UK), Canada and the USA, 214 SIT; to Australia and New Zealand, 434 SIT; and to most of Asia, 615 SIT. Rates are 20% cheaper between 7 pm and 7 am every day.

Slovenian call boxes do not display their telephone numbers so it's impossible for the other party to phone you back. The only 'country direct' service currently available is MCI WorldPhone to the USA – call ☎ 080-8808. Most telephone credit cards like Sprint and AT&T still can't be used from Slovenia.

To call Slovenia from abroad, dial the international access code, ☎ 386 (the country code for Slovenia), the area code (minus the initial zero) and the number. There are six area codes in Slovenia and these are listed in the header for each city and town in this book – see also the boxed text 'Ringing the Changes'. To call abroad, dial ☎ 00 followed by the country and area codes and then the number.

Telephone numbers you may find useful include:

☎ 981 – general information
☎ 988 – directory assistance for Slovenia
☎ 989 – international directory assistance
☎ 900 – domestic operator
☎ 901   international operator/collect calls
☎ 95 – time (in Slovene)

Mobile Phones Slovenia uses GSM 900, which is compatible with the rest of Europe and Australia but not with the North American GSM 1900 or the totally different system in Japan (though some North Americans have GSM 1900/900 phones that do work here). Coverage amounts to 98% of the country. If you have a GSM phone, check with your service provider about using it in Slovenia, and beware of calls being routed internationally (very expensive for a 'local' call). You can also rent one from Mobitel (☎ 01-472 22 00) at Brnik airport and at Vilharjeva cesta 23 in Ljubljana for 475 SIT a day (dropping to 370 SIT a day for 20 or more days). In this case you can't use your existing number, however.

Email & Internet Access
Travelling with a portable computer is a great way to stay in touch with life back home, but unless you know what you're doing it's fraught with potential problems. If you plan to carry your notebook or palmtop computer with you, remember that the power-supply voltage in Slovenia may vary from that at home, risking damage to your equipment. The best investment is a universal AC adaptor for your appliance, which will enable you to plug it in anywhere without frying the innards. You'll also need a plug adaptor for European outlets – often it's easiest to buy these before you leave home.

Also, your PC-card modem may or may not work once you leave your home country – and you won't know for sure until you try. The safest option is to buy a reputable 'global' modem before you leave home, or buy a local PC-card modem if you're spending an extended time in Europe. Keep in mind that the telephone socket in Slovenia

will probably be different from the one at home, so ensure that you have at least a US RJ-11 telephone adaptor that works with your modem. You can almost always find an adaptor that will convert from RJ-11 to the local variety. For more information on travelling with a portable computer, see www.teleadapt.com or www.warrior.com.

You might be able to log on from your hotel room for the cost of a local or long-distance call. Most newer, top-end hotels have Internet facilities for business customers, and rooms may have telephone jacks, usually USA standard (RJ-11). Adapters for older jacks can be found in electronic supply shops.

Major Internet service providers such as AOL (www.aol.com), CompuServe (www.compuserve.com) and AT&T (www.att business.net) have dial-in nodes throughout Europe; it's best to download a list of the dial-in numbers before you leave home. If

---

Ringing the Changes

In November 2000 Slovenia adopted a new system of telephone numbers. The old area codes of the form '06x' – a legacy of the former Yugoslavia – were replaced with two-digit area codes, and almost all land-line telephone numbers are now seven-digit. Mobile phone numbers have six digits and now use the codes 031, 040, 041 (Mobitel GSM) and 050 (Mobitel NMT).

All the telephone numbers in this book have been updated to the new system. However, if you have old contact numbers from a previous visit or from old publicity material, there are two ways of finding out their new equivalents. You can use the Internet and go to the Web page (in Slovene only) tis.telekom .si/Renum_si.htm – enter the old number in the box and click the button and the new one will be displayed. If you are in Slovenia, you can call the toll-free number ☎ 186, then the old number, and an automated service will read back the new number, first in Slovene and then in English

you access your Internet email account at home through a smaller ISP or your office or school network, your best option is either to open an account with a global ISP, like those mentioned above, or to rely on cybercafes and other public access points to collect your mail.

If you do intend to rely on cybercafes, you'll need to carry three pieces of information with you to enable you to access your Internet mail account: your incoming (POP or IMAP) mail server name, your account name and your password. Your ISP or network supervisor will be able to give you these. Armed with this information, you should be able to access your Internet mail account from any net-connected machine in the world, provided it runs some kind of email software (remember that Netscape and Internet Explorer both have mail modules). It pays to become familiar with the process for doing this before you leave home. A further option to collect mail through cybercafes is to open a free eKno Web-based email account online at www.ekno.lonelyplanet.com. You can then access your mail from anywhere in the world from any net-connected machine running a standard Web browser.

Most libraries in Slovenia have free Internet access terminals, as do an increasing number of mid-range and top-end hotels. Commercial cybercafes, where rates range from 400 to 800 SIT an hour, are limited to half a dozen in Ljubljana, and places in Bled, Kranjska Gora, Piran and Portorož.

INTERNET RESOURCES

The World Wide Web is a rich resource for travellers. You can research your trip, hunt down bargain air fares, book hotels, check on weather conditions or chat with locals and other travellers about the best places to visit (or avoid!).

There's no better place to start your Web explorations than the Lonely Planet Web site (www.lonelyplanet.com). Here you'll find succinct summaries on travelling to most places on earth, postcards from other travellers and the Thorn Tree bulletin board, where you can ask questions before

you go or dispense advice when you get back. You can also find travel news and updates to many of our most popular guidebooks, and the subWWWay section links you to the most useful travel resources elsewhere on the Web.

Useful Slovenian Web sites include:

www.slovenia-tourism.si The Slovenian Tourist Board site, where you can read and order brochures on various subjects
www.matkurja.com The Mat'Kurja (literally 'Mother Hen') site, a Yahoo-style directory of Slovenian Web resources
www.uvi.si/eng The Government Public Relations and Media Office site, full of facts and figures about Slovenia's politics, economy, culture and environment
www.sigov.si/mk The slick Ministry of Culture site, which has links to museums, galleries and other cultural institutions and news

BOOKS

Most books are published in different editions by different publishers in different countries. As a result, a book might be a hardcover rarity in one country while it's readily available in paperback in another. Fortunately, bookshops and libraries search by title or author, so your local bookshop or library is best placed to advise you on the availability of any given title.

There's no shortage of books in Slovenia but the big problem is price: printed material of any kind is terribly expensive here. An English-Slovene/Slovene-English pocket dictionary will set you back a whopping 9860 SIT, and even maps or simple town plans cost 950 to 1400 SIT each. Remember that Slovenes, who earn a lot less than many of us, have to pay those prices too. Slovenia is the third-smallest literature market in Europe and a fiction 'bestseller' in this country means 500 copies. It still manages to publish 15 books per 10,000 people a year, though, against the EU average of 10.

The books marked with prices in SIT can be purchased at most branches of Mladinska Knjiga or Cankarjeva Založba in Slovenia. See the Information section of individual towns for addresses.

Lonely Planet

Lonely Planet's *Slovenia* remains the only complete guidebook to the country in the English language and is available in most Ljubljana bookshops for 5585 SIT. LP's *Eastern Europe, Central Europe* and *Mediterranean Europe* guides all contain a chapter on Slovenia. Zoë Brân's *After Yugoslavia* (Lonely Planet Journeys series) recounts the author's trip through the former Yugoslavia.

The *Central Europe phrasebook* and *Eastern Europe phrasebook* both contain a Slovene chapter, with useful words and phrases.

Guidebooks

The only other guides devoted exclusively to the country are the Italian-language *Slovenia* (ClupGuide, Milan), the German *Slowenie* (Polyglott) and the French *Slovenie* (Le Petit Futé). Good local guides to the whole country are thin on the ground, but the colourful *Slovenia Tourist Guide* (Založba Mladinska Knjiga; 11,130 SIT) is a decent if expensive choice.

Walks in Old Ljubljana (Marketing 013 ZTP; 6267 SIT) by Ivan Stopar is an excellent source for the capital's history, while *Plečnik's Ljubljana* (Cankarjeva Založba; 1300 SIT) and *Outdoor Sculpture in Ljubljana* (DZS; 1490 SIT) by Špelca Čopič et al are good guides to architecture.

History & Politics

Janko Prunk's revised *Brief History of Slovenia* (Založba Grad; 2250 SIT) is a good start, but for something more in-depth, pick up a copy of *Independent Slovenia: Origins, Movements, Prospects* (Macmillan; UK£17.99) edited by Jill Benderly & Evan Craft. A dozen chapters written by Slovenian experts examine the country's history, political system and economy, both past and present. *Slovenia and the Slovenes: A Small State and the New Europe* (Indiana University Press; US$35.99) by Cathie Carmichael and James Gow was due to be published in the USA at the time of research.

Misha Glenny's excellent *The Fall of Yugoslavia* (Penguin; UK£7.99) is a thrilling, on-the-spot account of the war that led to Slovenia's independence, though it concentrates on events in Bosnia and Croatia and mentions Slovenia only in passing.

General

Art & Culture *Discover Slovenia* (Cankarjeva Založba; 3500 SIT) is not exclusively devoted to things artistic or cultural but contains very enlightening, easy-to-read sections on them and is updated annually. It also introduces the nation's history, geography and key cities and towns. *Traditional Arts & Crafts in Slovenia* (Domus; 6966 SIT) by Edi Berk is a lavishly illustrated guide to local folk craft and lore.

For something more specialised, the *Slovenia Art Guide* (Marketing 013 ZTP; 8100 SIT) by Nace Šumi is an excellent introduction to the architecture of Slovenia.

Picture Books There are plenty of these. The 80-page *Greetings from Slovenia* (Založba Mladinska Knjiga; 5979 SIT), available in English, German and Slovene, introduces the country's natural and cultural heritage with shots of daily life. The 244-page *Slovenia from the Air* (Založba Mladinska Knjiga; 13,620 SIT) by Matjaž Kmecl et al, in English, German and Slovene, has the standard 'Gosh!' photographs of Slovenia's mountains, lakes, coast and towns from on high. An excellent all-rounder, with superb photos and text that delves into Slovenian culture, history and folklore, is *Mountains of Slovenia* (Cankarjeva Založba; 3500 SIT), also by Kmecl et al. *Ljubljana* (Avante Garde; 6900 SIT) by Bogdan Kladnik & Daniel Rojšek is a basic introduction to the capital.

Language

The best compact dictionary is the English-Slovene/Slovene-English *Moderni Slovar/ Modern Dictionary* (Cankarjeva Založba; 9860 SIT) by Daša Komac. (Beware the seemingly cheaper orange paperback dictionaries – there are separate English-Slovene and Slovene-English volumes, so the total cost ends up much the same.)

If you're interested in learning Slovene on your own, then it's worth purchasing

Colloquial Slovene (Routledge, London; 11,300 SIT, UK£33.99), a course pack containing a 324-page book and two 60-minute cassettes. Another self-paced course is *Teach Yourself Slovene* (Hodder & Stoughton; UK£19.99), which includes a 196-page book and one cassette.

CD-ROMS

Two CD-ROMs available on Slovenia include *Slovenia: Facts and Figures* from Vitrum Publishing (7560 SIT), and *Slovenia: Museums & Galleries* (4820 SIT), with information and images from 47 museums and eight galleries around the country. Both are in English.

NEWSPAPERS & MAGAZINES

Slovenia counts four daily newspapers, the most widely read being *Delo (Work), Dnevnik (Daily)* and *Večer (Evening)*. Some 30 weeklies, fortnightlies and monthlies cover topics as diverse as agriculture, finance and women's fashion. *Mladina (Youth)* is a liberal weekly covering political and social issues.

There are no locally published English-language newspapers, but *Slovenia Weekly* (980 SIT), a 20-page political and business newsletter, is available. *Ljubljana Life* is an excellent bimonthly magazine with useful listings of restaurants, bars and nightlife. It's distributed free at Brnik airport and in hotels and tourist offices.

The Slovenian Emigrants' Centre (see Useful Organisations later in this chapter) publishes a glossy quarterly magazine in English called *Slovenija*. An annual subscription (four issues) for Great Britain is UK£17, including airmail postage. Write to: Slovenija Magazine, c/o SIM p.p.1548, Cankarjeva 1, 1001 Ljubljana, Slovenia.

Western newspapers available on the day of publication (late afternoon) at kiosks, hotels and bookshops in Ljubljana, Maribor and other tourist towns include the *International Herald Tribune*, the *Guardian International*, the *Financial Times* and *USA Today*. The European edition of the *Wall Street Journal* and the *Independent* are usually available the following day.

RADIO & TV

Radiotelevizija Slovenija (or RTV Slovenija for short) incorporates both radio and television. Radio Slovenija has three national channels (Radio Slovenija 1, 2 and 3), a regional one in Maribor (MM1) and special stations for the Hungarian minority in Murska Sobota (Radio Murski Val) and the Italian one in Koper (Radio Koper-Capodistria).

There's a nightly news bulletin in English and German year-round at 10.30 pm on Radio Slovenija 1. In July and August both Radio Slovenija 1 and 2 broadcast a report on the weather, including conditions on the sea and in the mountains, in English, German and Italian at 7.15 am. News, weather, traffic and tourist information in the same languages follow on Radio 1 at 9.35 am daily, except Sunday. Also in these months Radio 2 broadcasts weekend traffic conditions after each news bulletin from Friday afternoon through Sunday evening.

Radio 1 broadcasts on FM 88.0, 88.5, 89.0, 90.0, 90.9, 91.8, 92.0, 92.9, 96.4 and 100.1 MHz. Radio 2 can be found on FM 87.8, 91.6, 92.9, 93.5, 94.1, 95.3, 96.9, 97.6, 98.9 and 99.8 MHz.

Televizija Slovenija broadcasts on two channels, Slovenija 1 and Slovenija 2. A subsidiary called TV Koper-Capodistria broadcasts in Italian on the coast. There are three private commercial channels, including Kanal A, TV3 and the immensely popular Pop TV (which often show films and other programs in English with Slovene subtitles) and about 20 local cable stations in cities and towns across the country. In general, public television is not very good in Slovenia – you may have noticed all those satellite dishes on the roof tops pulling in Sky, BBC World, CNN and the Cartoon Network – with 'talking heads' droning on for hours about the state of privatisation and the like.

VIDEO SYSTEMS

If you want to record or buy video tapes to play back home, you won't get the picture if the image registration systems are different. Like most of Europe and Australia, Slovenia uses the PAL (Phase Alternative Line) system which is incompatible with the North American and Japanese NTSC standard or the SECAM system used in France.

PHOTOGRAPHY & VIDEO

Film and basic camera equipment are available throughout Slovenia, though the largest selection is in Ljubljana. Film prices vary, but a 36-exposure roll of 200 ASA Kodak, Agfa or Fuji colour print film will cost about 750 SIT, and a disposable camera about 1730 SIT. Slide film (36 exposures) is 1110 SIT. Kefo (✆ 01-438 40 00), in the lower level of the shopping arcade at Slovenska cesta 58 in Ljubljana, stocks a wide range of cameras and photographic equipment. It's open from 8 am to 7 pm weekdays and till 1 pm on Saturday.

There are processing labs in towns and cities nationwide where you can have your film developed and printed in a matter of hours. Print processing costs from 200 SIT per roll plus 55 SIT per print. Labs with fast processing in Ljubljana include Kodak Express at Slovenska cesta 55, and Foto Grad at Trg OF 13, opposite the train station. Both are open from 8 am to 7 pm weekdays and till 1 pm on Saturday.

Spare cassettes for video cameras are also widely available in photographic and electronic goods shops. A 60-minute 8mm cassette costs 850 SIT and a 90-minute Hi8 cassette is 2350 SIT.

TIME

Slovenia lies in the Central European time zone. Winter time is GMT/UTC plus one hour while in summer it's GMT/UTC plus two hours. Clocks are put forward one hour at 2 am on the last Sunday in March and turned back on the last Sunday in October. Without taking daylight savings time into account, the list below shows the time in various cities when it's noon in Ljubljana.

Los Angeles	3 am
New York	6 am
London	11 am
Paris	noon
Hong Kong	7 pm
Sydney	9 pm
Auckland	11 pm

Like a lot of other European languages, Slovene tells the time by making reference to the next hour – not the last one. Thus 1.15 is 'one quarter of two', 1.30 is 'half of two' and 1.45 is 'three quarters of two'.

ELECTRICITY

The electric current in Slovenia is 220V, 50Hz AC. Plugs are the standard European type with two round pins. Do not attempt to plug an American appliance into a Slovenian outlet without a transformer.

WEIGHTS & MEASURES

Slovenia uses the metric system exclusively. In supermarkets and outdoor markets, fresh food is sold by weight or by piece (kos). When ordering by weight, you specify by kilo or decagram (dekagram) – 50 decagrams is equal to half a kilo or roughly one pound. Fresh fish is almost always sold in restaurants by decagram, usually abbreviated as dag. For those who need help with the metric system, there's a conversion table at the back of this book.

Beer in a pivnica (pub) is served in either a 0.5L glass (veliko pivo, or large beer) or one measuring 0.3L (malo pivo, or small beer). Wine comes in 0.75L bottles or is ordered by the deci (decilitre, 0.1L). A 'normal' glass of wine is about 0.2L (dva deci), but no-one is going to blink an eye if you order three or more.

LAUNDRY

With 94% of all Slovenian households owning washing machines... well, good luck trying to find a self-service laundrette! The best place to look for do-it-yourself washers and dryers is at hostels, college dormitories and camping grounds, and there are a couple of places in Ljubljana that'll do your laundry reasonably quickly (see Laundry in the Information section of that chapter). Hotels will take care of it too, but at a price.

TOILETS

Finding a public lavatory is not always easy and when you do you'll probably have to pay anything from 30 to 50 SIT for the convenience. All train stations have toilets as do most shopping centres and department stores. The standard of hygiene is usually good.

HEALTH
Travel health depends on your predeparture preparations, your daily health care while travelling and how you handle any medical problem that does develop. While the potential dangers can seem quite frightening, in reality few travellers experience anything more than an upset stomach.

Tap water is 100% safe everywhere in Slovenia (though over-chlorinated on the coast). Mosquitoes can be a real pain around lakes and ponds – make sure you're armed with insect repellent, and wear long-sleeved shirts and long trousers around sundown.

The standard of medical care in Slovenia is adequate. Citizens of the UK have the right to free medical care in Slovenia upon submitting their passports. Austria, Belgium, Croatia, Germany, Hungary, Italy, Luxembourg, the Netherlands and Romania also have contractual arrangements with Slovenia for the guarantee of emergency medical assistance or treatment provided that the visitor submits the appropriate forms. In such cases, the medical assistance is free.

Check with your Ministry of Health or equivalent before setting out. Everyone else is entitled to treatment, but they must bear the cost.

Every city in Slovenia has a health centre where clinics operate from 7 am to 7 pm. Pharmacies are usually open from 7 am to 8 pm and at least one in each town or city is open round the clock.

A sign on the door of any pharmacy (*lekarna*) will help you find the nearest 24-hour service.

Predeparture Planning
Immunisations Although there are no official vaccination requirements for travellers to Slovenia, you should ensure that routine jabs for tetanus, diphtheria and polio etc, are up-to-date. Also, as Hepatitis A and rabies are both present, along with tick-borne encephalitis in forested areas, vaccinations against these should also be considered.

Plan ahead for getting your vaccinations as some require more than one injection, while some vaccinations should not be given together. Note that some vaccinations should not be given during pregnancy or to people with allergies – discuss with your doctor.

It is recommended you seek medical advice at least six weeks before travel. Be aware that there is often a greater risk of disease with children and during pregnancy. Discuss your requirements with your doctor (for more details about the diseases themselves, see the individual disease entries later in this section).

Diphtheria & Tetanus Vaccinations for these two diseases are usually combined and are recommended for everyone. After an initial course of three injections (usually given in childhood), boosters are necessary every 10 years.

Hepatitis A Hepatitis A vaccine (eg, Avaxim, Havrix 1440 or VAQTA) provides long-term immunity (possibly more than 10 years) after an initial injection and a booster at six to 12 months. Alternatively, an injection of gamma globulin can provide short-term protection against hepatitis A – two to six months, depending on the dose given. It is not a vaccine, but is ready-made antibody collected from blood donations. It is reasonably effective and, unlike the vaccine, it is protective immediately, but because it is a blood product, there are current concerns about its long-term safety. Hepatitis A vaccine is also available in a combined form, Twinrix, with hepatitis B vaccine. Three injections over a six-month period are required, the first two providing substantial protection against hepatitis A.

Polio Everyone should keep up to date with this vaccination, normally given in childhood. A booster every 10 years maintains immunity.

Rabies Vaccination should be considered by those who will spend a month or longer in Slovenia, especially if they will be cycling, caving or handling animals, and for children (who may not report a bite). Pretravel rabies vaccination involves having three injections over 21 to 28 days. If someone who has been vaccinated is bitten or scratched by an animal, they will require two booster injections of vaccine; those not vaccinated require more.

Health Insurance Make sure that you have adequate health insurance. See Travel

Insurance under Visas & Documents earlier in this chapter for details.

Other Preparations Make sure you're healthy before you start travelling. If you are going on a long trip make sure your teeth arc OK. If you wear glasses take a spare pair and your prescription.

If you require a particular medication take an adequate supply, as it may not be available locally. Take part of the packaging showing the generic name rather than the brand, which will make getting replacements easier. It's a good idea to have a legible prescription or letter from your doctor to show that you legally use the medication to avoid any problems.

Water Purification

If you are hiking or camping in Slovenia's mountains and are unsure about the water, the simplest way of purifying it is to boil it thoroughly. Chlorine tablets will kill many pathogens. Iodine is more effective and is available in tablet form. Follow the directions carefully and remember that too much iodine can be harmful.

Infectious Diseases

Hepatitis Hepatitis is a general term for inflammation of the liver. It is a common disease worldwide. There are several different viruses that cause hepatitis, and they differ in the way that they are transmitted. The symptoms are similar in all forms of the illness, and include fever, chills, headache, fatigue, feelings of weakness and aches and pains, followed by loss of appetite, nausea, vomiting, abdominal pain, dark urine, light-coloured faeces, jaundiced (yellow) skin and yellowing of the whites of the eyes. People who have had hepatitis should avoid alcohol for some time after the illness, as the liver needs time to recover.

Hepatitis A is transmitted by contaminated food and drinking water. You should seek medical advice, but there is not much you can do apart from resting, drinking lots of fluids, eating lightly and avoiding fatty foods. Hepatitis E is transmitted in the same way as hepatitis A; it can be particularly serious in pregnant women.

There are almost 300 million chronic carriers of **hepatitis B** in the world. It is spread through contact with infected blood, blood products or body fluids, for example through sexual contact, unsterilised needles and blood transfusions, or contact with blood via small breaks in the skin. Other risk situations include having a shave, tattoo or body piercing with contaminated equipment. The symptoms of hepatitis B may be more severe than type A and the disease can lead to long-term problems such as chronic liver damage, liver cancer or a long-term carrier state. Hepatitis C and D are spread in the same way as hepatitis B and can also lead to long-term complications.

There are vaccines against hepatitis A and B, but there are currently no vaccines against the other types of hepatitis. Following the basic rules about food and water (hepatitis A and E) and avoiding risk situations (hepatitis B, C and D) are important preventative measures.

HIV & AIDS Infection with the human immunodeficiency virus (HIV) may lead to acquired immune deficiency syndrome (AIDS), which is a fatal disease. Any exposure to blood, blood products or body fluids may put the individual at risk. The disease is often transmitted through sexual contact or dirty needles – vaccinations, acupuncture, tattooing and body piercing can be potentially as dangerous as intravenous drug use. HIV/AIDS can also be spread through infected blood transfusions. Fear of HIV infection should never preclude treatment for serious medical conditions.

Sexually Transmitted Diseases HIV/ AIDS and hepatitis B can be transmitted through sexual contact – see the relevant sections earlier for more details. Other STDs include gonorrhoea, herpes and syphilis; sores, blisters or rashes around the genitals and discharges or pain when urinating are common symptoms. In some STDs, such as wart virus or chlamydia, symptoms may be less marked or not observed at all, especially in women. Chlamydia infection can cause infertility in men and women before any symptoms have been noticed. Syphilis symptoms eventually disappear completely but the disease continues and can cause severe problems in later years. While abstinence from sexual contact is the only 100% effective prevention, using condoms is also effective. The treatment of gonorrhoea and syphilis is with antibiotics. The different sexually transmitted diseases each require specific antibiotics.

Cuts, Bites & Stings
See Less Common Diseases for details of rabies, which is passed through animal bites, and of tick-borne diseases.

Cuts & Scratches Wash well and treat any cut with an antiseptic such as povidone-iodine. Where possible avoid bandages and Band-Aids, which can keep wounds wet.

Bites & Stings Bee and wasp stings are usually painful rather than dangerous. However, in people who are allergic to them severe breathing difficulties may occur and require urgent medical care. Calamine lotion or a sting-relief spray will give relief and ice packs will reduce the pain and swelling.

Ticks You should always check all over your body if you have been walking through a potentially tick-infested area as ticks can cause skin infections and other more serious diseases. If a tick is found attached, press down around the tick's head with tweezers, grab the head and gently pull upwards. Avoid pulling the rear of the body as this may squeeze the tick's gut contents through the attached mouth parts into the skin, increasing the risk of infection and disease. Smearing chemicals on the tick will not make it let go and is not recommended.

Women's Health
Antibiotic use, synthetic underwear, sweating and contraceptive pills can lead to fungal vaginal infections, especially when travelling in hot climates. Fungal infections are characterised by a rash, itch and discharge and can be treated with a vinegar or lemon-juice douche, or with yogurt. Nystatin, miconazole or clotrimazole pessaries

or vaginal cream are the usual treatment. Maintaining good personal hygiene and wearing loose-fitting clothes and cotton underwear may help prevent these infections.

Sexually transmitted diseases are a major cause of vaginal problems. Symptoms include a smelly discharge, painful intercourse and sometimes a burning sensation when urinating. Medical attention should be sought and male sexual partners must also be treated. For more details see the section on Sexually Transmitted Diseases earlier. Besides abstinence, the best thing is to practise safer sex using condoms.

Less Common Diseases
The following diseases pose a small risk to travellers, and so are only mentioned in passing. Seek medical advice if you think you may have any of these diseases.

Lyme Disease This is a tick-transmitted infection which may be acquired throughout North America, Europe and Asia. The illness usually begins with a spreading rash at the site of the tick bite and is accompanied by fever, headache, extreme fatigue, aching joints and muscles and mild neck stiffness. If untreated, these symptoms usually resolve over several weeks but over subsequent weeks or months disorders of the nervous system, heart and joints may develop. Treatment works best early in the illness. Medical help should be sought.

Rabies This fatal viral infection is found in many countries. Many animals can be infected (such as dogs, cats and bats) and it is their saliva which is infectious. Any bite, scratch or even lick from an animal should be cleaned immediately and thoroughly. Scrub with soap and running water, and then apply alcohol or iodine solution. Medical help should be sought promptly to receive a course of injections to prevent the onset of symptoms and death.

Tick-Borne Encephalitis In the warmer months there is a risk of tick-borne encephalitis in forested areas. Encephalitis is inflammation of the brain tissue. Symptoms include fever, headache, vomiting, neck stiffness, pain in the eyes when looking at light, alteration in consciousness, seizures and paralysis or muscle weakness. Correct diagnosis and treatment require hospitalisation. Ticks may be found on the edge of forests and in clearing, long grass and hedgerows. A vaccine is available.

WOMEN TRAVELLERS
Travelling in Slovenia is no different from travelling in most Western European countries. If you can handle yourself in a less than comfortable situation, you'll be fine.

In the event of an emergency ring ☎ 080-124 or any of the following six numbers: ☎ 9780 to ☎ 9785.

GAY & LESBIAN TRAVELLERS
The gay association Roza Klub (☎ 01-430 47 40), at Metelkova ulica 6 in Ljubljana, organises a disco every Sunday night at the Klub K4 for gays and lesbians. Magnus (same phone number), the gay branch of the Student Cultural Centre (Študentski Kulturni Center; ŠKUC), puts out the monthly broadsheet *Kekec*. Lesbians can contact the ŠKUC-affiliated organisation LL (☎ 01-430 35 35), also at Metelkova ulica 6 in Ljubljana. It publishes a political, cultural and social review call *Lesbo*.

GALfon (☎ 01-432 40 89) is a hotline and source of general information for gays and lesbians. It operates from 7 to 10 pm daily. The Queer Resources Directory Web site (www.ljudmila.org/siqrd) contains a lot of information in English, but much of it is out of date.

DISABLED TRAVELLERS
Disabled facilities found throughout Slovenia include public telephones with amplifiers, pedestrian crossings with beepers, sloped pavements and ramps in government buildings, and reserved spaces in many car parks. An increasing number of hotels (mostly top-end, and mostly in Ljubljana) have rooms designed specially for wheelchair users; these are mentioned in the text.

Zveza Paraplegikov Republike Slovenije (☎ 01-432 71 38, fax 432 72 52), at Štihova

ulica 14 in Ljubljana, is a group that looks after the interests and special needs of paraplegics, and produces a special guide for its members (in Slovene only). Some cities produce useful brochures outlining which local sights and attractions are accessible for wheelchairs.

SENIOR TRAVELLERS
Senior citizens may be entitled to discounts in Slovenia on things like transport (eg, those over 60 years of age holding an international RES card get from 30% to 50% off on Slovenian Railways), museum admission fees etc, provided they show proof of their age. The minimum qualifying age is generally 60.

STUDENT TRAVELLERS
The Student Organisation of the University of Ljubljana (Študentska Organizacija Univerze Ljubljani; ŠOU; ☎ 01-433 70 10) at Kersnikova ulica 4 in the capital is a good place to mix with like-minded people. There's a small club/cybercafe there for socialising and surfing the net, and the organisation produces a useful brochure called *Slovenia for Foreign Students* in which, among lots of other things, the dates and locations of weekly student parties are listed. It's also on the Web at www.sou.uni-lj.si /mp/brochure. The Student Cultural Centre (ŠKUC; ☎ 01-430 47 40) at the same address organises cultural activities such as theatre productions.

Two agencies in Ljubljana – Erazem and Mladi Turist – deal specifically with students and young travellers. See Tourist Offices in the Ljubljana chapter for more information.

TRAVEL WITH CHILDREN
They may not have a whole lot of kids – the average family numbers just three people – but Slovenes love them and this is a very child-friendly country. The family goes everywhere together, and you'll see youngsters dining with their parents in even the poshest restaurants.

Successful travel with young children requires planning and effort. Don't try to overdo things; even for adults, packing too much into the time available can cause problems. And make sure the activities include the kids as well – balance that morning at Ljubljana's National Museum with an afternoon at the zoo on Rožnik Hill or a performance at the Puppet Theatre. Include children in the trip planning; if they've helped to work out where you will be going, they will be much more interested when they get there. Lonely Planet's *Travel with Children* is a good source of information.

Most car-rental firms in Slovenia have children's safety seats for hire for between €2.50 and €5, but it is essential that you book them in advance. The same goes for highchairs and cots (cribs); they're standard in some restaurants and hotels but numbers are limited. The choice of baby food, infant formulas, soy and other types of milk, disposable nappies (diapers) and the like is as great in Slovenian supermarkets as it is back home, but the opening hours may be different. Don't get caught out at the weekend.

USEFUL ORGANISATIONS

In addition to the organisations listed elsewhere in this chapter, the following may be helpful for visitors to Slovenia with special interests.

Archives of the Republic of Slovenia (Arhiv Republike Slovenije; ☎ 01-125 12 22, fax 216 551) Gruber Palace, Zvezdarska ulica 1, 1000 Ljubljana. If you are searching for your Slovenian roots, check first with the municipal government *(mestna občina)* or country office *(občina)*; they have birth and death certificates going back a century. Vital records beyond the 100-year limit are kept at the archives.

Slovenian Emigrants' Centre (Slovenska Izseljenska Matica; SIM; ☎ 01-126 32 84, fax 210 732) Cankarjeva ulica 1, 1000 Ljubljana. This office deals with ethnic Slovenes living abroad and publishes the quarterly magazine *Slovenija* in English (see Newspapers & Magazines earlier).

DANGERS & ANNOYANCES

Slovenia is not a violent or dangerous society. Firearms are strictly controlled, drunks are sloppy but docile and you'll see little of the vandalism that plagues cities like New York or London. The organised crime that is tormenting Russia and Eastern European countries has arrived in Slovenia, notably in Ljubljana and Maribor, but nowhere to the same degree.

Police say that 90% of all crimes reported in Slovenia involve thefts so take the usual precautions. Be careful of your purse or wallet in busy areas like bus and train stations, and don't leave it unattended on the beach, or in a hut while hiking. Lock your car at all times, park in well-lit areas and do not leave valuables visible.

In cities like Ljubljana, Maribor (sometimes called 'Mafiabor' because of organised crime based there) or Celje, you might be approached occasionally by beggars who ask for and then demand money. But it's usually nothing dangerous. One problem can be drunks on the road – literally or behind the wheel – especially around St Martin's Day (Martinovanje, 11 November) when grape juice (or *must*) legally becomes new wine and everybody has got to have a sip or three.

In the event of an emergency, the following numbers can be dialled nationwide:

Police (Policija)	☎	113
Fire (Gasilci)	☎	112
Ambulance (Reševalci)	☎	112
First Aid (Prva Pomoč)	☎	112
Automobile Assistance (AMZS)	☎	19 87

LEGAL MATTERS

The permitted blood-alcohol level for motorists is 0.5g/kg.

BUSINESS HOURS

The opening time *(delovni čas)* of shops, groceries and department stores is usually from about 7 or 8 am to 7 pm on weekdays and till 1 pm on Saturday. In winter they may close an hour earlier.

Bank hours vary but generally they're from 8 am to 5 or 6 pm weekdays (often with a lunchtime break of one or two hours) and till noon on Saturday. The main post office in any city or town (almost always the ones listed in the Information sections of the individual towns and cities) is open from 7 am to 8 pm weekdays, till 1 pm on Saturday and occasionally from 9 to 11 am on Sunday. Branch offices close earlier on weekdays and at noon on Saturday. They are always closed on Sunday.

Museums are usually open from 10 am to 6 pm Tuesday to Sunday from April to October; winter opening hours are shorter or at weekends only.

PUBLIC HOLIDAYS & SPECIAL EVENTS

Slovenia celebrates 14 holidays *(prazniki)* a year. If any of the following fall on a Sunday, then the Monday becomes the holiday.

New Year's holidays 1 & 2 January
Prešeren/Slovenian Culture Day 8 February
Easter & Easter Monday March/April
Insurrection Day 27 April
Labour Day holidays 1 & 2 May
National Day 25 June
Assumption Day 15 August
Reformation Day 31 October
All Saints' Day 1 November
Christmas Day 25 December
Independence Day 26 December

Though it's not a public holiday, St Martin's Day (11 November) is important as on this day, the winemakers' *must* (fermenting grape juice) officially becomes wine and can be sold as such. That evening families traditionally dine on goose and some restaurants offer a *Martinovanje* dinner of goose and young wine accompanied by folk music.

On Palm Sunday (the Sunday before Easter), people carry a complex arrangement of greenery and ribbons called a *butara* to church to be blessed. These *butare* end up as home decorations or are placed on the graves of relatives. On the eve of St Gregory's Day (11 March), children in certain Gorenjska towns and villages (eg, Tržič, Železniki) set afloat hundreds of tiny boats bearing candles.

Many towns celebrate Midsummer's Night (Kresna Noč; 23 June) with a large bonfire, and St John's Eve (30 April) is the night for setting up the maypoles and more bonfires. A *žegnanje* is a fair or some sort of celebration held on the feast day of a church's patron saint. Naturally a lot of them take place throughout Slovenia on 15 August, the Assumption of the Virgin Mary, especially at Ptujska Gora in Štajerska and at Sveta Gora, north of Nova Gorica.

Major cultural and sporting events are listed in the Special Events section of individual towns and cities. The following abbreviated list gives you a taste of what to expect.

January

Women's World Cup Slalom and Giant Slalom Competition (Golden Fox), Pohorje – one of the major international ski events for women, held on the slopes south-west of Maribor.

February

Kurentovanje, Ptuj – a 'rite of spring' celebrated for 10 days up to Shrove Tuesday and the most popular Mardi Gras celebrations in Slovenia (other important pre-Lenten festivals take place in Cerknica and Cerkno).

March

Ski Jumping World Cup Championships, Planica – three days of high flying on skis near Kranjska Gora.

April

International Kayak and Canoe Competition, Osilnica – five days of wild-water racing on the Kolpa River in Notranjska.
Day of Tulips, Volčji Potok (Kamnik) – Slovenia's largest flower and gardening show.

May

International Cycling Marathon, Novo Mesto – an international bicycle race which starts in Dolenjska.

June

Festival Lent, Maribor – a two-week extravaganza of folklore and culture held in late June/early July with stages set up throughout the old part of town.
Druga Godba, Ljubljana – a festival of world music.

July

International Summer Festival, Ljubljana – the nation's premier cultural event (music, theatre and dance) from mid-July through August.

Piran Musical Evenings & Primorska Summer Festival – concerts, theatre and dance events held in various locations in Piran, Koper, Izola and Portorož from early July to mid-August.
International Motocross Grand Prix of Slovenia, Orehova Vas (Štajerska).

August
Brežice Festival of Early Music, Brežice – a series of concerts of ancient music.

September
Kravji Bal (Cows' Ball), Bohinj – a zany weekend of folk dance, music, eating and drinking to mark the return of the cows from their high pastures to the valleys.

October
Dormouse Night (Polharska Noč), Cerknica – a celebration and feast during the very short dormouse-hunting season.
City of Women, Ljubljana – an international festival of contemporary arts, focusing on art and culture created by women.
Ljubljana Marathon – first run in 1996, this draws an increasingly international field.

December
Christmas concerts, Ljubljana and Postojna Cave.

ACTIVITIES
As 'Europe's activities playground', Slovenia offers an extensive range of outdoor activities, from the hedonistic (see the boxed text 'Taking the Waters') to the energetic (see the special section 'The Great Outdoors' for details of skiing, hiking, climbing, cycling, kayaking, caving and the like).

LANGUAGE COURSES
The most famous place to learn Slovene is the Centre for Slovene as a Second/Foreign Language (☎ 01-241 13 20, fax 425 70 55) at the University of Ljubljana's Faculty of Arts at Aškerčeva cesta 2. There are two-week winter courses in January/February for 70,000 SIT, four-week summer ones in July/August for 130,000 SIT, and an intensive course running from October to May for 436,000 SIT. Prices do not include room and board.

Other private schools offering courses in Slovene in Ljubljana include the Miklošič Educational Centre (☎ 01-231 69 78, fax 231 23 95) at Miklošičeva cesta 26 and the

---

Taking the Waters

Slovenia has 16 thermal spa resorts – two on the coast near Portorož and the others in the eastern half of the country in Štajerska, Dolenjska and Prekmurje. All are described in the relevant chapters of this book. They are excellent places not only for 'taking the cure' but also for relaxing and meeting people. Many resorts use the trendier Italian *terme* for 'spa' instead of the proper Slovene word *toplice* (thermal spring) or *zdravilišče* (health resort).

Only two – Dolenjske Toplice and Radenci – are really spa towns as such, with that distinctive *fin-de-siècle* feel about them. Others, like Atomske Toplice and Čatež Terme, are loud, brash places dedicated to all the hedonistic pursuits you care to imagine, complete with swimming pools, waterslides, tennis courts, saunas, beauty parlours and massage services. The Banovci spa near Veržej, about 13km south of Murska Sobota in Prekmurje, is reserved for naturists.

The Slovenian Tourist Board publishes a brochure entitled *Slovenian Spas*. Information on the resorts can be found on the Web at www.terme-giz.si.

Cene Štupar Center (☎ 01-234 44 00, fax 234 44 28) at Vojkova cesta 71. Courses of about 100 hours start at about US$450. The TIC in Ljubljana has a list of private tutors used to teaching foreigners.

WORK
Travellers on tourist visas in Slovenia are not supposed to accept employment, but many end up teaching English (going rate from €13 per hour) or even doing a little work for foreign firms without work permits. An organisation called MOST (☎ 01-425 80 67) at Breg 12 in Ljubljana, which is part of the Service International Civil (SIC), organises summer work camps in Slovenia on projects ranging from ecology research in Novo Mesto to working with Roma (Gypsies) near Murska Sobota.

[Continued on page 61]

THE GREAT OUTDOORS

Slovenes have a strong attachment to nature, and most lead active, outdoor lives from an early age. From skiing and climbing to caving and cycling, Slovenia has it all and it's always affordable. The Slovenian Tourist Board publishes specialist brochures on skiing, hiking, cycling, golfing and horse riding.

Skiing

Skiing is by far the most popular recreational pursuit in Slovenia, counting some 300,000 enthusiasts – the first written record of the sport in the 17th century refers to skiing on the Bloke Plateau in Notranjska province. Everyone seems to take to the slopes or trails in season (mainly December to March) and you can too at ski resorts across the country. They'e most crowded over the Christmas holidays and early February.

Slovenia's ski areas are small and unchallenging compared to the Alpine resorts of France, Switzerland and Italy, but the scenery is lovely and they do have the attraction of lower prices. For details of facilities at all of Slovenia's ski resorts, visit the Tourist Board's Web site at www.slovenia-tourism.si/skiing. You can also check piste maps and the latest weather and snow reports on the Web at www.smucisca.7-s.si, or call the Snow Hotline (Snežni Telefon; ☎ 040-940 100) – both in Slovene only.

The biggest downhill skiing area in Slovenia is Mariborsko Pohorje (altitude 336m to 1347m), in the hills immediately south of Maribor in Štajerska, with 64km of linked pistes suitable for skiers of all levels. It offers a ski and snowboard school, equipment rental and floodlit night skiing, as well as being a good starting point for ski touring in the forested hills of the Pohorje. Each year it hosts the Zlata Lisica (Golden Fox) competition, the opening event in the calendar of the women's slalom and giant slalom world championship. A day/week ski pass here costs 4300/18,800 SIT.

Kranjska Gora (810m to 1623m) in Gorenjska has 30km of pistes, but the skiing here is fairly dull and suited mostly for beginners and intermediates. It also suffers from a shortage of good restaurants and bars. Nevertheless, for foreign visitors, it is probably Slovenia's best-known and most popular ski resort, being easily accessible from Austria and Italy. It has a ski and snowboard school and equipment rental, and hosts the annual Vitranc Cup competition as part of the men's slalom and giant slalom world championship. A day/week pass will cost you 4200/24,700 SIT.

Krvavec (1450m to 1970m), in the hills north-east of Kranj in Gorenjska, is one of the best-equipped ski areas in the country, with ski (alpine

MARTIN HARRIS

and telemark) and snowboard schools, equipment rental, a good variety of piste and off-piste skiing, a freestyle mogul course, a speed-skiing track, a half-pipe and boarder-cross track, a ski shop and some good restaurants and bars. However, as it's only an hour's drive from Ljubljana, it's best avoided at the weekends unless you fancy sharing long queues with half the population of the capital. A day pass costs 4300 SIT (week passes are not available).

Many Slovenian skiers think that the Cerkno Ski Centre (900m to 1300m), north of Idrija in Primorska, offers some of the country's best downhill skiing. There are only 15km of marked pistes, served by five modern chairlifts and two tows, but all are covered by snow cannon which guarantee adequate snow cover throughout the season. There's a ski school, equipment rental and a self-service restaurant on the slopes, and a ski bus linking to the town of Cerkno 10km away. A day pass costs 3600 SIT.

For spectacular scenery, you can't beat Kanin (1600m to 2300m), Slovenia's highest ski resort, perched above Bovec in Primorska, and Vogel (570m to 1800m), above beautiful Lake Bohinj in Gorenjska. Both resorts enjoy stunning views north to Triglav and the Julian Alps, and from the top station at Kanin you can even see the Adriatic. Both have ski and snowboard schools and equipment rental, and are more suited to experienced skiers, with great opportunities for off-piste and ski-touring. A day/week pass at Kanin is 3400/13,600 SIT, and at Vogel 4000/23,000 SIT.

Snowboarders can find fun parks at Krvavec and Stari Vrh (near Škofja Loka in Gorenjska), and there are also half-pipes at Vogel and Rogla (near Zreče, north of Celje in Štajerska).

There are marked cross-country ski trails at most Slovenian resorts, but the major ones are at Kranjska Gora (40km), Rogla (30km), Mariborsko Pohorje (28km) and Logarska Dolina (15km). The forests of the Pokljuka Plateau west of Bled are crisscrossed with trails, and are host to annual world championship cross-country and biathlon events. International ski-jumping and ski-flying competitions are held at Planica, a few kilometres west of Kranjska Gora.

Hiking & Mountain Walking

Almost as many Slovenes hike as they do ski and one of the nicest things about this activity is that it gives you a chance to meet local people in an informal environment. Slovenia has an excellent system of trails – some 7000km of them – many of them waymarked with a red circle with a white centre. At crossings, there are signs indicating distances and walking times. The Julian Alps, the Kamnik-Savinja Alps and the Pohorje Massif are the most popular places for hiking, but there are some wonderful trails in the lower hills and valleys as well.

The E6 European Hiking Trail running from the Baltic to the Adriatic Seas enters Slovenia at Radlje in Koroška and continues for some 280km to a point south of Snežnik in Notranjska.

By air, foot, ski or bike, get out there and enjoy Slovenia's great outdoors, with its unparalleled scope for activities and sports.

The various faces of today's urban Slovenia, from sightseers to the chic, from cool dudes to crossword fans

The E7 European Hiking Trail, which connects the Atlantic with the Black Sea, crosses into Slovenia at Robič in Primorska, runs along the Soča Valley and then continues through the southern part of the country eastward to Bistrica ob Sotli in Štajerska before exiting into Croatia. The E6 and the E7 trails are marked by a red circle with a yellow centre.

The Slovenian Alpine Trail, which opened in 1953, runs from Maribor to Ankaran on the coast via the Pohorje Massif, the Kamnik-Savinja Alps, the Julian Alps and the Cerkno and Idrija hills. You can also follow the Slovenian Geological Trail (Slovenska Geološka Pot) in various parts of the country.

In 2000 Slovenia joined with Austria, Germany, Liechtenstein, Switzerland, Italy, France and Monaco to organise the development of the Via Alpina, a 150-day long-distance trail that will follow the entire arc of the Alps from Trieste to Monaco; it should be completed by 2006.

The Alpine Association of Slovenia (Planinska Zveza Slovenije; PZS; ☎ 01-434 30 22, fax 432 21 40, e info@pzs.si) at Dvoržakova ulica 9 in Ljubljana, the umbrella organisation of 231 local hiking and climbing clubs with 75,000 paid members, is the font of all information and can also organise mountain guides. It publishes hiking maps and a very useful list of the 165 mountain huts, refuges and bivouacs throughout Slovenia. It can tell you which huts are open and when, and whether you can book in advance via telephone. It also provides information about weather conditions and specific trails in Triglav National Park and elsewhere.

You can find more detailed information about the park and mountain huts in the Gorenjska chapter, or check the association's Web site (www.pzs.si) – it's mostly in Slovene, including the directory of mountain huts, but there are plans to translate it all into English.

MARTIN HARRIS

The guidebook *Walks in the Julian Alps* by Simon Brown (Cicerone, 1993; UK£8.99) describes 30 routes of varying difficulty around Bled, Bohinj, Kranjska Gora and Bovec.

Mountaineering & Rock Climbing

The peaks and rock faces of Slovenia's Julian Alps have nurtured some of the world's finest mountaineering talent. The most prominent achievement of recent years was Tomaž Humar's remarkable solo ascent of the south face of Dhaulagiri in the Himalayas in 1999.

The principal rock- and ice-climbing areas include Triglav's magnificent north face – where routes range from the classic Slovene Route (Grade II/III; 750m) to the modern Obraz Sfinge (Sphinx Face; Grade IX+/X-; 140m), with a crux 6m roof – and the impressive northern buttresses of Prisank overlooking the Vršič Pass. Currently the only mountaineering guidebook in English is *Julian Alps* (Cordee, 1990; UK£10.95) by Robin Collomb, which includes five classic routes on Triglav's north face.

Sport climbing *(športno plezanje)* is very popular here too – a new guidebook, *Plezalni vodnik Slovenije* (Slovenian Climbing Guide; Sidarta, 2000; 3990 SIT), covers all the sport-climbing crags in the country, with good topos and descriptions in English and German as well as Slovene. The nearest sport-climbing crags to Bled are only a few kilometres away at Bohinska Bela and Bodešče. Sidarta also publishes a series of regional climbing guides, in Slovene only, that covers all of Slovenia's mountaineering regions.

The ProMontana agency (see Adventure Sports in Bled's Activities section in the Gorenjska chapter) is a good source of information and advice on climbing in the Julian Alps. It also offers guided mountaineering and sport-climbing trips, and rents and sells equipment. Local climbers often meet for a beer in the Gostilna Pri Planincu in Bled.

Cycling

Slovenia is a wonderful country for cycling and mountain biking; the Slovenian Tourist Board publishes a cycling brochure and map detailing the most popular areas. There is also an English-language map *The Karst Regional Park by Bike,* available free from tourist offices, which describes a dozen different day trips.

You can rent mountain bikes at Bled and Bohinj, and the uncrowded roads around these resorts are a joy to cycle on. Other excellent areas for cycling are the Upper Savinja Valley in Štajerska, the Soča Valley, the Krka Valley and, in Koroška, the Drava Valley. Note that bikes are banned from the trails in Triglav National Park. Places where you can rent bikes are listed in the Getting Around sections of each town.

The Hotel Club Krnes (☎ 02-823 85 55, fax 823 81 14), in Črna na Koroškem in the Koroška region, sits at the centre of a network of marked forest and mountain trails ranging in length from 20km to 75km – some of which climb up to 1690m – and a downhill racecourse. It offers single or multiday guided mountain-bike tours, and organises training camps and competitions.

Kayaking, Canoeing & Rafting

River sports are hugely popular and practised anywhere there's running water, particularly on the Krka River in Dolenjska (at Žužemberk, Krka, Novo Mesto), the Kolpa in Bela Krajina (Vinica), the Sava River in Gorenjska (Šobec camping ground near Bled, Bohinj), the Savinja River in Štajerska (Logarska Dolina near Radmirje) and especially the Soča River in Primorska (Bovec).

The Soča is famed as one of the best white-water rafting and kayaking rivers in Europe, and is one of only a half-dozen rivers in the European Alps whose upper waters are still unspoiled. Agencies offering rafting and canoeing trips are detailed in the relevant regional chapters.

Caving

It is hardly surprising that the country that gave the world the word 'karst' is riddled with caves – around 6700 have been recorded and described. The deepest – Čehi II, on Jelenk peak north-west of Bovec – is 1370m deep. There are about two dozen show caves open to tourists, most of which – Škocjan, Postojna, Križna, Planina, Pivka, Predjama – are in the karst areas of Primorska and Notranjska.

The main potholing regions are the Notranjska karst, centred on Postojna, and the Julian Alps of Gorenjska and Primorska. The only English-language guidebook is *Cave Guide Slovenia* by Ian Bishop (UK£9), published in 1997 and available through caving shops in the UK.

Adventure sports agencies like ProMontana (see the Bled section in the Gorenjska chapter) and Soča Rafting (see the Bovec section in the Primorska chapter) can provide caving advice, equipment and guides.

Sailing & Windsurfing

Sailing is big on the Adriatic, but most yachties prefer the delights of Croatia's island-studded Dalmatian coast to the strictly limited attractions of Slovenia's 47km littoral. The country's main marina is at Portorož, where you can charter yachts and powerboats. Jonathan Yachting (☎ 05-677 89 35), at Solinarjev cesta 4, Portorož, has a range of boats for hire – a four- to six-berth Dufour 30 sailing yacht costs from €665 a week in winter to a high of €1175 a week in July and August.

You can rent sailing dinghies and windsurfers at several coastal locations, including the Portorož Marina, and Lake Bohinj in Gorenjska.

Fishing

Slovenia's mountain streams are teeming with trout and grayling, while its lakes and more sluggish rivers are home to pike, perch, carp and other coarse fish. The best rivers for angling are the Soča, the Krka, the Kolpa, the Sava Bohinjka near Bohinj and the Unica in Notranjska. The Soča is recognised as offering some of the finest trout fishing in Europe. But angling is not a cheap sport in Slovenia – a daily permit at the more popular rivers can cost you from 8000 to 14,000 SIT.

For information on licences and close seasons, contact the Fisheries Institute (Zavod za Ribištvo; ☎ 01-426 20 19, fax 425 51 85) at Župančičeva ulica 9 in Ljubljana. Its Web site (www2.arnes.si/~ljzavodri b6) is packed with useful information in English.

Horse Riding

Slovenia is a nation of horse riders. The world's most famous horse – the Lipizzaner of the Spanish Riding School in Vienna – was first bred at Lipica in Primorska. More than a dozen riding centres, registered with the Equestrian Association of Slovenia, rent horses and offer lessons, but there are just as many smaller stables and ranches renting privately.

One of the biggest – and most professional – outfits is the Kaval Horse Riding Centre (☎ 05-754 25 95, ☎/fax 754 27 10) at Prestranek Castle, about 6.5km south of Postojna. A weekend riding course, including on-site accommodation, costs 18,300 SIT; individual 45-minute lessons cost 5000 SIT.

Paragliding, Ballooning & Flying

Paragliding has really taken off in Slovenia, especially around Lake Bohinj and at Bovec in Gorenjska; at the latter you can take a tandem flight from the upper cable-car station on Kanin peak and descend some 2000m into the Bovec Valley. See Activities in the Bohinj (Gorenjska) and Bovec (Primorska) sections for more details.

You can take hot-air balloon flights at the Balonarski Center Barje (☎ 01-252 26 81) in Ljubljana – see the Activities section in the Ljubljana chapter for details.

Every self-respecting town or city in Slovenia seems to have an airstrip or aerodrome these days, complete with an enthusiastic *aeroklub* whose members will take you 'flight-seeing'. The Ljubljana-based Aeronautical Association of Slovenia (Letalska Zveza Slovenije; ☎ 01-422 33 33, fax 422 33 30) at Tržaška cesta 2 has a complete list, or see Activities in the following sections for details: Novo Mesto (Dolenjska), Lake Bled (Gorenjska), Slovenj Gradec (Koroška), Portorož (Primorska).

Bird-Watching

Although many Slovenes don't know it, Slovenia has some of the best bird-watching in Central Europe with well over 300 species spotted here. The Ljubljana Marsh (Ljubljansko Barje), Lake Cerknica and Sečovlje salt pans are especially good for sighting waterfowl and waders, and the arrival of the white storks in Prekmurje in April is a wonderful sight. There's no guidebook devoted specifically to the birds of Slovenia, but the *Collins Guide to the Birds of Britain and Europe* (UK£12.99) is very useful, as is *Where to Watch Birds in Eastern Europe* (Hamlyn; US$25) by Gerard Gorman.

Golf

There are 18-hole golf courses at Bled (Gorenjska), Mokrice Castle (Dolenjska) and Ptuj (Štajerska), and nine-hole courses at Lipica (Primorska), Volči Potok (Gorenjska), Atomske Toplice and Slovenske Konjice (both Štajerska), plus a tiny five-holer at Moravske Toplice.

By far the best course in the country – and one of the most beautiful in Europe – is the par 73 King's Course at Bled Golf & Country Club (☎ 04-537 77 00). See the Bled section in the Gorenjska chapter for details of green fees and equipment rentals.

[Continued from page 54]

ACCOMMODATION

Accommodation in Slovenia runs the gamut from riverside camping grounds, cosy *gostišča* (inns) and farmhouses to elegant castle hotels in Dolenjska and Štajerska. Slovenia counts some 78,000 beds in total – more than a third of them in hotels – so you'll seldom have trouble finding accommodation to fit your budget, except at the height of the season (July and August) on the coast, at Bled or Bohinj, or in Ljubljana.

Accommodation is never really cheap in Slovenia, and there are a lot of 'hidden' costs. First of all, virtually every municipality levies a tourist tax that can add 100 to 350 SIT to your bill (per person per night), and some places charge fees for registration and insurance (100 SIT or under). Many pensions and private rooms charge 30% extra for stays of fewer than three nights.

Accommodation owners are required by law to register foreign visitors with the local town hall, so many will insist on holding your passport or identity document during your stay. This can be a real pain when trying to change money, though most places are happy to return it to you after registering your details.

Camping

In summer, camping is the cheapest way to go, and there are conveniently located camping grounds *(kampi)* in all parts of the country. You don't always need a tent; some grounds have tents and inexpensive bungalows available for rent. The two best camping grounds for those who want to experience the mountains are Zlatorog on Lake Bohinj, and Špik at Gozd Martuljek near Kranjska Gora; on the coast, head for Jezero Fiesa near Piran. However, they can be crammed to bursting in summer. Prices vary according to the site and the season, but expect to pay anywhere between 700 and 1600 SIT per person a night. About one-third of the official camping grounds offer discounts of 5% to 10% to Camping Card International (CCI) holders.

It is forbidden to camp 'wild' in Slovenia, or to light fires outside recognised camping grounds and picnic areas.

Hostels & Student Dormitories

Only a half-dozen hostels in Slovenia are registered with the Holiday Association of Slovenia (Počitniška Zveza Slovenije; PZS), the national hostel organisation. There are two in Ljubljana and one each in Bled, Koper, Maribor and Rogla. Contact Mladi Turist (☎ 01-425 92 60) at Salendrova ulica 4 in Ljubljana for information. You are never required to have a Hostelling International (HI) card to stay at hostels here, but it sometimes earns you a discount or cancellation of the tourist tax.

A large portion of Slovenian pupils and students live away from home during the school year and sleep in a college dormitory *(dijaški dom)*. Some of the dorms in Ljubljana, Maribor, Idrija etc accept foreign travellers in summer for rates ranging from 1200 SIT for a bed in a dormitory to 2500 SIT for a single room.

Private Rooms & Apartments

The system of letting private rooms to travellers is not as developed or as widespread as it is in, say, Hungary, but you'll find them available through tourist offices and travel agencies at most tourist towns. Make sure you understand exactly where you'll be staying; in cities some private rooms are quite far from the centre.

You don't *have* to go through agencies or tourist offices; any house with a sign reading 'Sobe' or 'Zimmer frei' means that rooms are available. Of course, you have no recourse if things don't work out, but if you've seen the room and understand the price, what could go wrong?

In Slovenia, private rooms are ranked according to category. Category I rooms have their own shower or bath, Category II means running water in the room and a shower or bath in the corridor, Category III means no basin or tap in the room. Prices vary according to the town and season but typical rates range from 2000 to 3500 SIT per person per night.

The price quoted is usually for a minimum stay of three nights. If you're staying a shorter time (and you are usually welcome to), you'll have to pay 30% and sometimes as much as 50% more. The price of a private room never includes breakfast (600 to 900 SIT if available) or tourist tax. An extra bed in the room adds 20% on top.

Some agencies and tourist offices also have holiday apartments available that can accommodate up to six. One for two people could go for as low as 4500 SIT or as high as 8000 SIT per night.

Pensions & Guesthouses

Pensions and guesthouses go by several names in Slovenia. A *penzion* is, of course, a pension but more commonly it's called a *gostišče* – an inn or restaurant with accommodation *(prenočišče)* upstairs or somewhere out the back. They are more expensive than hostels but cheaper than hotels and often your only choice in small towns and villages. Generally speaking, a *gostilna* serves food and drink only, but some have rooms available as well. The distinction between a gostilna and a gostišče isn't very clear – even to most Slovenes.

Farmhouses

Over 230 working farms in Slovenia offer accommodation to paying guests, and for a truly relaxing break they can't be beaten. You either stay in private rooms in the farmhouse itself or in Alpine-style guesthouses somewhere nearby. Many of the farms offer activities such as horse riding, kayaking, trekking or cycling and allow you to help out with the farm work if you're interested.

The farms themselves can range from places where Old MacDonald would feel at home to not much more than a modern pension with a vegetable patch and orchard. The latter is especially true at tourist destinations like Bled and near the coast. You'll find much more isolated farmsteads with livestock and vineyards in Štajerska and Dolenjska.

ABC Farm and Countryside Holidays (☎ 01-510 43 20, fax 519 98 76, e infoabc@ siol.net) at Ulica Jožeta Jame 16 in Ljubljana

oversees much of the farmhouse accommodation in Slovenia. Its UK agent is Slovenia Pursuits (☎ 01767-631144), 14 Hay Street, Steeple Morden, Royston, Herts SG8 0PE.

Expect to pay about €15 per person in a room with shared bathroom and breakfast in the low season (from September to mid-December and from mid-January to June), rising to €25 per person for a room with private bath and meals in the high season (July and August). Apartments for groups of up to eight people are also available. There's no minimum stay but you must pay 30% more if it's fewer than three nights. Prices at very popular destinations like Bled and Logarska Dolina are higher.

Hotels

Slovenia's hotels are more expensive than other accommodation options. Rates vary seasonally, with July and August being the peak season and September/October and May/June the shoulder; ski resorts like Kranjska Gora and Maribor Pohorje also have a peak season from December to March. In Ljubljana, prices are constant all year. Many resort hotels, particularly on the coast, are closed in winter. As hotels seldom levy a surcharge for stays of one or two nights, they're worth considering if you're only passing through.

As with many other countries in the region, hotel standards in Slovenia vary enormously, and it's often difficult to tell what's what until you've stepped (or slept) inside. Many hotels have been privatised and/or renovated since 1998, sometimes leading to higher rates and occasionally to lower, more competitive ones. Among the finest and most expensive places to stay in Slovenia are the castle hotels at Otočec and Mokrice.

FOOD

The most important thing to remember about Slovenian food is that it is heavily influenced by its neighbours' cuisines. From Austria, there's sausage *(klobasa)*, strudel *(zavitek)* filled with fruit, nuts and/or curd cheese *(skuta)*, and Wiener schnitzel *(Dunajski zrezek)*. The ravioli-like *žlikrofi*, potato dumplings *(njoki)* and risotto *(rižota)* obviously have Italian origins, and Hungary has contributed *golaž* (goulash), *paprikaš* (piquant chicken or beef 'stew') and *palačinke,* thin pancakes filled with jam or nuts and topped with chocolate. Distinctively Slovenian dishes are often served with *žganci,* groats made from buckwheat, barley or corn, and make use of the country's excellent venison and game. Slovenian bread *(kruh)* is generally excellent, especially the braided loaves made around the holidays. A real treat is 'mottled bread' *(pisan kruh)* in which three types of dough (buckwheat, wheat and corn) are rolled up and baked.

Most Slovenian meals start with soup, usually chicken or beef broth with little egg noodles *(kokošja* or *goveja juha z rezanci)* and move on to a main course. This is for the most part meat *(meso)* with the favourites being pork *(svinjina),* veal *(teletina),* beef *(govedina)* and, in season, game like deer *(srna).* One excellent prepared meat is *pršut* – air-dried, thinly sliced ham that is nothing like the slimy Italian *prosciutto* from which it takes its name.

For some reason, chicken *(piščanec)* is not as common on a Slovenian menu as turkey *(puran)* and goose *(gos).* Slovenes are big eaters of fish *(riba)* and seafood – trout *(postrv)* from the Soča River is a real treat.

Slovenia is hardly a paradise for vegetarians, but this is changing and you're sure to find a few meatless dishes on any menu. Dumplings made with cheese *(štruklji)* and often flavoured with chives or tarragon are widely available as are dishes like *gobova rižota* (mushroom risotto) and deep-fried cheese *(ocvrti sir).* Another boon for vegies is that Slovenes love fresh salad *(solata)* – a most un-Slavic partiality – and you can get one any place, even in a countryside gostilna. In season (late summer and autumn) the whole country indulges in *jurčki* (wild cep mushrooms). A milk bar *(mlečna restavracija)* sells yogurt and other dairy products as well as *krofi* – tasty, jam-filled doughnuts.

Slovenian cuisine boasts two excellent and very different desserts. *Potica,* almost a national institution, is a kind of nut roll (though often made with savoury fillings too) eaten after a meal or with coffee or tea during the day. *Gibanica* from Prekmurje is a rich concoction of pastry filled with poppy seeds, walnuts, apples and/or sultanas and cheese and topped with cream. It's definitely not for dieters.

You should have no problem getting a snack between meals in Slovenia; many people eat a light meal *(malica)* at mid-morning. The most popular street food is a Balkan import called *burek* – flaky pastry stuffed with meat, cheese or even apple, not unlike Greek *tiropita,* and sold at outdoor stalls throughout the land. It is very cheap and filling but can be quite greasy.

It's customary to wish others at your table *'Dober tek!'* ('Bon appetit!') before starting your meal.

See the Food section of the Language chapter at the back of the book for a comprehensive glossary of menu items.

Places to Eat

Restaurants go by many names in Slovenia, but the distinctions are not always very precise. At the top of the heap, a *restavracija* is a restaurant where you sit down and are served by a waiter. A *gostilna* or *gostišče* has waiters too but it's more like an inn, with rustic decor and usually (but not always) traditional Slovenian dishes. A *samopostrežna restavracija* is a self-service establishment where you order from a counter and sometimes eat standing up. An *okrepčevalnica* and a *bife* serve simple, fast food like grilled meats and sausages; a *krčma* may have snacks, but the emphasis here is on drinking. A *slaščičarna* sells sweets and ice cream while a *kavarna* provides coffee and pastries.

Almost every sit-down restaurant in Slovenia has a multilingual menu with dishes translated into English, Italian, German and sometimes even French. But the translations are sometimes inaccurate or less than appetising; 'Beef Mouth in Salad' and 'Farinaceous Dishes' would have most would-be diners scratching their heads or running for the door. And then there are all those lists with 'daily recommendations' *('Danes priporočamo...')* that are frequently in Slovene only.

Many restaurants and inns have an inexpensive set lunch menu *(dnevno kosilo)* advertised on a blackboard outside. Three courses can cost less than 700 SIT.

It's important to remember that not many Slovenes eat in city-centre restaurants, unless they have to because of work or because they're entertaining. At the weekend, most will head 5km or 10km out of town to a gostilna or gostišče they know will serve them good, home-cooked food and local wine at affordable prices. For the traveller without a car, it can be difficult reaching these little 'finds' but this book includes as many as practical.

DRINKS
Wine

Slovenia has been making wine *(vino)* since the time of the Romans, and many of its wines today are of a very high quality indeed. Unfortunately, most foreigners know Slovenian wine – if at all – from the 'el cheapo' bottles of white Ljutomer Riesling or Laški Riesling served at college parties. For the most part, these are dull, unmemorable wines (the Ljutomer can be slightly sweet), but a trip to Slovenia will convince you that most of the best wines stay at home. For more detailed information, contact the Slovenian Academy of Wine (Slovenska Vinska Akademija; mobile ☎ 050-611 591, e sva-veritas@sva-veritas .si) at Grajska ulica 2, 2250 Ptuj, or get hold of the book *Wines of Slovenia* by Mišo Alkalaj (6690 SIT).

Slovenia counts 14 distinct wine-growing areas with some 22,000 hectares under cultivation, but there are just three major regions. Podravje ('on the Drava') extends from north-east Štajerska into Prekmurje and produces whites almost exclusively. Eschew the insipid Ljutomer and Laški Rizlings in favour of Renski Rizling (a true German Riesling), Beli Pinot (Pinot Blanc), Traminec (Traminer) or Šipon (Furmint), all whites.

Posavje is the region running from eastern Štajerska across the Sava River into Dolenjska and Bela Krajina. This region produces both whites and reds, but its most famous wine is Cviček, a dry light red, almost rosé wine that is distinctly Slovenian.

The Primorska wine region concentrates on reds, the most famous being Teran made from Slovenian Refošk grapes in the Karst region. It is a ruby-red, peppery wine with high acidity that goes perfectly with pršut and game. Other wines from this region are Malvazija, a yellowish white from the coast that is light and dry and good with fish, and red Merlot, especially the one from the Vipava Valley.

On a Slovenian wine label, the first word usually identifies where the wine comes from and the second the grape varietal: Vipavski Merlot, Mariborski Traminec etc. But it's not always like that. Some bear names according to their place of origin such as Jeruzalemčan, Bizeljčan, Haložan.

There is no *appellation contrôlée* as such in Slovenia; *kontrolirano poreklo* is a trademark protection that usually – but not in every instance – suggests a certain standard. When choosing wine, look for the words *vrhunsko vino* (premium wine) and a gold label, *kakovostno vino* (quality wine) and a silver one, and *namizno vino* (table wine) with a bronze-coloured label. They can be red, white or rosé and dry, semidry, semisweet or sweet. Vintage is not as important with most Slovenian wines as it is with French and Californian ones.

The best sparkling wine is Zlata Radgonska Penina from Gornja Radgona.

Slovenes usually drink wine with meals or socially at home; it's rare to see people sit down to a bottle at a cafe or pub. As elsewhere in Central Europe, a bottle or glass of mineral water is ordered along with the wine when eating. It's a different story in summer, when spritzers (wine coolers) of red or white wine mixed with mineral water are consumed in vast quantities.

All of the wine-producing areas have a 'wine route' *(vinska cesta)* or two – 20 in all – that you can follow in a car or on a bicycle. These are outlined on the useful *Slovenian Wine Map* (Imago) available from most bookshops in Ljubljana. Along the way, you can stop at the occasional cellar *(klet)* offering wine tastings or at a *vinoteka* in wine towns or cities (Maribor, Metlika, Ptuj, Rogaška Slatina, Dobrovo near Nova Gorica and Brežice).

Beer
Beer *(pivo)* is very popular in Slovenia, especially outside the home and among younger people. Štajerska hops *(hmelj)* grown in the Savinja Valley are used locally, and are also widely sought by brewers from around the world. They have been described as having the flavour of lemon grass.

Slovenia has three breweries: Union in Ljubljana, Laško in the town of that name south of Celje, and the small Gambrinus in Maribor. Union is lighter-tasting and sweeter than Zlatorog, the excellent and ubiquitous beer (it has about 50% of the market) brewed by Laško. Union also produces an alcohol-free beer called Uni, a decent stout called Črni Baron and a shandy called Radler. Laško's alcohol-free brew is called Gren and its shandy is called Roler. It also makes a 'light' beer called Lahko.

In a pub *(pivnica)*, draught beer is drunk in 0.5L mugs or 0.3L ones. Both locally brewed and imported beers are also available at pubs, shops and supermarkets in 0.5L bottles or 0.3L cans.

Other Drinks
An alcoholic drink as Slovenian as wine is *žganje,* a strong brandy or eau de vie distilled from a variety of fruits but most commonly apples, plums and cherries. Another type is *medeno žganje* (or *medica*) flavoured with honey, but the finest is Pleterska Hruška, a pear brandy (or *viljemovka*) made by the Carthusian monks at Pleterje Monastery near Kostanjevica na Krki in Dolenjska. They let a pear grow into a bottle that has been placed upside-down on a branch, then 'pick' bottle and pear together and pour brandy inside. Drink too much of this stuff and you'll see visions of the place the monks warn us all about.

Many Slovenes enjoy a *špička* – slang for a little glass of schnapps – during the day as a pick-me-up. You'll probably get the invitation *'Pridite na kupico'* ('Come and have a drop') more than once.

Most international brands of soft drinks are available in Slovenia, but mineral water *(mineralna voda)* from Radenci (Radenska) or Rogaška Slatina seems to be the most popular libation for teetotallers in pubs and bars. Juice *(sok)* is usually boxed fruit 'drink' with lots of sugar or a drink made with syrup.

Italian espresso is the type of coffee *(kava)* most commonly served but thick, sweet Turkish coffee is also popular, especially at home. If you don't want it too sweet, say *'Ne sladko, prosim'*. Coffee is good everywhere except at hotel breakfasts when you'll almost invariably be served a cup of lukewarm, milky, ersatz coffee.

Tea *(čaj)* is becoming an increasingly popular drink, a trend reflected in the number of tearooms – many called Čajnik (teapot) or Čajna Hiša (tea house) – that have sprung up all over the place.

There are more words and phrases in Slovene in the Language chapter and the Glossary at the back of the book.

ENTERTAINMENT
Discos & Clubs
Clubs are the most popular form of entertainment for young people and are always good fun. The biggest and most rollicking are in Ljubljana and on the coast, but you'll find them even in small provincial towns.

Classical Music, Opera, Ballet & Theatre
Slovenia has a lot of excellent, high-brow entertainment on offer – particularly classical music and theatre. Ljubljana alone counts seven theatres, an opera house where ballets are also performed, and two symphony orchestras. Maribor has a resident opera company as well as a symphony orchestra, a ballet company and two theatres. There are also theatres in Celje, Kranj and Koper. Many other towns have chamber orchestras and string quartets that perform in churches, castles, museums and civic centres.

Folk & Traditional Music
Folk-music performances are usually local affairs and are very popular in Dolenjska, Bela Krajina and even Bled (especially in

July and August during the Okarina World Music Festival). Črnomelj is the centre of Slovenian folk music and as many as 50 bands playing stringed instruments like the *tamburica,* the *berdo* (contrabass), the guitar-like *brač* and the *bisernica* (lute) are active in the area. Flyers and posters in these areas are always announcing folk nights at halls and cultural centres.

Cinema

Foreign films are never dubbed into Slovene but are shown in their original language with subtitles. The choice, even in Ljubljana, is not very great – each film usually travels from one cinema to the next – but you're sure to find something of interest.

SPECTATOR SPORTS

Slovenia – a land where skiing *(smučanje)* is king – has produced numerous world-class ski champions, including Roman Perko in cross-country racing, Mitja Dragšič in men's slalom and Špela Pretnar in women's slalom (World Cup winner in 1999/2000). But the national hero is the young Primož Peterka, the ski-jumping World Cup winner in 1996/97 and 1997/98. Peterka was the first ski-jumper to pass the 200m mark in Planica in 1994. Extreme skier Davo Karničar became a household name in 2000 when he succeeded in making the first uninterrupted descent of Mt Everest on skis.

Until recently Slovenia was one of the few countries in Europe where football *(nogomet)* is not a national passion, but interest in the sport has increased following the national side's plucky performance in the 2000 European championship.

Basketball *(košarka)* has always been more popular than soccer. The Union Olimpija team reigns supreme and one of its members, the slam dunker Marko Milič, was hunted by the American NBA in 1996. Other popular spectator sports are ice hockey *(hokej),* with Olimpija Ljubljana at the top, and volleyball *(rokomet),* with the team from Celje excelling.

Slovenia punches well above its weight when it comes to Olympic medals, regularly winning more gold medals per head of population than Russia or the USA. The first Olympic medal won by a Slovene was a silver won by Rudolf Cvetko at Stockholm in 1912 as part of the Austrian fencing team. But the most celebrated Slovenian Olympic athlete was the gymnast Leon Štukelj (1898–1999), who took two gold medals at Paris in 1924, a gold and two bronzes at Amsterdam in 1928 and a silver at Berlin in 1936. Štukelj was the oldest surviving Olympic champion in the world until his death at the age of 100.

Slovenia took two golds in the 2000 Sydney Olympics, in the men's double sculls and the 50m rifle shooting. These were added to an impressive tally that includes two bronze medals at Barcelona in 1992 (rowing) and two silvers at Atlanta in 1996 (white-water kayaking and 100m hurdles). At the 1994 Winter Olympics at Lillehammer in Norway, skiers Katja Koren, Alenka Dovžan and Jure Košir all won bronze medals.

SHOPPING

For folk crafts and other souvenirs it's best to go to the source where you'll find the real thing and not mass-produced kitsch – go to Idrija or Železniki for lace, Ribnica for wooden household utensils, Bohinj for carved wooden pipes with silver lids, Prekmurje for Hungarian-style black pottery, Kropa for objects made of wrought iron and Rogaška Slatina for crystal. Some people think they're tacky, but traditional beehive panels *(panjske končnice)* painted with folk motifs make original and unusual souvenirs – especially the ones showing a devil sharpening a gossip's tongue on a grindstone. We all know a few people back home who should hang that one up as an icon and light votive candles in front of it.

The silver-filigree jewellery you'll see for sale in shops all over the country, but especially on the coast, is not distinctively Slovenian but a good buy nonetheless. Almost all of the shops are owned and run by ethnic Albanians who brought the craft here from Kosovo.

Ski equipment and ski-wear are of very high quality. Elan skis and snowboards are made in Begunje na Gorenjskem near Bled and Alpina boots at Žiri, north-east of Idrija.

Natural remedies, herbal teas and apian products like beeswax, honey, pollen, propolis and royal jelly can be found in speciality shops around the country.

A bottle or two of Slovenian wine makes a great gift. Buy it from a vinoteka or a dealer with a large selection like Simon Bradeško or Vinoteka Movja (see the Ljubljana chapter). A couple of monasteries in Dolenjska – the Cistercian one at Stična near Ivančna Gorica and the Carthusian one at Pleterje – sell their own brand of firewater made from fruits and berries. It's fragrant but very potent stuff.

Getting There & Away

AIR
Airports & Airlines

While there are international airports at Maribor in Štajerska and Portorož in Primorska, only Brnik airport (☎ 04-202 27 00), 23km north-west of Ljubljana, receives regular scheduled flights. The airport is open from 6 am to 10 pm daily and has a hotel booking board with telephone in the arrivals hall and an information desk in the departures area. The Kompas travel agency has a representative office, and there are car-rental firms, including ABC, Avis, Budget, Europcar, F-Rent-a-Car, National and Hertz. There's also a post office, duty-free shop, and a la carte and self-service restaurants. You can change money in the departures area at the Nova Ljubljanska Banka branch (open 8 am to 3 pm weekdays) or at the newsagent (open from 7 am to 8 pm daily). In arrivals there's an SKB Banka ATM dispensing tolars and an automatic exchange machine that can change 15 different currencies into tolars.

The Slovenian national carrier, Adria Airways (airline code JP; ☎ 01-431 30 00 in Ljubljana, ☎ 04-236 34 62 at Brnik airport), flies nonstop to Ljubljana from more than 20 cities in Europe and the Middle East. It also has charters during summer months to several other destinations, including Athens, Barcelona, Istanbul and Malta. You can check the latest timetable on its Web site at www.adria.si.

Other airlines that serve Ljubljana include Aeroflot (SU) from Moscow, Austrian Airlines (OS) from Vienna, Lufthansa (LH) from Frankfurt and Munich, and Swissair (SR) from Zürich.

Departure Tax

A departure tax of 2700 SIT is collected from everyone leaving Slovenia by air. This is almost always included in the ticket price.

The UK & Continental Europe

Adria flies nonstop to Ljubljana from more than 20 cities, with daily flights from Brussels, Frankfurt, London (LHR), Munich, Paris (CDG), Pristina, Sarajevo, Skopje, Split, Vienna and Zürich, and one to three flights a week from Amsterdam, Copenhagen, Moscow, Ohrid (Macedonia), Stockholm and Tirana.

At the time of writing, the cheapest return excursion fare from London to Ljubljana was around UK£210 with Adria. If you can spare an extra day or so in travelling time, you can save money by taking a cheap flight from London Stansted to either Venice-Treviso (RyanAir; www.ryanair.com) or Venice-Marco Polo (Go; www.go-fly.com) and taking the train from there to Slovenia. By booking several months in advance and travelling midweek you can get a return flight to Venice for as little as UK£78 including taxes; the extra costs of the airport bus to Mestre train station (30 minutes) and

Air Travel Glossary

Cancellation Penalties If you have to cancel or change a discounted ticket, there are often heavy penalties involved; insurance can sometimes be taken out against these penalties. Some airlines impose penalties on regular tickets as well, particularly against 'no-show' passengers.

Courier Fares Businesses often need to send urgent documents or freight securely and quickly. Courier companies hire people to accompany the package through customs and, in return, offer a discount ticket which is sometimes a phenomenal bargain. However, you may have to surrender all your baggage allowance and take only carry-on luggage.

Full Fares Airlines traditionally offer 1st class (coded F), business class (coded J) and economy class (coded Y) tickets. These days there are so many promotional and discounted fares available that few passengers pay full economy fare.

Lost Tickets If you lose your airline ticket an airline will usually treat it like a travellers cheque and, after inquiries, issue you with another one. Legally, however, an airline is entitled to treat it like cash and if you lose it then it's gone forever. Take good care of your tickets.

Onward Tickets An entry requirement for many countries is that you have a ticket out of the country. If you're unsure of your next move, the easiest solution is to buy the cheapest onward ticket to a neighbouring country or a ticket from a reliable airline which can later be refunded if you do not use it.

Open-Jaw Tickets These are return tickets where you fly out to one place but return from another. If available, this can save you backtracking to your arrival point.

Overbooking Since every flight has some passengers who fail to show up, airlines often book more passengers than they have seats. Usually excess passengers make up for the no-shows, but occasionally somebody gets 'bumped' onto the next available flight. Guess who it is most likely to be? The passengers who check in late.

Promotional Fares These are officially discounted fares, available from travel agencies or direct from the airline.

Reconfirmation If you don't reconfirm your flight at least 72 hours prior to departure, the airline may delete your name from the passenger list. Ring to find out if your airline requires reconfirmation.

Restrictions Discounted tickets often have various restrictions on them – such as needing to be paid for in advance and incurring a penalty to be altered. Others are restrictions on the minimum and maximum period you must be away.

Round-the-World Tickets RTW tickets give you a limited period (usually a year) in which to circumnavigate the globe. You can go anywhere the carrying airlines go, as long as you don't backtrack. The number of stopovers or total number of separate flights is decided before you set off and they usually cost a bit more than a basic return flight.

Transferred Tickets Airline tickets cannot be transferred from one person to another. Travellers sometimes try to sell the return half of their ticket, but officials can ask you to prove that you are the person named on the ticket. On an international flight tickets are compared with passports.

Travel Periods Ticket prices vary with the time of year. There is a low (off-peak) season and a high (peak) season, and often a low-shoulder season and a high-shoulder season as well. Usually the fare depends on your outward flight – if you depart in the high season and return in the low season, you pay the high-season fare.

a return train ticket to Ljubljana (5½ hours) add less than UK£40 to the total.

Return flights from Frankfurt to Ljubljana with Adria or Lufthansa cost around €335 or €240 from Munich. You can fly from Paris (Adria) for €328, and from Vienna for €298 (Adria or Austrian Airlines). From Sarajevo to Ljubljana, expect to pay around €265 return.

The USA & Canada

Travellers from North America will get the best deal by flying into one of the major European hubs, like Frankfurt, London or Paris, and connecting there with a flight to Ljubljana. A return flight from New York to Ljubljana via Paris with Air France and Adria costs from US$1200. Return fares from Toronto begin at US$1150.

Australia

The best way to get to Slovenia is to fly Qantas from Sydney or Melbourne to Frankfurt or London, and connect there with an Adria flight to Ljubljana. Return fares begin at around A$3600.

The Middle East

Adria flies nonstop twice a week between Ljubljana and Tel Aviv, and has daily charter flights to Istanbul.

LAND

Slovenia is reasonably well connected by road and rail to its four neighbours. Note that many bus and train timetables use the Slovene names of foreign cities – eg, Benetke for Venice, Celovec for Klagenfurt, Budimpešta for Budapest – check the Alternative Place Names appendix at the back of this book.

Bus

Many international buses arrive and depart from Ljubljana bus station (for information, ring ☎ 01-434 38 38 or ☎ 090-4030), but you can also pick them up in cities and towns around Slovenia.

Italy Up to 17 buses a day run between Koper and Trieste (520 SIT, 30 minutes),

20km to the north-east, between 6 am and 7.30 pm on weekdays only – though there is also one bus at 7.30 pm on Saturday. There's a bus from Ljubljana to Trieste (1810 SIT, 1½ hours) at 6.25 am Monday to Saturday. The bus station in Trieste is immediately south-west of the train station in Piazza Libertà.

Nova Gorica is the easiest exit/entry point between Slovenia and Italy as you can catch up to five buses a day to/from the Italian city of Gorizia, just across the border, or simply walk across the border at Rožna Dolina (Casa Rossa in Italian). Tarvisio in north-east Italy is linked with Kranjska Gora by two buses, which run at 9.35 and 11.45 am Monday to Saturday (490 SIT, 25 minutes).

Croatia & Yugoslavia The coastal towns of Koper, Piran and Portorož are the best places for making your way to Croatian Istria by bus. Ideal Turist (☎ 05-639 86 08) in Koper runs an express minibus service in summer from Trieste to Belgrade via Koper and Ljubljana. It departs Koper at 4.30 am daily and Ljubljana at 6 am, arriving in Belgrade at 12.30 pm; the one-way Ljubljana-Belgrade fare is 17,800 SIT, and the Ljubljana-Koper leg is 2000 SIT. The return trip departs Belgrade at 3 pm daily, arriving in Koper at 11.15 pm.

There's a bus at 2.20 pm daily from Koper to Banja Luka (3960 SIT, six hours) in Bosnia-Hercegovina, and one at 4.25 pm daily from Piran to the Croatian coastal towns of Poreč, Pula and Rovinj. There's also a bus at 10.10 am Monday to Saturday from Koper to Rijeka.

From Ljubljana, three buses a day leave for Zagreb (2750 SIT, 2½ hours) and for Belgrade (6000 SIT, 7½ hours), and there are departures at 6.35 am on Saturday and Sunday to Varaždin (3390 SIT, four hours). A bus departs at 7.40 pm daily for Rijeka (1870 SIT, three hours) and Split (5250 SIT, 12 hours).

You can also count on four buses a day from Maribor and three a day from Ptuj to Varaždin and Zagreb, and one bus on Saturday (8.20 am) from Celje to Varaždin.

Germany & Austria Deutsche Touring
(☎ 069-79 03 50 in Frankfurt or ☎ 01-090
40 30 in Ljubljana) operates an overnight
bus between Frankfurt and Ljubljana (€70,
13 to 15 hours), leaving Frankfurt at 1.30 pm
daily and picking up at Stuttgart (4.30 pm),
Ulm (6 pm) and Munich (7.15 pm). The
northbound bus leaves Ljubljana at 7.30 pm
daily. Buy tickets at Ljubljana bus station
at least 24 hours in advance. A daily bus
(6.50 pm) also links Maribor with Munich
and Frankfurt.

There's a weekly bus from Ljubljana to
Klagenfurt (Celovec in Slovene) in Austria
(1680 SIT, 1¾ hours), departing at 6.15 am
Wednesday, and a daily bus (7.30 am) from
Maribor to Graz. One bus daily in summer
goes to Villach (Beljak in Slovene) from
Kranjska Gora, and there are daily buses to
Klagenfurt from Dravograd.

Hungary From Ljubljana you can catch a
bus to Budapest at 10 pm on Tuesday,
Thursday and Friday. There's also a service
at 5.30 am on Thursday to Lenti. Otherwise
take one of up to five daily buses to Lendava; the Hungarian border is 5km north.
The first Hungarian train station, Rédics, is
only 2km beyond the border. From Rédics,
there are up to 10 trains a day (1¼ hours,
49km) to Zalaegerszeg, from where there
are three direct trains (3¾ hours) and five
buses to Budapest.

Train
Slovenian Railways (Slovenske Železnice;
SŽ) links up with the European railway net-
work via Austria (Villach, Salzburg, Graz,
Vienna), Germany (Munich), Italy (Trieste,
Venice, Milan), Hungary (Budapest) and
Croatia (Zagreb, Karlovac, Rijeka, Pula).
SŽ trains are hardly luxurious, but they are
clean and punctual.

The international trains listed below are
expresses, and some require a seat reservation. The supplement on InterCity (IC) trains
is 200 SIT; the one EuroCity (EC) train
which serves Slovenia (the air-conditioned
Mimara linking Berlin and Zagreb via
Munich, Salzburg and Ljubljana) charges a
supplement of 564 SIT.

On some trains, including the *Venezia
Express, Lisinski* and *Opatija,* sleepers are
available in 1st and 2nd class, and couch-
ettes in 2nd class. Surprisingly not all express trains have dining or even buffet cars;
bring along some snacks and drinks as vendors can be few and far between.

To reduce confusion, specify your train
by the name and number listed on the
timetable when requesting information or
buying a ticket. You can do both at the train
stations, of course, but it is often easier to
deal with the less-harried staff at Slovenijaturist offices. They sell train tickets of all
types and have branches at Slovenska cesta
58 in Ljubljana, and at the train stations in
Celje and Maribor.

Tickets on SŽ trains are valid for two
months.

Tickets & Discounts Wasteels 26 (BIJ)
tickets, available to people under 26 for
2nd-class travel on selected routes, offer
discounts of between 30% and 40%. Sample Wasteels fares include Vienna (7463
SIT), Prague (12,373 SIT), Rome (9478
SIT) and Kraków (6498 SIT). BIJ tickets
must be purchased at Slovenijaturist offices
– not the regular ticket windows in the train
stations – or at the Wasteels office at the
Ljubljana train station. Fare reductions are
also available to children between six and
12 years of age (50%).

SŽ and Slovenijaturist sell Inter-Rail
passes to those under 26; older travellers
can get an Inter-Rail 26+ card, which is
about 40% more expensive. Theoretically,
you must have resided in the country of purchase for six months. Inter-Rail divides
Europe into seven zones (A to G). Passes
for one, two, three or all seven are available.
A 22-day pass valid in Zone G only, which
includes Slovenia, Italy, Greece and the
ferry companies serving the last two, costs
UK£129 (40,103 SIT). Other passes are
valid for a month. A two-zone pass is
UK£169 (53,053 SIT), three zones UK£195
(60,572 SIT) and a pass for all seven zones
(called Global) is UK£219 (69,136 SIT).

Inter-Rail cards should be treated as cash
for you can make no claims in the event of

loss or theft. Eurail passes and Flexipasses are neither valid nor sold in Slovenia.

Adult (26 or over) and youth (under 26) Euro Domino passes, allowing three to eight days of midnight-to-midnight travel over a one-month period, are also available. An eight-day adult/youth pass for use within Slovenia costs UK£53/41. Euro Domino passes are only available to those who have resided in Europe for at least six consecutive months prior to the date of purchase. A pass for Slovenia must be bought before your departure; it cannot be bought in Slovenia (although passes for use in other countries can).

Italy The *Venezia Express* and the IC *Drava* link Venice to Budapest via Trieste, Ljubljana and Zagreb, each train passing through the Slovenian capital once a day in each direction. Departures from Ljubljana to Venice (5940 SIT, 5½ hours) are at 3.20 am and 4.10 pm; from Venice to Ljubljana at 8.14 am and 9.22 pm.

Another daily train at 7.55 am links Ljubljana with Villa Opicina via Pivka year-round, with a 20-minute transfer by bus to Trieste train station (1810 SIT, three hours), where trains depart hourly to Venice.

Croatia & Yugoslavia There are six trains a day from Ljubljana to Zagreb via Zidani Most (2350 SIT, 2½ hours), two a day to Rijeka via Pivka (2250 SIT, 2½ hours), and two a day to Split, changing at Zagreb (7500 SIT, eight to 11 hours). Two trains a day go to Belgrade via Zagreb (7700 SIT, 8¾ hours).

Germany & Austria There are three trains a day between Munich (11,266 SIT, seven hours) and Ljubljana via Salzburg, two of which need a change at Villach. One more train makes the run between Ljubljana and Salzburg direct (6763 SIT, 4½ hours).

To get to Vienna (10,103 SIT, six hours) from Ljubljana, you have a choice between the morning IC *Rogla* from Zagreb (but you must change at Maribor) or the afternoon IC *Emona* from Rijeka. When travelling by train to Austria, you'll find it's somewhat cheaper to take a local train to Maribor or Jesenice and buy your ticket on to Vienna or Salzburg from there. Domestic fares in Slovenia are much lower than the international ones.

Hungary The *Venezia Express* and the IC *Drava* (see the Italy section earlier) link Ljubljana directly to Budapest (9000 SIT, 7½ hours) via Koprivnica.

Car & Motorcycle

Slovenia maintains some 150 border crossings with Italy, Austria, Hungary and Croatia, though not all are open to citizens of third countries.

The following is a list of border crossings with each of Slovenia's four neighbours that are open to all international traffic at present. They run clockwise from the southwestern border with Italy. The name of the Slovenian border post appears first, followed by its location in brackets. Those crossings marked with an asterisk (*) have a Kompas MTS office, which is authorised to make sales-tax refunds to foreigners (see Taxes & Refunds in the Money section of the Facts for the Visitor chapter).

International vehicle insurance is compulsory in Slovenia. If your car is registered in the EU it is assumed you have this, and Slovenia has concluded special agreements with Croatia, Hungary, Macedonia and Slovakia. Other motorists must buy a Green Card valid for Slovenia at the border (€26 for 15 days, €38 for a month).

Austria

Gederovci (10km west of Murska Sobota)
Gornja Radgona* (41km north-east of Maribor)
Holmec* (49km east of Klagenfurt)
Jezersko (35km north-east of Kranj)
Jurij* (13km north-west of Maribor)
Karavanke* (at the 7km tunnel between Jesenice and Villach)
Korensko Sedlo* (20km south-west of Villach)
Kuzma (28km north of Murska Sobota)
Ljubelj* (between Klagenfurt and Kranj)
Radlje (43km west of Maribor)
Šentilj* (17km north of Maribor)
Trate (16km east of Šentilj)
Vič* (between Klagenfurt and Maribor)

Croatia
Babno Polje (30km south-west of Cerknica)
Bistrica ob Sotli (9km north-east of Podsreda)
Čabar (25km south of Sodražica)
Dobova (8km south-east of Brežice)
Dobovec (7km south-east of Rogatec)
Dragonja* (between Koper and Buje)
Gruškovje* (18km south of Ptuj)
Jelšane* (between Ilirska Bistrica and Rijeka)
Križevska Vas (1km south of Metlika)
Obrežje* (3km south-east of Mokrice)
Ormož (25km east of Ptuj)
Petišovci (5km south of Lendava)
Petrina (between Kočevje and Rijeka)
Razkrižje (10km east of Ljutomer)
Rogatec (7km east of Rogaška Slatina)
Sečovlje* (7km south-east of Portorož)
Sočerga* (between Trieste and Rijeka)
Središče ob Dravi* (20km west of Čakovec)
Starod* (between Trieste and Opatija)
Vinica (18km south of Črnomelj)
Zavrč* (19km south-east of Ptuj)

Hungary
Dolga Vas* (between Lendava and Rédics)
Hodoš (60km west of Zalaegerszeg)

Italy
Kozina* (between Trieste and Rijeka)
Lazaret* (between Trieste and Ankaran)
Lipica* (near Trieste)
Predel* (13km south of Tarvisio)
Rateče* (12km east of Tarvisio)
Robič (32km north-east of Udine)
Rožna Dolina (between Gorizia and Nova Gorica)
Sežana* (between Trieste and Ljubljana)

Škofije* (between Trieste and Koper)
Učeja (16km south-west of Bovec)
Vrtojba* (near Nova Gorica)

SEA
An alternative way of travelling between Slovenia and Italy is by boat. Between March and November the *Prince of Venice,* a 40m catamaran seating 330 passengers, sails between Izola and Venice (8500 to 12,500 SIT return depending on season, 2½ hours). Another catamaran called *Marconi* links Trieste with Piran (2500 SIT one way, 35 minutes).

For more information on boat travel, see Things to See & Do in the Izola section, and Cruises in the Piran section, both in the Primorska chapter.

ORGANISED TOURS
In the UK, Slovenia Pursuits (☎ 01767-631144), 14 Hay Street, Steeple Morden, Royston, Herts SG8 0PE, is a long-standing specialist that can arrange farmhouse holidays in Slovenia and Croatia.

In the USA, Slovenia Travel Inc (☎ 212-358 9024, fax 358 9025, ⓔ info@sloveni atravel.com) at 345 East 12th Street, New York, NY 10003 offers all-inclusive package holidays to Slovenia, including a seven-day coach tour taking in Vienna, Slovenia and Venice (US$899) and an eight-day tour of the highlights of Slovenia and Croatia (US$890). Prices do not include flights.

Getting Around

AIR

Slovenia has no scheduled domestic flights, but a division of Adria called Aviotaxi (☎ 04-236 34 60 at Ljubljana's Brnik airport) will fly a chartered Piper Turbo Arrow (three passengers) on demand to airports and aerodromes around the country. Sample return fares for three passengers are 13,500 SIT to Bled, 22,000 SIT to Slovenj Gradec and 44,000 SIT to Portorož or Maribor.

BUS

Except for long journeys, the bus is preferable to the train in Slovenia and departures are frequent. In some cases you don't have a choice – bus is the only practical way to get to Bled, the Julian Alps and much of Dolenjska, Koroška and Notranjska. But for a large part of the rest of the country you do have a choice.

You can buy your ticket at the bus station (*avtobusna postaja*) or simply pay the driver as you enter the bus. In Ljubljana you should book your seat (200 SIT) a day in advance, particularly if you're travelling on Friday or to popular destinations in the mountains or on the coast on a public holiday. Be aware that bus services are severely restricted on Sunday and holidays (and sometimes on Saturday too). Plan your trip accordingly or you'll find yourself marooned until Monday morning.

A range of bus companies serve the country. It's Integral and ASAP in Ljubljana, Kambus in Kamnik, Alpetour in Škofja Loka and Kranj, Avrigo in Nova Gorica and I&I in Koper. But this means little to travellers, and prices are uniform when services overlap or compete. Fares are calculated according to distance – around 510 SIT for 25km, 960 SIT for 50km, 1630 SIT for 100km and 3280 SIT for 200km. For some sample domestic and international bus fares from the capital, see Getting There & Away in the Ljubljana chapter.

Some, but not all, bus stations have a left-luggage office (*garderoba*) and charge 200 SIT per piece per day. Be careful as some of them work almost banker's hours. A better (and safer) bet is to leave your luggage at the train station, which is usually nearby and has longer hours. If your bag has to go in the luggage compartment below the bus, it will be 230 SIT extra, though most drivers don't mind you carrying it on the bus if it will fit between your seat and the one in front of it.

Bus Timetables

Timetables in the bus station, or posted on a wall or column outside, list all destinations and departure times. If you cannot find your bus listed or don't understand the schedule, get help from the information or ticket window (usually combined). *Odhodi* means 'Departures' and *Prihodi* is 'Arrivals'. *Blagajna Vozovnice* is the place to buy tickets.

Slovenian bus timetables use coloured text or abbreviation footnotes to denote which days of the week and during what seasons the buses run. The following lists cover most of the combinations you'll encounter. (Please note that a different colour scheme may be in operation at some stations.)

Bus Timetable Colours

white or black	daily
green	Monday-Saturday
blue	Monday-Friday
orange	Monday-Friday and working Saturdays
yellow	days when school is in session
red	Sunday and public holidays

Bus Timetable Abbreviations

Č	Thursday	PP	Monday-Friday
D	workdays	So	Saturday
D+	Monday-Friday	SN	Saturday and Sunday
N	Sunday	ŠP	days when school is in session
NP	Sunday and holidays		
Pe	Friday	Sr	Wednesday
Po	Monday	To	Tuesday
		V	daily

TRAIN

Slovenian Railways (Slovenske Železnice, or SŽ) runs trains on just over 1200km of track, about 40% of which is electrified. Large stretches of the main lines need to be improved and though most SŽ rolling stock is not the most modern, the service is reliable, fairly punctual and inexpensive, if a little slow. Very roughly, figure on covering about 60km to 65km per hour.

The exception is the new, streamlined ICS express train which hurtles along the recently upgraded line between Ljubljana and Maribor (2050 SIT, 156km) in just 105 minutes, eight times a day. OK, at an average speed of 90km/h it's not the Bullet Train, but it's definitely an improvement.

Although many secondary lines link provincial cities and towns, all the main ones converge on Ljubljana and to get from A to B it's usually easier to go via the capital. Going from Maribor to Novo Mesto, for example, takes two or more changes if you refuse to backtrack. At the same time, large parts of the country (the Alps, Notranjska, western Dolenjska, central Primorska) are not served by rail, making the bus your only choice. Aside from Ljubljana, other important rail junctions are at Pivka, Divača, Zidani Most and Pragersko.

The provinces are served by regional trains (*regionalni vlaki;* RG) and city trains (*primestni vlaki),* but the fastest are InterCity trains (IC). IC trains levy a surcharge of 200 SIT. An 'R' next to the train number on the timetable means seat reservations are available. If the 'R' is boxed, seat reservations are obligatory,

Buy your ticket before you travel at the *železniška postaja* (train station), or at Mladi Turist, Erazem, or Slovenijaturist travel agencies in Ljubljana. If you weren't able to buy a ticket in advance, seek out the conductor who will sell you one and charge

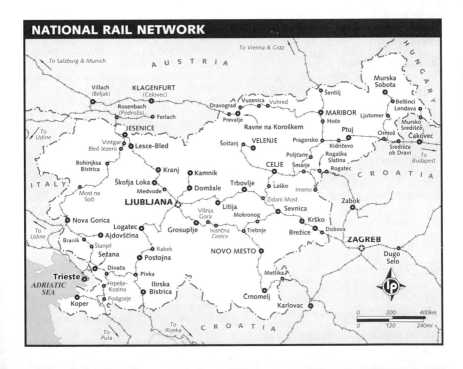

you a supplement of 200 SIT. The extra charge is not made if the ticket window at the station was closed (yes, the conductor will know) or your connecting train was late. An invalid ticket or trying to avoid paying will earn you a fine of 2500 SIT.

A return ticket (*povratna vozovnica*) costs 20% less than double the price of a one-way ticket (*enosmerna vozovnica*). A 1st-class ticket costs 50% more than a 2nd-class one.

Travelling by train is generally cheaper than going by bus – in rough terms, a 100km journey costs 1000 SIT in 2nd class and 1500 SIT in 1st class. See Getting There & Away in the Ljubljana chapter for sample fares to various destinations in Slovenia. Holders of ISIC, HI, GO25 and Euro<26 cards aged under 26 get a 30% discount; Euro Domino railpass holders (see under Train in the Getting There & Away chapter) get 25% off.

Left-luggage offices (*garderoba*) at over 30 stations around the country are supposed to be open 24 hours a day, but double-check the hours before you leave your bag behind. The charge is about 220 SIT per piece of luggage per day.

Train Timetables

Depending on the station, departures and arrivals are announced by loudspeaker or on an electronic board and are always on a printed timetable. The yellow one with the heading *Odhod* or *Odhodi Vlakov* means 'Departures' and the white one with the words *Prihod* or *Prihodi Vlakov* is 'Arrivals'. Other important train words that appear often are *čas* (time), *peron* (platform), *sedež* (seat), *smer* (direction) and *tir* (rail). Timetable symbols include:

✗ Monday-Saturday (except public holidays)

⊗ Monday-Friday (except public holidays)

✪ Monday-Saturday and public holidays

Ⓥ Saturday and Sunday

Ⓥ Saturday, Sunday and public holidays

Ⓟ Sunday and public holidays

7 no Sunday service

✝ holiday service

If you expect to use the train a lot in Slovenia, buy a copy of the official timetable, *Vozni Red Slovenske Železnice*, which is available at the Ljubljana train station for 800 SIT. It has explanatory notes in Slovene, German and French. Remember, too, when planning your trips that almost two-thirds of all rail passengers in Slovenia are commuters who only travel at peak times in the morning and late afternoon.

Scenic Routes

Slovenia's most scenic rail route runs from Jesenice (near the Austrian border) to Nova Gorica via Bled Jezero, Bohinjska Bistrica and Most na Soči. This 89km route through the Julian Alps and Soča River Valley opened for service in 1906. If you are travelling south, sit on the right-hand side of the train to see the cobalt-blue Soča at its most sparkling. A half-dozen local trains a day cover this route in each direction. The trip takes about two hours.

The 160km train ride from Ljubljana to Zagreb is also worth taking as the line follows the Sava River through a picturesque gorge. Sit on the right side if you're eastbound, the left side if you're westbound.

Steam Trains

SŽ has a stock of five steam locomotives and antique rolling stock – a train spotter's dream come true – and puts them to good use every year with its Oldtimer Train excursions in summer. See Activities in the Bled section of the Gorenjska chapter for details.

CAR & MOTORCYCLE

Roads in Slovenia are generally good if a bit narrow at times. Driving in the Alps can be hair-raising, with a gradient of up to 18% at the Korensko Sedlo Pass into Austria, and a series of 49 hairpin bends on the road over the Vršič Pass. Many mountain roads are closed in winter and early spring.

Motorways and highways are very well signposted, but secondary and tertiary roads are not; be sure to have a good map (see Maps under Planning in the Facts for the Visitor chapter) at the ready.

No less than US$4 billion is being invested in the expansion of Slovenia's motorway network, from 280km in 1997 to 600km by 2004. There are two main motorway corridors – between Maribor and the coast, and between Zagreb in Croatia and the Karavanke Tunnel to Austria – intersecting at the Ljubljana ring road, with a branch from Postojna to Nova Gorica. In early 2001 there were still major gaps in the network, notably between Ljubljana and Celje and Ljubljana and Zagreb. Motorways are numbered from A1 to A10 (for *avtocesta*), and a (relatively inexpensive) toll is payable – 230 SIT between Ljubljana and Brnik airport, for example.

Major international roads are preceded by an 'E'. The most important of these are the E70 to Zagreb via Novo Mesto, the E61 to Villach via Jesenice and the Karavanke Tunnel, and the E57 to Graz via Maribor. National highways contain a single digit and link cities. Secondary and tertiary roads

have two sets of numbers separated by a hyphen; the first number indicates the highway that the road runs into. Thus road No 10-5 from Nova Gorica and Ajdovščina joins the A10 motorway at Razdrto.

Private-car ownership in Slovenia (365 vehicles per 1000 inhabitants) is as high as it is in Germany and the UK so expect a lot of traffic congestion, especially in summer and on Friday afternoons when entire cities and towns head for the countryside. The roads between Ljubljana and Celje, Celje and Maribor and Ljubljana and Koper can get very busy, and traffic jams are frequent. Work is being carried out on major roads throughout the country so factor in the possibility of delays and diversions *(obvozi)*.

Petrol stations are usually open from about 7 am to 8 pm Monday to Saturday, though larger towns have 24-hour services on the outskirts. Fuel is relatively cheap by European standards: around 153.80/163.50 SIT per litre for EuroSuper 95/SuperPlus98 (both unleaded), 167.10 SIT for Super 98 (leaded) and 159.80 SIT for diesel. Credit cards are accepted at service stations on motorways and main roads – in the countryside you'll probably have to pay cash.

Road Distances (km)

	Bled	Bovec	Celje	Črnomelj	Koper	Kranjska Gora	Ljubljana	Maribor	Murska Sobota	Nova Gorica	Novo Mesto	Postojna	Ptuj	Slovenj Gradec
Bled	---													
Bovec	79	---												
Celje	126	205	---											
Črnomelj	167	246	107	---										
Koper	163	176	183	224	---									
Kranjska Gora	35	44	161	202	198	---								
Ljubljana	53	132	73	114	110	88	---							
Maribor	186	265	60	167	243	221	133	---						
Murska Sobota	246	325	120	227	303	281	193	60	---					
Nova Gorica	113	76	236	277	100	120	163	296	356	---				
Novo Mesto	122	201	92	45	179	157	69	152	212	232	---			
Postojna	105	140	125	213	58	140	52	185	245	64	111	---		
Ptuj	181	260	56	163	238	216	128	26	86	291	148	180	---	
Slovenj Gradec	152	231	38	145	209	187	99	73	133	262	130	151	99	---

Slovenia's national automobile club is the Avto-Moto Zveza Slovenije (AMZS). For emergency roadside assistance, motorists should call it on ☎ 19 87. For information on road and traffic conditions, contact the AMZS in Ljubljana (☎ 01-589 06 00, fax 534 23 78, ⓔ info.center@amzs.si). All accidents should be reported to the police (☎ 113) immediately.

Road Rules

You must drive on the right. Speed limits for cars and motorcycles are the same throughout the country: 60km/h in towns and villages; 80km/h on secondary and tertiary roads; 100km/h on highways; 120km/h on motorways. These limits are being more and more strictly enforced and should you exceed them you'll hit a speed trap for sure.

The use of seat belts is compulsory and motorcyclists must wear helmets. Neither they nor motorists are required by law to show their headlights throughout the day outside built-up areas, as is the case in some other European countries, but many do. The permitted blood-alcohol level for drivers is 0.5g/kg.

Parking

You must pay to park in the centre of most large towns in Slovenia, and illegally parked vehicles are routinely towed away, especially in Ljubljana and the historic towns on the coast. In general you'll have to seek out car parks (indicated on most maps by a 'P') where fees are charged (around 200 SIT per hour) or buy a special parking coupon from newsstands, kiosks or vending machines and place it on the dashboard.

A sign saying 'Plačilno Parkirnine' means you have to pay for parking; 'Brezplačno' means 'free'.

Car Rental

Car rentals from international firms like Budget, Avis and Hertz (all have offices in Ljubljana and in some provincial cities) vary widely in price, but expect to pay from 11,100/57,700 SIT a day/week with unlimited mileage. Check that any quoted rates include collision damage waiver (CDW), theft protection (TP), Personal Accident Insurance (PAI) and taxes.

Independent agencies like ABC and Unis Tours have more competitive rates – from 8500 SIT a day for unlimited mileage with all the extras. See Car & Motorcycle in the Getting Around section of the Ljubljana chapter for a list of agencies.

Travellers have reported that if you rent a car in Italy, you will not be allowed to drive it over the border into Slovenia. The Italian rental companies claim this is because there are high rates of car theft in Slovenia, but this is just not true. It is more likely a side effect of political tensions between Italy and Slovenia. There is no problem taking a car hired in Slovenia into Italy or any other neighbouring countries.

BICYCLE

Cycling is a popular leisure pastime in Slovenia, and bikes can be carried free of charge in the baggage compartments of InterCity and regional trains. On buses, you can put your bike in the luggage compartment, space permitting. Cycling is permitted on all roads except motorways. Many towns and cities, including Ljubljana, Maribor, Ptuj, Novo Mesto, Kranj and Škofja Loka, have bicycle lanes and some even have special traffic lights. See Cycling in the special section 'The Great Outdoors' for details on cycling in the countryside.

Bicycle rental places are not that widespread in Slovenia, and are concentrated in the more popular tourist areas like Ljubljana, Bled, Bovec and Piran. Look in the Getting Around sections of the relevant towns for details.

HITCHING

Hitchhiking is a popular way of getting around for young Slovenes. It's legal everywhere except on motorways and some major highways and is generally easy, except on Friday afternoon, before school holidays and on Sunday when all the best hitching places are taken and cars are often full. If you're heading north, don't count on many rides from Austrian motorists; they seem to have an aversion to this method of travel.

Hitching from bus stops is fairly common. Otherwise use motorway access roads or other areas where the traffic will not be disturbed. See Hitching in the Getting There & Away section of the Ljubljana chapter for the best routes out of the capital.

Hitching is never entirely safe in any country in the world, and we don't recommend it. Travellers who decide to hitch should understand that they are taking a small but potentially serious risk. People who do choose to hitch will be safer if they travel in pairs and let someone know where they are planning to go.

ORGANISED TOURS

The big travel agencies like Kompas and Globtour, as well as some smaller ones, organise excursions and tours for individuals and groups, usually out of Ljubljana. If you're pressed for time or want to squeeze in as much as possible over a short period, you can 'do' the entire country with Kompas in a week in summer for US$850 (single supplement US$160), including all meals, accommodation and transportation. Kompas also has several very good specialised tours, from horse riding in Rogla and rafting on the Soča River to thermal spa and castle tours.

Ljubljana

☎ 01 • postcode 1000 • pop 330,000

Despite its small size, Ljubljana is by far Slovenia's largest and most populous city. It is also the nation's political, economic and cultural capital. As such, virtually everything of national importance begins, ends or is taking place in Ljubljana.

But it can be difficult to get a grip on the place. In many ways the city whose name almost means 'beloved' *(ljubljena)* in Slovene does not feel like an industrious municipality of national importance but a pleasant, self-contented town with responsibilities only to itself and its citizens. You might think that way too, especially in spring and summer when cafe tables fill the narrow streets of the Old Town and street musicians (both free agents and hired help) entertain passers-by on Čopova ulica and Prešernov trg. Then Ljubljana becomes a little Prague without the crowds or a more manageable Paris.

With some 35,000 students attending Ljubljana University's 14 faculties and three art academies, the city feels young and offers all the facilities you'll need during your stay. And among the fine baroque churches, palaces and quaint bridges, you'll see a lot of greenery. A large park called Tivoli and the hills beyond it form the city's western border and willow-lined walkways follow the Ljubljanica River and its canals. A much longer trail, a legacy of WWII, completely encircles the city as a kind of pedestrian 'ring road' and is a boon for those who want to escape the early morning fog endemic to the city in autumn and winter.

HISTORY

Ljubljana first appeared in print in 1144 as the town of Laibach, but a whole lot more had taken place here before that. The area to the south, an infertile bog, was settled during the Bronze Age by marsh dwellers who lived in round huts on stilts sunk into the soggy soil. Remnants of these dwellings can be seen in the National Museum. These early people were followed by the Illyrians

Highlights

- Take a stroll up to Ljubljana Castle
- Relax on a warm summer's evening at the outdoor Kavarna Plочnik on Prešernov trg
- View the collection of 19th-century Slovenian art at the National Gallery
- Survey the Old Town from Nebotičnik (Skyscraper) on Slovenska cesta
- Take in a performance during the Ljubljana Summer Festival at the outdoor Križanke theatre
- Treat yourself to a night out at the Old Town pubs or Metelkova clubs
- Enjoy a special meal at the Pri Vitezu or Špaja restaurants
- Stroll along the willow-lined walkways of the Ljubljanica River

Ljubljana pp86-87
Central Ljubljana p90
Krakovo & Trnovo p97

HUNGARY

AUSTRIA

ITALY

Ljubljana

CROATIA

BOSNIA-HERCEGOVINA

and, in about 400 BC, the Celts, who settled along the Ljubljanica.

The first important settlement in the area, however, came with the arrival of the Romans who built a military camp here in the century preceding the birth of Christ. Within 100 years, what had become known as Emona was a thriving town and a strategic crossroads on the routes linking Roman Pannonia in the south with colonies at Noricum and Aquileia. Legacies of the Roman presence – walls, dwellings, early churches – can still be seen throughout Ljubljana.

Emona was sacked and eventually destroyed by the Huns, Ostrogoths and Langobards from the 5th century, but the 'Ljubljana Gate' remained an important crossing point between east and west. Tribes of early Slavs settled here in the 6th century.

Ljubljana changed hands frequently in the Middle Ages. In the 12th century the fortified town between Castle Hill and the Ljubljanica River was in the possession of the Dukes of Carinthia. Within 100 years, it was transferred to the rulers of the new Duchy of Carniola, who made it their capital. The last and most momentous change came in 1335 when the Habsburgs became the town's new rulers. Except for a brief interlude in the early 19th century, they would remain the city's (and the nation's) masters until the end of WWI in 1918.

The Habsburgs turned Ljubljana into an important trading centre and made it an episcopal seat; it would later become the centre of the Protestant Reformation in Slovenia. The town and its 12th-century hill-top castle were able to repel the Turks in the 15th century, but a devastating earthquake in 1511 reduced much of medieval Ljubljana to rubble. This led to a period of frantic construction in the 17th and 18th centuries which provided Ljubljana with many of its pale-coloured baroque churches and mansions – and the nickname 'Bela Ljubljana' (White Ljubljana). The town walls were pulled down to allow Ljubljana to expand, and the southern marsh was partly drained. But the most important engineering feat was the construction of a canal to the south and east of Castle Hill that regulated the flow of the Ljubljanica and prevented flooding.

When Napoleon established his Illyrian Provinces in 1809 in a bid to cut Habsburg Austria's access to the Adriatic, he made Ljubljana the capital, as it remained until 1813. In 1821 members of the Holy Alliance (Austria, Prussia, Russia and Naples) met at the Congress of Laibach to discuss measures to suppress the democratic revolutionary and national movements in Europe.

The railway linking Trieste and Vienna reached Ljubljana in 1849 and stimulated development of the town. By then Ljubljana had become the centre of Slovenian nationalism under Austrian rule. Writers and nationalists like France Prešeren and Ivan Cankar produced the bulk of their work here. Slovenes began to join the town government and emerged as a majority in 1882. But in 1895 another earthquake struck Ljubljana, forcing the city to rebuild once again. To Ljubljana's great benefit, the Secessionist and Art Nouveau styles were all the rage in Central Europe at the time, and many wonderful buildings were erected – structures the communists would later condemn as 'bourgeois' and 'decadent' and raze to the ground.

Slovenia and its capital joined the Kingdom of Serbs, Croats and Slovenes after WWI. During WWII the city was occupied by the Italians and then the Germans, who encircled the city with barbed-wire fencing creating, in effect, an urban concentration camp. Ljubljana became the capital of the Socialist Republic of Slovenia within Yugoslavia in 1945 and remained the capital after Slovenia's independence in 1991.

ORIENTATION

Ljubljana lies in the Ljubljana Basin (Ljubljanska Kotlina), which extends to the north and north-west along the Sava River to Kranj. The basin has two distinct parts: the Ljubljana Marsh (Ljubljansko Barje) to the south and the fertile Ljubljana Plain (Ljubljansko Polje) to the north and east. The city is wedged between the Polhov Gradec Hills to the west and Golovec Hills (including Castle Hill) to the east and south-east. The Ljubljanica River and the Gruber Canal have effectively turned a large part of central Ljubljana into an island.

All this geography is important in order to understand how the city has developed and continues to grow. If you look at a map or stand atop Ljubljana's landmark Skyscraper, you'll see that the city has had to expand fan-like to the north and east; hills and marshy ground have prevented growth in the other directions.

Ljubljana is traditionally divided into five districts, but only a few are of any importance to travellers. Center is the commercial area on the left bank of the Ljubljanica to the west and north of Castle Hill and the Old Town. Tabor and Poljane are the easternmost parts of Center, and Bežigrad, where the bulk of the university buildings are, lies to the north. Two old suburbs to the south of Center – Krakovo and Trnovo – retain a lot of their old character.

Certain streets and squares (Čopova ulica, Trubarjeva cesta, Prešernov trg) and much of the Old Town are reserved for pedestrians and cyclists. The Ljubljanica is crossed by a dozen vehicular bridges and footbridges and three of them – Shoemaker Bridge (Čevljarski Most), Triple Bridge (Tromostovje) and Dragon Bridge (Zmajski Most) – are historically important.

The train and bus stations are opposite one another on Trg Osvobodilne Fronte (known as Trg OF) at the northern end of Center. Slovenska cesta, the capital's main thoroughfare, is 250m to the west. To get to central Prešernov trg, head south on Miklošičeva cesta (600m).

Maps

The tourist office and many hotels hand out a free map of Ljubljana that should take care of most people's needs. If you intend staying longer in the capital or exploring it in depth, pick up a copy of the 1:20,000-scale *Ljubljana* published by the Geodesic Institute of Slovenia (GZS; 1350 SIT); it has an enlarged 1:6840 city-centre plan and a 1:75,000 regional map on the reverse. The 1:13,000 *Karta Mesta Ljubljana* from the Inštitut za Geodezijo in Fotogrametrijo is also widely available.

INFORMATION
Tourist Offices

The Tourist Information Centre (TIC; ☎ 306 12 15, fax 306 12 04, ⓔ pcl.tic-lj@ljubljana .si) – the best office anywhere for information, not just on Ljubljana but on all of

---

The Ljubljana Triangle

If you're feeling pretty good about yourself and the world in general while in Ljubljana, you might want to pay homage to the Union Brewery on Celovška cesta, but credit could go to the city's fabulous ley lines.

According to those who dibble-dabble in geomancy, which deals with an environment's invisible dimensions as well as its psychic and spiritual levels, Ljubljana is in the exact centre of Slovenia – not the geographical one (that's near Litija to the east) but at the axis of three energy currents (or ley lines) that cross Slovenia and meet to form the 'Ljubljana Triangle'.

Marko Pogačnik, a Ljubljana-based geomancer, says that the west-east ley line heading for Zagreb runs through Tivoli, down the Jakopičevo sprehajališče designed by Jože Plečnik and over the Triple Bridge and through the cathedral. The north-south one from Prague hits the east-west ley line in the park before carrying on to Trnovo Bridge and the Church of St John the Baptist. The current coming from Graz in the north-east meets the east-west line at the cathedral and travels south-west to the Trnovo church, where it mates with the north-south line.

So where can you feel all this energy at its buzziest best? The Trnovo Bridge, says Pogačnik, concentrates the forces of birth while Triple Bridge is the centre of creativity and maturing. The centre for the forces of transformation and destruction (read death) is in the little park called Navje, just north of the train station and east of the Slovenian Youth Theatre. This too was designed by Plečnik but is clearly outside the Ljubljana Triangle – at least according to my map. I'm happy to report that the Union Brewery, where my ley line is heading, is a mere 700m to the west.

Steve Fallon

Slovenia – is in the historical Kresija building on Stritarjeva ulica, just across the Triple Bridge from Prešernov trg. The Ljubljana Promotion Centre, which runs the TIC, employs students during summer months who are very enthusiastic about their country and your interest in it. Though they can book accommodation only in Ljubljana, they can help with information on all of Slovenia. The TIC is open from 8 am to 8 pm weekdays (to 6 pm from October to May), 10 am to 6 pm weekends and holidays.

The TIC branch office (☎/fax 433 94 75) in the central hall of the train station is open from 8 am to 9 pm daily in summer, and 10 am to 5.30 pm weekdays only from October to May. The TIC is worth visiting just to pick up its free maps and brochures especially the *Ljubljana City Map*, the *Where?* tourist guide, which contains suggested tours and historical background, and the *Ljubljana from A to Z* booklet, which lists hotels and services.

Backpackers and students should head for the Erazem travel office (☎ 433 10 76) at Trubarjeva cesta 7. The staff provide information, make bookings, sell Lonely Planet guidebooks and have a message board. They also sell ISIC cards for 900 SIT and, for those under 26 but not studying, FIYTO (Federation of International Youth Travel Organisations) cards for 700 SIT. Erazem is open from 10 am to 5 pm weekdays (from noon in winter). Mladi Turist (☎ 425 92 60), at Salendrova ulica 4 near the Municipal Museum, is the office of the Slovenian Youth Hostel Association and is open from 9 am to 3 pm Monday and Friday, 9 am to 5 pm Tuesday to Thursday.

The Cultural Information Centre (☎ 251 40 25) next to Trg Francoske Revolucije 7 can provide information on museums and galleries and exhibitions. It's open from 10 am to 6 pm weekdays and to 1 pm Saturday (and again from 4 to 7 pm in summer).

The main office of the Planinska Zveza Slovenije, or PZS (Alpine Association of Slovenia; ☎ 434 30 22), is at Dvoržakova ulica 9, a small house set back from the street. It has information about hiking and mountain huts throughout the country and some excellent maps and guides for sale. The office is open from 8 am to 2 pm weekdays (till 6 pm Monday).

Motorists in need of assistance or advice can contact the Avto-Moto Zveza Slovenije (AMZS; ☎ 534 13 41) at Dunajska cesta 128, about 3km north of Center. It's open from 7 am to 7.30 pm weekdays and till noon Saturday, and you can telephone for information between 5 am and 7 pm daily.

Money

There's a currency exchange desk in the train station next to the TIC office. It is open daily from 6 am to 10 pm. The *bureau de change* at the bus station is open from 5.30 am to 9 pm daily.

You'll find automatic teller machines (ATMs) scattered throughout the city; there's one next to the Noč in Dan shop on Masarykova cesta, directly opposite the bus and train stations. Next to the SKB Banka ATM on Trg Ajdovščina is a currency-exchange machine that changes the banknotes of 18 countries into tolars.

Some of the best rates of exchange in Ljubljana are available at Nova Ljubljanska Banka at Trg Republike 2. It is open from 8 am to 5 pm weekdays and 9 am till noon Saturday. Three other central Nova Ljubljanska Banka branches are at Šubičeva ulica 2 (open 8 am to 5 pm weekdays, till 6 pm Wednesday); in the beautiful Art-Nouveau City Savings Bank building (Mestna Hranilnica Ljubljanska) at Čopova ulica 3 (open 9 am to noon and 2 to 5 pm weekdays, till noon Saturday); and at Mestni trg 16 in the Old Town (open 9 am to noon and 2 to 5 pm weekdays, till 6 pm Wednesday).

Ljubljana is full of private exchange bureaus *(menjalnice)* taking no commission and offering good exchange rates. One called Hida has a branch in the Central Market at Pogarčarjev trg 1 open from 7 am to 7 pm weekdays and to 2 pm Saturday.

Credit Cards A Banka, with a branch at Slovenska cesta 50 (open from 8 am to 5 pm weekdays and till noon Saturday) and another to the south at Slovenska cesta 9 (open from 9 am to 4 pm weekdays and to

3 pm Friday), is a local rep for Visa and can issue a tolar cash advance on your card. It takes a 1% commission for cashing travellers cheques.

If you have problems with your Visa card when A Banka is closed, call the Visa Centre (☎ 433 21 32). Eurocard and MasterCard holders should go to Nova Ljubljanska Banka (☎ 425 01 55) at Trg Republike 2.

Atlas Express (☎ 430 77 20) at Kolodvorska ulica 20 is the Slovenian representative for American Express and can replace cards, make cash advances and hold clients' mail. It is open from 8 am to 5 pm weekdays and 9 am till noon Saturday.

Post & Communications
The main post office, where poste restante is held for 30 days only, is at Slovenska cesta 32 on the corner of Čopova ulica; it's open from 7 am to 8 pm weekdays and to 1 pm Saturday. You can make international telephone calls from booths and send faxes and telexes here.

To mail a parcel you must go to the special customs post office at Trg OF 5, due west of the train station and opposite the bus station. Make sure you bring your package open for inspection; the maximum weight is about 15kg, depending on the destination. This post office is open 24 hours a day for letter post, telephones and telegrams.

Email & Internet Access
Most of the middle and top-end hotels in town have data sockets in the rooms where you can plug in your laptop, and/or an Internet computer in the lobby. There are also half a dozen cafes and bars in Ljubljana offering Internet access, though most have only one or two machines. In these places you can usually use the computer for free for up to 15 minutes, as long as you buy a drink. Beyond that, the standard rate for access is 400 SIT an hour.

A.R.T. Cafe (☎ 421 94 20) Slovenska cesta 10. Open from 7 am to 11 pm daily (to midnight Friday and Saturday).
Čerin Kavarna (☎ 232 09 90) Trubarjeva cesta 52. Open from 9 am to 7 pm daily.

Klub K4 (☎ 431 70 10) Kersnikova 4. Open from 9 am to 9 pm weekdays only during the university term.
Klub Podhod (☎ 421 41 00) Plečnikov trg 1 (in the underpass). Open 9 am to 3 pm Monday to Thursday, 7 am to 8 pm Friday, 8 am to 1 am Saturday and 4 pm to 1 am Sunday.
Knjižnica Župančiča (☎ 291 23 26) Vilharjev podhod (the pedestrian underpass at the east end of the train station). Open from 7 am to 7 pm weekdays only.
Pr' Semaforju (☎ 426 52 45) Slovenska cesta 5. Open from 7 am to midnight weekdays only (computer is downstairs in the basement).

Internet Resources
You can find general tourist information about Ljubljana at www.ljubljana.si, while the University of Ljubljana site (www.uni-lj.si) has useful info for students. Details of cultural events can be found on the Cankarjev Dom (cultural and congress centre) site at www.cd-cc.si and the Križanke Festival site at www.festival-lj.si.

Sound of Ljubljana (www.soundoflj.com) has listings of what's happening on the rave/techno/house scene.

Ljubljana Digital Media Lab (www.ljudmila.org) contains links to alternative culture, music, venues and publications, including the Metelkova clubs (mail.ljudmila.org/metelko).

Travel Agencies
All of the big agencies have offices in Center. Kompas (☎ 200 61 00) is at Slovenska cesta 36 and has another office (☎ 432 10 53) at Miklošičeva cesta 11, while Globtour (☎ 251 38 43) is in the Maximarket passageway connecting Trg Republike with Plečnikov trg. Slovenijaturist (☎ 431 52 06) at Slovenska cesta 58 is your best source of information for details of rail travel. These offices are generally open from 8.30 or 9 am to 6 or 7 pm weekdays and till noon or 1 pm Saturday.

Bookshops
Mladinska Knjiga, upstairs at Slovenska cesta 29, is the biggest bookshop in Ljubljana and has coffee-table books, dictionaries, guidebooks and maps to every corner of

the country as well as fiction and nonfiction books in English. It is open from 8 am to 7.30 pm weekdays and to 1 pm Saturday. MK Konzorcij (as it's known) has several smaller branches in the city, including one opposite the train station at Miklošičeva cesta 40 and another at Nazorjeva ulica 1.

A smaller chain with knowledgeable and helpful staff is Cankarjeva Založba with an outlet at Slovenska cesta 37. It keeps the same hours as MK. Cankarjeva Založba's Oxford Center at Kopitarjeva ulica 2 stocks English-language titles only, including some novels, but is really aimed at Slovenes studying English. DZS, with branches at Šubičeva ulica 1a and Mestni trg 26, has academic titles and reference books. Knjigarna Novak at Wolfova 8 is a pleasant, old-fashioned place with chairs to sit in (open till 10 pm), and Knjigarna Philip Wilson at Gornji trg deals entirely in English-language books, both new and second-hand.

The best selection of maps in Ljubljana can be found at a shop called Kod & Kam – meaning roughly 'Whence & Whither' – at Trg Francoske Revolucije 7, opposite the Križanke. It stocks most city, regional and hiking maps produced in the country as well as imported maps and guides, including the Lonely Planet series. It is open from 9 am to 7 pm weekdays and 8 am to 1 pm Saturday. The Geographical Museum is also based here.

For foreign newspapers, go to the Ljubljanček gift shop in the lobby of the Grand Hotel Union, open from 8 am to 2 pm and 4 to 8 pm weekdays, 8 am to 1 pm and 2 to 6 pm Saturday, and 8 am to noon Sunday, or to the MK bookshop at Slovenska cesta 29.

Cultural Centres

The British Council (☎ 425 92 92) is at Cankarjevo nabrežje 27 and is open from 9 am to 8 pm Monday to Thursday, to 3 pm Friday, and 9 am to 1 pm on the first Saturday of every month.

The American Center (☎ 200 55 00) is at the US embassy at Prešernova cesta 31; you can visit by appointment only.

The Institut Français Charles Nodier (☎ 200 05 00) overlooks the river at Breg

12 and opens from 9 am to 5 pm Monday to Thursday, 10 am to 4 pm Friday and 9 am to 2 pm Saturday.

The Deutscher Lesesaal (☎ 476 37 25) is on the 2nd floor of the business centre at Trg Republike 3, next to Cankarjev Dom, and is open from 9 am to 6.30 pm weekdays only (till 2 pm Friday).

Laundry

Getting your clothes washed is a problem in Ljubljana, as it is everywhere in Slovenia. A couple of the student dormitories have washing machines and dryers that you can use – the Dijaški Dom Poljane at Potočnikova ulica 3, about 1.5km east of the Old Town, and the Dijaški Dom Kam (Building C) at Kardeljeva ploščad 14, north of the centre in Bežigrad and near the Dijaški Dom Bežigrad – as does the Ježica camping ground. Mehurček is a self-service place at Viška cesta 54 open from 8 am to 8 pm weekdays and to 1 pm weekdays, but it's about 3.5km south-west of Center (take bus No 6 to Vič). Chemo Express at Wolfova ulica 12 near Prešernov trg is an old-style laundry and dry cleaner open from 7 am to 6 pm weekdays.

Left Luggage

The left-luggage office in the train station is on platform No 1 (open 24 hours a day; 220 SIT per piece per day). The bus station also has a left-luggage office, which is open from 5.30 am to 8.30 pm.

Medical Services

You can see a doctor at the medical centre (klinični center; ☎ 433 62 36, 431 31 13) at Zaloška cesta 2–7, which is in Tabor east of Hotel Park. The emergency unit (urgenca; ☎ 232 30 60), on the north side of the centre at Bohoričeva 4, is open 24 hours a day. The dental clinic (☎ 431 31 13) is at Zaloška cesta 2.

The Centralna Lekarna (Central Pharmacy; ☎ 433 50 44), Prešernov trg 5, is open from 8 am to 7 pm weekdays and to 1 pm Saturday. The Lekarna Miklošič (☎ 231 45 58), Miklošičeva cesta 24, serves as the city centre's 24-hour duty pharmacy.

LJUBLJANA

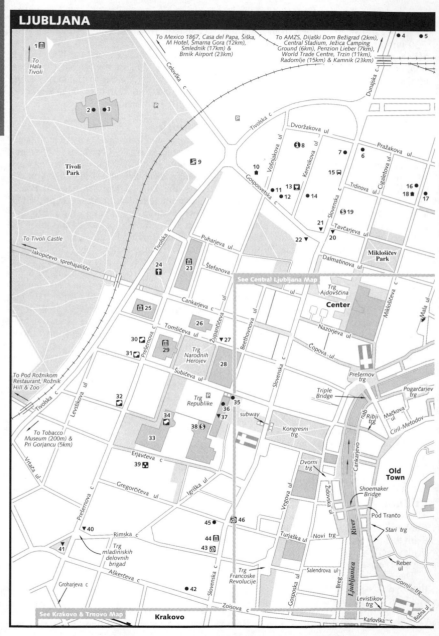

LJUBLJANA

1 🏛

To
Hala
Tivoli

To Mexico 1867, Casa del Papa, Šiška,
M Hotel, Smarna Gora (12km),
Smlednik (17km) &
Brnik Airport (23km)

To AMZS, Dijaški Dom Bežigrad (2km),
Central Stadium, Ježica Camping
Ground (6km), Penzion Lieber (7km),
World Trade Centre, Trzin (11km),
Radomlje (15km) & Kamnik (23km)

● 4   ● 5

Celovška c

Dunajska c

2 ●   ● 3

Tivoli
Park

Tivolska c

Dvoržakova ul

P

🛈 8

Vošnjakova ul

Kersnikova ul

7 ●   ● 6

Pražakova ul

Cigaletova ul

9

15 🖥

Trdinova ul

16 ●

Gosposvetska c

10 🖥

18 🏠   ● 17

To Tivoli Castle

Jakopičevo sprehajališče

Tivolska c

Puharjeva ul

Štefanova

24 ✝

23 🏛

Cankarjeva c

25 🏛

Tomšičeva ul

26

Prešernova

30 📷

31 📷

29 🏛

27 ▼

Trg
Narodnih
Herojev

Šubičeva ul

28

Beethovnova ul

● 11   13 🖥

12 ●   ● 14

🕓 19

Slovenska c

21 ▼

Tavčarjeva ul

20

22 ▼

Dalmatinova ul

See Central Ljubljana Map

Trg
Ajdovščina

Center

Nazorjeva ul

Copova ul

Miklošičev
Park

Miklošičeva c

Mala ul

To Pod Rožnikom
Restaurant, Rožnik
Hill & Zoo

To Tobacco
Museum (200m) &
Pri Gorjancu (5km)

Levstikova ul

Tivolska c

32

34 📷

33

Erjavčeva c

39 🎭

Gregorčičeva ul

40 ▼

41 ▼

Rimska c

Trg
mladinskih
delovnih
brigad

Groharjeva c

Aškerčeva c

Trg
Republike

P

35 ●

36 ●

37 ▼

38 🕓

subway

Slovenska c

Kongresni
trg

Triple
Bridge

Prešernov
trg

Pogačarjev
trg

Ribji
trg

nab

Mačkova c

Ciril-Metodov

Old
Town

Dvorni
trg

Vegova ul

Igriška ul

45 ●

46 🛑

44 🏛

43 🎞

42 ●

Trg
Francoske
Revolucije

Zoisova c

Slovenska c

Gosposka c

Turjaška ul

Novi trg

Salendrova ul

Breg

Krakovo

See Krakovo & Trnovo Map

Cankarjevo

Židovska ul

Shoemaker
Bridge

Pod Trančo

Stari trg

River

Ljubljanica

Reber
ul

Gornji trg

Levistikov
trg

Rožna c

Karlovška c

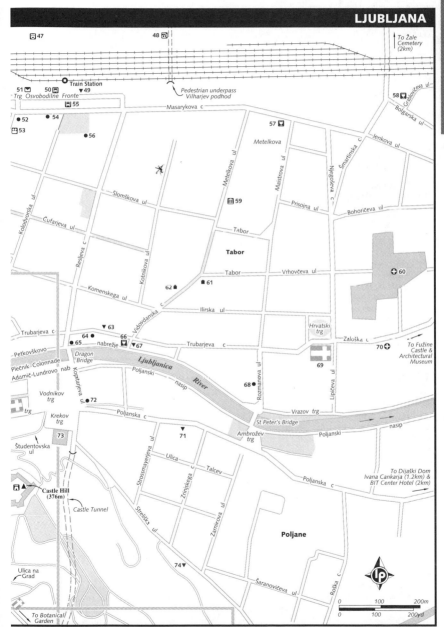

LJUBLJANA

LJUBLJANA

47

48

To Žale
Cemetery
(2km)

Train Station

51 50
▼49
Trg Osvobodilne Fronte

58

55

Masarykova c

Grablovičeva ul

Bolgarska ul

Pedestrian underpass
Vilharjev podhod

52   54

53

56

57

Metelkova

Jenkova ul

Šmartinska c

Njegoševa c

🗲

Slomškova ul

Metelkova ul

Maistrova ul

Prisojna ul

Bohoričeva ul

59

Čufarjeva ul

Kolodvorska ul

Resljeva ul

Tabor

Tabor

Tabor

Vrhovčeva c

60

Komenskega ul

Kotnikova ul

62   61

Ilirska ul

Hrvatski
trg

▼63

Trubarjeva c

Vidovdanska c

Zaloška c

70

To Fužine
Castle &
Architectural
Museum

64
65
66
nabrežje   ▼67

Petkovškovo

Plečnik Colonnade

Adamič-Lundrovo nab

Dragon
Bridge

Ljubljanica

River

Poljanski

nasip

Rozmanova ul

Lipičeva ul

69

68

Koptarjeva c

Vodnikov
trg

72

Poljanska c

Vrazov trg

St Peter's Bridge

Poljanski

nasip

Krekov
trg

73

Ambrožev
trg

Poljanska c

▼
71

To Dijaški Dom
Ivana Cankarja (1.2km) &
BIT Center Hotel (2km)

Študentovska
ul

Strossmayerjeva ul

Ulica

Talcev

Zrinjskega

Poljanska c

Castle Hill
(376m)

Castle Tunnel

Streliška ul

Zarnikova ul

Poljane

Ulica na
Grad

74▼

Šaranovičeva ul

Roška c

To Botanical
Garden

0   100   200m
0   100   200yd

LJUBLJANA

PLACES TO STAY
10 Lev Inter-Continental Hotel
18 Austrotel; Ljubljana Casino
61 Hotel Park
62 Dijaški Dom Tabor

PLACES TO EAT
20 Čajnik Tea House
21 Kavarna Evropa
22 Figovec
27 Operna Klet
37 Restavracija 2000; Maximarket Supermarket & Deli
40 Restavracija Lovec
41 Tramvaj Ekspress
49 McDonald's
63 Dalmatinska Konoba
67 Čerin Pizzeria & Cybercafe
71 Shang Hai Chinese Restaurant
74 Meson Don Felipe

THINGS TO SEE
1 Modern History Museum
23 National Gallery
24 Church of Sts Cyril & Methodius
25 Museum of Modern Art
26 Opera House
28 Parliament
29 National Museum
33 Cankarjev Dom (Cultural Centre)

39 Ferant Garden & Roman Ruins
44 Jakopič Gallery
59 Ethnographic Museum
69 Orthodox Church of St Peter

OTHER
2 Zlati Klub Sauna
3 Tivoli Recreation Centre
4 Vinoteka Simon Bradeško
5 Ljubljana Fairgrounds
6 Slovenijaturist Travel Agency; Burek Stand
7 Kodak Express
8 Alpine Association of Slovenia (PZS)
9 Ilirija Swimming Pool
11 Lovec Hunting Shop
12 Adria Airways; Lufthansa
13 Miriam's Pub
14 ŠOU Centre; Klub K4; K4 Cybercafe
15 City Bus Ticket Kiosks
16 Kompas Travel Agency; Hertz Car Rental
17 Kinoteka
19 A Banka
30 US Embassy; American Center
31 German Embassy
32 Austrian Embassy
34 UK Embassy; Deutscher Lesesaal; Adria Airways

35 DZS Bookshop
36 Globtour Travel Agency; SKB ATM
38 Nova Ljubljanska Banka
42 University of Ljubljana Faculty of Arts
43 Pr' Semaforju (Internet Cafe)
45 Mikrocop Kodak Express
46 A.R.T. Café
47 Slovenian Youth Theatre
48 Knižnica Župančiča
50 Airport Buses
51 Post Office (Customs)
52 Mladinska Knjiga Bookshop
53 Kompas Cinema
54 Noč in Dan 24-hour Shop; ATM; Foto Grad
55 Bus Station
56 Atlas Express (American Express)
57 Klub Tiffany; Monokel Klub
58 Propaganda Klub; Orto Bar
60 University Clinic Centre
64 Hard Rock Music Shop
65 Rec-Rec Music Shop
66 Birdland Jazz Cafe
68 Rog Bicycle Shop & Bike Rental
70 Medical Centre; Dental Clinic
72 Oxford Book Centre
73 Puppet Theatre & St James Theatre

THINGS TO SEE

The easiest way to see the best that Ljubljana has to offer and still enjoy a leisurely stroll is to follow the walking tour outlined here. It's broken up into eight sections which can be done individually or together with preceding or subsequent ones. If you run straight though them and make no stops, all eight shouldn't take much more than half a day. But count on a full day if you expect to see everything and even longer if you intend visiting all the museums too. Many sights have plaques outside identifying and providing historical information in four languages, including English.

Around Prešernov Trg

Begin the tour at **Prešernov trg**, a beautiful square that forms the link between Center and the Old Town and is always a hub of activity. Taking pride of place in the square is the **Prešeren monument** designed by Maks Fabiani and Ivan Zajc and erected in 1905 in honour of Slovenia's greatest hero. In summer, the steps at the base of the plinth (with motifs from Prešeren's poems) become a sitting-out area for Ljubljana's young bloods and foreigners alike.

To the east of the monument at No 5 is the Italianate **Central Pharmacy**, which was a famous cafe frequented by intellectuals in the 19th century, and to the north, on the corner of Trubarjeva cesta and Miklošičeva cesta, the delightful Secessionist **Urbanc** building (1903), now the Centromerkur department store. Diagonally across the square at No 1 is another Secessionist gem. The **Ura** building, now marred by a Citizen watch sign above it, was once a shop for painters and thus is very gaily decorated. Peer two doors down Wolfova ulica and at No 4 you'll see a terracotta figure peeking out

Ljubljana's Center district and Cathedral of St Nicholas

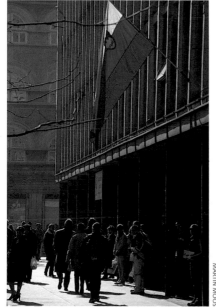

Flag down a bus on Slovenska cesta

Franciscan Church and Triple Bridge, Ljubljana

MARTIN MOOS

Dragon Bridge, Ljubljana

MARTIN MOOS

Reliefs adorning Parliament Building, Ljubljana

MARTIN MOOS

Willows grace the banks of the Ljubljanica River.

MARTIN MOOS

Door handle of the Plečnik-designed National Library, Ljubljana

NEIL WILSON

France Prešeren monument

from a 'window'. It's Julija Primic looking at the monument to her life-long admirer France Prešeren.

The 17th-century **Franciscan Church of the Annunciation** stands on the northern side of the square. The interior is not so interesting with its six side altars and enormous choir but to the left (west) of the main altar, designed by the Italian sculptor Francesco Robba, is a glass-fronted coffin with the spooky remains of a saint. Like many churches in Ljubljana, the Franciscan church is open from morning till dusk, but closes from about noon to 3 pm.

Attached to the church on the western side is the **Franciscan monastery**, with a very important library. Nearby in the southwestern corner of the square is a bronze **relief map** of the city.

Walk north along Miklošičeva cesta from the Urbanc building and don't miss the several fine buildings along the way. The cream-coloured **People's Loan Bank** (1908) at No 4 is topped with the figures of two women holding a beehive and a purse – symbols of industry and wealth. The **Cooperative Bank** at No 8 was designed by Ivan Vurnik, and the red, yellow and blue geometric patterns were painted by his wife Helena in 1922. Just opposite is the renovated **Grand Hotel Union**, the *grande dame* of Ljubljana hotels. A short distance to the north-west is **Miklošičev Park**, laid out by Maks Fabiani in 1902. All the buildings facing it are Art-Nouveau masterpieces, with the exception of the unspeakable Gorenjska Banka to the south on Dalmatinova ulica.

Market Area

From Prešernov trg, cross into the Old Town via the **Triple Bridge** (Tromostovje), once the Špital Bridge (built in 1842). The prolific architect Jože Plečnik added the two sides almost a century later to create something quite unique for Slovenia and the world. He also designed the elegant covered walkway along the river to the east, the **Plečnik Colonnade**, which forms part of the city's **Central Market**.

Walk through Pogarčarjev trg with its wonderful open-air market and old men and women selling everything from forest berries and wild mushrooms to honey and home-made cheeses like soft white *sirček*.

The strange **cone** in Pogarčarjev trg was erected in honour of Plečnik in 1993. It represents the Parliament building he designed, but never built, for the top of Castle Hill. The building on the southern side of Pogarčarjev trg is the Renaissance **Bishop's Palace** (Škofijski Dvorec) with a lovely arcaded courtyard. The **Seminary** (Semenišče; 1749) to the east, with its pockmarked Atlases outside, contains valuable baroque furnishings and a library with priceless incunabula and 16th-century manuscripts. It can be visited by appointment only. There's a market with meat, fish and dairy products on the ground floor.

Dominating the square is the **Cathedral of Saint Nicholas** (Stolnica Sv Nikolaj), dedicated to the patron of boatmen and fishermen (closed from noon to 3 pm). A church has stood here since the 12th century, but the existing twin-towered building is from the early 18th century. Inside it's a baroque palace of pink marble, white stucco and gilt with frescoes by Matevž Langus. Have a look at the magnificent carved choir stalls, organ and the sweet faces of the angels on the main altar, another Francesco Robba creation. The pietà in the glass case on the outside southern wall is a copy. Two stunning bronze doors were added in 1996 to commemorate the Pope's visit – the west one symbolises 1250 years of Christianity in Slovenia, while the six bishops on the south door depict the Ljubljana Diocese's history.

If you want a closer look at what Ljubljančani like to eat, continue east to Vodnikov trg where there's yet another **outdoor market** filled with fresh fruit and vegetables. From here you could cross Ciril-Metodov trg and begin walking up Študentovska ulica to the castle, a relatively steep, 15-minute climb. Instead, let's head west along Ciril-Metodov trg to one of the prettiest squares in the city.

Old Town

Mestni trg has two major landmarks. The **Magistrat** (Town Hall), seat of the city government, was erected in the late 15th century,

LJUBLJANA

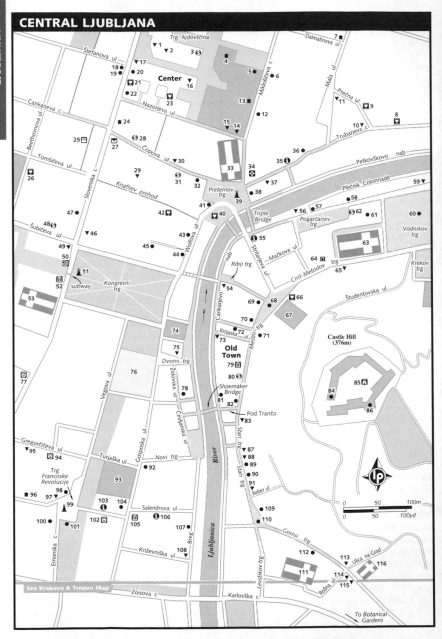

CENTRAL LJUBLJANA

Trg Ajdovščina

Dalmatinova ul — 7

Štefanova ul

▼1 ▼2 3 — 4 — 5 — 6

18 ▼17 Mala ul

19 ▼20 Prečna ul ▼11

21 Center ▼16 9

22 13 8

Cankarjeva c 23 12 10 ▼

Nazorjeva ul Trubarjeva c

24 15 ▼14

25 28 36

27 Čopova ul ▼30 35

Tomšičeva ul 29 33 34 Petkovškovo nab

26 31 32 ▼37 Plečnik Colonnade 59 ▼

Knafljev prehod Prešernov trg 38

47 42 39 58

48 40 Triple 56 57 62 61

Šubičeva ul ▼46 43 Bridge Pogačarjev 60

49 ▼ 44 45 55 trg

50 Mačkova ul 63 Vodnikov

51 Ribji trg 64 trg

52 subway Ciril-Metodov 65 ▼

53 Kongresni 54 Krekov

trg 69 68 66 trg

70 67 Študentovska ul

74 Krojaška 72 71

75 ▼ 73

76 Dvorni trg Old

Town Castle Hill

77 78 79 (376m)

80

Shoemaker 85 84

Bridge 81

82 Pod TranČo 86

Gregorčičeva ul ▼83

▼95 94 Star trg ▼87

Turjaška ul Novi trg ▼88

Trg 92 93 89

Francoske 90

Revolucije 91 Reber ul

96 98 Salendrova ul 109

97 99 110

100 101 103 104 Gornji trg

102 105 106

107 112 113 Ulica na Grad

108 ▼ 116

Križevniška ul 111 114

115

See Krakovo & Trnovo Map Zoisova c Karlovška c

To Botanical

Gardens

CENTRAL LJUBLJANA

PLACES TO STAY
4 Holiday Inn
7 Hotel Turist; Klub Central Disco
13 Grand Hotel Union
24 Hotel Slon Best Western
96 Gostilna Pri Mraku

PLACES TO EAT
1 Super 5 Fast-Food Restaurant
2 Skriti Kot Self-Service Restaurant
10 Kebapči
11 Napoli Pizzeria
14 Kavarna Union
15 Smrekarjev Hram
16 Papillon Restaurant & Club
17 Šestica
29 Gostilna As; As Pub
30 McDonald's
37 Zrno Store
46 Rio Ham Ham Fast-Food Restaurant
49 Tomato
54 Zlata Ribica
56 Ribca Seafood Bar
59 Plac
65 Vinoteka Sokol
73 Cafe Maček
75 Ljubljanski Dvor
83 Čajna Hiša Teahouse
87 Julija-sur-Seine
88 Nostalgija
91 Cafe Antico
95 Foculus Pizzeria
97 Le Petit Café
108 Pri Vitezu
113 Sichuan Chinese Restaurant
114 Špajza
115 Pri Sv Florianu

THINGS TO SEE
12 Bank Buildings
18 Nebotičnik (Skyscraper)
33 Franciscan Church of the Annuciation

34 Urbanc Building & Centromerkur Department Store
38 Central Pharmacy
39 Prešeren Monument
41 Ura Building
51 Citizen of Emona Statue
52 School Museum
53 Ursuline Church of the Holy Trinity
63 Cathedral of Saint Nicholas
64 Bishop's Palace
67 Town Hall
68 Robba Fountain
74 Filharmonija
76 Ljubljana University
79 Theatre Museum
82 Tranča
84 Belvedere Tower
85 Castle
86 Pentagonal Tower
89 Schweiger House
92 Academy of Arts & Sciences
93 National & University Library
99 Ilirija Column
100 New University Library Site
101 Križanke Ticket Office
102 Križanke; Plečnikov Hram Cafe
105 Municipal Museum
110 Hercules Fountain
111 Church of St James
116 Church of St Florian

OTHER
3 SKB Banka & Exchange Machine
5 Ljubljanček Gift Shop
6 Peko Shoe Shop
8 TrueBar
9 Patrick's Irish Pub
19 Cankarjeva Založba Bookshop; Little Gallery
20 Vino Boutique
21 Holidays Pub
22 Kompas Travel Agency

23 Tramontana Pub
25 Komuna Cinema
26 Gajo Jazz Club
27 Post Office (Poste Restante)
28 Hida Exchange Bureau
31 Art Nouveau City Savings Bank; Nova Ljubljanska Banka
32 Peko Shoe Shop
35 Erazem Travel Agency
36 Carniola Antiqua
40 Kavarna Pločnik
42 Cutty Sark Pub
43 Knjigarna Novak (Bookshop)
44 Big Bang Music Shop
45 Chemo Express Laundry
47 Mladinska Knjiga Bookshop
48 Nova Ljubljanska Banka
50 Klub Podhod
55 Tourist Office (TIC)
57 Pekarna Por (Bakery)
58 Pekarna Neža (Bakery)
60 Fruit & Vegetable Market
61 Covered Market; Seminary
62 Hida Exchange Bureau
66 Vinoteka Movja
69 Trubarjev Antikvariat Bookshop
70 Dom Crafts Shop
71 Mestna Galerija
72 Antikvariat Tizian
77 National Drama Theatre
78 Galerija Lala
80 Nova Ljubljanska Banka
81 British Council
90 Parazol Crafts Shop
94 Glej Theatre; Equrna Gallery
98 Musikalje Music Shop
103 Cultural Information Centre
104 Kod & Kam Bookshop; Geographical Museum
106 Mladi Turist
107 Institut Français Charles Nodier
109 Galerija ŠKUC
112 Knjigarna Philip Wilson (Bookshop)

but rebuilt in 1718. The Gothic courtyard inside, arcaded on two levels and boasting some lovely decoration, is where theatrical performances once took place. Above the south portal leading to a second courtyard you'll see a relief map of Ljubljana as it appeared in the second half of the 17th century.

The hall is topped with a golden dragon, a symbol of Ljubljana, but quite a recent one.

A wily mayor in the early 20th century apparently convinced the authorities in Vienna that Ljubljana needed a new crossing over the Ljubljanica River and the **Dragon Bridge** (Zmajski Most) was built to the north-east. City folk say the dragons wag their tails whenever a virgin crosses the bridge.

In the middle of Mestni trg stands the **Robba Fountain** (1751), modelled after one in Rome. But the Tritons with their gushing urns here represent something totally Slovenian, the three rivers of Carniola (the Sava, Krka and Ljubljanica). To protect it from decay, it may be moved to the courtyard between the old and new wings of the National Gallery and a copy put in its place.

From Mestni trg you can make a small detour west into **Ribji trg** with perhaps the oldest house (1528) in Ljubljana still standing at No 2 and a golden fountain with a girl in classical dress pouring water.

Mestni trg leads into **Stari trg**, the true heart of the Old Town. More of a street than a square, with 19th-century wooden shop fronts, quiet courtyards and cobblestone passageways, Stari trg is a positive delight to explore. From behind the houses on the eastern side, paths once led to Castle Hill, a source of water. The buildings fronting the river had large passageways built to allow drainage in case of flooding.

Tranča at No 4 was a prison until the 18th century and those condemned to death were executed at a spot nearby in some fairly unpleasant ways (strangulation, drowning, being burned at the stake). Later it became the city's monopoly bakery – the only place where bread could be sold. Unscrupulous bakers who cheated customers got a dunking in the cold waters of the Ljubljanica.

A small street called **Pod Trančo** just beyond leads to **Shoemaker Bridge** (Čevljarski Most). Like all the bridges here in the Middle Ages, this was a place of trade and a gateway to the town. Craftsmen worked and lived on the bridges (in this case 16 cobblers) to catch the traffic and avoid paying town taxes – a kind of medieval duty-free setup.

Between Stari trg 11 and 15 – the house that *should* bear the number 13 – there's a lovely rococo building called **Schweiger House** with a large Atlas supporting the upper balcony. The figure has his finger raised to his lips as if asking passers-by to be quiet. But the owner, whose name meant the 'Silent One' in German, might have had something other than self-promotion in mind. In this part of the world, bordellos were traditionally located at house No 13 of

a street and he probably got quite a few unsolicited calls.

In the middle of **Levstikov trg**, the southern extension of Stari trg, the **Hercules Fountain** is a favourite meeting place in summer. Perhaps that's why a copy has replaced the original 17th-century statue, which is now in the town hall.

The big church farther south off Stari trg is the **Church of St James**. Far more interesting than the main altar (1732) by Francesco Robba is the one in the church's **Chapel of St Francis Xavier** with statues of a 'White Queen' and a 'Black King'. The **Column of Mary** outside to the south of the church was designed by Janez Vajkard Valvasor (well, at least the statue on top was) and erected in 1682 in memory of the victory over the Turks at Monošter (now Szentgotthárd in Hungary) 18 years earlier.

Across Karlovška cesta is **Gruber Palace** (Gruberjeva Palača). Gabriel Gruber, who built the canal (Gruberjev Prekop) regulating the Ljubljanica, lived here until 1784. The palace is in Zopf style, a transitional art style between late baroque and neoclassicism, and now contains the national archives. If you look eastward on Karlovška cesta to No 1, you'll see a 'bridge of sighs' that was once the Balkan Gate, the easternmost point of the Old Town. From here the town walls ran halfway up Castle Hill. If you were to continue south-east along Karlovška cesta for 800m and cross the Ljubljanica, you'd reach the **Botanical Garden** (Botanični Vrt) at Ižanska cesta 15 with some 4500 species of plants and trees. It is open from 7 am to 7 pm April to October and to 5 pm the rest of the year. Entry is free. You can also reach here on bus No 3 (stop: Strelišče).

Gornji trg is the eastern extension of Stari trg. The fine **medieval houses** at Gornji trg 7 to 15 have narrow side passages where rubbish was once deposited so it could be washed down into the river. The most important building on this elongated square is the **Church of St Florian** built in 1672 and dedicated to the patron saint of fires after a serious blaze destroyed much of the Old Town. Beyond the church is an area of small houses once inhabited by Ljubljana's struggling artists. Venture into a courtyard or peer through an open door or window, and you'll see that they left their mark.

A footpath called Ulica na Grad leads from the Church of St Florian up to Castle Hill.

Ljubljana Castle

There have been fortifications of some kind or another on Castle Hill at least since Celtic times, but the existing Ljubljana Castle (Ljubljanski Grad) mostly dates from a 16th-century rebuild following the 1511 earthquake. It is now frequently used as a venue for concerts and other cultural activities, and as a wedding hall.

The climb up the double wrought-iron staircase (150 steps) of the 19th-century **Belvedere Tower** and a walk along the **ramparts** is worth the effort for the views down into the Old Town and across the river to Center. The ceiling in the **Chapel of St George** (1489) is covered in frescoes and the coats of arms of the Dukes of Carniola; the **Pentagonal Tower** of the southern wing hosts changing exhibits.

The castle and Pentagonal Tower are open from 11 am to 6 pm, but closed all day Saturday and Monday and till 1 pm Wednesday and Friday when weddings are being held. Admission is 200/100 SIT for adults/children. The Belvedere Tower is open from 10 am to dusk daily.

Center

A path from below the castle's Western Gate will bring you to Reber ulica and Stari trg. Return to Pod Trančo and cross Shoemaker Bridge; the very narrow street a few steps to the north-west called Židovska ulica was once the site of a synagogue and the centre of Jewish life in the Middle Ages.

A lot of this district on the left bank of the Ljubljanica is worth exploring. If you go south from Shoemaker Bridge to **Breg**, the city's port when the Ljubljanica was still navigable this far (a steamboat once called from Vrhnika), and then west up **Novi trg**, you'll pass the **Academy of Arts and Sciences** (Akademija Znanosti in Umetnosti) on your left at No 3, which was once the seat of the Provincial Diet under the Habsburgs. The **National and University Library** (Narodna in Univerzitetna Knjižnica; 1941), Plečnik's masterpiece, is across Gosposka ulica. To appreciate more of this great man's philosophy, enter through the main door on Turjaška ulica – you'll find yourself in near darkness, surrounded by black marble. But as you ascend the steps, you'll emerge into a colonnade suffused with light – the light of knowledge, according to Plečnik's plans. The reading room with huge glass walls has some interesting lamps, also designed by Plečnik.

The **Municipal Museum** (Mestni Muzej) is a few steps to the south-east at Gosposka ulica 15. It has a collection of well-preserved Roman artefacts (some of them recovered from the archaeological dig in the museum courtyard) and a scale model of Emona to help it all make sense. Upstairs rooms contain period furniture and household objects and one is devoted to the work of the poet Oton Župančič (1878–1949). The museum was closed for renovations at the time of research, and is not expected to reopen until late in 2002.

Diagonally opposite the museum in **Trg Francoske Revolucije** is the **Križanke**, a monastery complex that once belonged to the Knights of the Teutonic Order and now serves as the headquarters of the Ljubljana Summer Festival. Its outside theatre alone seats 2000 people. The **Ilirija Column** in the square is dedicated to Napoleon and his Illyrian Provinces (1809–13), when Slovene was taught in schools for the first time. Monsieur Bonaparte actually visited his 'capital' during this period and stayed at the Bishop's Palace. South-west of the square on Emonska cesta, where a new university library is being built, more archaeological excavations are in progress.

Vegova ulica runs north from Trg Francoske Revolucije past a row of busts of Slovenian writers, scientists and musicians to the central building of **Ljubljana University**, established in 1919. The proclamation of independence was announced from the balcony facing **Kongresni trg** in 1991.

Named in honour of the Congress of the Holy Alliance, convened by Austria, Prussia,

Jože Plečnik, Architect Extraordinaire

Few architects anywhere in the world have had as great an impact on their birthplace as Jože Plečnik – a name you'll hear again and again during your travels in Slovenia. And with good reason. His work is eclectic, inspired, unique – and found everywhere.

Born in Ljubljana in 1872, Plečnik was educated at the College of Arts in Graz and studied under the architect Otto Wagner in Vienna. From 1911 to 1921 he lived in Prague where he taught and later helped renovate Prague Castle.

Plečnik's work in Ljubljana began in 1921 and continued until his death in 1957. Almost single-handedly, he transformed the city, adding elements of classical Greek and Roman architecture with Byzantine, Islamic, ancient Egyptian and folkloric motifs to its baroque and Secessionist faces. The list of his creations and renovations are endless – from the National and University Library, the colonnaded Central Market and the cemetery at Žale in Ljubljana to the delightful churches in Bogojina in Prekmurje and Ribnica in Dolenjska.

MARTIN HARRIS

Plečnik was also a city planner and designer. Not only did he redesign the banks of the Ljubljanica River (including the Triple Bridge), entire streets (Zoisova ulica) and Tivoli Park, but he also set his sights elsewhere on monumental stairways (Kranj), public buildings (Kamnik) and outdoor shrines (Bled). An intensely religious man, Plečnik designed many furnishings and liturgical objects (especially chalices and candlesticks) for churches throughout the land (eg, Škofja Loka's Church of St James).

Plečnik's eclecticism and individuality alienated him from the mainstream of modern architecture during his lifetime. But in the 1980s he was 'rediscovered' and hailed as a prophet of postmodernism. Oddly, he remained more or less in favour under the communists because of his classicist phase.

One of Plečnik's designs that was never realised was an extravagant Parliament, complete with an enormous cone-shaped structure, to be built on Castle Hill after WWII. But such an extravagant building would have alarmed the federalist Josip Broz Tito and the Slovenes backed off.

Russia and Naples in 1821 and hosted by Ljubljana, Kongresni trg contains several important buildings. **Philharmonic Hall** (Filharmonija) sitting on the south-east corner is home to the Slovenian Philharmonic Orchestra – founded in 1701 and one of the oldest in the world. Haydn, Beethoven and Brahms were honorary members and Gustav Mahler was resident conductor for a season (1881–82). The **Ursuline Church of the Holy Trinity** (1726) to the west is the most beautiful baroque building in Ljubljana and contains a multicoloured altar by Robba made of African marble. The church is open from 7.30 to 9.30 am and 10.30 am to 4.30 pm daily.

As you descend into the pedestrian underpass at the western end of the square, keep an eye open for a small gilded statue on top of a column. It's a copy (the original is in the National Museum) of the **Citizen of Emona**, dating from the 4th century. It was unearthed nearby in 1836 and probably formed part of a Roman necropolis.

Trg Republike is Center's main square. Unfortunately it is basically a car park dominated by a pair of glowering, grey tower blocks. The ugly **Parliament Building** (1959), festooned with revolutionary reliefs, overlooks the north-eastern corner, and **Cankarjev Dom**, the city's cultural and congress centre, rises diagonally opposite.

To the south beyond Erjavčeva cesta in **Ferant Garden** are the remains of an early Christian church porch and baptistery with mosaics from the 4th century.

Museum Area

Ljubljana's three most important museums are situated to the north of Trg Republike.

The **National Museum** (Narodni Muzej) at Muzejska ulica 1, at the western end of park-like Trg Narodnih Herojev, has sections devoted to history and natural history as well as fine coin and mineral collections (the latter amassed by the philanthropic Baron Žiga Zois in the early 19th century). The Roman glass and the jewellery found in 6th-century Slavic graves is pretty standard fare; the highlight here is the **Vače situla**, a Celtic pail from the 5th or 6th century BC unearthed in a town east of Ljubljana. The relief around the situla shows men hunting stags, driving chariots, playing reed pipes and wrestling.

Other items on display – 16th-century crossbows, a tiny 17th-century strong box with a complicated locking system, an Art-Nouveau mirror from the early 20th century – are interesting but say little about Slovenian history and few are labelled in English. Still, the museum building (1885) itself is impressive. Check the ceiling fresco in the foyer featuring an allegorical Carniola surrounded by important Slovenes from the past and the statues of the Muses and Fates relaxing on the stairway banisters. The National Museum is open from 10 am to 6 pm Tuesday to Sunday (to 8 pm Wednesday). Admission is 500/300 SIT.

The graceful **Opera House** on Župančičeva ulica to the north-east was opened in 1892 as the Provincial Theatre, and plays in both German and Slovene were performed here. After WWI it was renamed the Opera House and is now home to the Slovenian National Opera and Ballet companies. No doubt you'll hear someone singing scales as you walk by. Two blocks east, at the junction of Štefanova ulica and Slovenska cesta, is the Art-Deco **Nebotičnik** (Skyscraper), designed by Vladimir Subič and built in 1933. It remained Ljubljana's tallest building for decades, but is now sadly in need of

renovation. The rooftop cafe was closed at the time of research, but may have reopened by the time you read this – check with the tourist office.

The **National Gallery** (Narodna Galerija; 1896) at Cankarjeva cesta 20 offers portraits and landscapes from the 17th to 19th centuries, copies of medieval frescoes and wonderful Gothic statuary in its old south wing. Although the subjects of the earlier paintings are the usual foppish nobles and lemon-lipped clergy, some of the later works are remarkable and provide a good introduction to Slovenian art. Take a close look at the works of the impressionists Jurij Šubic and Rihard Jakopič (eg, *Birches in Snow*), the pointillist Ivan Grohar *(Škofja Loka in the Snow)* and Slovenia's most celebrated woman painter Ivana Kobilca *(Summer)*. The bronzes by Franc Berneker are truly exceptional and, while you're here, have a look at the Art-Deco toilets, all black marble and green glass.

The gallery's newer north wing has a permanent collection of European paintings from the Middle Ages to the 20th century and is used for temporary exhibits. At the time of research the gallery was closed while a glassed-in area linking the two buildings was under construction; it should have reopened by the time you read this. The National Gallery is open from 10 am to 6 pm Tuesday to Saturday and to 1 pm Sunday. Admission is 500/300 SIT for adults/ seniors and children, but free on Saturday.

The **Museum of Modern Art** (Moderna Galerija) south-west of the National Gallery at Cankarjeva cesta 15 is in an ugly modern building that feels like stepping into a cold shower after walking around the other museums. The gallery shows part of its permanent collection of 20th-century Slovenian art, which helps put some of the socialist-inspired work of sculptors like Jakob Savinšek into artistic perspective. A large part of the building is given over to temporary exhibitions that a lot of people would consider 'fun' rather than 'serious' art. The museum hosts the International Biennial of Graphic Arts in odd-numbered years. It keeps the same hours as the National Gallery.

The interior of the Serbian Orthodox **Church of Sts Cyril and Methodius** north of the Museum of Modern Art is covered from floor to ceiling with colourful modern frescoes and has a richly carved iconostasis separating the nave from the sanctuary. It is open from 3 to 6 pm Tuesday to Saturday.

Tivoli Park

You can reach the city's leafy playground via a subway from Cankarjeva cesta. Straight ahead, at the end of a monumental promenade designed by Plečnik (Jakopičevo sprehajališče), is the 17th-century **Tivoli Castle** (Tivolski Grad) which contains the **International Centre of Graphic Arts** (Mednarodni Grafični Likovni Center) open from 10 am to 6 pm Tuesday to Saturday, to 1 pm Sunday.

Along with making use of the sports facilities at the Tivoli Recreation Centre (see Swimming & Sauna under Activities later in this chapter), you can climb to the top of **Rožnik Hill** (394m) for wonderful views of the city. The 45-hectare **Zoological Gardens** (Živalski Vrt), on the hill's southern slope along Večna pot, contain some 800 animals representing 120 species. The zoo is open from 9 am to 7 pm daily (except Monday) in summer, till 4 pm in winter. Admission is 600/350 SIT.

The **Museum of Modern History** (Muzej Novejše Zgodovine) at Celovška cesta 23, just beyond the Tivoli Recreation Centre, has gone from being a temple to the Partisans to an excellent museum tracing the history of Slovenia in the 20th century through multimedia. Note the contrast between the sober earnestness of the communist-era Red Room and the exuberant, logo-mad commercialism of the neighbouring industrial exhibit; a portrait of Stalin lies 'discarded' behind the door between the two. The museum is open from 10 am to 6 pm daily, except Monday, and admission costs 500/300 SIT (free on the first Sunday of the month).

Krakovo & Trnovo

These two attractive districts south of Center are Ljubljana's oldest suburbs and have a number of interesting buildings and historic sites. The Krakovo neighbourhood around Krakovska ulica with its two-storey cottages was once called the 'Montmartre of Ljubljana' because of all the artists living there.

If you walk along Barjanska cesta, the short southern extension of Slovenska cesta, you'll reach the **Roman Wall** (Rimski Zid) from Emona times running along Mirje. The **pyramid** is a Plečnik addition. Within the **Jakopič Garden** to the south-east at Mirje 4 where the impressionist painter once worked in his summerhouse, there are more **Roman ruins** including household artefacts and the remains of a sophisticated heating system. Ask at the Cultural Information Centre (see Tourist Offices under Information earlier in this chapter) about access to the garden.

Barjanska cesta ends at a picturesque canal called **Gradaščica**, which is a pleasant place for a stroll on a warm day. Spanning the canal to the east is the little **Trnovo Bridge**, designed by Plečnik in 1932. Birch trees actually grow on the bridge and the railings are topped with five curious pyramids. The **Church of St John the Baptist**, where France Prešeren met the love of his life, Julija Primic, is on the southern side.

Farther south at Karunova ulica 4 is the house where Jože Plečnik lived and worked for almost 40 years. Today it houses the Ljubljana Architectural Museum's **Plečnik Collection**, an excellent introduction to this almost ascetically religious man, his inspiration and his work. It is open from 10 am to 2 pm Tuesday and Thursday only. Admission costs 500/200 SIT.

Other Museums & Galleries

Ljubljana contains many other interesting museums besides the ones mentioned above, most notably the **Slovenian Ethnographic Museum** (Slovenski Etnografski Muzej) at Metelkova ulica 2, which houses the National Museum's collections of traditional Slovenian art, culture and handicrafts. It's open from 10 am to 6 pm Tuesday to Sunday; admission is 500/300 SIT (free on Sunday).

The following is a list of other museums in the Ljubljana area that may interest you. Some – but not all – can be visited while following the walking tours and are noted on the Ljubljana, Central Ljubljana and Krakovo &

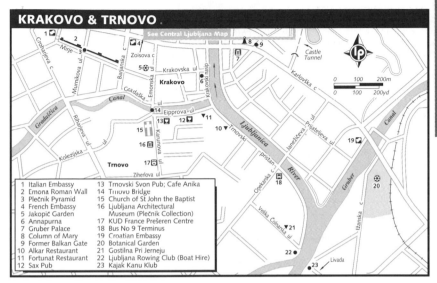

KRAKOVO & TRNOVO

1	Italian Embassy
2	Emona Roman Wall
3	Plečnik Pyramid
4	French Embassy
5	Jakopič Garden
6	Annapurna
7	Gruber Palace
8	Column of Mary
9	Former Balkan Gate
10	Alkar Restaurant
11	Fortunat Restaurant
12	Sax Pub
13	Trnovski Svon Pub; Cafe Anika
14	Trnovo Bridge
15	Church of St John the Baptist
16	Ljubljana Architectural Museum (Plečnik Collection)
17	KUD France Prešeren Centre
18	Bus No 9 Terminus
19	Croatian Embassy
20	Botanical Garden
21	Gostilna Pri Jerneju
22	Ljubljana Rowing Club (Boat Hire)
23	Kajak Kanu Klub

Trnovo maps. They can have very convoluted and abbreviated opening times so check with the TIC before setting out.

Architectural Museum (Arhitekturni Muzej) Fužine Castle, in the eastern suburb of Studenec (bus No 20 to Fužine)

Brewery Museum (Pivovarski Muzej) Pivovarniška ulica 2 (Union Brewery)

City Gallery (Mestna Galerija) Mestni trg 5

Equrna Gallery (Galerija Equrna) Gregorčičeva ulica 3

Jakopič Gallery (Jakopičeva Galerija) Slovenska cesta 9

Little Gallery (Mala Galerija) Slovenska cesta 35

Railway Museum (Železniški Muzej) Parmova ulica 35

Slovenian Film Museum (Slovenski Filmski Muzej) Kinoteka, Miklošičeva cesta 28

Slovenian School Museum (Slovenski Šolski Muzej) Plečnikov trg 1

Slovenian Theatre Museum (Slovenski Gledališki Muzej) Mestni trg 17

Tobacco Museum (Tobačni Muzej) Tobačna ulica 5 (bus No 6 to Tobačna)

ACTIVITIES
Swimming & Sauna
The Tivoli Recreation Centre (☎ 431 51 55) at Celovška cesta 25 in Tivoli Park has bowling alleys, tennis courts, an indoor swimming pool, a fitness centre, and a roller-skating rink (ice rink in winter). It also has a popular sauna called Zlati Klub with saunas, a steam room, cold and warm splash pools and a small outside pool surrounded by high walls so you can sunbathe *au naturel* (mixed sexes). The Zlati Klub is open from 10 am to 8 pm daily (to midnight Tuesday, Friday and Saturday). Entrance costs 1500 SIT (1800 SIT at weekends).

The Ilirija outdoor pool south-east of the Tivoli Centre at Celovška cesta 3 is open in summer from 10 am to 7 pm on weekdays, 9 am to 8 pm at weekends.

Hiking
If you fancy a long but easy walk, you could follow the marked Trail of Remembrance (Pot Spominov), which runs for some 34km around the city where German barbed wire once completely enclosed Ljubljana during WWII. Today it is especially popular with joggers. The easiest places to reach it from are the AMZS (Automobile Association of Slovenia) headquarters at Dunajska cesta 128, north of the Bežigrad student dormitory, or from Trg Komandanta Staneta just

north-west of the LPP (Ljubljanski Potniški Promet, the public transport authority) central office at Celovška cesta 160. You can also join it from the south-western edge of Tivoli Park near the zoo or the northern side of Žale Cemetery.

Boating & Rafting

You can rent rowing boats on the river from the Veslaški Klub Ljubljana (Ljubljana Rowing Club; ☎ 283 87 12) at Velika Čolnarska ulica 20 in Trnovo from 10 am to 7 pm mid-May to September. The Kajak Kanu Klub (☎ 427 12 88) at Livada 31, across the river from Trnovo (bus No 19), rents canoe equipment and leads kayak tours on the Ljubljanica (1000 SIT per person).

Skok Sport (☎ 512 44 02, e skoksport@ s5.net) at Marinovševa 8 in Šentvid, 8km north-west of Center (bus Nos 8 and 16), organises rafting trips on the Sava and Soča Rivers for 2200 to 5500 SIT per person.

Horse Riding

There are several riding clubs around the city. The nearest is the Ljubljana Equestrian Club (Konjeniški Klub Ljubljana; ☎ 568 73 52) at the hippodrome at Stožice 2, 5km north of Center (bus Nos 6 and 8). A 10-hour beginners' course costs 20,000 SIT, and individual lessons are 3000 SIT per hour.

Hot-Air Ballooning

Balonarski Center Barje (☎ 252 26 81) at Breg 2 offers one-hour flights over the city (for groups of three to eight people) for 15,000 SIT per person.

ORGANISED TOURS

From June to September, a two-hour guided tour in English (700/500 SIT adults/seniors, students and children) sponsored by the TIC departs at 5 pm daily from the town hall in Mestni trg. During the rest of the year there are tours at 11 am on Sunday only. Tours are also available in Italian, German, French, and several other languages on request.

SPECIAL EVENTS

The number one event on Ljubljana's social calendar is the International Summer Festival of music, theatre and dance held in venues throughout the city, but principally at the open-air theatre of the Križanke on Trg Francoske Revolucije. The festival, now in its fourth decade, begins in early July and runs through August. Visit the Web site at www.festival-lj.si.

A festival of alternative and world music called Druga Godba (Other Music) takes place in the Križanke in early June along with the Photo Antique Fair, where old photographs, cameras and other equipment are traded. There's a Jazz Festival at the Križanke in late June.

Vino Ljubljana is an international wine fair in April for the trade and general public alike. It takes place at the Ljubljana Fairgrounds (Gospodarsko Razstavišče) north of the train station at Dunajska cesta 10 and the opening is marked with the delivery of wine from the Vipava Valley to Ljubljana via the ancient *vinska magistrala* (wine trading route). Some restaurants, *gostilne* and bars serve special dishes and selected wines during the fair. They are identified by grape-shaped wreaths made of wood shavings.

Ljubljana is at its most vibrant in July and August during the so-called Summer in the Old Town season when there are three or four cultural events a week in the city's historic squares and courtyards. All are free. Trnfest, an arts festival organised by KUD France Prešeren (see Multicultural Centres under Entertainment later in this chapter), takes place in Trnovo in August.

The International Biennial of Graphic Arts, at the Museum of Modern Arts, the International Centre of Graphic Arts in Tivoli and other venues, takes place throughout the summer during odd-numbered years. The 24th and 25th take place in 2001 and 2003.

Mesto Žensk – Društvo za promocijo žensk v kulturi (City of Women – Association for the Promotion of Women in Culture), part of the Government Office for Women's Affairs (☎ 438 15 80, fax 438 15 85, e info@cityofwomen-a.si) at Kersnikova ulica 4, sponsors an international festival of contemporary arts, held every October, called City of Women. Visit the Web site at www.cityofwomen-a.si.

Numerous church concerts and street fairs are held throughout Ljubljana in December during the build-up to Christmas and the New Year.

PLACES TO STAY
Camping

The only camping ground convenient to Ljubljana is *Avtokamp Ježica* (☎ *568 39 13, fax 232 10 60,* e *acjezica@siol.net, Dunajska cesta 270)* on the Sava River about 6km north of the train and bus stations. You can reach it on bus No 6 or 8. Ježica, which is open all year, has an outdoor swimming pool, a fitness studio, bowling alley, tennis courts and a laundry room and costs 740 SIT per person with tent only, or 1200 SIT with tent and car. Bicycles are available for rent, and there are daily permits (1300 SIT) for fishing in the Sava. There are also three-dozen cramped little bungalows at 5500/8000/12,900 SIT for a single/double/triple.

Avtokamp Smlednik (☎ *362 70 02)* in Dragočajna, 17km north-west of Ljubljana, is located between two small lakes; the big attraction here seems to be the nudist beach. Smlednik, open from May to mid-October, charges similar rates to Ježica.

Hostels & Student Dormitories

Four student dormitories *(dijaški dom)* open their doors to foreign travellers in July and August and are clean, cheap and friendly places in which to stay.

The dormitory nearest to Center is *Dijaški Dom Tabor* (☎ *232 10 67, fax 232 10 60,* e *ssljddta1s@guest.arnes.si, Vidovdanska ulica 7),* which is affiliated to Hostelling International (HI) and can accommodate up to 60 people. It charges 3500 SIT for a single room with breakfast and 3000 SIT per person for a bed in a double, triple or quad (2450 SIT for HI members). As usual, toilets and showers are down the corridor, but all rooms have running water. Though there's a 'curfew' between 10 pm and 6 am, the security guard will let you in when you ring the bell. The Tabor is open late June to August. It is a 10-minute walk south-east from the bus and train stations.

The *Dijaški Dom Bežigrad* (☎ *534 28 67, fax 534 28 64, Kardeljeva ploščad 28)* is in the Bežigrad district 2km north of the train and bus stations. It has doubles/triples with shower and toilet for 2900/2400 SIT per person and rooms with one to three beds with shared facilities for 2000 SIT per person. None of the rates include breakfast. An HI card gets you about 10% off, and the hostel is open throughout the night. The Bežigrad has 70 rooms available from late June to late August but only about 20 (available at weekends only) for the rest of the year. There's a laundry in the Dijaški Dom Kam (Building C) at Kardeljeva ploščad 14 which is open from 8 am till noon and 2 to 6 pm weekdays and 8 am to 3 pm Saturday. To get here from Slovenska cesta, take bus No 6, 8 or 21 and get off at the Mercator/Triglavska stop.

A bit closer to town is the *Dijaški Dom Ivana Cankarja* (☎ *433 51 77, fax 432 03 69, Poljanska cesta 26–28, Building B),* about 1.2km east of Center in Poljane. It has 160 rooms and charges 3460/2800/2600 SIT per person for singles/doubles/triples. Rooms don't have running water, but there are showers, toilets and TVs on each floor. It is open mid-June to August, but you may be able to find a bed here on weekends at other times of the year. Take bus No 5 or 13 from Center.

Private Rooms & Apartments

The TIC has about 40 private rooms on its list, but just a handful are in Center. Most of the others require a bus trip north to Bežigrad. Prices start at 3500 SIT for singles and 5000 SIT for doubles. *Tour Da-La* (☎ *721 59 57, fax 721 63 84,* e *apartmaji@tour-da-la.si)* in Trzin has eight very comfortable apartments and two studios – four of which are central – for one to five people with prices ranging from 9900 to 17,200 SIT a night. Reception is at the Miredita agency (☎ *431 11 02, fax 431 10 96)* in the Ledina shopping centre at Kotnikova ulica 5.

Pensions & Guesthouses

The closest thing you'll find to a guesthouse in Ljubljana proper is the 30-room *Gostilna Pri Mraku* (☎ *421 96 00, fax 421 96 55,* e *mrak@daj-dam.si, Rimska cesta 4),* west of Trg Francoske Revolucije. It's newly renovated, and the restaurant downstairs has reasonably priced and generous Slovenian set menus, but the rooms are small and quite expensive – 10,450 SIT for a single with shower, TV and breakfast and 17,800 SIT for a double.

The 11-room *Penzion Lieber* (☎ *561 21 23, fax 537 28 62, Srednje Gameljne 32e*), 7km north of Ljubljana, charges from 6000 SIT for singles and from 8000 SIT for doubles. The Lieber has an excellent Maison de Qualité restaurant.

There are a dozen decent pensions around the towns of Domžale and Radomlje about 15km north-east of Ljubljana. One of the nicest is *Penzion Pri Špornu* (☎ *722 70 00, fax 722 71 35, Cesta Radomeljske Čete 1*) in Radomlje, with 11 rooms and three apartments. It is famed for its excellent restaurant.

Hotels – Budget

The best-value budget deal in Ljubljana is the *BIT Center Hotel* (☎ *548 00 55, fax 548 00 56,* e *hotel@bit-center.net, Litijska 57*), 2km east of the city centre. The 37 rooms are spartan but bright and comfortable, with private bathroom and TV. Singles cost 4190 SIT, doubles and triples are 6890 SIT. A good buffet breakfast is 700 SIT extra. Take bus No 9 from the train and bus station (eastbound) or No 13 from Kongresni trg and get of at the Emona stop.

The 120-room *Hotel Park* (☎ *433 13 06, fax 433 05 46,* e *tabor@siol.net, Tabor 9*) is where most people usually end up as it's the only budget hotel close to Center and the Old Town. Although the lobby has been spruced up, the rooms are still pretty basic. Singles/doubles are 5800/7200 SIT with private WC but shared shower, and 7200/9000 SIT with private shower and WC; add 700 SIT for a TV. Breakfast is included. Students with ISIC cards get a 20% discount.

Hotels – Mid-Range

The newly renovated 154-room *M Hotel* (☎ *513 70 00, fax 519 30 48,* e *info@m-ho tel.si, Derčeva ulica 4*) is 2km north-west of Center, set back from Celovška cesta. Take bus No 5 from Tavčarjeva ulica just north

of the Hotel Turist and alight at the Kino Šiska stop. Smart singles/doubles with bathroom, TV and Internet connection cost 9700/13,000 SIT, and there is one room designed for wheelchair users.

The 108-room *Hotel Turist* (☎ *234 91 30, fax 234 91 40,* e *info@hotelturist.si, Dalmatinova ulica 15*) is a mere 400m from the train and bus stations and only 200m from Prešernov trg. A rather unprepossessing six-storey block, it has undergone a much needed renovation and now offers central, four-star accommodation. Rates are 10,800 to 12,960 SIT for a single and 15,770 to 17,930 SIT for a double, including a generous breakfast buffet, depending on room and season.

Hotels – Top End

In the thick of things is the 171-room *Hotel Slon Best Western* (☎ *470 11 00, fax 251 71 64,* e *sales@h-slon-bw.si, Slovenska cesta 34*). The 'Hotel Elephant' has a history going back more than four centuries – it is said that this was the spot where a pachyderm presented to the Habsburg emperor by an African king tarried on its way to Vienna – though the present hotel dates from the 20th century. There are several categories of rooms, with prices ranging from 15,900 to 21,620 SIT for a single, and from 22,890 to 30,630 SIT for a double. Try to get an east-facing room with a view of Castle Hill. The Slon has a floor reserved for nonsmokers, and popular Slovenian and Italian restaurants.

The 62-room *Austrotel* (☎ *308 43 00, fax 230 11 81,* e *austrotel@magistrat.kompas .si, Miklošičeva cesta 9*) is a modern business hotel barely five minutes' walk from the train station. Singles/doubles cost from €82/128. Rooms facing Miklošičeva cesta can be noisy.

The most desirable place to stay in Ljubljana is the renovated Art-Nouveau *Grand Hotel Union* (☎ *308 12 70, fax 308 10 15,* e *hotel.union@gh-union.si, Miklošičeva cesta 1*), which was built in 1905. Singles range from €114 to €137, and doubles from €151 to €182. Try to get a room in the old part of the hotel, rather than the modern north wing. The hotel has a cellar restaurant (Unionska Klet) and a lovely garden restaurant, and guests get to use the swimming pool, sauna and fitness centre. The neighbouring *Holiday Inn* (☎ *308 11 70, fax 308 19 13,* e *holiday.inn@gh-union .si, Miklošičeva cesta 3)* is under the same management and charges similar rates, but feels like any Holiday Inn from Cleveland, Ohio, to Kuala Lumpur.

The five-star *Lev Inter-Continental* (☎ *433 21 55, fax 434 33 50,* e *ljubljana@ interconti.com, Vošnjakova ulica 1),* southeast of the landmark Pivovarna Union (Union Brewery), has metamorphosed in recent years from an old, nondescript hotel into Ljubljana's most luxurious and expensive accommodation. The 173 rooms cost 32,500 or 34,500 SIT for a single, and 40,500 SIT for a double or twin. There are two rooms for wheelchair users, at 35,500 SIT. The Lev is within easy walking distance of the stations and almost everything in Center.

PLACES TO EAT
Restaurants
Ljubljana has a lively restaurant scene, with a core of old favourites complemented by a range of new and innovative places. It is possible to eat well here without breaking the bank – even the more expensive restaurants offer an excellent-value set lunch *(dnevno kosilo)* for as little as 1200 to 1600 SIT.

Slovenian The *Vinoteka Sokol* (☎ *439 68 55, Ciril-Metodov trg 18)* opposite the cathedral is a delightfully rustic *gostilna,* popular with everyone from market vendors taking their morning coffee and *malica* to families out for an evening meal. Traditional dishes include *štruklji* (cheese pastries; 400 SIT) and *obara* (veal stew; 850 SIT); the set lunch is 1300 SIT. It's open from 6 am to 11 pm Monday to Saturday, 8 am to 10 pm Sunday.

An old stand-by – it's been around since 1776 – with national dishes is *Šestica* (☎ *251 95 75, Slovenska cesta 40).* It's a very popular place with local people and serves up plates of *goveji golaž* (beef goulash) and fat Kranjska sausage with cabbage. The set lunch is 1000 SIT, and supper is 1250 SIT. The back courtyard is

pleasant but gets a bit stuffy in summer. Šestica is open from 8 am to 11 pm Monday to Saturday.

Figovec (☎ *426 50 00, Gosposvetska cesta 1)* is a bustling, city-centre hostelry where a set lunch of beef soup, goulash and ice cream will set you back a mere 1150 SIT.

Restavracija Lovec (☎ *426 57 08, Trg mladinskih delovnih brigad 1)* has a pleasant summer garden and serves steaks and venison as well as pizzas, pastas and salad; main courses cost from 950 to 2600 SIT. It's open from 6.30 am to 11 pm Monday to Saturday, 9 am to 10 pm Sunday.

Arguably the poshest restaurant in Ljubljana is *Smrekarjev Hram* (☎ *308 19 07, Nazorjeva ulica 2),* an Art-Nouveau jewel run by the Grand Hotel Union. But without the rich aunt or uncle in tow, enter at your own peril as this place is very expensive. It's open from noon to 11 pm weekdays only. The atmospheric *Unionska Klet* (☎ *308 19 72, Miklošičeva cesta 1),* in the cellar of the Grand Hotel Union, is less of a strain on the wallet.

A couple of gostilne that are a bit out of the way but get rave reviews from both local and foreign residents alike are *Pri Jerneju* (☎ *283 87 35, Velika Čolnarska ulica 17),* about 400m south-east of Eipprova ulica and the Gradaščica canal, open noon to 11 pm daily, and *Pri Gorjancu* (☎ *423 11 11, Tržaška cesta 330),* 5km south-west of Center, open from noon to 10 pm Sunday to Friday.

International The *Špajza (The Pantry;* ☎ *425 30 94, Gornji trg 28)* is a labyrinth of rustic rooms with rough-hewn tables and chairs, wooden floors, low, frescoed ceilings and nostalgic bits and pieces. It's an ideal place for a romantic dinner, but expect to pay around 4500 SIT a head plus wine. The set lunch, from noon to 4 pm weekdays only, is 2000 SIT. Špajza is open from noon to midnight daily, except Sunday.

Pri Sv Florianu (☎ *251 22 14, Gornji trg 20)* is a bright and elegant eatery serving Slovene food with a modern slant, and a range of international cuisines from Latin

American to South-East Asian. It's open from noon to midnight daily, and the 1490 SIT set lunch is available until 4 pm daily.

Stylish *Pri Vitezu* (☎ 426 60 58, Breg 20) across the river from the Old Town, is the place for a special meal, whether in the vaulted cellar dining rooms or the riverside garden with its view of the castle. 'The Knight' specialises in Italian-style dishes and Adriatic seafood, and has an excellent wine list – allow 5000 to 6000 SIT a head for dinner, or 1600 SIT for the set lunch.

Ljubljanski Dvor (☎ 251 65 55, Dvorni trg 1), south-east of Kongresni trg, is both an upmarket restaurant serving decent international fare and a pizzeria (see Italian). It opens from noon till midnight daily, except Sunday.

Despite its official address, *Papillon* (☎ 426 21 26, Nazorjeva ulica 6) is entered from the Trg Ajdovščina shopping centre. This basement restaurant is made up to look like a prison, and has videos of the Steve McQueen film *Papillon* playing continuously. The mixed menu includes traditional Slovenian fare and international offerings like French onion soup and Mexican fajitas. It's open from 11 am to 10 pm weekdays, and from noon to 10 pm Saturday.

Pod Rožnikom (☎ 251 34 46, Cesta na Rožnik 18) – known to locals as 'Čad' – is famous for its southern Slav-style grills like *pljeskavica* (spicy meat patties) served with *ajvar* (roasted red peppers, tomatoes and eggplant cooked into a puree) and starters like *prebranac* (onions and beans cooked in an earthenware pot) and *šampinjoni na žaru* (grilled mushrooms). It's open from noon till 11 pm daily.

Italian If you hanker after real Italian cuisine, you should head for the upmarket *Ristorante Atrij* (☎ 470 11 00) in the Hotel Slon or, at a pinch, the *Fortunat* (☎ 283 52 94, Eipprova ulica 2) in Trnovo, open to 11 pm daily, except Saturday. Otherwise, 'Italian' in Ljubljana usually means pizza or a bit of pasta.

For pizza try the local favourites: *Napoli* (☎ 231 29 49, Prečna ulica 7), off Trubarjeva cesta (enter from Mala ulica), open to 11 pm Monday to Saturday, 10 pm Sunday; or *Ljubljanski Dvor* (☎ 251 65 55, Dvorni trg 1) north of Breg. But you can't beat the bustling *Pizzerija Foculus* (☎ 251 56 43, Gregorčičeva ulica 3) for original decor – the entire vaulted ceiling is painted with spring and autumn leaves. Small/large pizzas cost from 650/800 SIT and the salad bar from 450 SIT. It's open from noon till midnight daily. *Čerin* (☎ 232 09 90, Trubarjeva cesta 52) has good pizzas and an excellent salad bar where you pay by weight.

Spanish & Mexican The *Casa del Papa* restaurant (☎ 434 31 58, Celovška cesta 54a) is Spanish (and maybe a little Cuban – the 'Papa' refers to Ernest Hemingway) and is decorated in a hotchpotch of styles: Spanish here, French there and African somewhere over there. Somehow it all works and well-heeled Ljubljančani can't seem to get enough of the place. On the 1st floor is the Key West Bar and in the cellar the Cuban Room (see Entertainment). The restaurant is open from noon to 1 am daily.

Friendly *Meson Don Felipe* (☎ 434 38 62, Streliška ulica 22), south-east of Krekov trg, is Ljubljana's first – and only – tapas bar, where around 3000 SIT will get you four tapas and a glass of wine. It's open from noon till midnight daily.

There's authentic Mexican food on the menu at *Mexico 1867* (☎ 438 24 50, Medvedova cesta 18) north of the Union Brewery, open from 11 am to midnight Monday to Thursday, and to 2 am Friday and Saturday.

Chinese If you're looking for a fix of Chinese food, try the *Sichuan* (☎ 251 93 37, Gornji trg 23) below St Florian's Church, where main courses run from 950 to 1500 SIT. Another place with seriously over-the-top decorations and slightly lower prices is *Shang Hai* (☎ 433 80 54, Poljanska cesta 14). Both are open from 11 am to 11 pm daily.

Seafood For a quick and very tasty lunch, try the fried squid or *škarpina* fillet (both 1000 SIT) at *Ribca* (☎ 426 17 77, Adamič-Lundrovo nabrežje 1), a basement seafood bar below the Plečnik Colonnade in Poga-rčarjev trg. *Zlata Ribica (☎ 241 06 90, Cankarjevo nabrežje 5)*, a small pub-restaurant, serves simple fish dishes at lunch for 500 to 1000 SIT. It is open from 8 am to 10 pm weekdays, to 3 pm Saturday and 7 am to 3 pm Sunday.

Dalmatinska Konoba (☎ 432 80 47, Trubarjeva cesta 47) is an attractive base-ment restaurant specialising in seafood – the grilled sardines (600 SIT) and roast oc-topus (1000 SIT) are superb. It's open from 10 am to 11 pm daily, except Monday. The riverside bar-restaurant *Alkar (☎ 283 53 12, Trnovski prstan 4)* in Trnovo is another place worth checking, and is open from noon to 10 pm daily, except Sunday.

Operna Klet (☎ 251 47 15, Župančičeva ulica 4), near the Opera (enter from Tomši-čeva ulica), is a more upmarket seafood venue, open from noon till 10 pm daily, but at the top of the heap is *Gostilna As (☎ 425 88 22)* in Knafljev prehod, the passage be-tween Wolfova and Slovenska cesta. The 'Ace' is the place for a special occasion – seafood and classic Slovene dishes domi-nate the menu, and a three-course a la carte dinner with wine will set you back around 9000 SIT a head.

Vegetarian Most eating places in Ljub-ljana have at least one or two vegie dishes on the menu, but there are as yet no special-ist vegetarian restaurants in town. The *Zrno* store *(Trubarjeva cesta 8)* sells vegetarian and vegan sandwiches and snacks, and is open from 6.30 am to 7 pm weekdays and 7 am to 1 pm Saturday.

Cafes
The coffee house *(kavarna)* is nowhere near as much a part of the social fabric and daily routine in Ljubljana as it is in, say, Buda-pest or Vienna, but in recent years Stari trg in the Old Town has seen a flowering of cafe society, with street tables almost end to end in summer.

Ljubljana's classic cafes include the reno-vated *Kavarna Evropa (Gosposvetska cesta 2)* on the corner of Slovenska cesta, com-plete with crystal chandeliers, and the

Kavarna Union in the Grand Hotel Union, which is a little lacklustre. The *Art Cafe* in Hotel Slon is another popular haunt. *Kavarna Pločnik* beside the Triple Bridge on Prešernov trg, is one of the city's most popular outdoor cafes.

More interesting are Old Town cafes like *Nostalgija (Stari trg 9)*, with its retro-chic decor; the French-style *Julija-sur-Seine* next door; *Cafe Antico (Stari trg 17)*, with its frescoed ceilings and antique furniture; and the ultra-trendy *Cafe Maček (Krojaška ulica 5)* – the place to be seen on a sunny summer afternoon.

The *Plečnikov Hram (Trg Francoske Revolucije 1)* in the Križanke complex is a great meeting place, especially for a quiet tete-a-tete. *Le Petit Café (Trg Francoske Revolucije 4)*, across the square, is a pleas-ant, studenty little place offering a wide range of breakfast goodies, from muesli (300 SIT) and yogurt (150 SIT) to ham and eggs (450 SIT). It's open from 8 am to 11 pm Monday to Saturday and noon to 9 pm Sunday.

Tramvaj Ekspres (Trg mladinskih de-lovnih brigad 10) is worth a visit for the novelty of sipping your espresso in a vin-tage Ljubljana tram. It's open from 10 am to 11.30 pm weekdays, from noon Saturday and from 1 pm Sunday. If you're feeling peckish, it does pizzas too.

If tea is your drink, try the *Čajna Hiša (Stari trg 1)*, which serves a wide range of green and black teas for 270 SIT a pot. The 'Tea House' is open from 9 am to 11 pm daily, except Sunday (also closed from 3 to 6 pm Saturday). *Čajnik (Slovenska cesta 46)* has a smaller range of teas, but charges only 220 SIT a pot; the 'Teapot' is open from 7 am to 10 pm weekdays, 8 am to 10 pm Saturday and 8 am to 8 pm Sunday.

Cafe Anika (Eipprova ulica 19) in Trnovo is said to have the best ice cream in the city.

Cheap Eats
One of the best places in Ljubljana for a cheap meal is *Plac* in the Plečnik Colon-nade beside the market on Vodnikov trg, where you can get a tasty and filling set

lunch for only 500 or 600 SIT. It's open from 9 am to 3 pm weekdays and 8 am to 2 pm Saturday.

The best self-service restaurant in Ljubljana, according to cognoscenti, is *Skriti Kot (Trg Ajdovščina 4),* very much a 'Hidden Corner' in the arcade below the shopping centre. Hearty main courses start at 600 SIT, pork chops and mash cost only 700 SIT. It's open from 7 am to 4 pm weekdays and till 2 pm Saturday.

The gleaming glass, wood and chrome *Restavracija 2000 (Trg Republike 1),* a self-service restaurant in the basement of the Maximarket shopping arcade, is a bit more upmarket – it does a three-course lunch for 1100 SIT. It's open from 9 am to 7 pm weekdays, and till 4 pm Saturday.

Snacks & Fast Food

There are *burek stands* at several locations in Ljubljana, and one of the best is the one next to Slovenijaturist on Pražakova ulica. Cheese, meat or apple bureks go for 250 SIT. If you want something more substantial, head for *Super 5,* which faces Slovenska cesta from the shopping mall on Trg Ajdovščina. It serves cheap and cheerful Balkan grills like *čevapčiči* (600 SIT), *pljeskavica* (540 SIT) and *klobasa* and is open 24 hours.

Tomato (Šubičeva ulica 1) is a diner-style restaurant serving good sandwiches, salads and burgers for 300 to 800 SIT, open from 7 am to 9 pm weekdays and 8 am to 2 pm Saturday. For a taste of the Middle East, try a kebab from the *Kebapči (Trubarjeva cesta 17),* open from 9 am to 2 am daily.

If you *must* have Western-style fast food, there are *McDonald's* branches up the stairs at Čopova ulica 14, open from 9 am to 11 pm daily (from 10 am Sunday), and at the train station, open from 7 am to midnight daily. A local version of fast food is available at *Rio Ham Ham (Slovenska cesta 28).* It's open from 8 am to 10 pm weekdays, and from 10 am Saturday and Sunday.

Food Markets & Self-Catering

The large *outdoor market* in Vodnikov trg, selling mostly fresh fruit and vegetables, is open from 6 am to 5 or 6 pm Monday to Saturday in summer and to 4 pm in winter. The *fish market* is on the lower level of the Plečnik Colonnade overlooking the river. The *covered market* on the ground floor of the Seminary on Pogarčarjev trg – with a superb range of meats, charcuterie, fish and dairy products – is open from 6 am to 4 pm weekdays and to 2 pm Saturday. The outdoor stalls below the cathedral sell seasonal goods like wild mushrooms, honey, chestnuts, beeswax and fresh herbs.

The Plečnik Colonnade beside the market houses several excellent food shops – the *Pekarna Neža* is the best place to buy *potica,* while the *Pekarna Por* at the western end has superb bread baked in wood-fired ovens and a range of delicious cheeses.

The *supermarket* and *delicatessen* in the basement of the Maximarket shopping arcade on Trg Republike have the largest selection of food and wine in the city centre. They are open from 9 am to 8 pm weekdays and 8 am to 5 pm Saturday.

Noč in Dan (Trg OF 13), opposite the train station, sells groceries, sweets, drinks and hot snacks and is open 24 hours a day.

ENTERTAINMENT

Ljubljana enjoys a rich cultural and social life for its size, so ask the TIC for its monthly program of events in English *(Where to? in Ljubljana)* as well as any flyers it might have for various theatres and concert halls.

Classical Music, Opera & Dance

Concerts are held in various locations all over town, but the main venue – with up to 700 cultural events a year – is *Cankarjev Dom* (☎ 425 81 21, *Prešernova cesta 10).* It has two large auditoriums (the Gallus Hall has perfect acoustics) and a number of smaller ones. The ticket office (☎ 252 28 15), in the basement of the nearby Maximarket shopping arcade, is open from 10 am to 2 pm and 4.30 to 8 pm weekdays, 10 am to 1 pm Saturday and an hour before performances. Also check for concerts at the beautiful *Filharmonija (Kongresni trg 10).* Tickets run anywhere between 300 and 2000 SIT, but most are in the 600 to 900 SIT range.

The ticket office (☎ 425 48 40) of the **Opera House** *(☎ 425 46 80, Župančičeva ulica 1)*, which stages operas and ballets, is open from 2 to 5 pm weekdays, 6 to 7.30 pm Saturday, and an hour before performances.

For tickets to the Ljubljana Summer Festival and anything else staged at the **Križanke**, go to the booking office (☎ 252 65 44) opposite the Ilirija Column at Trg Francoske Revolucije 1-2. It is open from 11 am to 2 pm and 4 to 7 pm weekdays and 10 am to 1 pm Saturday. Tickets can be bought at the venue starting one hour before the performance.

Theatre

Ljubljana has a half-dozen theatres so there should be something for everyone. Slovenian theatre is usually quite visual with a lot of mixed media, so you don't always have to speak the lingo to enjoy the production.

The home of the national company is the **National Drama Theatre** *(Slovensko Narodno Gledališče or SNG;* ☎ 252 14 62, 426 45 49, Erjavčeva cesta 1); the box office (☎ 252 15 11) is open from 2 to 5 pm weekdays and from 6 pm till the performance begins. Tickets cost from 1100 to 2400 SIT (30% to 40% more for a first night). The **Slovenian Youth Theatre** *(Slovensko Mladinsko Gledališče;* ☎ 231 06 10, Vilharjeva ulica 11) in the Festival Hall (Festivalna Dvorana) has staged some highly acclaimed productions.

The **Glej Theatre** *(☎ 251 66 79, Gregorčičeva ulica 3)* is Ljubljana's foremost experimental theatre with three resident or affiliated companies, including Betontanc (dance) and Grapefruit (drama). They're often on tour and the theatre is closed in July and August; in other months, your best chance to see a performance is on Thursday or Friday night. The box office is open from 10 am to 2 pm and 5 to 7 pm weekdays and 10 am to 1 pm Saturday.

The **Café Teater** *(☎ 252 71 08, Miklošičeva cesta 2)* at the Grand Hotel Union, stages comedies and musicals, mainly on Friday and Saturday. The box office (in the Kavarna Union) is open from 3 to 7 pm Thursday and Friday. **Cankarjev Dom** (see Classical Music, Opera & Dance) regularly stages theatrical productions.

The **Ljubljana Puppet Theatre** *(Lutkovno Gledališče Ljubljana;* ☎ 300 09 70, Krekov trg 2) hosts the annual International Puppet Festival (Mednarodni lutkovo festival) in October, as well as staging its own shows throughout the year.

Cinemas

For first-run films, head for any of the following cinemas: **Komuna** *(☎ 421 24 60, Cankarjeva cesta 1);* **Kompas** *(☎ 432 01 40, Miklošičeva cesta 38);* or **Šiška** *(☎ 519 32 84, Trg prekomorskih brigad 3)* near the M Hotel. They generally have three screenings a day, and tickets cost 650 to 800 SIT.

Kinoteka *(☎ 433 02 13, Miklošičeva cesta 28)* shows art and classic films, with screenings at 6, 8 and 10 pm. Tickets here generally cost 300 to 500 SIT, and discounts are usually available on Monday.

Pubs & Bars

One of the most popular places for a drink, if you just want to sit outside and watch the passing parade, is the roped-off **Kavarna Pločnik** on the southern side of Prešernov trg. You'll probably bump into half the people you've met along the way in Slovenia here. It's open till at least midnight from June to October. A pleasant and congenial place for a *pivo* or glass of *vino* nearby is the **Cutty Sark** in the courtyard behind Wolfova ulica 6 on Knafljev prehod. The garden at the **As**, immediately opposite the Cutty Sark, is a popular meeting place, and its downstairs bar is one of the liveliest party pubs in town.

Trubarjeva cesta is a lively street with plenty of bars, cafes and late-night pizzerias. The **TrueBar** *(Trubarjeva cesta 23)*, open to 1 am nightly, is a favourite hangout, and **Patrick's Irish Pub** *(Prečna ulica 6)* nearby is also a pleasant place for a drink. Travellers have recommended the **Tramontana** *(Nazorjeva ulica 8)*, a courtyard bar, as a good place to meet people. It's open till 1 am daily (till 3 or 4 am Friday and Saturday). Or you can head for the wine bar in the **Vinoteka Movja** *(Mestni trg 1)* if you fancy whiling away an afternoon or evening sampling the best of Slovenian wine (see Shopping later in this chapter).

Holidays Pub (Slovenska cesta 36), next to the Kompas travel agency, is a very popular meeting place in the evening and can get very crowded; it's open till 3 am every night. A favourite place for students is **Miriam's Pub** *(Kersnikova ulica 5)* opposite the Študentska Organizacija Univerze Ljubljani (ŠOU; the Student Organisation of the University of Ljubljana). The well-heeled set smokes Havana cigars in the **Key West Bar** above Casa del Papa restaurant (see Places to Eat). It's open from 9 am to 5 am daily.

Trnovski Svon is in the same building as Cafe Anika in Trnovo (see Places to Eat), and has pleasant outdoor tables beside the canal. It isn't as much fun as the Sax (see Rock, Jazz & Blues) but is sometimes easier to get into.

Rock, Jazz & Blues
Ljubljana has a number of excellent music clubs and the ones listed below are highly recommended. The landmark **Orto Bar** *(☎ 232 16 74, Graboličeva ulica 1)*, a short distance north-east of Metelkova, hosts a wide range of local and foreign bands from rock, punk and blues to rap. The **Križanke** (see Classical Music, Opera & Dance) is also used as a rock venue.

The **Gajo Jazz Club** *(☎ 425 32 06, Beethovnova ulica 8)*, just up from the Parliament building, is Ljubljana's premier venue for live jazz and attracts both local and international talent. It's open from 10 am to 2 am weekdays and 7 pm to midnight Saturday and Sunday. **Birdland** *(☎ 231 79 37, Trubarjeva cesta 50)* is a new jazz cafe with a cool atmosphere and good food.

Hound Dog *(☎ 519 50 55, Trg prekomorskih brigad 4)*, in the basement of the M Hotel complex, is a great live music venue (rock, blues, reggae) that also hosts themed DJ nights when there's no band playing. The **Sax Pub** *(☎ 252 54 31, Eipprova ulica 7)* in Trnovo, decorated with colourful murals and graffiti, occasionally has live jazz.

Discos & Clubs
The most popular conventional discos are **Papillon** *(☎ 426 21 26, Nazorjeva ulica 6)*

above the restaurant of the same name (see Places to Eat), open till 3 am daily, and **Klub Central** *(☎ 252 12 92, Dalmatinova ulica 15)* next to the Hotel Turist.

Klub K4 *(☎ 431 70 10, Kersnikova ulica 4)*, in the basement of the Student Organisation of the University of Ljubljana, has a dance club on various nights during university terms. Two other venues that are popular with Ljubljana's young bloods are the **Cuban Room** *(☎ 434 31 58, Celovška cesta 54a)* below the Casa del Papa restaurant, with Latino and salsa music (open from 6 pm to 5 am daily), and the **Propaganda Klub** *(☎ 231 93 79, Grablovičeva ulica 1)*, which has house nights on Wednesday and Saturday and techno on Friday.

Gay & Lesbian Venues
Ljubljana may not be the gayest city in Central Europe, but there are a few decent options. For general information and advice, ring Roza Klub (☎ 430 47 40), the gay branch of the Student Cultural Centre (Študentski Kulturni Center; ŠKUC) at Kersnikova ulica 4, or the GALfon hotline (☎ 432 40 89; from 7 to 10 pm daily).

A popular spot for both gays and lesbians alike is the Sunday night **Roza Klub** disco at Klub K4 (see Discos & Clubs). The music takes no risks, but the crowd is lively and friendly. It's open from 11 pm to 4 am and costs 800 SIT (600 SIT for students).

In Metelkova – a former army barracks between Metelkova ulica and Maistrova ulica, now Ljubljana's answer to Christiania in Copenhagen – there's a friendly gay and lesbian cafe-pub called **Klub Tiffany**. It's in the small blue building to the left (east) as you enter the squat. Tiffany is open from 8 pm till midnight Sunday to Thursday and 10 pm to 4 am Friday and Saturday. There's also the lesbian-only **Klub Monokel** in the same building, open from 9 pm Thursday to Saturday.

The **Zlati Klub** sauna in Tivoli Park (see Swimming & Sauna under Activities earlier in this chapter) attracts a gay crowd.

If you prefer to meet friends *en plein air,* the walkways behind the Tivoli Recreation Centre and Modern History Museum in the park – as far as the Hala Tivoli sport centre – are notoriously cruisy after dark, as are the car parks just in front of the recreation centre and to the east across the train tracks along Tivolska cesta. The path along the Sava River near the Gostilna Žagar (Gameljska ulica 1) in Črnuče (bus No 6) is a popular meeting place in warmer weather.

Multicultural Centres
Klub K4 (see Discos & Clubs) is a popular venue featuring both canned and live music nightly – from hip-hop, rap and techno to acid jazz and folk. Ask for its monthly program and make your choices. It's open until 2 or 4 am and admission is 500 SIT (400 SIT for students) except on Friday and Sunday night when it costs 800/600 SIT respectively.

KUD France Prešeren (☎ 283 22 88, *Karunova ulica 14*), a 'noninstitutional culture and arts society' in Trnovo, stages concerts of all kinds and is the headquarters of the Ana Monro Theatre, the only street theatre in Slovenia. KUD also has a great high-tech pub-cafe, open from 3 to 10 pm daily, where you can meet people.

Galerija ŠKUC (☎ 251 65 40, *Stari trg 21*), run by the student cultural association, has information, music performances and art exhibitions, especially by the Neue Slowenische Kunst (NSK) multimedia group and the Irwin artists' cooperative.

Casinos
Ljubljana Casino (☎ 230 29 88, *Miklošičeva cesta 9*), next to the Austrotel, has American roulette, blackjack, poker and slot machines. It's open from noon to 2 am daily (to 3 am Friday and Saturday).

SPECTATOR SPORTS
For a schedule of sporting events in the capital, check the monthly *Where to? in Ljubljana* available from the TIC.

Football matches take place at the Central Stadium (Centralni Stadion) on Dunajska cesta, designed by Jože Plečnik in 1925. It's an easy bus ride (bus No 6, 8 or 21 to the Stadion stop) or a 20-minute walk north up Dunajska cesta from Center.

For basketball, ice hockey and volleyball, the venue is the Hala Tivoli sport centre in Tivoli Park.

SHOPPING
For general souvenirs and folk crafts, check what's on offer at Galerija Zibka in Hotel Slon, the Dom at Mestni trg 24, Parazol at Stari trg 15 and 365 at Mestni trg 9. They all have Slovenian things like Prekmurje black pottery, Idrija lace, beehive panels with folk motifs, decorated heart-shaped honey cakes, painted Easter eggs, Rogaška glassware and so on. The best place in town for distinctly Ljubljana souvenirs is the Ljubljanček gift shop in the lobby of the Grand Hotel Union.

Don't expect any bargains, but Carniola Antiqua at Trubarjeva cesta 9 and Antika Ferjan at Mestni trg 21 in the Old Town have superb antiques. Antikvariat Tizian at Ključavničarska 3 (an alley off Mestni trg) is an Aladdin's Cave of antiques and bric-a-brac, and at Mestni trg 25 there's a second-hand/antiquarian bookshop called Trubarjev Antikvariat. Galerija Lala at Židovska ulica 5 is one of the finest galleries in the capital, with both old and new art.

Big Bang at Wolfova ulica 12 is a music shop with CDs and cassettes of all kinds of music, including Slovenian folk, but Rec-Rec at Resljeva cesta 2 has a better selection. Another good place for music is the Hard Rock shop at Trubarjeva cesta 40.

Musikalje at Trg Francoske Revolucije 6, near the Križanke, is the place for classical music and scores. If you fancy buying or ordering a custom-made violin, then head for the workshop of Vilem Demšer in a passage at Mestni trg 11.

If you've forgotten your sleeping bag, ski poles, hiking boots or climbing gear, head for Annapurna at Krakovski nasip 10 in Krakovo. It's open from 8.30 am to 7 pm weekdays and to 1 pm Saturday. For those into ridin', fishin' and shootin', Lovec at Gosposvetska 12 has all the kit and equipment you'll need. It's open from 8 am to 7 pm weekdays and to 1 pm Saturday.

The city of Tržič, north-west of Ljubljana, has always been synonymous with quality shoes and the Peko branches at

Čopova ulica 1 and Miklošičeva cesta 12 (both open from 8 am to 7.30 pm weekdays, to 1 pm Saturday) stock a wide range.

Vinoteka Simon Bradeško at Dunajska cesta 18 has a selection of some 400 Slovenian wines. It's open from 10 am to 7 pm weekdays and 9 am to 1 pm Saturday. Vinoteka Movja, next to the Town Hall at Mestni trg 1, and Vino Boutique at Slovenska cesta 38, may not have as many choices, but are more conveniently located. Movja has an excellent wine bar where, with due ceremony and ritual, you can taste your way through some award-winning Slovenian wines (400 to 600 SIT for 0.1L, which can be shared between two). Recommended wines include the 1997 Movja Chardonnay (2100 SIT a bottle) and the 1994 Merlot (3000 SIT).

There's an interesting antiques flea market on Cankarjevo nabrežje from 8 am to 1 pm every Sunday. On the second Saturday of the month the same site hosts a pottery and ceramics market.

GETTING THERE & AWAY
Air
The main ticket office for Adria Airways (☎ 431 30 00) is at Gosposvetska cesta 6 near the Lev Inter-Continental Hotel, open from 8 am to 7 pm weekdays and to noon Saturday. A more convenient branch (☎ 426 22 62), open 8 am to 4 pm weekdays only, is on the ground floor of Trg Republike 3.

Other airlines with offices in Ljubljana include:

Aeroflot (☎ 231 33 50) Dunajska cesta 21
Austrian Airlines (☎ 436 12 83) Dunajska cesta 58
Lufthansa (☎ 232 66 69) Gosposvetska cesta 6
Swissair (☎ 569 10 10) World Trade Centre, Dunajska cesta 156

See the Getting There & Away chapter for details of flights to Ljubljana.

Bus
Buses to destinations both within Slovenia and abroad leave from the same bus station at Trg OF 4, opposite the train station. For information, ring ☎ 434 38 38 or ☎ 090-4030. There's an information window, inside the station across from the ticket desks, open from 5.30 am to 9 pm, and a big timetable board listing all departure times. The staff are multilingual and quite helpful.

For the most part, you do not have to buy your ticket in advance; just pay as you board the bus. But for long-distance trips on Friday, just before the school break and public holidays, you are running the risk of not getting a seat. Book one the day before and reserve a seat for 120 SIT.

You can reach virtually anywhere in the country by bus – as close as Kamnik (at least every half-hour) or as far away as Vinica in Bela Krajina (three a day). The timetable in the bus station lists all bus routes and times, but here are some sample frequencies and one-way fares (return fares are double): Bled (980 SIT, hourly), Bohinj (1480 SIT, hourly), Jesenice (830 SIT, hourly), Koper (1900 SIT, nine to 12 a day), Maribor (2050 SIT, every half-hour), Murska Sobota (3050 SIT, nine a day), Novo Mesto (1170 SIT, hourly), Piran (2120 SIT, six to 11 a day) and Postojna (900 SIT, hourly).

For details of international bus services from Ljubljana see the Getting There & Away chapter.

Train
All trains – both domestic and international – arrive at and depart from the train station (☎ 291 33 32 for information) at Trg OF 6. The lemon-yellow building houses a bar, cafe, *okrepčevalnica* (snack bar), McDonald's outlet (open 7 am to midnight daily) and general store. There's a currency-exchange bureau next to the TIC branch office, open from 6 am to 10 pm daily. Nearby is the Wasteels office for BIJ tickets (open from 9.15 am to 5 pm weekdays).

You can get information from window No 11, and buy domestic tickets from window Nos 3 to 8 and international ones from Nos 9 and 10. For Croatia, you'll need to go to window No 1.

The following are some one-way 2nd-class domestic fares from Ljubljana: Bled 760 SIT, Jesenice 690 SIT, Koper 1380

SIT, Maribor 1380 SIT, Murska Sobota 2080 SIT and Novo Mesto 760 SIT. Return fares are usually 20% cheaper than double the price, and there's a 200 SIT surcharge on domestic InterCity (IC) train tickets.

Sample one-way 2nd-class fares on international trains include: Budapest (8833 SIT, 72½ hours), Munich (11,266 SIT, seven hours), Trieste (3791 SIT, three hours), Salzburg (6763 SIT, 4½ hours) and Zagreb (6650 SIT, 2½ hours). Seat reservations (200 SIT) are mandatory on some trains and available on others. An extra 200 SIT is levied on foreign IC train tickets and 564 SIT on the one EuroCity (EC) train.

For more information on trains leaving Ljubljana, turn to the Getting There & Away and Getting Around chapters.

Hitching
If you are leaving Ljubljana by way of thumb, take one of the following city buses to the terminus and begin hitching there.

Postojna, Koper, Croatian Istria and Italy (Trieste) Bus No 6 south-west (stop: Dolgi Most)
Bled, Jesenice and Austria (Salzburg) Bus No 1 north-west (stop: Vižmarje)
Novo Mesto and Croatia (Zagreb) Bus No 3 south-east (stop: Rudnik)
Maribor and Austria (Vienna) Bus No 6 north-east (stop: Črnuče)

GETTING AROUND
To/From the Airport
City bus No 28 (450 SIT, 35 minutes) runs between Ljubljana and Brnik airport, 23km to the north-west. It departs from the bus station (stop No 28) on weekdays at 5.20 am then hourly from 6.10 am to 8.10 pm; on weekends at 6.10 am then every two hours from 9.10 am to 7.10 pm. From airport to city, departures are on the hour. There are also hourly buses to Kranj (10 minutes).

An Adria Airways bus (1000 SIT) also runs from the airport to the Adria city terminal (on Trg OF near the bus station) eight times daily between 6.30 am and 10 pm. The SuperShuttle service (mobile ☎ 041-887 766, ☎ 541 66 34) picks up and drops off passengers at the Slon, Holiday Inn,

Grand Union, Austrotel and Lev hotels between 6 am and 10 pm, but you must book in advance. The fare is 2500 SIT per passenger.

A taxi from the airport to Ljubljana will cost around 5000 SIT. To Bled, expect to pay about 6000 SIT and double that to Kranjska Gora.

Public Transport
Ljubljana's public transport system, run by LPP (Ljubljanski Potniški Promet), is very user-friendly. There are a total of 22 lines with five of them (Nos 1, 2, 3, 6 and 11) considered main services; these start at 3.15 am and run till midnight. The rest operate between 5 am and 10.30 pm. Buses on the main lines run about every five to 15 minutes throughout the day. Service is less frequent on other lines and on Saturday, Sunday and holidays.

The system is foolproof. You can pay on board, which costs 160 SIT (exact change only), or use a tiny plastic token (žeton) costing 115 SIT and available at many newsstands, kiosks and post offices.

Bus passes (as well as tokens, of course) can be purchased from LPP's central office (☎ 582 24 60) at Celovška cesta 160 or from the two kiosks marked 'LPP' on the pavement at Slovenska cesta 55 opposite the system's central stop (Bavarski Dvor). Passes are available for a day (dnevna vozovnica, 345 SIT) or a week (tedenska vozovnica, 1725 SIT). The LPP office on Celovška cesta is open from 6.45 am to 7 pm weekdays and to 1 pm Saturday. The kiosks on Slovenska cesta are open from 5.30 am to 8 pm Monday to Saturday and from 9 am Sunday.

From the bus or train stations, bus No 2 will take you down Slovenska cesta to Mestni trg (bus stop: Magistrat) in the Old Town. To reach Trnovo, catch bus No 9 to the terminus.

Car & Motorcycle
Parking is not easy in central Ljubljana and, if you're not prepared to pay in some form or another, you're bound to get a ticket, or even towed away. There are car parks

throughout the city and their locations are indicated on most maps. Charges range from 220 to 330 SIT per hour.

Car Rental The big international car-rental firms have offices in Ljubljana, including Avis (☎ 430 80 10) at Čufarjeva ulica 2, Budget (☎ 421 73 40) at the Holiday Inn, Miklošičeva cesta 3, and Hertz (☎ 231 12 41) at Miklošičeva cesta 11. However, you will get a much cheaper deal at one of these local firms:

ABC (☎ 510 43 20 or ☎ 04-236 79 90) Ulica
  Jožeta Jame 16, and Brnik airport
Avtoimpex (☎ 505 50 25) Celovška cesta 150
Unis Tours (☎ 425 00 08) Igriška 5

For sample rates and information on conditions, see the Car & Motorcycle section in the Getting Around chapter.

Taxi
Taxis can be hailed on the street or hired from ranks near the train station, at the tourist information centre, in front of Hotel Slon on Slovenska cesta, or on Mestni trg. You can call a taxi on any one of 10 numbers: ☎ 9700 to ☎ 9709.

Bicycle
Ljubljana is a city of cyclists and there are bike lanes and special traffic lights everywhere. You can rent bikes (mobile ☎ 041-696 515) from 9 am to 8 pm daily in summer, at the Cutty Sark pub (see Pubs & Bars under Entertainment earlier in this chapter) and Cafe Maček (see Cafes under Places to Eat) for 500 SIT an hour or 2500 SIT a day.

Rog (☎ 231 58 68), Rozmanova ulica 1, is a bicycle shop that also rents bikes for 1500 SIT a day. It's open from 8 am to 7 pm weekdays and till noon Saturday.

For information about organised bike tours, see Cycling in the special section 'The Great Outdoors' earlier in the book.

AROUND LJUBLJANA
Let's face it, an awful lot in little Slovenia is 'around Ljubljana' and most of the towns and cities in Gorenjska, Primorska and Notranjska could be day trips from the capital. You can be in Bled in an hour, for example, and on the coast in less than two. Škofja Loka, Kamnik and Velika Planina are less than 30km away, and Cerknica is only 50km to the south-west.

Žale
Another Plečnik masterpiece, the monumental **Žale Cemetery** (Pokopališče Žale), 3km to the north-east of Center, has a series of chapels dedicated to the patron saints of Ljubljana's churches, and the entrance is an enormous two-storey arcade. It is a very peaceful, green place and 'home' to a number of Slovenian actors, writers, painters and a certain distinguished architect – Gospod Plečnik himself. You can reach Žale on bus No 2 or 7 (stop: Žale).

Šmarna Gora
This 669m hill above the Sava River, 12km north-west of Ljubljana, is a popular walking destination from Ljubljana and a mecca for hang-gliders and paragliders. Take bus No 15 from Slovenska cesta or Gosposvetska cesta to the Medno stop and begin walking. Another way to go is via the Smlednik bus from the main station and then follow the marked path from the 12th-century **Smlednik Castle**. There's swimming and boating in **Zbilje Lake** nearby.

Gorenjska

Mountains and lakes are the big attraction in Gorenjska (Upper Carniola), the province that in many ways feels more 'Slovenian' than any other. The start of the Kamnik-Savinja Alps are a short drive from Ljubljana, and Triglav National Park contains most of Slovenia's share of the Julian Alps, with many peaks rising to well over 2000m. There's a lot of skiing here, and Gorenjska offers some of the best hiking in Europe. A mountain trek is an excellent way to meet other Slovenes in a relaxed environment so take advantage of this opportunity if you're in Gorenjska during the hiking season.

The lakes at Bled and Bohinj are also popular centres for any number of outdoor activities, but Gorenjska also has many of Slovenia's most attractive, historical towns. Škofja Loka, Kamnik, Kranj and Radovljica – to name just a few – are treasure-troves of Gothic, Renaissance and baroque art and architecture, and wonderful bases from which to explore this diverse and visually spectacular province.

Because of the difficulty of eking out a living in mountainous areas, the people of Gorenjska have a reputation in Slovenia for being on the, well, let's just say 'thrifty' side. You won't see evidence of this yourself, but you'll probably hear a fair few jokes like the ones made about the Scots.

KAMNIK
☎ 01 • postcode 1240 • pop 10,000
This historical town 'in the bosom of the mountains' just 23km north-east of Ljubljana is often given a miss by travellers en route to Bled or Bohinj. But Kamnik's tidy and attractive medieval core, with its houses and portals of hewn stone, balconies and arcades, is well worth a visit. It was declared a cultural and historical monument in 1986.

History
Established early in the 13th century under the Counts of Andechs and later claiming its own mint and school, Kamnik (Stein in Ger-

Highlights

- Take on the challenge of climbing Triglav, Slovenia's tallest peak
- Enjoy the trip by cable car to Velika Planina near Kamnik
- Admire the painted burgher houses of Mestni trg in Škofja Loka
- Visit the fascinating Beekeeping Museum at Radovljica
- Discover the ironmongering village of Kropa
- Marvel at the Church of St John the Baptist at Bohinj, the most beautiful and evocative house of worship in Slovenia
- Explore Vintgar Gorge near Bled
- Experience the hair-raising drive over the Vršič Pass in the Julian Alps

man) competed with Ljubljana and Kranj for economic and cultural dominance in Kranjska (Carniola) throughout the Middle Ages. The town was known for its large numbers of artisans and craftspeople, and it was on this rising middle class that Emperor Charles IV bestowed the massive forests around Kamniška Bistrica in the 14th century.

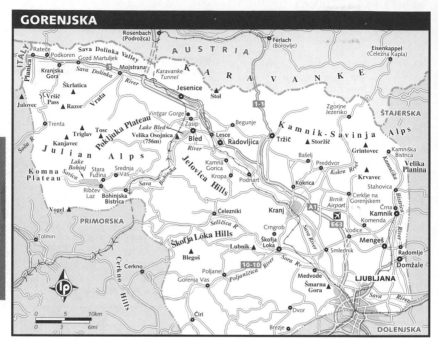

GORENJSKA

For centuries Kamnik controlled the pass in the Tuhinj Valley to the east that was indispensable for moving goods from the coastal areas to Štajerska and Koroška. But when the route was redirected via Trojane to the south-east in the 1600s, Kamnik fell into a deep sleep and only awakened in the late 19th century when the town was linked by rail to Ljubljana.

Kamnik became a mecca for holidaying Ljubljančani in the early 20th century due to easy access to the Kamnik Alps and their popular thermal baths. The baths were destroyed during WWI and, though it remained a gateway in subsequent decades for hikers and skiers headed for the Velika Planina to the north, Kamnik began to industrialise and expand.

Orientation

Kamnik lies on the west bank of the Kamniška Bistrica River and south of the Kamnik Alps, which form part of the Kamnik-

Savinja chain. The Old Town consists of two parts: medieval Glavni trg and the newer 'suburb' of Šutna, really just the southern continuation of the square.

Kamnik's bus station is near the river east of Glavni trg at the end of Prešernova ulica. The town has three train stations. The main one is on Kranjska cesta, south-west of Šutna. Kamnik-Mesto, which is convenient for the Old Town and its sights, is on Kolodvorska ulica west of the Little Castle. Kamnik-Graben station, the terminus of the Ljubljana-Kamnik line, is north-west of Glavni trg on Tunjiška cesta.

Information

Tourist Offices The tourist office (☎ 839 14 70, fax 831 74 43, ⓔ infocenter.kamnik@ siol.net) opposite the bus station at Tomši-čeva 23 can arrange bookings, find keys to locked sights and organise guides for excursions into the mountains. It also publishes a very useful English-language booklet called

What & Where – Guide to Kamnik and Environs. The office is open from 8 am to 6 pm daily June to September. During the rest of the year hours are 8 am to 4 pm weekdays and 9 am to 1 pm Saturday.

The Kamnik Alpine Society at Šutna 42 will advise you on hiking guides for walking in the Kamnik Alps and weather conditions there. The office is open from 8 am till noon weekdays (from 1 to 5 pm Wednesday).

Money The SKB Banka is at Glavni trg 13. It is open from 8.30 am till noon and 2 to 5 pm weekdays only. Just north, at No 14, you'll find a private exchange bureau called Publikum open 8 am to noon and 1 to 5 pm weekdays and from 8 am till noon Saturday.

Post & Communications The post office, open from 8 am to 7 pm weekdays and till noon Saturday, is at Glavni trg 27.

Things to See & Do
The **Franciscan monastery** (1492), a short distance to the west of the tourist office at Frančiškanski trg 2, has a rich library of theological, philosophical and scientific manuscripts and incunabula dating from the 15th to 18th centuries (including an original copy of the Bible translated by Jurij Dalmatin in 1584), and some valuable paintings by early Slovenian artists. Ask one of the priests in residence at the monastery if you can have a look – you'll need a minimum of five people for a tour.

Next door is the **Church of St James** with a chapel designed by Jože Plečnik, who also did the attractive beige-and-orange house with the glassed-in loggia (now the R Bar) on the eastern side of Glavni trg.

The **Little Castle** (Mali Grad), on a low hill above the southern end of Glavni trg, is Kamnik's most important historical sight. It has foundations going back to the 11th century, and this is where the town mint once stood. Behind the castle stand the ruins of a unique two-storey **Romanesque chapel** with 15th-century frescoes in its lower nave and wall paintings by Janez Potočnik (1749–1834) in the presbytery. The castle was undergoing renovation at the time of

research, but should be open to the public in summer 2001.

The Little Castle is home to Veronika, a legendary countess who was turned partly into a snake when she refused to help the Christian faithful build a church. Not only was the old gal mean, but she was spiteful too. In her rage at having been asked to contribute, she struck the entrance to the castle with her fist. If you look to the right of the portal as you go in, you'll see the imprint of her hand. Veronika continues to rule the treasure of the Little Castle and, in a way, the community of Kamnik too. She appears both on the town seal and on the licence plate of every car registered here.

From the Little Castle, a walk along the quiet and attractive main street of **Šutna** is a trip back in time; check the fine neoclassical house with columns at No 24, the stone relief of the Pascal lamb above the door at No 36 and the fresco indicating a butcher's shop sign at No 48.

In the centre of Šutna stands the **Parish Church of the Annunciation**, erected in the mid-18th century but with a detached belfry that shows an earlier church's Gothic origins. A short distance beyond at Šutna 33 is the **Sadnikar Collection**, a private museum – the first in Slovenia (1893) – of Gothic artwork, period furniture and paintings from the 18th century amassed by Josip Nikolaj Sadnikar (1863–1952), a local veterinarian and painter. It is open from 9 am to noon and 4 to 6 pm Tuesday to Saturday, and from 10 am to 1 pm Sunday; entry is 300 SIT.

Zaprice Castle, with towers, ancient stone walls and an interesting chapel at Muzejski pot 3, was built in the 16th century but later converted into a baroque manor house. Today it's the home of the **Kamnik Museum**, with some dullish exhibits devoted to Kamnik's glory days and 18th-century furniture. More interesting are the **granaries** from the 18th and 19th centuries outside that have been moved from the Tuhinj Valley. The museum is open from 9 am to noon Tuesday to Saturday and 4 to 6 pm Tuesday, Thursday, Friday and Saturday from May to September. During the rest of the year it opens in the morning

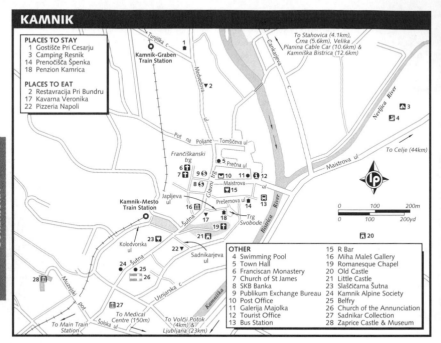

KAMNIK

PLACES TO STAY
1 Gostišče Pri Cesarju
3 Camping Resnik
14 Prenočišča Špenka
18 Penzion Kamrica

PLACES TO EAT
2 Restavracija Pri Bundru
17 Kavarna Veronika
22 Pizzeria Napoli

Kamnik-Graben Train Station

To Stahovica (4.1km),
Črna (5.6km), Velika
Planina Cable Car (10.6km) &
Kamniška Bistrica (12.6km)

To Celje (44km)

Kamnik-Mesto Train Station

To Medical
Centre (150m)

To Main Train
Station

To Volčji Potok
(4km) &
Ljubljana (23km)

OTHER
4 Swimming Pool
5 Town Hall
6 Franciscan Monastery
7 Church of St James
8 SKB Banka
9 Publikum Exchange Bureau
10 Post Office
11 Galerija Majolka
12 Tourist Office
13 Bus Station
15 R Bar
16 Miha Maleš Gallery
19 Romanesque Chapel
20 Old Castle
21 Little Castle
23 Slaščičarna Šutna
24 Kamnik Alpine Society
25 Belfry
26 Church of the Annunciation
27 Sadnikar Collection
28 Zaprice Castle & Museum

from Tuesday to Sunday and in the afternoon on Tuesday and Thursday only. Admission is 300 SIT.

The **Miha Maleš Gallery** on Glavni trg 1 contains works by the eponymous painter and graphic artist who was born in Kamnik in 1903. It keeps the same hours as the Kamnik Museum.

The **Old Castle** (Stari Grad), a 13th-century ruin on Bergantov Hill east of the centre, can be reached from the end of Maistrova ulica on foot in about 20 minutes. There are excellent views of the Alps and the town from the top of this 585m hill.

On a hill east of Stahovica, a village about 4.5km north of Kamnik, is the **Church of Sts Primus and Felician** with some of the best medieval frescoes in Slovenia. It's about a 40-minute walk up from the village of **Črna** but make this 'pilgrimage' only on Saturday and Sunday when the church door is open. The frescoes on the north wall depict the Flight into Egypt, the Adoration of

the Magi and Maria Misericordia – the Virgin Mary sheltering supplicants under her cloak in a scene similar to the one at the church in Ptujska Gora (see Around Ptuj in the Štajerska chapter). The painting on the south wall shows scenes from the life of Mary and is dated 1504.

Some 4km south of Kamnik is **Volčji Potok**, Slovenia's largest and most beautiful arboretum. With the heart-shaped park of a former castle as its core, the 88-hectare arboretum counts more than 4500 varieties of trees, shrubs and flowers from all over the world. Volčji Potok's greenery, ponds and nearby Kamniška Bistrica make it a lovely place to visit on a warm summer's day. It's open from 8 am to 7 pm daily March to October, and the entry fee is 800/550 SIT for adults/children. Though five buses a day arrive here directly from Kamnik on weekdays, there's only one on Saturday and Sunday. If you're stuck, take the Radomlje bus, which stops close by.

The outdoor **swimming pool** near the camping ground on Maistrova ulica is open from 10 am to 6 pm (9 pm at weekends) mid-June to mid-September. Licences for fishing in the Kamniška Bistrica are available at the *gostilna* Pri Planinskem Orlu (see Places to Stay) and cost 3000 SIT a day.

Special Events
The big events in Kamnik are the Medieval Days Festival on the second weekend in June, and the National Costumes Festival (Dnevi Narodnih Noš), held on the second weekend in September. A half-dozen stages are set up around town, and there's music, dancing, parades and general merrymaking. These events attract people from all over Slovenia. Kamnik Evenings is a four-day festival of concerts held in mid-October.

There are big flower and horticultural shows at Volčji Potok in late April/early May and in early September.

Places to Stay
The tiny *Camping Resnik* (☎ 831 73 14, Maistrova ulica 15) is north-east of the Old Town on the Nevljica River. Open from May to September, it charges 600/400/400 SIT per person/car/tent site. There's a tennis court and the public swimming pool is adjacent, as is a popular gostilna, *Pod Skalo*, open till 10 pm (midnight on weekends).

With Ljubljana so close, Kamnik doesn't seem to have much need for a hotel – or budget accommodation. *Prenočišča Špenka* (☎ 831 73 30, Prešernova ulica 14c) offers basic but very central accommodation in 11 rooms and breakfast for €23 per person. *Penzion Kamrica* (☎ 831 77 07, Trg Svobode 2) is also central and has similar rates. *Gostišče Pri Cesarju* (☎ 839 29 17, Tunjiška cesta 1), a 12-room guesthouse a bit farther afield, charges €34/58 for singles/doubles.

Other accommodation can be found at a couple of gostilne in Stahovica on the road to Velika Planina and the village of Kamniška Bistrica. *Pri Planinskem Orlu* (☎ 832 54 10) at No 20 in Stahovica charges €21 per person for B&B, and *Pri Gamsu* (☎ 832 55 88) at No 31 in Stahovica charges €35/46 for singles/doubles.

Places to Eat
The *Napoli* (Sadnikarjeva 5), a pizzeria south-west of the Little Castle, is open from 9 am to 10 pm Monday to Saturday and from 1 pm on Sunday. *Restavracija Pri Bundru* (☎ 831 12 35, Medvedova 24) is a good place for lunch or a dinner of traditional Slovene food. It's open from 9 am to 1 am weekdays, 10 am to 10 pm Saturday and 10 am to 3 pm Sunday.

Kavarna Veronika on the corner of Glavni trg and Japljeva ulica is a good place to cool your heels over a cup of something warm and a slice of cake. It's the most popular cafe in town and doubles as an art gallery; it's open from 8 am till midnight or 1 am daily.

Entertainment
Lira, Slovenia's first choir (founded in 1882 and still going strong), occasionally gives local concerts. Ask the staff at the tourist office for information.

There are a couple of good pubs in town, including the *R Bar* in the house that Plečnik built on Glavni trg, and *Slaščičarna Šutna* (Šutna 8), a pleasant cafe-bar on the old main street.

Shopping
Check the interesting old clockmaker's at Maistrova ulica 1 near the post office. At No 11 on the same street, the Galerija Majolka sells souvenirs, paintings, porcelain and antiques. It is open from 9 am till noon and 3 to 7 pm weekdays and till noon on Saturday.

Getting There & Away
Bus services are frequent – at least one departure every half-hour to and from Domžale, Ljubljana, Mengeš and Radomlje. You can also reach Gornji Grad on between two and six buses a day, Kamniška Bistrica (three), Kranj (seven on weekdays, two on Saturday), Šentjakob (five) and Volčji Potok (five on weekdays, one daily at weekends).

Kamnik is on a direct rail line from Ljubljana (45 minutes, 24km) via Domžale. Trains run hourly (leaving at 15 minutes past the hour) from 8.15 am to 9.15 pm, with a few earlier departures. The line terminates at the Kamnik-Graben station.

GORENJSKA

VELIKA PLANINA
☎ 01

The so-called Great Highlands area, which reaches a height of 1666m, is a wonderful place to explore and is accessible to 1418m by cable car *(žičnica)* from the lower station 11km north of Kamnik. The six-minute ride is not for the skittish! You can also walk to Velika Planina from Stahovica, taking in the Church of Sts Primus and Felician above Črna along the way, in about three hours.

Velika Planina is where traditional dairy farmers graze their cattle between June and September. If you follow the road from the upper station up the hill for about 2km, you'll reach a highland plain filled with more than 50 shepherds huts and a small church dedicated to Our Lady of the Snows. The low-lying rounded buildings with conical roofs are unique to Velika Planina, and the design may be a legacy of ancient shepherds dating back as far as the Bronze Age. Today's silver-grey huts are replicas; the originals from around the early 20th century were burned to the ground by the Germans in WWII.

A circular walk of the plain and **Mala Planina** (1569m) to the south will take only a few hours. In summer, the friendly shepherds in their pointed green felt hats will sell you curd, sour milk and white cheese.

Velika Planina is a popular ski area with 6km of slopes. When it's skiable, a chairlift ferries skiers up to Gradišče from the upper cable-car station daily between December and April, when up to six T-bars may be running. For information, contact the tourist office in Kamnik.

Places to Stay & Eat
There's quite a choice of accommodation in Velika Planina. Among the mountain lodges offering accommodation, daily between June and September and at the weekend during the rest of the year, are *Domžalski Dom na Veliki planini* (mobile ☎ 050-647 523) and *Dom na Mali Planini* (mobile ☎ 041-843 172), each with nine multibed rooms.

At the lower cable-car station you'll find something to eat at the simple *Bife Pri Žičnici* (along with picnic tables and barbecue pits) open from 7.15 am to 8 pm (10 pm at weekends). In Velika Planina, there's an *okrepčevalnica* (snack bar) at Zeleni Rob about 1km up the hill, open daily in season.

Getting There & Around
The cable-car station can be reached from Kamnik on three buses a day. From mid-June to September, the cable car runs every half-hour from 8 am to 6 pm Monday to Thursday and till 8 pm Friday to Sunday. In winter (mid-December to March) the daily schedule is from 8 am to 6 pm. During the rest of the year it goes at 8 and 8.30 am, noon and 12.30, 4.30 and 5 pm Monday to Thursday and every hour from 8 am to 7 pm Friday to Sunday. A return ticket costs 1000/700 SIT for adults/children.

KAMNIŠKA BISTRICA
This pretty little settlement in a valley near the source of the Kamniška Bistrica River is 3km north of the Velika Planina lower cable-car station, and the *Dom v Kamniški Bistrici* (☎ 01-832 55 44) offers hostel-like accommodation in multibed rooms. Check-in is from 7 am to 9 pm in summer, 8 am to 8 pm in winter.

Kamniška Bistrica is the springboard for some of the more ambitious and rewarding Kamnik Alps treks such as the ones to **Grintovec** (2558m; 11 hours return), **Brana** (2251m; eight hours) and **Planjava** (2394m; 10 hours).

The most popular hikes, though, are the easier, 3½-hour ones north-west to the mountain pass or saddle at **Kokra Saddle** (Kokrško Sedlo; 1791m) and north to **Kamnik Saddle** (Kamniško Sedlo; 1903m). On the other side of the latter lies Rinka Waterfall and Logarska Dolina (see the Upper Savinja Valley section of the Štajerska chapter). Each saddle has a mountain hut: *Cojzova Koča* (mobile ☎ 050-635 549) on Kokrško Sedlo and *Kamniška Koča* (mobile ☎ 050-611 367) on Kamniško Sedlo. Both are open 20 June to 10 October.

The main trails in the Kamnik Alps are well marked and pass numerous springs, waterfalls and caves. Guides are available from the tourist office in Kamnik, but the less energetic may be content to picnic around the lake near the hostel, cooling their drinks (or feet) in the blue Alpine water.

Kamniška Bistrica can be reached from Kamnik on three buses a day, leaving at 7 and 11.30 am and 4.35 pm (only the first and last run at weekends).

ŠKOFJA LOKA
☎ 04 • postcode 4220 • pop 12,500

Škofja Loka – 'Bishop's Meadow' – vies with Ptuj and Piran for being among the oldest settlements in Slovenia. Today the Old Town is protected as a historical and cultural monument (since 1987) and is among the most beautiful in Slovenia. When the castle and other old buildings are illuminated at night at the weekend, Škofja Loka takes on the appearance of a fairy-tale village.

History
In 973 German Emperor Otto II presented the Bavarian Bishops of Freising with the valleys along the Poljanščica and Selščica Rivers. The point where the two tributaries merge to form the Sora River began to develop as a town.

The Freising bishops held control over Škofja Loka (Bischofflack in German) for more than eight centuries – and two actually met their maker in the town. Bishop Leopold drowned in the late 14th century when his horse slipped off the new bridge (no guard rails in those days) and Conrad was murdered three decades later by a greedy footman who wanted the bishop's 5000 gold ducats.

In the Middle Ages Škofja Loka developed as a trade centre along the Munich-Klagenfurt-Trieste route, doing particularly well in iron, linen and furs. A circular wall with five gates protected by guard towers was built around the town in 1318 to ensure that this success continued.

But it was all for naught. An army of the Counts of Celje breached the wall and burned the town to the ground in 1457; two decades later the Turks attacked. Then natural disasters struck: an earthquake in 1511 badly damaged the town, and several great fires at the end of the 17th century reduced most of Škofja Loka's finest buildings to ashes.

In 1803 the Habsburgs took possession of the town, and the advent of the railway later in the century put Škofja Loka on the road to industrialisation, especially in the field of textiles.

Orientation
The new part of Škofja Loka – without any redeeming qualities except that things of a practical nature are centred on Kapucinski trg – lies north of the Selščica River. The Old Town to the south consists of two squares – long streets really – called Mestni trg and Spodnji trg, which run south from Cankarjev trg and the river. Mestni trg, which is the more beautiful and historically important, bans cars altogether while Spodnji trg (also known as Lontrg) is a busy thoroughfare.

Škofja Loka's bus station is in Kapucinski trg at the footbridge leading to Cankarjev trg. The train station is 3km to the north-east, at the end of Kidričeva cesta, in the industrial suburb of Trata.

Information
Tourist Offices Škofja Loka's tourist office (☎/fax 512 02 68, ⓔ td-skofja.loka@siol.net) is at Mestni trg 5 and opens from 8.30 am to 7.30 pm weekdays and till 12.30 pm Saturday year-round. It also opens from 8.30 am to 12.30 pm and 5 to 7 pm on Saturday and Sunday from June to August. The office sells maps and souvenirs and has a series of handouts on a wide range of subjects – from the history of the town and local lace-making to hiking, fishing and what farms in the area offer accommodation. It also offers guided tours of the town and Loka Museum (5000 SIT for a group, with an English-speaking guide).

Money Gorenjska Banka, next to Kompas and the Hotel Transturist at Kapucinski trg 7, is open from 8 am to 6 pm weekdays and till noon Saturday. An SKB Banka branch, at Kapucinski trg 3 in the same building as the Nama department store, is open from 8.30 am till noon and 2 to 5 pm weekdays only.

Post & Communications The post office, Kapucinski trg 9, is open from 7 am to

GORENJSKA

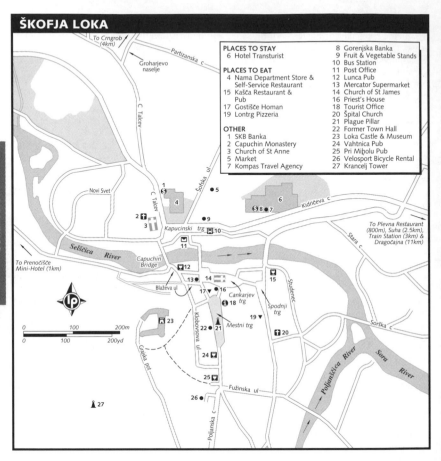

ŠKOFJA LOKA

PLACES TO STAY
6 Hotel Transturist

PLACES TO EAT
4 Nama Department Store &
   Self-Service Restaurant
15 Kašča Restaurant &
   Pub
17 Gostišče Homan
19 Lontrg Pizzeria

OTHER
1 SKB Banka
2 Capuchin Monastery
3 Church of St Anne
5 Market
7 Kompas Travel Agency

8 Gorenjska Banka
9 Fruit & Vegetable Stands
10 Bus Station
11 Post Office
12 Lunca Pub
13 Mercator Supermarket
14 Church of St James
16 Priest's House
18 Tourist Office
20 Špital Church
21 Plague Pillar
22 Former Town Hall
23 Loka Castle & Museum
24 Vahtnica Pub
25 Pri Miholu Pub
26 Velosport Bicycle Rental
27 Krancelj Tower

7 pm weekdays and till noon Saturday. It's just west of the bus station between the footbridge and Capuchin Bridge.

Travel Agencies Kompas (☎ 512 40 27) has an office next to the Hotel Transturist at Kapucinski trg 8. It is open from 9 am to 7 pm weekdays and till noon Saturday.

Old Town
Parts of the **Parish Church of St James** in Cankarjev trg date back to the 13th century, but its most important elements – the nave, the presbytery with star vaulting (1524) and

the tall bell tower (1532) – were added over the next three centuries. On either side of the choir are black marble altars designed in about 1700. These are very unusual for a time and place when baroque-style gilded wood and gypsum were all the rage. On the vaulted ceiling are bosses with portraits of the Freising bishops, saints, workers with shears and a blacksmith, who probably contributed handsomely to the church. Two crescent moons in the presbytery are reminders of the Turkish presence in Škofja Loka. The dozen or so modern lamps and the baptismal font were designed by Plečnik.

Opposite the church's main entrance on the south side is the **Priest's House**, part of a fortified aristocratic manor house built in the late 16th century. Below the rounded projection on the corner are strange consoles of animal heads.

The colourful 16th-century burgher houses on **Mestni trg**, rebuilt after that terrible earthquake in 1511, have earned the town the nickname 'Painted Loka'. Almost every one is of historical and architectural importance, and plaques in English and Slovene explain their significance. Among the more impressive is **Homan House** at No 2 with bits of frescoes of St Christopher and of a warrior. The **former town hall** at No 35 is remarkable for its three-storey Gothic courtyard and the 17th-century frescoes on its facade. **Martin House** at No 26 leans on part of the old town wall. It has a wooden 1st floor, a late Gothic portal and a vaulted entrance hall. The **plague pillar** erected in the square in 1751 was renovated a few years ago.

Klobovsova ulica, a narrow street west of Homan House, leads to Loka Castle and the remains of **Krancelj Tower**.

Spodnji trg to the east of Mestni trg was where the poorer folk lived in the Middle Ages; after the devastating fire of 1698, most of them couldn't afford to rebuild the square so the houses remained two-storey and relatively modest. Of interest at the northern end at No 2 is the 16th-century **granary** *(kašča),* where the town's grain stores, collected as taxes, were once kept. It now contains a pub and winery, a bank and the **France Mihelič Gallery**, with the works of the artist born in nearby Virmaše in 1907 (open from noon to 5 pm Tuesday to Sunday). The **Špital Church** at Spodnji trg 9 has an opulent baroque gold altar. The church was built in 1720 around the town's almshouse, and the poor lived in the cells of the courtyard building behind.

Loka Castle

The town castle, which looks down over Škofja Loka from a grassy hill west of Mestni trg at Grajska pot 13, was built in the 13th century, but extensively renovated after the earthquake. Today it houses the **Loka Museum** (Loški Muzej), which has one of the best ethnographical collections in Slovenia. The area around Škofja Loka was famous for its smiths and lace-makers, and there are lots of ornate guild chests on display. The copies of the 15th-century frescoes from the churches at Crngrob and Suha (see Around Škofja Loka later in this chapter) in the corridors are much clearer than most of the originals *in situ*. Have a good look at these before you make the trip – and don't miss the spectacular **Golden Altars** taken from a church destroyed during WWII in Dražgoše, north-west of Škofja Loka.

The Loka Museum is open from 9 am to 5 pm daily, except Monday, April to October. It's open on Saturday and Sunday only during the rest of the year. Entry is 350/250 SIT for adults/children or 450/350 SIT if you want a guided tour.

Other Attractions

The 18th-century **Capuchin monastery** west of the bus station at Kapucinski trg 2 has a priceless **library** of medieval manuscripts, including the *Škofja Loka Passion,* a processional with dramatic elements, from around 1720. The library can be visited by prior arrangement. Contact the tourist office or the monastery directly (☎ 512 09 70).

The stone **Capuchin Bridge** leading from the monastery's **Church of St Anne** (1710) dates from the 14th century and is an excellent vantage point for the Old Town and castle as well as the river with its deep gorge, dams, abandoned mills and 18th-century barracks. The area north-west of the bridge is called Novi Svet (New World) because it was settled after the Old Town. The statue on the bridge is of St John Nepomucen, a Bohemian prelate who was martyred in the 14th century by being thrown from Charles Bridge in Prague, the city where executioners usually favoured windows.

A dry-goods **market** is held on Mestni trg and Cankarjev trg on the second Wednesday of every month.

Activities

The Škofja Loka Hills to the west, a region of steep slopes, deep valleys and ravines, is an excellent area for day-long walks or

GORENJSKA

Škofja Loka's medieval castle overlooks the town.

hikes of a longer duration and there are several huts with accommodation in the area. Before you set out, buy a copy of the 1:50,000 hiking map *Škofjeloško in Cerkljansko Hribovje* (Škofja Loka and Cerkno Hills) available from the tourist office for 1350 SIT, and ask the tourist office for a copy of its *Crngrob-Planica-Križna Gora* hiking pamphlet in English.

One of the easiest trips is to **Lubnik**, a 1025m peak north-west of the Old Town, which can be reached on foot in two hours via Vincarje or the castle ruins near Gabrovo. Start the walk from Klobovsova ulica in Mestni trg. A mountain hut near the summit, *Dom na Lubniku* (☎ *512 05 01),* has 18 beds and is open daily from April to December and weekends from January to March.

A hike to 1562m **Blegoš** farther west would be much more demanding, but it only takes about three hours from Hotavlje, a village about 2km from Gorenja Vas and accessible by bus from Škofja Loka. There are two huts in the area. *Koča na Blegošu* (*mobile* ☎ *050-614 587)* has 61 beds and is open daily from June to September and at weekends in May and October. *Zavetišče GS na Jelencih* (☎ *518 12 40),* about 2km to the south-west, has 20 beds and is open at weekends only from November to April.

The ski centre at **Stari Vrh**, 12km west of Škofja Loka, is situated at an altitude of 1200m and covers 65 hectares of ski slopes and 3km of trails. There are four T-bar tows and a chairlift.

Special Events

A music festival called Pod Homanovo Lipo takes place under the big linden trees in front of Homan House on Mestni trg every Friday evening in July and August.

Places to Stay

Smlednik camp site (☎ *512 70 02)* in Dragočajna, 11km to the east, is the closest camping ground to Škofja Loka. It is situated between two small lakes and has a nudist beach. Open from May to mid-October, it charges 950 SIT per person per night.

Škofja Loka is not overly endowed with places to lay your weary head. The tourist office can organise *private rooms*, including one (☎ *512 05 09, Grajska pot 8*) for 2500 to 3500 SIT per person, but it has a very short list. There are lots of *farmhouses* with accommodation, but most are around Poljane, 13km to the south-west.

Prenočišče Mini-Hotel (☎ *515 05 40*), a 10-bed guesthouse in the suburb of Vincarje (house No 55) about 1km west of the bus station, has rooms with showers for about 3600 SIT per person. It's the building beside the tennis courts, cunningly disguised as a sports centre. The 48-room *Hotel Transturist* (☎ *512 40 26*, fax *512 40 96*, e *info@alpetour-thp.si, Kapucinski trg 9*) is tall, grey, depressing and relatively expensive. Singles with breakfast and shower are 6900 SIT, doubles 10,800 SIT.

Places to Eat

There's a *self-service restaurant* (*Kapucinski trg 1*) on the 2nd floor of the Nama department store opposite the post office, where you can get lunch for under 1000 SIT; enter from Cesta Talcev. *Plevna* (*Kidričeva cesta 16*), a 'gallery restaurant' about 800m to the east, is a very popular spot with Lokans. Dishes are simple but tasty and inexpensive. Plevna is open from noon to 11 pm Wednesday to Sunday. It closes in August.

Gostišče Homan (☎ *512 30 47, Mestni trg 2*) in historical Homan House has a pub and cafe on the ground floor that serves pizza and salads too – in warm weather, tables are set out on Mestni trg under the giant linden trees. Upstairs is a restaurant serving quality food and wine. Homan is open from noon to 11 pm daily (6 pm on Sunday), except Monday. There's more pizza available at the *Lontrg* (*Spodnji trg 33*). It's open from 9 am to 10 pm daily.

Kašča (☎ *512 43 00, Spodnji trg 2*) in the 16th-century town granary is an excellent pub and wine bar that also serves good local food. It's open from noon till midnight daily (to 2 am Friday and Saturday) except Sunday.

There are *fruit and vegetable stands* on Kapucinski trg across from the bus station; the *market* is held on Tuesday, Thursday and Saturday mornings on Šolska ulica. The *Mercator supermarket* (*Cankarjev trg 16*)

is open from 6 am to 7 pm weekdays and 7 am to 1 pm Saturday.

Entertainment

Škofja Loka has a number of pleasant pubs, open till about 11 pm daily, including *Lunca* (*Blaževa ulica 10*) and *Pri Miholu* (*Mestni trg 24*), built into part of the defence walls at Poljane Gate. *Vahtnica* (*Mestni trg 31*) is a trendy cafe-bar frequented by the local youth, with an atrium garden and art gallery.

Getting There & Away

Count on at least hourly buses (between 5 am and 9 pm) to Kranj and Ljubljana but otherwise the bus service from Škofja Loka is only adequate. Other destinations are: Radovljica (one bus a day, at 1.37 pm), Cerkno (one to three), Sorica (two), Soriška Planina (two at the weekend), Zali Log (five), Železniki and Žiri (six to 10).

Škofja Loka can be reached by up to 12 trains a day from Ljubljana (20 minutes, 20km) via Medvode. An equal number continue to Kranj, Radovljica, Lesce-Bled and Jesenice (50 minutes, 44km). About four of these cross the border for Villach in Austria.

Getting Around

Local buses make the run between the train station in Trata and the bus station on Kapucinski trg. You can order a taxi on mobile ☎ 041-625 875, 041-676 516. Velosport at Poljanska cesta 4 rents mountain bikes and bicycles. It's open from 9 am till noon and 4 to 7 pm weekdays, and Saturday morning.

AROUND ŠKOFJA LOKA
Suha

The 15th-century **Church of St John the Baptist** at Suha, about 2.5km east of the bus station in Škofja Loka, is unexceptional except for the presbytery which has an interior completely covered with amazing **frescoes** by Jernej of Loka. The paintings on the vaults show scenes from the life of Christ, the coronation of Mary and various Apostles. The panels below depict the five wise and five foolish virgins (the latter forgot to put oil in their lamps and were thus excluded from the wedding celebrations,

GORENJSKA

according to Christ's parable reported in the Gospel of St Matthew). Inside the arch is a frightening scene from the Last Judgment.

If the church is locked, request the key from the house at No 45, the first building on the right as you enter Suha village and about 150m beyond the church.

Crngrob

The **Church of the Annunciation** at Crngrob, about 4km north of Škofja Loka, has one of the most priceless frescoes in Slovenia. Look for it on the outside wall under a 19th-century portico near the church entrance. Called **Holy Sunday** (Sveta Nedelja) and produced in the workshop of Johannes de Laibaco (John of Ljubljana) in 1470, it explains in pictures what good Christians do on Sunday (pray, go to Mass, help the sick) and what they do *not* do (gamble, drink, play bowls or fight). The consequence of doing any of the latter is damnation – vividly illustrated with souls being swallowed whole by a demon. On the south wall there's a large fresco of St Christopher from the same era.

The interior of the church, which was built and modified between the 14th and 17th centuries, contains more medieval frescoes on the north wall as well as the largest gilded altar in Slovenia, built by Jurij Skarnos in 1652. The spectacular organ was made around the same time. The stellar vaulting of the presbytery, painted in light red, blue and yellow, has a number of bosses portraying the Virgin Mary, the Bishops of Freising, and a man on a horse, probably a benefactor.

The people at the house (No 10) nearest the church hold the keys. You can eat at *Gostišče Crngrob* (☎ 04-513 16 01) at house No 13, which is open till 11 pm daily, except Wednesday, and there is accommodation at the four-room *Pri Marku farmhouse* (☎ 04-513 16 26) at house No 5, which also has horses for hire.

Crngrob is easily accessible on foot or by bicycle from Škofja Loka via Groharjevo naselje, which runs north from the Capuchin monastery and Cesta Talcev. An alternative is to take the bus bound for Kranj, get off at the village of Dorfarje and walk west for about 1.5km.

KRANJ

☎ 04 • postcode 4000 • pop 37,000

Situated at the foot of the Kamnik-Savinja Alps with the snowcapped peak of Storžič (2132m) and others looming to the north, Kranj is Slovenia's fourth largest and most industrialised city with its share of unemployment and graffiti. But the casual traveller needn't know anything about all that. The attractive Old Town, sitting on an escarpment above the confluence of the Sava and Kokra Rivers that barely measures 1km by 250m, contains everything of interest in Kranj.

History

A secondary Roman road linking Emona (Ljubljana) and Virunum (near today's Klagenfurt in Austria) ran through Kranj until about the 5th century; 100 years later the Langobards established a base here. They were followed by the early Slavs, whose large burial grounds can be partly seen below the floor of the Gorenjska Museum.

In the 11th century, Kranj (Krainburg in German) was an important border stronghold of the German Frankish counts in their battles with the Hungarians, and the town gave its name to the entire region – Kranjska (Carniola in English). It was also an important market and ecclesiastical centre and, within 200 years, Kranj was granted town status by the new rulers, the Bavarian Counts of Andechs. More wealth came with the development of iron mining and foundries and when the progressive Protestant movement reached Gorenjska, it was centred in Kranj.

Kranj grew faster after the arrival of the railway in 1870 and is home to much of Slovenia's textile industry and Iskra, the electrical appliance company. As was the case in the Middle Ages, Kranj is known for its trade and industrial fairs.

Orientation

Kranj's Old Town is essentially three pedestrian streets running north to south. The main one begins as Prešernova ulica at Maistrov trg and changes its name to Cankarjeva ulica at Glavni trg, the main square and market place in medieval times. Cankarjeva ulica

GORENJSKA

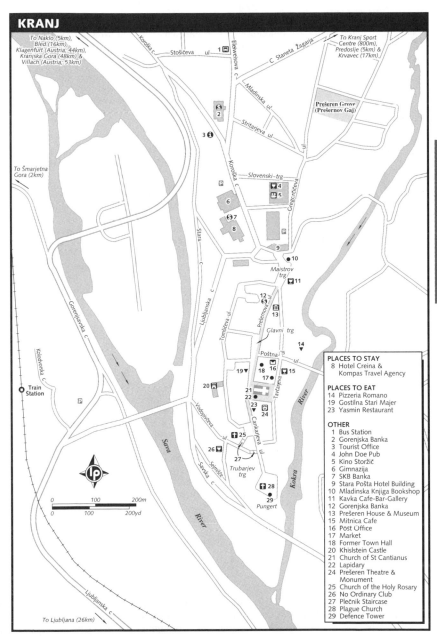

KRANJ

To Naklo (5km),
Bled (16km),
Klagenfurt (Austria: 44km),
Kranjska Gora (48km) &
Villach (Austria: 53km)

To Kranj Sport
Centre (800m),
Predoslje (5km) &
Krvavec (17km)

To Šmarjetna
Gora (2km)

Stošičeva ul

Koroška c.

Eliewešova c.

Mladinska ul

C. Staneta Žagarja

Prešeren Grove
(Prešernov Gaj)

Stritarjeva ul

Koroška c.

Slovenski trg

Gregorčičeva

Maistrov
trg

Stara c.

Ljubljanska c.

Gorenjska c.

Kolodvorska c.

Train
Station

Sava

Tomšičeva ul

Prešernova ul

Glavni trg

Poštna

ul

Tavčarjeva

River

Kokra

Vodopivčeva ul

Savska c.

Semiče

Cankarjeva ul

Trubarjev
trg

Pungert

River

Ljubljanska c.

To Ljubljana (26km)

Ljubljanska c.

0   100   200m
0   100   200yd

PLACES TO STAY
8 Hotel Creina &
   Kompas Travel Agency

PLACES TO EAT
14 Pizzeria Romano
19 Gostilna Stari Majer
23 Yasmin Restaurant

OTHER
1   Bus Station
2   Gorenjska Banka
3   Tourist Office
4   John Doe Pub
5   Kino Storžič
6   Gimnazija
7   SKB Banka
9   Stara Pošta Hotel Building
10 Mladinska Knjiga Bookshop
11 Kavka Cafe-Bar-Gallery
12 Gorenjska Banka
13 Prešeren House & Museum
15 Mitnica Cafe
16 Post Office
17 Market
18 Former Town Hall
20 Khislstein Castle
21 Church of St Cantianus
22 Lapidary
24 Prešeren Theatre &
    Monument
25 Church of the Holy Rosary
26 No Ordinary Club
27 Plečnik Staircase
28 Plague Church
29 Defence Tower

ends, like everything else, at Pungert, the 'Land's End' at the tip of the promontory.

'New Kranj' spreads in every direction but especially northward to Zlato Polje and to the south-east to Planina. Brnik airport is 15km south-east of Kranj.

Kranj's bus station is about 600m north of Maistrov trg on Stošičeva ulica. The train station lies below the Old Town to the west, on the west bank of the Sava. To reach the Old Town from the station, follow Kolodvorska cesta south then east, cross the bridge over the Sava and walk up Vodopivčeva ulica to the Plečnik stairway. If you're headed for the Hotel Creina, continue north along Ljubljanska cesta after crossing the bridge.

Information

Tourist Offices The tourist office (☎ 236 30 30, fax 236 30 31, @ td.kranj@siol.net) at Koroška cesta 29 is open from 8 am to 7 pm weekdays and till 1 pm Saturday. The office stocks the rather out-of-date English-language *Tourist Guide of Kranj & Its Environs* (500 SIT), which could be useful if you plan to spend a fair bit of time in this part of Gorenjska. It has eight motoring day trips.

Money Gorenjska Banka has a branch at Prešernova ulica 6, open from 9 to 11.30 am and 2 to 5 pm weekdays and till 11 am Saturday. The main branch on Bleiweisova cesta near the tourist office is open from 8 am to 6 pm weekdays and till noon Saturday. SKB Banka in the Hotel Creina building at Koroška cesta 5 is open from 8.30 am till noon and 2 to 5 pm weekdays.

Post & Communications The main post office in Kranj is several hundred metres north-east of the bus station at Dražgoška ulica 8. A more convenient branch is at Poštna ulica 4 east of Glavni trg, open from 7 am to 7 pm weekdays and till noon Saturday.

Travel Agencies Kompas (☎ 222 41 00) at the Hotel Creina opens from 8 am to 7 pm weekdays and till noon Saturday.

Bookshops Mladinska Knjiga at Maistrov trg 1 has maps as well as English-language guides and books. It is open from 8 am to 7 pm weekdays and till 3 pm Saturday.

Walking Tour

You can see virtually everything of note in Kranj by following Prešernova ulica and Cankarjeva ulica to Pungert and returning to Maistrov trg via Tomšičeva ulica. Most of the important sights have plaques in English and are also marked with numbers. These correspond to the map included with the *Tourist Guide of Kranj & Its Environs.*

Maistrov trg was the site of the upper town gates in the 15th century and was the most vulnerable part of Kranj; the steep Kokra Canyon protected the town on the eastern side and thick walls did the trick on the west from Pungert as far as the square. The **Špital Tower**, one of seven along the wall, forms part of a shop at Maistrov trg 3. The unusual Art-Deco building with the three statues facing the square to the north is the **former Stara Pošta hotel** built in the 1930s.

Prešeren House (Prešernova Hiša) at Prešernova ulica 7 was home to the poet France Prešeren (1800–49) for the last two years of his life, and he died in the front bedroom. The **Prešeren Memorial Museum** contained in five rooms here is devoted to his life and work but, sadly, the explanatory notes next to his letters, diaries and manuscripts are in Slovene only. The house was closed for renovation at the time of research, but should be open by 2002. Prešeren is buried in the parish cemetery, now called **Prešeren Grove** (Prešernov Gaj), about 500m to the north.

Glavni trg is a beautiful square of Gothic and Renaissance buildings; the ones on the western side with their painted facades, vaulted hallways and arched courtyards are masterpieces. The 16th-century one (actually *ones* as they were formerly two houses joined together) opposite at Glavni trg 4 was once the town hall. Below the floor of the vaulted vestibule, **Slavic tombs** from the 9th and 10th centuries can be seen through glass panels.

Glavni trg's pride and joy, though, is the **Church of St Cantianus** (Sveti Kancijan), which was built onto part of an older church starting in about 1400. It is the best example of a hall church – one with nave and aisles of equal height – in Slovenia and was the model for many others. There are some 15th-century frescoes of angels with musical instruments on the stellar vaulting of the nave. The Mount of Olives relief in the arch above the main portal is worth a look, as is the modern altar designed by Ivan Vurnik (1884–1971).

Below the northern side of the church there are more old bones from early Slav graves and a medieval **ossuary**. On the south wall is a **lapidary** of medieval tombstones and nearby the **Fountain of St John Nepomucen**, with a stone statue of the 14th-century Bohemian martyr complete with a doleful looking octopus.

The **Prešeren Theatre** is across the plaza at Glavni trg 6. The portico near the **Prešeren Monument** (showing a rather rugged-looking and heroic Dr France) was designed by Jože Plečnik in the early 1950s.

Walk down Cankarjeva ulica and you'll pass the **Church of the Holy Rosary**, built in the 16th century and a Protestant sanctuary during the Reformation. The church was 'attacked' by neo-Gothic restorers in 1892 and 'so renovated that it is of little importance artistically or historically', we are told on the outside. Beside the church are arcades, a fountain and a **staircase** designed in the late 1950s by Plečnik to give Kranj a monumental entrance up from the Sava River. This was where the lower town gates once stood.

Pungert is the end of the line for the Old Town. Here you'll find another old church, sometimes called the **Plague Church**, built during a time of pestilence in the 1470s. It contains some important artwork, including a painting dedicated to the three 'intercessors against the plague' – Sts Rok, Fabian and Sebastian – by the Austrian baroque artist Martin Johann Kremser-Schmidt (1718–1801). It is now used by Serbian Orthodox Christians. A three-storey **defence tower**, the only one in Kranj entirely preserved, was built in the 16th century.

If you return to the Church of the Holy Rosary and head north on Tomšičeva ulica, you'll come to a restored section of the **town wall** and **Khislstein Castle** at No 44. Part of this stronghold was built during the Turkish invasions of the 15th century, but

mostly it's Renaissance. Today it houses the offices of several cultural institutes, and also the history and folk art collections of the **Gorenjska Museum**. Among the eye-catching bits and bobs lying around is a large porcelain stove topped with a Turk's turbaned head, an embroidered sheepskin coat called a *kožuh* and a child's toy of a devil sharpening a gossip's tongue on a grindstone (a common motif in Slovenian folk art and one that always makes you wonder whether Slovenes perhaps like a bit of gossip). The museum is open from 10 am to noon and from 5 to 7 pm (4 to 6 pm from October to April) Tuesday to Friday, and on mornings only at weekends. Entry is 300/150 SIT for adults/children.

Activities
The Kranj Sport Centre (☎ 221 11 76) at Partizanska cesta 37, about 1.5km north-east of Maistrov trg, has tennis courts and both a covered and an outdoor swimming pool.

A very easy destination for a walk is **Šmarjetna Gora**, a 643m hill 3km northwest of the Old Town, where a fort stood during the Hallstatt period. The reconstructed **Church of St Margaret** is atop the hill. The views from here of Kranj, the Alps and the Sava River are astonishing; on a clear day you might be able to see Bled and Ljubljana, each some 30km away in opposite directions.

Special Events
It may sound like a bit of a schlep but if you're in Kranj in mid-July, follow the flocks to **Jezersko** for the annual Shepherds' Ball (Ovčarski Bal). It's a day and evening of folk music, dancing and drinking *žganje* (brandy) – an ovine alternative to the bovine event in Bohinj (see Special Events in that section later in this chapter). Jezersko, on the Austrian border 28km north-east of Kranj and easily accessible by car or bus, was a popular health resort before WWII. Today it is an unspoiled area in the shadow of Grintovec with a delightful Alpine lake, hiking trails, old farmhouses and mountain huts. A good hiking map for this area is the 1:50,000 *Karavanke* from PZS, the Alpine Association of Slovenia.

Places to Stay

The tourist office can arrange *private rooms* from 2600 SIT per person, but most are in Naklo, 5km north-west of the town centre. *Gostišče Marinšek (☎ 257 22 20, fax 257 11 15, Glavna 2)* in Naklo has pleasant doubles for 5000 SIT, and also sells home-made beer from its own brewery.

The brick-and-timber *Hotel Creina (☎ 202 45 50, fax 202 24 83, e hotel.creina@siol.net, Koroška cesta 5)* with 89 rooms is vastly superior in comfort and style – at a price; this is the place for Austrian business people, tour groups headed for the Alps and airline crews who don't want to travel all the way to Ljubljana from Brnik. Singles with shower and breakfast are €38 to €48, doubles €51 to €72. Most rooms have TV and direct-dial telephones. There's a wine cellar *(vinoteka)* in the basement which is open from noon to 11 pm Monday to Saturday.

Hotel Bellevue (☎ 270 00 00, fax 270 00 20) atop Šmarjetna Gora has 31 beds and a very pleasant restaurant open 9 am till midnight (to 2 am Friday and Saturday).

Places to Eat

Pizzeria Romano (Tavčarjeva ulica 31), north-east of the post office, serves a novel triumvirate: pizza, pasta and 'dishes made from horsemeat'. It's open from 7 am to 11 pm (from 4 pm on Sunday). The stick-to-the-ribs Slovenian dishes at *Gostilna Stari Majer (Glavni trg 16)* will keep you going for longer than you'd think. Set lunches here are 600 and 800 SIT.

A favourite place to eat is the *Yasmin (Cankarjeva ulica 1),* a combined cafe and restaurant, which serves well-prepared Continental food with a Slovenian touch and some good vegetarian dishes; try the cheese *štruklji* (dumplings). The cafe is open from 8.30 am till 10.30 pm daily (midnight on Friday and Saturday), and the restaurant from noon.

The large *market* selling fruit and vegetables north-east of the Church of St Cantianus is open from 6 am to 6 pm from mid-March to mid-October and from 7 am to 3 pm during the rest of the year.

Entertainment

The *Prešeren Theatre (☎ 202 27 01, Glavni trg 6)* is very active, staging four plays with up to 200 performances a year. Concerts – both classical and popular – are held in the courtyard of Khislstein Castle in summer and sometimes at the Church of St Cantianus during the year.

Kino Storžič, in the passageway south of the John Doe pub on Slovenski trg, is the place to catch the latest films.

Maistrov trg and Prešernova ulica are home to a number of pleasant pubs and cafes. One of the more unusual ones is *Kavka (Maistrov trg 8),* a lively upstairs cafe-bar-gallery. It is open from 8 or 9 am till midnight Monday to Saturday and from 6 pm on Sunday. *Mitnica (Tavčarjeva ulica 35),* a lovely *kavarna* in the basement of a 16th-century toll house, is just the place to relax in Kranj on a warm afternoon. There's live music from 6 pm Thursday and Sunday. Another decent pub, popular with a younger crowd, is *John Doe* on Slovenski trg.

The mature and well-heeled set frequents the *Trezor* disco at the Hotel Creina (from 9 pm to 4 am Thursday to Saturday), but Kranj clubbers head for *No Ordinary Club*, on a side street just off Vodopivčeva near the foot of the Plečnik stairs (10 pm till 4 am Friday and Saturday).

Getting There & Away

Bus Frequent buses leave Kranj for Bled, Bohinj, Brnik airport, Ljubljana, Medvode, Piran, Predoslje, Radovljica, Rateče-Planica via Kranjska Gora, Škofja Loka, Tržič and Vodice. You can also reach Bohinjska Bistrica (one a day), Bovec via Kranjska Gora and the Vršič Pass (one bus a day in July and August), Brezje (one a day from May to September), Jezersko (five), Kamnik (two), Kropa (one or two) and Maribor (one at weekends). As well, there's an early-morning bus to Varaždin in Croatia on Saturday and Sunday.

Train Up to 14 trains a day pass through Kranj from Ljubljana (30 minutes, 29km) via Medvode and Škofja Loka. They carry on to Radovljica, Lesce-Bled and Jesenice

(40 minutes, 35km), where eight cross the border for Villach in Austria.

Getting Around
Local buses make the run from the train station to the bus terminus on Stošičeva ulica if you don't feel like walking. You can ring a local taxi on ☎ 232 38 20, or pick one up at the bus station. Valy (☎ 204 50 07) at Cesta na Brdo 52, north-east of the Old Town, rents bikes for 1200 SIT a day.

AROUND KRANJ
Brdo Castle
Until recently, 16th-century Brdo Castle at Predoslje, about 5km north-east of Kranj, was for official state guests only. Though it is still managed by the State Protocol Service of the Republic of Slovenia (Servis za Protokolarne Storitve), now anyone can visit or even stay, provided they have the dosh.

The castle was long the property of the aristocratic and philanthropic Zois (sometimes spelled Cois) family, the Slovenian equivalent to the Széchenyi clan in Hungary. It has two towers on the northern side, corridors crammed with artwork and a library containing a priceless copy of the Bible translated by Protestant reformer Jurij Dalmatin (1547–89). Brdo is surrounded by lovely parkland and a protected 500-hectare forest. You can fish in one of 11 lakes stocked with trout, carp and pike (1500 SIT per day), play tennis or ride horses for 1000 SIT per hour (1500 SIT for a one-hour lesson). Visitors not staying at Brdo may have to pay a fee of 500 SIT to enter the park.

Accommodation for most people here is at the 68-room *Hotel Kokra (☎ 04-260 10 00, fax 202 15 51),* where very run-of-the-mill singles are €49 to €65 and doubles €69 to €107. Of course if you're not 'most people' and are very flush indeed, a 1st-class suite in *Brdo Castle (same ☎/fax)* can be had for around €1023. State guests, who are still put up here, probably get a discount.

Krvavec
The ski centre at Krvavec (☎ 04-252 11 80 or ☎ 202 25 79 in Kranj), 17km to the north-east of Kranj, is one of the most popular

(and crowded) in Slovenia. A cable car transports you up to the centre at 1450m and a dozen chairlifts and T-bar tows serve the 25km of slopes and 6km of cross-country runs. Krvavec is also an excellent starting point for hikes in summer to **Kriška Planina** or **Jezerca**, about an hour's walk from the upper station of the cable car.

RADOVLJICA
☎ 04 • postcode 4240 • pop 6200
A charming town full of historical buildings, Radovljica enjoys an enviable position atop an outcrop 75m above a wide plain called the Dežela (Country). A short distance to the west, two branches of the Sava join to form Slovenia's longest and mightiest river.

Radovljica (Ratmansdorf in German) was settled by the early Slavs and grew into an important market town by the early 14th century. With increased trade on the river and the iron forgeries at nearby Kropa and Kamna Gorica, Radovljica expanded and the town was built around a large rectangular square fortified with a wall and defence towers. Radovljica's affluence in the Middle Ages can be seen in the lovely buildings still lining Linhartov trg today.

Radovljica is an easy day trip from Bled, just 6km to the north-west.

Orientation
The centre of old Radovljica is Linhartov trg, a protected historical and cultural monument; everything of importance in Radovljica is on it. The new town extends primarily northward along Gorenjska cesta toward Lesce. Radovljica's bus station is 500m north-west of Linhartov trg on Kranjska cesta. The train station is below the town on Cesta Svobode. To reach the square from the train station, walk up steep Kolodvorska ulica and then turn right (eastward).

Information
The tourist office (☎/fax 531 53 00) is at Kranjska cesta 13. It is open from 8 am to 6 pm daily, except Sunday.

There's an SKB Banka branch at Gorenjska 10, open from 8.30 am till noon and 2 to 5 pm weekdays only. About 150m north

GORENJSKA

at No 16 of the same street is a Gorenjska Banka open from 8 am to 6 pm weekdays and till noon Saturday. The post office beside the bus station at Kranjska cesta 1 is open from 7 am to 7 pm weekdays, and till noon Saturday.

Beekeeping Museum

Though it may not sound like a crowd-pleaser, the Beekeeping Museum (Čebelarski Muzej; ☎ 531 51 88) at Linhartov trg 1 is one of the most fascinating in Slovenia, and there isn't a whole lot you won't know about things apiarian after an hour inside.

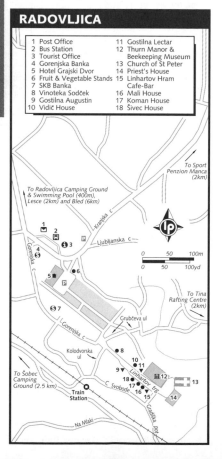

RADOVLJICA

1	Post Office	11	Gostilna Lectar
2	Bus Station	12	Thurn Manor &
3	Tourist Office		Beekeeping Museum
4	Gorenjska Banka	13	Church of St Peter
5	Hotel Grajski Dvor	14	Priest's House
6	Fruit & Vegetable Stands	15	Linhartov Hram
7	SKB Banka		Cafe-Bar
8	Vinoteka Sodček	16	Mali House
9	Gostilna Augustin	17	Koman House
10	Vidič House	18	Šivec House

To Sport Penzion Manca (2km)

To Radovljica Camping Ground & Swimming Pool (400m), Lesce (2km) and Bled (6km)

Kranjska c.

Ljubljanska c.

Gorenjska c.

0   50   100m
0   50   100yd

To Tina Rafting Centre (2km)

Grubčeva ul

Gorenjska c.

Kolodvorska ul

To Šobec Camping Ground (2.5 km)

Train Station

Linhartov trg

C. Svobode

Gradiška pot.

Na Mlaki

The museum is housed in **Thurn Manor**, the largest and most important public building on the historical square and worth a look in itself. Thurn Manor began life as Ortenburg Castle in the early Middle Ages but was rebuilt with a large hall on the ground floor after the earthquake of 1511. Subsequent alterations and expansions gave it the appearance of a large baroque manor house. The cream-and-white structure has interesting reliefs and stucco work on its facade.

The museum's exhibits take a close look at the history of beekeeping in Slovenia (which was at its most intense in the 18th and 19th centuries), the country's unique contribution to the industry with the development of the Carniolan grey bee species *(Apis mellifera carnica)* and the research of men like Anton Janša (1734–73), who set up a research station in the Karavanke and is considered around the world to be the father of modern beekeeping. And the museum doesn't fail to pass on a few 'fun facts to know and tell'. Did *you* realise that bees cannot see the colour red but go gaga over yellow? The museum's collection of illustrated beehive panels *(panjske končnice)* from the 18th and 19th centuries, a folk art unique to Slovenia, is the largest in the country. Gratefully, everything here is labelled in English and German along with Slovene.

The Beekeeping Museum has extremely complicated hours but this much is certain – it is always closed in January and February. It is open from 10 am to 1 pm and 3 to 6 pm daily, except Monday, May to August. It is open from 10 am till noon and 3 to 5 pm on Wednesday, Saturday and Sunday only in March, April, November and December. It's open from 10 am till noon and 3 to 5 pm daily, except Monday, in September and October. The entry fee is 300/200 SIT for adults/children.

Linhartov Trg

Radovljica's main square, named in honour of Slovenia's first dramatist and historian, Anton Tomaž Linhart (1756–95), who was born here, is lined with painted houses mostly from the 16th century and is an absolute delight to explore. The sad part, however, is that you'll frequently find it jammed with cars. It has been called 'the most homogeneous old town core in Slovenia' and has interesting details at every step.

Several lovely buildings are opposite the Beekeeping Museum, including **Koman House** at No 23 with a baroque painting on its front of St Florian, the patron saint of fires (he douses, not sets, them) and **Mali House** at No 24 with a picture of St George slaying the dragon. But the most important one is 16th-century **Šivec House** at No 22.

Šivec House is an interesting hybrid – Renaissance on the outside and Gothic on the inside. The fresco on the exterior shows the Good Samaritan performing his corporal work of mercy; inside there is a vaulted hall on the ground floor and a wood-panelled drawing room with a beamed ceiling on the first. The hall is now used as a gallery and the drawing room as a wedding hall. The gallery is open from 10 am to noon and 4 to 6 pm.

East of Thurn Manor, in an oddly shaped, shady courtyard, is the Gothic **Parish Church of St Peter**, a hall church modelled after the one in Kranj. The three portals are flamboyant Gothic and the sculptures inside were done by Angelo Pozzo in 1713. The building with the arcaded courtyard south of the church is the **Priest's House**. Parts of the old **town wall** can still be seen nearby.

North-west at Linhartov trg 3 is the 17th-century **Vidič House** with a corner projection and colourfully painted in red, yellow and blue. Past the city park on Gorenjska cesta is the former **Savings Bank building** (1906) with a marvellous mosaic flowering tree, in Secessionist style, decorating the front.

Find out all about Slovenia's Carniolan grey bee species at the Beekeeping Museum.

Activities

A public swimming pool is open in summer near the camping ground at the northern end of Kopališka cesta, with tennis courts nearby.

The Sport Riding Centre at Podvin Castle (☎ 538 88 11) in Mošnje, about 4km southeast of Radovljica, has horses available for riding individually or with an instructor. The centre also has a covered hippodrome.

Radovljica-based Tina Raft (☎ 531 50 05 or mobile ☎ 041-646 255) offers a number of rafting trips on the Sava Dolinka and Sava Bohinjka Rivers lasting between one hour and five hours. You can also rent two-person canoes. The rafting centre is on the Sava River, about 2km south of the town centre.

Places to Stay

Radovljica's tiny *camping ground* (☎ 531 57 70) is next to the public swimming pool on Kopališka cesta. It is open from June to mid-September and costs between 800 and 1200 SIT per person, with an extra 300 SIT charged for a tent.

The largest (and some say the best equipped) camping ground in Slovenia, *Šobec* (☎ 535 37 00, fax 535 37 01, ☒ sobec@siol .net), is in Lesce, about 2.5km north-west of Radovljica. Situated on a small lake near a bend of the Sava Dolinka River, the camping ground is huge – 20 sq hectares – and can accommodate up to 1500 people, which this popular place often does in summer. Šobec is open from May to September and costs from 1530 to 1800 SIT for adults and 1190 to 1400 SIT for children, depending on the month. There are bungalows costing 10,800 SIT for one night, 21,600 SIT for two nights, and 8300 SIT a night for three nights or more.

You'll find lots more budget accommodation in nearby Bled, but if you're determined to stay in Radovljica, the town's only hotel, a four-storey concrete block called *Hotel Grajski Dvor* (☎ 531 15 85, fax 531 58 78, ☒ info@hotel-grajski-dvor.si, Kranjska cesta 2), is opposite the bus station and the tourist office. Rooms with shower and breakfast cost 4500 to 5500 SIT per person. The hotel has 60 rooms and a swimming pool.

Sport Penzion Manca (☎ 531 41 20, fax 531 41 40, ☒ info@manca-sp.si, Gradnikova

GORENJSKA

The Boards & the Bees

The keeping of honeybees (species *Apis*) has been an integral part of Slovenian agriculture since the 16th century when buckwheat *(ajda)* was first planted on fallow ground to allow the more intensive use of farm land. Bees favour buckwheat and Slovenia, especially the Alpine regions of Carniola (Kranjska), was soon awash with honey for cooking and beeswax for candles. Valvasor discussed the subject at some length in *The Glory of the Duchy of Carniola*, published in 1689.

Originally bees were kept in hollow logs or woven baskets, but the entire hive was damaged when the honeycomb was removed. The invention of the *kranjič* hive, with removable boxes that resembled a chest of drawers, solved the problem by creating individual hives. It also led to the development of Slovenia's most important form of folk art.

Kranjič hives have front boards *(panjske končnice)* above the entrance, and painting and decorating these panels with religious motifs soon became all the rage. Ethnographers are still out to lunch over whether the illustrations were religious appeals to protect the hives from fire or disease, meant to guide the bees – they can distinguish colour – back home or to help beekeepers identify their hives.

The first panels (from the mid-18th century) were painted in a 'folk baroque' style, with subjects taken from the Old and New Testaments (Adam and Eve, the Virgin Mary, St Florian and St George and, especially, patient Job, the patron of beekeepers) and history (the Turkish invasions, the Counter-Reformation with Martin Luther being driven to hell by a devil, Napoleon and the Illyrian Provinces). The most interesting panels show the foibles, rivalries and humour of the human condition. A devil may be sharpening a gossip's tongue on a grindstone or two women fighting over a man's trousers (ie, his hand in marriage). A very common illustration shows the devil exchanging old wives

TAMSIN WILSON

The *kranjič* hive's removable boxes create a series of individual hives.

cesta 2), a couple of kilometres north of Linhartov trg, has singles with shower and breakfast for €38, and doubles for €56.

If money is no object, you might treat yourself to a night at *Hotel Grad Podvin* (☎ 538 88 81, fax 538 88 85) in Podvin Castle, a rather boxy affair about 4km southeast of Radovljica in the village of Mošje. Depending on the season, singles with shower and breakfast are 10,000 to 12,000 SIT while doubles are 12,000 to 14,000 SIT. Podvin Castle is surrounded by a lovely park and has tennis courts and a popular horse riding centre. Its restaurant gets high marks.

Places to Eat
Gostilna Augustin (Linhartov trg 14) has a terrace out the back with stunning views towards Triglav; the set lunch is 800 SIT. *Gostilna Lectar (Linhartov trg 2),* in yet

another historical building, comes highly recommended by locals, and is open from 11 am till 11 pm daily, except Tuesday. Across from Thurn Manor is *Linhartov Hram (Linhartov trg 26),* a cafe-pub with snacks. There's a small *fruit and vegetable market* opposite the Hotel Grajski Dvor.

Shopping
There's an excellent selection of Slovenian wines at Vinoteka Sodček, Linhartov trg 8. It's open from 9 am to 7 pm weekdays and 8 am to noon Saturday.

Getting There & Away
Buses leave Radovljica almost every half-hour between 7 am and 10 pm for Bled and Ljubljana. They go hourly to Bohinj (via Bled), Kranj, Kranjska Gora and Kropa. Other destinations, and daily frequencies,

The Boards & the Bees

for nubile young women – to the delight of the husbands. Another – in a 'world turned upside down' – has gun-toting deer and bears laying the hunter in his grave.

It is important to remember that these paintings were not 'art for art's sake'; the painters were primarily concerned with content and subject matter. But in their attempt to express the simple world around them, ordinary people and artisans between jobs produced some beautiful work.

A typical beehive panel *(panjska knočnica)* illustrated with folk motifs

The painting of beehive panels in Slovenia enjoyed its golden age between about 1820 and 1880; after that the art form went into decline. The introduction of a new and much larger hive by Anton Žnidaršič at the end of the 19th century obviated the need for small illustrations and the art form degenerated into kitsch.

Nowadays you'll see the best examples of painted panjske končnice in museums (eg, in Radovljica and Maribor), but there are still a few traditional – and protected – ones around, such as those at Muljava in Dolenjska. An interesting twist is the beehive at Brdo Castle near Kranj, painted in the 1970s by some of Slovenia's most outstanding artists. Nowadays, the most common hives are the large box ones painted bright yellow (a colour bees like) and the 'hives on wheels', which can be moved into the sun or to a promising meadow.

Bees are still kept in Slovenia for their honey and wax but much more lucrative are by-products like pollen, propolis and royal jelly, used as elixirs and in homeopathic medicine. Propolis is a brownish, waxy substance collected from certain trees by bees and used to cement or caulk their hives. Royal jelly, so beloved by the European aristocracy of the 1920s and 1930s and by the Chinese, is the substance fed to the queen bee by the workers.

include: Bovec via Kranjska Gora and the Vršič Pass (one bus a day in summer), Brezje (one), Jesenice via Vrba (six), Novo Mesto (one), Škofja Loka (one), Tržič (up to four) and Zagreb in Croatia (one).

Radovljica is on the rail line linking Ljubljana (50 minutes, 48km) with Jesenice (20 minutes, 16km) via Škofja Loka, Kranj and Lesce-Bled. Up to 14 trains a day pass through the town in each direction. About eight of the northbound ones carry on to Villach in Austria.

KROPA
☎ 04 • postcode 4245 • pop 1025

While in Radovljica, don't miss the chance to visit Kropa, a delightful little village tucked away in a narrow valley below the Jelovica Plateau some 10km to the southeast. Kropa (Cropp in German) has been a

'workhorse' for centuries, mining iron ore and hammering out the nails and decorative wrought iron that can still be seen in many parts of Slovenia. Today Kropa has turned its attention to screws – the Plamen factory is based here – but artisans continue their work, clanging away in the workshop on the village's single street, and the work of their forebears is evident in ornamental street lamps shaped like birds and dragons, weather vanes and shutters.

Blacksmith Museum

The fascinating collection at the Blacksmith Museum (Kovaški Muzej; ☎ 533 67 17) at house No 10 traces the history of iron mining and forging in Kropa and nearby Kamna Gorica in English, German and Slovene from the 14th to the early 20th centuries. Nail manufacturing was the town's main industry for most of that period, and it is difficult to imagine that so many different types of nails existed, never mind that they were all made here. From giant ones that held the pylons below Venice together to little studs for snow boots, Kropa produced some 130 varieties in huge quantities. In Kropa you did not become a master blacksmith until you could fit a horseshoe around an egg – without cracking the shell.

The museum has working models of forges, a couple of rooms showing how workers and their families lived in very cramped quarters (up to 45 people in one house) and a special exhibit devoted to the work of Joža Bertoncelj (1901–76), who turned out exquisite wrought-iron gratings, candlesticks, chandeliers and even masks. The museum shows a fascinating black-and-white documentary film about the town and its work produced in the very socialist 1950s. It's a real period piece.

The house itself was owned by a 17th-century iron baron called Klinar and contains some valuable furniture and paintings. Among the most interesting pieces is a 19th-century wind-up 'jukebox' from Bohemia. Ask the friendly caretaker to insert one of the large perforated rolls and watch the piano, drums, triangle and cymbals make music.

The Blacksmith Museum keeps the same hours as the Beekeeping Museum in Radovljica, including winter closure. The entrance charge is 300/200 SIT for adults/children.

Other Attractions

The **UKO forgers' workshop** across from the museum at house No 7b is open for visits from 7 am to 2 pm on weekdays and from 9 am till noon on Saturday. The artisans sell their wares – none of them even approaching the work of Master Bertoncelj – at the shop next door (No 7a), open the same hours.

An 18th-century furnace called **Purgatory Forge** (Vigenj Vice) lies a short distance north of the museum near the Kroparica, a fast-flowing stream that once turned the wheels that powered the furnaces for the forges. Close by is the birthplace of the Slovenian painter Janez Potočnik (1749–1834), whose work can be seen in the baroque

Church of St Leonard on the hill to the east and in Kamnik. Kropa has many other lovely old houses, including several around Trg Kropa, the main square, which also has an interesting old wayside shrine.

A 13th-century medieval smelter – the so-called **Slovenian Furnace** – is at Jamnik, about 3.5km south of Kropa along a tortuously twisting road. There are trails from Trg Kropa into the Jelovica Hills to the west, an area once rich in iron ore and timber for charcoal. In the early 19th century over 800 charcoal burners worked in this area alone.

Places to Eat

There's no accommodation in Kropa, which is just as well as you'd never get any sleep with all the banging and clanging going on. However, you can eat at *Gostilna Pri Kovač* just north of the museum at house No 30 or *Pri Jarmu*, a gostilna at the southern end of Kropa in house No 2.

BLED

☎ 04 • postcode 4260 • pop 5664

With its emerald-green lake, picture-postcard church on an islet, medieval castle clinging to a rocky cliff and some of the highest peaks of the Julian Alps and the Karavanke as backdrops, Bled is Slovenia's most popular resort and its biggest tourist money-spinner. Not surprisingly, it can be overpriced, swarming with tourists and often less than welcoming. Many travellers make a beeline for the larger and far less developed Lake Bohinj, 26km to the south-west.

But as is the case with many popular destinations around the world, people come in droves – and will continue to do so – because the place *is* special. On a clear day you see Stol (2236m) to the north-east and Slovenia's highest peak, Triglav (2864m), in the distance and then the bells start ringing from the belfry of the little island church. You should visit Bled too – at least for a look.

History

Bled was the site of a Hallstatt settlement in the early Iron Age but, as it was far from the main trade routes, the Romans gave it short shrift. More importantly, from the 7th century the early Slavs – no doubt attracted by the altitude (501m), the mild climate and the natural protection afforded by the mountains – came in waves, establishing themselves at Pristava below the castle, on the tiny island and at a dozen other sites around the lake. Bled has been linked with the myths and legends of these people for centuries, particularly the ancient Slavic goddess Živa, the priestess Bogomila and the man who loved her, Črtomir. Prešeren gave this relationship new life in his epic poem *Krst pri Savici* (Baptism by the Savica Waterfall) in 1836.

In 1004 the German Emperor Henry II presented Bled Castle and its lands to the Bishops of Brixen in South Tyrol, who retained secular control of the area until the early 19th century when the Habsburgs took it over. By that time a number of small villages, including Mlino, Želeče and Rečica, had grown up around the lake.

Bled's beauty and its warm waters were well known to medieval pilgrims who came to pray at the island church; the place made it into print in 1689 when Janez Vajkard Valvasor described the lake's thermal springs in *The Glory of the Duchy of Carniola,* his seminal work on Slovenian geography, history and culture. But Bled's wealth was not fully appreciated at that time, and in the late 18th century the keeper of the castle seriously considered draining Lake Bled and using the clay to make bricks.

Fortunately, along came a Swiss doctor named Arnold Rikli who saw the lake's full potential. In 1855 he opened baths where the casino now stands, taking advantage of the springs, the clean air and the mountain light. With the opening of the railway from Ljubljana to Tarvisio (Trbiž) in 1870, more and more guests came to Bled and the resort was a favourite of wealthy Europeans from the early 20th century right up to WWII. In fact, under the Kingdom of Serbs, Croats and Slovenes, Bled was the summer residence of the Karadžordževići, the Yugoslav royal family.

Orientation

'Bled' refers both to the lake and the settlements around it, particularly the built-up area to the north-east where most of the hotels are located. Bled's main road, Ljubljanska cesta, runs eastward from here. Footpaths and a road called Cesta Svobode (south of the lake) and Kidričeva cesta (north) circle the lake.

Bled's bus station is at the junction of Cesta Svobode and Grajska cesta, just up from the Hotel Jelovica. There are two train stations. The station called Lesce-Bled is 4km to the south-east on the road to Radovljica and on the line linking Ljubljana with Jesenice and Austria. Bled Jezero station, on Kolodvorska cesta north-west of the lake and the Zaka Regatta Centre, connects Jesenice to the north with Nova Gorica, Sežana and Italy to the south-west.

Information

Tourist Offices Bled's tourist office (☎ 574 11 22, fax 574 15 55, e td-bled@g-kabel .si), next to the Park Hotel at Cesta Svobode 15, is essentially a souvenir shop with information, maps and guides. It also does currency exchange (3% commission) and sells fishing licences for the lake. Ask for the helpful English-language publication *Bled Tourist Information* (250 SIT). The office is open from 8 am (10 am Sunday) to 10 pm daily in July and August; and 8 am to 8 pm (10 am to 6 pm Sunday) daily in June and September. It's open 8 am to 7 pm (9 am to 5 pm Sunday) daily in October, April and May; and 9 am to 5 pm (to 2 pm Sunday) daily from November to March.

An important office to visit if you are headed for *the* mountain is the Triglav National Park information centre (☎ 574 11 88) in the Vila Rog at Kidričeva cesta 2 on the lake's northern shore. It is open from 8 am to 3 pm weekdays only. The staff can provide information about the park and on climbing Triglav, and can arrange guides.

Money Gorenjska Banka in the Park Hotel shopping complex on Cesta Svobode is open from 9 to 11.30 am and 2 to 5 pm on weekdays and 8 to 11 am on Saturday. SKB Banka has a branch in the Bled Shopping Centre at Ljubljanska cesta 4. It is open from 8.30 am till noon and from 2 to 5 pm weekdays only.

GORENJSKA

BLED

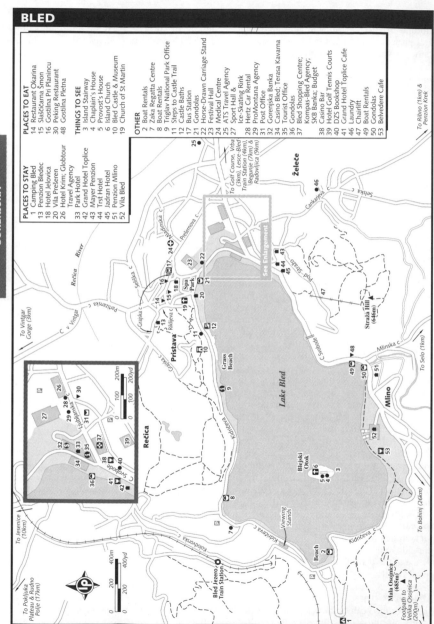

PLACES TO STAY
1 Camping Bled
13 Pension Bledec
18 Hotel Jelovica
20 Vila Prešeren
26 Hotel Krim; Globtour
    Travel Agency
33 Park Hotel
42 Grand Hotel Toplice
43 Mayer Penzion
44 Trst Hotel
45 Jadran Hotel
51 Penzion Mlino
52 Vila Bled

PLACES TO EAT
14 Restaurant Okarina
15 Slaščičarna Šmon
16 Gostilna Pri Planincu
30 Peking Restaurant
48 Gostilna Pletna

THINGS TO SEE
3 Island Stairway
4 Chaplain's House
5 Provost's House
6 Island Church
10 Bled Castle & Museum
19 Church of St Martin

OTHER
2 Boat Rentals
7 Zaka Regatta Centre
8 Boat Rentals
9 Triglav National Park Office
11 Steps to Castle Trail
12 Castle Baths
17 Bus Station
21 Gondolas
22 Horse-Drawn Carriage Stand
23 Festival Hall
24 Medical Centre
25 ATS Travel Agency
27 Sport Hall &
    Ice-Skating Rink
28 Hertz Car Rental
29 ProMontana Agency
31 Post Office
32 Gorenjska Banka
34 Casino Bled; Terasa Kavarna
35 Tourist Office
36 Gondolas
37 Bled Shopping Centre;
    Kompas-Bled Agency;
    SKB Banka; Budget
38 Casino Bar
39 Hotel Golf Tennis Courts
40 DZS Bookshop
41 Grand Hotel Toplice Cafe
46 Laundry
47 Chairlift
49 Boat Rentals
50 Gondolas
53 Belvedere Cafe

Post & Communications The main post office, Ljubljanska cesta 10, is open from 7 am to 7 pm weekdays and till noon Saturday.

You can check your email at the tourist office, which charges 500 SIT for 10 minutes, 1100 SIT for 30 minutes and 2000 SIT for an hour. Guests can get free Internet access at the terminals in the lobbies of the Hotel Krim and the Grand Hotel Toplice (see Places to Stay later in this section).

Travel Agencies Kompas (☎ 574 15 15) has an office in the Bled Shopping Centre at Ljubljanska cesta 4. It is open from 8 am to 7 pm daily (to 8 pm Sunday from June to September, and 8 am till noon and 4 to 8 pm Sunday from October to May). Globtour (☎ 574 18 21) is in the eastern wing of the Hotel Krim at Ljubljanska cesta 7. It is open from 8 am to 7 pm Monday to Saturday and noon to 4 pm Sunday.

Bookshops The DZS bookshop opposite the Grand Hotel Toplice on Cesta Svobode has maps of the region and some guidebooks in English. It is open from 7.30 am to 7 pm weekdays and till noon Saturday.

You can find English-language newspapers in the kiosk at the east end of the Bled Shopping Centre; it's open from 8 am to noon and 3 to 7 pm daily (9 to 11 am and 3 to 5 pm Sunday).

Laundry If you're running low on clean laundry, Bled is the place to wash those dirty clothes. A machine load washed and dried should only cost about 600 SIT at the Penzion Bledec, and there's a laundry south of the centre at Cankarjeva cesta 23c, open from 6 am to 2 pm.

Medical Services Bled's medical centre (☎ 574 14 00) is at Mladinska cesta 1.

Bled Castle

Perched on a steep cliff more than 100m above the lake, Bled Castle (Blejski Grad) is how most people imagine medieval forts to be – with towers, ramparts, moats and a terrace offering magnificent views on a clear day. The castle, which is built on two levels, dates back to the 11th century (though most of what stands here now is from the 16th century) and for 800 years was the seat of the Bishops of Brixen, who apparently redecorated the place regularly.

The baroque southern wing houses a **museum collection** that traces the history of Lake Bled and its settlements from the Bronze Age to the mid-19th century. None of the furniture is original to the castle, but it helps give you an idea of how the leisured class lived in the Middle Ages.

There's a large collection of armour and weapons (swords, halberds and firearms from the 16th to 18th centuries), jewellery found at the early Slav burial pits at Pristava, and a few interesting carvings, including a 16th-century one of the overworked St Florian, dousing yet another conflagration. The small 16th-century **chapel**, strewn with coins and notes left by favour-seekers, contains a painting of Henry II and his wife Kunigunda above the altar.

The castle is open from 8 am to 7 pm daily March to October, and from 9 am to 4 pm during the rest of the year. Admission costs 600/400 SIT for adults/children.

You can reach the castle via two trails: from behind the Penzion Bledec (see Places to Stay) or from just north of the neo-Gothic **Parish Church of St Martin** on Riklijeva cesta – both trails are signposted 'Grad'. The church (1905) was designed by Friedrich von Schmidt, who also did the city hall and Votive Church in Vienna. The frescoes illustrating the Lord's Prayer were painted by Slavko Pengov in the 1930s. Outside there's a small shrine designed by Jože Plečnik and the remains of defence walls built to subdue the Turks in the 15th century.

Bled Island

Tiny, tear-shaped Blejski Otok, the only true island in Slovenia, has been the site of a Christian church since the 9th century. But excavations have shown that the early Slavs worshipped at a pagan temple here at least a century before that.

Getting to the island is half the fun. The easiest way is to climb aboard a hand-propelled gondola (*pletna* in Slovene) – there are jetties next to the casino, to the east of the Castle Baths pool complex and in Mlino, on the south shore. The return fare is 1500 SIT, and you get about half an hour to explore the island; in all, the trip takes about 1½ hours. Alternatively, you can rent a rowing boat at the Castle Baths (see Swimming & Boating under Activities) at Mlino or at the large beach at the south-west end of the lake. You can even swim to the island, but if you choose that method you're going to have to drag some clothes along in a plastic bag. The powers-that-be will not let you into the island church in your swimming gear.

The boat sets you down on the island's south side at a monumental stairway built in 1655; as you walk up you'll pass the **Chaplain's House** and the **Provost's House** from the 17th and 18th centuries with the Brixen bishops' coat of arms on the facade.

The baroque **Church of the Assumption** contains some fresco fragments from the 14th century, a large gold altar and, under the floor of the nave, part of the apse of the **pre-Romanesque chapel**, the only one in Slovenia. Models in the porch illustrate the development of the site from an 8th-century wattle-and-daub structure to the 17th-century church standing here today. Outside is a 15th-century **belfry** with a 'wishing bell' that visitors can ring if they want to ask a favour. Naturally everyone and their grandmother does it – again and again and again. The church is open from 8 am to dusk daily.

Lake Walk

Lake Bled is not a large body of water – it measures only 2km by 1380m – and the second-best way to see it is from the shore. A walk around the lake (6km) shouldn't take much longer than an hour or so, and it is at its best in the early morning. Along the way, you'll pass linden, chestnut and willow trees hanging over the water, boat slips, wooden walkways, innumerable anglers, the start of several hikes and a couple of interesting sights. Start at the Grand Hotel Toplice and walk clockwise.

On the south shore you'll pass through the hamlet of Mlino, then leave the road for a path that passes beneath the grand edifice of the Hotel Vila Bled. Around the far end of the lake and past the camping ground is the **Zaka Regatta Centre** where a rowing competition is staged in June. The bronze statue of the *Boatman* by Boris Kalin is attractive but does little to distract attention from the dreadful concrete viewing stands to the south, built for an international rowing championship in 1989 – they're *very* unpopular in these parts. The **Triglav National Park office** at Kidričeva cesta 2 has a small exhibit concerned with mountain ecology and what you might encounter in the park. You're unlikely to spot Zlatorog, the fearsome and immortal 'golden horn' chamois *(Rupicara reupicara)* who guards the golden treasure of Triglav (see the boxed text 'Zlatorog & His Golden Horns'). The **Castle Baths** are a bit farther on.

An alternative to circling the lake on foot is to rent a bicycle (see Getting Around) or to take a horse-drawn carriage *(fijaker)* from the stand near the Festival Hall (☎ 574 16 24) on Cesta Svobode. A twirl around the lake for five people costs 4000 SIT, and it's the same price for two or three people up to the castle. You can even get a carriage for four to Vintgar (8000 SIT for a two-hour round trip).

Activities

Hiking There are many good, short, way-marked hikes around Bled (numbered signs correspond to numbered routes on the local hiking maps). One of the best is trail No 6 from the south-west corner of the lake to the summit of Velika Osojnica (756m). The view from the top – over the lake, island and castle, with the peaks of the Karavanke in the background – is stunning, especially towards sunset. The climb to the first summit is steep, but the round trip, returning via Ojstrica (610m), takes only three hours or so.

See also Adventure Sports later in this section for details of longer treks.

Swimming & Boating Bled's warm (23°C at source), crystal-clear water makes it suitable for swimming well into the autumn, and there are decent beaches around the lake, including a big gravel one near the camping ground and a grass lido with a big water slide to the east of the Triglav National Park office.

Just beyond the latter is the large Castle Baths (Grajsko Kopališče) complex with an indoor pool and protected enclosures in the lake itself where you can splash around. Entry is 600/400 SIT for adults/children with cabins costing 600 SIT. The baths are open from 7 am to 7 pm from mid-April to October.

This is also one place to rent rowing boats for getting to the island or just potter-ing about (motor boats are banned here); others are at Gostilna Pletna in Mlino, or farther west near the entrance to the camping ground; the cost is 1000 to 1500 SIT per hour. At the Pletna, you can also rent kayaks for 800 SIT an hour.

Four hotels in Bled have indoor pools filled with thermal water as well as saunas: the Grand Hotel Toplice, the Park, the

Zlatorog & His Golden Horns

The oft-told tale of Zlatorog, the mythical chamois (*gams* in Slovene) with the golden horns who lived on Mt Triglav and guarded its treasure, almost always involves some superhuman (or, in this case, super-antelopine) feat that drastically changed the face of the mountain. But don't let Slovenes fool you into believing that their ancient ancestors passed on the tale. The Zlatorog story first appeared in the *Laibacher Zeitung (Ljubljana Gazette)* in 1868 during a period of Romanticism and national awakening. This one tells of how the chamois created the Triglav Lakes Valley, a wilderness of tumbled rock almost in the centre of Triglav National Park.

Zlatorog roamed the valley (at that time a beautiful garden) with the White Ladies, good fairies who kept the mountain pastures green and helped humans whenever they found them in need.

Meanwhile, down in the Soča Valley near Trenta, a greedy plot was being hatched. It seemed that an innkeeper's daughter had been given jewels by a rather wealthy Venetian merchant. The girl's mother demanded that her daughter's lover, a poor but skilled hunter, match the treasure with Zlatorog's gold which was hidden under Mt Bogatin and guarded by a multiheaded serpent. If not, he was at least to bring back a bunch of Triglav 'roses' (actually pink cinquefoils) to prove his fidelity – an impossible task in mid-winter.

The young hunter, seething with jealousy, climbed the mountain in search of the chamois, figuring that if he were to get even a piece of the golden horns, the treasure of Bogatin – and his beloved – would be his. At last the young man spotted Zlatorog, took aim and fired. It was a direct hit.

The blood gushing from Zlatorog's wound melted the snow and up sprang a magical Triglav rose. The chamois nibbled on a few petals and – presto! – Zlatorog was instantly back on his feet. As the chamois leapt away, roses sprang up from under his hooves, luring the hunter onto higher and higher ground. But as they climbed, the sun caught Zlatorog's shiny horns. The hunter was blinded, lost his footing and plunged into a gorge.

The once kind and trusting chamois was enraged that a mere mortal would treat him in such a manner. In his fury he gored his way through the Triglav Lakes Valley, leaving it much as it looks today. He left the area with the White Ladies, never to return.

And the fate of the others? The innkeeper's daughter waited in vain for her lover to return home. As spring approached, the snow began to melt, swelling the Soča River. One day it brought her a sad gift – the body of her young swain, his lifeless hand still clutching a Triglav rose. As for the innkeeper's rapacious wife, we know nothing. Perhaps she learned Italian and moved to Venice.

Observant travellers will see the face of Zlatorog no matter where they go in Slovenia. It's on the label of the country's best beer.

MICHELLE STAMP

Jelovica and the Golf (Cankarjeva ulica 6). The pool in the Hotel Jelovica is open from noon to 10 pm and costs about 900/500 SIT for adults/children (free for hotel guests).

Adventure Sports The friendly and helpful ProMontana agency (☎/fax 574 26 05, e bled@promontana.si), Ljubljanska cesta 1, organises a wide range of outdoor activities, including trekking, mountaineering, rock climbing, ski touring, cross-country skiing, mountain biking, rafting, kayaking, canyoning and caving. It can also provide guides and instructors, and rent and sell equipment.

A two-day, guided ascent of Triglav from Pokljuka, Vrata Valley or Kot Valley costs 21,000 SIT for one person, plus 12,000 SIT for each additional person; the price includes everything except food and transport. A longer trip, descending through the Triglav Lakes Valley to Bohinj, costs 29,000/16,000 SIT. A more challenging, five-day, mountaineering traverse of the main peaks of the Julian Alps, starting from the Tamar Valley and taking in Prisank (2547m), Razor (2601m), Bovški Gamsovec (2392m) and Triglav, and finishing via Triglav Lakes, is 40,000/25,000 SIT.

If you don't fancy scaling the summits, then a three-day trek through the Alpine meadows south of Triglav, from Pokljuka to the Soča Valley in the west costs 32,000 SIT plus 19,000 SIT per additional person.

A two-hour rafting trip down the Sava Bohinjka River costs 3500 SIT per person, a three-hour canyoning descent is 10,000 SIT, and a two-day intensive kayaking course is 8000 SIT. A half-day tour of the (easy) Bobji Zob cave near Bohinjska Bela is 1500/1000 SIT for adults/children (six persons minimum), while the more challenging Simnovo Brezno cave (including a 50m abseil descent) takes all day and costs 12,000 SIT, including equipment rental.

If you want to go it alone, you can hire a kayak and accessories for 3500 SIT a day, cross-country skis and boots for 2500 SIT a day, climbing gear for 2000 SIT a day, or a Scott USA mountain bike for 500/1000/1800 SIT an hour/half-day/day.

Tennis There are four tennis courts at the Zaka Regatta Centre at the western end of the lake, and more at the Hotel Golf, just south of Bled Shopping Centre, open March to November.

Golf The 18-hole, par 73 King's Course at Bled Golf & Country Club (☎ 537 77 00), about 3km to the east of the lake near Lesce, is Slovenia's best golf course and one of the most beautiful in Europe. There's also a nine-hole, par 36 course. The club is open from 8 am to 7 pm daily April to October. Green fees for a round are €33, a set of clubs costs €10 to rent, a hand cart €3. There's also a driving range (€2 for 36 balls) and a pro who gives lessons for €18 to €25 per hour. Miniature golf is available at the Bife Mini Golf opposite the Lovec hotel for 350 SIT.

Flying The Alpine Flying Centre (Alpski Letalski Center; ☎ 533 34 31) at Begunjska cesta 10 in Lesce has panoramic flights over Bled (10,000 SIT for three people), Bohinj (15,000 SIT) and even Triglav (21,000 SIT), or anywhere you want for 28,000 SIT an hour. And if you're feeling brave, you can take a tandem skydive for 26,000 SIT.

Ice Skating The lake itself usually freezes in winter but if you're in Bled during a warm spell or in summer and feel like cutting up the ice, visit the ice-skating rink (drsališče) in the Sport Hall (Športna Dvorana) at Ljubljanska cesta 5 in the park behind the Hotel Krim, open August to May.

Skiing The closest 'real' ski resort to Bled is **Zatrnik** (☎ 574 11 33) on the slopes of the Pokljuka Plateau, 8km west of Bled, with skiing up to 1250m, a chairlift and four T-bars. But beginners will be content with the miniski centre at **Straža** (☎ 576 60 40) southwest of the Grand Hotel Toplice. A chairlift takes you up the 646m hill in three minutes; you'll be down the short slope in no time.

Steam Train In the warmer months (roughly from June to September) Slovenian Railways' Oldtimer Train (Muzejski Vlak; ☎ 572 10 32) offers excursions in

vintage carriages hauled by a steam locomotive. Trains run between Jesenice, 13km
to the north-west, and Most na Soči, stopping at Bled Jezero and Bohinjska Bistrica.
The fare for a round trip is 3900/1900 SIT
for adults/children under 13, or 8900/4900
SIT including lunch and side trips. Ask the
tourist office about departure times.

Special Events
A number of special events take place during the summer in Bled, including the International Rowing Regatta in early June,
the Okarina/No Borders Music Festival in
July and August, and Rikli's Days, a multi
media festival in late July when there are
fireworks and the entire lake is illuminated
by candlelight. In winter, the Pokljuka
Plateau west of Bled is the venue for the
Biathlon (cross-country skiing and rifle
shooting) World Championship.

Summertime concerts (most often on
Monday afternoon and Friday evening) take
place at the castle, the island church and the
parish church. While the island is a far more
romantic venue for Bach or Handel, don't
miss a concert at the Church of St Martin –
it has one of the finest organs in Slovenia.

In October 2002 Bled will host the Chess
Olympics, when some 2000 players will
descend on the resort, and in April 2004 the
town will celebrate the 1000th anniversary
of its founding.

Places to Stay
Befitting a resort of such popularity, Bled
has a wide range of accommodation – from
Slovenia's first youth hostel to a five-star
hotel in a villa that was once the summer
retreat of Tito. The lake and surrounding
areas count some 4000 beds, more than 5%
of the total available in Slovenia.

Camping At *Camping Bled (☎ 575 20 00)*,
a six-hectare camping ground in a quiet
valley at the western end of the lake, about
2.5km from the bus station, there is accommodation for 750 people. The location is
good, and there's a decent beach, tennis
courts, a large restaurant facing the lake and
a supermarket, but the site fills up very

quickly in summer. It's open from April to
October and costs about €5/3.50 to €7.50/
5.50 per adult/child aged seven to 13, depending on season (children aged six and
under can stay for free).

Šobec, Slovenia's largest camping ground,
is in Lesce. See Places to Stay in the Radovljica section earlier in this chapter for details.
It is strictly forbidden to camp elsewhere on
the lake, and the law is enforced.

Hostels The HI-affiliated *Penzion Bledec
(☎ 574 52 50, Grajska cesta 17)* is open year-
round, except November. It has 56 beds in 13
rooms and costs 3000 SIT per person (10%
discount for HI members). Check-in is from
7 am to 10 pm, and you'll be given a key to
the front door if you expect to return late.

Private Rooms Dozens of private rooms
and apartments are listed with *Kompas,
Globtour* and the *ATS travel agency (☎ 574
17 36, Kajuhova cesta 1)*. Low-season prices
per person for a room without breakfast
range from 1900 to 3200 SIT, depending on
category. In July and August you'll pay between 2300 and 3800 SIT. Apartments for
two range from 4700 to 7400 SIT. You'll
pay 30% more if you stay in a private room
or apartment for fewer than three days.

If you want to do your own investigating
and strike a private deal, there are lots of
houses advertising 'sobe' (rooms available)
around Bled, particularly to the north in
Rečica. It's not exactly in the centre of
things but it's a quiet area.

Farmhouses Believe it or not, you can
actually stay at a farm very close to Bled. It
may not exactly be a Štajerska-style spread,
but it will be a working farm nonetheless.
Selo, a village 1km south of Mlino, has several farmhouses with accommodation, including *Povšin (☎ 574 23 43)* at No 22 with
eight rooms and *Stojan (☎ 574 46 17)* with
four rooms at No 20. Prices range from
about €18 to €24.50 per person, depending
on the season and room category.

Pensions The *Penzion Mlino (☎ 574 14 04,
Cesta Svobode 45)*, better known for its

restaurant than its accommodation, has 15 rooms. Singles, with shower and breakfast, are €25.50 to €30.50 and doubles €36 to €46. The attractive *Vila Prešeren* (☎ *574 16 08, fax 574 11 38, Kidričeva cesta 1)*, with only six rooms and two suites facing the lake, charges from €38/66 for singles/doubles.

Delightful *Mayer Penzion* (☎ *574 10 58, fax 576 57 41,* e *penzion@mayer-sp.si, Želeška 7)*, set in a renovated 19th-century house, is more upmarket. Its 12 rooms have en suite bathrooms and TV, and cost 7020 to 8100 SIT for a single, 9720 to 12,960 SIT for a double. *Penzion Krek* (☎ *574 17 01, fax 574 54 05,* e *krek@krek.si, Savska 5)* is 2km from Bled, in Ribno. It has 15 rooms, all en suite with TV, costing 5500/8800 SIT for singles/doubles including breakfast.

Hotels Not surprisingly, the cheaper hotels in Bled are a bit away from the water and on noisy streets. The sprawling *Hotel Krim* (☎ *579 70 00, fax 574 37 29,* e *prodaja@ hotel-krim.si, Ljubljanska cesta 7)* with 215 beds charges €32 to €42 for singles, €48 to €79 for doubles. Close to the bus station and fronting a pretty park above the lake, the 188-bed *Hotel Jelovica* (☎ *579 60 00, fax 574 15 50,* e *jelovica@hotel-jelovica.si, Cesta Svobode 8)* has singles for 7935 to 9085 SIT and doubles for 11,270 to 13,570 SIT.

Bled's largest hotel, the 400-bed *Park Hotel* (☎ *579 30 00, fax 574 15 05,* e *info@ gp-hoteli-bled.si, Cesta Svobode 15)*, is opposite the casino and the lake, and about as central as you are going to get. Singles are 11,100 to 16,800 SIT while doubles are 15,400 to 22,800 SIT, depending on season and whether or not you have a lake view.

If you really want to splurge, or have the rich uncle or aunt in tow, there are two choices – both of them on the lake. The 205-bed *Grand Hotel Toplice* (☎ *579 10 00, fax 574 18 41,* e *toplice@hotel-toplice.si, Cesta Svobode 12)* is Bled's 'olde worlde' hotel, with attractive public areas (though some rather dark rooms) and superb views of the lake on its northern side. Singles are €46 to €66, depending on the season and view, while doubles are from €77 and €112. The hotel's two extensions opposite – the *Trst*

(Cesta Svobode 19) and the more attractive *Jadran (Cesta Svobode 23)* on the hill – are about one-third cheaper.

West of Mlino village, the 70-bed *Vila Bled* (☎ *579 15 00, fax 574 13 20,* e *vilabl ed@robas.si, Cesta Svobode 26)*, where Tito and his foreign guests once put their feet up and their heads down, is even more expensive: US$95 to US$115 for a single, US$135 to US$155 for a double, or lay out US$350 a night for the presidential suite. Vila Bled is surrounded by a large park and has its own private beach and boat dock.

Places to Eat

Bled is blessed with many restaurants – good, bad and indifferent. For pizza and vegetarian food, head for the large garden cafe and pub called the *Pod Kostanji* at the Hotel Jelovica. The restaurant at *Penzion Bledec* (see Hostels under Places to Stay) has everything from vegetarian dishes to steak, sausage and *cevapci,* with affordable prices around 700 to 800 SIT.

The *Peking* *(Ulica Narodnih Herojev 3)* is a – come on now, guess – Chinese restaurant almost opposite the Hotel Krim. The *hui guo rou* (twice-cooked pork) and *ma po doufu* (spicy bean curd) aren't exactly what you'd get in Chengdu but this is Slovenia after all; main courses cost around 950 to 1300 SIT. Peking is open till 11 pm daily.

There are a couple of *gostišča* in Mlino, the main village on the lake's southern shore: *Pletna (Cesta Svobode 37)*, with a decent lunch menu for 950 SIT and open from 8 am to 11 pm daily, and *Mlino (Cesta Svobode 45)*. The latter, open till 11 pm, has decent Slovenian dishes with an emphasis on fish. The *Mayer Penzion* (see Places to Stay) has an excellent, rustic restaurant that dishes up hearty Slovenian fare, including sausage, trout, roast pork and *skutini štruklji* (cheese curd pastries), accompanied by the best Slovenian wines; allow 2000 to 3000 SIT a head. Mayer is open from 5 pm to midnight weekdays, and from noon at weekends.

A favourite restaurant in Bled remains the homely, pub-like *Gostilna Pri Planincu (Grajska cesta 8)* just down the hill from the Penzion Bledec. Excellent mushroom soup and roast chicken with chips and salad shouldn't cost much more than 1650 SIT and the grilled Balkan specialities like *čevapčiči* (spicy meatballs of beef or pork) and the tasty *pljeskavica z kajmakom* (Serbian-style meat patties with mascarpone-like cream cheese; 1100 SIT) are very well prepared. Pri Planincu is open from 9 am to 11 pm daily.

Slightly uphill and a long way upmarket is **Restaurant Okarina** *(Riklijeva cesta 9)*. It has a lovely, torch-lit back terrace, and is decorated with traditional musical instruments (an *okarina* is a small clay flute). But it's not cheap: soups and starters range from 800 to 1500 SIT, with mains (some of them vegetarian) from 1900 to 2500 SIT. As well as Slovenian favourites like *jota* and roe-deer venison with buckwheat dumplings, the Okarina has a *tandoor* oven and serves Indian food – chicken tikka (2100 SIT), masala (1900 SIT) and naan bread (800 SIT). It's open from noon to midnight daily.

Bled's culinary speciality is the *kremna rezina* (cream cake) – a layer of vanilla custard topped with whipped cream, and sandwiched neatly between two layers of flaky pastry. One of the best places in town to try it is the **Slaščičarna Šmon** *(Grajska cesta 3)*.

Entertainment

Several pubs have lovely terraces with great views open in the warmer months. Two of the better ones are the Park Hotel's **Terasa Kavarna** above the casino on Cesta Svobode and the **Grand Hotel Toplice cafe** *(Cesta Svobode 12a)*. But nothing beats the **Belvedere**, a cafe on top of a tall tower near the Vila Bled. It closes in winter though. More down to earth – in every respect – is the **Casino Bar** *(Cesta Svobode 19a)* opposite the Grand Hotel Toplice cafe.

Casino Bled *(☎ 574 11 50, Cesta Svoboda 15)*, with roulette, blackjack, baccarat and 80 slot machines, is open every day of the week – from 7 pm Monday to Thursday and from 5 pm Friday to Sunday – till late.

Getting There & Away

Bus There are buses every 30 to 40 minutes to Radovljica (via both Lesce and Begunje), and there is at least one an hour to Bohinj,

Kranj and Ljubljana. Other destinations served from Bled include: Bovec via Kranjska Gora and the Vršič Pass (one bus a day in July and August, on Saturday and Sunday in June and September), Celje (one, at 11.40 am), Jesenice (10), Kranjska Gora (nine), Piran (one a day in summer), Pokljuka (one or two from late June to October) and Škofja Loka (one, at 6.14 am). One bus daily heads for Zagreb in Croatia via Ljubljana.

Train Lesce-Bled station gets up to 16 trains a day from Ljubljana (55 minutes, 51km) via Škofja Loka, Kranj and Radovljica. They continue on to Jesenice (15 minutes, 13km), from where eight cross the border for Villach in Austria.

Up to seven daily trains from Jesenice via Podhom pass through Bled Jezero station on their way to Bohinjska Bistrica (20 minutes, 18km), Most na Soči and Nova Gorica (1¾ hours, 79km), from where you can make connections for Sežana, 40km to the southeast, and Italy. This mountain railway is one of the most picturesque in Slovenia. If you are headed south-west to Nova Gorica, sit on the right-hand side of the train to see the valley of the cobalt-blue Soča River at its best.

Car Hertz (☎ 574 15 19) rents cars from its office beneath the Hotel Krim at Ljubljanska cesta 7. It is open from 7 am till noon and from 5 to 7 pm weekdays. It closes at 1 pm on Saturday. Budget (☎ 576 64 00) has an office in the Bled Shopping Centre at Ljubljanska cesta 4, but F-Rent A Car (☎ 574 15 15), in the Kompas-Bled travel agency in the shopping centre, is cheaper, with small cars available from 3160 SIT a day plus 21.70 SIT a kilometre, or 9650 SIT a day with unlimited mileage (not including tax).

Getting Around

From mid-June to September, a tourist bus leaves daily from the Hotel Jelovica at 9.30 am and heads for Vintgar, stopping at Mlino, the far end of the lake and Bled Castle, returning from Vintgar at 11.45 am.

Parking in Bled is restricted to seven city-maintained car parks around the resort and costs 500 SIT (or 1000 SIT right on the lake) per day. You can order a local taxi on mobile ☎ 041-631 629.

Kompas, Globtour and ATS rent bicycles and mountain bikes. Prices are 600 SIT an hour, 1200 SIT a half-day and 1800 SIT a day. Kompas has the biggest selection.

AROUND BLED

The area around Bled offers endless possibilities for excursions, notably the forests and meadows of the **Pokljuka Plateau** below Triglav to the west. Here you can explore the 1km-long Pokljuka Gorge (Pokljuška soteška) just north of the small ski resort of Zatrnik, 7km west of Bled. Well-marked trails crisscross the plateau and are outlined on the 1:30,000 map *Bled* (1200 SIT) and the 1:50,000 *Gorenjska* map (1000 SIT) from GZS, both available from the tourist office.

The village of **Vrba**, 3km north-east of Bled, is where poet France Prešeren was born (house No 2), and is the site of the Romanesque-Gothic Church of St Mark with its 14th-century frescoes. **Begunje**, 7km east, has the ruins of Kamen Castle, the Church of St Peter (containing some of the most valuable medieval frescoes in Gorenjska, painted by Jernej of Loka), and the Hostages Museum (Muzej Talcev) in an old manor house (house No 55), dedicated to over 12,000 people held here by the Gestapo during WWII.

Vintgar Gorge

One of the easiest and most satisfying day trips is to Vintgar Gorge, a mere 4km north-west of Bled. A wooden walkway built in 1893 hugs the rock walls of the gorge for 1600m along the Radovna River, crisscrossing the raging torrent four times over rapids, waterfalls and pools before reaching **Šum Waterfall**. The entire walk is spectacular though it can get pretty wet and slippery. There are little snack bars at the beginning and the end of the walkway and picnic tables at several locations along the way. Admission to the gorge costs 400/200 SIT for adults/children, and it is open from 8 am to 8 pm mid-April to October.

It's an easy walk to the gorge from Bled. Head north-west on Prešernova cesta then north on Partizanska cesta to Cesta v Vintgar.

This will take you to Podhom, where signs show the way to the gorge entrance. To return, you can either retrace your steps or, from Šum Waterfall, walk eastward over Hom (834m) to the ancient pilgrimage **Church of St Catherine**, which retains some 15th-century fortifications. From there it's due south through Zasip to Bled.

Those unable or unwilling to walk all the way can take the bus or the train (from Bled Jezero station) to Podhom. From there it's a 1.5km walk westward to the main entrance. From mid-June to September a tourist bus makes the run from Bled's bus station daily at 9.30 am, stopping at the castle car park, and returns at 11.45 am; one way is 200 SIT.

BOHINJ
☎ 04

Bohinj, a larger and much less developed glacial lake 26km to the south-west of Bled, is a wonderful antidote to the latter. OK, so it doesn't have a romantic little island or a castle looming high on a rocky cliff. But it does have Triglav itself visible from the lake when the weather clears and a wonderful naturalness that doesn't exist at Bled. The Bohinj area's handful of museums and historical churches will keep culture vultures busy during their visit, and for action types there are activities galore – from kayaking and mountain biking to scaling Triglav via one of the southern approaches. The only drawback is the lake's propensity for attracting fog, especially in the morning.

History

Bohinj (Wochain in German) was densely settled during the Hallstatt period due to the large amounts of iron ore in the area, and a trade route linked the lake with the Soča Valley and the Adriatic Sea via a pass at Vrh Bače, south-east of Bohinjska Bistrica. During the Middle Ages, when the area fell under the jurisdiction of the Bishops of Brixen at Bled, Bohinj was known for its markets and fairs, which were held near the Church of St John the Baptist. Here peasants from the Friuli region around Trieste traded salt, wine and foodstuffs with their Slovenian counterparts for iron ore, livestock and butter. As the population grew, herders went higher into the Julian Alps in search of pasture land while charcoal burners cleared the upper forests for timber to fuel the forges.

The iron industry continued to flourish here until the late 19th century when it moved on to Jesenice. But all was not lost for Bohinj; a railway connecting the Sava Valley with Gorica and the coast opened in 1906, providing Bohinj with its first modern communications link.

Triglav was 'conquered' from Bohinj for the first time in the late 18th century. Bohinj has also figured prominently in Slovenian literary history. The poet Valentin Vodnik (1758–1819) lived and worked in nearby Gorjuše and even left his name in pencil on the back of the high altar at the Church of St John the Baptist. And most of the events in France Prešeren's epic poem *Baptism at the Savica Waterfall*, including the demise of our hero Črtomir, take place around Bohinj. For those reasons Bohinj enjoys a much more special place than Bled in the hearts and minds of many Slovenes.

Orientation

Lake Bohinj, some 4.5km long and up to 45m deep, lies in a valley basin 523m above sea level on the southern edge of Triglav National Park. The Savica River flows into the lake from the west while the Sava Bohinjka flows out from the south-eastern corner.

There is no town called Bohinj; the name refers to the entire valley, its settlements and the lake. The largest town in the area is Bohinjska Bistrica (population 3080; postcode 4264), 6km to the east of the lake. Small villages on or near the southern and eastern shores include: Ukanc; Ribčev Laz; Stara Fužina at the mouth of the Mostnica Gorge; Studor, a veritable 'village of hayracks'; and Srednja Vas. There are no settlements on the northern side.

You'll find everything of a practical nature in Ribčev Laz – more specifically in the shopping complex south-east of the Jezero Hotel. In Ribčev Laz, buses stop near the tourist office and in Bohinjska Bistrica on Triglavska cesta near the police station/post office and at the train station. Bohinjska

Bistrica's train station is about 700m north-east of the town centre at Triglavska cesta 1.

Information

Tourist Offices The helpful and very efficient tourist office (☎ 574 60 10, fax 572 33 30, 🄴 tic@bohinj.si) at No 48 in Ribčev Laz is open from 7 am to 8 pm daily, July through mid-September. It is open from 8 am to 7 pm Monday to Saturday and 8 am to 3 pm Sunday the rest of the year.

Money The tourist office can change money but the rate is not good and it takes a 3% commission. The post offices in Ribčev Laz and Bohinjska Bistrica give a better rate. There's an ATM outside the post office in Ribčev Laz, and Gorenjska Banka has a branch in Bohinjska Bistrica at Trg Svobode 2b, about 100m east of Slovenijaturist. It is open from 9 to 11.30 am and 2 to 5 pm weekdays and 8 to 11 am Saturday.

Post & Communications The post office at No 47 in Ribčev Laz is open from 8 am to

Old Mr Three Heads

The 2864m-limestone peak called Triglav has been a source of inspiration and an object of devotion for Slovenes for more than a millennium. The early Slavs believed the mountain to be the home of a three-headed deity who ruled the sky, the earth and the underworld, but no-one managed (or dared) to reach the summit until the late 18th century. Today Triglav (the name means, literally, three heads) figures prominently on the national flag and seal.

As the statue of four men at Ribčev Laz constantly reminds visitors, Triglav's summit was first reached from Lake Bohinj by an Austrian mountaineer and his three Slovenian guides in 1778 on the initiative of Žiga Zois (1747–1819), an iron magnate and patron of the arts. Under the Habsburgs in the 19th century, the 'pilgrimage' to Triglav became, in effect, a confirmation of one's Slovenian identity, and this tradition continues to this day – a true Slovene is expected to climb Triglav at least once in their life.

6 pm weekdays with a couple of half-hour breaks and till noon Saturday. Bohinjska Bistrica's post office, just east of Slovenijaturist at Triglavska cesta 35, is open nonstop from 8 am to 6 pm weekdays, till noon Saturday.

Travel Agencies The staff at the Alpinum travel agency (☎ 572 34 41) can provide accommodation of all grades and organise any number of sporting activities. The agency is a couple of doors along from the tourist office at No 50 in Ribčev Laz, and is open from 7 am to 7 pm weekdays and till 3 pm at weekends. The Alpinsport kiosk (☎ 572 34 86) at No 53, Ribčev Laz, to the right just before you cross the stone bridge to the Church of St John the Baptist, primarily rents equipment. It is open from 9 am to 7 pm daily June to August and 10 am to 6 pm the rest of the year. Another outdoor sports agency is PAC Club (☎ 572 34 61), whose services are available at the Bohinj and Pod Voglom Hotels, and through Alpinum.

Slovenijaturist (☎ 572 10 32) has a branch in Bohinjska Bistrica at Triglavska cesta 45. It is open from 8 am to 8 pm Monday to Saturday and 9 am till noon Sunday in summer. The hours are 8 am till noon and 2 to 6 pm Monday to Saturday in winter. It also opens on Sunday morning.

Church of St John the Baptist

Ribčev Laz's Church of St John the Baptist on the northern side of the Sava Bohinjka, across the stone bridge from the Hotel Jezero, is what every medieval church should be: small, on a lake and full of exquisite frescoes. It is perhaps the most beautiful and evocative church in all of Slovenia, with the possible exception of the Church of the Holy Trinity at Hrastovlje in Primorska.

The nave is Romanesque while the Gothic presbytery dates from about 1440. A large portion of the latter's walls, ceilings and arches are covered with 15th- and 16th-century **frescoes** too numerous to appreciate in one viewing. As you face the arch from the nave, look for the frescoes on either side depicting the beheading of the church's patron saint. On the opposite side of the arch to the left is Abel making his offering to

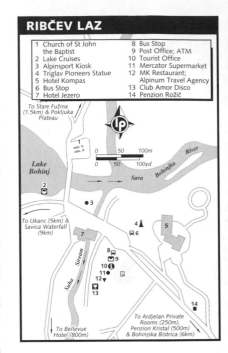

RIBČEV LAZ

1 Church of St John the Baptist	8 Bus Stop
2 Lake Cruises	9 Post Office; ATM
3 Alpinsport Kiosk	10 Tourist Office
4 Triglav Pioneers Statue	11 Mercator Supermarket
5 Hotel Kompas	12 MK Restaurant; Alpinum Travel Agency
6 Bus Stop	13 Club Amor Disco
7 Hotel Jezero	14 Penzion Rožič

God and, to the right, Cain with his inferior one. Upon the shoulder of history's first murderer sits a white devil – a very rare symbol. Behind you on the lower walls of the presbytery are rows of angels with vampire-like teeth; look for the three men above them singing. Some of them have goitres, once a common affliction in mountainous regions due to the lack of iodine in the diet. The carved wooden head of – guess who? – on one of the side altars dates from 1380.

Several paintings on the outside southern wall, one dating back to the early 14th century, depict St Christopher. In the Middle Ages people believed they would not die on the day they had gazed upon an icon of the patron saint of travellers. No fools our ancestors, they painted them on churches near roads and villages, but apparently they forgot to look at least once in their lives as they're all now dead. (The 18th-century **Church of the Holy Spirit**, a couple of kilometres to the west on the lake shore, also

View from trail above Vršič Pass

Poštarski Dom, Vršič Pass

Bled Island's picturesque Church of the Assumption (Gorenjska)

Bled Castle perches on a cliff above Lake Bled (Gorenjska).

Roadside memorial near Kranj

Full of architectural and historical interest, Slovenia's cities have a relaxed, unhurried feel and little of the madding crowds of many other European cities.

has a painting of St Christopher on the outside.) The Church of St John the Baptist is open from 9 am till noon and 3 to 6 pm daily, mid-June to mid-September. At other times a staff member from the tourist office will accompany you (150 SIT).

Museums

The **Alpine Dairy Museum** (Planšarski Muzej) at house No 181 in Stara Fužina, about 1.5km north of Ribčev Laz, has a small collection related to Alpine dairy farming in the Bohinj Valley, once the most important such centre in Slovenia. Until the late 1950s large quantities of cheese were still being made on 28 highland pastures, but a modern dairy in nearby Srednja Vas does it all now.

The four rooms of the museum, a cheese dairy itself once upon a time, contain a mock-up of a 19th-century herder's cottage, fascinating old photographs, cheese presses, wooden butter moulds, copper rennet vats, enormous snowshoes and sledges, and wonderful hand-carved crooks. It is open from 11 am to 7 pm daily, except Monday, in July and August. The hours are 10 am till noon and 4 to 6 pm Tuesday to Sunday the rest of the year (except for November and December, when it is closed). Admission is 300/160 SIT for adults/children.

While you're in Stara Fužina, take a walk over to the village of **Studor**, a couple of kilometres to the east. **Oplen House** (Oplenova Hiša) at No 16 is an old peasant's cottage with a chimney-less 'smoke kitchen' that has been turned into a museum (same hours and admission as the Alpine Dairy Museum). But Studor's real claim to fame is its many *toplarji*, double-linked hayracks with barns or storage areas at the top. Look for the ones at the entrance to the village, which date from the 18th and 19th centuries.

The **Tomaž Godec Museum** (Muzej Tomaža Godca) in Bohinjska Bistrica at Zoisova ulica 15, about 100m south of Triglavska cesta, is a mixed bag of a place that does have its moments. Housed in a reconstructed tannery owned by Mr Godec (1905–42), a Partisan who played a role in the formation of the Yugoslav Communist Party, the exhibits trace the history of iron forging in the

valley from earliest times, explain the long process of making leather – the small mill over the Bistrica River here still turns – and examine the life of Comrade Godec.

Above the mill there is a small but fascinating collection dealing graphically and often very poignantly with the horrors of the Isonzo Front in the Soča Valley during WWI. Along with weapons and bombs are many personal items from soldiers, including models of churches made from matchsticks by Russian prisoners of war and Italian helmets with holes punched into them for use as colanders when making pasta. It's really a peace museum and in many ways more moving and immediate than the much-promoted museum in Kobarid. Josip Tito, who spent a few days in Bohinjska Bistrica in 1939, returned 40 years later to open the museum – something the curator is very proud of. The Tomaž Godec Museum is open from 10 am till noon and 4 to 6 pm Tuesday to Sunday from May to October. It is open the same hours, but on Wednesday, Saturday and Sunday only, from January to April. Admission is 300/150 SIT.

Savica Waterfall

Savica is one of the reasons people come to Bohinj – to hike to this magnificent 60m waterfall cutting deep into a gorge and perhaps carry on to the Triglav Lakes Valley or even Triglav itself.

The waterfall, the source of Slovenia's longest and mightiest river, is 4km from the Hotel Zlatorog in Ukanc and can be reached by footpath from there. Cars (and the bus in summer) continue via a gravel road to a car park beside the Savica restaurant, from where it's a 20-minute walk over rapids and streams to the falls. Entrance to the trail costs 300/150 SIT and it is open from 9 am to 5 pm (to 6 pm in July and August) from April to October. It costs 400 SIT to park.

The falls are among the most impressive sights in the Julian Alps, especially after a heavy rain, but bring something waterproof or you may be soaked to the skin by the spray. Two huts to the west at just over 1500m, *Dom na Komni* (☎ *572 14 75 or*

mobile ☎ *050-611 221)* and ***Koča pod Bog-**
***atinom** (mobile* ☎ *050-621 943)*, can be
reached in about 2½ hours. Both have accommodation and food; the former is open
year-round, the latter late June to September.

Activities

Hiking A circular walk around the lake
(12km) from Ribčev Laz should take between three and four hours. Or you could
just do parts of it by following the hunters'
trail in the forest above the south shore of
the lake to the Hotel Zlatorog and taking the
bus back, or walking along the more tranquil northern shore under the cliffs of
Pršivec (1761m). Much more strenuous is
the hike up to **Vogel** (1922m) from the cable
car's upper station (see Skiing later in this
section). Take a map and compass, and
don't set out if it looks stormy; Vogel is
prone to lightning strikes. The whole trip
should take about four hours. For information about climbing Triglav from Bohinj see
the boxed text 'Approaches to Triglav' later
in this chapter.

The Bohinj area map available at the
tourist office lists 10 excellent walks. The
Alpinum agency can arrange guides and excursions for €15 to €20.

Adventure Sports PAC Club (see Travel
Agencies under Information earlier in this
section) offers a range of activities, including canyoning (10,000 SIT), hydrospeed
(5000 SIT), minirafting (in two-person rafts;
5000 SIT) and tandem paraglider flights
(10,500 SIT). You can also rent a mountain
bike for 800/3000 SIT an hour/day.

Swimming & Boating Some of the
beaches on Lake Bohinj's northern shore are
reserved for nude bathing in summer. Two
hotels – the Zlatorog and Jezero – have their
own indoor swimming pools, should the fog
drive you inside. Outsiders can use the former seven days a week between 3 and 8 pm
and from 9 am till noon on Saturday and
Sunday morning. Admission is 600 SIT; for
400 SIT more you can use the sauna as well.

PAC Club and Alpinsport rent kayaks and
canoes for 800 SIT an hour or 3000 to 3800

SIT a day. As at Bled, no motor boats of any
kind are allowed on the lake, but you can
rent a sailing dinghy for 4000 SIT a day.

An old paddle steamer offers trips along
the lake, between Ribčev Laz and the Hotel
Zlatorog, departing every two hours between 10 am and 6 pm in summer. You can
buy tickets at the tourist office for 1000/500
SIT for adults/children.

Fishing Lake Bohinj is home to lake trout
and char, and the jade-coloured Sava Bohinjka River is rich in brown trout and
grayling; together they are among the most
popular places for angling in Slovenia. But
don't expect licences to come cheaply;
you'll pay 4000 SIT a day for the lake and
8000 SIT for the river as far as Soteska
(about 25% cheaper for catch-and-release
licences). The season on the lake extends
from March to September, depending on
the fish, while on the river it's from May to
October. The Alpinum travel agency sells
the permits.

Tennis The tennis courts at the Kompas,
Bellevue and Zlatorog Hotels and Danica
camping ground cost between 800 and 1200
SIT per hour to hire. Two rackets and balls
are about 600 SIT.

Skiing The main skiing station for Bohinj
is **Vogel** (☎ 574 60 60), some 1540m above
the lake's south-western corner and accessible by cable car. With skiing up to 1840m,
the season can be long, sometimes from late
November to early May. Vogel has 36km of
ski slopes and cross-country runs served by
three chairlifts and five T-bar tows. A ski
pass costs 4000/18,100 SIT for a day/week,
ski or snowboard equipment costs about
2200 to 3000 SIT a day, and an individual
lesson costs 3700 SIT for an hour. There is
accommodation near the cable car's upper
station at the 63-bed ***Hotel Ski*** *(☎ 572 14*
71, fax 572 34 46), with singles/doubles
with shower at 8600/15,000 SIT.

The cable car's lower station is about
250m up the hill south of the Hotel Zlatorog
in Ukanc, about 5km west of Ribčev Laz. The
cable car runs every half-hour from 7.30 am

to 6 pm (till 8 pm in July and August) year-round, except in November. Adults/children pay 1000/700 SIT for a return ticket.

The smaller and lower (up to 1480m) ski centre of **Kobla** (☎ 574 71 00) is about 1km east of Bohinjska Bistrica. It has 23km of slopes and 10km of cross-country runs with three chairlifts and three T-bars.

Horse Riding The Mrcina Ranč (mobile ☎ 041-790 297 or ☎ 041-629 804) in Studor offers a range of guided tours on sturdy Icelandic ponies, lasting from one hour to three days. Prices are around €10/25/51 an hour/half-day/day.

Steam Train The Oldtimer Train run by Slovenijaturist has several excursions in summer that pass through Bohinjska Bistrica to or from Jesenice and Most na Soči. For details see the earlier Bled section.

Special Events
The Cows' Ball (Kravji Bal) is a wacky event staged every year, on the third weekend in September, in a field north of the Hotel Zlatorog. Although it traditionally marked the return of the cows to the valley after a spring and summer on highland pastures of up to 1700m, the ball has now degenerated into a day-long knees-up of folk dance and music, eating and drinking and haggling over baskets, painted beehive panels and bowls carved from tree roots. Of course, if you want to say you've seen cows dance, then by all means go.

On Midsummer's Night (Kresna Noč; 23 June) everyone goes out on the lake in boats with candles and there are fireworks.

Places to Stay
Camping The Bohinj area has two camping grounds. On the lake near the Hotel Zlatorog, the large *Camping Zlatorog* (☎ 572 34 82, or ☎ 572 34 41 out of season) costs 800 to 1600 SIT per person per night, depending on the season (mid-May to September). Campers opt for the tennis courts at the Hotel Zlatorog. *Camping Danica* (☎ 572 10 55, or ☎ 574 60 10 out of season), some 200m west of the bus stop in Bohinjska

Bistrica, is open from May to September and costs 1000 to 1400 SIT per person.

Private Rooms The tourist office can arrange private rooms in Ribčev Laz, Stara Fužina and neighbouring villages for as little as 1570 SIT per person per night in the low season and 2330 SIT in July and August (though there's a 30% surcharge for stays of fewer than three days and guests on their own pay an additional 20%). Breakfast usually costs about 950 SIT more, though you can sometimes use the kitchen yourself.

Two of the best places to stay are at the *Ardjelan* (☎ 572 32 62) at No 13 in Ribčev Laz and the *Planšar* (☎ 572 30 95), better known for its fabulous cheeses (see Places to Eat), at No 179 in Stara Fužina. The latter offers accommodation in three rooms and one apartment for 2300 SIT per person.

Apartments for two/four people arranged through the tourist office run from 5260/7840 SIT to 8100/12,850 SIT, depending on the season and category. The Alpinum travel agency and Slovenijaturist in Bohinjska Bistrica also have apartments for rent.

Farmhouses Several farmhouses in the area offer accommodation, including the four-room *Agotnik* (☎ 572 30 14) at No 145 in Stara Fužina, and *Pri Andreju* (☎ 572 35 09) with three apartments for two, four or six people at No 31 in picturesque Studor.

Pensions Travellers have recommended the *Penzion Rožič* (☎ 574 61 11, e rozic@ siol.net), at No 42 in Ribčev Laz, 200m south-east of the tourist office, where B&B costs 2800 to 5000 SIT per person depending on season. Another favourite is the *Penzion Kristal* (☎ 572 33 42, e kristal@ cc-line.si), another 500m south of the Rožič at No 4a in Ribčev Laz, which offers B&B for 3500 to 5500 SIT per person.

The nine-room *Penzion Stare* (☎ 572 34 03), north of the Hotel Zlatorog on the Sava Bohinjka River at No 128 in Ukanc, has singles with shower and breakfast for €22.50 to €31.50, depending on the season, and doubles for €35 to €43. There are discounts of 5% and 15% for Euro<26 and

GORENJSKA

Climbing the Big One

The tradition that all true Slovenes should climb Triglav at least once (see the boxed text 'Old Mr Three Heads' earlier in this chapter) has led to the belief that anyone – even those whose experience of climbing extends no further than clambering onto a bar stool – can climb Slovenia's highest peak. But it's not true. Despite the fact that on a good summer's day over 100 people will reach the summit, Triglav is not for the unfit or faint-hearted. In fact, its popularity is one of the main sources of danger on the final approach to the summit, where there are often dozens of people clambering along a rocky, knife-edge ridge in both directions, trying to pass each other and kicking loose stones down on those below.

The shortest route to the summit (from Rudno Polje – see the boxed text 'Approaches to Triglav' later in this chapter) involves a round trip of 25km and an ascent of over 1500m, which would take a fit and experienced mountaineer around eight to 10 hours of continuous hiking. And although the difficult, final sections of the climb are protected with metal spikes and cables, if you are not used to moving on steep, rocky ground above a high drop, you may find the summit ridge a terrifying place to be.

But if you are fit and confident, and have a good head for heights, then by all means hire a guide and go for it. Guides can be hired through the tourist office in Bohinj and the Triglav National Park office or the ProMontana agency in Bled, or booked in advance through the Alpine Association of Slovenia (see Hiking & Mountain Walking in the special section 'The Great Outdoors'). Only experienced mountain walkers with full equipment – including good hiking boots, warm clothes and waterproofs, map and compass, whistle, head torch, first-aid kit, and emergency food and drink – should consider making the ascent without a guide. Take care – people die on Triglav every year.

Triglav is usually inaccessible to hikers from late October to early June. June and July are the rainiest (and sometimes snowiest) summer months so August and particularly September and October are the best times to go. Patches of snow and ice can linger in the higher gullies until late July, and the weather can be very unpredictable at altitudes above 1500m, with temperatures varying by as much as 20°C and violent storms appearing out of nowhere.

Before you attempt the climb, pick up a copy of How to Climb Triglav, a superb booklet which describes a dozen of the best routes (published by Planinska Založba). This 63-page publication, available in bookshops and tourist offices for about 650 SIT, also has an illustrated section on Triglav's remarkable Alpine flora.

Several maps to the area are available. Freytag and Berndt's 1:50,000-scale Julische Alpen Wanderkarte covers the whole of Triglav National Park. The Alpine Association publishes a two-sheet 1:50,000-scale map of the Julian Alps; for Triglav and the park you want the eastern part (Julijske Alpe – Vzhodni Del). The most useful map for the ascent of Triglav is the Alpine Association's 1:25,000 Planinska Karta Triglav, with all the trails and huts clearly marked, and a panoramic drawing of the view from the summit on the reverse.

ISIC card-holders respectively. If you really want to get away from it all without having to climb mountains, this is the place.

Hotels Bohinj has no shortage of hotels but the cheapest, the 49-room *Hotel Pod Voglom* (☎ 572 34 61, fax 572 34 46) on the lake's southern shore at No 60 in Ribčev Laz, is not that nice. It has singles with shared showers for 4800 to 6500 SIT per person, depending on the season, and doubles for 7400 to 10,800 SIT.

In Ribčev Laz proper, you have a choice of three hotels. The 50-room *Hotel Jezero* (☎ 572 33 75, fax 572 34 46), used by the Gestapo during WWII, is the most central – a few steps from the tourist office and the lake at No 51. Single rooms with shower and breakfast start at 8800 to 11,900 SIT and doubles at 13,200 to 19,400 SIT. The 59-room *Hotel Bellevue* (☎ 572 33 31, fax 572 36 84), with a beautiful location on a hill about 800m south of the Jezero at No 65, charges a minimum of 6200 to 9100

SIT for singles and 10,200 to 16,000 SIT for doubles. The 55-room **Hotel Kompas** (☎ 572 34 71, fax 572 31 61), above the road to Bohinjska Bistrica north-east of the post office at No 45, will be closed for renovation until at least September 2001.

Out of the way and pleasant for that is the 43-room **Hotel Zlatorog** (☎ 572 33 81, fax 572 33 84) at No 64 in Ukanc, with lots of activities available. Singles start at 9200 to 12,500 SIT, doubles at 14,000 to 20,600 SIT.

Places to Eat
The **MK Restaurant**, a pizzeria next to the Alpinum travel agency at No 50 in Ribčev Laz, is one of the most popular places to eat and a good place to hang out.

If you've got wheels of any sort, head for **Gostišče Rupa** (☎ 572 34 01) at No 87 in Srednja Vas, about 5km from Ribčev Laz. It has excellent home-cooked food, including spectacular Bohinj trout and *ajdova krapi,* crescent-shaped dumplings made from buckwheat and cheese.

In Stara Fužina, the **Gostilna Mihovc** (☎ 572 33 90) at No 118 is a popular place – not least for its home-made brandy – and opens daily from 11 am till midnight. But if you want something light, head for **Planšar** (☎ 572 30 95) opposite the Alpine Dairy Museum at No 179. It specialises in home-made dairy products – hard Bohinj cheese, a soft, strong-tasting cheese called *mohant,* cottage cheese, curd pie, sour milk etc – and you and a friend can taste a variety of them for about 700 to 900 SIT, or make a meal of cheese and different types of grain dishes like *žganci* (buckwheat), *ješprenj* (barley) or *močnik* (white corn). Other dishes available include *štruklji* (cheese dumplings) and *jota* (a thick soup of beans and salt pork). Planšar is open from 10 am to about 8 pm Tuesday to Sunday, but only at weekends in winter. It's a taste sensation and highly recommended.

The **Zoisov Grad** (Grajska ulica 14) in Bohinjska Bistrica, about 200m east of the Tomaž Godec Museum, is a standard Slovenian restaurant in an old manor house with set menus from 1100 SIT and pizzas. It's open from 11 am till midnight daily.

Another place with pizza and cheaper set menus (from 550 SIT) in Bohinjska Bistrica is the **Bistrica** (Trg Svobode 1).

The **Mercator supermarket** at No 49 in Ribčev Laz is open from 7 am to 6.30 pm weekdays and to 5 pm Saturday.

Entertainment
The only late-night venue in these parts is **Club Amor**, a disco next to the MK Restaurant and Alpinum travel agency.

Shopping
The traditional craft of Bohinj is a small, handcarved wooden pipe with a silver cover (gorjuška čedra) for smoking tobacco or whatever. The real thing isn't so easy to find these days, but the tourist office sells them and can tell you which masters are still carving.

Getting There & Away
Bus Services from Ribčev Laz to Ljubljana via the Hotel Zlatorog, Bohinjska Bistrica, Bled, Radovljica, and Kranj are frequent. There are also about six buses a day to Bohinjska Bistrica via Stara Fužina, Studor and Srednja Vas. From mid-June to September a bus leaves Bled bus station daily at around 10 am for Savica Waterfall, returning at about 12.45 pm; one way costs 300 SIT.

Train Lake Bohinj is not on a train line, though Bohinjska Bistrica is on the scenic one linking Jesenice (35 minutes, 28km) and Bled Jezero to the north-east and Most na Soči and Nova Gorica (1¼ hours, 61km) to the south-west. Up to eight trains a day pass through Bohinjska Bistrica in each direction. From Nova Gorica you can carry on another 40km south-east to Sežana from where there are trains to Italy.

Getting Around
From mid-June to mid-September, four buses daily run from Bohinjska Bistrica to Savica Waterfall via Ribčev Laz. From Monday to Saturday there's one departure in the morning and three in the afternoon. On Sunday, there's an extra early morning run. The timetable is on display at the tourist

office. Alpinsport rents bicycles and mountain bikes from 700/2900 SIT per hour/day.

KRANJSKA GORA
☎ 04 • postcode 4280 • pop 2800

The town of 'Carniolan Mountain', 40km north-west of Bled, is the largest and best-equipped ski resort in the country, but somehow it just doesn't seem Slovenian. The fact that the Italian *and* Austrian borders are a half-dozen kilometres to the west and north-west might help explain that impression. But there's a clinical feel here too – one that speaks with a Teutonic accent rather than a Slavic one.

Kranjska Gora is situated at 810m in the Sava Dolinka Valley separating the Karavanke range from the Julian Alps. The valley has been an important commercial route between Gorenjska and Koroška for centuries; the 853m pass at Rateče is the lowest Alpine link between the Sava and Drava Valleys. The first railway in Gorenjska – from Ljubljana to Tarvisio (Trbiž) in Italy – made use of this pass when it opened in 1870.

Kranjska Gora was just a small valley village called Borovška Vas until the late 19th century, when skiing enthusiasts began to flock here. Planica (south of Rateče), the cradle of ski jumping, helped put the town on the world map earlier in the 20th century. Kranjska Gora is at its best under a blanket of snow, but its surroundings are wonderful to explore in warmer months as well. There are endless possibilities for hiking and mountaineering in Triglav National Park on the town's southern outskirts, and there aren't many travellers who won't be impressed by a trip over the Vršič Pass (1611m), the gateway to the Soča Valley and the province of Primorska.

Orientation
Kranjska Gora sits at the foot of Vitranc (1631m) and in the shadow of two higher peaks (Razor and Prisojnik/Prisank) that rise above 2600m. Rateče and Planica, famous for ski-jumping championships, are some 6km to the west while Jasna Lake, Kranjska Gora's doorway to Triglav National Park, is 2km south.

Kranjska Gora is a very small town with some unattractive modern buildings around its periphery and a more romantic older core along Borovška cesta. As you walk along this street you might see tanners clipping and scraping sheepskins behind one of the farmhouses. The chairlifts up to the ski slopes on Vitranc are at the western end of Borovška cesta.

The town's bus station (just a couple of stops and a shelter) is 150m west of the big TGC shopping centre at the main entrance to the town from the motorway.

Information
Tourist Offices The tourist office (☎ 588 17 68, fax 588 11 25) is at Tičarjeva cesta 2, a few steps east of the Hotel Prisank. It has quite a few useful handouts on various activities and sells maps and guides to the surrounding areas (including Triglav National Park). The office is open from 8 am to 2 pm and 3 to 7 pm Monday to Saturday and 9 am to 1 pm Sunday from December to March and in July and August. The hours are 8 am to 3 pm daily in April, October and November.

You'll find English-language newspapers at the kiosk just west of the tourist office.

Money SKB Banka has a branch next to the ski school at Borovška cesta 99a. It is open from 8.30 am till noon and 2 to 5 pm weekdays only. Gorenjska Banka is in the building behind the ski school and southwest of the entrance to Hotel Prisank. It is open from 9 to 11.30 am and 2 to 5 pm weekdays and 8 to 11 am Saturday. You can also change money at the tourist office (3% commission) and post office.

Post & Communications Kranjska Gora's post office, next to the Mercator supermarket on Borovška cesta, is open from 8 am to 7 pm weekdays and till noon Saturday. During the high seasons (July and August, and December to March), the hours may be extended to 7 pm on Saturday.

You can check your email at the Gostilna Frida, beside the bus station, from 10 am to 11 pm daily; the cost is 10 SIT per minute.

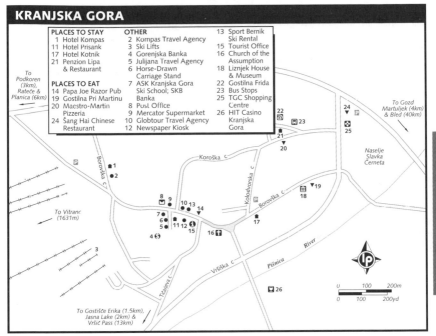

KRANJSKA GORA

PLACES TO STAY
1 Hotel Kompas
11 Hotel Prisank
17 Hotel Kotnik
21 Penzion Lipa
  & Restaurant

PLACES TO EAT
14 Papa Joe Razor Pub
19 Gostilna Pri Martinu
20 Maestro-Martin
  Pizzeria
24 Šang Hai Chinese
  Restaurant

OTHER
2 Kompas Travel Agency
3 Ski Lifts
4 Gorenjska Banka
5 Julijana Travel Agency
6 Horse-Drawn
  Carriage Stand
7 ASK Kranjska Gora
  Ski School; SKB
  Banka
8 Post Office
9 Mercator Supermarket
10 Globtour Travel Agency
12 Newspaper Kiosk

13 Sport Bernik
  Ski Rental
15 Tourist Office
16 Church of the
  Assumption
18 Liznjek House
  & Museum
22 Gostilna Frida
23 Bus Stops
25 TGC Shopping
  Centre
26 HIT Casino
  Kranjska Gora

To Podkoren (3km), Rateče & Planica (6km)

To Gozd Martuljek (4km) & Bled (40km)

Naselje Slavka Černeta

To Vitranc (1631m)

Koroška c

Kolodvorska c

Borovška c

River

Pišnica

Vršiška c

Tkalčeva c

To Gostišče Erika (1.5km), Jasna Lake (2km) & Vršič Pass (13km)

GORENJSKA

Travel Agencies Most of the big agencies are represented in Kranjska Gora, including Globtour (☎ 588 10 55) on the corner of Koroška cesta at Borovška cesta 90 and Kompas (☎ 588 16 61) at Borovška cesta 98–100. In season, Globtour is open from 9 am to 4 pm daily (till noon Sunday). Kompas' hours are 7.30 am to 7 pm daily (8 am till noon Sunday).

Liznjek House

One of the very few sights in Kranjska Gora, this late-18th-century house at Borovška cesta 63 contains quite a good collection of household objects and furnishings peculiar to this area of Gorenjska. But don't for a minute think that this 'folk baroque' house was typical of the place and time; it belonged to an immensely rich landowner and was probably considered a palace in rural Slovenia 200 years ago. Among the various exhibits here are some excellent examples of trousseau chests covered in folk paintings,

some 19th-century icons painted on glass and a collection of linen tablecloths (the valley was famed for its flax and its weaving).

In the main room are two shuttered 'safes' for valuables; one was meant for the man of the house and one for the woman. The tiny fireplace was intended for light only. The chimneyless 'black kitchen' was used to smoke meat.

Antique carriages and a sledge are kept in the massive barn in the back, which once housed food stores as well as pigs and sheep. The stable reserved for cows below the main building now contains a **memorial room** dedicated to the life and work of Josip Vandot (1884–1944), a writer born in Kranjska Gora who penned the saga of *Kekec,* the do-gooder shepherd boy who, together with his little playmate Mojca and his trusty dog Volkec, battles the evil poacher and kidnapper Bedanec. It's still a favourite among Slovenian kids (and was made into several popular films). Kekec has become something of a symbol for Kranjska Gora, and there's a wooden statue of the tyke outside the tourist office on Borovška cesta.

Liznjek House is open from 10 am to 5 pm Tuesday to Saturday (to 4 pm Saturday and Sunday) year-round, except in April and November. Admission costs 350/250 SIT.

Church of the Assumption

In the nameless little square with the giant linden, opposite Borovška cesta 78, is this baroque-looking church. While the date on it says 1758, the net vaulting of the nave inside reveals its true age – the early 16th century. Most of the church is, in fact, late Gothic, and the belfry is even older.

Skiing

The snow-covered slopes of the Sava Dolinka Valley, running for almost 11km from Gozd Martuljek to Rateče and Planica, are effectively one big piste. But the main ski centres are in Kranjska Gora and Podkoren, 3km to the west, with ski jumping concentrated at Planica. The season usually lasts from mid-December to early March. New chairlifts were installed for winter 2000/2001, and new snow-cannons and floodlighting have enabled night skiing.

Skiing in Kranjska Gora is on the eastern slopes of Vitranc, and some runs join up with those at Podkoren on Vitranc's northern face to an altitude of about 1600m. Kranjska Gora has two chairlifts and 10 tows; Podkoren, site of the Men's World Cup Slalom and Giant Slalom Competition (Vitranc Cup) in late December, has another two chairlifts and five tows. Generally, skiing is easier at Kranjska Gora than at Podkoren, where the two most difficult slopes – Ruteč and Zelenci – are located. In all, the two centres have 30km of pistes and 40km of cross-country courses.

The ski-jumping centre at **Planica** across the motorway from Rateče has six jumps with lengths of 25m, 120m and 180m. The short lift near the Dom Planica hut reaches an altitude of 900m. There are also good possibilities at Planica for tobogganing and for cross-country skiing in the Tamar Valley. The Ski Jumping World Championships

are held here every year in March. The 100m mark was reached here by Austrian Josef Bradl in 1936 and the 200m one by the Slovenian teenage champion Primož Peterka in 1994.

Ski passes for Kranjska Gora/Podkoren are 4200/3600/2600 SIT a day for adults/ students and seniors/children aged 14 and under, with a full seven days costing 24,700/ 20,600/15,100 SIT.

Needless to say, there are a lot of places offering ski tuition and rental equipment, but it's best to stick with the tried and true. Both Kompas and Sport Bernik (☎ 588 14 70) at Borovška cesta 88a next to Globtour have skis and snowboards for hire; a complete kit should cost about 1800 SIT a day or 10,500 SIT a week. Bernik opens from 8 am to 6 pm daily in season. For skiing and snowboarding lessons contact the ASK Kranjska Gora Ski School (☎ 588 53 00) opposite the post office on Borovška cesta. It does both Alpine and cross-country tuition in groups and individually. For one-on-one instruction, expect to pay about 4800 SIT for an hour, or 7500 SIT for two people.

Hiking

The area around Kranjska Gora is excellent for hikes and walks ranging from the very easy to the difficult. One of the best references available is *Walking in the Julian Alps* (UK£8.99) by Simon Brown, published by Cicerone Press in the UK. It also includes excursions from Bled and Bohinj in Gorenjska and Bovec in Primorska. Another possible source is the dated *Julian Alps* (UK£10.95) by Robin G Collomb, published by West Col Publishing (Reading, Berkshire).

Between Podkoren and Planica is a beautiful area called **Zelenci** with a turquoise-coloured lake, the source of the Sava River. You can easily walk here on a path from Kranjska Gora via Podkoren and on to **Rateče** – both attractive Alpine villages with medieval churches, wooden houses and traditional hayracks – in about two hours. If you want to go further, there's a well-marked trail via Planica to *Dom v Tamarju* (☎ 587 60 55) in the **Tamar Valley** 6km to the south. The walk is spectacular, in the shadow of

Mojstrovka (2366m) to the east and **Jalovec** (2645m) to the south. The Tamar hut is open every day and has a restaurant and accommodation for 70 people. From here, the **Vršič Pass** is less than three hours away on foot.

Another great walk from Kranjska Gora, and quite an easy one, takes you north and then east through meadows and pasture land to the traditional village of **Srednji Vrh** and **Gozd Martuljek** in a couple of hours. The views of the Velika Pisnica Valley and the Martuljek range of mountains to the south are breathtaking. From Gozd Martuljek, it's only 9km east to **Mojstrana**, the starting point for the northern approaches to Triglav. In Mojstrana, the **Triglav Museum Collection** (Triglavska Muzejska Zbirka) in an old inn at Triglavska cesta 50 deals with the early history of mountaineering and is open from 10 am till noon and 2 to 5 pm daily, except Monday, from mid-May to mid-September. Entry costs 200/100 SIT.

Other Activities

Four hotels in Kranjska Gora have indoor swimming pools and saunas, including the Larix (Borovška cesta 99), the Kompas, the Lek (Vršiška cesta 38) and the Relax (Vršiška cesta 23). You can hire one of several tennis courts at the Hotel Kompas.

Horse-drawn carriages (☎ 588 10 82, 588 12 41) seating four people can be hired from the stand behind the ski school on Borovška cesta. Prices range from 1500 SIT for a trip to Jasna Lake to 5000 SIT for one to Planica. Horses for riding are available at the Porentov Dom (☎ 588 14 36) just east of Kranjska Gora on the main road at Čičare 2.

Fishing is possible in the Sava Dolinka and Jasna Lake but as always it's not for the budget-conscious. A day licence for a total of three fish (the daily limit from the Sava) will cost you 4000 SIT. See Kompas for fishing licences for the river and the Gostišče Jasna (beside Jasna Lake) for the lake.

Places to Stay

Camping The closest camping ground is *Autocamp Špik* (☎ 588 01 20) near the Hotel Špik in Gozd Martuljek, 4km east of Kranjska Gora. The eight-hectare site is on the left bank of the Sava Dolinka below the peaks of the Martuljek range, and there's an outdoor swimming pool on the grounds. The overnight rate per person is 1200 to 1500 SIT, depending on the season.

Kamp Kamne (☎ 589 11 05) in Mojstrana, 13km east of Kranjska Gora, is a more convenient base for the northern approaches to Triglav.

Private Rooms The tourist office has singles for 2500 to 3100 SIT and doubles for 3000 to 4200 SIT, depending on the category and the time of year. Breakfast is 800 SIT extra, and there's a 20% supplement for stays of fewer than three nights. Apartments for two/four people run between 4700/8200 SIT and 5600/9300 SIT. If the office is closed or you want to check the premises before you hand over your money, there are a lot of houses with rooms available (look for 'sobe' or 'Zimmer frei' signs) in the development called Naselje Slavka Černeta, south of the TGC centre. There are also lots of private rooms and apartments available in Rateče. Globtour can also arrange private rooms.

Farmhouses If you want to go rural, you'll have to head out of Kranjska Gora in the direction of Rateče. On the Planica side of the road, the *Kvabišar house* (☎ 587 61 13) at No 120 in Rateče has three rooms. *Skubr* (☎ 588 17 86), with four rooms, is at No 78 in Podkoren. Both are open all year.

Pensions The attractive *Penzion Lipa* (☎ 582 00 00, fax 582 00 25, @ perkolic@ g-kabel.si, Koroška cesta 14) beside the bus station has B&B at 3500 to 6500 SIT per person. *Gostišče Erika* (☎/fax 588 14 75, Vršiška cesta 76), 1.5km south of the centre, is cheaper at 1500 to 2000 SIT per person.

Hotels Kranjska Gora has about 10 hotels within easy walking distance of the ski lifts. Among the cheapest is the *Hotel Prisank* (☎ 588 44 76, fax 588 44 82, @ info@htp-go renjka.si, Borovška cesta 95) with a total of 320 beds in two buildings. Prices range from 3700 to 6300 SIT per person for half-board, depending on the season.

GORENJSKA

The newly renovated, pension-like *Hotel Kotnik* (☎ 588 15 64, fax 588 18 59, e *kotnik@siol.net, Borovška cesta 75)* is located in the centre of town. It has 15 double rooms costing from 5200 to 6500 SIT per person for B&B, depending on the season. Single rooms at the 156-room *Hotel Kompas* (☎ 588 16 61, fax 588 11 76, e *info@hoteli-kompas.si, Borovška cesta 98–100),* Kranjska Gora's biggest hotel, start at 6900 to 10,700 SIT, with double rooms from 11,800 to 19,400 SIT.

Places to Eat
One of the cheapest places for a quick meal in Kranjska Gora is the *Papa Joe Razor* pub *(Borovška cesta 86)* opposite the tourist office, where you can get sandwiches and burgers for 400 to 650 SIT. It's open from 8 am till after midnight daily. For pizza, try the lovely glassed-in cafe-restaurant in the *Penzion Lipa (Koroška cesta 14),* open from 11 am to 11 pm daily, or *Maestro-Martin (Koroška cesta 16)* opposite. The latter has dozens of varieties of pizza and a good choice of fish dishes. The *Gostilna Pri Martinu* (☎ 582 03 00, *Borovška cesta 61)* is one of the best places in town to try local specialities like venison, trout, *telečja obara* (veal stew) and *vampi* (tripe). It's open from 10 am to 11 pm daily.

The restaurant at *Hotel Kotnik* (☎ 588 15 64), one of Kranjska Gora's better eateries with bits of painted dowry chests on the walls, serves grilled meats (pepper steak a speciality) for about 1200 SIT that should keep you going for a while. If you fancy a change from local fare, try the *Šang Hai* (☎ 588 13 46) Chinese restaurant, in the lower level of the TGC shopping centre, facing the car park on the north side. Starters are 800 to 1000 SIT, mains are around 1200 SIT, and it's open from noon to midnight daily.

The huge *Mercator supermarket* across from the Hotel Prisank on Borovška cesta is open from 7 am to 8 pm weekdays, till 7 pm Saturday, and from 8 am till noon Sunday. The *Delikatesa supermarket* in the TGC shopping centre at Naselje Slavka Černeta 33 has a better selection of meats, cheeses and

fruit. It is open from 8 am to 7 pm Monday to Saturday and to 11 pm Sunday.

Entertainment
The *Papa Joe Razor* pub (see Places to Eat) is Kranjska Gora's most popular late-night venue, with live music every weekend and daily in high season, when it stays open till 5 am. The *HIT Casino Kranjska Gora* (☎ 587 80 00), south of the town centre on the road to Jasna Lake, is open 24 hours a day (gaming tables from 3 pm to 3 am). Entry is 1500 SIT, dress code is smart-casual, you must be over 18, and you'll need your passport or ID card.

Getting There & Away
Buses depart frequently for Rateče-Planica (via Podkoren) and Jesenice and once an hour for Ljubljana via Mojstrana, Jesenice, Lesce, Radovljica and Kranj. Other destinations include Villach in Austria (daily during the summer), Tarvisio in Italy (twice a day, except Sunday) and Zagreb in Croatia (one a day).

On Saturday and Sunday in September and daily from late June to August, a bus from Ljubljana links Kranjska Gora with Bovec via the Vršič Pass. The first bus departs at 7.30 am and the last one leaves Bovec for Kranjska Gora at 5.30 pm.

Getting Around
Bernik, Kompas and Julijana (☎ 588 13 25), a small travel agency in a kiosk west of the Hotel Prisank, all rent bicycles. Julijana's rates are 500/1200/1800 SIT per hour/half-day/day. Bernik's bikes cost a bit less.

TRIGLAV NATIONAL PARK
Though there are three dozen protected landscape parks in Slovenia, this is the country's only gazetted national park and it includes almost all of the Julian Alps lying within Slovenia. The centrepiece of the park is, of course, Triglav – Slovenia's highest mountain – but there are many other peaks here reaching above 2000m as well as ravines, canyons, caves, rivers, streams, forests and alpine meadows. Triglav National Park (Triglavski Narodni Park) is especially rich

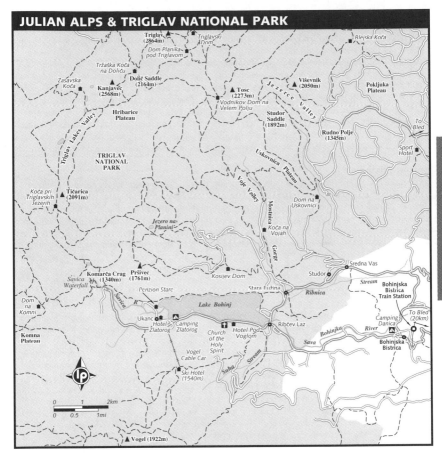

JULIAN ALPS & TRIGLAV NATIONAL PARK

in fauna and flora, including blossoms like the pink Triglav rose, blue Clusi's gentian, yellow hawk's-beard, Julian poppy and purple Zois bell flower.

The idea for a park was first mooted in 1908 and realised in 1924, when 14 hectares in the Triglav Lakes Valley were put under temporary protection. The area was renamed Triglav National Park in 1961 and expanded 20 years later to include most of the eastern Julian Alps. Today the park covers about 84,000 hectares and stretches from Kranjska Gora in the north to Tolmin in the south and from the Italian border in the west almost to Bled in the east. The bulk of the park lies in Gorenjska province, but once you've crossed the awesome Vršič Pass and begun the descent into the Soča Valley, you've entered Primorska.

Excellent marked trails in the park lead to countless peaks and summits besides Triglav, and favourite climbs include **Mangart** (2678m) on the Italian border (the 12km road that descends to the Predel Pass is the highest road in Slovenia), the needlepoint of **Jalovec** (2645m) in the north, and the sharp ridge of **Razor** (2601m) south-east of Vršič. But the Triglav National Park is not

GORENJSKA

Approaches to Triglav

There are about 20 different ways to reach the top of Triglav (2864m), with the main approaches from the south (Bohinj and Pokljuka) and the north (Mojstrana and the Vrata Valley). They offer varying degrees of difficulty and have their pluses and minuses. Experienced hikers tend to go for the more forbidding northern approaches, descending via one of the gentle southern routes. Novices usually ascend and descend near Bohinj. The western route from Trenta in the Soča Valley is steep and less frequented due to its relatively remote start. Most treks require one or two overnights in the mountains.

On public transport, Mojstrana is the easiest trailhead to get to from Ljubljana – hourly buses between Kranjska Gora and the capital stop here. In summer, there's also a daily bus from Bled to Rudno Polje. If you're driving, there are parking areas at Rudno Polje and at the head of the Vrata Valley near Aljažev Dom, though the latter can only be reached on an unsurfaced road with gradients up to 1:4.

From Pokljuka

The route from Rudno Polje (1340m) on the Pokljuka Plateau (18km south-west of Bled) is the shortest way to the summit – a round trip of 25km, with 1500m of ascent. A very fit and experienced mountain walker could do this in one day, but most mortals overnight at a hut. The route follows a well-marked trail under Viševnik (2050m) and over the Studorski saddle (1892m), before contouring around the slopes of Tosc to the **Vodnikov Dom na Velem Polju** (mobile ☎ 050-615 621) at 1819m (three hours). Another two hours' climbing leads to **Dom Planika pod Triglavom** (mobile ☎ 050-614 773) at 2401m from which a further hour of steep climbing and scrambling along the summit ridge takes you to the top. Don't be surprised if you find yourself being turned over and your bottom beaten with a birch switch – it's a long-established tradition for Triglav 'virgins'.

From Bohinj

The approaches from Bohinj (550m) are longer and involve more ascent, but are more gently graded than those in the north and west. They are more often used for descent. However, the following route would make a good three-day loop.

From the Savica Waterfall a path zigzags up the steep Komarča Crag (there's an excellent view of Lake Bohinj from the top of this 1340m-high cliff). Three to four hours' hike north from the falls is the **Koča pri Triglavskih Jezerih** (mobile ☎ 050-615 235) at 1685m, a 104-bed hut at the southern end of the fantastic Triglav Lakes Valley where you spend the first night. If you want a good view over the valley and its seven permanent lakes (the others fill up in spring only), you can climb to Tičarica (2091m) to the north-east in about an hour. An alternative – though longer – route from the waterfall to the Triglav Lakes Valley is via **Dom na Komni** (☎ 04-572 14 75 or mobile ☎ 050-611 221) and the Komna Plateau, a major battlefield in WWI.

On the second day you hike north along the valley, which the immortal chamois Zlatorog is said to have created, then north-east to the desert-like Hribarice Plateau (2358m). You then descend to the Dolič Saddle (2164m) and the **Tržaška Koča na Doliču** (mobile ☎ 050-614 780), about four hours from Koča pri Triglavskih Jezerih. You could well carry on to **Dom Planika pod Triglavom** (see From Pokljuka), about 1½ hours to the north-east, but this 80-bed hut is often packed; it's better to stay where you're sure there's a bed unless you've booked ahead. From Dom Planika it's just over an hour to the summit of Triglav.

only about climbing mountains. There are easy hikes through beautiful valleys, forests and meadows too. Two excellent maps are the PZS 1:50,000-scale *Triglavski Narodni Park* and Freytag and Berndt's 1:50,000 *Julische Alpen Wanderkarte*.

The park has a number of rules and regulations and most of the don'ts are as clear as Triglav on a sunny day: no littering, no picking flowers, no setting fires etc. But also remember that this is a very fragile landscape, and there is no wild camping, mountain

Approaches to Triglav

You could return the way you came, but it's far more interesting to go back to Bohinj via Stara Fužina. This way passes the **Vodnikov Dom na Velem Polju** (see From Pokljuka) less than two hours from Dom Planika, where there are two routes to choose from: down the Voje Valley, or along the Uskovnica ridge, a highland pasture to the east. The former takes about four hours; the route via Uskovnica is a little longer but affords better views. The trail to Rudno Polje and the road to Bled branches off from the Uskovnica route.

From Mojstrana

This approach, which is dominated by the stupendous northern face of Triglav, is popular with experienced climbers, and is often combined with a leisurely descent along the Triglav Lakes Valley to Bohinj. From the village of Mojstrana, which has a camping ground and a small supermarket (open from 7 am to 7 pm weekdays, till 11 am Saturday and from 8 to 11 am Sunday), a (mostly unsurfaced) road leads in 11km to the **Aljažev Dom v Vratih** (☎ 04-589 10 30) at 1015m. Walking here should take about three hours, including time for a look at Peričnik Waterfall on the way. You'll probably want to spend the night here as it is among the most beautiful sites in the park, with a perfect view of Triglav's north face. Nearby is a 10m boulder called Mali Triglav (Little Triglav) where you can practise your ascent of The Big One.

Five minutes' walk beyond the hut is a monument to the mountaineers who died during WWII, in the shape of a giant piton and carabiner. From here, the steep and exposed Tominšek Trail leads via the north-west flank of Cmir and below Begunjski Vrh to Begunjski Studenec, a spring with excellent drinking water at 2100m (three hours). Much of this trail is a *via ferrata* (iron way) protected with iron spikes and cables.

From the spring you can choose to walk to either **Dom Valentina Staniča** (mobile ☎ 050-614 772) 30 minutes to the south-east at 2332m, or to **Triglavski Dom na Kredarici** (☎ 04-202 31 81) an hour to the south. The latter is the main hut serving the northern routes and at 2515m is the highest accommodation in the land; the summit is two hours away. While Triglavski Dom has 126 beds it is often full; the best idea is to spend the night at Staniča Dom and make the ascent in the morning (two hours from hut to summit). Side trips from Staniča Dom via marked and secure trails include Begunjski Vrh (2461m; 30 minutes), Cmir (2393m; two hours), Spodnja Vrbanova Špica (2299m; 1½ hours) and Rjavina (2532m; two hours).

From Trenta

Because Trenta is harder to get to from the population centres of Ljubljana and southern Austria, the western approach to Triglav is quieter than the other routes. It's a long climb, though, starting from an altitude of only just over 600m.

From Trenta, an hour's hike eastward along the Zajdnica Valley leads to the foot of Triglav's massive western face, where you begin zigzagging monotonously up an easy but seemingly neverending trail for four more hours to the Dolič saddle and the **Tržaška Koča na Doliču** (2151m). From here, you can follow the normal route to the summit via Dom Planika pod Triglavom (see From Pokljuka), or take the slightly more difficult west ridge (2½ hours), passing the ruined Morbegna barracks built by the Italian army in WWII at 2500m.

bikes are banned from trails and the park tradition is to greet everyone you pass. That can get a bit tiresome after a while but a simple *'Dober dan'* (Hello) and/or a smile will suffice. You may notice that the roads running through the park aren't in such great shape. The park commission refuses to upgrade them for fear that half of Europe would descend on this little paradise. For more information about Triglav, see the boxed texts 'Old Mr Three Heads' and 'Approaches to Triglav' earlier in this chapter.

Kranjska Gora to Soča Valley

One of the most spectacular – and easy – trips in Triglav National Park is simply to follow the paved road, open from May to October, from Kranjska Gora via the Vršič Pass to Bovec, about 50km to the south-west. Between June and September, you can do the trip by bus. At other times, you'll need your own transport – be it a car or mountain bike.

The first stop from Kranjska Gora is **Jasna Lake**, about 2km south of town. It's a beautiful, almost too-blue glacial lake with white sand around its rim and the little Pivnica River flowing alongside. A bronze statue of that irascible old goat Zlatorog stands guard.

As you zigzag up to just over 1100m, you'll come to the **Russian Chapel** erected on the site where more than 400 Russian prisoners of war were buried in an avalanche in March 1916. The POWs were in the process of building the road you are travelling on, so spare a moment in remembrance. The little wooden church is on a small hill and very simple inside. Services in memory of the victims were held here jointly by the Russian patriarch and the archbishop of Ljubljana, Alojzij Šuštar, for the first time in 1994.

The climbing then begins in earnest as the road meanders past a couple of huts and corkscrews up the next few kilometres to **Vršič Pass** (1611m), about 13km from Kranjska Gora. The area was the scene of fierce fighting during WWI, and a high percentage of the dead lay where they fell (at 1525m there's a **military cemetery** to the east of the road). The Tičarjev Dom mountain hut is also east of the road, just before it begins to drop down the far side (roadside parking at the summit of the pass costs 600 SIT). To the west is Mojstrovka (2366m), to the east Prisank (2547m), and to the south the valley of the Soča River points the way to Primorska. A hair-raising descent of about 10km ends just short of the **Julius Kugy Monument**. Kugy (1858–1944) was a pioneer climber and author whose books eulogise the beauty of the Julian Alps. He is shown meditating on the Trenta Mountains to the north-west.

From here you can take a side trip along the Soča Trail (Soška Pot) of about 2.5km north-west to the **source of the Soča River** (Izvir Soče). Fed by an underground lake, the infant river bursts from a dark cave before dropping 15m to the rocky bed from where it begins its long journey to the Adriatic.

Not long after joining the main road again you'll pass the entrance to the **Alpinum Juliana**, a botanical garden established in 1926 and showcasing the flora of all of Slovenia's Alps (Julian, Kamnik, Savinja and Karavanke) as well as the Karst. The elongated mountain village of **Trenta** (662m) is about 4km to the south.

Trenta has a long tradition of mountain guides; shepherds and woodsmen made the first ascents of the Julian Alps possible in the 19th century and their bravery and skill is commemorated in a plaque just below the botanical garden. Na Logu, in the upper part of Trenta, is the gateway to the western approach to Triglav – a much less frequented and steeper climb than most of the others. In lower Trenta at house No 34 the Dom Trenta contains the Triglav National Park Information Centre (☎ 05-388 93 30) and the **Trenta Museum** (500/400/300 SIT for adults/students/children), dedicated to the park's geology and natural history, and to the Trenta guides and the pioneers of Slovenian alpinism.

The equally long village of **Soča** (480m) is another 8.5km downriver. The **Church of St Joseph** from the early 18th century has paintings by Tone Kralj (1900–75). Completed in 1944 as war still raged in Central Europe, one of the frescoes depicts Michael the Archangel struggling with Satan and the foes of humanity, Hitler and Mussolini. The colours used are those of the Slovenian flag. Outside stands a lovely old linden tree and opposite, through the potato fields, the narrowing Soča flows past.

Bovec, the recreational centre of the Upper Soča Valley (Gornje Posočje), is 12km west of Soča. For details, see the Primorska chapter.

Places to Stay & Eat The *Gostišče Jasna* overlooking Jasna Lake is a great place for

Mountain Huts

The Alpine Association of Slovenia (Planinska Sveza Slovenije, or PZS; see Hiking & Mountain Walking in the special section 'The Great Outdoors') maintains 165 mountain huts across the country, providing accommodation for hikers and climbers. Some are very basic, others come close to hotel-style accommodation.

A bivouac *(bivak)* is the most basic hut, providing shelter only, while a refuge *(zavetišče)* has refreshments, and sometimes accommodation, but usually no running water. A hut *(koča)* or house *(dom)* can be a simple cottage or a fairly grand establishment, like some of those close to Triglav.

A bed for the night runs from 1320 to 2750 SIT in a Category I hut, depending on the number of beds in the room, and from 1000 to 1760 SIT in a Category II. (A hut is Category I if it is more than 1km away from motorised transport – everything closer is Category II.) Ten of the highest huts, including most of those around Triglav, are more expensive – from 1450 to 3025 SIT. Members of the PZS, and visitors with a UIAA-affiliated club membership card, get a 30% discount. Holders of a Hostelling International card may also get a small discount.

Food prices at PZS huts are regulated as well. A simple meal of *jota*, *ričet*, *špageti* or *golaž* (see Food in the Language chapter) should cost between 500 and 800 SIT in a Category I hut, from 400 to 600 SIT in a Category II. Tea is 100 to 150 SIT, 1L of mineral water 400 to 600 SIT and 0.5L of beer 300 to 550 SIT.

There are around 50 mountain huts in the Julian Alps, most of them open between June and September. But others may extend their season a month in either direction and some huts at lower altitudes are open all year. Huts are never more than five hours' walk apart at the most. You'll never be turned away if the weather looks bad, but some huts on Triglav can be unbearably crowded at weekends – especially in August and September. Try to plan your hikes for midweek if possible, and phone ahead – most huts take bookings.

a meal or a drink before pushing on for the Vršič Pass and beyond. A lovely terrace at the back is open in the warmer months.

There are several mountain huts on or near the Vršič road. *Mihov Dom na Vršiču (mobile ☎ 041-717 396)*, a hut with food and accommodation at 1085m on the Vršič road and just before the Russian Chapel, is open most of the year. The next one – at 1525m – is *Erjačeva Koča (mobile ☎ 041-610 031)*, also open all year. *Tičarjev Dom na Vršiču (mobile ☎ 041-634 571)*, right on the pass, is open from May to October. A bed in a room for three is 2100 SIT, 1500 SIT in rooms with four to six beds and a bed in the attic is only 1050 SIT.

Beyond the Tičarjev Dom at 1688m is the *Poštarski Dom (mobile ☎ 050-610 029)*. Near the source of the Soča River at 886m,

the *Koča pri Izviru Soče (☎ 04-586 60 70)* is open from May to October.

Trenta and Soča count a number of camping grounds, including *Bolčina (mobile ☎ 041-615 966)*, open all year, at No 60a in Trenta and charging 770 SIT per person; *Komac (☎ 05-388 93 18)* at No 8 in Soča, open May to September and charging 675 to 805 SIT; and *Korita (☎ 05-388 93 38)* at No 38 in Soča, open June to October and charging 600 to 800 SIT. *Kamp Klin (☎ 05-388 93 56)*, about 4.5km to the south-west of Soča at the start of the Lepena Valley, is open May to September and charges 750 to 850 SIT.

The staff at the Dom Trenta (☎ 05-388 93 30), No 34 in Trenta, can book *private rooms* and *apartments*, while *Penzion Julius (☎ 05-388 93 55)* at No 31 in Soča has accommodation and there's also a decent restaurant.

Primorska

It may come as a surprise to many that Primorska, the long slender province that extends from Austria and Triglav National Park to Istria and the Adriatic Sea, means 'Littoral' in Slovene. With Slovenia's coastline measuring only 47km long, why such an extravagant name?

It all has to do with weather. Almost all of Primorska gets warm winds from the coast that influence the valleys as far as Kobarid and Bovec and inland. So the climate and the flora here are distinctly Mediterranean right up to the foothills of the Alps. Yet the province has four distinct regions: the Soča Valley (partly covered in the Triglav National Park section of the Gorenjska chapter); central Primorska with its rolling Cerkno and Idrija Hills; the unique Karst region; and the coast (also called Slovenian Istria).

Primorska is a magical province offering unlimited activities and sights; it really is 'Europe in miniature'. In one day you can climb mountains or kayak in the Soča Valley, tour the wine-growing areas of the Vipava Valley or Brda Hills near Nova Gorica, explore the Škocjan Caves or ride Lipizzaners in the Karst, or laze on the beaches of Piran or Portorož. Primorska is also an excellent gateway to Italy (eg, from Nova Gorica or Ankaran) and to Croatian Istria from Sečovlje and Sočerga.

The Soča Valley

The Soča Valley region (Posočje) stretches from Triglav National Park to Nova Gorica, including Bovec, Kobarid, Tolmin and Most na Soči. Its most dominant feature is the 96km Soča River, which is famous for its deep, almost unreal, turquoise colour. The valley has more than its share of historical sights and important artwork but most people come here for such recreational pursuits as rafting, hiking and skiing.

The Soča Valley has been an important trade route between the Friulian Plain and

the Alpine valleys since early times. It was the site of several Hallstatt settlements, evidenced by the rich archaeological finds unearthed at Most na Soči, Tolmin and Kobarid. During Roman times the valley was on the important Predel road between Noricum and the province of Histria, but it lost its importance when the Romans left.

160

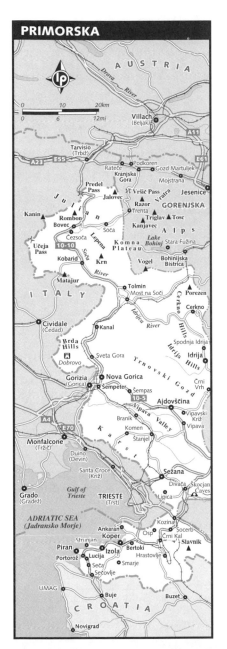

The proximity of Venice and the Napoleonic wars of the late 18th and early 19th centuries restored the valley's strategic role. The railway to Bohinj brought modern transport between the Sava Valley and Gorica for the first time in 1906 and during WWI millions of troops were brought here to fight on the battle front stretching from the Karst to Mt Rombon. Between the wars, Primorska and the Soča Valley fell under Italian jurisdiction. Many Italians were expelled or left the province voluntarily after WWII.

BOVEC
☎ 05 • postcode 5230 • pop 1775

Bovec, 483m above sea level, lies in a broad basin called the Bovška Kotlina at the meeting point of the Soča and Koritnica Valleys. Towering above are several peaks of well over 2000m including Rombon (2208m) and Kanin (2587m). The Soča River flows past Bovec 2km to the south at Čezsoča. The Italian border is 16km to the south-west via the pass at Učeja and 17km north at Predel.

The 'capital' of the Upper Soča Valley (Gornje Posočje), Bovec has a great deal to offer adventure-sports enthusiasts. With the Julian Alps above, the Soča River below and Triglav National Park at the back door, you could spend a week hiking, kayaking, mountain biking and, in winter, skiing at Slovenia's highest ski station without ever doing the same thing twice.

History

The area around Bovec (Plezzo in Italian; Pletz in German) is first mentioned in documents dating back to the 11th century. At that time it was under the direct rule of the Patriarchs of Aquileia but was later transferred to the Counts of Gorica and, in about 1500, to the Habsburgs. The Turks passed through the basin on their way to the Predel Pass in the 15th century, and on two occasions (in 1797 and again in 1809) Napoleon's army·attacked Austria from here.

Bovec suffered terribly in the fighting around the Soča Valley during WWI. Much of the town was destroyed, but its reconstruction by the architect Max Fabiani in the 1920s gave Bovec an interesting combination of traditional and modern buildings. Further reconstruction took place after a severe earthquake in 1976.

Except for a period in the 17th and 18th centuries when the Bovec area was a centre of iron mining and forging, the people here have traditionally worked as sheep and goat herders, climbing high into the mountains in search of pasture. The knowledge of these herders was highly prized by early Alpinists, and many of them became guides – a tradition that continues to this day.

Orientation

The centre of Bovec is Trg Golobarskih Žrtev, about the only named 'street' in Bovec. Actually it's a long square that forms the main east-west drag and runs northward to the neo-Romanesque Church of St Urh and the holiday village of Kaninska Vas. Buses stop on Trg Golobarskih Žrtev in front of the Letni Vrt restaurant at No 1.

Information

The Bovec tourist office (☎ 384 19 19, ℯ info.lto@bovec.si) is just downhill from the post office, and is open from 9 am to 5 pm weekdays year-round, and until 9 pm daily in high season.

There's a Komercialna Banka branch next to the Alp Hotel at Trg Golobarskih Žrtev 47, open from 8 am to 6 pm weekdays and till noon Saturday. The post office is at Trg Golobarskih Žrtev 8 at the foot of the hill leading to the church and Kaninska Vas. It is open from 8 am to 6 pm on weekdays and till noon Saturday.

The knowledgeable staff at the Alpkomerc agency (☎ 388 63 70) in the Hotel Kanin can organise many outdoor activities. The Avrigo travel agency (☎ 389 60 23), between the Alp Hotel and the bank, can do the same and is particularly good with accommodation and transport. It's open from 8 am to 6 pm Monday to Saturday (to 8 pm in July and August) and from 9 am till noon Sunday, but from 9 am to 4 pm weekdays only in winter.

Activities

Rafting & Canoeing Rafting, kayaking and canoeing on the beautiful Soča River

(10% to 40% gradient; Grades I to VI) attract many people to Bovec. The largest group dealing with these pursuits is Soča Rafting (☎ 389 62 00), located about 100m uphill from the post office. It is open from 9 am to 6 pm daily.

You can also book through the Bovec Rafting Team (☎ 388 61 28) in the small kiosk on Trg Golobarskih Žrtev opposite the Martinov Hram restaurant. It is open from 8.30 am to 8 pm daily June to late September, and 10 am to 6 pm weekends only in April and May and from late September to mid-October.

The season for river sports lasts from mid-April to October, but organised excursions are available daily only from May to September. At other times, they take place on Saturday and Sunday. You go rafting in groups of six to eight (leaving at 10 am, 2 pm and 4 or 5 pm) while you can canoe or kayak individually or with a guide.

Rafting trips on the Soča of about 1½ hours over a distance of 10km cost from 4790 to 6480 SIT (including neoprene long johns, windcheater, life jacket, helmet and paddle). You should bring along a swimsuit, T-shirt and towel. A canoe for two is 3780 SIT for the day and a kayak is 3770 SIT (4630 SIT with life jacket, helmet etc). There are also a number of kayaking courses on offer in summer (eg, a two-day course for beginners for 9180 to 11,470 SIT).

Skiing The Kanin ski centre (☎ 388 60 22) in the mountains north-west of Bovec has skiing up to almost 2300m – the only real high-altitude Alpine skiing available in Slovenia. As a result, the season can be long (God and Jack Frost providing) with good spring skiing in April and even May. The ski area – 14km of pistes and some 12km of cross-country runs served by three chairlifts and two T-bars – are reached by a cable car in three stages. The bottom station is some 600m south-west of the centre of Bovec on the main road. Skiing at Kanin is generally more difficult than at centres like Kranjska Gora in Gorenjska and Rogla in Štajerska. A ski pass costs 3400 SIT for a day, or 12,800 for five days. You can rent

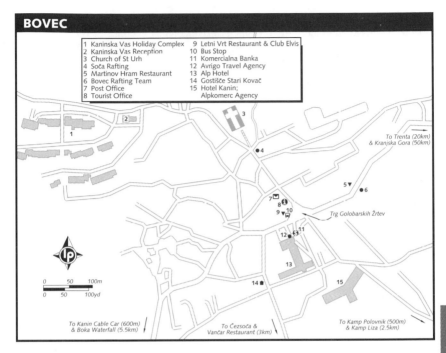

BOVEC

1 Kaninska Vas Holiday Complex	9 Letni Vrt Restaurant & Club Elvis
2 Kaninska Vas Reception	10 Bus Stop
3 Church of St Urh	11 Komercialna Banka
4 Soča Rafting	12 Avrigo Travel Agency
5 Martinov Hram Restaurant	13 Alp Hotel
6 Bovec Rafting Team	14 Gostišče Stari Kovač
7 Post Office	15 Hotel Kanin;
8 Tourist Office	Alpkomerc Agency

To Trenta (20km)
& Kranjska Gora (50km)

Trg Golobarskih Žrtev

0   50   100m
0   50   100yd

To Kanin Cable Car (600m)
& Boka Waterfall (5.5km)

To Čezsoča &
Vančar Restaurant (3km)

To Kamp Polovnik (500m)
& Kamp Liza (2.5km)

PRIMORSKA

the complete kit (skis, poles, boots) for 1800 SIT a day from the Alp Hotel.

The cable car (fitted with new cabins in December 2000) runs constantly during the skiing season; in July and August it runs hourly from 8 am to 4 pm and every second hour from Thursday to Sunday in June and September.

It's a lovely place to go when the weather is clear, and walks lead from the cable car's upper station (see Hiking).

Hiking The 1:25,000-scale map called *Bovec z Okolico (Bovec and Surroundings)* lists a number of walks and hikes ranging from a two-hour stroll south to **Čezsoča** and the protected gravel deposits in the Soča to an ascent of **Rombon** (2208m), which would take a good four hours one way. *Walks in the Julian Alps* by Simon Brown (see Hiking & Mountain Walking in the special section 'The Great Outdoors') also lists half a dozen walks in the area, includ-

ing an easy one to the source of the Soča River and the difficult ascent of Kanin.

From the ski-centre cable car's upper station you could make the difficult three-hour climb of Kanin (2587m) or reach the **Prestreljenik Window** (2499m) in about 1½ hours. For your troubles, you'll see all the way to Trieste and the Julian Alps.

The Alp Hotel also offers guided walks, such as the one to the **Mangrt Saddle** (2072m) along the highest road in Slovenia and to **Krn Lake** above the Lepena Valley. They're expensive at about €23 per person, but you certainly won't get lost. The hotel also has a mountain-walking tour of medium difficulty that follows the Soča Front lines (see Kobarid later in this chapter) to Rombon, passing trenches, old caverns, bunkers and observation posts. It takes between eight and 10 hours and costs €46.

The most popular do-it-yourself walk in the area is to **Boka Waterfall** some 5.5km to the south-west of Bovec. The waterfall drops more than 100m from the Kanin Mountains into the valley and is almost 30m wide – it's an impressive sight, especially in late spring when the snow melts. To get there you can either walk along the main road toward Tolmin, which more or less follows the Soča, or take the bus and get off after the Gostilna Žikar, a small restaurant and pub in Pod Čela. The trip up to the falls (850m) and back takes about 1½ hours but the path is steep in places and can be very slippery. Those of you who are not up for climbing can stand at the bridge on the main Bovec-Tolmin road and look up at the falls which are on full – but distant – display.

Fishing The Alpkomerc and Avrigo agencies sell two types of fishing licences for hooking the famous Soča trout. One for the area east of Čezsoča, as well as the Lepenjica River, costs €61 per day. To fish in the Soča below Bovec, where there is a lot more kayaking and boating, you'll pay €46 a day. The season lasts from April to October.

Canyoning A 3km canyoning trip with Soča Rafting (lasting two hours) costs from 6550 to 8340 SIT. You can also learn to pothole – descending with a guide into the bowels of the earth – in the Kanin Mountains. This is real adventure stuff – there are no pretty stalactites or stalagmites or easy trails to keep you going here. A one-hour trip costs around 4000 to 5000 SIT per person.

Paragliding In winter you can take a tandem paraglider flight (ie, as a passenger accompanied by a qualified pilot) from the top of the Kanin cable car, 2000m above the valley floor. The cost of a flight is around 14,500 SIT per person – ask for details at Soča Rafting, or the Bovec Paragliding Club (Klub za jadralno padalstvo; ☎ 388 68 40, fax 388 65 20).

Places to Stay

The closest camping ground to Bovec is the *Kamp Polovnik* (☎ 388 60 69) about 500m south-east of the Hotel Kanin. It's small but is in an attractive setting. Polovnik, which is open from April to September, costs

between 850 and 1000 SIT per person, depending on the month.

The little *Kamp Liza* (☎ 388 60 73) is farther afield in Vodenca, some 2.5km southeast of the town centre at the point where the Koritnica River meets the Soča. It charges 980 SIT per person and is open from April to mid-October. Nearby and right on the river is the *Kayak Kamp Toni* (☎ 388 64 54).

Private rooms are easy to come by in Bovec and the agencies have more than 300 beds on their lists. A room costs around 2540 SIT per person, but this falls to 2000 SIT for stays of more than three nights.

The attractive *Gostišče Stari Kovač* (☎ 388 67 40), just west of the Alp Hotel, has single guest rooms available for 3000 SIT, and doubles from 4000 to 6000 SIT depending on season. It can also offer comfortable apartments with bathroom and kitchen for two to five people costing from 5500 to 9000 SIT.

The 103-room *Alp Hotel* (☎ 388 63 70, fax 389 63 87, e hotelalp1@siol.net, Trg Golobarskih Žrtev 48) was taken over by a new owner in 2000 and lowered its charges to 6200 to 8300 SIT for singles with shower and breakfast, depending on the season, and 9400 to 13,800 SIT for doubles. Use of the Hotel Kanin's pool is included.

The *Hotel Kanin* (☎ 388 60 22, fax 388 60 81, e hoteli.bovec@siol.net), about 150m south-east of the Alp, is in slightly quieter surrounds and has an indoor swimming pool and a sauna. It has 122 rooms. Single rates are 7700 to 10,300 SIT, depending on the season and whether your room has a balcony. Doubles are 11,200 to 16,400 SIT.

The *Kaninska Vas holiday complex* (same contact details as Hotel Kanin), just north-west of the centre, has apartments for two people for between 6000 and 8500 SIT, depending on the season.

Places to Eat

The *Letni Vrt* (Summer Garden; ☎ 388 63 83) opposite the Alp Hotel has pizza, grilled dishes and trout at affordable prices. Its garden is lovely in summer and there is also the Club Elvis disco here, if you want to kick up your heels after dark. *Martinov Hram* (☎ 388 62 14, Trg Golobarskih Žrtev 27) specialises in seafood and grills. It is open from 10 am to 11 pm daily except Monday.

If you want to go where local people do, head for *Vančar* (☎ 388 63 30) in Čezsoča (house No 48), about 3km south of Bovec. It is open from 11 am to 10 pm but closed Monday and Tuesday.

Getting There & Away

Buses are frequent to Kobarid and Tolmin, with some eight departures a day (a lot fewer at the weekend). There are also four buses a day to Ljubljana via Tolmin and Most na Soči and three to Nova Gorica. In July and August there are up to five daily buses to Kranjska Gora via the Vršič Pass, one of which carries on to Bled. They depart every two hours or so, and the fare is 1000 SIT.

Getting Around

Alpkomerc and Soča Rafting rent bicycles and mountain bikes. The latter charges 1200 SIT for a half-day, 1800 SIT for a full day and 7200 SIT for five days.

KOBARID
☎ 05 • postcode 5222 • pop 1460

Kobarid, some 21km south of Bovec, lies in a broad valley on the west bank of the Soča River. Though it is surrounded by mountain peaks of more than 2200m, Kobarid feels more Mediterranean than Alpine. The Italian border at Robič is only 9km to the west and Cividale, where a good many people from Kobarid commute to work every day, is another 18km to the south.

Only a few things have changed since the American writer Ernest Hemingway described Kobarid (then Caporetto) in his novel depicting the horror and suffering of WWI, *A Farewell to Arms* (1929). It was 'a little white town with a campanile in a valley,' he wrote, 'a clean little town and there was a fine fountain in the square'. The bell in the tower still rings on the hour, but the fountain has disappeared; you can locate it (and hear the water rushing below) in the courtyard behind Trg Svobode 15, north of the rather striking statue of the poet and priest Simon Gregorčič (1844–1906), who was born in nearby Vrsno.

Kobarid did have a history before WWI and things have happened since. It was a military settlement during Roman times, was hotly contested in the Middle Ages and hit by a devastating earthquake in 1976 which destroyed some historical buildings and farmhouses with folk frescoes (now preserved in the Kobarid Museum). But the world will always remember Kobarid as Caporetto and the decisive battle of 1917 in which the combined forces of the Central Powers defeated the Italian army.

Orientation & Information

The centre of Kobarid is Trg Svobode, dominated by the Gothic Church of the Assumption and that famous bell tower. Buses stop in front of the Bife Kramar on the eastern side of the square at No 9. There is a schedule posted.

The tourist office (☎/fax 388 50 55) is on the ground floor of the Kobarid Museum at Gregorčičeva ulica 10 and keeps the same hours as the museum. There's a Banka Vipa branch on Markova ulica, open from 8 to 11.30 am and 2 to 5 pm weekdays and from 8.30 to 11 am Saturday. The post office, to the west of the church at Trg Svobode 2, is open from 8 am to 6 pm weekdays, with a couple of half-hour breaks, and till noon Saturday.

Kobarid Museum

This museum (Kobariški Muzej), which opened to great fanfare in 1990 and has won several European awards, is located in the 18th-century Mašer House at Gregorčičeva ulica 10. It is devoted almost entirely to the Soča Front and deals with the tragedy of the 'war to end all wars'.

Among the collection are 500 photographs documenting the horrors of the Soča or Isonzo Front (see the boxed text 'Soča (Isonzo) Front' later in this section), military charts, diaries and maps and two large relief displays showing the front lines and offensives through the Krn Mountains and the positions in the Upper Soča Valley the day before the decisive breakthrough.

There's also a 22-minute 'multivision presentation' (slides with commentary) which

PRIMORSKA

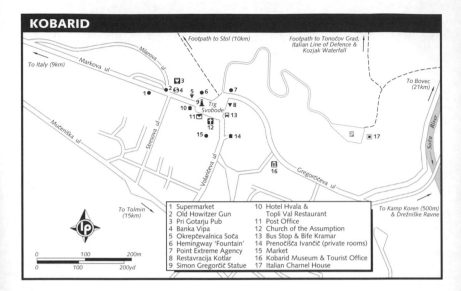

KOBARID

Footpath to Stol (10km)

Footpath to Tonočov Grad,
Italian Line of Defence &
Kozjak Waterfall

To Italy (9km)

Milanova ul

Markova ul

To Bovec
(21km)

Mučeniška ul

Streova ul

Trg
Svobode

Volaričeva ul

Gregorčičeva ul

Soča River

To Tolmin
(15km)

To Kamp Koren (500m)
& Drežniške Ravne

1	Supermarket	10	Hotel Hvala &
2	Old Howitzer Gun		Topli Val Restaurant
3	Pri Gotarju Pub	11	Post Office
4	Banka Vipa	12	Church of the Assumption
5	Okrepčevalnica Soča	13	Bus Stop & Bife Kramar
6	Hemingway 'Fountain'	14	Prenočišča Ivančič (private rooms)
7	Point Extreme Agency	15	Market
8	Restavracija Kotlar	16	Kobarid Museum & Tourist Office
9	Simon Gregorčič Statue	17	Italian Charnel House

0   100   200m
0   100   200yd

describes the preparations for the final battle, the fighting and its results. The observations made by soldiers on both sides are the most enlightening parts.

The museum is divided into about 18 rooms on three floors and the displays are labelled in four languages, including English. The entrance hall on the ground floor has photographs of soldiers, tombstone crosses, mortar shells and the flags of all the countries involved in the conflict.

The rooms on the 1st and 2nd floors have themes: the **Black Room** shows horrible photographs of the dead and dying; the **White Room** describes the particularly harsh conditions of waging war in the mountains in the snow and fog; and the **Rear Lines Room** explains what life was like for soldiers during pauses in the fighting and for the civilian population uprooted by war and famine. The **Breakthrough Room** deals with the events over the three days (24–27 October 1917) when the combined Austrian and German forces met up near Kobarid and defeated the Italian army. In one room an Italian soldier sits in his cavern shelter writing a letter to his father while the war rages outside.

The Kobarid Museum is open from 9 am to 6 pm daily. Admission costs 500/400 SIT for adults/students and children.

Historical Walk

A leaflet available from the museum describes the Kobarid Historical Walk (Kobariška Zgodovinska Pot), which begins at a map and signpost on the north side of Trg Svobode. From here, a winding road lined with the Stations of the Cross climbs up to the **Italian Charnel House**. This huge ossuary (*kostnica* in Slovene), containing the bones of more than 7000 Italian soldiers killed on the Soča Front, stands on the **Hill of St Anthony** east of Trg Svobode.

After the war Austrian, German and Italian cemeteries littered the entire Soča Valley. During the Italian occupation of Primorska between the wars, the authorities in Rome decided to collect what Italian remains they could and bury them at the charnel house. The dedication in September 1938 was attended by Benito Mussolini.

The charnel house comprises three stacked octagons, each smaller than the one before it, and is topped with the 17th-century **Church of St Anthony**, which was moved here in 1935. Only one of several frescoes painted by Jernej Vrtav (1647–1725) survived the move.

From the ossuary, a path leads north (take the left-hand fork after a minute's walk) for just over 1km to **Tonočov Grad**, an ancient fortified hilltop where an archaeological project has uncovered the remains of houses and churches dating from the 5th and 6th centuries.

The path then descends through the remains of the **3rd Defence Line** built by the Italians in 1915, past cleared trenches, gun emplacements and observation posts, before crossing the Soča over a copy of the bridge that was originally built by the French during the period of the Illyrian Provinces in the early 19th century. Though the original was destroyed in May 1915, it is still called the **Napoleon Bridge**.

On the far side of the river, the path leads up a side valley to a series of walkways that take you to the foot of the spectacular **Kozjak Waterfall**. The route then returns to

Soča (Isonzo) Front

The breakthrough in the Soča Front (more commonly known to historians as the Isonzo Front) by the combined Austrian, Hungarian, German and Slovenian forces near Kobarid in October 1917 was one of the costliest battles in terms of human life that the world has ever known. By the time the fighting had stopped 17 days later, hundreds of thousands of soldiers lay dead or wounded, writhing and screaming in the blood-drenched earth, gassed and mutilated beyond recognition, with limbs and faces torn away.

In May 1915, Italy declared war on the Central Powers and their allies and moved its army across the south-western border of Austria to the strategically important Soča Valley. From there, they hoped to move eastward to the heart of Austria-Hungary. By then, however, the Austrians had fortified the lines with trenches and bunkers for some 80km from the Adriatic and the Karst to the mountain peaks overlooking the Upper Soča Valley as far north as Mt Rombon. The First Offensive launched by the Italians was successful and they occupied Kobarid and Mt Krn to the north-east, where they would remain for 29 months.

The Italians, commanded by General Luigi Cadorna, launched another 10 offensives over the ensuing months, but the difficult mountain terrain turned it into a war of attrition between two entrenched armies. Territorial gains were minimal but the fighting was horrific, involving a total assault of light artillery, anti-aircraft guns, trench mortars and gas-mine throwers. With the stalemate, much of the fighting shifted to Gorica (Gorizia) on the edge of the Karst.

On 24 October 1917 the stalemate was broken. By then the Italians had become dispirited by their lack of success and the weaker Austrian forces knew this. So the Austrians formulated an unusual plan of attack based on surprise and moved hundreds of thousands of troops, arms and materiel (including six German divisions) into the area between Trnovo and Kobarid. The 12th Offensive – the first by the Austrians – began with heavy bombardment.

The 'miracle of Kobarid' routed the Italian army and pushed the fighting back to the Friulian Plain as far as the Piave River, where the war continued for another year. The sketches of the breakthrough by one Lieutenant Erwin Rommel, who later became known as the 'Desert Fox' while commanding Germany's North African offensive in WWII, are invaluable for understanding the battle. But nothing is more vivid than the description of the Italian retreat in Ernest Hemingway's *A Farewell to Arms*. The novelist himself was wounded on the Gorica battlefield in the spring of 1917 while driving an Italian ambulance.

The 12th Offensive was the greatest breakthrough in WWI. It was also the most difficult mountain battle and the first successful 'lightning war' (blitzkrieg) in the history of European warfare. The Italians alone lost 500,000 soldiers and another 250,000 were taken prisoner. But if we count the casualties on the Soča Front for the entire 1915–17 period, that number grows to almost a million, including soldiers on the battlefields and men, women and children behind the lines.

PRIMORSKA

Kobarid along the east bank of the Soča. Allow three hours for a leisurely circuit.

Activities

A footpath to the left of the start of the Kobarid Historical Walk offers hikers a steep climb up onto the high ridge that runs west from Kobarid, affording stunning views of the upper Soča Valley and the peaks of Triglav National Park. The summit of Stol (1673m), 10km away, can be reached in four hours.

The Point Extreme agency (mobile ☎ 041-692 290), at the north end of Trg Svobode, offers a wide range of outdoor activities, including rafting, kayaking, canyoning, hydrospeed and trekking. You can take a tandem paraglider flight from the summit of Stol for €61, or join a full-day guided mountain-bike expedition for €36.

Places to Stay

Wherever you stay in Kobarid that infamous church bell is likely to keep you awake at least part of the night. Not only does it ring on the hour every hour but two minutes later as well!

The small *Kamp Koren* (☎ 388 53 12) is about 500m north of Kobarid on the east bank of the Soča and just before the turn to Drežniške Ravne, a lovely village with traditional farmhouses at the foot of Krn peak. Koren is open from mid-March to October and costs 900 SIT per person.

In Kobarid, the tourist office has a short list of families offering private rooms, including *Prenočišča Ivančič* (☎ 388 53 07, *Gregorčičeva ulica 6c*), between the museum and Trg Svobode (but enter via the driveway from Volaričeva ulica south of the main square). It charges 2500 SIT per person without breakfast.

The only hotel in town is the delightful 32-room *Hotel Hvala* (☎ 389 93 00, fax 388 53 22, e *topli.val@siol.net*) at Trg Svobode 1. It has a bar, one of the best restaurants in the country, a back garden which is open in summer and it even sells permits for fishing in the Soča. Singles are 6700 to 8300 SIT, depending on the season, and doubles are 9800 to 13,000 SIT.

Places to Eat

The *Okrepčevalnica Soča*, opposite the Hotel Hvala at Trg Svobode 12, has drinks and snacks, including pizza. A more salubrious sit-down option is the *Restavracija Kotlar* at Trg Svobode 11, open to 11 pm Thursday to Monday (to midnight Friday and Saturday).

One of Slovenia's finest restaurants is in Kobarid – the *Topli Val* at the Hotel Hvala, open from noon to midnight daily. With a name meaning 'Warm Wave' and owners from Portorož, the speciality here has got to be seafood. It's excellent but not cheap: a shellfish starter for two is 2200 SIT and Soča trout and other fish main courses cost around 2500 SIT. Expect to pay about 9000 SIT for two with a decent bottle of wine (eg, Goriška Chardonnay).

There's a large *supermarket* at Markova ulica 1, open from 7 am to 7 pm daily (to 3 pm Thursday and 8 pm daily in summer).

Entertainment

The *Pri Gotarju* pub in a shady garden at the start of Milanova ulica is a pleasant place for a drink – especially in the courtyard in summer. In the grassy area near the petrol station opposite is a rusting 150mm Howitzer weighing more than 5000kg and built by Krupp-Eassen in 1911. It was fished out of the Soča River after WWI.

Getting There & Away

Buses are frequent to Bovec and Tolmin, 15km to the south-east. Other destinations include Cerkno (up to five a day), Ljubljana via Idrija (six) and Nova Gorica (four).

NOVA GORICA

☎ 05 • postcode 5000 • pop 17,000

Nova Gorica sits on a broad plain south of the Soča River. Across the Italian region of Goriziano to the north-west are the Brda Hills (Goriška Brda). The Vipava Valley (Vipavska Dolina) lies to the south-east. The Karst region is south and south-east of Nova Gorica.

When the town of Gorica, capital of the former Slovenian province of Goriška, was awarded to the Italians under the Treaty of

Paris in 1947 and became Gorizia, the new socialist government in Yugoslavia set itself to building a model town on the eastern side of the border 'following the principles of Le Corbusier', the Swiss functionalist architect who has a lot to answer for. Appropriately enough they called it 'New Gorica' and erected a chain-link barrier between the two towns.

'Where the Latin and the Slavic worlds shake hands in the name of friendship' and other tourist-brochure malarkey notwithstanding, Nova Gorica itself offers travellers little more than a game of chance and an easy doorway into or out of Slovenia. With the Italian frontier running right through what was once united Gorica and a couple of flashy casino-hotels dominating the place, most people arrive here to try their luck or move on – sometimes both and in that order. But Nova Gorica isn't all bad. It's a surprisingly green place with a couple of lovely parks and gardens, and its

immediate surrounds – eg, the Franciscan monastery at Kostanjevica nad Gorico to the south and the ancient settlement of Solkan in the north, with several baroque manor houses – offer some startling contrasts. Slovenian, Venetian, Friulian and Austrian influences can be felt everywhere in the hinterland.

Nova Gorica straddles two important wine-growing areas: the Brda Hills to the north-west and the wide Vipava Valley to the south-east. It's also an excellent springboard for some of Slovenia's most popular destinations: the Soča Valley, Bled and Bohinj in Gorenjska and the beautiful Karst region leading to the coast.

Orientation

Nova Gorica is an unusually long town, running about 5km from the border crossing at Rožna Dolina (Casa Rossa) in the south to Solkan in the north. The bus station is in the centre of town at Kidričeva ulica 22,

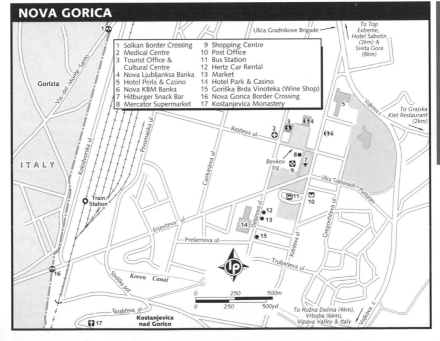

NOVA GORICA

1	Solkan Border Crossing
2	Medical Centre
3	Tourist Office & Cultural Centre
4	Nova Ljubljanksa Banka
5	Hotel Perla & Casino
6	Nova KBM Banka
7	Hitburger Snack Bar
8	Mercator Supermarket
9	Shopping Centre
10	Post Office
11	Bus Station
12	Hertz Car Rental
13	Market
14	Hotel Park & Casino
15	Goriška Brda Vinoteka (Wine Shop)
16	Nova Gorica Border Crossing
17	Kostanjevica Monastery

PRIMORSKA

some 400m south-west of the Hotel Perla. The train station is on Kolodvorska ulica, about 1.5km to the west. To get to the train station from Kidričeva ulica, walk south-west on Erjavčeva ulica. When you reach the Italian border and checkpoint follow Kolodvorska ulica north to No 6.

Neither this border checkpoint nor the one farther north at Solkan is open to foreigners (ie, non-Slovenes and non-Italians). To cross into Italy you must travel 4km south to Rožna Dolina or another 2km to Vrtojba (Santa Andrea).

Information

The tourist information office (☎ 333 03 26, fax 333 03 28) is in the Kulturni Dom (Cultural Centre) at Bevkov trg 4, and is open from 9 am to 7 pm daily.

Nova Ljubljanska Banka is next to the Kulturni Dom, and opens from 9 am to noon and 2 to 5 pm weekdays only. The Nova KBM bank near the Hotel Perla at Kidričeva 11 is open from 7.30 am to 6 pm weekdays and till noon Saturday.

The post office is opposite the bus station at Kidričeva ulica 19. It's open from 7 am to 7 pm weekdays, to 1 pm Saturday and from 9 to 11 am Sunday. Nova Gorica's medical centre (☎ 302 21 22) is at Rejčeva ulica 4.

Things to See

Neither the neobaroque **basilica** built in 1927 nor yet another **WWI museum** perched atop **Sveta Gora** (Monte Santo) 8km north of Nova Gorica is worth the trip; you can see the church from the town anyway. But if you do walk up the 681m hill on a clear day, you'll be able to see the Soča Valley to the north and the impossibly blue ribbon that is the Soča River, and across the Friulian Plain to the Gulf of Trieste. The museum is open from noon to 5 pm (to 4 pm in winter) Wednesday to Friday, and from 11 am to 7 pm (to 4 pm in winter) Saturday and Sunday.

The **Kostanjevica Monastery**, on another hill 800m south of the train station, was founded by the Capuchin Franciscans in the early 17th century and has a wonderful library which can be visited. The narrow,

single-nave **church** nearby has interesting stuccos and in the spooky **crypt** lie the mortal remains of the last members of the French house of Bourbon, including Charles X (1757–1836), who was overthrown in the July Revolution of 1830 in Paris. The monastery is open from 9 am till noon and from 2 to 5 pm Monday to Saturday.

Activities

If you have the time to spare and always did want to try bungee jumping, Top Extreme (☎ 330 00 90 or mobile ☎ 041-620 636) at Vojkova ulica 9 in Solkan will have you flying from the Solkan Bridge over the Soča River in a few hours. The minicourse and jumps are organised on Saturday and Sunday between April and October, and cost 7000 SIT. Top Extreme also organises rafting, kayaking and canyoning on the Soča.

Places to Stay

Decent and affordable accommodation is at a premium in this transient town and if it's value for money you want, hop on the next train or bus out. The tourist office can organise *private rooms* from around 2500 SIT per person, but most are located out of town.

In Rožna Dolina, south of town, *Prenočišče Pertout* (☎ 303 21 94, mobile ☎ 041-624 452, Ulica 25 Maja 23) has singles/doubles for 3300/5000 SIT. The house is scarcely 200m from the border crossing.

All the hotels in town are owned by the casino group HIT. The best value is the *Hotel Sabotin* (☎ 300 54 24, fax 300 54 25, e info@hit.si, Cesta IX Korpusa 35), in an old baroque manor in Solkan, about 2km north of the bus station. It has singles with shower and TV from 6700 SIT and doubles from 11,000 SIT, including breakfast. Better-quality renovated single/double rooms cost 7700/13,400 SIT.

The *Hotel Park* (☎ 336 20 00, fax 302 23 81, e hotel.park@hit.si, Delpinova ulica 5) is the cheaper of the two big central hotels, charging 12,000 SIT for a single with shower and breakfast and 17,500 SIT for a double. The flashiest place in town – and arguably in all of Slovenia – is the 105-room *Hotel Perla* (☎ 336 30 00, fax 302 88 86, e *hotel.perla@hit.si, Kidričeva ulica 7).* A favourite with Italians, this place could be anywhere – Hong Kong, Las Vegas, Disneyland Paris – and it's something local people are just a wee bit proud of. For 16,500 SIT for a single and 22,500 SIT for a double you get the run of the place (pool, sauna, tennis courts, casino) and breakfast.

Places to Eat

The Sabotin and Perla hotels (see Places to Stay) both have good restaurants – the former Chinese and the latter (surprise, surprise) Italian.

The shopping centre north of the bus station is a warren of cafes, pubs and fast-food places, including the ever-popular *Hitburger*. There's also a large *Mercator supermarket* here, open from 6.30 am to 7 pm Monday to Friday, to 1 pm Saturday, and from 8 am to noon Sunday. The outdoor *market* is just off Delpinova ulica east of the Hotel Park. The *Goriška Brda Vinoteka* next door, open 10 am to 5 pm weekdays and 8 am to 1 pm Saturday, has an excellent selection of local wines.

If you win big at the casino, the place to celebrate is the *Grajska Klet (☎ 302 71 60)* in Kromberk Castle, about 3km east of the town centre. The best restaurant in the region, it specialises in using fresh local produce, including Adriatic seafood and Soča trout, and will happily cater for vegetarians. But don't expect much change from 6500 SIT per person. It's open from noon to 10 pm, and is closed Wednesday and Thursday.

Entertainment

The *HIT Casino Perla (☎ 303 36 30, Kidričeva ulica 7)* is the company store – nothing makes more money in this town, and it's all in lire from Italians across the border. So if you want to gamble along with thousands of Italiani, by all means beat a path to it – it's open 24 hours a day. The *HIT Casino Park (☎ 336 26 33)* is also open 24 hours with the exception of the roulette tables (open 3 pm to 4 am).

Both casinos offer all the usual games – roulette, blackjack, poker, baccarat – with a total of almost 800 slot machines. There are also concerts, cabarets and Las Vegas-style floor shows. Admission to either casino costs 500 SIT Monday to Thursday and 1000 SIT Friday to Sunday.

Getting There & Away

Bus From Nova Gorica you can expect buses to Ajdovščina, Ljubljana, Postojna, Šempeter and Tolmin at least once an hour. Other destinations and their daily frequencies include: Bovec (four), Celje and Maribor (one, leaving at 8.45 am), Dobrovo (three), Idrija via Tolmin or Ajdovščina (three, all in the afternoon), Koper (three), Piran (one, at 5.30 am) and Sežana via Komen or Branik (six). In July and August there is one bus a day to Kranjska Gora via Bovec and the spectacular Vršič Pass (departs 5.50 am).

Up to five buses a day cross the Italian border to Gorizia. There's also a daily departure at 7.15 am for Rijeka in Croatia.

Train About half a dozen trains head northeast each day for Jesenice (1¾ hours, 89km) via Most na Soči, Bohinjska Bistrica (70 minutes, 61km) and Bled Jezero (1½ hours, 79km) on what is arguably the country's most beautiful train trip. In the other direction, an equal number of trains go to Sežana (55 minutes, 40km), where you can change for Ljubljana or Trieste in Italy.

Nova Gorica is linked to Ajdovščina, 26km to the south-east, by two trains a day from Monday to Saturday, year-round except during school holidays.

Getting Around

Local buses serve Solkan, Rožna Dolina, Šempeter and Vrtojba from the main station. Hertz (☎ 302 87 11) at Delpinova ulica 12 rents cars and is open from 7 am to 7 pm weekdays and to 1 pm Saturday. You can order a taxi on ☎ 303 51 11 or mobile ☎ 041-632 428.

AROUND NOVA GORICA

If you want to have a look at **Goriška Brda**, the hilly wine region that stretches from Solkan west to the Italian border, catch a bus to **Dobrovo**, 13km to the north-west. The town has a **Renaissance castle** dating from about 1600 that is filled with period furnishings and exhibits on the wine industry. Dobrovo Castle on Grajska cesta also has a very good restaurant and a vinoteka where you can sample the local vintages: white Rebula and Chardonnay or the Pinot and Merlot reds. The very full red Teran (made from the grape varietal Refošk) is more closely associated with the Karst region than here. Goriška Brda is also known for its fabulous cherries in early June.

This area has been under the influence of northern and central Italy since time immemorial and you'll think you've crossed the border as you go through little towns with narrow streets, houses built of karst limestone and the remains of feudal castles. One good example is **Šmartno** (San Martino), a pretty little fortified village with stone walls and a tower from the 16th century.

South-east from Nova Gorica is the wide and fertile **Vipava Valley**, also famous for its wines; indeed, the first wine cooperative in Slovenia was established here in 1894. Some of the reds here are world-class and Vipava Merlot is among the best wines in Central Europe. They also do a decent rosé. The valley's mild climate encourages the cultivation of delicate stone fruits like peaches and apricots and in autumn, when the red sumac changes colour, the valley can look as if it is in flames.

The Vipava Valley is where the Romans first launched their drive into the Danube region, and it was overrun by the Goths, Huns and Langobards from the 4th to 6th centuries before the arrival of the early Slavs. Along the way through the valley, about 22km south-east of Nova Gorica, is **Vipavski Križ** (Santa Croce), a walled medieval village with a ruined castle, a Gothic church and a 17th-century monastery with some wonderful illuminated medieval manuscripts.

Another 4km to the west is **Ajdovščina** (Aidussina). This was the site of Castra ad Fluvium Frigidum, a Roman fort on the River Frigidus (Vipava) and the first important station on the road from Aquileia to Emona (Ljubljana). The border between Goriška and Kranjska (Carniola) provinces once ran nearby.

The town of **Vipava** (Vipacco), the centre of the valley 6km to the south-east, is full of stone churches below **Mt Nanos**, a karst plateau from where the Vipava River springs. Be sure to make a side trip 2km to **Zemono Palace** (☎ 05-366 51 29), a summer mansion built around 1700 by one of the Counts of Gorica. Today the mansion, built in the shape of a cross inside a square with arcaded hallways and a raised central area, houses a posh restaurant and wine cellar and is used for wedding ceremonies and banquets. Have a peek at some of the **baroque murals** near the entrance. They portray a phoenix and a subterranean cave – symbols of fire and water. There are some excellent views down into the fertile valley from Zemono.

Central Primorska

This is an area of Primorska often overlooked by travellers heading for the 'sexier' Alps, Karst or beaches.

Central Primorska is a land of steep slopes, deep valleys and innumerable ravines with plenty of good hiking, the lovely Idrijca River and a couple of interesting towns.

The region is dominated by the Cerkno and Idrija Hills, which eventually join the Škofja Loka Hills in Gorenjska to the east. They are foothills of the Julian Alps. A major tectonic fault line runs below the region and Idrija was the epicentre of the catastrophic quake of 1511.

It was at the time no more than an upstart mining town of wooden buildings and the quake damage was not as severe as that at Škofja Loka.

Nowhere in Slovenia can cultivated fields be found on such steep slopes and human dwellings in such remote locations as in the regions around Idrija and Cerkno. The ravines and valleys were very useful to the Partisans during WWII and the region is dotted with monuments testifying to their presence: the hospitals of Pavl and Franja (near Cerkno), and the Partisan printing house called Slovenija at Vojsko, some 14km north-west of Idrija.

IDRIJA

☎ 05 • postcode 5280 • pop 7000

Idrija sits snugly in a deep basin at the confluence of the Idrijca and Nikova Rivers. Surrounding the valley are the Idrija and Cerkno Hills which eventually join the Škofja Loka Hills in Gorenjska to the east.

When most Slovenes think of Idrija, three things come to mind: *žlikrofi*, lace and mercury. The women of Idrija have been taking care of the first two for centuries, stuffing the crescent-shaped 'Slovenian ravioli' with a savoury mixture of bacon, potatoes and chives as fast as they spin their web-like lace, *čipka*. The men, on the other hand, went underground to extract the 'quicksilver' *(živo srebro)* that would make this town one of the richest in medieval Europe.

History

Mercury was first discovered here in 1490 at the site where the Church of the Holy Trinity now stands. The legend is that a man who made *suha roba,* or traditional wooden products, was busy at work on some tubs he was going to sell at the market in Škofja Loka. After he'd finished soaking them in a spring to ensure they wouldn't leak, he tried to lift one up but it was too heavy. At the bottom was a mass of silvery material that he'd never seen before. But some of the people at the market in Loka where he took the stuff had seen mercury before and the 'mercury rush' to Idrija (Ydria in German) began.

The first mine opened at Idrija in 1500, making it the second-oldest mercury mine in the world after the one in Almadén in central Spain. By the 18th century, Idrija was producing 13% of the world's mercury, thought to be the purest and of the best quality. Its biggest markets were Venice, Trieste, Amsterdam and towns in Germany.

All that meant money – for both Idrija and the imperial court in Vienna. Because of the toxic effects of mercury, doctors and lawyers flocked here to work. The Idrija miners faced many health hazards, but the relatively high wages attracted workers from all over the Habsburg Empire. In 1769, Idrija built Slovenia's first theatre and later could boast two of its finest schools. By the turn of the century, Idrija was second in size only to Ljubljana among the towns of Carniola.

The mercury market bottomed out in the 1970s and production of this once precious element has now ceased in Idrija. The last pit has been shut down and most miners now work in factories north of town at Spodnja Idrija or Cerkno.

The mine has left the town a difficult and expensive legacy. Idrija sits on something like 700km of shafts that go down 15 levels to 32m below sea level. The first four have now been filled with water and more have to be loaded with hard core and debris to stabilise the place. Otherwise the town might sink.

Some destinations in Slovenia just have the right feel, and Idrija is one of them. Walking through the shaft where miners toiled for almost five centuries, across Mestni trg to the town's well-preserved castle or along the Idrijca River and its canal to pristine Wild Lake on a warm summer's evening, you might just think so too.

Orientation

The centre of Idrija is Mestni trg but everything of a practical nature is to the east on Lapajnetova ulica. The bus station is nearby between Vodnikova ulica and Prešernova ulica.

Information

Idrija's tourist office (☎ 377 38 98) is at Lapajnetova ulica 7, a few steps west of the post office. It is open from 9 am to 3 pm weekdays and, from June to August, from 9 am to 5 pm Saturday and Sunday as well. The staff at Kompas (☎ 377 17 00), to the east of the post office on Lapajnetova ulica, may also be able to help. It is open from 8 am to 5 pm weekdays and till noon Saturday.

The Nova KBM Banka in the shopping centre opposite the bus station at Lapajnetova ulica 13 is open from 7.30 am to 6 pm weekdays and till noon Saturday. There's an SKB Banka at Ulica Svete Barbare 3 open from 8.30 am till noon and 2 to 5 pm weekdays only. The post office at Lapajnetova ulica 3 is open from 8 am to 7 pm weekdays and till noon Saturday.

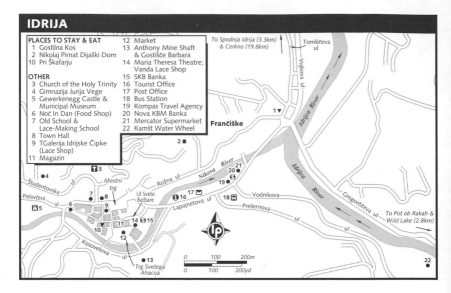

IDRIJA

PLACES TO STAY & EAT
1 Gostilna Kos
2 Nikolaj Pirnat Dijaški Dom
10 Pri Škafarju

OTHER
3 Church of the Holy Trinity
4 Gimnazija Jurija Vege
5 Gewerkenegg Castle & Municipal Museum
6 Noč In Dan (Food Shop)
7 Old School & Lace-Making School
8 Town Hall
9 TGalerija Idrijske Čipke (Lace Shop)
11 Magazin

12 Market
13 Anthony Mine Shaft & Gostišče Barbara
14 Maria Theresa Theatre; Vanda Lace Shop
15 SKB Banka
16 Tourist Office
17 Post Office
18 Bus Station
19 Kompas Travel Agency
20 Nova KBM Banka
21 Mercator Supermarket
22 Kamšt Water Wheel

Municipal Museum

This excellent museum (Mestni Muzej; ☎ 377 11 35), which won the coveted Micheletti Prize for 'Best Technical Museum in Europe' in 1997, is housed in the enormous Gewerkenegg Castle on top of the hill to the west of Mestni trg at Prelovčeva ulica 9. Because the castle was purpose-built for the mine administration in 1533, local people call it Rudniški Grad from the Slovene word *rudnik* for mine. Visit the museum before you go into the Anthony Mine Shaft; you'll understand a whole lot more.

The collections, which deal with mercury and lace but, sadly, not žlikrofi, are exhibited in three wings centred around a courtyard. The **rococo frescoes** of plants, scrolls and columns framing the windows and arcades date from the 18th century.

Mercury (symbol Hg, from its Latin name *hydrargyrum*) is the only metal that exists in a liquid state at room temperature. The silvery metal is extracted from the mercury ore – a bright-red mineral called cinnabar (mercuric sulphide) – by smelting at a high temperature. As the wood-worker discovered, mercury is a very heavy metal, much denser than iron, and in the castle's

north wing, amid a jungle of minerals and fossils, is a large cauldron of mercury with an iron ball floating in the middle.

Part of the **ethnographical collection** in this wing shows rooms in a typical miner's house at various times in history (including the 1960s). A miner's job carried status and they earned more than double the average wage in this part of Slovenia; the furnishings are more than adequate. The miners were well organised and socialism was popular in the late 19th and early 20th centuries.

In the Rondel Tower of the east wing there's a mock-up of the 'call man', the unspeakable so-and-so who summoned miners to work every day at 3.30 am in the town centre by hitting a hollow log with a mallet. There's also an ingenious 'walking tour of Idrija' set up here. Paintings and old photographs spaced between the windows allow you to compare old Idrija with the town that now lies below you. At the bottom of the new **Mercury Tower** at the start of the south wing is a 320kg plexiglass cube filled with drops of mercury.

One large room in the south wing is given over entirely to *klekljana čipka,* the **bobbin lace** woven in broad rings with distinctive patterns. Motifs, numbering up to 40, run the gamut from the usual hearts and flowers to horseshoes, crescents and lizards. Check the table covering measuring 3m by 1.80m. It took 5000 hours to make and was intended for Madame Tito until she was banished into political limbo after the death of her husband in 1980.

Another room is dedicated to the life and work of the novelist France Bevk (1890–1970), born in the village of Zakojca near Cerkno. One of Bevk's finest works is *Father Martin Čedermac* about the persecution of an Italian-Slovene priest and his struggle against the Fascists just before WWII.

The Municipal Museum is open from 9 am to 6 pm daily year-round. Admission is 500/300 SIT for adults/students and children.

Anthony Mine Shaft

Antonijev Rov, a 'living museum' on Kosovelova ulica south of Trg Svetega Ahacija, allows you to get a brief feel for what working conditions were like for the mercury miners of Idrija. The entrance is the Anthony Shaft, sunk in 1500, which led to the first mine: 1.5km long, 600m wide and 400m deep.

The tour, lasting about 1¼ hours, begins in the 'call room' of an 18th-century building where miners were selected each morning and assigned their duties. Just imagine sitting on those hard, cold benches at 4 am with 10 hours' toil underground to look forward to.

There's an excellent 20-minute video in several languages (including English) describing the history of Idrija and the mine.

On the Wings of Mercury

Why was mercury so important in the Middle Ages when they hadn't yet invented the thermometer? Well, mercury (or quicksilver as it was then called in English) had a lot of other important uses – as it still does today.

Alchemists, who named it after the fleet-footed messenger of the Roman gods because of its fluidity, were convinced that all metals originated from mercury. They used it extensively in their search to obtain gold from other metals. But the biggest boon came in the 16th century, when amalgam processes for obtaining silver and gold were introduced by the *conquistadores* in Mexico and Peru. Since mercury bonds as an alloy to many metals, it could separate gold or silver from the rock or ore.

Mercury was used as a medicine – it was an early antidote to syphilis – and in another form as an antiseptic. The Venetians needed it to make their famous mirrors and later milliners used it to lay felt for making hats. Mercury is a highly toxic substance and can affect behaviour; occupational mercurialism from vapours and absorption by the skin is a serious disorder. As a result many milliners went crazy and this was the inspiration for the Mad Hatter in *Alice's Adventures in Wonderland* by Lewis Carroll (1865). Idrija's miners weren't immune to mercurialism and one of the largest mental hospitals in the country is in the hills to the north of town.

In modern times, mercury has been used in industry to obtain caustic soda and chlorine and to make drugs. It is an important element in certain light bulbs, batteries, laboratory monitoring equipment and power control switches. It has a role in the electrical industry, as a conductor, and in the paper industry and has been used with silver to make amalgam for tooth fillings.

Its uses have not always been for peaceful purposes; it is a crucial ingredient in some detonators and bombs. Indeed, during the Vietnam War the USA was one of the biggest importers of Idrija mercury from what was then socialist (and neutral) Yugoslavia.

Mercury mining in Idrija is coming to an end for several reasons. The use of heavy metals has been abandoned by many industries in favour of more environmentally friendly substances, and protective measures have been in place in some countries since the 1970s. More importantly, a 2.5L flask (about 34kg) of mercury that went for approximately US$800 in the 1970s was worth only $100 a decade later. Such prices no longer even covered production costs.

PRIMORSKA

Before entering the shaft, you must don coats with the miners' insignia, helmets with torches attached and wish each other 'Srečno!' ('Good luck!'), the traditional miners' farewell. You'll be thankful for those helmets every time you knock your head against one of the support beams.

As you walk into the shaft there's a good display of the mine's levels done with glass and light underfoot. As you follow the circular tour you'll see samples of live mercury on the walls that the miners painstakingly scraped to a depth of about 5cm, as well as some cinnabar ore. The 18th-century **chapel** in the shaft is dedicated to St Barbara, patron of miners, and St Ahac, on whose feast day (22 June) rich deposits of cinnabar were discovered.

You can visit the mine with a guide at 10 am and 4 pm only, on weekdays. On Saturday and Sunday, tours depart at 10 am, and 3 and 4 pm. Admission is 700/500 SIT for adults/children.

Other Attractions

There are several fine neoclassical buildings on Mestni trg, including the **town hall** at No 1. To the west of the square opposite Prelovčeva ulica 1a is the **Lace-making School** (Čipkarska Šola) in the Stara Šola (Old School), built in 1876. Lace-making is still a required subject for girls in elementary school in Idrija. Visitors are welcomed from noon to 4 pm daily. The **Gimnazija Jurija Vege** (1901), to the north-west on Študentovska ulica, educated many Slovenes who later rose to national prominence, including the painter Božidar Jakac (1899–1989).

The large 18th-century building on the north side of Trg Svetega Ahacija, the centre of town in the Middle Ages, is the **Magazin**, a granary and warehouse where the miners, who were paid in food as well as in cash, kept their stores. It now houses a gallery and the city library. To the east, at Trg Svetega Ahacija 5, is the **Maria Theresa Theatre**, the oldest in the country. Today it functions as a cinema.

Laid out across the slopes encircling the valley are Idrija's distinctive **miners' houses**. Large wooden A-frames with cladding and

dozens of windows, they usually had four storeys with living quarters for three or four families. They must have appeared massive when they were first built in the 17th century.

North of Mestni trg is the **Church of the Holy Trinity** (1500) on the site where mercury was first discovered by our friend the tub-maker more than 500 years ago. To the north-east off Grilčeva ulica in the district of **Frančiške** was the last working mine in Idrija – it closed in 1999. A warehouse nearby contains a mass of mining equipment from before WWI that works on compressed air. If you're interested, ask the staff at the Municipal Museum about a tour.

One of the most interesting bits of mining technology that still exists is the **Kamšt**, a 13.6m water wheel made of wood that was used to pump the water out of the flooded mines from 1790 until 1948. It is about 1.5km south-east of Mestni trg off Vodnikova ulica. You could combine a visit here with a walk along the Idrijca River Canal to Wild Lake, about 3km south.

Wild Lake

An excellent trail called Pot ob Rakah follows the Idrijca River Canal from the Kamšt to Wild Lake (Divje Jezero), a tiny, impossibly green lake fed by a karst spring more than 80m under the surface. After a heavy rainfall, water gushes up from the tunnel like a geyser and the lake appears to be boiling. Perhaps that's not quite the right word; the surface temperature never exceeds 10°C. Three cave divers have drowned at Wild Lake – two in 1995 and one in 1997 – trying to find the source.

The lake has been declared a natural monument and little signboards around the shore (which should take you about 15 minutes to circle if you go at a snail's pace) identify the plants and trees and point out the lake's unique features. That body of water flowing from Wild Lake into the Idrijca just happens to be the shortest river in Slovenia. The Jezernica River is a mere 55m long.

If you followed the canal for 15km to the south-west you'd come to the first of the barriers (klauže) of stacked wood and stones that dammed the Idrijca and Belca

The bell tower of the Church of St George overlooks Piran's waterfront (Primorska).

Giuseppe Tartini, Piran

Beautiful Lipizzaners, Lipica stud farm (Primorska)

Fruit, herbs, confectionery, even sausage stew – whatever your taste, it's all there on the streets of Slovenia.

Rivers to float timber in the old days. They were once called 'Slovenian pyramids' because of their appearance. Wood was an important commodity for two reasons. First, something had to support those 700km of mine shafts, and second, the heat needed to extract mercury from cinnabar required a lot of fuel. The dams continue for some 12km down the Belca River.

The area of the Idrijca near the suspension bridge is good for swimming in summer, when the water averages about 20°C.

Special Events

The big event in Idrija is the annual Lace-making Festival in late August. The highlight is a contest in which up to 100 people compete.

Places to Stay & Eat

In summer the *Nikolaj Pirnat Dijaški Dom* (☎ 377 105 2, *Ulica IX Korpusa 6*) has 56 beds available in multibed rooms for around 2000 SIT per person.

The only standard accommodation in Idrija is the six-room *Gostišče Barbara* (☎/fax 377 11 42, *Kosovelova ulica 3*) above the mine shaft museum. Singles/doubles with shower are 5200/8000 SIT.

If you're looking for somewhere romantic to stay, head for the friendly five-star *Hotel Kendov Dvorec* (☎ 372 51 00, fax 375 64 75, e *kendov-dvorec@s5.net*) in Spodnja Idrija, about 4km north of Idrija on the road towards Cerkno. The hotel is a converted family mansion – the oldest part of which dates from the 14th century – fitted with 19th-century antique furniture, and enjoys stunning views along the Idrijca Valley. The 11 rooms cost from €61 to €102 per person, depending on season.

Pri Škafarju ('At the Sign of the Tub'; *Ulica Svete Barbare 9*) is a friendly restaurant, open to 10 pm weekdays and Sunday and to 11 pm Friday and Saturday. Pizza baked in a beautiful wood-burning tile stove is why most people come here, but there are plenty of other things on the menu as well. Pri Škafarju does decent enough žlikrofi, but the best place to have this most Idrijan of specialities is at *Gostilna Kos* (*Tomšičeva*

ulica 4), a little pub and restaurant. It is open to 3 pm Monday, to 10 pm Tuesday to Saturday.

There's a large *Mercator supermarket* (*Lapajnetova ulica 45*), open from 7 am to 7 pm weekdays, to 5 pm Saturday and from 8 am to noon Sunday. The 24-hour *Noč in Dan* shop (*Prelovčeva ulica 5*) sells food, drinks and snacks. A *market* is held in Trg Svetega Ahacija on the 15th and 20th of every month.

Entertainment

Evenings of classical, folk and jazz concerts take place in the courtyard of Gewerkenegg Castle every second Friday or so in July, August and September. Contact the museum (☎ 377 11 35) for schedules and information.

Shopping

Idrija lace is among the finest in the world and a small piece, though not cheap, makes a great gift or souvenir. The best place to buy it is at a shop called Galerija Idrijske Čipke at Mestni trg 16. It is open from 10 am till noon and 4 to 7 pm weekdays and on Saturday morning. The Vanda shop at Trg Svetega Ahacija 7 has a smaller selection. It is open from 9 am till noon and 4 to 7 pm weekdays and on Saturday morning.

Getting There & Away

Idrija is not the easiest place in the world to reach. The town is not on a train line and the bus service is fairly limited. There are at least hourly departures to Cerkno and Ljubljana, about three buses a day to Bovec, eight to Črni Vrh, eight to Tolmin, three to Ajdovščina and one (at 5.30 am) to Nova Gorica, which then carries on into Italian Gorizia.

CERKNO

☎ 05 • postcode 5282 • pop 2170

Cerkno lies in the Cerknica River Valley 4km north-east of the main road linking Idrija with the Soča Valley.

Until recently this town could not claim the historical importance of its celebrated neighbour Idrija, 20km to the south. But with the recent discovery of what is considered to be the oldest known musical instrument on earth (see the boxed text 'Stone-Age Music' later in this section), that has changed.

In any case, Cerkno has two other claims to fame. It is the home of the Laufarija, the ancient Shrovetide celebration in which the key players wear artfully crafted wooden masks and 'execute' the Old Year. If you don't get a chance to come to Cerkno for Mardi Gras to see the famous show, you'll have to be content with looking at the masks in the town's museum. Cerkno is also known for its strange dialect in a land where there are something like 50 of them. People from outside the Cerkno region (Cerkljanska) always seem to smile when they hear what is the equivalent of an American southern drawl.

Orientation & Information

Glavni trg is the main square, and is where the buses stop. At the time of research there was no tourist office in Cerkno, but the helpful and knowledgeable staff at the Hotel Cerkno can provide tourist information. The Nova KBM bank branch (open from 8 am to 6 pm weekdays and till noon Saturday) is at Glavni trg 5. The post office, in Sedejev trg

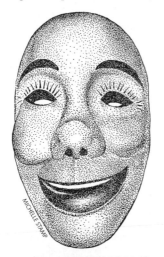

Laufarji masks are part of a tradition that can be traced to South Tyrol in Austria.

next to the Hotel Cerkno, keeps the same hours as the bank, with a couple of half-hour breaks in the morning and afternoon.

Cerkno Museum

The Cerkno Museum (Cerkljanski Muzej) is about 150m south-west of Glavni trg at Bevkova ulica 12. A large section of this small museum is given over to the work of the WWII Partisans in secret hospitals and printing presses around the region, but those displays are black, white and grey at best and labelled in Slovene only. Step into the room with the Laufarji masks. It's a lot brighter.

Ethnologists believe that the Laufarija celebration (see the boxed text 'The Laufarija Tradition') and the masks came from Austria's South Tyrol hundreds of years ago. *Lauferei* means 'running about' in German and that's just what the players do as they nab their victim. The masks with the crazy, distorted faces on display here are originals bought from one of the Laufarji clubs. Only one elderly man in Cerkno still makes them.

The Cerkno Museum shows a dated video of the Laufarija in Slovene, but it is entertaining and illustrates how the masks and costumes are made and how events unfold at Mardi Gras. The museum is open from 9 am to 2 pm daily, except Monday, and admission is 300/200 SIT for adults/children.

Franja Partisan Hospital

This hospital (Partizanska Bolnišnica Franja), hidden in a canyon near Dolenji Novaki about 5km north-east of Cerkno, treated wounded Partisan soldiers from Yugoslavia and other countries from late 1943 until the end of WWII. Franja Hospital really has nothing to do with political or economic systems; it is a memorial to humanity, courage and self-sacrifice. It is a moving and very worthwhile place to visit, and the most popular WWII museum in Slovenia.

The complex, named after its chief physician, Dr Franja Bojc-Bidovec, was built in December 1943 for the needs of the IX Corps which included seven brigades and a large number of companies – a total of some 10,000 soldiers. By May 1945 it

The Laufarija Tradition

Groups of boys and young men (and now a few girls and women) belonging to Laufarji societies (like the Mardi Gras clubs in New Orleans) organise the Laufarija celebration every year in late February/early March and about two dozen perform. Those aged 15 and over are allowed to enter, but they must prove themselves worthy apprentices by sewing costumes. These costumes – though not masks – must be made fresh every year because many of them are made out of leaves, pine branches, straw or moss stitched onto a burlap (hessian) backing and can take quite a beating during the festivities.

The action takes place on the Sunday before Ash Wednesday and again on Shrove Tuesday (Pustni Torek). The main character is the Pust, whose mask is horned and who wears a moss costume weighing up to 100kg. He's the symbol of winter and the old year – he must die.

The Pust is charged with a long list of crimes – a bad harvest, inclement weather, lousy roads – and, of course, is found guilty. Some of the other two dozen Laufarji characters represent crafts and trades (the Baker, the Thatcher, the Woodsman), while the rest have certain character traits or afflictions such as the Drunk and his Wife, the Bad Boy, Sneezy and the Sick Man, who always plays the accordion. The Old Man, wearing Slovenian-style lederhosen and a wide-brimmed hat, executes the Pust with a wooden mallet and the body is rolled away on a caisson.

counted some 13 structures, including treatment sheds, operating theatres, X-ray rooms and bunkers for convalescence. More than 500 wounded were treated here with a mortality rate of only about 10%.

The complex, hidden in a ravine by the Pasica Stream with steep walls riddled with caves, had an abundance of fresh water that was also used to power a hydroelectric generator. Because of the hospital's isolated position, noise was not a problem. Local farmers and Partisan groups provided food that was lowered down the steep cliffs by rope; medical supplies were diverted from hospitals in occupied areas or later air-dropped by the Allies. The hospital came under attack by the Germans twice – once in April 1944 and again in March 1945 – but it was never taken.

The Franja Partisan Hospital is open from 9 am to 6 pm daily April to September and to 4 pm in March, October and November. From December to February it is open from 9 am to 4 pm Saturday, Sunday and holidays only. Admission costs 500/300 SIT.

Ravne Cave

The snow-white aragonite crystals in the Ravne Cave (Ravenska Jama) at Ravne, about 7km south-west of Cerkno, are a very rare phenomenon. They are formed by karst springs containing magnesium as well as calcium and are very beautiful, resembling ice, needles, even hedgehogs. The cave is a total of 682m long and you get to see about half of it in three galleries. But to visit, you must seek permission from the Srečko Logar Caving Club (no telephone) at Ljubljanska cesta 5 in Idrija or from the Municipal Museum (☎ 377 11 35).

Hiking

The Cerkno Hills (Cerkljansko Hribovje) are tailor-made for hiking and the English-language *Cerkno Map of Local Walks*, available from Hotel Cerkno, lists eight walks, most of them pretty easy. They include walks to the **Franja Partisan Hospital** (No 7; 3½ hours return) and **Ravne Cave** (No 2; four hours). The highest peak in the area is **Porezen** (1632m) to the north-east, which has a mountain hut called *Dom na Poreznu (1590m;* ☎ *377 51 35)* with accommodation. It is open daily from June to September and at the weekend only during the rest of the year.

Skiing

The **Cerkno Ski Centre** (☎ 371 74 20), 10km north-east of Cerkno, is situated on Črni Vrh (1290m) and covers 50 hectares of ski slopes. In normal snow conditions five chairlifts and two tows operate and there are cannons for making artificial snow. The

PRIMORSKA

Stone-Age Music

The image of our Neanderthal ancestors sitting around a campfire making beautiful music together is not an easy one to conjure up, but it's a lot easier now, following a major discovery in a mountain cave near Cerkno.

Paleontologists were messing around in the area in 1995 and collecting Stone-Age tools when a local pundit who happened to pass by told them he knew where they'd find lots more. He led them to Divje Babe, a cave some 200m above the main road linking Cerkno with the Tolmin-Idrija highway, and they began digging. Among the buried tools was a piece of cave-bear femur measuring 10cm long and perforated with four aligned holes – two intact and two incomplete – at either end. It looked exactly like a flute.

Because objects of such antiquity cannot be dated by the usual radiocarbon techniques, the flute was sent to the City University of New York to undergo electron spin resonance, which measures the small amounts of radiation absorbed by objects from the time of their burial. And the verdict? According to the researchers, the flute is anywhere between 45,000 and 82,000 years old, depending on how much moisture – which inhibits the absorption of radiation – the cave floor had been exposed to. One thing is certain, however – Slovenia can now claim the oldest known musical instrument on earth. The flute will eventually be put on display at the Cerkno Museum and – just in case you were wondering – it still works.

facilities include a ski school, equipment rental and a self-service restaurant. The closest accommodation is at Cerkno or Dolenji Novaki so you'll have to make it a day trip via one of the special ski buses.

Special Events
The Laufarija festival in late February/early March takes place outdoors both in Glavni trg and Sedejev trg near the Hotel Cerkno.

Places to Stay & Eat
The 75-room *Hotel Cerkno* (☎ 374 34 00, fax 374 34 33, e hotel.cerkno@siol.net, Sedejev trg 8) is in a modern building in the heart of town. It's a comfortable enough place with an indoor pool (900 SIT for nonresidents), sauna, gym and three clay tennis courts. Singles with breakfast and shower are €41, while doubles are €72. The hotel offers discounts for stays of more than two nights.

The *Gostilna V Logu* (☎ 374 51 88) in Dolenji Novaki (house No 1), not far from the Franja Partisan Hospital, is very popular with local people, particularly for lunch at the weekend. It is open from 11 am to 11 pm Wednesday to Sunday. V Logu also has four rooms where you can stay for about €13 per person.

Getting There & Away
There are hourly departures by bus to Idrija (six a day on Saturday and Sunday), up to five a day to Ljubljana and three to Bovec via Most na Soči, Tolmin and Kobarid. Another eight or so (two at the weekend) go just to Tolmin, where you can change for Nova Gorica and the coast.

Karst Region

The Karst region is a limestone plateau stretching from Nova Gorica south-east to the Croatian border, west to the Gulf of Trieste and east to the Vipava Valley. Because it was the first such area to be researched and described in the 19th century, it is called the Classic, Real, True or Original Karst and always spelled with an upper-case 'K'. Other karst areas (from the Slovene word *kras*) around the world are similar but they get only a lower-case 'k'.

The thick layers of limestone deposits were laid down millions of years ago. Earth movements then raised the limestone above sea level, where it could be attacked by mildly acidic rainwater. Over hundreds of thousands of years, this slow, chemical erosion has produced the typical features of karst scenery – limestone pavements, dry valleys, sinkholes, springs and, of course, vast subterranean networks of caves and tunnels.

Rivers, ponds and lakes can disappear and then resurface in the porous limestone through sinkholes and funnels. Some rivers have created large underground caverns like the caves at Škocjan. Calcium carbonate dissolved in the water dripping from the roofs of caves creates stalactites (the ones that grow downward) and stalagmites (the ones that grow upward). When these underground caverns collapse – and they do periodically – they form a depression *(polje)* which collects soil (mostly red clay, the *terra rossa* of the Karst) and then vegetation. These fertile hollows are cultivated by local farmers but, because of the proximity of underground rivers, they tend to flood quickly after heavy rain.

The Karst, with its olives, ruby-red Teran wine, air-dried *pršut* ham, old stone churches and red-tiled roofs, is some people's favourite region of Slovenia. You can explore Rihemberk Castle near Branik or the walled village of Štanjel with its magnificent Ferrari Gardens to the north, but the areas with the most to see and do are to the south.

Though the weather is very pleasant for most of the year, with lots of sun and low humidity, don't be fooled into thinking it's sweetness and light all the time. The *burja,* a fiercely cold north-easterly wind, can do a lot of damage in winter, ripping off roofs, uprooting trees and blowing away topsoil. It is said to give the pršut its distinctive taste, though.

ŠKOCJAN CAVES
☎ 07 • postcode 6215

The karst caves at Škocjan are far more captivating and 'real' than the larger one at Postojna, some 33km to the north-east in Notranjska province. If you can imagine climbing the concrete Matterhorn at Disneyland and then scaling the real thing, you'll get the picture. For many travellers, a visit here will be one of the highlights of their trip to Slovenia – a page right out of Jules Verne's *A Journey to the Centre of the Earth.* Heed the words of a French speleologist who wrote in 1955: 'In the Postojna Cave the speleologist sees everything he could desire, but the Škocjan Caves have no comparison in the world.'

The Škocjan Caves (Škocjanske Jame), 5km long and 250m deep, were carved out by the Reka River, which originates in the foothills of Snežnik (1796m) to the south-east. The Reka enters the caves in a gorge below the village of Škocjan (San Canziano in Italian) and eventually flows into the Dead Lake (Mrtvo Jezero), a sump at the end of the cave where it disappears. It surfaces again – this time as the Timavo River – at Duino in Italy, some 40km to the north-west, before emptying into the Gulf of Trieste.

The caves – or at least their entrances – were known by prehistoric people who sheltered in them or used them to make sacrifices to the gods of the underworld. Janez Vajkard Valvasor described the caves and the phenomenon of the disappearing Reka in his encyclopaedic work *The Glory of the Duchy of Carniola* in the late 17th century, but real exploration did not start until the mid-19th century. Organised visits followed soon afterward, but the caves never became the tourist mecca that Postojna did; electric lighting was not even installed until 1959. Today, visitors can explore about 2km of these spectacular caves.

Unesco included the Škocjan Caves and surrounding nature reserve in its World Heritage Sites list in 1986.

Orientation & Information
The caves lie about 1.5km east of the main Ljubljana-Koper highway. The closest town of any size is Divača (population 1750), about 5km to the north-west. Divača's train station, where buses stop as well, is on Trg 15 Aprila about 600m west of this highway.

The information office (☎ 763 28 40) at the caves' reception area is open from 9 am until the last tour departs. The small shop opposite sells a few good guides and maps (including a Unesco 1:5000-scale one) to the caves and surrounding areas. There's a

ŠKOCJAN CAVES

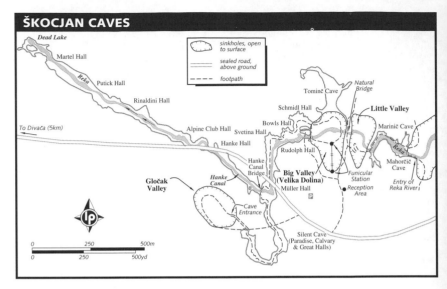

Legend:
- sinkholes, open to surface
- sealed road, above ground
- footpath

Map labels:
Dead Lake
Martel Hall
Reka
Putick Hall
Rinaldini Hall
To Divača (5km)
Alpine Club Hall
Svetina Hall
Hanke Hall
Hanke Canal Bridge
Gločak Valley
Hanke Canal
Cave Entrance
Tominč Cave
Schmidl Hall
Bowls Hall
Rudolph Hall
Natural Bridge
Little Valley
Marinič Cave
Reka
Mahorčič Cave
Big Valley (Velika Dolina)
Müller Hall
Funicular Station
Reception Area
Entry of Reka River
Silent Cave (Paradise, Calvary & Great Halls)

Scale: 0 – 250 – 500m / 0 – 250 – 500yd

post office in Divača at the start of Kraška cesta and a Banka Koper branch just west of the Risnik pension.

The Caves

If you have some time to spare before your tour departs, follow the path leading north and down some steps from the reception area for 300m to the **lookout** (it is sign-posted 'Razgledišče/Belvedere' in Slovene and Italian). Extending before you is a superb vista of the Velika Dolina (Big Valley) and gorge where the Reka starts its subterranean journey (and where you will emerge from the caves). Across the 180m-deep gorge to the east is the village of **Škocjan** and the 17th-century **Church of St Cantianus**. St Cantianus is the protector against evil spirits and floods and is also the caves' namesake. He's a good man to know in this volatile part of Slovenia.

Visitors to the caves assemble around the picnic tables across from the restaurant at the reception area and walk with their guides for about 500m down a gravel path to the main entrance in the Gločak Valley. Through an artificial tunnel built in 1933, you soon reach the head of the **Silent Cave**

(Tiha Jama), a dry branch of the underground canyon that stretches for 500m. The first section, called **Paradise**, is filled with beautiful stalactites, stalagmites and flow stones; the second part (called **Calvary**) was once the river bed. The Silent Cave ends at the **Great Hall** (Velika Dvorana), 120m wide and 30m high. It is a jungle of exotic dripstones and deposits; keep an eye open for the stalagmite called the **Giant** and the one named the **Organ**.

The sound of the Reka River rushing through cascades and whirlpools below signals your entry into the astonishing **Müller Hall**, with walls 100m high. To get over the Reka you must cross **Hanke Canal Bridge**, 45m high, narrow, and surely the highlight of the trip. Count your blessings as you do (or don't) look down – the catwalk that allowed visitors to cross over into long, narrow **Svetina Hall** before this bridge was built 60 years ago was 20m higher. You can see the remains of the old bridge up to the left as you cross.

Only experienced speleologists are allowed to explore the 5km of caves and halls that extend to the north-west ending at Dead Lake. Every century or so the siphon gets blocked and the caves are flooded. This happened most recently in 1965.

From Svetina Hall you climb up a path hewn into the stone to **Bowls Hall**, remarkable for its rare bowl-like potholes which were formed when water flooding the cave churned and swirled up to the ceiling. They look like troughs or rice terraces.

The final section, **Schmidl Hall**, emerges into the Velika Dolina. From here you walk past **Tominč Cave**, where finds from a prehistoric settlement have been unearthed, and over a walkway near the **Natural Bridge** to the funicular, which carries you 90m up the rock face to near the reception area.

You may be surprised to learn that the Škocjan Caves are home to an incredible amount of flora and fauna: 250 varieties of plants and five different types of bats. The temperature in the caves is constant at about 13°C so you should bring along a light jacket or sweater. Good walking shoes (the path can get pretty wet and slippery in the high humidity) and a torch (flashlight) are also recommended.

The caves can be visited seven times a day (at 10 and 11.30 am and on the hour from 1 to 5 pm) from June to September. In April, May and October there are tours at 10 am and at 1 and 3.30 pm. From November to March, visits are allowed at 10 am and 3 pm only on Sunday and holidays. The entry fee is 1500/700 SIT for adults/children. The tours, much less structured than at Postojna Cave, are given in five different languages (the guides will separate you into groups) and take about 1½ hours.

Other Caves The 803m-long **Vilenica Cave** (Jama Vilenica) is a couple of kilometres north-west of Lokev, halfway between Divača and Lipica. It was the first karst cave to open to the public in the early 19th century and still welcomes guests at 3 pm every Sunday. **Divača Cave** (Divaška Jama), about 3km north-east on the road to Divača, is open only by arrangement. It is only 672m long but has excellent dripstones and rock formations. Inquire about these caves at the Škocjan Caves or the Lipica Stud Farm reception areas.

Horse Riding

The Farma Diomed (☎ 766 00 03) in Lokev (house No 230), west of Divača, has horses for hire. An excellent short excursion would be to ride to the Vilenica Cave, or the Divača Cave (see the preceding paragraph).

Places to Stay & Eat

The closest camping ground to the caves is *Avtokamp Kozina* (☎ 714 66 11), 7km south of Divača. It's a tiny place, with only 25 sites, and is full of caravans and cars. It's open from May to September and costs 900 SIT per person.

Divača is the only place to stay near the caves unless you want to head for Lipica (see the Lipica section later in this chapter). In Divača, the *Penzion Risnik* (☎ 763 00 08, Kraška cesta 24), about 400m north of the main highway to the caves and the coast, has 10 dark and dingy rooms for which it asks an outrageous 4500/6900 SIT for singles/doubles. With the highway so close, a busy petrol station opposite and buses and trains heading for the station, it is very noisy here. *Gostilna Malovec* (☎ 763 02 00, Kraška cesta 30) is cheerier but charges similar rates.

Both the Risnik and the Malovec have restaurants that serve fairly decent food, open from 8 am to 10 pm daily. A more pleasant place to eat in Divača is the *Okrepčevalnica Klunov Hram* (Kraška cesta 32), a cellar restaurant next to the Malovec. It has some good pasta dishes like *njoki* and pizza (around 1100 SIT) as well as its own home-made Teran wine. The Klunov Hram is open from 11 am to 10 pm daily (though the pesky minicasino adjoining the dining room stays open to 2 am).

There's a restaurant called *Pri Jami* at the caves' reception area open from 9 am to 8 pm daily.

Getting There & Away

The Škocjan Caves are about 5km by road south-east of the Divača train station. Getting to the caves by public transport can be tricky, but the driver of any bus heading along the highway to/from the coast will let you off at the access road if you ask in

PRIMORSKA

advance (there are huge signs announcing the caves). From there you can walk the remaining 1.5km to the caves' entrance. All in all, it's probably easier to take the train to Divača and walk along the 3km path (signposted 'Park Škocjanske Jame') from Divača train station through the village of Dolnje Ležeče to Matavun. You can pick up a free map from the ticket office at the station. Alternatively:

Go through Dolnje Ležeče on the main road out of town, turn right at the Gradišče sign and follow that road until you see a small clearing on your right with a trail marker (white dot and red circle), and follow this trail directly to the caves. This is a slightly longer route, but easier to follow than the signposted Škocjanske Jame trail...The trail you're supposed to follow isn't marked for the first part, and you end up in a meadow with nowhere to go if you don't know where to turn into the bushes to find the start of the trail.
Brendan Hickey, Canada

About half a dozen buses a day (12 in July and August) pass through Divača from Ljubljana and Postojna on their way to the coast and destinations in Croatia. The first leaves Divača at 5.40 am, the last at 8.15 pm. There are four buses a day to Lipica, the first at 6.10 am and the last at 2.38 pm.

Divača is on the rail line linking Ljubljana (1½ hours, 104km) with Sežana (10 minutes, 9km), with around 20 trains a day in each direction. Divača is also the railhead for four trains a day to Koper (50 minutes, 49km) via Hrpelje Kozina, with two daily connections to Buzet and Pula in Croatia.

LIPICA
☎ 05 • postcode 6210 • pop 125

Lipica lies 2km north-east of the Italian border and about 9km south-west of Divača. Its impact on the world of sport has been far greater than its tiny size would suggest. In 1580, in what was then called Lipizza, the Austrian Archduke Charles, son of Ferdinand I, established a stud farm *(kobilarna)* to breed horses for the Spanish Riding School in Vienna.

The riding school had been founded eight years earlier to train horses for the imperial court and was looking for a lighter, more elegant breed for parades and military purposes (which would later lead to the development of dressage). Andalusian horses from Spain were coupled with the local Karst breed that the Romans had once used to pull chariots – and the Lipizzaner was born. But they weren't quite the snow-white beauties we know today. Those didn't come about for another 200 years when white Arabian horses got into the act.

It's easy to see why both Charles and the nags liked the place. Though very much part of the region, this 'oasis in the barren Karst' (as Lipica is called) feels like Eden after all that limestone. Indeed, the word *lipica* in Slovene means 'little linden', after the trees that grow in such profusion here. The moderate, dry climate provides ideal conditions for breeding horses with speed, strength and stamina.

The stud farm remained the property of the court in Vienna until the end of WWI when the Italians took control of Primorska province. The horses were moved to Hungary and then Austria but the change in climate took its toll. In 1943, with WWII still raging, the Germans moved more than 200 horses to the Sudetenland in Bohemia (now the Czech Republic). When the area was liberated by American forces in 1945, most of the horses and the stud farm's archives were shipped off to Italy. Sadly, only 11 horses returned when operations resumed at Lipica in 1947.

Today, there are 200 Lipizzaners remaining at the original stud farm while 'genuine' Lipizzaners are bred in various locations around the world: Croatia, Hungary, Italy, Slovakia and even in the American state of Illinois. The stud farm at Piber, north-east of Graz in Austria, now breeds the horses for the Spanish Riding School.

Orientation & Information

The centre of everything in Lipica, of course, is the stud farm in the south-west corner of the village and the two hotels nearby. The tourist information office (☎ 739 15 80, fax 734 63 70, @ lipica@siol.net) at the entrance to the stud farm can change money, but it takes a 2% commission.

Lipica Stud Farm

Tours of the 311-hectare stud farm (Kobilarna Lipica) begin opposite the information and ticket office; simply wait by the sign bearing the name of the language you want to hear it in (English, German, French, Italian or Slovene). The guide will find you. A visit covers the stables, one of which dates from 1703, and the riding halls to give you an idea of what it's like to learn dressage and control a very large animal. But frankly, the tour is a little boring with endless facts, figures and horse pedigrees.

The highlight of a visit (if you time it right) is the performance of these elegant horses as they go through their complicated paces with riders *en costume*. It's not as complete a show as the one at the Spanish Riding School in Vienna or in such ornate surroundings, but watching great white horses pirouetting and dancing to Viennese waltzes sort of makes up for it. If you miss the show, at least try to be around when the horses are moved from the stables to pasture (usually before 9 am) and again in the late afternoon. It's stunning to see them gallop past.

Dancing Horses of Lipica

Lipizzaners are considered to be the finest riding horses in the world – sought after for *haute école* dressage – and with all the trouble that's put into producing them, it's not surprising. They are very intelligent, sociable horses, quite robust and graceful.

Breeding is paramount, and it is carried out with all the precision of a well-organised crime. A half-dozen equine families with 16 ancestors can be traced back to the early 18th century and their pedigrees read like those of medieval royalty. When you walk around the stables at Lipica you'll see charts on each horse stall with complicated figures, dates and names like 'Maestoso Allegra' and 'Neapolitano'. It's all to do with the horse's lineage.

Lipizzaners foal between January and May and the colts and fillies suckle for six or seven months. They remain in the herd for about three years. They are then separated for training, which takes another four years.

Lipizzaners are not white when they are born but grey, bay or even chestnut. The celebrated 'imperial white' does not come about until they are between five and 10 years old, when their hair loses its pigment. Think of it as just part of the old nag's ageing process. Their skin remains grey, however, so when they are ridden hard enough to sweat, they become mottled and are not so attractive.

A fully mature Lipizzaner measures about 15 hands (about 153cm) and weighs between 500kg and 600kg. They have long backs, short, thick necks, silky manes and expressive eyes. They live for 25 to 30 years and are particularly resistant to disease. They will nuzzle you out of curiosity if you approach them while they graze.

Lipizzaners are bred at Lipica, in Austria and in the USA as riding and show horses; they are known for their beauty, elegance and agility. Lipizzaners bred at Szilvásvárad near Eger in Hungary and at Jakovo near Osijek in Croatia, however, are raised primarily as carriage horses and are bigger and stronger.

MARTIN HARRIS

PRIMORSKA

You can visit the Lipica Stud Farm throughout the year and it's open from 8 am to 6 pm. From April to October, tours, which are mandatory, leave at 10 and 11 am and then hourly from 1 to 5 pm weekdays with an additional tour at 9 am at the weekend. In July and August there are tours on the hour seven days a week from 9 to 11 am and 1 to 6 pm. In March, weekday tours are at 11 am and 1, 2 and 3 pm and at the weekend at 10 and 11 am and hourly from 1 to 4 pm. From November to February there are four tours (at 11 am and 1, 2 and 3 pm) every day of the week. Tickets cost €4 to €5 for adults, depending on the season, and €2 or €2.5 for children.

Exhibition performances take place at 3 pm on Tuesday, Friday and Sunday from May to September; in April and October they are at 3 pm on Friday and Sunday only. Admission to the performance, which includes the tour of the stud farm, is €10/5 for adults/children.

Activities

Some 60 horses are available for riding both in the ring and the open countryside at 8.30 and 9.30 am and then at 4.30 and 5.30 pm from April to September and at 8.30 and 9.30 am and 2.30 and 3.30 pm from October to March. The cost for riding in a guided group is €15 per hour. There is also a large choice of courses including group classes for beginners and intermediate riders (both €20) and individual dressage classes (€56). There are week-long courses too: six two-hour lessons for beginners and classes for advanced riders (both €221), and dressage classes (€304; minimum L-level). For kids of 10 and under there are pony rides (€7.50). Half-hour/hour carriage jaunts are €18/36.

The nearby Lipica Golf Course (☎ 734 63 73) has nine holes for a par 36, a driving range and a couple of putting greens. The green fees are €18/24 on weekdays/weekends for nine holes, or €26/34 for 18 holes, and you can rent a half-set of clubs for €10.

Renting one of the five tennis courts near the Hotel Maestoso costs between €6.5 and €7.5, depending on the time and day. Racquet hire costs €3 per hour.

Places to Stay & Eat

There are two hotels in Lipica, both managed by the same company. The 65-room *Hotel Maestoso* (☎ 739 17 90, fax 734 63 70, e lipica@siol.net) has most of the amenities, including an indoor swimming pool, sauna and tennis courts nearby. Singles with bathroom, TV and breakfast are €46 to €61, depending on the season, and doubles €72 to €93. But these prices are discounted heavily for stays of a week or more if you are taking a riding course.

The 80-room *Hotel Klub* (☎ 739 15 70, same fax and email as for Maestoso) is generally for those staying for longer periods. It has a sauna and fitness centre and is slightly closer to the stud farm. Rates are €37 to €48 for single rooms and €59 to €75 for doubles.

The Maestoso has a **snack bar** with a terrace cafe open from 8 am to 11 pm. The best (and most expensive) eatery in the complex is the *Lipica* wine cellar restaurant.

Entertainment

The *Casino Lipica* (☎ 739 11 11) at the Hotel Maestoso is open from 3 pm to 3 or 4 am Monday to Saturday (from 2 pm to 3 am Sunday).

Getting There & Around

Most people visit Lipica as a day trip from Divača or Sežana, both of which are on the rail line to Ljubljana. You can reach them on up to five buses a day during the school year, between two and three buses in summer and on holidays.

The Maestoso hotel has bicycles for rent for €2.5/7.5 per hour/day.

HRASTOVLJE
☎ 05 • postcode 6275 • pop 425

Hrastovlje lies near the source of the Rižana River, whose valley effectively forms the boundary between the Karst and the coast. From here, northward to the village of Črni Kal and on to Osp, a row of fortresses was built below the limestone plains during the Bronze Age, which the Illyrian tribe of Histrians later adapted to their needs. The valley and the surrounding areas would prove to be safe havens for later inhabitants during the Great Migrations and the Turkish invasions.

The Romanesque church in this tiny village in a valley between the Karst region and the Slovenian coast is the Istrian equivalent of St John the Baptist's Church in Bohinj. OK, so it's not on a lake. But it is small, surrounded by medieval walls with corner towers and covered inside with extraordinary 15th-century frescoes.

Church of the Holy Trinity

This church (Cerkev Sv Trojica), with a nave and two aisles, was built between the 12th and 14th centuries in the southern Romanesque style though the fortifications were added in 1581 in advance of the Ottomans. As you approach this structure of grey Karst stone at the south-eastern end of the village, just imagine the fear in the hearts of the men, women and children who scrambled to protect what they must have considered to be the most important thing in their lives.

The sombre exterior does not prepare you for what's inside; the complete interior of the church is festooned with **narrative frescoes** painted by Johannes de Castuo (John of Kastav near Rijeka) around 1490. The paintings are a *Biblia pauperum* – a 'Bible of the poor' – to help the illiterate understand the Old Testament stories, the Passion of Christ and the lives of the saints. It is a unique way to see and understand how our ancestors viewed their lives, joys, hopes and sufferings some five centuries ago. Spare the 20 minutes it takes to listen to the taped commentary that will guide you around the little church in English, German, Italian or Slovene. It's dull with a capital 'D', but there are a lot of things you'd miss otherwise.

Facing you as you enter the church is the main altar, carved in the 17th century, and the central apse with scenes from the Crucifixion on the ceiling and portraits of the Trinity and the Apostles. On the arch, Mary is being crowned Queen of Heaven. To the right of the central aisle are episodes from the **seven days of Creation**, to the left the

story of Adam and Eve, as well as the murder of Abel by Cain – all easy stories for an unschooled 15th-century peasant to comprehend.

On the ceilings of the north (left) and south (right) aisles are scenes from daily life (sowing, hunting, fishing, making wine) as well as the **calendar year** and its seasonal duties. **Christ's Passion** is depicted at the top of the southernmost wall, including his descent into hell, where devils are attacking him with blazing cannons.

Yes, the best bit has been saved for last. Below the Passion is what attracts most people to Hrastovlje and its little church – the famous **Dance of Death fresco** (also called the Danse Macabre) showing 11 skeletons leading the same number of people forward to a freshly dug grave, a pick and shovel at the ready. A 12th skeleton holds a list of the 'invited'. The line-up includes a child, a beggar, a soldier, a banker, a merchant, a monk, a bishop, a nun, a queen, a king and an emperor. Under the nun you can see graffiti left by a visitor in 1640.

Ghoulish and strange though the Dance of Death may appear to be at first, it carries a simple message – we are all equal in the eyes of God no matter how important we (or others) think we are in this mortal life. It was a radical concept, perhaps, for the late 15th century in a remote part of Europe, and it remains a sobering and thought-provoking one today.

Out in the courtyard, have a look around at the two corner towers and ancient walls, which are at least 1m thick. The strange cliffs of loose rock to the north make up the Kraški Rob – the very 'Edge of the Karst' – above the village of Črni Kal, marking the end of the stony limestone plateau and the start of a green valley leading to the sea. Could it be that this little church between two worlds was placed in this geographical limbo on purpose?

Entry to Holy Trinity Church costs 300/150 SIT for adults/students and children. It is usually open from morning to dusk every day but should you find it locked, get the key from house No 30 in the village. It's a five-minute walk from the church.

PRIMORSKA

Getting There & Away

Hrastovlje is 31km south-west of Divača off the main highway to the coast; Koper is 18km to the north-west. Any bus travelling this road in either direction will drop you off just west of Črni Kal, but it's still another 6km south to Hrastovlje. One of the three daily buses from Koper to Buzet in Croatia could get you closer, but without a car or bicycle (or a horse or bullock cart) the only sure way of making it to Hrastovlje is by train.

Unfortunately, the trains do not have a very extensive or flexible schedule. A train leaves Divača daily at 7.30 am, arriving at Hrastovlje station at 8.03 am; the church is about 1km to the north-west. The next train of any kind through this backwater is the 7.08 pm from Koper, which gets into Hrastovlje 16 minutes later. The train carries on to Divača, Postojna and Ljubljana.

If you're driving south to the coast on highway No 10, take the first left after Črni Kal, which is the road heading south for Buzet and Pula in Croatia, and follow the signs for Hrastovlje.

The Coast

Slovenia's very short coast (47km) on the Adriatic Sea is both an area of history and recreation. Three important towns full of Venetian Gothic architecture and art (Koper, Piran, Izola) will keep even the most indefatigable of sightseers busy, and there are beaches, boats for rent and rollicking discos in those towns as well as at Portorož and Ankaran.

But the coast is not everybody's cup of tea. It is very overbuilt, jammed from May to September and the water is not especially clean. Many Slovenes give it a miss in favour of the unspoiled beaches of Istria or Dalmatia, leaving it to German, Italian and Austrian tourists. If you want solitude, head for the hinterland to the south or east where 'Slovenian Istria' still goes about its daily life. Or spend an afternoon at the eerily tranquil salt pans of Sečovlje.

The Koper wine-producing area is known for its white Malvazija and Chardonnay and red Refošk. A number of cultural events take place during the Piran Musical Evenings and Primorska Summer Festival in Koper, Izola, Piran and Portorož in July and the first half of August.

Bear in mind that many of the region's hotels, camping grounds, tourist offices and restaurants close down during the off-season (lasting from November to March or as late as April).

KOPER

☎ 05 • postcode 6000 • pop 27,000

Koper is a workaday port city that hardly gives tourism a second thought. It is much less crowded and uppity than its ritzy cousin Piran, 17km down the coast, but despite the surrounding industry, container ports and high-rise buildings, Koper has managed to preserve its compact medieval centre. Its recreational area, the seaside resort of Ankaran, is to the north across Koper Bay.

History

Koper has been known by many names through its long and turbulent history. As an island separated from the mainland by a canal, it was called Aegida by ancient Greek sailors, Capris by the Romans (who found it being used to raise goats) and Justinopolis by the Byzantines. The Patriarchs of Aquileia, who took over the town in the 13th century and made it the base for their estates on the Istrian peninsula, renamed it Caput Histriae – 'Capital of Istria' – from which its Italian name Capodistria is derived. They fortified the town and erected some of Koper's most beautiful buildings, including its cathedral and palaces.

Koper's golden age, though, came during the 15th and 16th centuries under the domination of the Venetian Republic. Trade increased and Koper became the administrative and judicial centre for Istria as far as Buzet to the south-east and Novigrad on the coast. It also had a monopoly on salt, which Austria so desperately needed. But when Trieste, some 20km to the north-east, was proclaimed a free port in the early 18th century and the Habsburgs opened a railway line between Vienna and Trieste in 1857,

PRIMORSKA

Koper's fate was sealed. Many of the coastal people moved inland to raise grapes, olives and stone fruits.

Between the two world wars, Koper was administered by the Italians, who launched an aggressive program of Italianisation, closing bilingual schools and keeping close tabs on Slovenian intellectuals. After the defeat of Italy and Germany in WWII, the disputed area of the Adriatic coast – the so-called Free Territory of Trieste – was divided into two zones. Under the London Agreement of 1954, Zone B and its capital Koper went to Yugoslavia while Zone A, including Trieste, fell under Italian jurisdiction.

Up to 25,000 Italian-speaking Istrians fled to Trieste, but 3000 stayed on in Koper and other coastal settlements. Today Koper is the centre of the Italian ethnic community of Slovenia and Italian is widely spoken here.

Koper has developed rapidly since the 1950s. Not only is it Slovenia's sole port (and Austria's main shipping outlet) but also a business and industrial centre. It is the largest town by far on the coast.

Orientation

Koper's semicircular Old Town was an island until the early 19th century when it was joined to the mainland by a causeway and later by landfill. Today it's difficult to imagine it as a separate entity as you travel from the combined bus and train station just over 1km to the south-east at the end of Kolodvorska cesta.

The centre of the Old Town is Titov trg, a marvellous Gothic-Renaissance square with Venetian influences. The marina and tiny city beach are to the north-west.

Information

Tourist Offices Koper's tourist office (☎ 663 10 10, fax 663 10 11) is at Ukmarjev trg 7, opposite the marina. In summer it's open from 9 am to 7 pm Monday to Saturday, and till 1 pm Sunday; in winter the hours are 9 am to 2 pm and 5 to 7 pm Monday to Friday.

Money Banka Koper has a branch at Kidričeva ulica 14 near the regional museum. It

is open from 8.30 am till noon and from 3 to 5 pm weekdays, and on Saturday morning. There's a Nova Ljubljanska Banka at Pristaniška ulica 45, open from 8.30 am to noon and 3.30 to 6 pm weekdays only. There are also a couple of private exchange offices on Pristaniška ulica, including Maki at No 13 next to the Hertz office, and Ilirika, in the east wing of the large shopping complex and market across the street. Both are open from 7 am or 7.30 am to 7 pm weekdays and Saturday to 1 pm.

Post & Communications The main post office is next to the train and bus station. It is open from 7 am to 8 pm weekdays, to 7 pm on Saturday and from 8 am till noon Sunday. Much more convenient is the post office branch at Muzejski trg 3 near the Regional Museum. It is open from 7 am to 7 pm weekdays and till 1 pm Saturday.

Travel Agencies Kompas (☎ 627 23 46) opposite the outdoor market at Pristaniška ulica 17 is open from 8 am to 7.30 pm weekdays and to 1 pm on Saturday. Capris Time (☎ 631 15 55) has a counter inside the train station open from 8 am to 1 pm and 4 to 6 pm weekdays, and from 8 am to noon Saturday.

Bookshops If you're looking for maps, head for the Mladinska Knjiga bookshop, opposite the outdoor market on Pristaniška ulica. It's open from 7.30 am to 7 pm weekdays, and till 1 pm Saturday.

Consulates The Italian Consulate is at Belveder 2 opposite the bath house. It's open from 8.30 am to 1 pm weekdays.

Walking Tour

The easiest way to see almost everything of interest in Koper's Old Town is simply to walk from the marina on Ukmarjev trg east along Kidričeva ulica to Titov trg and then south down Čevljarska ulica, taking various detours along the way.

The first stop is **Carpacciov trg** behind the Taverna restaurant where the **Column of St Justin** commemorates Koper's contribution

PRIMORSKA

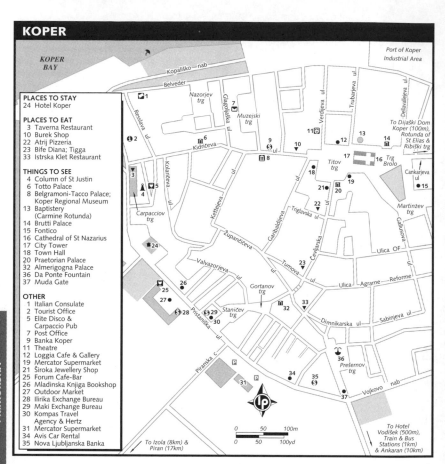

KOPER

PLACES TO STAY
24 Hotel Koper

PLACES TO EAT
3 Taverna Restaurant
10 Burek Shop
22 Atrij Pizzeria
23 Bife Diana; Tigga
33 Istrska Klet Restaurant

THINGS TO SEE
4 Column of St Justin
6 Totto Palace
8 Belgramoni-Tacco Palace;
  Koper Regional Museum
13 Baptistery
  (Carmine Rotunda)
14 Brutti Palace
15 Fontico
16 Cathedral of St Nazarius
17 City Tower
18 Town Hall
20 Praetorian Palace
32 Almerigogna Palace
36 Da Ponte Fountain
37 Muda Gate

OTHER
1 Italian Consulate
2 Tourist Office
5 Elite Disco &
  Carpaccio Pub
7 Post Office
9 Banka Koper
11 Theatre
12 Loggia Cafe & Gallery
19 Mercator Supermarket
21 Široka Jewellery Shop
25 Forum Cafe-Bar
26 Mladinska Knjiga Bookshop
27 Outdoor Market
28 Ilirika Exchange Bureau
29 Maki Exchange Bureau
30 Kompas Travel
  Agency & Hertz
31 Mercator Supermarket
34 Avis Car Rental
35 Nova Ljubljanska Banka

– a galley – to the Battle of Lepanto in which Turkey was defeated by the European powers in 1571. Nearby is a large Roman covered basin.

On the north side of Kidričeva ulica you'll pass several disued churches and, at No 20, the 16th-century **Totto Palace** with a relief of the winged lion of St Mark taken from Koper's medieval fortress. Opposite, at Kidričeva ulica 33, are some wonderful old **medieval town houses** with protruding upper storeys painted red, gold and green.

The **Koper Regional Museum** in the 16th-century Belgramoni-Tacco Palace, at Kidričeva ulica 19, displays old maps and photos of the port and coast, 16th- to 18th-century Italianate sculptures and paintings, and copies of medieval frescoes. And take a look at the wonderful bronze door knocker of Venus arising from a seashell. The museum is open from 9 am to 1 pm weekdays (and again from 6 to 8 pm in July and August), and till noon Saturday. Admission is 300/150 SIT for adults/children.

Titov trg, the centre of old Koper, is a beautiful square full of interesting buildings; mercifully, like much of the Old Town's core, it is closed to traffic. On the north side is the arcaded Venetian Gothic **Loggia** built in 1463. It now contains a coffee house and art gallery. To the south, directly opposite at No 3, is the white **Praetorian Palace**, a mixture of Venetian Gothic and Renaissance styles dating from the 15th century and now the symbol of Koper. The facade of the palace, once the residence of Koper's mayor who was appointed by the doge in Venice, is chock-a-block with medallions, reliefs and coats of arms of the rich and famous. The Praetorian Palace was once two separate buildings with the Loggia in the centre. When the latter was moved across the square to its current location, the two wings of the palace were joined and the battlements added later.

On the square's western side at No 4, the **town hall** occupies what was an armoury some four centuries ago. Opposite is the **Cathedral of St Nazarius** and its belfry, now called the **City Tower**. You can climb this 36m tower between 10 am and 1 pm and again between 4 and 7 pm daily.

The cathedral, partly Romanesque and Gothic but mostly dating from the 18th century in its present state, is the sixth church on this spot. It has a white classical interior with a feeling of space and light that belies the sombre exterior. The **carved stone sarcophagus** behind the main altar is that of the cathedral's (and town's) patron, a 6th-century bishop. Among the furnishings are choir stalls made from olive wood, an ornate 18th-century **bishop's throne** on the north side and **paintings by Vittore Carpaccio** (1465–1526), a native of Koper. The cathedral doors are open from 7 am till noon and from 3 to 7 pm daily.

Behind the cathedral to the north is a circular Romanesque **Baptistery** (also called the Carmine Rotunda) dating from the 12th century.

Trg Brolo, which links to Titov trg on its western side, is another square of fine old buildings, including the baroque **Brutti Palace** to the north, and on the eastern side, at No 4, the **Fontico**, a granary where the town's wheat was stored in the 14th century. **Ribiški trg**, a 10-minute walk to the northeast from here, is an old fishing quarter with narrow streets and houses dating back to the 14th century. To get there from Trg Brolo, walk east along Cankarjeva ulica and turn north on to Dijaška ulica. Along the way you'll pass the **Rotunda of St Elias**, a pre-Romanesque structure that could date back as far as the 9th century. Bosadraga ulica, the next street on the right, leads into Ribiški trg.

From Titov trg continue the tour by walking south along **Čevljarska ulica** (Shoemaker's Street). As you walk under the arch of the Praetorian Palace, have a look to the right. The little hole in the wall with the Italian inscriptions was the town's so-called lion's mouth, where anonymous denunciations of officials and others could be made.

Čevljarska ulica, a narrow pedestrian street, leads into Župančičeva ulica (Mayor's Street). Just below it, down the stairs in Gortanov trg at No 13 is the **Almerigogna Palace**, a painted Venetian Gothic palace and arguably the most beautiful building in Koper. It's now a pub.

The Italian family who erected the **fountain** in Prešernov trg in the 17th century was named Da Ponte; thus it is shaped like a bridge (*ponte* in Italian). At the southern end is the **Muda Gate**, erected in 1516 and the last of a dozen such entrances to remain standing. On both sides of the archway you'll see the city seal – the face of a youth in a sunburst.

Activities
Koper's tiny – and dirty – beach is on the north-west edge of the Old Town on Kopališko nabrežje. It has a small bath house, a grassy area for lying in the sun, a restaurant and a snackbar. It's open from 8 am to 8 pm daily in season; entry is 450/300 SIT for adults/children.

Places to Stay
Camping The closest camping grounds are at Ankaran, about 10km to the north by road, and at Izola, 8km to the west. See those later sections for details.

Private Rooms The tourist office and Kompas have private rooms available for 2000 to 2500 SIT, depending on the category and the season. Apartments for two cost from 6400 to 7335 SIT. There is a surcharge if you stay for fewer than three days. The vast majority of the rooms are in the new town beyond the train station but not all; the family at Kidričeva ulica 16 has great rooms for rent in an old town house.

Hostels Koper has one of Slovenia's six official hostels. *Dijaški Dom Koper* (☎ 627 32 52, Cankarjeva ulica 6), a modern five-storey building in the Old Town, about 150m east of Trg Brolo, rents beds in triple rooms at 2380 SIT per person, including breakfast, in July and August. The rest of the year only a handful of beds is available, but the price is only 1400 SIT without breakfast. An HI card will get you a 10% discount.

Hotels The only hotel in the Old Town is the recently renovated 65-room *Hotel Koper* (☎ 210 05 00, fax 210 05 94, [e] koper@ terme-catez.si, Pristaniška ulica 3). Singles with shower, TV and breakfast are 9200 to 11,100 SIT, depending on the season, and doubles 14,800 to 17,800 SIT.

The *Hotel Vodišek* (☎ 639 24 68, fax 639 36 68, Kolodvorska 2), halfway between the Old Town and the train station, is slightly more affordable at 8480/13,356/16,960 SIT for a single/double/triple with bathroom, TV, air-con and a buffet breakfast.

Places to Eat

For fried dough on the go, head for the *burek shop* (Kidričeva ulica 8), open daily from 7 am to 10 pm. A decent place for a cheap and fast meal is the little *Bife Diana* (Čevljarska ulica 36), with čevapčiči, hamburgers and so on. It's open to 10 pm daily. *Tigga*, next door, has sandwiches and kebabs for 250 to 350 SIT, and is open from 7 am to 8 pm daily except Sunday. A pizzeria called *Atrij* (Triglavska ulica 2) is open from 9 am (10 am Sunday) till 10 pm daily.

One of the most colourful places in Koper for a meal is the *Istrska Klet* (☎ 627 67 29, Župančičeva ulica 39) in an old palace. Filling set lunches go for 1000 SIT, and there's draught wine straight from the barrel. Istrska Klet is open from 6.30 am to 9 pm daily.

The *Taverna* (☎ 627 60 50, Pristaniška ulica 1), in a 15th-century salt warehouse almost opposite the marina, is one of Koper's more upmarket restaurants and serves some decent fish dishes, with set lunch menus at 850 and 1000 SIT.

There's an outdoor *market* (open from 7 am to 2 pm most days), on Pristaniška ulica. A block south on the same street is a *Mercator supermarket*, open from 7 am to 7 pm weekdays and till 1 pm Saturday. There's a smaller branch of *Mercator* on the east side of Titov trg, open the same hours but also 8 am to noon Sunday.

Entertainment

Koper's *theatre* (Gledališče Koper; ☎ 663 13 81, Verdijeva ulica 3), north of Titov trg, puts on plays, dance performances and concerts.

Koper often feels more Italian than Slovenian and at dusk, as in most cities and towns across the Adriatic, the *passaggiata* – a lot of strolling and strutting – begins. You can watch some of it while enjoying a *real* cappuccino from the lovely *Loggia Cafe* (Titov trg 1), open to 10 pm Monday to Saturday, but the outdoor *Forum* cafe-bar at the west side of the market on Pristaniška ulica facing a little park and the marina, is where you'll see most of the action.

The *Elite* (Carpacciov trg 6) is a high-class nightclub and disco, closed Sunday. The *Carpaccio Pub* next door is pleasant for a drink.

Shopping

Koper has some fine shops selling jewellery, textiles and folkcraft at the eastern end of Kidričeva ulica near Titov trg. Most shops close for siesta between about 1 and 4 pm (or even later). The Široka jewellery shop (open 9 am to 1 pm and 4 to 8 pm weekdays and from 8 am till noon Saturday) at Čevljarska ulica 4 has lovely Art Deco pieces in silver, onyx, amber, coral etc.

Getting There & Away

Bus Although train departures are limited, the bus service to and from Koper is excellent. There are departures almost every 20

PRIMORSKA

minutes on weekdays to Izola, Strunjan, Piran and Portorož and every 40 minutes at the weekend. The buses start at the train and bus station and stop at the market on Pristaniška ulica before continuing on to Izola. The information kiosk at the bus station is open from 6 am to 1 pm daily except Sunday.

About nine buses a day leave Koper for Ankaran and Lazaret and about six for Ljubljana via Divača and Postojna. Other destinations include: Branik (one or two buses a day), Celje (two), Ilirska Bistrica (four), Maribor (one, at 2.38 pm), Murska Sobota (two), Nova Gorica (three), Sežana (three) and Velenje (two).

Frequent service (up to 17 buses a day Monday to Saturday, but none on Sunday) to and from nearby Trieste makes Koper an easy entry/exit point for Italy. Buses run from 6 am to 7.30 pm weekdays (at 7.30 pm only on Saturday). The bus station in Trieste is immediately south-west of the train station in Piazza Libertà.

Koper also provides an excellent springboard for Istria. Destinations on the Croatian peninsula and their daily departures include: Buzet (three), Poreč (two to three), Pula (one or two), Rijeka (one, at 10.10 am) and Rovinj (one). There are also two buses a day to Zagreb (at 4.56 and 6.22 am) and one to Banja Luka (at 2.20 pm).

The Capris Time travel agency in the train station sells tickets for an express minibus service that runs between Koper and Ljubljana three times a week, continuing to Zagreb and Belgrade. It departs Koper on Tuesday, Friday and Saturday at 4.30 am, and the one-way fare to Ljubljana is 2000 SIT.

Train Koper is on a minor rail line linking it with Ljubljana (2¼ hours, 153km) via Postojna and Divača. There are three or four direct trains a day, and the one-way fare is 1220 SIT.

To get to Buzet and Pula in Croatia from Koper, you must change at Hrpelje-Kozina for one of two trains a day.

Car Hertz (☎ 627 41 34) has rental cars available from its office at Pristaniška ulica 15,

open from 7 am to 3 pm weekdays. Avis (☎ 630 13 50) is down the street at Pristaniška 45, open 8 am to 4 pm weekdays and till noon Saturday. Parking in much of the Old Town is restricted – or banned – between 6 am and 8 pm. Generally, you can only park in the pay car parks on Pristaniška ulica.

Getting Around
Local bus Nos 1, 2 and 3 go from the main bus and train station to the eastern edge of Cankarjeva ulica in the Old Town with a stop not far from Muda Gate.

To order a taxi in Koper ring ☎ 080-1141.

ANKARAN
☎ 05 • postcode 6280 • pop 2820

With Koper concerned primarily with container ships, the role of city playground has fallen to Ankaran (Ancarano in Italian), a seaside holiday village 10km by road to the north. The town lies on the southern side of the hilly Milje Peninsula which is shared between Slovenia and Italy. There's not much at Ankaran apart from a large tourist complex with a camping ground, hotels and a shopping centre. But it's a lush, very green place with a mild subtropical climate, and Italy is right around the corner. Just follow the main road north-west for 3.5km to the checkpoint at Lazaret (Lazzaretto). Trieste is directly across Muggia Bay (Miljski Zaliv) to the north.

Orientation
The 'town' is essentially a stretch of the road (Jadranska cesta) leading from the coastal highway to Italy and the scattered houses and vineyards above it. Buses stop in front of the shopping centre on Jadranska cesta. The Adria resort and camping ground are opposite.

Information
There's a tourist office (☎ 652 05 60) at the uphill end of the shopping centre at Regentova ulica 2, open from 9 am to 1 pm and 3 to 7 pm weekdays, and on Saturday mornings. Alternatively, get help from the reception desk at the entrance to the Adria Ankaran resort complex.

PRIMORSKA

Banka Koper has a branch in the shopping centre open from 8.30 am till noon and 3 to 5 pm weekdays and on Saturday morning. The post office is on the western side of the shopping centre at Regentova ulica 1. It is open from 8 am to 7 pm weekdays and to noon Saturday.

Activities

The Adria holiday village, which can accommodate up to 700 people at its hotel, cottages, bungalows and camping ground, has a small pebble beach below a cement promenade, two large swimming pools (one faces south-east to the Istrabenz refinery; 1200 SIT) and sporting facilities, including tennis courts, minigolf, table tennis, basketball court and a fitness centre.

Ankaran is the start (or finish) of the Slovenian Alpine Trail that goes all the way to Maribor (see Hiking & Mountain Walking in the special section 'The Great Outdoors'). One of the first stops on the trail is **Mt Slavnik** (1028m), which is about 8km north-east of Hrastovlje. There's accommodation at the *Tumova Koča na Slavniku* mountain hut *(mobile ☎ 041-428 280)* near the summit.

Places to Stay

Camp Adria Ankaran (☎ 652 83 23) extends over an area of 12 hectares on the eastern side of the Adria Ankaran resort and down to the sea. The price per person ranges from 1100 to 1600 SIT depending on the season, and guests get to use all the facilities at the resort. Adria Camping is open from May to September.

The *Adria Ankaran resort complex* *(☎ 652 84 44, fax 652 83 21, ⓔ adria.hoteli@ siol.net)* contains a half-dozen different types of accommodation, ranging from cottages with balconies to self-contained seaside bungalows. The cheapest place to stay at the resort just happens to be the most interesting. It's a two-storey hotel dead in the centre called the *Adria Convent*. It was once a Benedictine monastery and later became the summer residence of the aristocratic Madonuzza family from Koper. The price for a single is 3800 to 6300 SIT for a room with breakfast and shower, and 5600 to 9600 SIT for a double; the differential depends on the season and the direction in which your room faces. The five-person bungalows cost from 11,000 to 16,500 SIT per night. The Convent is open year-round; most of the other accommodation at the resort is available from May to September only. The reception desk here caters for all the accommodation in the resort except for the camping ground.

The flashy 14-room *Hotel Andor (☎ 652 60 55, fax 652 60 58, Jadranska cesta 86a)*, 800m west of the shopping centre and opposite the large (and quite famous) orthopaedic hospital, charges from 6500 to 8300 SIT for a single, depending on the season. Doubles cost 10,600 to 13,000 SIT, and four-person apartments start at 20,000 SIT and jump to 25,000 SIT in July and August. All rooms have private bath, air conditioning, direct-dial telephones and satellite television. There's a fitness centre, sauna, casino and night club here as well.

Places to Eat

The *Biffe Adria (Regentova ulica 2)* next to the tourist office has light meals and snacks, but the emphasis is on liquid refreshment. The *Mercator supermarket* behind the post office is open from 8 am to 7 pm weekdays, to 1 pm Saturday and to 11 am Sunday.

Have you ever eaten a pizza in church? The desanctified monastery chapel at the Adria Convent hotel is now the *Pizzeria Convent*, where decent pizzas cost around 1000 SIT.

The *Gostilna-Trattoria Ankaran (Jadranska cesta 66)*, about 500m west of the Adria Ankaran resort, is one of the few independent eateries on the peninsula and popular with local people. It's open from 9 am to 11 pm daily.

Entertainment

There are a couple of popular night spots at the Adria Ankaran resort including the *Disco Club* near the entrance, with its own huge car park, open from 10 pm, and the *Taverna* restaurant with music near the seafront looking out over the Adriatic.

The *Korta* and *Luna* bars in the shopping-centre square are also good places for a drink. The *Casino Andor*, next door to the Hotel Andor, is open 24 hours a day.

Getting There & Away

Buses make the run from the centre of Ankaran to the Italian border crossing at Lazaret between eight and 11 times a day. Up to nine buses go to Koper. If you're heading for Trieste from Ankaran you'll have to change buses just over the border. All in all, it's probably easier to catch a direct bus from Koper.

IZOLA

☎ 05 • postcode 6310 • pop 10,300

Izola, a somewhat scruffy fishing port 7km south-west of Koper, is the poor relation among the historical towns on the Slovenian coast, but it wasn't always that way. The Romans built a port called Haliaetum at Simon's Bay (Simonov Zaliv) south-west of the Old Town, and they say you can still see parts of the original landing when the tide is very low.

History

The vicissitudes of Izola in the Middle Ages are closely tied to those of Koper and, to a lesser degree, Piran. Struggle among various groups (and a brief period of independence in the 13th century) led to the supremacy of Venice. At first, Izola – at that time an island (*isola* is Italian for 'island') – flourished, particularly in the trading of olives, fish and its celebrated wine, which was distributed as far away as Germany. But a devastating plague in the 16th century and the ascendancy of Trieste as the premier port in the northern Adriatic destroyed the town's economic base. During the period of the Illyrian Provinces in the early 19th century, the French pulled down the town walls and used them to fill the channel separating the island from the mainland. Many of the medieval churches and buildings were also razed.

After several fish canneries were opened at Izola in the 20th century, the town began to industrialise. It remains the country's foremost fishing port, but its glory days seem a million years ago as you walk through the narrow streets whose crumbling houses look as if they could topple over in the slightest of winds. Still, Izola has its charms along with some of the best seafood in Slovenia. It's definitely worth a visit as long as you don't mind a slight fishy smell and some very fat cats underfoot.

Orientation

Almost everything of a practical nature is centred on Trg Republike. Buses stop in front of the Slavnik Koper transport office at Cankarjev drevored 2 on the square's south-eastern edge.

To reach the Old Town and its main square, Veliki trg, which faces a circular inner harbour, walk north along the waterfront promenade called Sončno nabrežje.

Information

The tourist office (☎ 640 10 50) at Sončno nabrežje 4 is open from 8 am to 7 pm weekdays and till noon Saturday.

Banka Koper has a branch at Drevored 1 Maja 5 open from 8.30 am to noon and from 3 to 5 pm weekdays and till noon Saturday. A Banka at Pittonijeva ulica 1, the side street next to the bus office, is open from 8 am to noon and 4 to 6 pm weekdays and from 9 to noon Saturday.

The post office, open from 7.30 am to 7 pm weekdays, to noon Saturday, is opposite Slavnik Koper at Cankarjev drevored 1.

Things to See & Do

Izola isn't overly endowed with important historical sights; Napoleon's finest took care of that. But there are one or two things worth a brief look, such as the 16th-century **Church of Saint Maurus** and its detached bell tower on the hill above the town, the **Municipal Palace** on Veliki trg and the renovated Venetian Gothic **Manzoli House** (1470), owned by a chronicler of Istria in the 16th century, on Manzoli trg near the waterfront.

Izola's most beautiful building, though, is the rococo **Besenghi degli Ughi Palace** on the corner of Gregorčičeva ulica and Bruna ulica below the church. Built between 1775 and 1781, the mansion has windows and

PRIMORSKA

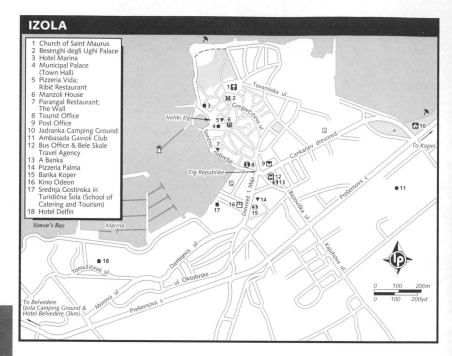

IZOLA

1 Church of Saint Maurus
2 Besenghi degli Ughi Palace
3 Hotel Marina
4 Municipal Palace (Town Hall)
5 Pizzeria Vida; Ribič Restaurant
6 Manzoli House
7 Parangal Restaurant; The Wall
8 Tourist Office
9 Post Office
10 Jadranka Camping Ground
11 Ambasada Gavioli Club
12 Bus Office & Bele Skale Travel Agency
13 A Banka
14 Pizzeria Palma
15 Banka Koper
16 Kino Odeon
17 Srednja Gostinska in Turistična Šola (School of Catering and Tourism)
18 Hotel Delfin

balconies adorned with stuccos and wonderful wrought-iron grilles painted light blue. Inside, a stairway decorated with illusionist paintings leads to a salon with a curious wooden balcony running just below the ceiling. The palace is now a music school and headquarters of the local Italian Society.

There are pebbly **beaches** to the north and south-east of the Old Town, but the best one is at Simon's Bay about 1.5km to the south-west. It has a grassy area for sunbathing and a water slide.

The **Prince of Venice** is a 40m high-speed catamaran that runs day trips between Izola and Venice. It departs Izola at 8 am and arrives in Venice at 10.30 am; the return journey departs at 5.30 pm and arrives back at Izola at 8 pm. There are sailings on Saturday from March to November; on Friday, Saturday and Sunday from April to October; and on Tuesday, Friday, Saturday and Sunday from late June to mid-September. A return ticket costs 8500 to 12,500 SIT

depending on season, and includes a guided tour of Venice. Tickets can be purchased at the Kompas travel agency in Portorož and various other agencies along the coast.

Places to Stay

Camping There are two camping grounds within easy reach of Izola. *Jadranka* (☎ 640 23 00, Polje cesta 8), a small site on the waterfront 1km east of the Old Town, is open from May to October. But it's right off the noisy coastal road and fills up quickly in summer. The per-person charge is 650 to 1000 SIT, depending on the month.

Belvedere Izola (☎ 660 51 00), on a bluff 3km west of Izola with wonderful views of the town and the Adriatic, is larger than Jadranka, covering an area of three hectares and accommodating 700 happy campers among the trees. It is open from May to October and costs from 7500 to 1300 SIT. The holiday village surrounding the camp has a large swimming pool.

Private Rooms The tourist office can arrange private rooms and apartments throughout the year, but the biggest choice is available in summer. Single rooms are 2300 to 3000 SIT, depending on the category and the season, while doubles are 2900 to 5500 SIT. Apartments for two start at 6500 SIT. Breakfast (when available) is usually 900 SIT extra, and you must pay a surcharge of 50% if your stay is fewer than three days.

Hotels Izola's cheapest hotel accommodation is in the four-storey *Srednja Gostinska in Turistična Šola (School of Catering and Tourism;* ☎ *641 71 59, fax 641 54 95, Prekomorskih Brigad ulica 7)* overlooking the marina. The catch is that its 174 beds are only available from mid-June to August; the rest of the year it serves as a dormitory for the school's students. Singles/doubles with breakfast and communal shower are 3650/5960 SIT.

The most central place in town is the 45-room *Hotel Marina (*☎ *660 41 00, fax 660 44 99, Veliki trg 11).* Singles start at 6800 SIT in the low season, rising to 10,500 SIT in July and August. Doubles are 8800 to 14,000 SIT.

If you don't mind being a bit out of the centre but still near the water, the *Hotel Delfin (*☎ *660 74 00, fax 660 74 20, Tomažičeva ulica 10),* beside the new marina complex, may be for you. It's a pleasant enough place on a hill about 1km south-west of Trg Republike and has its own pool. But it's big, with well over 100 rooms, caters largely to tour groups and is not cheap. Prices range from 6600 to 8350 SIT for a single with bathroom and breakfast, and from 10,200 to 17,700 SIT for a double.

The *Hotel Belvedere (*☎ *660 51 00),* beside the Belvedere camping ground 3km west of town, has singles with bath and breakfast from 6600 to 10,500 SIT and doubles from 9200 to 14,000 SIT. In the off season (October to May) there are two/three-person apartments available for 6400/7500 SIT a night (in summer these have to be booked for at least a week).

Places to Eat
Pizzeria Palma (Drevored 1 Maja 3) next to the Banka Koper has decent pizza but *Pizzeria Vida (Alietova ulica 3),* with garden seating out the back, is a better bet. Pizzas and pasta dishes here cost around 700 to 950 SIT.

Why not skip a meal and have a blow-out at one of Izola's fish restaurants? There is a large selection but not all are reasonably priced or even very good. Stick with the local favourites: *Parangal (*☎ *641 74 40, Sončno nabrežje 20)* just up from the tourist office or *Ribič (*☎ *641 83 13, Veliki trg 3),* both of which are open to about 11 pm daily. A lunch of deep-fried prawn tails at the Parangal will cost no more than 1500 SIT including a drink.

But do be careful when you order (especially at Ribič) and ask the exact price of the fish. As seafood is sold by decagram (abbreviated as *dag* on most menus), you may end up eating (and paying) a lot more than you expected. For a list of fish dishes see the Language chapter. Be sure to have a glass or two of Malvazija, the pale yellow local white that is light and reasonably dry.

Entertainment
The Wall pub, next to the Parangal Restaurant, is a lively spot for a drink. It's open from 7 am to 11 pm daily except Sunday, and also serves fast-food snacks. If you fancy watching a film, head for the *Kino Odeon* on the corner of Drevored 1 Maja and Prekomorskih Brigad ulica.

The top rave centre on the coast is Izola's *Ambasada Gavioli,* which features some of the top DJs and bands in the country. It's in the industrial area south-west of the port on Industrijska cesta and opens from midnight on Saturday night to 9 am Sunday only. Such talent doesn't come cheap, though, and you'll pay 2500 SIT to get in, including the first drink. For information on coming events call ☎ 641 82 12 or check the club's Web site at www.ambasada-gavioli.com.

Getting There & Away
Buses leave for Koper and for Strunjan, Piran and Portorož every 20 minutes during the week and every 40 minutes on Saturday

and Sunday. Other destinations from Izola (via Koper) include: Celje (two buses a day), Ljubljana (up to 12), Maribor (one), Murska Sobota (one) and Nova Gorica (two).

International routes include eight buses a day (weekdays only) to Trieste in Italy and two early morning departures to Pula and Zagreb in Croatia.

Like most of the towns on the coast, parking is severely restricted in Izola and you'll have to pay about 120 SIT per hour for the privilege.

Getting Around

From June to August a minibus does a continuous loop from the Belvedere Izola holiday village west of the Old Town to Simon's Bay, Izola Marina, Trg Republike and the Jadranka camping ground and back.

The Bele Skale travel agency (☎ 641 82 00) near the bus office at Cankarjev drevored 2 rents bicycles for 1000 SIT per day. It is open from 6 am to 7 pm weekdays and from 6.30 am till noon Saturday.

AROUND IZOLA
Strunjan
☎ 05

For centuries, the people who lived at Strunjan, a peninsula halfway between Izola and Piran, were engaged in making salt, and you'll see the disused pans spread out before you as you descend along the main road from the Belvedere tourist complex. Today the area, protected as a landscape park, attracts large numbers of waterfowl.

Though there has been much development around Strunjan Bay to the southwest, much of the peninsula is remarkably unspoiled. It is bounded by a high cliff – **Cape Ronek** (Rtič Ronek) – at its northernmost point and there are plans to turn the area into a nature reserve. The 16th-century **Church of St Mary** nearby is a place of pilgrimage on 15 August.

The **Strunjan Health Resort** (Zdravilišče Strunjan; ☎ 676 41 00, fax 678 20 36) has all types of accommodation on offer, but the nearby **Hotel Salinera Bungalows** (☎ 676 31 00, fax 676 32 08, ℮ salinera@ hoteli-piran.si) are cheaper – a bungalow

for two starts at 5400 SIT during the low season and rises to 10,400 SIT in summer. Along with a beach, the resort has an indoor pool filled with heated sea water as well as tennis courts and other sport facilities. Much use is made of the salty mud found nearby for beauty and therapeutic purposes. The **Strunjan camping ground** (☎ 672 20 76), which is open all year, has space for 350 campers. It charges 1000 to 1200 SIT per person, 450 SIT per car and 450 SIT for a caravan.

Frequent bus services link Strunjan with Izola, Koper, Piran and Portorož; see those sections for details.

PIRAN
☎ 05 • postcode 6330 • pop 4800

Picturesque Piran (Pirano in Italian) – everyone's favourite town on the Slovenian coast – sits on the tip of a narrow peninsula, the westernmost point of Slovenian Istria. Strunjan Bay is to the north; Piran Bay and Portorož, Slovenia's largest beach resort, lie to the south.

Piran's Old Town is a gem of Venetian Gothic architecture and full of narrow streets, but it can be mobbed at the height of summer. Some people might find the best thing to do at that time of year is to get out of the town, but others enjoy the buzz and bustle of the crowds.

History

Piran has been settled since ancient times, and it is thought that the town's name comes from the Greek word for fire (pyr). In those days, fires were lit at Punta, the very tip of the peninsula, to guide ships to the port at Aegida (now Koper). The Romans established a settlement here called Piranum after their victory over the Illyrians and Celts. They, in turn, were followed by the early Slavs, the Byzantines, the Franks and the Patriarchs of Aquileia.

Venetian rule began in the late 13th century and lasted in one form or another for more than 500 years. Unlike Koper and Izola, whose citizens rose up against the Venetians time and time again, Piran threw its full support behind Venice in its struggles with

Aquileia and Genoa. (The fact that Venice was Piran's biggest customer for the salt it produced was certainly an incentive.) The Venetian period was the town's most fruitful, and many of its most beautiful buildings and its fortifications were erected then.

Economic stagnation under Austrian and, particularly, Italian rule from the early 19th century until after WWII meant Piran was able to preserve – at a price to the affluence of its citizens – its medieval character. Today it is one of the best preserved historical towns anywhere on the Adriatic and is entirely protected as a cultural monument.

Orientation

Tartinijev trg, north of Piran Harbour and the small marina, is the centre of the Old Town today but in the Middle Ages the focal point was Trg 1 Maja (also written Prvomajski trg) in what is the oldest part of the Old Town. The bus station is along the waterfront, about 400m to the south of Tartinijev trg at Dantejeva ulica 6. There is no left-luggage office here.

Information

Tourist Offices Piran's helpful new tourist office (☎ 673 02 20, fax 673 02 21, ℮ info .piran@siol.net) is on the main square at Tartinijev trg 2. It is open from 9 am to 1.30 pm and 3 to 9.30 pm daily in July and August; the rest of the year the hours are 9 am to 4 pm (10 am to 2 pm Sunday), closed Thursday.

Money Banka Koper at Tartinijev trg 12 changes travellers cheques and cash from 8.30 am till noon and 3 to 5 pm weekdays and on Saturday morning.

Post & Communications The post office at Cankarjevo nabrežje 5 is open from 8 am to 7 pm weekdays and till noon Saturday (till 8 pm weekdays and 5 pm Saturday in July and August).

Cyber Point 1 is a student-run Internet cafe on the top floor of the Študentek building at Župančičeva ulica 14. It's open from 1 to 9 pm weekdays, and from 3 to 9 pm weekends; Internet access costs 800 SIT an hour.

You can find English-language newspapers in the newsagent beside the Hotel Tartini on Tartinijev trg.

Travel Agencies The helpful and knowledgeable staff at the Maona travel agency (☎ 673 12 90) at Cankarjevo nabrežje 7 can organise private rooms, an endless string of activities and boat cruises (see the Cruises section). From April to October, it's open from 9 am to 8 pm weekdays, from 10 am to 1 pm and 5 to 8 pm Saturday, and from 10 am to 1 pm Sunday. In winter, the opening hours are 9 am to 6 pm daily except Sunday.

Sergej Mašera Maritime Museum

This museum (Morski Muzej Sergej Mašera) in a lovely 17th-century palace on the waterfront at Cankarjevo nabrežje 3 is named in honour of a Slovenian naval commander whose ship was blown up off the Croatian coast in WWI.

The museum's excellent exhibits, labelled in Slovene and Italian only, focus on the three 'Ss' that have been so important to Piran's development over the centuries: the sea, sailing and salt-making. The salt pans at Sečovlje, south-east of Portorož, get most of the attention downstairs. There are some excellent old photographs showing salt workers going about their duties in coolie-like straw hats, as well as a wind-powered salt pump and little wooden weights in the form of circles and diamonds that were used to weigh salt under the Venetian Republic.

The **antique model ships** upstairs are very fine (especially the 17th-century galleon and 18th-century corvette); other rooms are filled with old figureheads and weapons, including some very lethal-looking blunderbusses. The folk paintings are **votives** that were placed by sailors on the altar of the pilgrimage church at Strunjan for protection against shipwreck.

The palace, with its lovely moulded ceilings, parquet floors and marble staircase, is worth a visit in itself. The museum is open from 9 am till noon and from 3 to 6 pm every day, except Monday, from April to June and in September and October. In July

PIRAN

GULF OF TRIESTE

Bathing Area

Prešernovo nabrežje

Presernovo nabrežje

Vegova

Bonifacijeva ul

Adamičeva ul

Gregorčičeva ul

Židovski trg

Trg 1 Maja

Verdijeva ul

Kosovelova ul

Obzidna ul

Tomažičev trg

Tartinijev trg

Tomažičeva ul

Steljkova ul

Bathing Area

Kidričevo nabrežje

Marina

PIRAN BAY

Piran Harbour

Kajuhova ul

Rozmanova ul

UL Svobode

Cankarjevo nabrežje

Bidovčeva ul

Gortanova ul

Town Walls

Customs Wharf

Trg Bratsva

Župančičeva ul

Tomšičeva

Grudnova ul

Dantejeva ul

To Car Park (200m) & Portorož (5km)

0   50   100m
0   50   100yd

Trail to Beaches, Fiesa, Hotel Fiesa & Camping Jezero Fiesa (700m)

THINGS TO SEE
1 Punta Lighthouse
2 Church of St Clement
5 Old Pharmacy
6 Cistern
10 Dolphin Gate
12 Church of St George
13 Bell Tower
14 Baptistery
15 Church of St Francis & Monastery
16 Our Lady of the Snows Church
19 Venetian House
20 Tartini Memorial Room; Intermezzo Cafe
22 Church of St Peter
23 Tartini Memorial
24 Town Hall
26 Court House
30 Aquarium
33 Sergej Mašera Maritime Museum

OTHER
11 Market
17 Pri Benečanki Bar
25 Tourist Office
27 Bus Stop
28 Banka Koper
32 Tartini Theatre; Teater Cafe-Bar
34 Marina Boat Tours
35 Post Office
36 Maona Travel Agency
39 Cyber Point 1
40 Jestvina Supermarket
42 Customs Office
43 Bus Station

PLACES TO STAY
4 Penzion Val
29 Hotel Tartini
31 Hotel Piran

PLACES TO EAT
3 Punta & Flora Pizzerias
7 Tri Vdove Restaurant
8 Pavel & Pavel 2 Restaurants
9 Delfin Restaurant
18 Galerija Cafe
21 Gostilna Mario
37 Neptun Restaurant
38 Gostišče Pri Obzidju
41 Surf Bar Restaurant

PRIMORSKA

and August the afternoon hours are from 6 to 9 pm. The admission charge is 400/300 SIT for adults/children.

Tartinijev Trg

The statue of the nattily dressed gentleman in the centre of this oval-shaped, marble-paved square, which was the inner harbour until a landfill in 1864, represents local composer and violinist Giuseppe Tartini (1692–1770). To the east and opposite the **Church of St Peter** (1818), Tartini's birthplace at No 7 contains the **Tartini Memorial Room** on the 1st floor, open in summer only

from 8 am till noon and 4 to 7 pm weekdays and from 8 am till noon Saturday; entry costs 250 SIT.

The red **Venetian House** (Beneške Hiša), a lovely Venetian Gothic structure from the 15th century with tracery windows and a balcony, is at No 4. There is a story attached to the stone relief of the lion with a ribbon in its mouth and the inscription *Lassa pur dir* above it. A wealthy merchant from Venice fell in love with a beautiful local girl. But she soon became the butt of the local gossips. So to shut them up and keep his lover happy, the merchant built her this little red palace complete with a reminder for loose-lipped neighbours: 'Let them talk'.

The classical 19th-century **town hall** and the **court house** with two 17th-century doors are to the west. The **aquarium**, less than 100m west along the harbour at Tomažičeva ulica 4, may be small, but there's a tremendous variety of sealife packed into its two dozen tanks. It's open from 10 am to noon and 2 to 7 pm daily and costs 350/250 SIT.

The two 15th-century **flagpoles** at the entrance to the square bear Latin inscriptions praising Piran as well as the town's coat of arms, and reliefs of St George, the patron, to the left, and St Mark with the lion symbol, on the right.

Church of St George & Around

This Renaissance and baroque church (Cerkev Sv Jurji), Piran's most eye-catching structure, stands on a ridge north of Tartinijev trg above the sea. To the east runs a 200m stretch of the 15th-century **town walls**. Climb them for superb views of Piran and the Adriatic. The walls once ran from the sea all the way to the harbour and seven crenellated towers remain pretty much intact.

The church was founded in 1344 and was rebuilt in baroque style in 1637. It's wonderfully decorated with paintings, a magnificent altar and a statue of St George slaying the dragon, with a woman curiously holding the monster by a lead.

The freestanding **bell tower** (1609) was modelled on the campanile of San Marco in Venice and can be climbed daily for excellent views of the town and harbour. Next to it, the octagonal 17th-century **Baptistery** contains altars, paintings and a Roman sarcophagus from the 2nd century later used as a baptismal font.

On your way up to the church from Tartinijev trg, have a quick look inside **Our Lady of the Snows Church** (Sveta Marija Snežna). It contains a wonderful 15th-century painting of the Crucifixion on the arch before the presbytery.

The large complex opposite is the former **Franciscan monastery** with a wonderful cloister and the **Church of St Francis**, built originally in the early 14th century but enlarged and renovated over the centuries. Inside is a giant clam shell for donations.

Trg 1 Maja

This was the centre of Piran until the Middle Ages and the surrounding streets are a maze of pastel-coloured 'overhanging' houses, vaulted passages and arcaded courtyards. The square is surrounded by interesting baroque buildings including the former town **pharmacy** on the north side (now a restaurant). In the centre of the square is a large **cistern** that was built in the late 18th century to store fresh water; rainwater from the surrounding roofs flowed into it through the fish borne by the stone cherubs in each corner.

If you're going to Tartinijev trg, walk along Obzidna ulica, one of Piran's oldest streets, which passes under the 15th-century **Dolphin Gate** (Dolfinova Vrata). **Židovski trg**, the centre of Jewish life in Piran in the Middle Ages, is about 200m to the northwest of here.

Beaches

Piran has several 'beaches' – rocky areas along Prešernovo nabrežje – where you might dare to get your feet wet. They are a little better on the north side near Punta, the 'point' with a lighthouse and an old church, but you're better off to keep walking eastward for just under 1km to **Fiesa**. Watch your step, however, as you walk under the bluffs, especially at night; the path can be slippery. There are a number of nudist swimming areas between Piran and Fiesa and Fiesa and Strunjan.

The beach at Fiesa is one of the cleanest on the Slovenian coast, essentially because boating is very restricted here. It is terribly small, though, and is positively jammed with bathers in summer. From here you can see Strunjan and on a really clear day the Miramare Castle in Trieste and even Grado in Italy. Kayaks and canoes are available by the hour on the beach.

Cruises

If you would like a quick tour of Piran Harbour (1000 SIT), board the taxi boat *Marina* (mobile ☎ 041-676 359) at the small pier on

PRIMORSKA

Cankarjevo nabrežje just south of the Maritime Museum. It sails daily in summer.

Maona (see Travel Agencies earlier) and several other travel agencies in Piran and Portorož can book you on any number of longer cruises – from a loop that takes in the towns along the coast to day-long excursions to Trieste, Brioni National Park in Croatia, or Venice.

The chunky catamaran *Big Red* (mobile ☎ 041-639 178) sails back and forth along the Slovenian coast between Portorož and Ankaran (1½ hours), stopping at Portorož's Bernardin holiday complex, Piran, Izola and Koper, making from one to four round trips a day depending on season. A return ticket from Piran to Portorož costs 400 SIT, to Koper 1000 SIT.

From late May to September, on Wednesday, Friday and Sunday the large, sleek *Marconi* (☎ 673 12 90) cruises down the Istrian coast of Croatia as far as the Brioni Islands and the national park there (9500 SIT return, or 12,500 SIT including lunch; 2¼ hours), with a stop at Rovinj (5000 SIT return; 1¼ hours). The boat leaves at 10 am and returns to Piran at 6.35 pm, except in September when it departs and returns 20 minutes earlier. At 8.35 pm on the same days, the *Marconi* glides between Piran and Trieste (35 minutes), returning the following morning; the journey costs 2500 SIT one way.

For day trips to Venice, see Things to See & Do in the Izola section earlier in this chapter.

Special Events
Some of the events in the Piran Musical Evenings/Primorska Summer Festival in July and the first half of August take place on Friday in the vaulted cloister *(križni hodnik)* of the former Franciscan monastery.

Places to Stay
Camping The closest camping ground is *Camping Jezero Fiesa* (☎ 674 62 30) at Fiesa, 4km by road from Piran (but less than 1km if you follow the coastal trail east of the Church of St George). It's in a quiet valley by two small, protected ponds and close to the beach, but it gets very crowded in summer. There's a small supermarket here open from 7 am to 7 pm daily in summer. The camp is open from June to September.

Private Rooms The Turist Biro (open from 9 am to 1 pm and 4 to 8 pm daily in summer) in the Hotel Piran and the Maona travel agency can arrange private rooms and apartments throughout the year, but the biggest choice is available in summer. Single rooms cost from 2300 to 3600 SIT, depending on the category and the season, while doubles are 3300 to 5500 SIT. Apartments for two/four start at 6000/10,000 SIT. You usually have to pay a surcharge of 50% if your stay is fewer than three days.

Pensions One of the cheapest places to stay in Piran – and very central – is the hostel-like *Penzion Val* (☎ 673 25 55, fax 673 25 56, Gregorčičeva ulica 38) on the corner of Vegova ulica. Open from late April to October, it has about two dozen rooms with shared shower for 3000 SIT per person including breakfast.

Hotels Piran has only two central hotels. The cheaper of the two, the *Hotel Piran* (☎ 673 24 64, fax 673 24 72, ⓔ info@ hoteli-piran.si, Stjenkova ulica 1), has about 80 rooms and 10 apartments, many of them facing the sea. Singles/doubles with breakfast and shower start at 4500/5800 SIT in the lowest season but jump to 8500/11,000 SIT in July and August.

The attractive, 42-room *Hotel Tartini* (☎ 671 10 00, fax 671 16 01, ⓔ info@ hotel-tartini-piran.com, Tartinijev trg 15) has singles/doubles with air-con and TV for 12,500/20,000 SIT in the high season, but only 7500/12,000 SIT in the lowest season (October to December).

Though not in Piran itself, one of the nicest places to stay in the area is the *Hotel Fiesa* (☎ 674 68 97, fax 674 68 96), a 22-room hotel overlooking the sea near the Jezero Fiesa camping ground. This pleasant four-storey hotel charges 4000/7180 SIT for singles/doubles in the low season, rising to 5200/10,400 SIT in July and August. The hotel's restaurant is excellent.

Places to Eat

Have a pizza at **Punta** or **Flora** east of the Punta lighthouse along Prešernovo nabrežje and enjoy the uninterrupted views of the sea. There are also several pubs in the area.

The **Surf Bar** restaurant (*Grudnova ulica 1*), on a small street north-east of the bus station, is a good place for a meal or drink. It has a 'photo-album menu' with some 60 dishes and lots of pizzas; the staff are multilingual. It's open from 10 am to 11 pm daily.

Gostilna Mario (*Kajuhova ulica 6*) is a pleasant little restaurant with an outside terrace up the steps from St Peter's Church. It specialises in fish dishes and is open until 11 pm daily except Wednesday. The set lunch is 1100 SIT, and dinner will cost about 3000 SIT a head.

Piran has a heap of seafood restaurants along Prešernovo nabrežje but most, including **Pavel**, **Pavel 2** and **Tri Vdove**, are fairly pricey; expect to pay about 6000 SIT for a meal for two, with drinks. Instead, try the local favourites **Delfin** (*Kosovelova ulica 4*) near Trg 1 Maja, or the more expensive **Neptun** (*Županičeva ulica 7*). Both are open from 11 am to 11 pm daily.

Gostišče Pri Obzidju (☎ 673 31 11, *Ulica IX Korpusa 29*) is a bit of a hike uphill from Tartinijev trg, but it's worth it for the traditional Istrian fish and meat dishes and a lovely setting beneath the old town walls. It's open from 9 am to 11 pm daily, and there's free parking across the road.

Two decent cafes to check are the **Galerija** near the Venetian House on Tartinjev trg and the clubby, Italian **Intermezzo** in the Tartini House (enter from Kajuhova ulica 12). The latter is open from 9 am till noon and 6 to 9 pm Tuesday to Sunday.

There's an outdoor **market** in the small square behind the town hall. The **Jestvina supermarket** opposite Trg Bratsva 8 is open from 7 am to 8 pm weekdays, till 1 pm Saturday and till 11 am Sunday.

Entertainment

The newly restored **Tartini Theatre** (*Gledališče Tartini;* ☎ 673 44 78) on Kidričevo nabrežje hosts a program of classical concerts throughout the year.

The **Pri Benečanki** bar (*Ulica IX Korpusa 9*), open 8 am to 10 pm, is a popular meeting place, but the **Teater** cafe-bar, next to the Tartini Theatre is probably the liveliest spot in town, with a good people-watching terrace overlooking the promenade.

Getting There & Away

Bus Buses head for Portorož and for Strunjan, Izola and Koper about every 20 minutes in season and every 40 minutes at the weekend. Other destinations that can be reached from Piran include: Beli Križ near Fiesa (up to seven a day), Celje (two), Ljubljana via Postojna (six to 10 a day), Maribor and Murska Sobota (one, at 2.05 pm), Nova Gorica (two, at 2.20 and 5.35 pm) and Sečovlje via Seča (10).

About six buses go to Trieste in Italy on weekdays, and there are two daily departures for the Croatian capital of Zagreb, at 4.25 and 5.49 am. One bus a day heads south for Croatian Istria, leaving at 4.25 pm, stopping at the coastal towns of Umag, Poreč and Rovinj.

Car Traffic is severely restricted in Piran and spaces are at an absolute premium. All cars must pay a stiff parking fee if they intend to stay in the town for more than an hour. It's best to leave your car in the municipal car park south of the bus station which charges 110 SIT per hour up to 1200 SIT for a full day.

Getting Around

Bus Minibuses run by a company called I&I go from Piran to Portorož every 15 minutes and as far as the camping grounds at Lucija continuously year-round; the fare is 210 SIT. In summer there is also a service to the beach and camping ground at Fiesa.

Taxi For a taxi in Piran call ☎ 674 55 55.

PORTOROŽ

☎ 05 • postcode 6320 • pop 2980

Every country with a sea coast has got to have a honky-tonk beach resort – a Blackpool, a Bondi or an Atlantic City – and Portorož is Slovenia's very own. The 'Port of

PRIMORSKA

Roses' skirts a sandy bay about 5km south-east of Piran. It is essentially a solid strip of high-rise hotels, restaurants, bars, travel agencies, shops, discos, parked cars, beaches with turnstiles and tourists, and it is not to everyone's liking. A senior Slovenian tourism official called it 'Portobeton' (Port of Cement) while another said he hasn't been there for over three decades, preferring, like the vast majority of Slovenes, to holiday in Croatian Istria or along the Dalmatian coast.

But Portorož (Portorose in Italian) isn't all bad. The sandy beaches are the largest on the coast and relatively clean, there is a pleasant spa where you can take the waters or cover yourself in curative mud, and the list of other activities goes on and on. If you take it for what it is and let your hair down, Portorož can be a fun place to watch Slovenes, Italians, Austrians, Germans and others at play and in various states of undress. You may just want to join in the fun.

History
Portorož may look as if it was born yesterday, but that's not the case. Though most of the development along the main drag Obala (Beach Road) dates from the late 1960s and 1970s, the settlement was first mentioned in the 13th century and its sheltered bay was fiercely contested over the next 200 years. In 1689, Portorož Bay was the centre of a pan-Istrian sailing competition in which over 100 galleons participated.

But Portorož didn't achieve real fame until the late 19th century when Austro-Hungarian officers came here to be treated with the mud collected from the salt pans at Sečovlje (see Around Portorož). Word spread quickly and the Palace Hotel (1912) was established. This once-luxurious pile is just opposite the main beach on Obala and is currently in limbo, awaiting someone with enough money to complete its renovation.

Orientation
Portorož's main development looks onto the bay from Obala, but there are satellite resorts and hotel complexes to the north-west at Bernardin and south near the Portorož Marina at Lucija.

The bus station is opposite the main beach on Postajališka pot.

Information
Tourist Offices The tourist office (☎ 674 02 61, fax 674 02 31) is at Obala 16, a short distance west of the bus station. It's open from 9 am to 9 pm daily in summer and 10 am to 5 pm in winter.

Money Banka Koper, below the Slovenija hotel at Obala 33, is open from 8.30 till noon and 3 to 5 pm weekdays and on Saturday morning. There are private exchange offices everywhere. There's an exchange bureau opposite the old Palace Hotel at Obala 14b that's open from 9 am to 7 pm seven days a week in season.

Post & Communications The post office is located at K Stari cesta 1 just west of the Palace Hotel building. It is open from 7.30 am to 7 pm weekdays and till noon Saturday.

The Cyber Point 2 Internet cafe is in the student residence at Obala 11. It's open from 1 to 9 pm weekdays, and from 3 to 9 pm weekends, and Internet access costs 800 SIT an hour.

Travel Agencies Almost all of the big Slovenian travel agencies are represented here, including Kompas (☎ 674 70 32) at Obala 41 below the post office, open in summer from 9 am to 8 pm daily (closed 1 to 5 pm at weekends) and from 9 am to 7 pm daily (to 1 pm weekends) in winter, and Atlas (☎ 674 50 77) at Obala 55 just south of the bus station, which is the local representative for American Express.

Maona (☎ 674 64 23) is next door at Obala 53, open from 9 am to 8 pm daily in summer, and from 9 am to 3 pm daily except Sunday in winter, and Rosetour (☎ 674 91 70) is in the Bernardin tourist complex at Bernardinska Reber 3B.

Things to See
The **Maritime Museum Collection** in the Villa San Marco, Obala 58, is a branch of the museum in Piran. This time, though, the emphasis is on the Slovenian shipping company

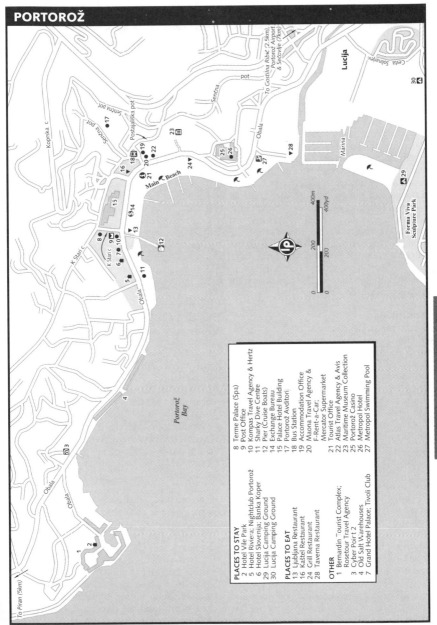

PORTOROŽ

PRIMORSKA

PLACES TO STAY
2 Hotel Vile Park
3 Hotel Riviera; Nightclub Portorož
5 Hotel Slovenija; Banka Koper
29 Lucija Camping Ground
30 Lucija Camping Ground

PLACES TO EAT
13 Ljubljana Restaurant
16 Kaštel Restaurant
24 Grill Restaurant
28 Taverna Restaurant

OTHER
1 Bernardin Tourist Complex;
  Rosetour Travel Agency
3 Cyber Point 2
4 Old Salt Warehouses
7 Grand Hotel Palace; Tivoli Club

8 Terme Palace (Spa)
9 Post Office
10 Kompas Travel Agency & Hertz
11 Sharky Dive Centre
12 Pier (Cruise Boats)
14 Exchange Bureau
15 Palace Hotel Building
17 Portorož Avditori
18 Bus Station
19 Accommodation Office
20 Maona Travel Agency &
   F-Rent-a-Car;
   Mercator Supermarket
21 Tourist Office
22 Atlas Travel Agency & Avis
23 Maritime Museum Collection
25 Portorož Casino
26 Metropol Hotel
27 Metropol Swimming Pool

Splošna Plovna Piran and its contribution to the development of the coast. It contains lots of ship models and naval paraphernalia – a collection only for the devoted sea dog. At the time of research the museum could only be visited by special arrangement – ask at the tourist office.

Forma Viva atop the Seča (Sezza in Italian) Peninsula near the Lucija camping ground is an outdoor sculpture garden with over 100 works of art carved in stone. This is just one of several in Slovenia. They were international exhibitions where sculptors worked with local materials: stone at Portorož, wood at Kostanjevica in Dolenjska, iron at Ravne in Koroška and – God help us – concrete in Maribor. This one, which is vaguely reminiscent of a cemetery, dates from 1961 and many of the sculptures are in sad shape. To be honest, the real reasons for coming are the fantastic views of Portorož and Piran Bays and, if you walk a short distance to the south, the salt pans at Sečovlje. The peninsula is an excellent place for a picnic.

Activities

Swimming The beaches at Portorož, including the main one accommodating some 6000 fried and bronzed bodies, are 'managed', so from April to September you'll have to pay 380 SIT (320 SIT after 1 pm) to use them. They have water slides, outside showers, beach chairs and umbrellas for rent (320 SIT) and are open from 8 am to 8 pm in season. On a hot summer's day they can be real zoos. The privately managed beach opposite the Metropol Hotel is smaller but nicer.

The large outdoor Metropol swimming pool next to the beach is open in summer (800/400 SIT admission). In the sports field attached there's minigolf, tennis courts and bowling (10 am to midnight daily).

Diving The Sharky Dive Center (mobile ☎ 041-635 763), in the little round building near the beach opposite the Riviera hotel, rents scuba equipment, organises guided boat dives and gives lessons; you can make arrangements with the diving instructor between 9 and 10 am daily in season. The

Discover Scuba one-day course for absolute beginners costs €26. Remember, though, that you're diving mainly for the sport here; there ain't a whole lot to see in these waters.

Boating & Cruises The Maona travel agency rents out boats and you can also hire them on the grassy beach area directly west of the Metropol Hotel. The *Big Red* catamaran (see Cruises in the earlier Piran section) cruises along the Slovenian coast between Portorož and Ankaran.

If you'd like to see what's *below* the water rather than on or above it, board the *Subaquatic* (mobile ☎ 041-636 371) at the Bernardin tourist complex at 10 am or at 2, 4.15, 6.30 or 9 pm daily in season. The trip costs 2200/1100 SIT for adults/children.

The Kompas travel agency can book day trips to Venice aboard the *Prince of Venice,* a 40m Australian-made catamaran seating 330 passengers (see Things to See & Do in the Izola section earlier in this chapter).

Spas The Terme Palace spa (☎ 696 90 01), located on K Stari cesta next to the post office, is famous for thalassotherapy, treatment using sea water and by-products like mud from the salt flats. The spa offers warm sea-water baths (2600 SIT per half-hour), brine baths (3700 SIT), Sečovlje mud baths (3700 SIT), massage (4100 SIT for 40 minutes) and a host of other therapies and beauty treatments. It is open from 7 am to 7 pm Monday to Saturday. The palatial indoor swimming pool here is open from 7 am to 9 pm daily; entry for nonguests costs 800/1400 SIT for four hours on weekdays/weekends.

Panoramic Flights Sightseeing by ultralight plane is available at the Portorož airport (☎ 672 25 25) near Sečovlje from April to September from 8 am to 8 pm and between 3 and 5 pm the rest of the year. Flights over Portorož and Piran or the whole coast (15 minutes) cost €26 (minimum two passengers). There are also 45-minute flights taking in places farther afield like Lipica and the Škocjan Caves and the Julian Alps and Triglav.

Special Events
Istrian Night in early August – an evening of celebration and fireworks – recalls the sailing competition held in the bay here in the 17th century. Many special events in summer are held in the large open-air theatre at the Portorož Avditorij (☎ 676 67 00), an auditorium at Senčna pot 12, a block behind the bus station.

One very unusual event held in Portorož is the Mariners' Baptism of new recruits to the naval school held in early September. It involves a lot of pageantry.

Places to Stay
Camping The *Lucija camping ground* (☎ 690 60 00) has two locations. The 2nd-category ground is south-east of the marina at the end of Cesta Solinarjev less than 2km from the bus station. The 1st-category site, 500m to the west, is beside the water. Both camps are open from May to September and get very crowded in summer. The charge per person ranges from 1400 to 1600 SIT, depending on the site and the month.

Private Rooms The Maona travel agency has private rooms and apartments. You can also book them through the accommodation office (☎ 674 03 60) at the bus station, open 9 am to 5 pm daily (Sunday till noon). Generally rooms cost from 3800 to 4300 SIT per person, depending on the category and the season, rising to 4900 to 5400 SIT in July and August. Some of the rooms are up on the hillside, quite a walk from the beach. Getting a room for fewer than three nights (for which you must pay a 50% supplement) or a single any time can be difficult, and in winter many owners don't want to rent at all due to the low off-season rates.

Hotels Portorož counts some 20 hotels, not including the 'olde worlde' Palace, the Art-Nouveau hotel that put Portorož on the map (currently under renovation at Obala 45). Hotels in Portorož can be very expensive during the warmer months. Many close for the winter in October or November and do not reopen until April or even May.

The cheapest hotels in Portorož are the central *Riviera* (☎ 692 00 00, fax 692 31 80, Obala 33) and *Slovenija (same ☎/fax and address)*, side by side, and the *Vile Park* (☎ 695 00 00, fax 674 64 10) in the Bernardin tourist complex. The Riviera charges from 9100 to 13,500 SIT for singles, depending on the season and category, and from 11,800 to 19,800 SIT for doubles; the Slovenija is about 30% more expensive. The Vile Park – that's the plural of 'villa' in Slovene, not a comment on the establishment's quality – has singles for 7000 to 12,500 SIT and doubles for 9500 to 17,000 SIT. The Riviera is closed from January to March and the Vile Park from mid-October to mid-April. The Slovenija is open all year.

Places to Eat
Fast-food and pizza/pasta restaurants line Obala. If you want a proper sit-down meal, the terrace at the *Taverna (Obala 22)* in the sports field looks out over the marina and the bay. It's open from 11 am till midnight daily. The *Grill* restaurant *(Obala 20)*, often with something large being roasted on a spit near the entrance, faces the main beach. Main courses start at 1000 SIT. The *Kaštel* restaurant sits under an enormous marquee in the warmer months almost opposite the tourist office on Obala. The *Ljubljana (Obala 14)*, opposite the post office, has pizzas and pastas for 850 to 1200 SIT, and delicious wild mushroom dishes in autumn.

The *Gostilna Ribič* in Seča (house No 143), south of the Forma Viva sculpture park, has a wonderful setting and good fish dishes. It is open from noon to 11 pm daily but closes in February.

The *Mercator supermarket* is a few steps away from the bus station. It is open from 7 am to 7 pm weekdays, to 6 pm Saturday and from 8 am to 11 am Sunday.

Entertainment
The *Nightclub Portorož* below the Riviera hotel and the *Tivoli Club* at the Grand Hotel Palace are the main nightspots, but there are countless lively bars and cafes along Obala where you can sip a drink and watch the world go by.

PRIMORSKA

Salt of the Sea

Although salt-making went on for centuries along the Slovenian coast at places like Sečovlje and Strunjan, the technique changed very little right up to 35 years ago when harvesting on a large scale came to an end.

Traditionally, sea water was channelled via three in-flow canals – the 'salt roads' – into shallow ponds separated by dikes, which were then dammed up with small wooden paddles. Wind-powered pumps removed some of the water and the rest evaporated in the sun and the wind as the salt crystalised from the remaining brine. To stop the salt from turning into a foul-tasting, reddish-brown material, workers lined the pans with a hard, compressed material of microorganisms and gypsum called *petola* so that the salt would not mix with the mud and clay. The procedure dated back to the 13th century.

The salt was collected, drained, washed and, if necessary, ground and iodised. It was then loaded onto to a heavy wooden barge called a *maona* and pulled to salt warehouses at various locations on the coast. Examples of these old *skladišča soli* can still be seen on Obala between Portorož and the Bernardin tourist complex.

Salt is necessary for the human body to enable it to retain water. Once, salt was one of the only things which could preserve meat. Sea salt later became prized because it tastes stronger and more pleasant than mined salt, which can be somewhat metallic, and because it dissolves more quickly. Sea salt was used in the 19th century to treat rheumatism and other muscular disorders at the thermal spa at Portorož and elsewhere.

The lifestyle of the salt workers didn't change much over the years. Salt harvesting was seasonal work, lasting from April to September, when the autumn rains came. During that time most of the workers (both those who controlled the water and those who harvested the salt) lived with their families in the houses you see lining the canals at Sečovlje. They rented the houses and their 'salt funds' – the pans around each house – and divided the profits equally with the landowner.

The set-up of each house was pretty much the same. The large room downstairs served as a store-house and had two doors so that salt could come in from the fields and then be carried out again on boats in the canal. Upstairs there were two bedrooms and a combination living room and kitchen. All the windows and doors opened on both sides so that workers could observe changes in the weather – as crucial to them as to sailors. Rain and wind could wipe out the entire harvest if the salt was not collected in time.

In September or during rainy periods, the workers returned to their villages to tend their crops and vines. For this reason – and because they lived both on the land and 'at sea' – Slovenian salt workers were said to be 'sitting on two chairs'.

KELLI HAMBLET

A wind-powered pump, used in the salt-making process to drain the saltwater ponds

The *Portorož Casino* (☎ 674 69 34) at the Metropol Hotel, popular with Italian day-trippers, is open from 5 pm daily.

Getting There & Away

Bus Buses leave Portorož station for Piran, Strunjan and Izola about every 20 minutes on weekdays in season and every 40 minutes on Saturday and Sunday.

Other destinations from Portorož and their daily frequencies are the same as for Piran (see Getting There & Away in the earlier Piran section). The morning bus for Zagreb leaves at 5.55 am, and the bus for Maribor is at 2.11 pm.

Getting Around

Bus I&I minibuses make the loop from the Lucija camping grounds to central Portorož and Piran throughout the year. For details see Getting Around in the Piran section.

Taxi For a local taxi in Portorož ring ☎ 674 55 55 or ☎ 677 07 00, or pick one up at the rank by the post office.

Car & Motorcycle The main car rental companies – Hertz (☎ 674 69 71) at Obala 41, Avis (☎ 674 05 55) at Obala 55 and Budget (☎ 674 03 13) at Obala 2 – are all represented in Portorož. There are quite a few smaller agencies along Obala so stroll along and compare prices – F-Rent-A-Car at the Maona travel agency offers cars from 6900 SIT a day.

Parking space is tight, and you must 'pay and display' to park in Portorož. One hour costs 110 SIT, a full day 1200 SIT.

Atlas and Rosetour rent motor scooters for 8000 SIT a day (or 4000 SIT for two hours).

Bicycle Atlas rents bicycles for 3500 SIT a day, or 1500 SIT for two hours.

AROUND PORTOROŽ
Sečovlje

The abandoned salt pans at Sečovlje, stretching some 650 hectares from Seča to the Dragonja River on the Croatian border, have been turned into a landscape park and

nature reserve. In the centre is the wonderful **Saltworks Museum**, ranked in the top 12 by the European Museums Association.

The area, crisscrossed with dikes, channels, pools and canals, was once a hive of activity and was one of the biggest money-spinners on the coast in the Middle Ages. Today, it looks like a ghost town with its empty grey stone houses and pans slowly being taken over by hardy vegetation. Part of a **nature park**, Sečovlje is eerily quiet except for the occasional cry of a gull, an egret or a heron – among the 150 species that flock here.

Sečovlje is right on the border with Croatia and to reach it you must pass through Slovenian immigration and customs first (don't forget your passport). Before you cross the Croatian checkpoint, though, you make a sharp turn to the right (east) and continue along an unsealed road for just under 3km. The two museum buildings stand out along one of the canals; they are the only renovated houses of the many still standing at Sečovlje.

The exhibits relate to all aspects of salt-making and the lives of salt workers and their families: tools, weights, water jugs, straw hats, baking utensils and the seals used to mark loaves of bread baked communally. They are not in themselves very interesting, but the surroundings are and you do begin to get a feeling of how the *solinarji* (salt workers) lived and worked (see the boxed text 'Salt of the Sea'). Out among the pans south of the museum is a **wind-powered pump** (just follow the earthen dikes to reach it) that still twirls in the breeze. The museum staff make use of it and other tools to produce a quantity of salt – about 180 tonnes – every year, in the traditional way.

The museum is open from 9 am till noon and 4 to 7 pm Tuesday to Sunday. Admission is 400/300 SIT for adults/children.

Getting There & Away Buses stop at the town of Sečovlje (Sicciole in Italian), about 1.5km north of the border, so it's best to catch a bus heading into Istria if you can and get off just before the Croatian frontier.

PRIMORSKA

Notranjska

'Inner Carniola' is the least developed of Slovenia's eight traditional provinces. It is largely covered in forest – the setting of many of the country's myths and legends (see the boxed text 'Big Men for Big Times') – but the region's most distinguishing characteristic is its karst caves below the ground.

Notranjska is the most typical Dinaric region of Slovenia, but its karst is different from that of Primorska. Abundant rain and snow fall here, but the ground is like a great Gruyere cheese – the water vanishes into the ground and resurfaces on the fringes of karst fields called *polje*. Notranjska is also known for its underground rivers (eg, Unica, Pivka, Ljubljanica, Rak) and the 'intermittent' lakes at Cerknica and Planina.

Notranjska had – and to a certain extent still has – poor communications links, which stunted development. Transport through the deep forests and valleys of this isolated province has been difficult for centuries and when the railway linking Trieste and Ljubljana opened in 1857, much of Notranjska was sidestepped. Notranjska was hit by massive emigration (especially around Cerknica) from the early 20th century up to WWII. Today much of the province is given over to logging, especially on the Bloke Plateau – the birthplace of skiing in Europe, according to some – and in the Lož Valley.

A 40,000-hectare area around Lake Cerknica – west to Postojna, east to Snežnik and south to the border with Croatia – has been declared a regional park (Notranjski Park). Much of the country's wildlife and most aggressive animals) lives in this region. There are also protected landscape parks at the Rakov Škocjan Gorge and around Snežnik Castle.

BISTRA CASTLE

☎ 01 • postcode 1353

The **Technical Museum of Slovenia** (Tehniški Mujez Slovenije) at Bistra Castle near Vrhnika, 22km south-west of Ljubljana, is

Highlights

- Discover Predjama Castle, built into a mountain cave
- View Lake Cerknica in winter
- Try dining on dormice – for the intrepid only – on Polharska Noč (Dormouse Night) in late September at Snežnik Castle
- Treat yourself to a musical program at the Concert Hall in Postojna Cave
- Enjoy the four days of the famous Cerknica Carnival

one of the country's most interesting museums. Housed in a former monastery, its extensive collection includes pre-WWII motor vehicles and bicycles, working examples of water-driven and horse-powered mills, and a wide range of implements used in agriculture, weaving, forestry, fishing and hunting. There are also carpenters, cabinet-makers and blacksmiths workshops where modern artisans preserve ancient skills. It's open from 8 am to 4 pm Tuesday to Friday, till 5 pm Saturday, and 10 am to 6 pm Sunday. The museum is an easy day trip from Ljubljana – there are frequent buses to Vrhnika (30 minutes), and six trains a day to

NOTRANJSKA

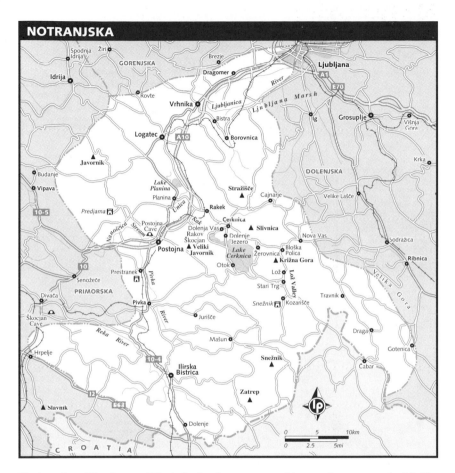

Verd station (30 minutes, 32km), both of which are about 3km west of Bistra Castle.

POSTOJNA
☎ 05 • postcode 6230 • pop 8200

The karst cave at Postojna, one of the largest in the world, is among Slovenia's most popular attractions. As a result, it is very commercialised and crammed most of the year with coaches and tour groups; many travellers prefer the less-visited caves north of the town or the ones at Škocjan in Primorska. It's not the end of the world if you miss Postojna; go to Škocjan and you'll

see something much more wonderful. The Postojna Cave (Postojnska Jama) system, a series of caverns, halls and passages some 27km long and two million years old, was hollowed out by the Pivka River, which enters a subterranean tunnel near the cave's entrance. The river continues its deep passage underground, carving out several series of caves, and emerges again as the Unica River. The Unica meanders through a sunken field of porous limestone – the Planinsko Polje (Planina Plain) – which becomes Lake Planina in the rainy season. But, as is the nature of what is called a

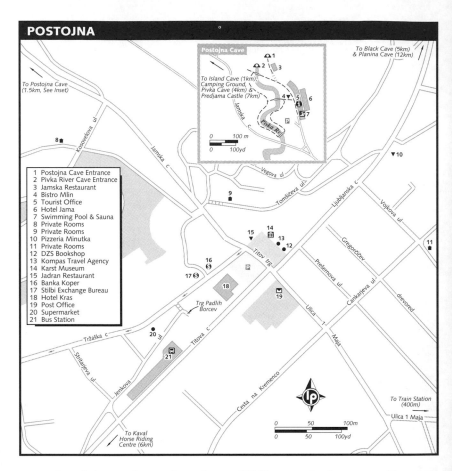

POSTOJNA

1 Postojna Cave Entrance
2 Pivka River Cave Entrance
3 Jamska Restaurant
4 Bistro Mlin
5 Tourist Office
6 Hotel Jama
7 Swimming Pool & Sauna
8 Private Rooms
9 Private Rooms
10 Pizzeria Minutka
11 Private Rooms
12 DZS Bookshop
13 Kompas Travel Agency
14 Karst Museum
15 Jadran Restaurant
16 Banka Koper
17 Stilbi Exchange Bureau
18 Hotel Kras
19 Post Office
20 Supermarket
21 Bus Station

ponor river, it is soon lost to the underground. It reappears near Vrhnika as the Ljubljanica River and continues its journey northward to the capital.

History

The town of Postojna (Adelsberg in German) dates back to the 12th century, but there's little of interest here beyond a very small collection in the Karst Museum at Titov trg 2.

Postojna Cave has been known – and visited – by residents of the area for centuries; one need only look at the graffiti dating back seven centuries in the Gallery of Old Signatures by the entrance. But people in the Middle Ages knew only the entrances. The inner parts were not explored until April 1818, just days before the arrival of Habsburg Emperor Franz I (ruled 1792–1835). The following year the Cave Commission accepted its first organised tour group, including Archduke Ferdinand, and Postojna's future as a tourist destination was sealed.

Even in those early days, the very poor region of Notranjska saw the potential economic benefits, and in 1823 a guidebook to Postojna was published, which also included the Škocjan and Vilenica caves and the mercury mine at Idrija. Since then more than 27 million people have visited Postojna.

Orientation

The town of Postojna lies in the Pivka Valley at the foot of Sovič Hill (677m). The Pivka River, once lined with water mills, and the entrance to the cave are about 1.5km north-west of Titov trg, the centre of town.

Postojna's bus station is at Titova cesta 36, about 250m south-west of Titov trg. The train station is on Kolodvorska cesta about 1km to the south-east of the square. If you're walking, the fastest way to get to the town centre from the train station is to go down the steps at the southern end of the station and follow Pod Kolodvorom to Ulica 1 Maja, which leads into Titov trg.

Information

Tourist Offices The tourist office (☎ 726 51 82, fax 720 16 10) in the shopping complex beneath the Hotel Jama, is open from 9 am to 6 pm daily, April to October only. For information specific to the cave, and for booking tickets, call ☎ 700 01 00. In the town centre, the staff at Kompas (see Travel Agencies) and Stilbi (see Money) will provide tourist information.

For maps, try the DZS bookshop next door to Kompas on Titov trg; it's open from 7 am to 7 pm weekdays and 8 am till noon Saturday.

Money Banka Koper has a branch at Tržaška cesta 2. It is open from 8.30 am till noon and 3 to 5 pm weekdays and on Saturday morning. The Stilbi exchange bureau at Tržaška cesta 4 changes money without taking a commission. It is open from 8 am to 6 pm weekdays and till noon Saturday. You can also change money at Kompas, but the commission there is 3%.

Post & Communications The post office is at Ulica 1 Maja 2a, a short distance south of Titov trg. It is open from 7.30 am to 7 pm weekdays and 8 am till noon Saturday.

Travel Agencies Kompas (☎ 726 42 81) at Titov trg 2a is open from 8 am to 7.30 pm

weekdays (to 6 pm in winter) and 9 am to 1 pm Saturday.

Postojna Cave

Visitors get to see about 5.7km of the cave on 1½-hour tours, but the lazy or infirm shouldn't fret – about 4km of this are covered by an electric train that will shuttle you through the so-called Old Passage. The remaining 1700m is on foot. Before you enter the cave, have a look at the Pivka River opposite the cave entrance, where it finds its way underground. That river has created everything you are about to see.

First you board the minitrain, just beyond the entrance, that runs as far as the **Big Mountain** (Velika Gora) cavern. Here you stand under one of the five signs identifying your language, and a guide escorts you through halls, galleries and caverns.

These are dry galleries, decorated with a vast array of white stalactites shaped like needles, enormous icicles and even fragile spaghetti. The stalagmites take familiar shapes – pears, cauliflower and sand castles – but there are also bizarre columns, pillars and translucent curtains that look like rashers of bacon. All in all, it could be a nightmare for anyone who saw monsters in the dark as a child.

Many of the dripstones are stained orange and brown by iron salts contained in the water that formed them. Only one of the halls is completely devoid of them. It was here that the Partisans blew up a Nazi fuel dump in 1944, and you can still see the blackened walls.

From the Velika Gora cavern you continue across the **Russian Bridge**, built by prisoners of war in 1916, through the 500m-long **Beautiful Caves** (Lepe Jame) filled with wonderful stalactites and stalagmites shaped like ribbons. In case you were wondering, it takes 30 years to produce 1mm of a stalactite. The halls of the Beautiful Caves are the farthest point you'll reach; from here a man-made tunnel stretches to the **Black Cave** (Črna Jama) and **Pivka Cave**, but you'll have to visit them from the entrance at the Pivka Jama camping ground to the north of Postojna.

The tour continues south through the **Winter Hall** (Zimska Dvorana) past the **Brilliant Stalagmite** and the **Pillar Column**, which have become the symbols of the cave (and which look pretty silly when reproduced graphically on the guides' badges and on bumper stickers). You then enter the **Concert Hall** (Koncertna Dvorana), which is the largest in the system and can accommodate 10,000 people for musical performances.

One of the last things you'll see before boarding the train for the trip back is a tank filled with pink salamanders. These bizarre (and rather rude-looking) little things are *Proteus anguinus,* a unique 'human fish' that was first described by Janez Vajkard Valvasor as the 'dragon's offspring' (see the boxed text 'Proteus Anguinus, the Human Fish' for details). The salamander is just one of 190 species of fauna (including beetles, bats, cave hedgehogs etc) found in the cave and studied at the Biospeleological Station here.

The cave has a constant temperature of 8°C and humidity of 95% so a waterproof jacket is essential. Don't worry if you haven't brought one along; green-felt cloaks can be hired at the entrance for 300 SIT. Shoes are not as big an issue here as they are at the Škocjan Caves and a torch (flashlight) is not necessary; the cave has been lit by electricity since 1884 when many European cities were still using gas.

From May to September, tours leave on the hour between 9 am and 6 pm daily. Admission is 2100/1050 SIT for adults/students and children. In March and April and again in October there are tours at 10 am, noon, 2 and 4 pm with an extra daily one at 5 pm in April and tours at the weekend in October at 11 am and 1, 3 and 5 pm. Between November and February, tours leave at 10 am and 2 pm weekdays with extra ones added at noon and 4 pm at the weekend and public holidays.

Other Caves

To the north of Postojna lie several smaller but equally interesting caves created by the Pivka River and still part of the Postojna system. They too are open to the public.

Island Cave (Otoška Jama), a half-hour walk north-west from Postojna Cave, is very small (632m in total) and the tour takes only 45 minutes, but its stalagmites and stalactites are very impressive. There's no electric lighting so you'll need a torch and the temperature is also 8°C.

The most popular caves after Postojna – **Pivka Cave** (Pivka Jama) and **Black Cave** (Črna Jama) – are about 5km to the north and the entrance is in the Pivka Jama camping ground. You reach the 4km-long system by descending a couple of hundred stairs. A walkway has been cut into the wall of a canyon in Pivka Cave, with its two siphon lakes and a tunnel, and a bridge leads to Black Cave. This is a dry cavern and, as its name implies, its dripstones are not white. A tour of both caves takes 1½ hours.

Planina Cave (Planinska Jama), 12km to the north-east near the unpredictable Lake Planina, is the largest water cave in Slovenia and a treasure-trove of fauna (including *Proteus anguinus*). This is where the Pivka and Rak join forces to form the Unica River. The cave's entrance is at the foot of a 100m rock wall. It's over 6km long and you get to visit about 900m of it in an hour. There are no lights so take a torch. Many parts of the cave are accessible only in low water or by rubber raft.

These caves are all open from June to September and can be visited between two and four times every day (weekends only at the Island Cave). For information about the caves, ask at the tourist office or call the guide, Janez Margon (mobile ☎ 041-584 011). Admission is 1000/500 SIT for adults/students and children for each cave.

Horse Riding

The Kaval Horse Riding Centre (☎ 754 25 95) at Prestranek Castle, about 6.5km south of Postojna, is one of the most professional stables in Slovenia and an excellent place for learning to ride or improving your skills. (The history of horse breeding at the castle goes back to the early 18th century.) The centre is open from 9 to 11 am and 4 to 8 pm daily in summer, and 10.30 am to 12.30 pm and 2 to 5 pm in winter.

Special Events

Musical performances are staged in the Concert Hall at Postojna Cave in summer and on various holidays throughout the year, especially the week between Christmas and New Year. This is also the time when the 'Live Christmas Crib' – the Christmas story performed by actors – takes place in the cave.

Places to Stay

Camping The *Kamp Pivka Jama* (☎ 726 53 82) is located on a 2.5-hectare site in a pine forest near the entrance to Pivka and Black Caves. The camping ground is open from May to September and costs 1400 SIT per person. The 20 box-like bungalows with four beds each are 10,000 SIT, apartments for four are 12,000 SIT. If you're in a group this is a pleasant, friendly place to stay, and there's a swimming pool. You can walk from Postojna along a marked trail through the forest to the camping ground in about 45 minutes.

Private Rooms Kompas can organise private rooms in and around Postojna for about 2400 SIT per person. The most central rooms available are at Tomšičeva ulica 3

Proteus Anguinus, the Human Fish

Proteus anguinus is one of the most mysterious creatures in the world. It's a kind of salamander, but related to no other amphibian and is the largest permanent cave-dwelling vertebrate known to man. The blind little fellow lives hidden in the pitch black for up to a century and can go years without food. *Proteus anguinus* is now the symbol of Postojna and has been added to the town seal (just below the imperial eagle).

The 17th-century chronicler Valvasor wrote about the fear and astonishment of local people when an immature 'dragon' was found in a karst spring near Vhrnika, but he judged it to be 'an underground worm and vermin of the kind that is common in some parts'. Several other reports about this four-legged 'human fish' (*človeška ribica* as it's called in Slovene) were made, before a doctor in Vienna realised its uniqueness in 1768. In announcing its existence to the scientific world, he called it 'Proteus anguinus', after the protector of Poseidon's sea creatures in Greek mythology and the Latin word for 'snake'.

Proteus anguinus measures about 25cm to 30cm long and is a little bundle of contradictions. It has a long tail fin that it uses for swimming, but also can propel itself with its four legs (the front pair have three little 'fingers' and the back have two 'toes'). Though blind, with atrophied, almost invisible eyes, *Proteus anguinus* has an excellent sense of smell and is sensitive to weak electric fields in the water. It uses these to move around in the dark, locate prey and communicate. It breathes through frilly, bright-red gills at the base of its head when submerged, but also has rudimentary lungs for breathing when it is outside the water. The human-like skin has no pigmentation whatsoever but it looks pink in the light due to blood circulation.

The question that scientists have asked themselves for three centuries is: How do they reproduce? This has never been witnessed in a natural state, and the crafty little things haven't been very cooperative in captivity. But it is almost certain that they hatch their young from eggs and that they don't reach sexual maturity until the age of 16 or 18.

Animal-rights activists will be happy to learn that the beasties in the tank in Postojna Cave call it home for only two or three months and are then returned to the 'wild'. Others aren't so lucky. The export of live *Proteus anguinus* is banned in Slovenia, but that hasn't stopped unscrupulous dealers, and the little creatures keep appearing for sale in aquariums and pet shops in other European countries. The biggest customers, it is said, are scientists.

MARTIN HARRIS

above Titov trg, Vojkova ulica 15 and Vilhajova 17.

Hotels The only hotel in Postojna town centre is the slightly tatty 54-room *Hotel Kras* (☎ *726 40 71, fax 726 44 31)* facing Titov trg at Tržaška cesta 1. Singles with breakfast and shower start at 6000 SIT, doubles at 9000 SIT.

Some 200m south-east of the entrance to Postojna Cave, the sprawling *Hotel Jama* (☎ *728 25 00, fax 728 44 31, Jamska cesta 28)* was undergoing renovation, but should be open later in 2001. Singles/doubles with shower cost 6730/10,560 SIT for B&B, but there is little reason to stay out here unless you want to be the first person in the cave in the morning. The hotel has an indoor swimming pool, sauna and fitness centre.

Places to Eat

The *Jadran* restaurant on Titov trg in Postojna town, has a good selection of fish dishes, but they can be pricey. *Pizzeria Minutka*, with a terrace outside at Ljubljanska cesta 14, is a local favourite. Pizzas cost around 1000 SIT, and it's open to 11 pm daily. The *supermarket (Tržaška cesta 9)* has sandwiches, minipizzas etc available from 7.30 am to 7 pm daily.

There are many places to eat in the tourist complex near Postojna Cave, including a *pizzeria* and two *self-service restaurants*. The *Jamska* restaurant in a 1920s-style building next to the cave entrance, has three-course set menus for 1200 and 1500 SIT. The *Bistro Mlin*, overlooking the river, is a pleasant spot for a drink or snack; it's open from 11 am to 6 pm daily.

Getting There & Away

Bus All the buses travelling between Ljubljana and the coast stop at Postojna. Count on a bus about every half-hour to the capital and hourly to Pivka, a town south of Postojna (not the camping ground of the same name).

Other destinations and their daily frequencies include: Celje (three), Cerknica (four during school term), Koper (10), Maribor (two), Murska Sobota (one), Nova Gorica (14), Piran (eight), Sežana (three to five) and Stari Trg pri Lož (one).

International destinations include Poreč (one a day, at 2.40 pm), Rijeka (one, at 9 am) and Zagreb (two, at 6.07 and 7.32 am) in Croatia, and Trieste (two, at 6.50 and 7.40 am) in Italy.

Train Postojna is on the main line linking Ljubljana (one hour, 67km) with Sežana and Trieste via Divača (40 minutes, 37km), and is an easy day trip from the capital. As many as 20 trains a day make the run from Ljubljana to Postojna and back. You can also reach here from Koper (1½ hours, 86km) on one of up to four trains a day.

Getting Around

For a taxi in Postojna, call ☎ 726 30 02 or mobile ☎ 041-266 941. The Pivka Jama camping ground has bicycles for rent.

PREDJAMA CASTLE
☎ 05 • postcode 6230

Situated in the gaping mouth of a cavern halfway up a hillside, about 9km north-west of Postojna, this four-storey castle has one of the most dramatic settings anywhere. Although traces of other structures can be dated back to the early 13th century, the castle as you see it today dates from the 16th century. Then – as now – it looked unconquerable, perched in the centre of a 123m cliff.

Ah, but along came one Erazem Lueger, a 15th-century robber baron who, like Robin Hood, waylaid wagons in the deep forest, stole the loot and handed it over to the poor. During the wars between the Hungarians (under good King Matthias Corvinus) and the Austrians (behind the wicked Frederick III), Lueger supported the former. He holed himself up in the castle and continued his daring deeds with the help of a secret passage that led out from behind the rock wall. Frederick was livid.

In the autumn of 1483, the Austrian army attacked the castle but it proved impregnable for months. All the while Erazem mocked the soldiers and showered them with fish, the occasional roast ox and even cherries to prove that he came and went as he pleased.

But Erazem proved to be too big for his breeches and met an ignoble fate. Having gone 'to where even the sultan must go alone' (as Valvasor described it), Erazem was hit by a cannon ball as he sat on the toilet. A turncoat servant, it seems, had betrayed his boss by marking the location of the water closet with a little flag for the Austrian soldiers.

The castle's eight **museum rooms** contain little of interest except for a portrait of Erazem and an oil painting of the 1483–84 siege. But Predjama's striking position and the views of the valley below are incomparable. And it does have all the features a castle should have: a drawbridge over a raging river, holes in the ceiling of the entrance tower for pouring boiling oil on intruders, a very dank dungeon, a 16th-century chest full of treasure (unearthed in the cellar in 1991) and an eyrie-like hiding place at the top called **Erazem's Nook**. Just watch out when walking and climbing over the very uneven surfaces.

The **cave** below the castle, carved out by the Lokva and Nanoščica streams, is actually a 7km network of galleries spread over five levels. Much of it is open only to speleologists, but casual visitors can see about 900m-worth. There is no electric lighting, and the trail is only partially constructed so you will need to don rubber boots and carry torches, both of which are available at the entrance. For information, contact Postojna Cave (☎ 700 01 00) or the castle directly (☎ 751 60 15).

Predjama is open daily year-round. The hours are 9 am to 7 pm from June to August; the castle closes an hour earlier in May and September. Daily hours are 10 am to 5 pm in March and April and again in October. It opens from 10 am to 4 pm Tuesday to Friday and to 5 pm at the weekend in winter – November to February. Admission is 700/350 SIT for adults/students and children. Short circular tours of Predjama Cave leave at 11 am and at 1, 3 and 5 pm from May to September and cost 700/350 SIT or 1200/600 SIT for both the castle and the cave. Longer tours – to the end of the cave's Eastern Passage (4500 SIT) or Erazem's

Gallery (Erazmov Rov; 2100 SIT) – are available by prior arrangement only.

If you want or need to stay out here (transport is tricky), the nearest accommodation is at the *Motel Erazem* (☎ 751 54 45) about 3km south-east near the village of Belsko, where a double room costs €41 including breakfast. *Gostilna Požar* near the ticket kiosk serves meals and is open from 10 am to 10 pm daily, except Wednesday.

Predjama is difficult to reach by public transport. As close as you'll get by local bus from Postojna (and during the school year only) is Bukovje, a village about 2km northeast of Predjama. A taxi from Postojna plus an hour's wait at the castle will cost you 10,000 SIT.

CERKNICA

☎ 01 • postcode 1380 • pop 3500

This is the largest town on the lake that isn't always a lake – one of Slovenia's most unusual natural phenomena. Cerknica itself is not important as a destination, but it is close to the 'intermittent' Lake Cerknica, the landscape park around Rakov Škocjan Gorge, Mt Snežnik and Snežnik Castle.

The area around the lake has been settled since prehistoric times, and a trade route once ran over the Bloke Plateau to the east, linking Slovenia and Croatia. During the Roman period, Cerknica (Cirkniz in German) was a stopover on the road leading from Emona (Ljubljana) to the coast. Cerknica was given town status in the 11th century.

But Cerknica is a good example of how important communication lines are for the development of a town. The railway linking Trieste and Ljubljana opened in 1857, but it dodged Cerknica in favour of Rakek, 5km to the north-west. The highway from Ljubljana toward the coast follows the same route, and Cerknica remains something of a backwater. With some of Notranjska's most beautiful forests and their fragile ecosystems in the town's back yard, that may not be such a bad thing.

Orientation & Information

Cerknica lies north of Lake Cerknica and about 16km north-east of Postojna. Cesta 4

Maja, the main street, is the centre of town. The bus station is on Čabranska ulica about 100m to the south-west.

Cerknica's tourist office (☎ 709 16 36) is on the ground floor of the Notranjska Ecology Centre (Notranjski Ekološki Center) at Cesta 4 Maja 51. It is open from 7.30 am to 3 pm weekdays and 8 am till noon Saturday.

Nova Ljubljanska Banka has a branch in the Mercator shopping centre at Cesta 4 Maja 64. It is open from 8 to 11 am and 2 to 5 pm weekdays and on Saturday morning. SKB Banka, open from 8.30 am till noon and 2 to 5 pm weekdays only, is at Partizanska cesta 1. The post office, next door to the tourist office at Cesta 4 Maja 52, is open from 8 am to 7 pm weekdays and till noon Saturday.

Parish Church of Our Lady

Sitting atop a gentle slope 200m north of Cesta 4 Maja, this church is the only real attraction right in Cerknica. To reach it, walk up the street called simply Tabor, which runs to the east of the shopping centre. This was called 'Road of the Patriarchs' in medieval times when Cerknica was the centre of Aquileia's estates in the area.

The church sat in the middle of a fortified settlement, and the ramparts and two towers, built to withstand Turkish raids in the late 15th century, remain intact. On the Latin plaque in the wall, the number 4 of the year 1472 is written with a loop – the top half of an 8 – because 4 was considered unlucky in the Middle Ages, as it still is in much of Asia.

Completed in the early 16th century, this is a hall church – with nave and aisles of equal height – and not unlike the one at Kranj in Gorenjska. In the 18th century two side chapels were added, and the bell tower was given its baroque dome.

Lake Cerknica

Since ancient times this periodic lake has baffled and perplexed people, including the Greek geographer and historian Strabo (63 BC–AD 24) who called the mysterious on-and-off body of water Lacus Lugeus (Mourning Lake). However, it wasn't until Valvasor explained how the water system worked at the end of the 17th century that it was fully understood. For his efforts, in 1697 this great Renaissance man was made a member of the Royal Society in London, the premier scientific institution in the world at the time.

Cerknica is a polje, a field above a collapsed karst cavern full of sinkholes, potholes, siphons and underground tunnels that can stay dry for much of the year but then floods. From the south, the polje is fed by another one of those disappearing ponor rivers, the Stržen, and to the east and west it collects water underground from the Bloke Plateau and the Javornik Mountains. During rainy periods in the autumn and spring, all this water comes rushing into the polje. Springs emerge and the water begins to percolate between the rocks, as though it were boiling. The sinkholes and siphons cannot handle the outflow underground and the polje becomes Lake Cerknica – sometimes in less than a day.

The surface area of Lake Cerknica can reach almost 40 sq km (Lake Bohinj in Gorenjska is a quarter that size), but it is never more than a few metres deep. During dry periods (usually July to September), farmers drive cattle down to the polje and haymakers come to work in the sunshine.

Lake Cerknica is a beautiful place – whether dry and under cultivation, full of water (and anglers and windsurfers and swimmers) or frozen solid. In fact, it is in winter that the lake becomes most glorious. The waves of the lake freeze into eerie ice formations, and mallard ducks and wild geese drift to and fro. A lot of people skate here then.

The lake really begins at the village of Dolenje Jezero about 2.5km south of Cerknica, where you will find the **Jezerski Hram Museum**. The museum's most famous exhibit is a 5m by 3m, 1:2500 scale working model of Lake Cerknica, showing how the underground hydrological system works. There are 45-minute tours of the museum at 3 and 5 pm for individual visitors at weekends only; entry costs 400/350 SIT for adults/children.

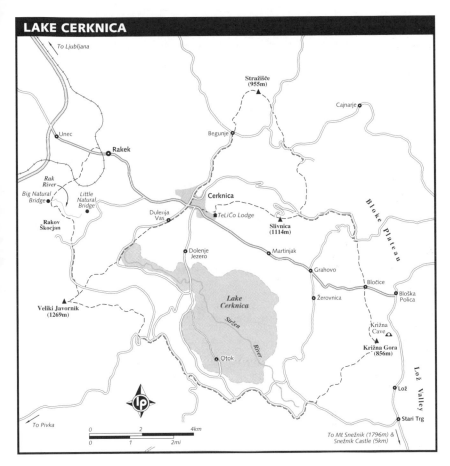

LAKE CERKNICA

To Ljubljana

Stražišče (955m) ▲

Cajnarje ●

Unec ●

Begunje ●

Rakek ■

Rak River

Big Natural Bridge ●

Little Natural Bridge ●

Cerknica ●

Rakov Škocjan

Dulenja Vas ●

■ TeLiCo Lodge

Slivnica (1114m) ▲

Bloke Plateau

Dolenje Jezero ●

Martinjak ●

Grahovo ●

Bločice ●

Bloška Polica ●

Veliki Javornik (1269m) ▲

Žerovnica ●

Lake Cerknica

Stržen River

Križna Cave ∩

Križna Gora (856m) ▲

Otok ●

Lož Valley

Lož ●

To Pivka

Stari Trg ●

0   2   4km
0   1   2mi

To Mt Snežnik (1796m) & Snežnik Castle (5km)

Rakov Škocjan

This gorge 6km west of Cerknica has been under protection as a landscape park since 1949. The Rak River, en route to join the Pivka at Planina Cave, sculpted out 2.5km of hollows, caves, springs and the big and little natural bridges – the **Veliki Naravni Most** and the **Mali Naravni Most**. To the south lie the Javornik Mountains, the tallest peak being **Veliki Javornik** (1269m). There are several hiking trails through and around the gorge.

Coming from Rakek, you can reach the Gostišče Rakov Škocjan restaurant on foot from the train station in about an hour.

Activities

When it's full, Lake Cerknica becomes a vast playground for boaters, anglers and swimmers. Ask the tourist office in Cerknica about fishing licences and boat rentals.

The tourist office can also help arrange tours of the lake by horse-driven carriage. The Kontrabantar farmhouse (☎ 709 22 53) in Dolenja Vas (house No 72), a village 2km south-west of Cerknica, has half a dozen horses for rent for 1500 SIT per hour from Thursday to Sunday as well as offering lessons and guided coach tours into the countryside. It's difficult to imagine a more

Big Men for Big Times

Slovenian folklore and tales are rife with fairies, witches and things that go bump in the night, but among the most common stories are those describing the derring-do of 'supermen' whose strong wills and unusual strength enabled them to overcome evil and conquer their enemies.

The legends are not limited to one geographical area. Peter Klepec, who swept away his enemies with trees uprooted with his bare hands, lived on the Kolpa River and is associated with Bela Krajina province. Another hero called Kumprej ruled the Upper Savinja Valley in Štajerska with his mighty voice and fearsome blade. His shoes were five times larger than those of the average person and when he disappeared a poor couple made footwear for their entire family from them.

But perhaps the most popular stories revolve around the feats of Martin Krpan, the hero of the Bloke Plateau in Notranjska. Krpan's traits and characteristics are familiar. He is an outlaw with a big heart hunted by the imperial guard for smuggling salt. When he is arrested, Martin Krpan proves his superhuman strength to the emperor in Vienna by picking up and carrying his horse.

Realising his fortune at having such a powerful giant under his control, the emperor sets Martin Krpan on Berdavs, the local scourge and personification of the marauding Turk. Martin Krpan defeats Berdavs and chops off his head with his magic axe – complete with a handle made of linden wood. For his pains the imperial court confers on him the privilege of the free transport and sale of salt.

The tales of Martin Krpan are traditional but reached a wider audience when the writer Fran Levstik collected and published them under the title *Martin Krpan* in 1858. This was during the period of national revival when authors around Europe were writing romantic stories, raising the status of local legends and, in doing so, the local language. Thanks to Levstik, Slovenia had for the first time a hero that all Slovenes could admire.

enjoyable way of exploring Lake Cerknica and the surrounding hills.

The area around Cerknica is excellent for hikes, and the **Cerknica Mountain Trail** will lead you to the most interesting peaks in a very full two-day walk. The trail heads south-west from Cerknica to thickly forested Veliki Javornik; from here you can take a side trip of about two hours to the gorge at Rakov Škocjan. The trail then skirts the southern shore of Lake Cerknica and carries on north to Križna Gora (856m) and its nearby cave and north-west to Slivnica (1114m). Slivnica, home of the witch Uršula and other sorcerers, has accommodation in a mountain hut. The next day you walk north to Stražišče (955m) and back to Cerknica.

If you prefer, you can do just parts of the walk, such as the stages to Rakov Škocjan or Veliki Javornik, or you can climb Slivnica from Cerknica in about an hour. Cerknica's tourist office sells a useful 1:25,000-scale map of the area around the lake for 1000 SIT.

Special Events

Cerknica is famous for its Carnival (Pustni Karneval), which takes place for four days before Ash Wednesday in February or early March. This is the time when the enormous masks of Uršula, who makes her home on Mt Slivnica, and a half-dozen other legendary characters are dusted off and paraded up and down Cesta 4 Maja while being provoked by upstarts with pitchforks. It wasn't such a laughing matter during the Reformation, though. Valvasor reports that this part of Notranjska was the centre of witch-hunting and executions even in his day.

Places to Stay

The choice of accommodation in Cerknica is very limited. The *Turšič guesthouse* (☎ 709 13 54, Partizanska ulica 14) between the tourist office and the Church of Our Lady, has two basic rooms with shared shower for 2000 SIT per person, as well as a large *apartment* with five beds in Dolenje Jezero for 8500 SIT a night. The tourist office will direct you to the *TeLiCo Lodge*

(☎ 709 41 18, Brestova 9) on the eastern edge of town. It has two double rooms with shared bath and WC, stunning views over the lake, and charges 2200 SIT per person.

If you have your own transport, then the *Apartma Dialog* (☎ 705 41 07) at No 9 in Hruškarje, near the village of Cajnarje (about 13km north-east of Cerknica), has delightfully rustic rooms for 2200 SIT per person including breakfast.

The *Dom na Slivnici* mountain hut (☎ 709 41 40) on Slivnica has 37 beds and is open year-round, except in July.

Places to Eat

Cerknica has a couple of decent restaurants, including *Valvasorjev Hram* (☎ 709 37 88) with its own wine cellar, opposite the tourist office at Partizanska cesta 1, and the *Gostilna Peščenek*, some 250m east of the centre on the main road. The *Mercator supermarket* in the shopping centre is open from 7 am to 7 pm weekdays, to 1 pm Saturday and 8 am till noon Sunday. There's a very basic *self-service restaurant* in the supermarket.

Getting There & Away

Bus The bus service to and from Cerknica is not great. Buses run hourly to Ljubljana and up to five times a day to Lož, Rakek and Stari Trg, but other destinations are few and far between. They include Bloška Polica (two buses a day), Hrib-Loški Potok (one on weekdays), Nova Vas (up to three), Postojna (three) and Snežnik Castle (one or two).

Train Luckily, there's a train station at Rakek, about 5km to the north-west of Cerknica, and it's on the line connecting Ljubljana with Sežana. About nine trains a day to or from the capital stop at Rakek. Heading south, all of these stop at Postojna and Pivka, but only about half carry on to Divača and Sežana.

Getting Around

The Notranjska Ecology Centre (☎ 709 16 36), above the tourist office at Cesta 4 Maja 51, rents bicycles for 1000/2000/2700/5000 SIT for a half-day/full day/three days/five days.

SNEŽNIK CASTLE

This 16th-century Renaissance castle below the village of Kozarišče, some 21km southeast of Cerknica, is one of the loveliest and best-preserved castles in Slovenia. Because of its secluded position in the Lož Valley (Loška Dolina), it has been able to escape the fate of most other castles in the country, and it looks almost exactly the way it did more than four centuries ago.

Things to See & Do

Snežnik Castle (Schneeberg in German), which houses a **museum**, stands in a large and protected park. The entrance is through a double barbican with a drawbridge and a moat. The exhibits in the main building are essentially the entire household inventory of the Schönburg-Waldenburg family, who used the castle as a summer residence and hunting lodge until WWII. The castle is full of tasteful period furniture; one room is done up in Egyptian handicrafts presented to Herman Schönburg-Waldenburg by a friend early in the 20th century. The castle also contains an **art gallery**.

Adjacent to the castle, a 19th-century building that once served as a dairy now contains a small **Dormouse Museum** (see Special Events). There's not much you won't know about this incredible-edible fellow's life and habits after a visit here.

Snežnik Castle is open from 10 am to 1 pm and 3 to 6 pm Wednesday to Friday from mid-April to October. It is open from 10 am to 6 pm on Saturday and Sunday. Admission is 500/450 SIT for adults/students and children.

Snežnik Castle would make an excellent bicycle trip from Cerknica. If you make the necessary preparations in advance, you could stop at **Križna Cave**, about a kilometre or so after you turn off the main Cerknica road. The cave, which was carved out by water from the Bloke Plateau, is 8.5km long and counts some 22 underground lakes filled with green and blue water as well as a unique 'forest' of ice stalagmites near the entrance.

This is one of the most magnificent water caves in the world and can be explored by

NOTRANJSKA

rubber raft. But in order to do so you must contact the guide, Alojz Troha (mobile ☎ 041-632 153), in Bloška Polica (house No 7) in advance; a tour costs 500 SIT per person. It's a long tour if you elect to do the entire cave. You should be dressed warmly and carry a torch as Križna Cave does not have electric lighting.

Lož, the next village, is a picturesque place in a valley with the ruins of a mighty 13th-century castle and a fortified church.

A stage of the E6 European Hiking Trail leads from near Snežnik Castle to **Snežnik** (1796m), whose peak remains snowcapped until well into the spring. Snežnik, about 15km south-west of Kozarišče, is the highest non-Alpine mountain in Slovenia and on a clear day you can see forever (well, as far as Trieste and Venice, the Julian Alps, the Karavanke on the Austrian border and the Pohorje Massif). There is accommodation at the ***Zavetišče na Velikem Snežniku*** *(mobile ☎ 050-615 356),* open on Saturday, Sunday and holidays from June to October and daily in August.

Special Events

Summer concerts are held as part of the Snežnik Evenings festival from July to September. Contact the tourist office (☎ 01-709 16 36) in Cerknica for details. The big occasion in these parts is Dormouse Night (Polharska Noč), held in late September during the brief period when it's open season to trap the edible dormouse or loir *(polh)*. This tree-dwelling nocturnal rodent, not unlike a squirrel, grows to about 30cm and sleeps through several months of the year. The dormouse is a favourite food in Notranjska (in fact, it was once a staple), and the hunting and eating of it is tied up with a lot of tradition. According to one Slovenian belief, the dormouse is shepherded by Lucifer himself and thus deserves its fate in the stew or goulash pot.

Getting There & Away

Snežnik's isolation makes it tough to reach by public transport. Without a car, bicycle or horse, you'll have to take a bus (up to five a day) to Stari Trg pri Lož and walk 4km.

Dolenjska

'Lower Carniola' is a charming area of gently rolling hills, vineyards, forests and the Krka River flowing south-eastward into Croatia. Those white hill-top churches with their red tile roofs, which you'll see everywhere, once protected the people from marauding Turks and other invaders; the ones on the flat lands are newer – built in the baroque style and painted the mustard colour ('Maria Theresa yellow') so common in Central Europe. The castles along the Krka are some of the best preserved in Slovenia as are the many monasteries and abbeys. You can't miss the distinctive 'double hayracks' *(toplarji)* of Dolenjska; they're here in spades.

Many people say that the 'purest' Slovene is spoken in Dolenjska – around the village of Rašica, south of the town of Krka, to be precise. But this may have more to do with the fact that Primož Trubar (1508–86), the 'father of the Slovenian literary language', was born here.

Dolenjska is the cycling centre of Slovenia. The E6 and E7 European Hiking Trails pass through Dolenjska, and there are lots of chances to do some kayaking or canoeing on the Krka. The province is also famous for its thermal spas.

History

Dolenjska was settled early on and is well known for its Hallstatt ruins and tombs, especially near Stična, Šmarjeta and Novo Mesto. The Romans eventually made the area part of the province of Upper Pannonia (Pannonia Superior) and built roads connecting Emona (Ljubljana) with smaller settlements at Praetorium Latobicorum (Trebnje), Acervo (Stična) and Neviodunum (Drnovo).

In the Middle Ages, the people of Dolenjska clustered around the many castles along the river (eg, at Žužemberk and Otočec) and at parish centres like Šentvid. Monasteries sprang up at Stična, Kostanjevica na Krki and near Šentjernej. Much of the region was

Highlights

- View the Cistercian abbey at Stična and its wonderful mix of architectural styles
- Explore the virgin forests of Kočevski Rog
- Enjoy an afternoon in the thermal spa at Dolenjske Toplice
- Marvel at the painted Knights' Hall at Brežice Castle
- Visit Bogenšperk Castle and Janez Vajkard Valvasor's study
- Sample the *viljemovka* (pear brandy) at Pleterje Monastery

part of the Slovenska Krajina, the 'Slovenian March' that became part of Carniola (Kranjska) in the 13th century.

Dolenjska declined after the Middle Ages and progress only came in the late 19th century when a railway line linked Novo Mesto with Ljubljana. This was extended (via Bela Krajina) to Karlovac in Croatia in 1914.

RIBNICA

☎ 01 • postcode 1310 • pop 3300

Though Ribnica is the oldest and most important settlement of western Dolenjska and just over the hills from the border with

DOLENJSKA

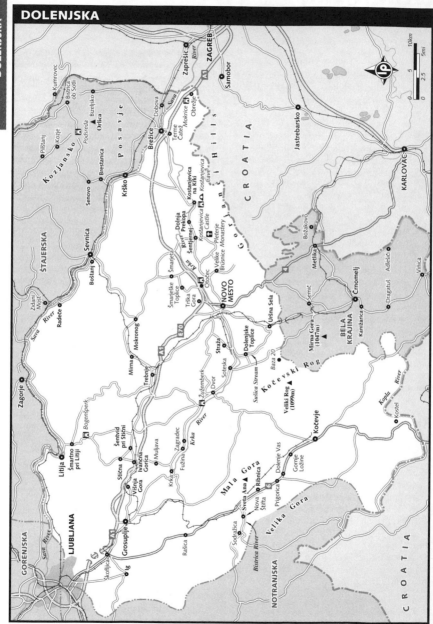

Notranjska, people in this region have traditionally affiliated with neither province. As far as they are concerned, this is Kočevsko, a forested, sparsely inhabited area with a unique history.

Ribnica is 16km north-west of the town of Kočevje, another gateway to Kočevski Rog (see Around Dolenjske Toplice), and on highway No 6 to the Croatian port of Rijeka.

History

Ribnica was an important feudal centre during the Middle Ages and was ruled by a succession of lords, including the Counts of Celje, before the Habsburgs arrived. It was also the centre of a large missionary area during the Christianisation of Slovenia. Like neighbouring Notranjska and Bela Krajina to the south-east, Kočevsko suffered greatly from the Turkish invasions of the 15th century. Bonfires would be lit atop peaks like Sveta Ana near Ribnica to warn the townspeople.

Among the inhabitants of the area at the time and up until the early days of WWII were many German-speaking Kočevarji who had been brought to Kočevsko by feudal lords a century before. Because the karst soil was too poor to make an adequate living from farming year-round, the Kočevarji supplemented their income with wooden products (*suha roba,* literally 'dry goods') that they produced at home: pails, sifters, baskets and kitchen utensils. The men sold these products throughout the Habsburg Empire, and even the advent of the railway in 1893 did not put an immediate end to this itinerant way of life. Until well into the 20th century the sight of the suha roba pedlar – his products piled high on his back and a staff in hand – was as Slovenian as a *kozolec* (hayrack). Woodcarving remains an important cottage industry today.

Orientation

The town lies in the Ribnica Valley sandwiched between two ridges called Velika Gora and Mala Gora. The main street, Škrabčev trg, lies on the east bank of the tiny Bistrica River and runs parallel to it. Buses stop near the Church of St Stephen.

Information

There's an inconspicuous tourist office, called 'TIC-a' (☎ 836 93 35, e obcina-ribni ca@siol.net), hidden upstairs at Škrabčev trg 40. The office is open from 9 am to 2 pm weekdays only.

Nova Ljubljanska Banka has a branch next to the Church of St Stephen at Škrabčev trg 9h. It is open from 8.30 to 11 am and 2 to 5 pm weekdays (3 to 6 pm Wednesday). SKB Banka, at the Ideal shopping centre on Kolodvorska ulica 9a, opens from 8 am till noon and 2 to 5 pm weekdays.

The main post office is at Kolodvorska ulica 2 opposite the shopping centre. It is open from 8 am to 7 pm weekdays and till noon Saturday.

Things to See

Ribnica Castle, on the west bank of the Bistrica at Gallusovo nabrežje 1, was originally built in the 10th century but was transformed and expanded over the centuries. Only a small section – a Renaissance wall and two towers – survived the WWII bombing. Today the castle houses a small **ethnographic collection** showcasing the traditional wood crafts and pottery made in the area. More interesting, perhaps, than the articles themselves are the tools that made them. The castle, set in an attractive semicircular park with memorial statues and markers to Slovenian greats, is a popular venue for weddings.

The **Parish Church of St Stephen** on Škrabčev trg, built in the latter part of the 19th century on the site of an earlier church, would not be of much interest were it not for the two striking towers added by Jože Plečnik after WWII. As usual, Plečnik mixed every conceivable style – to great success.

The plaque on the house opposite the church, **Šteklič House** (Šteklčkova Hiša) at Škrabčev trg 26, tells us that the 19th-century poet and patriot France Prešeren spent two years here (1810–12) in what was then the region's best-known school, attracting students from throughout Slovenia as well as from Trieste and Croatia.

The cultural centre at Miklova Hiša (☎ 836 19 38), a lovely cream and white building

DOLENJSKA

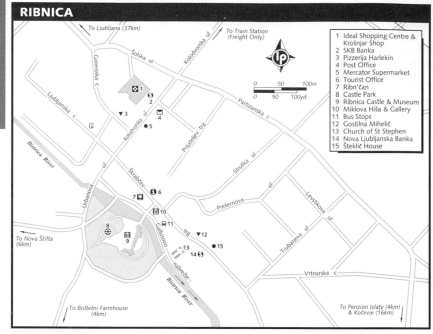

RIBNICA

To Ljubljana (37km)

Šolska ul.

Kolodvorska ul.

To Train Station (Freight Only)

Gorenjska c.

Ljubljanska c.

Kolodvorska ul.

Partizanska c.

Prijateljev trg.

Struška ul.

Bistrica River

Škrabčev

Urhanova ul.

Levstikova ul.

Prešernova

Trubarjeva ul.

Callisovo

nabrežje

Bistrica River

Vrtnarska c.

To Nova Štifta (6km)

To Bolletni Farmhouse (4km)

To Penzion Izlaty (4km) & Kočevje (16km)

0 50 100m
0 50 100yd

1 Ideal Shopping Centre & Krošnjar Shop
2 SKB Banka
3 Pizzerija Harlekin
4 Post Office
5 Mercator Supermarket
6 Tourist Office
7 Ribn'čan
8 Castle Park
9 Ribnica Castle & Museum
10 Miklova Hiša & Gallery
11 Bus Stops
12 Gostilna Mihelič
13 Church of St Stephen
14 Nova Ljubljanska Banka
15 Šteklič House

dating from 1858, has a small **gallery**. It is open from 10 am to noon and 4 to 6 pm.

Activities

Ribnica is the base for several excellent walks. A well-marked 'educational' trail leads north of the town for about 4.5km to the summit of Stena (963m), with fantastic views over the Ribnica Valley. Along the way you'll pass the entrance to France Cave, the hill-top Church of St Anne (Sveta Ana) and two huts selling food and drink.

From the Jasnica recreational centre (on the way to Kočevje), where horses are available for hire, a more difficult path leads north about 6km to the junction with the Ribnica Alpine Trail. This eventually joins up with the E7 European Hiking Trail about 5km west of Velike Lašče.

A trail into the Velika Gora ridge west of Ribnica that leads to a comfortable mountain hut is more easily accessible from Nova Štifta (see the Around Ribnica section).

Special Events

Ribnica's main event is the Dry Goods and Pottery Fair (Ribniški Semenj Suhe Robe in Lončarstva) held on the first Sunday in September, though the entire weekend is given over to music, drinking and, of course, buying and selling.

Places to Stay

The only accommodation near Ribnica is the *Penzion Izlaty* (☎ 836 45 15) in Prigorica (house No 115), which is about 4km south-east of Ribnica on the road to Kočevje. Singles with shower and breakfast are 3500 SIT, doubles 6000 SIT. Prigorica is less than 1km from Dolenja Vas, a town noted for its clay pottery and clay whistles. But if you've come this far, continue another 4km to the *Penzion Jasnica* (☎ 895 41 01) with 27 rooms in Gornje Ložine (house No 26) near the recreational centre. Singles/doubles cost 5200/8100 SIT. The *Boltetni Farmhouse* (☎ 836 02 08) at house

No 8 in Dane, 4km west of Ribnica, offers accommodation in July and August. Prices are around 3500 SIT per person.

Places to Eat

Ribnica's catering options are not much better than its accommodation. One of the very few central places for a meal is *Gostilna Mihelič* (☎ *836 31 31, Škrabčev trg 22)* opposite St Stephen's Church. It is open from 9 am till 10 pm (closed Sunday). *Pizzerija Harlekin (Gorenjska cesta 4)* is north of the centre and serves pizzas and salads from 10 am to 11 pm Monday to Saturday and noon to 10 pm Sunday.

There's a big *Mercator supermarket* on Kolodvorska ulica, south-west of the post office, open from 7 am to 6.30 pm weekdays and to 5 pm Saturday.

Entertainment

The convivial *Ribn'čan (Škrabčev trg 21)*, a 'garden pub' opposite the tourist office, is a popular hang-out for members of local motorcycling clubs.

Shopping

You'll see a fair number of wooden household articles for sale in Ribnica and the odd piece of pottery from nearby Dolenja Vas. The Krošnjar shop in the Ideal shopping centre at Kolodvorska ulica 9a has a large selection as well as handwoven baskets. It's open from 8 am till noon and 4 to 7 pm weekdays and Saturday morning.

Getting There & Around

Buses run at least once an hour north to Ljubljana and south to Kočevje. The bus to Sodražica is good for Nova Štifta.

Ribnica is no longer served by passenger train. The Grosuplje-Kočevje line that passes through Ribnica handles freight only – mostly timber. You can order a taxi in Ribnica on ☎ 836 31 20.

AROUND RIBNICA
Nova Štifta

The **Church of the Assumption** at Nova Štifta, in the foothills of the Velika Gora 6km west of Ribnica, is one of the most important pilgrimage sites in Slovenia. Completed in 1671 during the Counter-Reformation on a hill top where mysterious lights had been seen, the baroque church is unusual for its shape – both the nave and the presbytery are in the form of an octagon. The arcade on the west side fronting the entrance accommodated extra pilgrims on important holy days. The church proved so popular that the enclosed stairway on the north side was added in 1780 to allow even more of the faithful to reach the clerestory, the upper storey of the nave.

The interior of the church, with its three golden altars and pulpit carved by Jurij Skarnos, is blindingly ornate. Look for the painting of an aristocratic couple on stained glass on the north side of the presbytery. In the courtyard opposite the Franciscan monastery (where the church key is kept) stands a linden tree, planted in the mid-17th century, complete with tree house.

Dom na Travni Gori (☎ *01-836 63 33 in Ravni Dol),* a guesthouse 890m up with restaurant and accommodation, can be reached in about 1½ hours on a marked trail heading south-west from Nova Štifta. In winter one of Slovenia's smallest ski centres, **Travna Gora**, operates nearby with a 200m-long piste and one T-bar tow.

STIČNA

☎ 01 • postcode 1295 • pop 1150

The abbey at Stična (Sittich in German) is the oldest monastery in Slovenia and one of the country's most important religious and cultural monuments. At only 35km from Ljubljana and within easy walking distance of the train station at Ivančna Gorica (population 2060), Stična can be visited on a day trip from the capital or en route to Novo Mesto, the valley of the lower Krka or Bela Krajina. The monastery was established in 1136 by the Cistercians, a branch of the Benedictines that had been founded less than four decades before in France. The monks worked as farmers, following a vow of silence and communicating only through sign language. It became the most important religious, economic, educational and cultural centre in Dolenjska.

The lives of the monks were disrupted continuously in the second half of the 15th century during the Turkish invasions. Ultimately the abbey was surrounded by 8m-high walls and fortified with towers. But more damaging to the Cistercians was the edict issued by Emperor Joseph II in 1784 dissolving all religious orders – many of them very powerful and corrupt – in the Habsburg Empire. Stična was abandoned, and the order did not return until 1898.

Stična monastery has undergone steady reconstruction since WWII – much of it paid for by the government – and today almost the entire complex is again in use. There are five priests (including the abbot) and seven monks in residence.

Orientation & Information

The village of Stična is about 2.5km north of Ivančna Gorica, where the train station is located. The monastery office (☎ 787 71 00) will be able to help you if you need information.

Stična Abbey

The entrance to the walled abbey, an incredible combination of Romanesque, Gothic, Renaissance and baroque architecture, is on the east side across a small stream. This leads on to a large open courtyard bordered on the west by the Abbey Church and to the north by the Old Prelature, a Renaissance building dating from about 1600. The **Old Prelature**, once the administrative centre of

Under the Linden Trees

If cities can have municipal animals – where would Rome be today without the she-wolf that suckled Romulus and Remus? – and American states proclaim 'official drinks' (like tomato juice in New Jersey), why can't a country have a national tree? It's the linden (or common lime) in Slovenia and its heart-shaped leaf is often used as a symbol.

The stately linden (*lipa* in Slovene) can be found in abundance in Central Europe and was the most common tree in England thousands of years ago. Normally it grows slowly for about 60 years and then suddenly spurts upward and outwards, living to a ripe old age. It is said that a linden grows for 300 years, stands still for another 300 and takes 300 years to die.

Linden wood was used by the Romans to make shields and, as it is easy to work with, artisans in the Middle Ages carved religious figures from it, earning linden the title *sacrum lignum*, or 'sacred wood'. Tea made from the linden flower, which contains aromatic oils, has been used as an antidote for fever and the flu at least since the 16th century.

But the linden's ubiquity, longevity and many uses are not the only reasons it is so honoured by the Slovenes. For them, its past is even more important.

From earliest times, the linden tree was the focal point of any settlement in Slovenia – the centre of meetings, arbitration, recreation and, of course, gossip. The linden tree always stood in the middle of the village and important decisions were made by town elders at a table beneath it. The linden, which could never be taller than the church spire, was also the place to gather after Mass on Sunday.

So sacred has the linden tree become to Slovenes that its destruction is considered a serious offence. In discussing the barbarous acts committed by the Italians during the occupation of Primorska between the wars, one magazine article passionately points out that 'Kobarid had to swallow much bitterness ... The Fascists cut down the linden tree etc.' Arbicide, it would appear, is a grave crime in these parts.

In today's Slovenia, the linden represents not just hospitality but democracy too – something that has not been lost on seekers of high office. Few politicians facing an election fail to waltz around Slovenia's oldest linden, the Najevska Lipa under Mt Peca in Koroška.

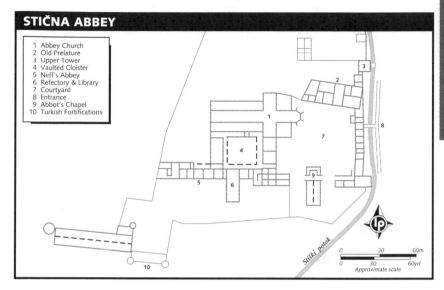

STIČNA ABBEY

1 Abbey Church
2 Old Prelature
3 Upper Tower
4 Vaulted Cloister
5 Neff's Abbey
6 Refectory & Library
7 Courtyard
8 Entrance
9 Abbot's Chapel
10 Turkish Fortifications

Stiški potok

0   30   60m
0   30   60yd
Approximate scale

the abbey, contains exhibition rooms on two floors. The collection is a hotchpotch of antique clocks, paintings, furniture and farm implements mixed with chalices, monstrances and icons. (One particularly gruesome statue shows Saint Perpetua holding her two amputated breasts on a platter.) There are a few 16th-century missals and medical texts in Latin and German, but all the medieval documents are facsimiles of the originals carted off to libraries in Vienna and Ljubljana when the order was banned in the 18th century, including the 15th-century *Stična Manuscript,* one of the earliest writings in Slovene. It is now kept at the National University Library in the capital.

One room is devoted to the accomplishments of the missionary Frederick Baraga (1797–1868), who was born in Trebnje to the south-east. Baraga taught among the Chippewa (or Ojibwa) Indians of Michigan and composed the first grammar of their language in 1843.

The video that the abbey shows visitors at the start of their tour is well produced and available in five languages, including English.

If you want to drop out of the tour early, you can exit under the **Upper Tower**, which is a few steps to the north-east of the Old Prelature. Just make sure you look up as you pass through. The ceiling is covered in stuccos from 1620 showing scenes of Christ's Passion and the Last Judgment.

Otherwise, across the courtyard to the west of the Abbey Church, a door leads to Stična's celebrated **vaulted cloister**, which mixes Romanesque and early Gothic styles. The cloister, which was once made of wood with stone corner pillars, served as an ambulatory for monks in prayer and connected the church with the monastery's other wings. The arches and vaults are decorated with frescoes of the prophets and Old Testament stories as well as allegorical subjects like the Virtues, the Four Winds etc. Look for the carved stone faces on the west side that were meant to show human emotions and vices – upon which the clergy were expected to reflect.

On the south side of the cloister is a typically baroque monastic **refectory** with an 18th-century pink ceiling and decorative swirls and loops made of white stucco. One floor above is the much impoverished library. **Neff's Abbey**, built in the mid-16th century by Abbot Volbenk Neff, runs to the west. The arches in the vestibule on the ground floor are painted with a dense network of leaves, blossoms, berries and birds. You can gain access to the church through a doorway in the cloister's north-east corner.

The **Abbey Church**, consecrated in 1156, was built as a buttressed, three-nave Romanesque cathedral. But except for the small windows at the top, you'd be hard-pressed to see much of that style today through all the baroque reconstruction that took place in the early 17th century and again in the mid-18th century, just a few decades before the order was forced to quit the premises. Apart from the ornate main altar and 11 side ones, the church contains several interesting elements. Look for the Renaissance red-marble tombstone of Abbot Jakob Reinprecht (who initiated the first baroque reconstruction) in the north transept and the blue organ cupboard with eight angels (1747) in the choir loft. But the greatest treasures here are the **Stations of the Cross** painted by Fortunat Bergant in 1766. The artist signed the last one – 'Jesus is Laid into the Sepulchre' – spelling his surname with a 'W'.

One final building worth a look is the outer wing **Abbot's Chapel** closing off the southern portion of the courtyard. Built in the late 18th century as a kind of replacement for the grandiose halls seen in palaces and some larger monasteries, it contains a double staircase and a hall chapel of incredible lightness and vivacity.

The abbey can be visited from 8 am to noon and 2 to 6 pm Tuesday to Saturday and on Sunday afternoon. Guided tours (available in Slovene, English and German) leave at 8.30 and 10 am, and 2 and 4 pm Tuesday to Saturday and at 2 and 4 pm Sunday and holy days. The entry charge is 400/200 SIT for adults/students and children. The abbey can be very crowded with visiting school children from April to June and September to November.

Places to Stay & Eat
It is possible to spend the night at the *monastery guesthouse* (☎ 787 71 00) for less

than 2500 SIT per person, but you should make prior arrangements with the abbot.

Much more comfortable is *Grofija* (☎ 787 81 41), a 19th-century farmhouse with accommodation, scarcely 1km south-east of Stična in the village of Vir pri Stični (house No 30). Its four rooms cost about €17 per person for B&B. Grofija (meaning 'county') is a working farm and horses are available for hire. Of historical note, a major Hallstatt settlement dating from 800 BC once stood near the site of the tennis court at Grofija. The farmhouse can also be reached directly from Ivančna Gorica (2.5km) on the Šentvid bus.

The *Krčma Deseti Brat (Tenth Brother Tavern;* ☎ 787 80 62), just uphill from the monastery entrance, serves up dishes of game, Dolenjska sausage, wild mushrooms and *štruklji* (dumplings). It's open from 8 am to 10 pm, but closed Monday.

In Ivančna Gorica, about 150m west of the train station, *Gostilna Krjavelj* (☎ 787 71 10, Ljubljanska cesta 38) serves local Dolenjska favourites to an appreciative local crowd. It's open from 8 am till midnight daily.

Shopping
The Cistercians sell many home-made products under their own label – bread, honey, wine, herbal teas and liqueurs – in a small shop in the Old Prelature. It's open from 8 am to 12.30 pm and 1 to 4 pm Monday to Saturday (to 3 pm Saturday).

Getting There & Away
Stična is served by up to 14 buses a day from Ljubljana, reducing to 12 on Saturday, and eight on Sunday.

Ivančna Gorica is on the rail line linking Ljubljana with Novo Mesto, Črnomelj and Metlika in Bela Krajina and Karlovac in Croatia. Up to 14 trains a day leave the capital, and the 37km trip to Ivančna Gorica takes about one hour.

BOGENŠPERK CASTLE
About 20km north of Stična is Bogenšperk Castle, in many respects the secular equivalent of Stična Abbey. Here the Slovenian polymath Janez Vajkard Valvasor (see the

boxed text 'Valvasor, Slovenia's Renaissance Man') spent the most productive two decades of his life, writing and eventually publishing *The Glory of the Duchy of Carniola* (1689), his encyclopaedic work on Slovenian history, geography and culture. Note that Bogenšperk is only accessible from Ivančna Gorica by car or bicycle; even the public transport options from Ljubljana, 40km to the west, are not good. Frequent trains and buses go to Litija, but it's still another 7km south to Bogenšperk – much of it uphill.

Bogenšperk Castle was built in the Renaissance style in the early 16th century by the aristocratic Wagen family, who named the place Wagensberg. Valvasor bought Bogenšperk in 1672 and installed his printing press, engraving workshop and extensive library here. But due to the enormous debts incurred in getting his *magnum opus*

published, he was forced to sell the castle in 1692. He died a year later in Krško.

The castle passed from family to family and the last owners, the Windisch-Grätz family, left it in 1943. During WWII, Bogenšperk was spared the total destruction that befell other castles in the area like Lichtenberg, Pogonik and Slatna since German soldiers were billeted here.

The castle, with its rectangular courtyard and three towers (the fourth burned down in Valvasor's time), was renovated in 1972 and today houses a museum devoted to the great man, his work and Slovenian culture. Valvasor's **library** is now used as a wedding hall (complete with a cradle, as is traditional in Slovenia), but his **study**, with its beautiful parquetry and painted ceiling, is pretty much the way he left it when he did his last alchemy experiments here. Other rooms contain examples of Valvasor's cartography

Valvasor, Slovenia's Renaissance Man

Most of our knowledge of Slovenian history, geography, culture and folklore before the 17th century comes from the writings of one man, Janez Vajkard Valvasor, and more specifically his *The Glory of the Duchy of Carniola*. Not only did this truly great Renaissance man map large areas of Carniola and its towns for the first time, he also explained the mystery of disappearing karst lakes and rivers, 'discovered' the unusual amphibian *Proteus anguinus*, introduced the world to Erazem Lueger, the 15th-century Robin Hood of Slovenia, and catalogued early Slovenian folk tales and dress.

Valvasor, whose name comes from the *valvassores*, the burghers who lived in the towns of the Holy Roman Empire in the early Middle Ages, was born in Ljubljana in 1641 of a noble family from Bergamo. After a Jesuit education there and in Germany, he joined Miklós Zrínyi, the Hungarian count and poet, in the wars against the Turks. Valvasor travelled widely for a man of his time, visiting Germany, Italy, North Africa, France and Switzerland. He collected data on natural phenomena and local customs as well as books, drawings, mineral specimens and coins.

In 1672 Valvasor installed himself, his books and his precious collections at Bogenšperk Castle, where he conducted scientific experiments (including alchemy) and wrote. In 1689 he completed his most important work. Published in German at Nuremburg under the title *Die Ehre des Herzogthums Crain* it ran into four volumes, containing 3500 pages with 535 maps and copper engravings. *The Glory of the Duchy of Carniola* remains one of the most comprehensive works published in Europe before the Enlightenment, a wealth of information on the Slovenian patrimony that is still explored and studied to this day.

As is so often the case with great men and women in history, Valvasor did not live to enjoy the success of his labour. Publishing such a large work at his own expense ruined him financially and he was forced to leave Bogenšperk in 1692. Valvasor died a year later at Krško, a town 65km to the east on the Sava River.

TAMSIN WILSON

and etching, four original volumes of his work donated by a Slovene from Trieste in 1993, a printing press similar to the one Valvasor used (the real one is in Munich) and the inevitable collection of hunting trophies, including a 132kg brown bear shot in Kočevski Rog in 1978.

The most interesting exhibits, though, are the ones that deal with folk dress (life-size mannequins sport costumes modelled exactly on Valvasor's illustrations, right down to the boots that have neither a right nor a left), superstition and folk medicine through the ages in Slovenia. There are endless recipes to break spells, red crosses to ward off witches, votives and good-luck charms and vials of herbs and elixirs. The **Knights' Hall** situated on the ground floor is often used for banquets and conferences, and the **castle chapel** near the entrance has been renovated.

Autumn Serenade concerts take place at the castle at 5 pm every Sunday throughout September.

Bogenšperk is open from 9 am to 3 pm Tuesday to Friday and till 5 pm at weekends (closed Monday) from March to October. At other times, tours can be made by arrangement (☎ 01-898 76 64, ⓔ bogensperk@ siol.net). The entrance fee is 500/400/350 SIT for adults/students/children.

KRKA RIVER VALLEY

The Krka River springs from a karst cave south-west of Stična, near the village of Trebnja Gorica, and runs to the south-east and east until it joins the mightier Sava River near Brežice. At 94km, it is Dolenjska's longest and most important waterway and one of the cleanest rivers in Slovenia.

If you are continuing on to other towns in Dolenjska and/or Bela Krajina and have your own transport, the ideal way to go is to follow the road along the Krka, which cuts a deep and picturesque valley along its upper course. The road is also excellent for cycling.

From Ljubljana most buses and the train heading for Dolenjska follow the old medieval road, today's route No 1 (E70). Opt instead for the bus going to Žužemberk.

Muljava

☎ 01 • postcode 1295 • pop 706

This picturesque town of double hayracks and beehives (a few with their original painted panels) is about 5km south of Ivančna Gorica and just north of a tributary of the Krka. Muljava's claim to fame is twofold: it is the birthplace of the writer Josip Jurčič (1844–81), whose *The 10th Brother* is considered the first full-length novel in Slovene, and is home to a small Gothic church with 15th-century frescoes.

Things to See & Do The **Church of the Assumption** lies east of the main road at the start of the village, and the key is available from the woman who lives next door (she's the bell ringer too). Not all of the paintings in the presbytery and on the vaulted arches are very clear – they show Cain and Abel making their sacrifices, symbols of the Apostles (including the winged lion of St Mark) and St Margaret – but the fresco depicting the death of the Virgin Mary on the south wall is still vibrant. The frescoes are signed by Johannes de Laibaco (John of Ljubljana) and dated 1456. The gilded main altar portraying the Assumption dates from the late 17th century.

Josip Jurčič's birthplace, a small cottage typical of the region, is west of the main road and open from 8 am to noon and 1 to 5 pm Tuesday to Friday, and afternoons only on Saturday and Sunday. Entry is 400/300 SIT. In front of the house is a beehive with painted front panels (*panjske končnice*) from the 19th century; behind it is an open-air theatre in a dell where some of Jurčič's works are staged in summer.

One of Slovenia's most popular places for fishing is the 9km stretch of the Krka from its mouth to Zagradec, about halfway to Žužemberk. The season lasts from March to November and brown and rainbow trout and grayling abound. But it's not a sport for the poor – a daily fishing licence costs 12,000 SIT. Permits are available from Gostišče Pod Lipo (☎ 07-308 70 07) in Žužemberk.

Places to Eat If you're hungry, *Gostilna Pri Obrščaku* serves up hearty Slovenian fare like *klobasa in zelje* (sausage with sauerkraut). It is on the main road in the village centre (house No 22) and is open to 10 pm daily, except Wednesday.

Krka Cave
Krka Cave, 2km from the main road and just west of the village of Trebnja Gorica, ain't in the same league as the Postojna or Škocjan Caves (see the Notranjska and Primorska chapters), but you do get to see some stalactites shaped like ribbons and fragile-looking 'spaghetti', a 100-year-old specimen of the *Proteus anguinus* amphibian in a tank (see the boxed text 'Proteus Anguinus, the Human Fish' in the Notranjska chapter) and a siphon lake that is the source of the Krka River.

From the kiosk marked 'Pri Izviru', a guide will escort you through fields to the entrance of the cave and as far as the lake (190m – a bit more than half the total length). The depth of the lake is 17m, but in winter – depending on the rain and the snowfall – the lake can rise almost as high as the ceiling. Krka Cave is open from 9 am to 7 pm daily March to October. Hours are 11 am to 3 pm during the rest of the year. Admission is 300/200 SIT for adults/students and children. Bring a jacket with you as the temperature is a constant 9.6°C and the humidity is high.

Žužemberk
☎ 07 • postcode 8360 • pop 3930
Once the site of a mighty fortress from the early Middle Ages perched on a cliff over the Krka, Žužemberk is about 17km from Muljava. The castle was completely rebuilt and the old walls fortified with round towers in the 16th century, but all but flattened during more than 20 air raids in WWII. Only two round towers have been reconstructed, but the sheer immensity and might of the place can still be seen from the opposite bank of the Krka. Note the iron well in the town's central square. It came from Dvor, a town to the south-east known for its ironwork.

Activities The fast-flowing Krka River offers excellent kayaking and canoeing, and

Žužemberk is a good spot from which to set out. The Žužemberk Kayak and Canoe Club (☎ 308 70 55) in Prapreče (house No 1a), 1km north-west of Žužemberk, can help with rentals and routes. Or contact the larger Rafting Club Gimpex (☎ 308 31 71) near Straža (Pod Srobotnikom 12) or Carpe Diem (☎ 01-780 60 11) in Krka (house No 27).

Special Events The Summer Castle Performances (Poletne Grajske Prireditve) are a series of concerts held in the Castle Cellar (Grajska Klet) from June to September.

Places to Eat The *Gostilna Župančič (Grajski trg 5)* is a pizzeria with an outside terrace overlooking the Krka and is open from 7 am till 10 pm (to 11 pm Friday and Saturday) daily, except Tuesday. The *Gostišče Pod Lipo (Grajski trg 4)* sits under a rather sick-looking linden in front of the castle and is open till 10 pm daily.

Getting There & Away The bus stop is near the post office at Grajski trg 28. Up to five buses a day go to Ljubljana (all depart by 12.30 pm), and four on weekdays to Novo Mesto (at 6.36 am, and 2.36, 3.30 and 7.10 pm).

DOLENJSKE TOPLICE
☎ 07 • postcode 8350 • pop 800
Within easy striking distance of Novo Mesto (13km to the north-east), this thermal resort is the oldest and one of the few real spa towns in Slovenia. Located in the karst valley of the Krka River below the wooded slopes of Kočevski Rog, Dolenjske Toplice is an excellent place in which to hike, cycle, fish or simply relax.

History
Although the curative powers of the thermal springs were known as early as the 14th century, the first spa was not built until 1658 when Ivan Vajkard, a member of the aristocratic Auersperg family, opened the Prince's Bath. The Kopališki Dom (Bathers' House), complete with three pools, was built in the late 18th century when the first chemical analysis of the thermal waters was done.

Within a century, Dolenjske Toplice had 30 rooms, basic medical facilities and its very own guidebook, but tourism did not really take off until 1899 with the opening of the Zdraviliški Dom (Health Resort House). Strascha Töplitz, as it was then called (after the nearby town of Straža), was a great favourite of Austrians from around the early 20th century up to WWI.

The complex was used as a military treatment centre in the 1920s and 1930s and part of it was a Partisan hospital during WWII.

Orientation & Information

Dolenjske Toplice lies about 1.5km south of the Krka River on an undulating stream called the Sušica. Virtually everything – including the two hotels of the thermal resort – is on or just off the main street, Zdraviliški trg. Buses stop just south of or opposite the post office. Dolenjske Toplice is not on a rail line.

The K2M tourist agency (☎/fax 306 68 30, ℮ k2m@k2m.si) at Pionirska cesta 3 can provide information and book accommodation in local pensions. The helpful staff at the Hotel Vital (☎ 391 94 00) will answer all your questions about the spa and surrounding area. Dolenjska Banka has a branch at Zdraviliški trg 8 and is open from 8 am to noon and 2 to 4.30 pm weekdays; its ATM is south of the church, beside the bridge over the river. The post office is north across the car park at No 3. It is open from 8 am to 5 pm weekdays (but closed 9.30 to 10 am) and till noon Saturday.

Thermal Spas

Taking the waters is the *sine qua non* of Dolenjske Toplice, and you don't have to be a hotel guest to do so; outsiders pay 1000 SIT a day for the privilege. It's actually taken very seriously. The warm mineral water (36° to 38°C) gushing from 1000m below the two covered pools at Kopališki Dom is ideal for ailments such as rheumatism, but a recreational soak is still a lot of fun and can avert backache. The health resort also offers any number of other types of therapy, from underwater massage (1800 SIT) to acupuncture (2000 SIT).

The outdoor thermal pool *(športni bazen)* is 300m north of the two hotels, reached via a lovely little park. The unusual carved wooden statues of curling snakes and elongated (and shackled) human figures suggest the traditional occupations of this area: logging and woodcarving. The pool, open from 9 am till 7 pm in summer, has 27°C water. Admission for a full day is 1100 SIT on weekdays and 1200 SIT at the weekend.

Hiking

A number of short (under 5km) and easy walks can be made from Dolenjske Toplice, or you might consider hiking in the virgin forests of Kočevski Rog, with Baza 20, the Partisan nerve centre during WWII, or even Veliki Rog (1099m) as your destination (see the Around Dolenjske Toplice section).

Walks marked on the Dolenjske Toplice town map include a 3km one south through the forest to Cerovec Hill (276m), with the Church of the Holy Trinity atop, affording pleasant views of the town, and a hike of 4km west to Cvinger (263m), where Hallstatt tombs and iron foundries have been unearthed. Nature lovers may be interested in the 'educational forest walk' just west of Podturn (2km), which also takes in a small cave and the ruins of Rožek Castle.

Other Activities

The tennis courts on the hill north-west of the camping ground can be hired for 1000 SIT (600 SIT for hotel guests) per hour between 7 am and 8 pm. See the staff at the Hotel Vital about renting racquets.

Daily permits (4100 SIT) valid for fishing in the Sušica and the middle course of the Krka, famous for its salmon and trout, are available from the hotels.

The ski centre of Rog-Črmošnjice (☎ 302 52 50), 16km south of Dolenjske Toplice, has five T-bar tows on the slopes of Mt Gače at altitudes of between 730m and 930m. It's open between December and the end of March (depending on the snowfall).

Places to Stay

The three-hectare *Dolenjske Toplice camping ground* (☎ 306 60 12) is just off the

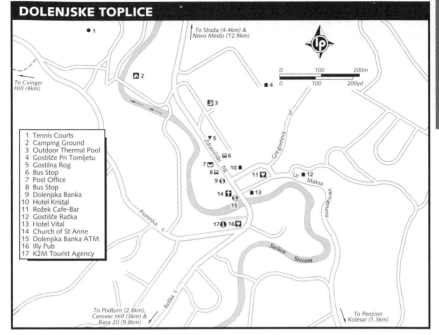

DOLENJSKE TOPLICE

To Straža (4.4km) &
Novo Mesto (12.9km)

To Cvinger
Hill (4km)

To Podturn (2.8km),
Cerovec Hill (3km) &
Baza 20 (9.8km)

To Penzion
Kolesar (1.3km)

1 Tennis Courts
2 Camping Ground
3 Outdoor Thermal Pool
4 Gostišče Pri Tomljetu
5 Gostilna Rog
6 Bus Stop
7 Post Office
8 Bus Stop
9 Dolenjska Banka
10 Hotel Kristal
11 Rožek Cafe-Bar
12 Gostišče Rača
13 Hotel Vital
14 Church of St Anne
15 Dolenjska Banka ATM
16 Illy Pub
17 K2M Tourist Agency

northern end of Zdraviliški trg, more or less opposite the outdoor swimming pool. It is open from May to September and can accommodate up to 120 guests. Daily charges are 700 to 900 SIT per person, 450 SIT per car and per tent.

Gostišče Rača (*π/fax 306 55 10, Ulica Maksa Henigmana 13*), in a renovated village house to the east of the centre, has two-, three- and four-bed rooms with bathroom and TV for 4000 SIT per person (3500 SIT if you stay three or more nights).

Gostišče Pri Tomljetu (*π 306 50 23, Zdraviliški trg 24*) is a cosy guesthouse behind the open-air pool. None of the eight rooms has its own bathroom but all have sinks, and cooking facilities are available. Singles/doubles including breakfast cost 2750/5000 SIT.

The eight-room ***Penzion Kolesar*** (*π 306 50 03*) is an even better deal – 4000 SIT for a double with bathroom and breakfast – and there's a very popular *gostilna* on the ground

floor. But it's in Dolenje Sušice (house No 22), about 2km south-east of Dolenjske Toplice, with no chance of catching a late-night bus.

The newly renovated, four-star spa hotels ***Vital*** and ***Kristal*** (*π 391 94 00, fax 306 56 62,* *e* *dolenjske.marketing@krka-zdravilisca.si, Zdraviliški trg 11*) share the same facilities, including two indoor thermal pools, two saunas and a fitness centre. Both charge from 10,100/15,800 SIT for a single/double room with breakfast, and both offer discounted weekend and week-long packages.

Places to Eat

The health resort's main restaurant is the ornately decorated dining room of the ***Hotel Kristal*** where most guests on half or full board take their meals. Otherwise the choice in the immediate area is limited to two gostilne: the ***Gostilna Rog*** (*Zdraviliški trg 22*) on the edge of the park near the outdoor pool has decent salads and is open to

10 or 11 pm daily; the *Gostišče Račka* (see Places to Stay) serves decent pizza and pasta until 1 pm daily.

If you've got two or more wheels or don't mind walking 3km, head south-west for *Gostilna Štravs* (☎ 306 53 90) in Podturn (house No 28). It's one of the best small restaurants in the area, specialising in freshwater fish and game, and also has accommodation.

Entertainment

The *Rog* has Slovenian folk music from 8 pm Tuesday to Friday. Otherwise it's generally early to bed and early to rise in this health-conscious town. The *Rožek* is a small, glassed-in cafe-bar in the plaza between the two hotels (open 7 am to 9 pm), though Dolenjske Toplice's young bloods tend to congregate at the *Illy Pub* just across the bridge at the start of Pionirska cesta.

Getting There & Around

There are hourly buses to Novo Mesto between 6 am and 9.20 pm and six or seven a day to Žužemberk.

You can hire bikes from the K2M tourist agency for 300 SIT per hour or 1500 SIT per day.

AROUND DOLENJSKE TOPLICE
Kočevski Rog

One of the most pristine areas in Slovenia, Kočevski Rog has been a protected nature area for more than 100 years, and six virgin forests, covering an area of more than 200 sq hectares, are preserved here.

The region was – and still is – so remote and filled with limestone caves that during the early days of WWII the Partisans, under the command of Marshal Tito, headquartered here, building bunkers, workshops, hospitals and schools, and even setting up printing presses. The nerve centre was the so-called **Baza 20** (Base 20), about 10km south-west of Dolenjske Toplice, which was reconstructed and turned into a national monument after the war.

During the former regime, Baza 20 was a favourite 'pilgrimage' spot for many Slovenes and other Yugoslavs, and busloads of 'the faithful' paid their respects daily.

Nowadays Baza 20 is a shadow of its former self – its two dozen buildings are ramshackle, the access trail unkempt and the indicator maps all but illegible. Still, as an indication of how Slovenes view the recent past, both under communism and now, it's worth a visit.

A plaque erected near the site in 1995 diplomatically pays homage to everyone involved in the 'national liberation war', presumably including the thousands of Domobranci (Home Guards) murdered here by the Partisans in 1945.

There is no scheduled bus service to Baza 20, but it is easily reached by sealed road on foot or bicycle from Podturn, 7km away. From the car park and *Gostišče Baza 20* (open 10 am to 10 pm daily), it's a 15-minute walk up a mountain path to the site. The road south to Črmošnjice is unsealed and pretty rough; if you're heading for Črnomelj or Metlika, it's easier to return to Podturn first.

The range's tallest peak, **Veliki Rog** (1099m), is about 5km to the south-west. The area is a popular hunting ground (brown bear, wild cat, boar etc) for rich Italian tourists and was a favourite of Tito and his cronies.

NOVO MESTO

☎ 07 • postcode 8000 • pop 25,000

Situated on a sharp bend of the Krka River, the inappropriately named 'New Town' is the political, economic and cultural capital of Dolenjska and one of its prettiest towns. For Slovenes, Novo Mesto is synonymous with the painter Božidar Jakac (1899–1989), who captured the spirit of the place on canvas, and the writer Miran Jarc (1900–42) who did the same in prose with his autobiographical novel *Novo Mesto*. For the traveller, Novo Mesto is an important gateway to the historical towns and castles along the lower Krka, the karst forests of the Gorjanci Hills to the south-east, Bela Krajina and Croatia. Indeed, Zagreb is a mere 74km east of Novo Mesto via route No 1 (E70).

Today's Novo Mesto shows two faces to the world: the Old Town, which is perched high up on a rocky promontory above the left bank of the Krka, and a new town to the north and south, which thrives on the business of Krka, a large pharmaceutical and chemical company, as well as Revoz, which produces Renault cars and is the country's largest exporter.

History
Novo Mesto was settled during the late Bronze Age around 1000 BC, and helmets and decorated burial urns unearthed in surrounding areas suggest that Marof Hill above the Old Town was the seat of Hallstatt princes during the early Iron Age. The Illyrians and Celts came later, and the Romans maintained a settlement in this region until the 4th century AD, when it was then overrun by Germanic tribes during the Great Migrations.

During the early Middle Ages, Novo Mesto flourished as a market because of its location and later became the centre of the estates owned by the Cistercian abbey at Stična. In 1365, Habsburg Archduke Rudolf IV raised it to the status of a town, naming it Rudolphswert. By the 16th century, some 15,000 loads of freight passed through Novo Mesto each year. But plague, fires and raids by the Turks on their way to Vienna took a toll on the city and within a hundred years Novo Mesto's main square had become grazing land for cattle. Despite Novo Mesto's decline, Janez Vajkard Valvasor wrote in his opus *The Glory of the Duchy of Carniola* that it was still 'the most remarkable town of the duchy after Ljubljana'.

Prosperity returned in the 18th and 19th centuries: a college was established in 1746, Slovenia's first National Hall (Narodni Dom) opened here in 1875 and a railway line linked the city with Ljubljana in the 1890s. After the capitulation of the Habsburgs in 1918, Novo Mesto began to industrialise. Bombardments during WWII, particularly in 1941 and 1943, severely damaged the city.

Orientation
Almost everything of interest in Novo Mesto is in the toe-shaped Old Town above the Krka River and dominated by the belfry of the Chapter Church. Glavni trg is a large, cobbled square – bigger than any square in Ljubljana, locals like to point out – lined with arcaded shops and public buildings. A bridge at its southern end leads to the suburbs of Kandija, Šmihel and Grm.

The bus station is south-west of the Old Town across the Krka on Topliška cesta; to reach Glavni trg, follow Kandijska cesta east for 800m and cross the bridge. Novo Mesto has two train stations: the main one about 2km north-west of the Old Town and tiny Novo Mesto-Center, at the start of Ljubljanska cesta at the western edge of the Old Town. From here it's a five-minute walk eastward to Novi trg, which has been converted into a pedestrian mall and business centre. Another 350m along Rozmanova ulica will take you to Glavni trg.

Information
Tourist Offices The tourist office (☎ 393 92 63) is hidden away in an office building at Seidlova cesta 1, just west of Novi trg. It's open from 7 am weekdays only, closing at 3 pm Monday and Tuesday, 5 pm Wednesday and 2 pm Thursday and Friday. Try to get the Slovenian Tourist Board's free pamphlet *Europe's Sleeping Beauty: Heritage Trails through Dolenjska & Bela Krajina,* which lists more than two dozen of the top sights in the region.

Money The most centrally located banks are the SKB Banka branches at Glavni trg 10 and Novi trg 3. They are open from 8.30 am to noon and 2 to 5 pm weekdays only. A Banka's Novo Mesto branch at Rozmanova ulica 38, just north of Novi trg, is open from 8 am to 5 pm weekdays and till 11 am Saturday.

Post & Communications The main post office, with a bank of cardphones, is at Novi trg 7 and open from 7 am to 8 pm weekdays, to 1 pm Saturday and 9 to 11 am Sunday.

Travel Agencies Agencies in Novo Mesto include Kompas (☎ 332 13 38) at Novi trg 10 and Emona Globtour (☎ 332 33 76) at Rozmanova ulica 19, both of which are open from 7 or 8 am until 4 pm weekdays and till noon Saturday.

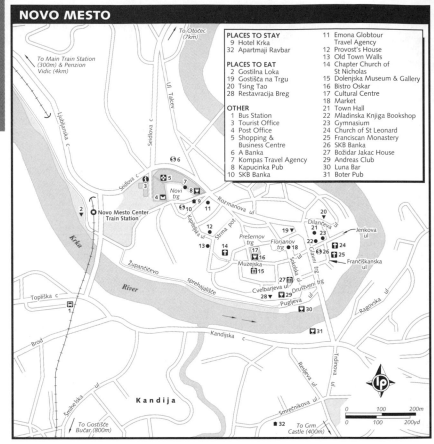

NOVO MESTO

PLACES TO STAY
9 Hotel Krka
32 Apartmaji Ravbar

PLACES TO EAT
2 Gostilna Loka
19 Gostišča na Trgu
20 Tsing Tao
28 Restavracija Breg

OTHER
1 Bus Station
3 Tourist Office
4 Post Office
5 Shopping &
Business Centre
6 A Banka
7 Kompas Travel Agency
8 Kapucinka Pub
10 SKB Banka
11 Emona Globtour
Travel Agency
12 Provost's House
13 Old Town Walls
14 Chapter Church of
St Nicholas
15 Dolenjska Museum & Gallery
16 Bistro Oskar
17 Cultural Centre
18 Market
21 Town Hall
22 Mladinska Knjiga Bookshop
23 Gymnasium
24 Church of St Leonard
25 Franciscan Monastery
26 SKB Banka
27 Božidar Jakac House
29 Andreas Club
30 Luna Bar
31 Boter Pub

Bookshops Mladinska Knjiga at Glavni trg 9, open from 7 am till 7 pm weekdays and till noon Saturday, sells regional maps and guides.

Chapter Church of St Nicholas

Perched above the Old Town on Kapiteljska ulica, this Gothic church is Novo Mesto's most visible historical monument. And, with a 15th-century presbytery and crypt, painted ceiling, a belfry that had once been a medieval defence tower and an altar painting of the eponymous saint supposedly done by the Venetian master Jacopo Tintoretto

(1518–94), it is also the city's most important. But what strikes many visitors most is the nave; it actually doglegs by some 17 degrees before reaching the main altar.

The cream-coloured building to the northwest of the church is the **Provost's House**, built in 1623. If the church is locked, you'll find the key here. A section of the town's **medieval walls** can be seen just west of the church. It dates from the 14th century.

Dolenjska Museum

Below the Chapter Church about 100m to the east at Muzejska ulica 7, the Dolenjska

Museum complex is divided into five parts. The oldest building, which once belonged to the Knights of the Teutonic Order, houses a valuable collection of archaeological finds unearthed in the southern suburb of Kandija in the late 1960s. The museum is divided into four periods: the Neolithic and Bronze ages; the Hallstatt (early Iron Age) period; the Celtic era; and Roman Dolenjska.

You can't miss the Hallstatt helmet dating from 800 BC with two enormous axe blows at the top, the fine bronze situlae (or pails) from the 4th century BC embossed with battle and hunting scenes, and the Celtic ceramics and jewellery (particularly the bangles of turquoise and dark-blue glass) from Beletov Vrt.

The **Dolenjska Gallery** hosts the Biennial of Slovenian Graphic Art, held during even-numbered years (the 4th Biennale was in 1996, the 5th in 1998 etc), which occasionally accepts non-Slovenian guests. The gallery's permanent collection includes regional works from the 16th to 20th centuries.

Other collections in the complex include one devoted to the Liberation Front and the Partisans during WWII and a small but excellent **ethnographic collection** with farm implements, commemorative jugs presented at weddings, decorated heart-shaped honey cakes and icons painted on glass. Take a look at the almost life-size wooden statue of a French soldier from the Illyrian Provinces era. It was used as a beehive.

The museum also administers **Božidar Jakac House** about 100m east at Sokolska ulica 1. The peripatetic and prolific Jakac visited dozens of countries in the 1920s and 1930s, painting and sketching such diverse subjects as Parisian dance halls, Scandinavian port towns, African villages and American city skylines. But his best works are of Novo Mesto: markets, people, churches and rumble-tumble wooden houses clinging precariously to the banks above the Krka. One unusual work is the almost surreal *Odkrivanje* (Revelation) of a man hiding his face before a parted curtain.

The Dolenjska Museum is open from 8 am (10 am Saturday) to 5 pm Tuesday to Saturday and 9 am till noon Sunday during summer. Hours are 8 am to 4 pm weekdays, 9 am to 1 pm Saturday and 9 am till noon Sunday during winter. The Božidar Jakac House is open from 9 am to 1 pm Tuesday to Saturday (from 10 am Saturday). Entrance to the Dolenjska Museum is 300/150 SIT for adults/students and children, or 500/300 SIT for both the museum and Božidar Jakac House.

Other Sights

Novo Mesto's other interesting buildings are mostly on or just off Glavni trg. At No 6 the neo-Renaissance **town hall**, out of step with the square's other arcaded buildings, ostentatiously calls attention to itself at all hours with its bells and odd facade. The coat of arms on the front is that of Archduke Rudolf IV, the town's founder.

South of the town hall on Frančiškanska ulica, is the **Church of St Leonard**, which was originally built by Franciscan monks fleeing the Turks in Bosnia in 1472, but with an unusual neo-Gothic/Moorish gable added in the 19th century, and the **Franciscan monastery**. The monastery library's collection of rare manuscripts, including many important 12th-century incunabula, are now in Ljubljana. The **Gymnasium** founded by Maria Theresa in 1746 is to the north at Jenkova ulica 1. Today it houses a music school, a public library and the provincial archives.

The only historical structure of note on the south side of the Krka is **Grm Castle**, a manor house at Skalickega ulica 1, with an ornately stuccoed central hall. It contains some government offices, but is still in a general state of disrepair.

Activities

Boating The Luna bar (☎ 332 16 12) rents canoes during the summer months (see Entertainment). Don't expect to get very far along the Krka from this point; you can only paddle about 2km upstream and 200m downstream.

Flying The Novo Mesto Aeroclub (☎ 332 11 07) at Prečna, 5km west of Novo Mesto, offers sightseeing flights over Novo Mesto

DOLENJSKA

and the Krka Valley in Cessna 172s and Piper 28-Warriors between 9 am and 7 pm daily. A 15-minute flight costs 6000 SIT for three passengers. Flying lessons are also available. The airfield is just over 1km from the centre of Prečna, which is served by bus from Novo Mesto.

Horse Riding The Novo Mesto Sport Equestrian Centre (☎ 302 81 66) in the village of Češča Vas, about 3km south of Prečna, has Holsteiners and Arabians for riders of all levels. You can ride on any day, but you should book first. There's also horse riding at the Struga Riding Centre near Otočec Castle, 7km to the north-east (see Otočec later in this chapter).

Places to Stay

The accommodation options in Novo Mesto are not great and can be quite expensive. The closest *camping grounds* are at Otočec and Dolenjske Toplice, 7km and 12km away respectively. Emona Globtour has a few *private rooms* on its books for around 3000 SIT per person, but they are quite a distance from town.

Apartmaji Ravbar (☎ 334 27 00, Smrečnikova ulica 15–17), a family-run guesthouse across the Krka (signposted from Kandijska cesta), has five modern, spotlessly clean apartments with kitchen and two rooms for about €18 per person. It's a very quiet area, full of trees and people walking their dogs. Farther afield (about 4km north-west of the Old Town), *Penzion Vidic* (☎ 332 18 22, Ljubljanska cesta 51) charges €26/41 for singles/doubles.

The only place to stay in the centre of town is the *Hotel Krka* (☎ 332 22 26, fax 331 30 00, Novi trg 1), a 53-room business hotel. Comfortable, modern singles with shower, TV, air-con and breakfast are 12,000 SIT, doubles 15,000 SIT. The Krka has a decent restaurant and a pub open till 10 pm.

Places to Eat

The *Tsing Tao* (☎ 332 43 88, Dilančeva ulica 7), tucked away in a cellar, is a Chinese restaurant where main courses like chicken with chilli and peanuts cost around

950 SIT including rice. It's open from 11 am to 11 pm daily.

Gostišča na Trgu (☎ 332 18 82, Glavni trg 30), the 'Inns on the Square', have three eateries and a *kavarna*. On the ground floor there's a cafe with a sidewalk terrace, a pizzeria (pizzas from 690 SIT) and an ice-cream parlour. Upstairs the 'classic' restaurant has set-lunch menus from 850 SIT. The self-service restaurant on the same floor, with pleasant seating on a narrow balcony overlooking a courtyard, is much cheaper.

For better (and more expensive) food, head deeper into the Old Town for the *Restavracija Breg* (☎ 332 12 69, Cvelbarjeva ulica 7), birthplace of Božidar Jakac and once an important spot for artists and writers. Try *kurja obara z ajdovimi žganci* (chicken stew with buckwheat groats) or *pečenica in zelje* (bratwurst with sauerkraut) along with a glass or two of Cviček, the uniquely Slovenian light red wine from Dolenjska. There's garden seating available in the warmer months. Expect to pay about 1600 SIT for two courses and a drink.

Gostilna Loka (Župančičevo sprehajališče 2) is on the Krka with restful views across the river. The speciality here is fish, particularly trout, and the restaurant is open from 9 am till midnight daily.

There is an outdoor *market* on Monday, Wednesday and Friday selling fruit and vegetables on Florjanov trg in the centre of the Old Town.

Entertainment

The *cultural centre* (☎ 332 12 14, Prešernov trg 3–5) has a cinema (screenings at 8 pm) and sponsors occasional theatrical and musical performances. Ask the staff about summer concerts held in the atrium of the Provost's House.

Like the province of Bela Krajina to the south, Dolenjska has a tradition of folk music, and flyers and posters around town are always announcing folk ensemble performances at music halls and cultural centres in neighbouring towns and villages.

Glavni trg has a number of small pubs and cafes (eg, at No 14) with outside terraces that would be pleasant in the warm months

Pivka River near its entry to the Postojna Cave (Notranjska)

Spectacular Predjama Castle (Notranjska)

Veliki Naravni bridge, Rakov Škocjan Gorge

Žužemberk Castle (Dolenjska)

Knights' Hall, Brežice Castle (Dolenjska)

The Three Parishes, pilgrimage churches in Rosalnice (Bela Krajina)

if the traffic through the square wasn't so heavy. Leave them behind and head for **Luna** *(Pugljeva ulica 2)* or **Boter** behind Kandijska cesta 4, two outdoor cafe-pubs on opposite sides of the river. The Luna, with its lovely back garden, is more pleasant, but the Boter has better views of the Old Town from across the Krka. They could be straight out of a Jakac painting.

The **Andreas Club** next to the Breg restaurant on Cvelbarjeva ulica and the **Kapucinka** pub at the eastern end of Novi trg opposite Rozmanova ulica 32 are decent late-night places for a drink. Another recommended venue is the **Bistro Oskar** opposite the Dolenjska Museum on Muzejska ulica. It's open till 11 pm daily.

Getting There & Away
Bus Bus service to and from Novo Mesto is good. There are frequent departures to Dolenjske Toplice, Otočec, Šentjernej and Šmarješke Toplice and at least 10 a day to Brežice, Kostanjevica na Krki and Ljubljana (via Trebnje or Žužemberk). Other destinations served from Novo Mesto include: Bled (one bus a day), Celje (one), Črnomelj (six), Kranjska Gora (two), Metlika (four), Trebnje (eight) and Vinica (five). You can also reach Zagreb on three buses a day.

Train Up to 15 trains a day serve Novo Mesto from Ljubljana (1¾ hours, 75km) via Ivančna Gorica and Trebnje. Many of these continue on to Črnomelj (45 minutes, 32km) and Metlika (one hour, 47km), where there are up to five connections a day with Karlovac in Croatia. To reach anywhere else of importance in Slovenia by train from Novo Mesto, you have to go via Ljubljana.

OTOČEC
☎ 07 • postcode 8222 • pop 1885
The castle at Otočec (Wördl in German), on a tiny island in the middle of the Krka River, 7km north-east of Novo Mesto, is one of Slovenia's loveliest and most complete fortresses. Unfortunately, someone else thought so too and turned it into an upmarket and very expensive hotel. But the area around Otočec, the gateway to the

lower Krka and the Posavje region, has become something of a recreational centre, and there is a wide choice of accommodation and activities.

History
The first castle at Otočec almost certainly stood on the right (south) bank of the river. But during the Mongol onslaught in the mid-13th century (or even a century later during the wars with the Hungarians), a canal was dug on the south side, thereby creating an artificial island. The present structure probably lost its military significance almost as soon as it was built in the early 16th century, since the frontier had moved southward by then. In 1560 the castle was purchased by Ivan Lenkovič, the commander of the Vojna Krajina (Military March) who went on to defeat the Turks at Kostanjevica na Krki three years later.

Orientation
The castle – now the posh Hotel Grad Otočec – is 1km east of Otočec village on a secondary road running parallel to route No 1 (E70) and the river. You reach the castle via a rickety wooden bridge that probably should not handle cars. Cheaper accommodation is available up the hill a few steps north of the bridge and across the main road. The camping ground is south-west of the island on the south bank.

Information
Staff at the reception of the castle hotel (☎ 307 56 99) can provide information about the recreational facilities at Otočec and help with equipment rentals. You can change money here, at the reception of the Hotel Šport, at the camping ground or at the post office in Otočec village.

Otočec Castle
Though you probably won't be staying at the castle hotel, there's no harm in having a look around this historical site and perhaps having a drink or a coffee at the terrace cafe in the courtyard, if the weather is warm. The castle, with elements of late Gothic and Renaissance architecture, consists of two

wings connected by a wall. There are four squat, rounded towers with very thick walls and narrow loopholes at each end.

Activities

Otočec (and the Krka Valley in general) is a cycling centre. The tennis centre by Hotel Šport rents bicycles and mountain bikes for 600 SIT per hour. The tennis centre has three indoor courts (2000 to 3000 SIT per hour) and six outdoor ones (700 to 900 SIT) as well as a sauna and steam room (1100 SIT) and fitness centre (700 SIT per hour).

The camping ground rents canoes, rowing boats and rafts for use on the Krka. (The best areas for rowing are downstream from Struga.) The per-hour fee is 700 SIT.

While not as rich as the upper Krka, the river around Otočec is a popular fishing spot and more than likely will yield a couple of pike, perch or carp. Fishing permits from the hotel cost 3200 SIT per day.

The Struga Riding Centre (☎ 307 56 27) on the south bank of the river, about 1.5km north-east of the Otočec camping ground, has a number of horses available for dressage, cross-country riding and coach excursions. One hour of riding is 3000 SIT, lessons are 4000 SIT per hour and a one-hour ride in an old coach is 5000 SIT. The centre, which is housed in another medieval castle complete with chapel, is open from 8 to 11 am and 5 to 9 pm daily, except Tuesday. To get there from the castle, cross the second bridge, walk east for 600m on the sealed road and then 900m north on the unsealed one.

Places to Stay

Kamp Otočec (☎ 307 57 00) camping ground is on a two-hectare strip of land running along the south bank of the Krka and can accommodate 200 people. To reach it from the castle, cross the second bridge, turn left (east) and walk for 300m. It has its own tennis court and pool and there's a 'beach' along the river. Daily charges are 600 SIT per person, 300 SIT per car, 400 SIT per tent and 400 SIT per caravan. It is open from May to September.

An unattractive area across the main road from the castle includes *Hotel Šport* (☎ 307

57 00, fax 307 54 20, Grajska cesta 2), a concrete-and-glass box with a cocktail bar, disco and 78 rooms. Singles with shower and breakfast are 12,500 SIT, doubles are 17,000 SIT. The *bungalows* in the nearby complex cost 7500/13,000 SIT, while the *motel* rooms are cheaper at 5600/9200 SIT.

The *Hotel Grad Otočec* (☎ 307 51 68, fax 307 54 60, e booking.otocec@krka-zdravilisca.si) is one of the most attractive and luxurious hotels in Slovenia. Its two dozen enormous rooms have polished parquet floors, Oriental carpets, marble-topped tables and large baths. But don't expect all that to come cheap – singles with bath and breakfast are 19,500 SIT, doubles 26,000 SIT.

If you want something a bit more rural and affordable, the *Šeruga Farmhouse* (☎ 308 56 56) in the village of Sela pri Ratežu (house No 15), about 2km south of Otočec village, has doubles and triples (some with kitchen) for about €18 per person for B&B.

Places to Eat

The *Restavracija Otočec* north of the castle has a large terrace that is very popular in summer. If you can't handle the crowds, try the small eatery at the camping ground or the one at the Struga Riding Centre.

The *Castle* and the smaller *Knights' Hall* restaurants at the Hotel Grad Otočec will be out of most people's price range, but the ancient stone walls, chandeliers and game and fish specialities make them worth a splurge.

Entertainment

Diskoteka Otočec at Hotel Šport is open till late on Thursday, Friday and Saturday. *Casino Otočec* (☎ 332 25 96), with blackjack, poker, American roulette and slot machines, is open from 5 pm to 2 am daily.

Getting There & Away

The bus linking Novo Mesto and Šmarješke Toplice stops at the bridge leading to the castle about once an hour on weekdays, but less frequently at the weekend.

AROUND OTOČEC

There are a couple of excellent excursions accessible from Otočec on foot, mountain bike or even horseback. The first is to the vincyards of **Trška Gora** (428m), which can be reached by road and trail from Mačkovec, about 5km south-west of Otočec on the main road to Novo Mesto. The walk (or ride) is quite straightforward from there. Follow the road north for 1km to Sevno and then continue along the winding track for 2km to Trška Gora and the **Church of St Mary**. From here there are wonderful views of the Gorjanci Hills, Kočevski Rog and the Krka Valley. Below the church is Krkin Hram, a 100-year-old wine cellar open to groups only.

Farther afield is **Gospodična** (828m) in the Gorjanci Hills and the **_Dom Vinka Paderšiča na Gorjancih_** (☎ 07-302 49 20), a mountain lodge with a restaurant and accommodation, open daily from May to September and at weekends only the rest of the year. Gospodična and the lodge are about 13km south-east of Otočec in the shadow of **Trdinov Vrh** (1178m), the highest peak in the Gorjanci. This densely forested area is known for its mushrooms and a 'magic spring' in which first-time visitors are supposed to wash. The route from Otočec goes for 5km south-east to **Velike Brusnice**, famous for its cherries and cherry festival in spring, then to Gabrje (4.5km) and to Gospodična (3.5km).

ŠMARJEŠKE TOPLICE
☎ 07 • postcode 8220 • pop 1860

If all that Cviček wine is taking its toll on you, consider taking a break at Šmarješke Toplice, a spa in a small, lush valley about 5km north of Otočec. While it doesn't have anything close to the history or atmosphere of Dolenjske Toplice, 25km to the southwest, it has lovely grounds and more than enough facilities to keep you busy and help recharge those batteries.

The three natural pools that once stood on the site of the spa were used by local people as far back as the 18th century and were collectively known as the Lake Spa. Development did not come until 1950, when the first hotel was built, but even that remained a rather exclusive facility reserved for the _nomenklatura_ (communist honchos) with ailing hearts. Only in the last decade has Šmarješke Toplice really made

it on the map as a serious therapy centre for those with cardiovascular problems as well as promoting relaxation and a healthier lifestyle.

Orientation & Information
The spa complex and its hotels are north of the tiny village of Šmarješke Toplice; the road to it passes a thermal stream and a pond with giant water lilies. Buses stop in front of and opposite the Gostilna Prinovec, a restaurant and grocery store. The post office, where you can change money, is nearby and open from 8 am to 5 pm weekdays and till noon Saturday.

Activities
The spa counts four pools fed by 32°C spring water rich in carbon dioxide and minerals. Two are indoor ones at the hotel complex and used for therapy. Nearby is a sauna, solarium and modern gym.

The larger outdoor pool is below the sports centre. Visitors not staying at the spa pay 1000 SIT (1100 SIT at weekends). Because the basin of the older (and smaller) pool nearby is made of wood, the water temperature is 2°C warmer.

The sports centre has four clay tennis courts available for hire and racquets can be rented. One of the courts is covered and illuminated at night. There are also facilities for table tennis, minigolf and lawn bowls.

The wine-growing areas surrounding Šmarješke Toplice make for some excellent walking and there are trails and footpaths south-west to Trška Gora and north-east to Vinji Vrh.

Places to Stay
All the accommodation at Šmarješke Toplice has the same numbers: ☎ 307 32 30, fax 307 31 07. The main complex is divided into three hotels. The **_Krka II_**, dating from 1950, is normally reserved for long-term guests with more serious medical problems. The **_Krka I_**, the middle section built in 1983, costs from 11,000 SIT per person with full board. The **_Šmarjeta_**, the newest (1991) and most attractive of the three hotels, costs 14,100 SIT for single rooms,

23,600 SIT for double rooms with full board, or 12,200/19,800 SIT for B&B. Some of the rooms at the Krka I and the Šmarjeta have small balconies with views of nearby hills and forests.

The new *Apartmaji na Dobravi*, about 1km west of the main complex, has luxury four-person apartments for 11,000 to 13,000 SIT per person, and its own steam bath, sauna, solarium and massage pool.

A cheaper alternative to staying at the spa is the 18-room *Penzion Domen (☎ 307 30 51)* in Družinska Vas (house No 1), about 1.5km south-east of Šmarješke Toplice. Singles/doubles are 4000/8000 SIT without breakfast. The Domen has a tennis court, a football pitch and a decent restaurant.

Places to Eat
Most guests take all their meals at the huge hotel restaurant, but if you're visiting or not staying on a full-board program, try the *Topliška Klet* cellar restaurant in the complex.

In Šmarješke Toplice village, *Gostilna Prinovec* is a pleasant, inexpensive place for a meal with an outside grill in summer and open till 11 pm or midnight. The *grocery* next door is open from 7.30 am to 7 pm Monday to Saturday and 8 am till noon Sunday. The restaurant at the *Penzion Domen* is open from 10 am till 10 pm daily, except Tuesday.

Getting There & Around
Bus service is frequent to Novo Mesto and Otočec, Šmarjeta and Brežice. There's also at least one bus daily to Ljubljana and Sevnica. The sports centre and the Penzion Domen rent bicycles for about 500 SIT per hour.

KOSTANJEVICA NA KRKI
☎ 07 • postcode 8311 • pop 765
Situated on an islet just 500m long and 200m wide in a loop of the Krka River, Kostanjevica is Slovenia's smallest town. And with a charter that dates back to 1252, it is also one of its oldest.

Kostanjevica was an important commercial centre in the Middle Ages and even had its own mint in the 13th century called Moneta Landestrostensis (Kostanjevica is still called Landstrass in German). Its coins

were in circulation as far as what is now western Romania. In 1563, after repeatedly attacking the town, the Turks were defeated by Ivan Lenkovič, supreme commander of the Military March.

Kostanjevica's glory days have long since passed, however, and today the town is so sleepy it is almost comatose. Though it is dubbed 'the Venice of Dolenjska' by the tourist industry and under full protection as a cultural monument, many of its buildings are in poor condition. Still, Kostanjevica is an important art centre and its location is magical. If you don't manage to flag down a helicopter to view the town from on high, at least take a look at the photographs of the town in *Slovenia from the Air* (Založba Mladinska Knjiga) by Matjaž Kmecl et al.

Orientation & Information
Though most of Kostanjevica's historical sights are on the island, some others and things of a more practical nature are on the mainland to the north-west or south-east, reached by two small bridges. Buses stop opposite the Green Bar.

There is a helpful tourist office (☎ 498 71 08, e tic.kktpkostanjevica@s5.net) on the island at Talcev ulica 20, open from 10 am to 4 pm daily, year-round.

Nova Ljubljanska Banka has a branch near the bus stop on Ljubljanska cesta. It's open from 8 to 11 am and 2 to 5 pm weekdays only. The post office is at Kambičev trg 5 and is open from 8 am to 5 pm weekdays (closed 9.30 to 10 am) and till noon Saturday.

Walking Tour
No-one is going to get lost or tired on a walking tour of Kostanjevica – some 400m up one street and 400m down another and you've seen the lot.

On Kambičev trg, across the small bridge from the bus stop and splitting the street in two, stands the **Church of St Nicholas**, a tiny late-Gothic structure dating from the late 16th century. The brightly coloured frescoes in the presbytery of scenes from the Old and New Testaments were painted by Jože Gorjup (1907–32). You can see more of this expressionist's work, including the wonderful

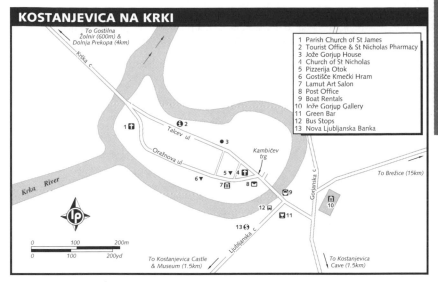

KOSTANJEVICA NA KRKI

To Gostilna
Žolnir (600m) &
Dolnja Prekopa (4km)

Krka c.

Talcev ul

Oražnova ul

Krka River

Kambičev
trg

Gorjanska c.

To Brežice (15km)

Ljubljanska c.

To Kostanjevica Castle
& Museum (1.5km)

To Kostanjevica
Cave (1.5km)

0   100   200m
0   100   200yd

1 Parish Church of St James
2 Tourist Office & St Nicholas Pharmacy
3 Jože Gorjup House
4 Church of St Nicholas
5 Pizzerija Otok
6 Gostišče Kmečki Hram
7 Lamut Art Salon
8 Post Office
9 Boat Rentals
10 Jože Gorjup Gallery
11 Green Bar
12 Bus Stops
13 Nova Ljubljanska Banka

Bathers series, at the **Jože Gorjup Gallery** back over the bridge at Gorjanska cesta 2; it's open from 8 am to 2 pm weekdays only.

If you walk north-west along Oražnova ulica for about 100m, you'll reach a 15th-century manor house at No 5 that now contains the **Lamut Art Salon** (open from 10 am to 6 pm weekdays only). The painter and graphic artist Vladimir Lamut (1915–62) completed a large portion of his work here.

Continue along Oražnova ulica, passing a lovely *fin-de-siècle* house at No 24, to the **Parish Church of St James**, a 13th-century Romanesque building at the island's north-western tip with a mostly baroque interior. Above the carved stone portal on the western side, you can just make out geometric shapes and decorative plants and trees. On the north side is a 15th-century depiction of Jesus rising from the tomb.

Talcev ulica, the island's other street, leads south-east back to St Nicholas Church and is lined with crumbling but quite attractive 'folk baroque' houses. About half-way down on the left is the 200-year-old **St Nicholas Pharmacy**, which now houses the tourist office. The **birthplace of Jože Gorjup** is farther along at No 8.

Kostanjevica Castle

The former Cistercian monastery – what most people here call Kostanjevica Castle – was begun in the mid-13th century and, through donation deeds from the rulers of Hungary and Bosnia, remained a very wealthy institution in the Middle Ages. It was abandoned by the order in the late 18th century and was severely damaged during WWII and again in an earthquake in 1984. Today it houses a large and important art gallery. The castle is about 1.5km south-west of the town at Grajska cesta 45.

The main entrance through two painted towers leads to an enormous courtyard enclosed by a **cloister** with some 260 arcades on three floors. To the west stands the disused **Church of the Virgin Mary** containing elements from the 13th to 18th centuries – and a lot of free-flying sparrows. A set of steps near what was once the altar leads to the **museum**.

The **Božidar Jakac Gallery** contains 16th-century frescoes taken from the church below, works by such Slovenian artists as the impressionist Jakac and the brothers France (1895–1960) and Tone Kralj (1900–75). There is also a permanent collection of

Old Masters from the Carthusian monastery at Pleterje. Much of Jakac's work here consists of line drawings done while documenting the underground Partisan movement in 1943. Of all the artists, the expressionist France Kralj was the most versatile and prolific, turning out hundreds of works in oil, ink, bronze and wood; don't miss his sculptures *The Reapers* and *Mother and Child*. Some of Tone Kralj's early work (like *Veined Sunset*) is almost surreal, but his later move to a kind of socialist realism obliterates all traces of it. The collection from Pleterje features works by French, German, Italian and Flemish artists of the 16th and 18th centuries. The oils are almost all portraits of saints and church noteworthies and pretty sombre stuff.

The castle grounds are used to exhibit over 100 large wooden sculptures from Forma Viva, an international exhibition once held in several places in Slovenia from 1961 to 1988 whereby sculptors worked with materials associated with the area. Here it was oak, in Portorož stone, iron at Ravne in Koroška and (shudder) concrete in Maribor. The castle is open from 9 am till 6 pm daily, except Monday, from April to October. During the rest of the year it closes at 4 pm. The entry fee is 400/200 SIT for adults/students and children.

Kostanjevica Cave

This small cave, on an unsealed road about 1.5km south-east of town, has half-hour tours (700/400 SIT) from 10 am to 6.30 pm at weekends between mid-April and October (daily from June to August). The guide will lead you some 300m in (only 1550m of the cave have been fully explored), past a small lake, several galleries full of stalactites and stalagmites and, no doubt, a couple of specimens of *Paladilhiopsis kostanjevicae,* a snail unique to the cave that seems to thrive in the 12°C temperature. There's a shaded picnic area in front of the cave on tiny Studena Stream.

Boating

The little ice-cream kiosk next to the bridge, just before you cross over to the island,

rents canoes and kayaks (600/3000 SIT per hour/day) for excursions on the Krka from April to September.

Places to Stay

Not surprisingly, accommodation is very limited in a town as small as Kostanjevica. The *Gostilna Žolnir* (☎ 308 71 33, *Krška cesta 4)*, about 700m north-east of the island, has 12 rooms, including shower and breakfast, costing 4300 SIT for singles, 6200 SIT for doubles.

Places to Eat

There are a couple of bare-bones places for a quick meal or drink on the island, including *Pizzerija Otok* and the old-style *Gostišče Kmečki Hram*, both on Oražnova ulica. The *Green Bar* in an attractive old baroque building opposite the bus stop is a pleasant place for a drink.

The best place to eat is at the *Gostilna Žolnir* (see Places to Stay), whose owners are very serious about the food and wine they serve. It's open till 10 pm daily. A speciality of Kostanjevica is duck served with little *mlinci* pancakes and, of course, accompanied by Cviček wine.

Getting There & Away

There are departures from Kostanjevica to Novo Mesto, Brežice and Šentjernej. Other destinations and their daily frequencies include Ljubljana (six), Krško (two) and Orešnje (one).

PLETERJE MONASTERY

You'll see more of the treasures of Pleterje, a huge monastery just over 3km south of Šentjernej, at Kostanjevica Castle than you will *in situ*. Pleterje (Pletariach in German) belongs to the Carthusians, the strictest of all Roman Catholic monastic orders. The Gothic **Holy Trinity Church** (also called the Old Monastery Church) is the only part of the complex open to the general public. But the monastery's location in a narrow valley between slopes awash in vines and the Gorjanci Hills is so attractive and peaceful, it's worth a visit. The Pleterje Trail is a 1½-hour walk in the hills around the complex.

The monastery was founded in 1407 by Herman II, one of the Counts of Celje, and its construction was supervised by an English abbot called Prior Hartman. The complex was fortified with ramparts, towers and a moat during the Turkish invasions and all but abandoned during the Protestant Reformation, which swept Dolenjska in the 16th century. The Carthusian order, like all monastic communities in the Habsburg Empire, was abolished in 1784. When the monks returned to Pleterje over a century later, they rebuilt the complex according to the plans of the order's charterhouse at Nancy in France.

You may catch a glimpse of the dozen or so white-hooded monks quietly going about their chores – they take a strict vow of silence and are vegetarians – or hear them singing their offices in the old monastery church at various times of the day. But the ubiquitous signs reading *Klavzura – Vstop Prepovedan* (Seclusion – No Entry) remind you that everything apart from the church – the ornate chapels, the inner courtyard, the cloisters and the library rich in medieval manuscripts – is off limits.

Above the ribbed main portal of the austere church, built in 1420 and one of the most important Gothic monuments in Slovenia, is a fresco depicting Mary and the Trinity. Inside, the rib-vaulted ceiling with its heraldic bosses and the carved stone niches by the altar are worth a look, but what is most interesting is the medieval rood screen, the low wall across the aisle that separated members of the order from the rest of the faithful.

At the monastery office in the main sand-coloured building, the monks sell some of their own products, including packs of beeswax candles (600 SIT), honey (1000 SIT), propolis (400 SIT for a small flask), cheese (1300 SIT per kilogram), Cviček and Chardonnay wines (380 SIT and 6500 SIT a litre) and four types of brandy: *sadjevec* (apple; 1000 SIT), *slivovka* (plum; 1200 SIT), *brinovec* (juniper; 2000 SIT) and – everyone's favourite – *hruška* (pear; 3200 SIT). If you're wondering how they got that whole pear inside the bottle, it's simple – the bottle is placed over the immature fruit while still on the tree. When the pear ripens inside, the bottle is removed and filled with brandy. The shop is open from 8 am to 5 pm Monday to Saturday.

Šentjernej is 6km west of Kostanjevica and can be reached on the Novo Mesto bus (return to Kostanjevica on one of two direct daily buses or on any of the dozen or so headed for Brežice). There are also up to six buses a day to Ljubljana and one each to Krško and Zagreb. Buses stop in front of the *Gostilna Majzelj (Trg Gorjanskega Bataljona 5)*, which is open till 10 pm daily, except Tuesday (to 1 pm Sunday). Accommodation can be arranged in town or in a vineyard cottage. You'll have to make your way on foot to Pleterje from the bus stop, though, as there is no local service; it's just over 3km. The post office, where you can change money, is on the square opposite the gostilna. It is open from 8 am to 6 pm weekdays and till noon Saturday.

POSAVJE REGION
Most of what is called Posavje, the area 'on the Sava River' as far as the border with Croatia, is in Štajerska, the large province north of Dolenjska. But historically and geographically, Posavje is closely tied to Dolenjska and easily accessible from many of its towns.

History
Like Dolenjska, Posavje was settled early and is rich in archaeological finds from the Hallstatt, Celtic and Roman periods. The Sava, of course, was paramount and, while Jason and the Argonauts probably did not navigate the 'Savus' upstream as legend tells us, the Romans certainly did, building a major port called Neviodunum near today's Drnovo. Slavic graves unearthed in the area date from the 7th century.

Posavje took centre stage during the Turkish invasions starting in the 15th century – which explains the large number of heavily fortified castles in the region – and again 100 years later during the Slovenian-Croatian peasant uprisings and the Protestant Reformation. River traffic increased in the 19th century after a 20km stretch of the Sava was regulated, and the arrival of the railway in 1862 linking Ljubljana and Zagreb helped the region develop industrially.

Posavje had more than its share of suffering during WWII. In a bid to colonise the area, the occupying German forces engaged in a brutal program of 'ethnic cleansing' and expelled more than 15,000 Slovenes. Many of them were interned at a camp in Rajhenburg Castle at Brestanica before being deported to Serbia, Croatia or Germany.

Brežice
☎ 07 • postcode 8250 • pop 6900

Brežice is not the largest town in Posavje – that distinction goes to Krško, 12km upriver – but from a traveller's point of view, it is the most interesting. The town lies between the Orlica Hills to the north and the Gorjanci to the south, and opens onto a vast plain to the east. The climate is milder and drier than elsewhere in Dolenjska.

History Situated in a basin just north of where the Krka flows into the Sava, Brežice (Rhain in German) was an important trading centre in the Middle Ages and was granted a town charter in 1354. Brežice's dominant feature has always been its castle, mentioned in documents as early as 1249, with a strategic position some 400m from the Sava. In the 16th century the original castle was replaced with a Renaissance fortress to strengthen the town's defences against the Turks and marauding peasants who, during one uprising, beheaded nobles at the castle and impaled their heads on poles.

The castle was built with the help of Italian masters and is not dissimilar to the ones at Otočec, Sevnica and Mokrice in design. Over a century later, the castle's new owners, the Counts of Attems, renovated the building in the baroque style and added several sumptuous rooms, including the largest function room in Slovenia. Today the castle houses the Posavje Museum.

Orientation & Information Brežice's main street is Cesta Prvih Borcev. Heading south it becomes Prešernova cesta and

crosses the Sava. Going north it changes names to Trg Izgnancev and Cesta Bratov Milavcev. The main artery going eastward is Bizeljska ulica.

The bus station is behind the big shopping centre on Cesta Svobode, 200m north of Bizeljska ulica. The train station is farther afield on Trg OF, about 2.5km north of the town centre.

There is no tourist office in Brežice, but the staff at the Posavje Museum will help you with any questions you have. There's a Nova Ljubljanska Banka branch at Cesta Prvih Borcev 31, open from 8 am to 5 pm weekdays and till noon Saturday. SKB Banka is farther north at No 39. The post office is at Trg Izgnancev 1a and is open from 7 am to 7 pm weekdays and till noon Saturday.

Posavje Museum Housed in the Renaissance castle at Cesta Prvih Borcev 1, this is one of provincial Slovenia's best museums, and its archaeological and ethnographic collections are particularly rich.

From the courtyard you ascend a staircase whose walls and ceiling are illustrated with Greek gods, the four Evangelists and the Attems family coat of arms. The first rooms contain bits and pieces from earliest times to the arrival of the Slavs; don't miss the skeletons from the 9th century BC unearthed near Dobova, the 5th-century BC bronze bridle, the Celtic and Roman jewellery and a dented helmet that suggests the legionnaire wearing it got kicked in the head by a mule. In the ethnographic rooms, along with the carved wooden bowls, decorated chests and plaited loaves of bread, is a strange beehive in the shape of a soldier from the early 1800s. On the top he's French and on the bottom Croatian.

Other rooms cover life in the Posavje region in the 16th century (focusing on the peasant uprisings in the area and the Protestant Reformation) and the time of the two world wars, with emphasis on the deportation of Slovenes by the Germans during WWII. There's also a collection of baroque oil paintings. Check the ornate tile stoves in many of the rooms.

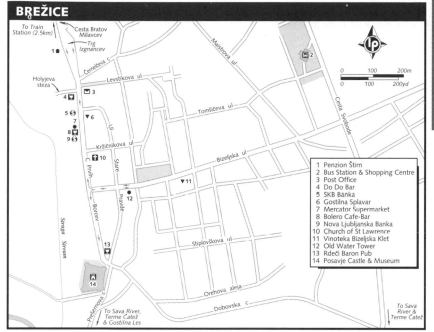

BREŽICE

To Train
Station (2.5km)

Cesta Bratov
Milavcev

Trg
Izgnancev

Cernelceva c

Levstikova ul

Holyjeva
steza

Maistrova ul

Cesta Svobode

Tomšičeva ul

Kržičnikova ul

Bizeljska ul

Stare

Prvih

Pravde

Borcev

Stiplovškova ul

Struga
Sirnom

Orehova aleja

Dobovska c

To Sava River,
Terme Čatež
& Gostilna Les

To Sava
River &
Terme Čatež

0   100   200m
0   100   200yd

DOLENJSKA

1 Penzion Štirn
2 Bus Station & Shopping Centre
3 Post Office
4 Do Do Bar
5 SKB Banka
6 Gostilna Splavar
7 Mercator Supermarket
8 Bolero Cafe-Bar
9 Nova Ljubljanska Banka
10 Church of St Lawrence
11 Vinoteka Bizeljska Klet
12 Old Water Tower
13 Rdeči Baron Pub
14 Posavje Castle & Museum

But the museum's real crowd-pleaser is the **Knights' Hall** (Viteška Dvorana), an Italian baroque masterpiece where everything but the floor is painted with landscapes, gods and heroes from Greek and Roman mythology, allegories, the Muses etc.

The Posavje Museum is open from 8 am to 1 pm Monday to Saturday and 9 am till noon Sunday. Entry is 300/150 SIT for adults/children and students.

Terme Čatež Rheumatics have been bathing in the thermal spring at Čatež (population 1005), 3km south-east of Brežice, since the late 18th century. Today, while the huge spa complex still attracts those suffering from such aches and pains, it is every bit as much a recreational area. The spa counts nine thermal-water (27° to 36°C) outdoor pools with huge slides, fountains and artificial waves over an area of 8000 sq metres. The indoor Termalna Riviera complex measures 1200 sq metres with a water temperature of about 32°C. The outdoor complex is open from 9 am to 8 pm April to September and admission is 1500 to 1700 SIT depending on the day of the week. The indoor pools are open all year and entry costs 1700 to 2100 SIT. The spa also has saunas, a steam room, Roman bath, solarium, gym, a jogging track along the river and tennis courts. A guide is made available to guests between 9 and 11 am daily; tell the guide where you want to go and what you want to see and you're off.

Activities At Čatež, along with taking the waters, you can rent a boat or a bicycle (1350 SIT a day, 5000 SIT a week). In the nearby town of Čatež ob Savi, horses can be hired from the Zean Club at Rimska cesta 22 and ridden up Šentvid Hill (386m).

The Penzion Štirn in Brežice (see Places to Stay) can organise any number of activities in the area, including canoeing on the Krka, fishing in the Sava or Krka, horse riding and tennis.

Special Events The Festival of Early Music, which for many years had been held in Radovlje in Gorenjska, is a series of concerts of ancient music held in Brežice during the first half of August and one of the country's most prestigious cultural events. The concerts take place in the Knights' Hall.

Places to Stay The huge *Kamp Terme Čatež* (☎ 493 50 00), at Čatež, is not cheap at 1900 to 2100 SIT per person, depending on the season, but campers get free use of the outdoor swimming pools. It is open from April to October. There are also *bungalows* nearby costing 6500/9200 SIT to 7100/10,200 SIT for singles/doubles, depending on the season, and *apartments* for up to five people from 9900 to 15,500 SIT.

In Brežice, *Penzion Štirn* (☎ 496 56 13, Trg Izgnancev 7) is an attractive little guesthouse with 22 beds that's been around for more than 70 years. Expect to pay about €14 per person including breakfast. It's on a rather busy street so ask for one of the back rooms. *Gostilna Les* (☎ 496 11 00, Rimska cesta 31) in Čatež ob Savi has single/double rooms with breakfast and shower for 3800/6500 SIT.

The *Terme Čatež spa complex* (☎ 493 50 00, fax 493 55 20, e info@terme-catez.si, Topliška cesta 35) has three hotels. The *Zdravilišče*, with 130 beds, is generally reserved for those who are taking the spa seriously. Depending on the season, rooms cost 8500/12,200 to 9200/13,400 SIT for singles/doubles. The *Terme*, with over 250 beds, charges from 12,600/16,800 SIT to 13,300/17,800 SIT. The newest hotel, the 48-bed *Toplice*, charges 10,800/14,400 SIT year-round.

Places to Eat The *Vinoteka Bizeljska Klet* (Bizeljska ulica 10), just past the old water tower (1914), serves food and wine from the Bizeljsko-Sremič wine region to the north and west of Brežice. Another possibility is *Gostilna Splavar* (Cesta Prvih Borcev 40).

The gostilna at the *Penzion Štirn* specialises in fish and seafood. The Laški Rizling, a slightly fruity, medium-dry wine from Bizeljsko, is not a bad accompaniment.

The gostilna is open to 9 pm daily for lunch and dinner (except Sunday).

The *Mercator supermarket* (Cesta Prvih Borcev 35) is open from 7 am to 4 pm weekdays and till noon Saturday.

Entertainment The *Knights' Hall* in the Posavje Museum has near-perfect acoustics and concerts are held there throughout the year. The *Rdeči Baron* pub (Cesta Prvih Borcev 2) and the *Bolero* cafe-bar (Cesta Prvih Borcev 33) are popular places for a drink, open to 11 pm or midnight daily. The *Do Do* bar (Holyjeva steza 1) attracts a very young crowd. It's open till late.

Getting There & Away Buses run every two hours from Brežice to Bizeljsko, Kostanjevica, Novo Mesto and Terme Čatež, and up to eight times a day to Ljubljana. Other destinations and their daily frequencies include: Celje (one bus a day on weekdays, at 12.05 pm), Orešje (three) and Senovo (three). Some of these buses, like the ones to Čatež, can be boarded at the train station in Brežice. There's a bus to Munich on Tuesday and Thursday at 5.27 pm and on Sunday at 2.42 pm.

As many as 15 trains a day serve Brežice from Ljubljana (1¾ hours, 107km) via Zidani Most, Sevnica and Krško. Many of these trains then cross the Croatian border near Dobova and carry on to Zagreb.

Getting Around Buses run between the bus station and the train station every half-hour throughout the day.

Mokrice Castle

Mokrice, about 10km south-east of Brežice, is the loveliest castle in the Posavje region and has been completely renovated and turned into a 30-room luxury hotel. With one of Slovenia's few golf courses, a large stable with horses for rent, a 20-hectare 'English park' full of rare plants, and a large orchard of pear trees, it makes a delightful excursion from Brežice.

The castle as it stands today dates from the 16th century, but there are bits and pieces going back to Roman times (inscription stones, part of a tower etc) built into the structure. Like many other castles in the region, it was built as a defence against the Turks and later turned into a baronial manor. The 19th-century German writer Count Friedrich von Gagern was born here, and some of his novels are set in the castle and surrounds.

There are a couple of interesting stories about the castle, one of which tells of a 17th-century countess named Barbara who fell in love with a sailor called Marko. When he went to sea and failed to return, poor Barbara committed suicide. Her ghost still stalks the castle's secret passageways and staircases at night, and she is particularly active on the feast day of St Barbara (4 December). The castle's coat of arms may strike you as odd; it portrays a raven with an arrow piercing its throat. Apparently a Turkish janissary shot the bird as it squawked to warn the inhabitants of an invasion in the 15th century.

The small Gothic **Chapel of St Ann** in the castle grounds, not far from the drawbridge, has some interesting baroque stucco work inside. The park is filled with baroque statues.

If you want to stay at the ***Hotel Golf Grad Mokrice*** (☎ *07-495 70 00, fax 495 70 07,* e *info@terme-catez.si)* be prepared to shell out a minimum of €83 for a single with breakfast and €90 for a double. One of the 240-sq-metre suites goes for €186. The rooms have beamed ceilings and period furniture, and some suites have fireplaces. The castle restaurant is pretty formal with fancy game and fish dishes and classical music; the cellar has 60 different Slovenian wines available by the glass or bottle. Try some *viljamovka,* Mokrice's famous pear brandy.

The green fee for a round of golf at Mokrice's 18-hole course is €32 on weekdays and €35 at weekends (less for hotel guests). A half-set of clubs costs €8 to rent. There's also a pro giving lessons (€23 an hour). Horse riding is available and a carriage ride to Čatež Terme (7km) and back costs €20 per person.

You can reach Mokrice on the bus to Obrežje, but the ideal way to go would be by bicycle from Čatež, following the secondary road running parallel to route No 1 (E70).

Bizeljsko-Sremič Wine District

Cycling all the way to **Bizeljsko** (Wisell in German; population 1940) through the heart of the Bizeljsko-Sremič wine country might be pushing it for some (it's 18km from Brežice), but there's a bus leaving every hour or so, allowing you to get off whenever you see a gostilna or wine cellar (*vinska klet*; marked by a red, yellow and brown sign) that takes your fancy. In Bizeljsko, try some of the local medium-dry whites and reds at the ***Vinska Klet Pinterič*** at house No 115 or at ***Gostilna Šekoranja*** at No 72, or visit the *Istenič* cellars in the nearby village of **Stara Vas** (house No 7). They are open from noon to 7 pm Monday, Wednesday and Thursday and till 9 pm Friday to Sunday. A tour and a wine tasting costs 1000 SIT.

From Bizeljsko you can either return to Brežice or continue north for 7km past Bizeljska Vas and the ruins of the 15th-century **Bizeljsko Castle** to Bistrica ob Sotli. From here, buses go north-west to Kozje via the village of **Podsreda**, the site of the oldest castle in Slovenia (see the Štajerska chapter).

Bela Krajina

The 'White March' of south-eastern Slovenia takes its name from the endless stands of birch trees that cover this little province. It is a treasure-trove of Slovenian folklore, and you'll see more traditional dance and hear more music here than anywhere else in the country, particularly around Črnomelj and Adlešiči. Many of the stringed instruments – the *tamburica,* the *berdo* (contrabass), the guitar-like *brač* and the *bisernica* (lute) – are unique to the region or originated here.

Like Dolenjska, Bela Krajina is famous for its Hallstatt and Roman sites; a 3rd-century shrine to the god Mithra (or Mithras) near the village of Rožanec is one of the best preserved in Europe. In the Middle Ages, Bela Krajina was the most remote part of Slovenia, and in some ways it still feels like that. Many of the peasant uprisings of the 15th and 16th centuries started here or across the border in Croatia.

METLIKA
☎ 07 • postcode 8330 • pop 3300

One of Bela Krajina's two most important towns, Metlika (Möttling in German) lies in a valley at the foot of the Žumberak Hills and is surrounded by Croatia on three sides. The Kolpa River is 2km to the south.

History

The area around Metlika was inhabited during prehistoric times, and there was a major Hallstatt settlement here during the early Iron Age. The Romans came too, establishing an outpost here, and Metlika was on a road leading to the important river port of Sisak in Croatia. In medieval times *reggio que Metlica dicitur* (the region called Metlika) included most of today's Bela Krajina, and the Metlika March was an important frontier region. Only a few kilometres from the pilgrimage site of Tri Fare at Rosalnice, Metlika grew into a market town and was given a charter in 1365.

Metlika was in the front lines during the wars with the Hungarians in the 14th century.

Highlights

- Visit the Three Parishes pilgrimage churches in Rosalnice
- Experience the Jurjevanje festival in Črnomelj in mid-June
- Go kayaking on the rapid-water run on the Kolpa River from Stari Trg to Vinica
- Discover Bela Krajina folk music, especially around Adlešiči
- Track down the Mithraic shrine in the woods near Rožanec

The Turks attacked some 17 times, beginning in 1408, and actually occupied the town in 1578 – something its rival Črnomelj points out never happened to it. For many years, Metlika was the last outpost of Christianity in this part of Europe. Prosperity came briefly during the Protestant Reformation, but the Žumberak Hills sheltered outlaws and brigands from Croatia, who would continue to harass the town for centuries.

The Italians occupied Metlika during WWII, and by the end of the war some 120 buildings had been burned to the ground. Though the kernel of the Old Town counts some buildings which date back several centuries, most of the town of Metlika was rebuilt after 1945.

Orientation

Metlika's Old Town, consisting of three squares, stands on a ridge between a small stream called the Obrh and the main street, Cesta Bratstva in Enotnosti (Avenue of Fraternity and Unity). You can reach it from the main street by walking up Ulica na Trg to Trg Svobode and then Mestni trg.

The modern bus station is 650m south of the Old Town on Cesta XV Brigade. To get to the train station, walk south along Cesta XV Brigade for 600m and then turn east on Kolodvorska ulica.

Information

There is a tiny tourist office (☎ 363 54 70) at Mestni trg 1. It's open from 9 am to 2 pm weekdays, and till noon Saturday.

Dolenjska Banka has a branch at Trg Svobode 7, and another one in the shopping complex opposite the bus station; both have ATMs and are open from 8 am till noon and 2 to 4.30 pm weekdays only. The post office, open from 7 am to 7 pm weekdays and till noon Saturday, is in the same shopping centre. The medical centre (☎ 305 82 59) is at Cesta Bratstva in Enotnosti 71.

Things to See

Metlika Castle, with its L-shaped arcaded courtyard at Trg Svobode 4, houses the **Bela Krajina Museum**. The collection, exhibited in 18 rooms, includes archaeological finds taken from the area such as Hallstatt buckles, bracelets and amulets from Pusti Gradac south of Črnomelj and a copy of the Mithraic relief from the Roman period found at Rožanec near Črnomelj. Artefacts collected from more recent periods are displayed in a mock-up of an old pharmacy and photo studio.

Much emphasis is placed on agriculture in Bela Krajina – everything you've ever wanted to know about beekeeping, fruit cultivation, viniculture, fishing and animal husbandry is here – as well as folk art peculiar to the region, including decorated Easter eggs, glass paintings and religious

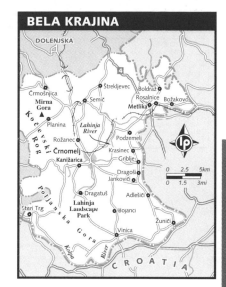

icons in bottles. The artist and sculptor Alojzij Gangl, who was born in Metlika, is given pride of place.

The Bela Krajina Museum is open from 9 am to 4 pm weekdays, till 2 pm Saturday and 9 am till noon Sunday; entry is 300/200 SIT for adults/children.

A small building west of the castle entrance (Trg Svobode 5) contains the **Fire Brigades Museum**. Metlika was the first town in Slovenia to have a fire brigade and has thus earned the right to such a shrine. It's a lot more interesting than it sounds, displaying old fire trucks with enormous wheels, ladders and buckets, but no Dalmatians (on four legs anyway). Firefighters, by the way, are considered the 'party animals' of Slovenia, hosting dances, fetes and other booze-ups outside the *gasilski dom* (fire stations) throughout summer. (Some Slovenes say that's all they ever seem to do.) The **defence tower** opposite the Fire Brigades Museum dates from the 16th century.

The Fire Brigades Museum is open from 9 am to 1 pm Monday to Saturday and till noon Sunday; entry is free.

Mestni trg is a colourful, leafy square of 18th- and 19th-century buildings, including

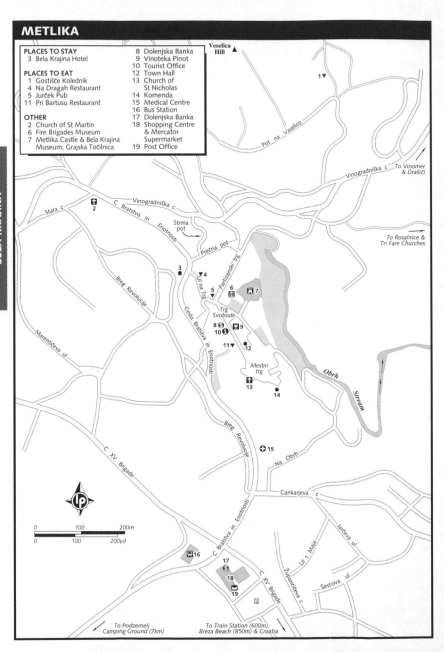

METLIKA

PLACES TO STAY
3 Bela Krajina Hotel

PLACES TO EAT
1 Gostišče Kolednik
4 Na Dragah Restaurant
5 Jurček Pub
11 Pri Bartusu Restaurant

OTHER
2 Church of St Martin
6 Fire Brigades Museum
7 Metlika Castle & Bela Krajina
   Museum; Grajska Točilnica

8 Dolenjska Banka
9 Vinoteka Pinot
10 Tourist Office
12 Town Hall
13 Church of
   St Nicholas
14 Komenda
15 Medical Centre
16 Bus Station
17 Dolenjska Banka
18 Shopping Centre
   & Mercator
   Supermarket
19 Post Office

the neo-Gothic **town hall** (1869) at No 24. At the southern end of the square is the so-called **Komenda** (Commandery), which once belonged to the Knights of the Teutonic Order (note the Maltese cross painted on the outside wall) and is now a rest home. The interior of the **Church of St Nicholas** (1759), which is modelled on the Križanke's Church of the Virgin Mary in Ljubljana, has sobering frescoes of the Day of Judgment by Domenico Fabrio.

The Gothic **Church of St Martin** at the northern end of Cesta Bratstva in Enotnosti is one of the oldest structures in Metlika, but is cracking from the bottom up and is no longer in use. It contains late-Renaissance tombs with reliefs. Outside is a wayside shrine with a barely recognisable fresco.

Activities

The Kolpa is a clean and very warm (up to 28°C) river so you might want to go for a dip at Breza at the end of Cesta XV Brigade, about 2km south of the Old Town across from Croatia. You can also swim in the Kolpa at the Podzemelj camping ground. The Kolpa is known for its grayling, carp and brown trout, but the area around Vinica, farther south, is richer. You can purchase fishing licences, valid for a day, at the Podzemelj camping ground.

There are a lot of walks in the surrounding areas. A very easy one is up to **Veselica**, a small hill less than 1km north of Metlika, with great views over the town.

Be sure to get a copy of the 1:50,000 *Bela Krajina* map from GZS.

Special Events

Metlika's main event is the Vinska Vigred wine festival in mid-May. The town also holds musical evenings in the castle from early July to early September. Ask for a program at the museum or the town hall.

Places to Stay

The *Kamp Podzemelj ob Kolpi* (☎ 306 95 72) is about 7km south-west of Metlika on the Kolpa River. It measures 1.5 hectares in size and can accommodate 70 tents. The charge is 900 SIT per person, and it is open

Hallstatt Culture in Slovenia

Hallstatt is the name of a village in the Salzkammergut region of Austria where objects characteristic of the early Iron Age (from about 800 to 500 BC) were found in the 19th century. Today, the name is used generically for the late Bronze and early Iron Age cultures that developed in Central and Western Europe from about 1100 to 450 BC.

Many parts of Slovenia were settled during this period, particularly Bela Krajina and Dolenjska. Burial grounds and forts have yielded swords, helmets, jewellery and especially situlae – pails (or buckets) that are often richly decorated with battle and hunting scenes.

Hallstatt art is very geometric, and typical motifs include birds and figures arranged in pairs. It was not until the advent of the late Iron Age La Tène culture (450–390 BC) of the European Celts that S-shapes, spirals and round patterns developed.

Situla decorated with Hallstatt art

from June to mid-September. Buses headed for Črnomelj and Griblje will let you off close to the site.

The *Pri Bregarjevih Farmhouse* (☎ 305 83 02) at Boldraž (house No 6), 4km north-east of Metlika, has one large apartment, with kitchen, that can accommodate up to six people for around 2500 SIT per person. The *Bela Krajina Hotel* (☎/fax 305 81 23, ✉ gostinstvo-turizem@gtm-metlika.si, Cesta

Bratstva in Enotnosti 28), the only hotel in town, has 24 fairly shabby rooms and charges 2700/5000 SIT for single/double rooms with shared shower and 4200/7000 SIT for rooms with private showers. Prices include breakfast.

Places to Eat

Pri Bartusu (Mestni trg 6) is a pleasant place for a meal and centrally located. It is open from 7 am until 10 pm daily, except Thursday (till midnight Friday). The town's largest restaurant is *Na Dragah (Cesta Bratstva in Enotnosti 45)*, opposite the Bela Krajina Hotel. It's open to 10 pm Sunday to Thursday, and to 11 pm Friday and Saturday.

The *Jurček* pub *(Partizanski trg 21)* has cheap pizzas from 525 SIT. The *Grajska Točilnica* in the castle courtyard is a good place for coffee and ice cream.

There's a wonderful restaurant called *Gostilna Veselič* (☎ 305 71 56) in Podzemelj (house No 17), not far from the camping ground. It's a favourite of local people and has accommodation.

If you want to try some Bela Krajina wine but don't have time to get out into the country, head for *Vinoteka Pinot (Trg Svobode 28)*, where you can sample Pinot Blanc, Chardonnay, Rieslings and sweet Gold Muscatel. A tasting, with cheese, costs 800 SIT. It's open from 7 am to 11 pm daily (till 5 pm Sunday).

There's a large *Mercator supermarket* in the shopping complex opposite the bus station, open from 6.30 am to 8 pm weekdays, to 5 pm Saturday and 8 am to 11 pm Sunday.

Getting There & Away

Destinations served by bus from Metlika include Božakovo (one bus a day, at 1.20 pm), Črnomelj (nine, between 6.15 am and 4.10 pm), Drašiči (three on weekdays), Karlovac in Croatia (three on weekdays), Novo Mesto (four, at 6.45, 7 and 11.25 am and 1.15 pm) and Vinica (one, at 3.05 pm).

Metlika is served by up to eight trains daily from Ljubljana (2¾ hours, 122km) via Novo Mesto and Črnomelj. Five trains a day head for Karlovac in Croatia (one hour).

AROUND METLIKA
Rosalnice

The **Three Parishes** (Tri Fare) in this village, 2.5km east of Metlika, is a row of three graceful little churches that have been important pilgrimage sites for seven centuries. Though they were originally built in the late 12th century by the Templars, today's churches date from the 14th and 15th centuries. The one to the north – the largest of the three – is the **Church of the Sorrowful Virgin** and has a Gothic presbytery. The church in the middle – **Ecce Homo** – has a large tower rising above its porch. The one on the south with the buttresses and another Gothic presbytery is the **Church of Our Lady of Lourdes**. Many of the gravestones in the churchyard are decorated with carved vines and grape leaves.

To the west of the churchyard entrance at house No 80 is *Gostilna Pri Treh Farah*, a pleasant place for lunch or a snack.

There is actually a train station in Rosalnice south of the Three Parishes and the bus to Božakovo stops here, but it is just as easy to walk from Metlika. From the Old Town, head north-east along Navratilova pot and follow Ulica Janka Brodariča eastward for 600m, then turn south. After 200m turn east and continue on straight to the churches.

Metlika Wine District

The hills to the north and north-east of Metlika are one of the most important wine-producing areas in Bela Krajina and produce such distinctive wines as Metliška Črnina, a very dark red – almost black – wine and a late-maturing sweet 'ice wine'. They are also superb areas for easy walking.

On the way to **Vinomer** and **Drašiči**, two important wine towns about 4km and 6km respectively from Metlika, you'll walk through *steljniki*, stands of birch trees growing among ferns in clay soil. For Slovenes, these 'forests' are the very symbol of Bela Krajina.

Drašiči is famous for its folk architecture – old peasant houses built over wine cellars. You can sample some local wines at several places, including the *Mavretič Farmhouse* (☎ 07-305 86 44) at No 2b in Drašiči. Call in advance as everyone might be out in the vineyards.

ČRNOMELJ
☎ 07 • postcode 8340 • pop 5400

The capital of Bela Krajina and its largest town, Črnomelj (pronounced cher-**no**-mel) is situated on a promontory in a loop where the Lahinja and Dobličica Rivers meet. The town is not overly endowed with important sights, but it is Bela Krajina's folk 'heart' and its Jurjevanje festival attracts hundreds of dancers and singers from around the region.

Legend has it that Črnomelj (a corruption of the words for 'black mill') got its name when a beggar, dissatisfied with the quality of the flour he'd been given, put a curse on the local miller. Perhaps the town's symbol – a smiling baker holding a pretzel – knew better than the miller the real threat of a 'beggar's curse'.

History
Like Metlika, Črnomelj (Tschernembl in German) was settled very early on, and the Roman presence is evident from the Mithraic shrine at Rožanec, about 4km north-west of the town. Črnomelj was an important market town and a bishopric as early as the 13th century, and was given a charter in 1407.

During the Turkish invasions in the 15th and 16th centuries, the town was attacked incessantly but, due to its strong fortifications and excellent hill-top lookouts at Stražnji Vrh and Doblička Gora to the west, it was never taken. In fact, trade thrived under such protection, and Črnomelj enjoyed something of a golden age in the 16th century. With the establishment of the Military March and the fort at Karlovac in Croatia in 1579, however, Črnomelj lost its military significance and prosperity. The town did not begin to develop again until 1914 with the opening of the railway between Novo Mesto and Karlovac.

Črnomelj played an important role during WWII. After Italy's surrender in 1943, the town functioned for a time as Slovenia's capital and was the centre of the Slovenian National Liberation Council and of Partisan activity.

Orientation & Information
Buses to and from Črnomelj stop on Trg Svobode in the heart of the Old Town. The train station is about 200m north of the Hotel Lahinja at Kolodvorska cesta 1.

The local tourist office (☎ 306 11 42, ⓔ turizem@crnomelj.si) is in Črnomelj Castle at Trg Svobode 3. It is open from 9 am to 3 pm weekdays only. Keep your eyes open for the freebie pamphlet *Europe's Sleeping Beauty: Heritage Trails through Dolenjska & Bela Krajina* which is produced by the Slovenian Tourist Board.

Dolenjska Banka has a branch at Kolodvorska cesta 32b, next to the post office, open from 8 am till noon and 2 to 4.30 pm weekdays only. There's an SKB Banka in the shopping centre just off Belokranjska cesta at Zadružna cesta 16.

The post office, Kolodvorska cesta 30, is open from 7 am to 7 pm weekdays and till noon Saturday. Črnomelj's medical centre (☎ 305 11 31) is at Delavska pot 4.

For local hiking maps, try the DZS bookshop on Ulica Staneta Rozmana. It's open from 7 am to 7 pm weekdays, and till noon Saturday.

Things to See & Do
Črnomelj Castle (Črnomaljski Grad), parts of which date from the late 12th century, houses government offices, a restaurant and the **Town Museum Collection** of items and documents related to the history of Črnomelj and Bela Krajina. It is open from 9 am to 3 pm weekdays only.

The foundations of **Stonič Castle** (Stoničev Grad), to the south at Ulica Staneta Rozmana 4, go back to the 12th century as well; this is where the town's original castle stood. The **Komenda** (Commandery) of the Teutonic knights, to the south-east across Trg Svobode, is a more recent structure, originally built in 1655 with alterations made in the 19th century.

The history of the **Parish Church of St Peter**, almost opposite Stonič Castle on Ulica Staneta Rozmana, also goes back more than seven centuries, but what you'll see today is a standard-issue baroque structure with a single spire. You can still see

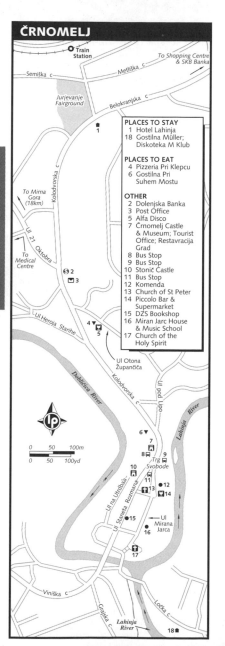

CRNOMELJ

Train Station

To Shopping Centre & SKB Banka

Semiška c.

Metliška c.

Jurjevanje Fairground

Belokranjska c.

1

Kolodvorska c.

To Mirna Gora (18km)

Ul 21 Oktobra

To Medical Centre

2
3

Ul Heroja Starihe

4
5

Dobličica River

Ul Otona Župančiča

Kolodvorska c.

Ul pod Lipo

Lahinja River

0   50   100m
0   50   100yd

6
7
8   9
Trg Svobode
10
11
12
13   14

Ul na Utrdbah

Ul Staneta Rozmana

15
Ul Mirana Jarca
16

17

Viniška c.

Lahinja River

Gribska c.

Lokca c.

18

PLACES TO STAY
1 Hotel Lahinja
18 Gostilna Müller; Diskoteka M Klub

PLACES TO EAT
4 Pizzeria Pri Klepcu
6 Gostilna Pri Suhem Mostu

OTHER
2 Dolenjska Banka
3 Post Office
4 Alfa Disco
7 Črnomelj Castle & Museum; Tourist Office; Restavracija Grad
8 Bus Stop
9 Bus Stop
10 Stonič Castle
11 Bus Stop
12 Komenda
13 Church of St Peter
14 Piccolo Bar & Supermarket
15 DZS Bookshop
16 Miran Jarc House & Music School
17 Church of the Holy Spirit

Roman tombstones built into the walls, and the fresco on the western exterior of St Christopher, the patron saint of travellers, was meant to remind passers-by that they, too, walked with God.

The **Church of the Holy Spirit** (1487) at the southern end of Ulica Mirana Jarca is still undergoing extensive renovations. The novelist and poet Miran Jarc (1900–42) was born in the house at No 3 of the same street; it is now a music school.

One of the most popular hikes in this part of Bela Krajina starts at the northern end of Ulica 21 Oktobra and carries on over hill and dale for 18km north-west to **Mirna Gora** (1047m).

A popular wine road *(vinska cesta)* runs from Tanča Gora, 5km south-west of Črnomelj, northward through Dobliačka Gora, Stražnji Vrh and Ručetna Vas to Semič. Try some of the local Bela Krajina wines, especially the Chardonnay.

Semič (population 753), 9km north of Črnomelj, is an attractive little town with the ruins of a castle, the 13th-century **Church of St Stephen** and, to the south-east, the **source of the Krupa River**.

Special Events
Jurjevanje, a three-day festival in mid-June of music, dance and bonfires held at the fairground near the train station, is one of the most important celebrations of folklore in Slovenia. This is the time of the Zeleni Jurij (Green George), when boys dressed in greenery go from house to house singing. Another big event is the Florjanovo, the firefighters' festival on 4 May. For information about both events ring ☎ 336 10 00.

There are concerts in Črnomelj Castle in July and August.

Places to Stay
The *Kamp Podzemelj ob Kolpi* camping ground on the Kolpa River is about 10km north-east of Črnomelj; see Places to Stay under Metlika earlier in this chapter.

If you tackle the hike up to Mirna Gora, accommodation there is available year-round at the *Planinski Dom na Mirni Gori* (☎ 306 85 73).

The only hotel in Črnomelj is the nondescript 30-room *Hotel Lahinja* (☎ *306 16 50, fax 306 16 40, Kolodvorska cesta 60*) near the train station. It charges 3000/5300 SIT for singles/doubles with shared shower and 5500/8000 SIT for rooms with private bath and TV. Prices include breakfast. The hotel's terrace cafe is a pleasant enough meeting place in warm weather.

A better option would be the 12-bed *Gostilna Müller* (☎ *305 10 97, Ločka cesta 6*), across the river to the south of the Old Town. It has bright, attractive rooms for around 3000 SIT per person.

Places to Eat

The *Restavracija Grad* in the castle at Trg Svobode 3 is an old-style eatery that hasn't changed a lot since the 1960s, and still serves pretty solid fare. For pizza, try the *Pri Klepcu* on Ulica Otona Župančiča, next to the Alfa disco. Another option for snacks is the *Gostilna Pri Suhem Mostu* (*Kolodvorska cesta 5*), open from 7 am to 11 pm daily.

The best place for a meal in Črnomelj is the *Gostilna Müller* (see Places to Stay). Its restaurant serves fish and traditional Slovene dishes, including *žlikrofi* (ravioli of cheese, bacon and chives), and is open from 7 am to 11 pm daily, except Monday, but is sometimes crowded with coach tour parties at lunchtime.

Entertainment

Črnomelj has several popular late-night venues, including the *Alfa Disco* (*Ulica Otona Župančiča 6*), open till 1 am Monday to Thursday and till 4 am Friday and Saturday, and *Diskoteka M Klub* at the Gostilna Müller (see Places to Stay), open till 11 pm daily, except Monday, and till 4 am Saturday. The *Piccolo* (*Trg Svobode 1a*) beneath the supermarket, at the start of Ulica Mirana Jarca, is the most popular place in town for a quiet drink. It's open from 8 am to 11 pm daily (till 1 am Friday and Saturday).

Getting There & Away

Departures by bus to Metlika and Vinica via Dragatuš are frequent, with up to 10 a day. Other destinations with less frequent bus service include Adlešiči (five), Novo Mesto (one, at 5.30 am) and Semič (four).

Črnomelj is served by up to a dozen trains a day from Ljubljana (2½ hours, 107km) via Novo Mesto and Semič. Four trains daily depart Črnomelj for Karlovac in Croatia.

AROUND ČRNOMELJ
Rožanec

About 5km north-west of Črnomelj on the road to Dolenjske Toplice is the little village of Rožanec (turn left just after Lokve). From a parking place in the village centre, a sign points the way along a trail that leads in 650m to the **Mithraeum** (Mitrej in Slovene).

This temple to the god Mithra (see the boxed text 'Mithra & the Great Sacrifice'), dating from the 2nd century AD, is no more than a natural hollow in the limestone set on a wooded hillside. But on one of the exposed limestone faces is a 1.5m-high carved relief of Mithra sacrificing the sacred bull, watched by Sol (the Sun, at top left) and Luna (the Moon, at top right), with a dog, serpent and scorpion at his feet.

Lahinja Landscape Park

This 200-hectare park, about 9km south of Črnomelj, is a protected karst area and the source of the Lahinja River, with trails crisscrossing the area. Two small swamps in the park are home to a number of endangered plants and animals, especially birds like orioles, nightingales and kingfishers, and the area around **Pusti Gradac** is a treasure-trove of prehistoric finds and caves. *Župančičev Hram* (☎ *07-305 73 47*), a farmhouse with restaurant and accommodation at house No 22 in Dragatuš, 3km to the north-west, is an excellent starting point for walks in the park. The park information centre (☎ 07-305 74 28) is in Veliki Nerajec at house No 18a.

KOLPA RIVER VALLEY
☎ 07

The 118km-long Kolpa, which forms Slovenia's south-eastern border with Croatia, is the warmest and one of the cleanest rivers in the country. As a result, it has become a popular recreational area for swimming,

BELA KRAJINA

BELA KRAJINA

Mithra & the Great Sacrifice

Mithraism, the worship of the god Mithra, originated in Persia. As Roman rule extended into Asia, the religion became extremely popular with traders, imperial slaves and mercenaries of the Roman army and spread rapidly throughout the empire in the 1st and 2nd centuries AD. The Roman emperors eventually accepted the new faith and Mithraism was the principal rival of Christianity until Constantine came to the throne in the 4th century.

Mithraism was a mysterious religion and its devotees were sworn to secrecy. What little is known of Mithra, the god of justice and social contract, has been deduced from reliefs and icons found in temples, like the ones at Rožanec near Črnomelj and at Ptuj in Štajerska. Most of these portray Mithra clad in a Persian-style cap and tunic sacrificing a white bull in front of Sol, the sun god. From the bull's blood and semen sprout grain, grapes and living creatures. Sol's wife Soma, the moon, begins her cycle and time is born.

Mithraism and Christianity competed strongly because of a striking similarity in many of their rituals. Both religions involved the birth of a deity on 25 December, shepherds, death and resurrection and a form of baptism. Devotees of Mithraism knelt when they worshipped and a common meal – a 'communion' of bread and water – was a regular feature of the liturgy.

MARTIN HARRIS

Mithra with sacrificial bull

fishing and boating, especially around the village of **Vinica**. Farther downstream is **Adlešiči**, known for its vibrant folk culture and easy walks.

Things to See
In Vinica (population 2288), the **Oton Župančič Memorial Collection** is in the house at No 9 where the celebrated Slovenian poet was born in 1878, and the tower of the partially preserved **castle** from the 16th century has an interesting Gothic chapel and offers commanding views of the valley and Croatia. But most people visit Vinica (Weinitz in German) to go swimming, fishing or boating on the Kolpa.

The ruins of **Pobrežje Castle** about 1.5km north-east of Adlešiči (population 938) are worth exploring. While passing through the village of Purga after Adlešiči, visit the **Čebelar Adlešič** farmhouse at house No 5. The family here are beekeepers and, while there is no accommodation and meals are only prepared for groups, they will be happy

to show you around. They will explain all things apiarian and give you a sample of their honey or *domača medica*, home-made mead that has a kick like a donkey.

Activities
Kamp Vinica (☎ 306 40 18) in Vinica is the best source of information for all sporting activities in the area, and there is a decent grass beach adjacent to it. Žagar, a company with an office at the camping ground, rents canoes and water scooters. The ambitious, though, will look into making the rapid-water kayak run from Stari Trg, 20km upriver, to Vinica. Fishing is good, especially around Dol to the north-west, and the Kolpa is particularly rich in grayling and brown trout. You can buy a daily fishing licence at the camping ground.

From Adlešiči, two easy hikes to nearby hills afford great views of the Kolpa, vineyards and surrounding towns. To get to **Mala Plešivica** (341m), walk south along a marked trail for about half an hour. A short distance to the west is a sinkhole with a water source called **Vodenica** which, according to local lore, was walled in by the ancient Illyrians. Steps lead down to the source, where you'll find a large stone vault.

Velika Plešivica (363m) is about an hour's walk north-west of Adlešiči. At the foot of the hill is a chapel dedicated to Mary; during attacks by the Turks, the faithful hid in the cave below it. On top of Velika Plešivica is another church dating back to the 12th century. This one is dedicated to St Mary Magdalen.

You can rent horses from the RIM farmhouse (☎ 307 05 16) in Jankoviči (house No 12) for about €11 per hour. There is a swimming area on the Kolpa just south of Pobrežje Castle.

Places to Stay
There are several camping grounds in the area. The **Kamp Vinica** (☎ 306 40 18), on the river at No 19a in Vinica, covers an area of about 1.5 hectares and can accommodate up to 300 people. The charge is 980 SIT per person, and the camping ground is open from April to mid-October. The **Kamp ba Kopališču** (☎ 305 78 14) on the Kolpa, at the southern end of Adlešiči (No 24a), is open from June to September, as is **Kamp Dragoši** (☎ 305 77 87) to the north at No 4 in Dragoši, between Jankoviči and Griblje.

Among the accommodation in Adlešiči is the **Grabrijanovi Farmhouse** (☎ 305 77 15) at house No 5. It has four rooms and is open year-round.

Places to Eat
Kamp Vinica has a full restaurant as well as a pub/snack bar open till 11 pm weekdays and till midnight at the weekend.

In the centre of Adlešiči, **Gostilna Milič** (☎ 307 00 19) at house No 16a is one of the oldest eateries in Bela Krajina. Its drawing card is a large baker's oven that produces anything from pizzas to roast suckling pig.

Gostilna Kapušin (☎ 305 71 54) in Krasinec (house No 55), about 2km north of Griblje, has excellent fish dishes and is highly recommended by locals. It is closed Monday. It has accommodation in six rooms.

Shopping
At the Čebelar Adlešič farmhouse (see Things to See) you can buy honey, mead, beeswax and pollen. An interesting souvenir is a vial of propolis, the sticky substance collected from certain trees by bees to cement their hives. It is supposed to be an elixir.

The RIM farmhouse (see Activities) contains a gallery of locally produced leather goods as well as some hand-woven linen, painted Easter eggs and other folk craft. It also has a range of local wines (including the sweet 'ice' variety) and brandies in beautifully crafted hand-blown bottles.

Getting There & Away
Bus connections with Črnomelj, Metlika and Novo Mesto from Vinica are good. There are five buses a day making the run from Črnomelj to Adlešiči, 12km to the south-east.

BELA KRAJINA

Štajerska

It is difficult to characterise Štajerska (Styria in English, Steiermark in German). Though it is Slovenia's largest province, it does not have as much variety as Gorenjska and Primorska. A lot of Štajerska is field, but there are plenty of mountains too, such as the Pohorje Massif. Štajerska has more big farms than any other part of Slovenia (hops for making beer are an important crop, as are wheat, potatoes and grapes for the province's excellent wines), but it also contains some of the country's largest and most historical cities and towns: Maribor, Celje and that little gem, Ptuj.

Štajerska has been at the crossroads of Slovenia for centuries and virtually everyone has 'slept here' – at least for a time: Celts, Romans, early Slavs, Habsburgs and Nazi German occupiers. In the 14th century the Counts of Celje were among the richest and most powerful feudal dynasties in Central Europe and challenged the Austrian monarchy's rule for 100 years. Štajerska suffered terribly under the black leather boot of Nazism in WWII and many of its inhabitants were murdered, deported or forced to work in labour camps.

Some Slovenian guidebooks divide up Štajerska simply as the 'Maribor area' and the 'Celje area'. Here we've split it into many more sections: the Kozjansko region in the south-east; the spa town of Rogaška Slatina above Kozjansko; historic Ptuj; Maribor, Slovenia's second largest city; the Pohorje Massif; the central city of Celje; and the Upper Savinja Valley bordering Gorenjska.

The geographical centre of Slovenia is at Spodnja Slivna, north of Litija in Štajerska.

KOZJANSKO REGION

Kozjansko is a remote region along the eastern side of the Posavje Mountains and the 80km-long Sotla River, which forms the border with Croatia. It is an area of forests, rolling hills, vineyards and scattered farms.

Highlights

- Go hiking, cycling or riding in the beautiful Logarska Dolina
- Discover Ptuj, one of the oldest towns in Slovenia
- Visit Podsreda Castle in the Kozjansko region
- View the 15th-century carved Misericordia statue at the church in Ptujska Gora
- Enjoy a farm holiday in the central Pohorje region
- Tour the Jeruzalem-Ljutomer wine road, with frequent stops, from Ormož to Ljutomer

AUSTRIA

Maribor p281

Logarska Dolina (Logar Valley) p298

Ptuj p273

Rogaška Slatina p269

Celje p291

Podčetrtek Area p265

CROATIA

Kozjansko's isolation made it suitable for settlement during the Great Migrations. In the Middle Ages it became the frontier region between Austrian Styria and Hungarian Croatia, which accounts for the large number of castles (eg, at Podsreda, Podčetrtek, Bistrica ob Sotli) and it became Slovenia's 'stormy corner' during the peasant uprisings of the 16th century.

Today, Kozjansko remains an underdeveloped region but with much to offer travellers: spas, castles, hiking and excellent wine.

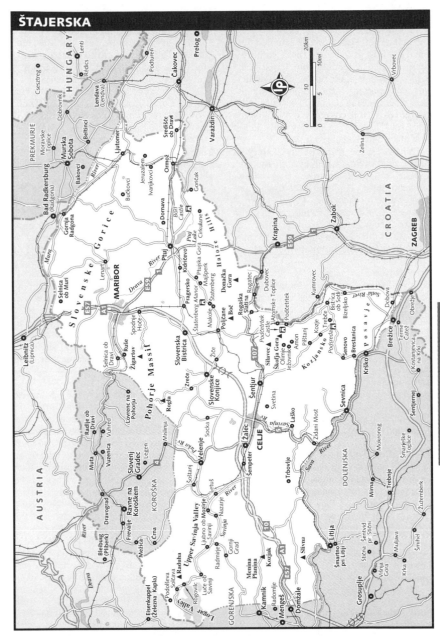

Podčetrtek

☎ 03 • postcode 3254 • pop 474

The village of Podčetrtek is situated less than 1km west of the Sotla River on a little bump of land extending into Croatia. Its castle, originally built in the 12th century, was an important fortification during the wars with the Hungarians 300 years later. Podčetrtek's name comes from the Slovene word for Thursday – the day the market took place and the court sat.

The castle, the Minorite monastery at Olimje and wonderful hikes into the surrounding hills are Podčetrtek's major drawcards, but most people visit the town these days to relax at the Terme Olimia thermal spa a short distance from the centre (note that the spa was until recently known as Atomske Toplice and this former name may still appear on signs and maps).

Orientation The centre of Podčetrtek is at the junction of four roads: to the west is Olimje; to the north-west, the castle; to the north-east, the Terme Olimia spa complex; and to the south, the town of Bistrica ob Sotli.

All buses stop at the crossroads as well as at the spa and the camping ground. There are three train 'stations'. For the village centre and the castle, get off at 'Podčetrtek'. 'Atomske Toplice' is good for the hotel, Vas Lipa and the Terme pool complex. 'Podčetrtek Toplice' is the correct stop for the camping ground.

Information The tourist office (☎/fax 582 94 50, e tic@podcetrtek.si) is next door to the fire station in Podčetrtek village. It's open from 9 am to 6 pm weekdays and till 1 pm Saturday, year-round. The staff at the Hotel Breza (☎ 829 70 00) can also answer questions, make bookings and change money.

The post office, open from 8 am to 6 pm weekdays (but closed 9.30 to 10 am and 3.30 to 4 pm) and 8 am till noon Saturday, is at Trška cesta 23, about 150m north of the tourist office. It too has exchange facilities.

Podčetrtek Castle The giant castle on the hill top to the north-west of town is not the original one that was built by the Krško bishops in the 13th century but razed in the 15th century during the wars with the Hungarians. The present castle went up some time in the mid-16th century but it too was badly damaged – this time by an earthquake in 1974. The castle can be easily reached on foot by a trail from town marked 'Grad'. Along the way you'll pass the **Church of St Lawrence** with baroque frescoes inside.

Terme Olimia Formerly known as Atomske Toplice, this 'health and holiday resort' about 1200m north-east of Podčetrtek is a serious thermal spa in its own right (the 28° to 36°C water is full of magnesium and calcium and recommended for those recovering from surgery or trying to cure rheumatism). But these days it puts most of the emphasis on recreation, with a total of eight pools, sauna, steam room, solarium and sports facilities. The indoor and outdoor pools connected by an underwater passage at the Terme complex alone cover an area of 2000 sq metres, and there's a section reserved for naturists. The only drawback to the complex is that it overlooks a rather busy road. The complex (☎ 829 70 00, fax 582 90 24, e info@terme-olimia.com) is at Zdraviliška cesta 24.

Minorite Monastery The Minorite monastery 3km west of Podčetrtek in Olimje was built as a Renaissance-style castle in about 1550. When Pauline monks took over what was then called Wolimia in German about a century later, they added the baroque **Church of the Assumption**, which retains its original ceiling paintings in the presbytery and the unbelievably ornate **Chapel of St Francis Xavier**. On the ground floor of one of the four corner towers is the monastery's greatest treasure: a 17th-century **pharmacy** – the third oldest in Europe – painted with religious and medical scenes. One of the best ones shows the cunning serpent tempting a rather plump Eve with Adam in attendance. The church and the pharmacy are open from 10 to 11 am and 1 to 2 pm daily, except Wednesday. Admission is 200/100 SIT for adults/children.

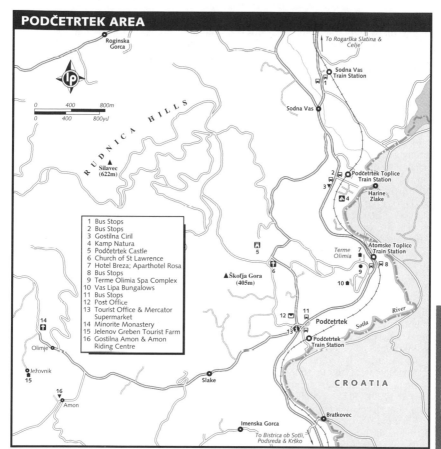

PODČETRTEK AREA

1 Bus Stops
2 Bus Stops
3 Gostilna Ciril
4 Kamp Natura
5 Podčetrtek Castle
6 Church of St Lawrence
7 Hotel Breza; Aparthotel Rosa
8 Bus Stops
9 Terme Olimia Spa Complex
10 Vas Lipa Bungalows
11 Bus Stops
12 Post Office
13 Tourist Office & Mercator Supermarket
14 Minorite Monastery
15 Jelenov Greben Tourist Farm
16 Gostilna Amon & Amon Riding Centre

Horse Riding Some 2.5km from Podčetrtek on the road to Olimje and another 500m south is the Amon Riding Centre (☎ 582 90 42) at Olimje 23 with horses for both beginners and the advanced. An hour in the paddock costs 1500 SIT, riding in the open countryside costs 2500 SIT per hour and half-hour lessons are 3000 SIT.

Hot-Air Ballooning Jelenov Greben (☎ 582 90 46), near Olimje, offers 50-minute sightseeing flights in a hot-air balloon for 15,000 SIT per person. The basket holds up to three people plus the pilot.

Hiking & Cycling Some of the most rewarding hikes and bike trips in Slovenia can be made in this area and the 1:18,000-scale *Podčetrtek-Atomske Toplice Tourist Map* lists dozens of excursions for walkers, cyclists and mountain bikers. The easiest walks on marked trails take an hour or two (though the circuitous one north-east to the hill-top Church of St Emma lasts about four hours) and there are bicycle routes all the way to Kozje, Podsreda and Rogaška Slatina. The more demanding mountain-bike routes head north to the forest-covered Rudnica Hills in the 600m range, but there are some easier ones down through the Olimje forest and through the vineyards of Virštanj, Selo and Imeno.

Places to Stay The *Kamp Natura (☎ 829 7000, ☎/fax 582 90 24, [e] info@terme-olimia .com – for all accommodation at the spa)* is just under 1km north of the main spa complex on the edge of the Sotla River; if you've checked in and you've got a guest card, you can take the shortcut to the spa through Croatia! The camping ground covers an area of two hectares and can accommodate 500 guests. It's far enough off the main road and the train line running close by doesn't get much use. For the daily fee of 1900 to 2100 SIT per person (depending on season), campers get to use the site's three outdoor thermal pools as well as the pools at the spa complex. The camping ground is open from Easter to August.

The 150-room *Hotel Breza* is a strange, five-storey structure with roofs sloping off every which way. Singles in this expensive place cost from 10,500 to 11,000 SIT, doubles 16,200 to 17,200 SIT, for bed and breakfast. The hotel has its own indoor thermal pool.

The nearby *Aparthotel Rosa* has 94 apartments with living room, bedroom, kitchen, bathroom and satellite TV. Prices start at 12,800 SIT per night for an apartment that sleeps two to three people.

Vas Lipa is a tourist 'village' south-west of the main hotel complex that does not look unlike an American suburban development; if that's what you want there are 25 houses with 136 apartments. One for two people (including kitchen, bathroom, bedroom and TV) costs 9800 SIT.

The tourist office has a list of families offering *private rooms* in Podčetrtek and Sodna Vas, 2km north of the spa complex. Prices range from 1750 to 4500 SIT per person per night. The other private rooms on the list are in Harine Zlake, a hop over the narrow Sotla and a few paces inside Croatia. There is no border check here.

The *Jelenov Greben tourist farm (☎ 582 90 46, fax 582 92 91, [e] jelenov.greben@siol .net)*, 500m south of Olimje at Ježovnik,

has 13 rooms at 4500 SIT per person (including breakfast), and four four-person apartments at 10,000 SIT per night (breakfast 500 SIT per person extra).

Places to Eat *Gostilna Ciril (Zdraviliška cesta 10)* on the main road across from the entrance to the camping ground is a popular grill restaurant frequented by local Slovenes and their Croatian neighbours. The vine-covered terrace is lovely on a warm evening. *Gostilna Amon* at the Amon Riding Centre (see Horse Riding earlier in this section) has better food, but it can get very crowded in the evening. *Jelenov Greben tourist farm* (see Places to Stay) has a popular restaurant that is famous for its venison and wild mushroom dishes.

There's a *Mercator supermarket* beside the tourist office in Podčetrtek village. It's open from 7 am to 7 pm weekdays, till noon Saturday and till 11 am Sunday.

Getting There & Around Up to eight buses a day cruise by Podčetrtek and Terme Olimia on their way to Bistrica ob Sotli and Celje. You can also reach Kozje (one bus a day), Maribor (three) and Virštanj (one).

Podčetrtek and Atomske Toplice are on the rail line linking Celje (via Stranje) with Imeno. Up to six trains leave the main Podčetrtek station every day for Celje (45 minutes, 47km) and Imeno (four minutes, 3km).

You can call a taxi on ☎ 582 93 82 or ☎ 581 39 24. There's also a van service available at Hotel Breza's reception (☎ 829 7000) to points of interest in the area.

Podsreda
☎ 03 • postcode 3257 • pop 672
If you're heading south to Bizeljsko, Brežice in Posavje or to Dolenjska, be sure to stop at Podsreda about 20km south-west of Podčetrtek, site of the best-preserved Romanesque castle in Slovenia. Getting to Podsreda from Podčetrtek is tricky if you don't have your own wheels: catch the bus to Kozje, change there for the one headed for Bistrica ob Sotli and get off at Podsreda village. The bus between Krško and Celje also stops here. The castle is perched on a

475m hill south of the village. A rough, winding road (5km) leads to the castle, but you can also reach it via a relatively steep 2km trail from Stari Trg, less than 1km south-east of Podsreda village.

Podsreda Castle (Grad Podsreda; Herberg in German) looks pretty much the way it did when it was built in about 1200. A barbican on the southern side, with walls some 3m thick, leads to a central courtyard. The rooms in the castle wings, some with beamed ceilings and ancient chandeliers, now contain a dull glassworks exhibit (crystal from Rogaška Slatina, vials from the Olimje pharmacy, green Pohorje glass), but the tiny Romanesque chapel is worth the wait, and there's a wonderful collection of prints of Štajerska's castles and monasteries taken from *Topographii Ducatus Stiria* (1681) by Georg Mattäus Vischer (1628–96). The view from the castle windows of the surrounding countryside and the pilgrimage church on Svete Gore above Bistrica ob Sotli are superb. A Musical Summer festival takes place in July and August.

The castle is open from 10 am to 6 pm (to 4 pm from October to April) daily, except Monday. The entry fee is 500/350 SIT for adults/children. If you've built up an appetite climbing up and down those hills, there's a small gostilna called *Pri Martinu* in Podsreda village that has a vine-covered terrace.

Kozjanski Park, some 2.5km north-east of Podsreda at Trebče, honours the Partisan effort during WWII and the pivotal role played by Josip Tito. Tito was born in the Croatian village of Kumrovec just over the border from Bistrica ob Sotli in 1892 to a Slovenian mother and a Croatian father.

ROGAŠKA SLATINA
☎ 03 • postcode 3250 • pop 8586

Rogaška Slatina is Slovenia's oldest and largest spa town, a veritable 'cure factory' with almost a dozen hotels, therapies ranging from 'pearl baths' to dreadful-sounding 'lymph drainage' and some 30,000 visitors a year. It's an attractive place set among scattered forests in the foothills of the Macelj range, whose two highest peaks, Boč and Donačka Gora, are visible from

the centre. The border crossing into Croatia at Rogatec is 7km to the east.

Legend tells us that the magnesium-rich spring was discovered by the Muses' winged horse Pegasus when Apollo advised the steed to eschew the 'make believe and glitter' of the magic Hippocrene fountain on Mt Helicon and drink instead at Roitschocrene. And the rest is history.

Well, not really. While it's true that the spring was known in Roman times, Rogaška Slatina didn't make it onto the map until 1574 when the governor of Styria, one Wolf Ungnad, took the waters, on the advice of his physician. A century later a publication entitled *Roitschocrene* examined the curative properties of the Slatina springs and claimed they had helped the ailing viceroy of Croatia. The news spread to Vienna, visitors started to arrive in droves and inns were opened. By the early 19th century, Rogaška Slatina (Rohitsch-Sauerbrunn in German) was an established spa town.

Today this 'Vichy of Slovenia' is as popular as a recreational and beauty resort as it is for health treatments, with a host of sporting facilities available. But Rogaška Slatina is still caught up in the continuing process of being privatised and sold, so standards may vary among establishments. Hiking and cycling in the area is particularly good.

Orientation
The heart of Rogaška Slatina is the spa complex, an attractive – and architecturally important – group of neoclassical, Secessionist and Plečnik-style buildings surrounding a garden. This is called Zdravilíški trg or 'Health Resort Square'. The unattractive hotels and Terapija building to the north and north-east are late 1960s and 1970s vintage and not in keeping with the rest of the lovely square.

Rogaška Slatina's bus station is south of Zdravilíški trg on Celjska cesta, not far from the post office. The train station is about 300m farther south on Kidričeva ulica.

Information
The helpful tourist office (☎ 811 57 31, fax 811 57 30) at Zdravilíški trg 1 is open from

9 am to 4 pm weekdays year-round and till noon Saturday.

Banka Celje is at Kidričeva ulica 5 and is open from 8 am to noon and 2 to 5 pm weekdays. On Saturday it closes at 11.30 am. Otherwise, try the Srečko exchange office in the little pavilion just opposite, open from 7.30 am to 6 pm (4 pm in winter) weekdays, till noon Saturday. The post office next door to Banka Celje at Kidričeva ulica 3 has exchange facilities and is open from 8 am to 7 pm weekdays and till noon Saturday.

Rogaška Spa

First and foremost, the mineral water (called Donat Mg here) found at Rogaška Spa (Zdravilišče Rogaška; ☎ 811 73 21, fax 811 73 20, e mail@rogaska.com) is for drinking. The stuff is bottled and sold throughout Slovenia for both curative and refreshment purposes, but you might find the real thing here a bit too salty and metallic. The water, which also contains calcium, sulphates, lithium and bromide, is said to eliminate stress, aid digestion and stimulate weight loss. The magnesium alone, it is claimed, regulates 200 bodily functions (most of which you probably didn't know were working for you).

You can engage in a 'drinking cure' of your own at the Pivnica, the round, glassed-in drinking hall where mineral water is dispensed directly from the springs. It's just beyond the gazebo-like Tempel, which was built in the early 19th century above the central Slatina spring. A pass admitting you to the Pivnica, valid for three days, costs 1200 SIT, but be sure you follow the advice in the pamphlet entitled *Catch Your Drop of Health* – you wouldn't want to overdo it. The Pivnica is open from 7 am to 1 pm and from 3 to 7 pm daily (7 am to noon and 4 to 6 pm Sunday).

The centre of real action at the spa is the 12-storey Terapija building where those pearl baths are being taken and those lymphs (shudder) are being drained. Between the Hotel Donat and the Zdravilíški Dom there's a beauty centre as well as an indoor thermal pool (750 SIT), sauna, steam room and gym. A 30-minute body massage costs 3300 SIT.

A day pass for the outdoor swimming pool complex (Termalna Riviera) next to the modern Sonce shopping centre at Celjska cesta 7 costs 1300/900 SIT for adults/children; a three-hour pass costs 900/800 SIT. It's open from 9 am to 8 pm daily (to 11 pm Saturday).

The former administration building at Zdravilíški trg 4, the oldest structure at the spa, houses the little Museum of Graphic Arts (Muzej Grafične Umetnosti), a collection of etchings and drawings from the 16th to the 19th centuries that was donated by a satisfied Swiss patient named Kurt Müller. It's open from 10 am till noon and from 4 to 6 pm Tuesday, Thursday and Saturday only. Entrance is 300/200 SIT for adults/children.

Other Attractions

The sports centre (☎ 811 63 86), a couple of hundred metres east of the Hotel Donat and up the hill, has six outdoor and four indoor tennis courts available for hire. Prices range from €6.50 to €13 depending on whether you're outside or inside and the time of day. A racquet and balls costs €1.5, and there's a squash court for hire at €3.50. Bicycles cost €3/5/6.50 per hour/half-day/day. There's also minigolf, table tennis, archery and lawn bowling. There's a nine-hole pitch and putt course (☎ 811 64 79) open daily in summer on Cesta na Bellevue.

South of the sports centre on Janina Hill is a tiny ski slope with 3km of trails and two tows. A day pass costs about 1200 SIT; skis, poles and boots are another 800 SIT.

There are 10 marked walking trails which fan out from Rogaška Slatina into the surrounding hills and meadows, and the hikes can be as short as 2km or as long as 20km. No 8, for example, leads 14km to the Church of St Florian, on a hill north-east of the spa, and to Ložno, from where you can continue on another 4km to Donačka Gora (883m). If you want to do it an easier way, take a bus or train to Rogatec, then walk to Donačka Gora in about two hours. Accommodation there is at the *Rudljev Dom* (☎ 882 71 28, mobile ☎ 050-331 001) at 590m. It's open weekends and holidays from May to the end of January.

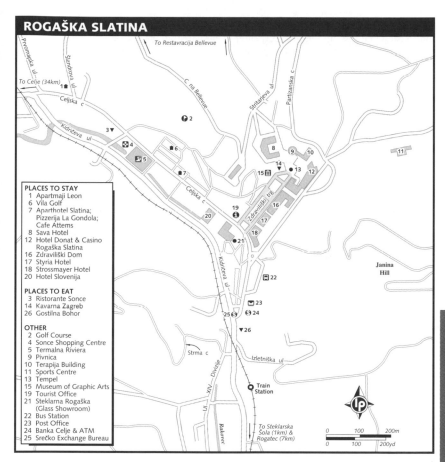

ROGAŠKA SLATINA

PLACES TO STAY
1 Apartmaji Leon
6 Vila Golf
7 Aparthotel Slatina;
   Pizzerija La Gondola;
   Cafe Attems
8 Sava Hotel
12 Hotel Donat & Casino
   Rogaška Slatina
16 Zdraviliški Dom
17 Styria Hotel
18 Strossmayer Hotel
20 Hotel Slovenija

PLACES TO EAT
3 Ristorante Sonce
14 Kavarna Zagreb
26 Gostilna Bohor

OTHER
2 Golf Course
4 Sonce Shopping Centre
5 Termalna Riviera
9 Pivnica
10 Terapija Building
11 Sports Centre
13 Tempel
15 Museum of Graphic Arts
19 Tourist Office
21 Steklarna Rogaška
   (Glass Showroom)
22 Bus Station
23 Post Office
24 Banka Celje & ATM
25 Srečko Exchange Bureau

ŠTAJERSKA

In **Rogatec** (population 1621), one of the oldest towns in Slovenia, there's an interesting **open-air ethnographic museum** with traditional Pannonian farmhouses on display.

The walk to **Boč** (979m) north-west of Rogaška Slatina takes about four hours, though you can drive as far as *Dom na Boču* (☎ *882 46 17)*, a mountain hut a couple of kilometres south of the peak.

Special Events

The Rogaška Musical Summer is a series of concerts held in the Crystal Hall (Kristlana Dvorana) of the Zdraviliški Dom, where Franz Liszt tickled the ivories in 1846, and in the Pivnica. Other concerts are held *en plein air* at the Tempel pavilion. Concerts take place every two to three days at 8.30 pm from late June to late September. The tourist office or the festival information office (☎ 811 64 24) on the 2nd floor of the Zdraviliški Dom (Zdraviliški trg 11) will provide you with a list.

Places to Stay

The tourist office can arrange *private rooms* in the town and surrounding area for between €7.50 and €13 for a single and €13 and €20 for a double, depending on the season (busiest time is July and August) and the room category. There's a list of private accommodation in the window if the office is closed.

With the exception of the high-priced *Sava Hotel Complex* (☎ 811 40 00, fax 811 47 32) and *Hotel Donat* (☎ 811 30 00, fax 811 37 32), two enormous and modern hotels with over 400 rooms at the north end of Zdraviliški trg, prices at most of the spa hotels are standard: from €25 to €31 per person for a double with shower and breakfast and €29 to €35 for a single, including half-board. Bed and breakfast only costs 10% less.

The *Zdravilíški Dom*, *Styria* and *Strossmayer* hotels (☎ 811 20 00, fax 811 27 11) are gradually being renovated, but many of their rooms look out on to the lovely park. Choose instead the 90-room *Hotel Slovenija* (☎ 811 50 00, fax 811 57 32, Celjska cesta 1), which is central to everything. For any of the above hotels you can send email inquiries to e mail@rogaska.com.

The attractive *Aparthotel Slatina* (☎ 818 27 00, fax 818 27 49, e zerak@siol.net, Celjska cesta 6), in a restored late-19th-century spa building, has two- to four-person apartments with bed-sitting room, bathroom, kitchenette and cable TV for €36 per person. The nearby *Vila Golf* is more stylish and more expensive, and can be booked through the Dober Dan agency (☎ 819 02 00, fax 819 02 01).

If you're in a group, you might try *Apartmaji Leon* (☎ 581 50 99, fax 547 16 52, Šlandrova ulica 1a), a pension with apartments for five people costing €66 to €87, depending on the season.

Places to Eat

Gostilna Bohor (Kidričeva ulica 23) has fish dishes and pizzas in the 800 to 1000 SIT range. The 'Farmer's Pizza' (Kmečka Pizza), with virtually everything from the barnyard on it, is good. The *Pizzerija La Gondola* is a delightful cubbyhole beneath the Aparthotel Slatina (see Places to Stay), serving good pizzas, pastas, salads and delicious cumin-scented kebabs for around 800 to 1000 SIT. Both establishments are

open from 9 am to 10 or 11 pm daily (from 11 am at weekends).

One of the most pleasant places for a drink and a snack in the spa complex is the *Kavarna Zagreb* (Zdraviliški trg 5) in what used to be the Zagreb Hotel next to the Museum of Graphic Arts. It's open from 10 am till midnight daily. The *Ristorante Sonce* (Celjska cesta 9) is an Italian restaurant specialising in seafood, open from 7 am to 11 pm daily except Sunday.

The best restaurant in town is the *Restavracija Bellevue* (☎ 581 48 70) on top of the hill about a kilometre north of the Sava Hotel Complex. It serves Slovenian specialities and enjoys a panoramic view of the surrounding countryside. It's open from 11 am to 11 pm daily (to 10 pm Sunday).

There's a *supermarket* (Clejska cesta 7) in the Sonce shopping centre, open from 9 am to 6 pm weekdays, from 8 am to noon Saturday.

Entertainment

The *Casino Rogaška Slatina* (☎ 881 49 60) at the Hotel Donat is open from 8 pm till 3 am nightly (from 6 pm Friday and Saturday). The *Kavarna Zagreb* has ballroom dancing to 11.30 pm daily, and there are regular concerts in the elegant *Crystal Hall* in the Zdravilíški Dom.

Most visitors to Rogaška Slatina spend their evenings in the hotel bars and cafes; *Cafe Attems* at the Aparthotel Slatina (see Places to Stay) is popular with a younger crowd.

Shopping

Rogaška Slatina is almost as celebrated for its crystal as it is for its mineral water. The Steklarna Rogaška showroom at Zdravilíški trg 23 has a large selection of stemware, vases and bowls. It is open from 8 am to 7 pm weekdays, and till noon Saturday (also 3 to 7 pm from May to September).

The Steklarska šola (Glass School; ☎ 818 20 00), south of the town centre at Steklarska ulica 1, also has a wide range of lead crystal, and can make items to order. It's open from 8 am to 7 pm weekdays, and till 1 pm Saturday.

Getting There & Away

Buses to Celje and Rogatec leave Rogaška Slatina at least once an hour. Otherwise, the bus service is no more than adequate. There are six buses a day to Maribor (between 5 am and 6.40 pm) and two to Ljubljana (at 4.47 am and 2.39 pm).

The following destinations can also be reached from Rogaška Slatina: Bistrica ob Sotli (one bus a day), Dobovec and the Croatian border (up to six a day), Gornja Radgona (one), Ormož (two), Podčetrtek (one) and Ptuj (one, at 6.50 am).

Rogaška Slatina is on the train line linking Celje via Dobovec with Zabok in Croatia, where you can change for Zagreb. Up to six trains a day go to Celje (45 minutes, 36km) with the same number heading eastward for Rogatec and Dobovec.

PTUJ

☎ 02 • postcode 2250 • pop 19,000

Ptuj, one of the oldest towns in Slovenia, equals Ljubljana in terms of historical importance. Ptuj's compact medieval core, with its castle, museums, monasteries and churches, can easily be seen in a day. But there are so many interesting side trips and activities in the area that you may want to base yourself here for a while. To the south of Ptuj are the Haloze Hills, among the best wine-growing regions in Slovenia.

History

Ptuj, which, when pronounced in English, sounds vaguely like someone spitting from a great distance, began life as a Roman military outpost on the right (or southern) bank of the Drava River and later grew into a civilian settlement on the opposite side called Poetovio. Unlike so many other Slovenian towns, Ptuj doesn't have to put a spade into the ground to prove its ancient origins; Tacitus mentioned it by name in his *Historiae* as having been in existence as early as AD 69.

Poetovio, then the largest Roman township in what is now Slovenia, lay on a major road linking Pannonia and Noricum provinces. It was famous for its large stone bridge spanning the Drava near today's Dominican monastery. An aqueduct brought water down from the distant Pohorje Massif. In the 2nd and 3rd centuries, Ptuj was the centre of the Mithraic cult, a new religion with origins in Persia that was popular among Roman soldiers and slaves (see the boxed text 'Mithra & the Great Sacrifice' in the Bela Krajina chapter). Several complete temples have been unearthed in the area.

But all this came to a brutal end when the Goths attacked the town in the 5th century. They were followed by the Huns, Langobards, Franks and then the early Slavs.

The hill-top castle at Ptuj (Pettau in German) was attacked by the Magyars in the 10th century but was not taken. Ptuj received its town rights in 977 and over the next several centuries it grew rich through trade on the Drava. By the 13th century it was competing with the 'upstart' Marburg (Maribor), some 26km upriver, in both crafts and commerce. Two monastic orders – the Dominicans and the Franciscan Minorites – settled here and built important monasteries. The Hungarians attacked and occupied Ptuj for most of the 15th century though each of the half-dozen raids by the Turks were thwarted.

When the railway reached eastern Slovenia from Vienna on its way to the coast in the mid-19th century, the age-old rivalry between Maribor and Ptuj turned one-sided – the former was on the line and the latter missed out altogether. Though Ptuj was rescued from oblivion in 1863 when the railway line to Budapest passed through it, the town remained essentially a provincial centre with a German majority and very little industry until WWI.

Orientation

Ptuj is on the north bank of the swift-flowing Drava, which widens into the artificial Ptuj Lake (Ptujsko Jezero) to the south-east. The castle, with its irregular shape and ancient walls, dominates the town from a 300m hill to the north-west. Though there is no real centre to Ptuj, much of historical interest lies on or near Slovenski trg while Minoritski trg could be considered the gateway to the town. Terme Ptuj, a spa and recreational area across the river, is a tempting place to visit on one of Ptuj's very hot summer days.

ŠTAJERSKA

The bus station is about 450m north-east of Minoritski trg on Osojnikova cesta. The train station is another 200m farther along the same street.

Information

Tourist Offices The tourist office (☎ 771 56 91, fax 787 62 31) is located at the bottom of the City Tower at Slovenski trg 14. It is open from 8 am to 6 pm weekdays, from 8 am till noon and 1 to 6 pm Saturday, and from 10 am to 3 pm Sunday. It can organise guided tours for 500 SIT per person (minimum five people). Anyone planning to spend more than a day or two in Ptuj should pick up a copy of *Ptuj: A Guide to the Town* (2000 SIT) from the tourist office. It contains a wealth of information on Ptuj and neighbouring areas.

The Ptuj Alpine Society (☎ 777 15 11) at Prešernova ulica 27 has information about hiking in the area, but it is only open from 4 to 6 pm Tuesday and Friday.

Money Nova Ljubljanska Banka has a branch and ATM next to the Garni Hotel Mitra at Prešernova ulica 6. It is open from 8.30 am till noon and from 2.30 to 5 pm weekdays. SKB Banka at Trstenjakova ulica 2 is open from 8 am to noon and 2.30 to 5 pm weekdays and till 11 am Saturday.

Post & Communications The main post office is at Vodnikova 2. It is open from 7 am to 7 pm weekdays and to 1 pm Saturday, and has exchange facilities and counter phones.

Ptuj Castle

Parts of the castle complex (Grad Ptuj) date back to the first half of the 12th century (notably the tower on the western edge of the hill), but what you see here is an agglomeration of styles from the 14th to the 18th centuries put into place by one aristocratic owner after another. The castle houses the collection of the **Ptuj Regional Museum** on its three arcaded floors, but a trip is worth it for the views alone.

As you enter the castle, you can't help but notice the red marble **tombstone of Frederick V**, the last lord of Ptuj who died in 1438. It was brought here from the Dominican

monastery. The ground-floor castle contains a fascinating exhibition of musical instruments from the 17th to 19th centuries – flutes, horns, drums, lutes, violas, harps, clavichords etc. As you approach each case, a tape plays the music the instruments make.

The 1st floor is given over to period rooms, each with its own style, as well as an impressive **Knights' Hall**. The rooms are treasure-troves of tapestries, painted wall canvases (many from Dornava Castle, 8km to the north-east of Ptuj), portraits, weapons and furniture left by the castle's last occupants, the Herbertsteins. You'll probably notice a coat of arms containing three buckles and the motto 'Grip Fast' in English. It belonged to the Leslies, a Scottish-Austrian family who owned the castle from 1656 to 1802. The buckles are said to have been added to the family escutcheon when one of their number saved a countess who had fallen into a well by pulling her up with belts buckled together.

Among some of the more interesting bits and pieces are the chinoiserie decorations and wallpaper (whose figures have curious European features), the beautiful porcelain stoves fuelled through pipes from the outside corridors and the large collection of clocks, including an astronomical one from the 18th century, in the Music Room.

The 2nd floor is a **gallery** of Gothic statues and oil paintings from the 16th to the 19th centuries. Have a look at the scene of Ptuj in winter by Franc Jožef Fellner (1721–70). There is also one from the early 19th century of the Church of St George, marred by graffiti in German. Two fine statues – one of St Catherine (with a wheel) and the other of St Barbara (with a tower) – carved from sandstone in about 1410 in the 'soft' Gothic style, are among the museum's most priceless possessions. Check the faces of the guards torturing Christ in the crucifixion scene nearby; they really seem to be enjoying themselves.

The museum also has the largest collection of **Turkerie portraits** in Europe. They are paintings of Turkish aristocrats, generals and courtiers commissioned by Count Johann Herbertstein in 1665 and painted in

Podsreda Castle (Stajerska)

Vineyard near Maribor

Stari Most spans the Drava River, Maribor (Stajerska).

View from castle walls of Ptuj (Stajerska)

Maribor apartment block

The easy way to take in the sights of Maribor (Stajerska)

Costumes, colour and commotion – it's the traditional Kurentovanje festival, Ptuj (Stajerska).

Centuries-old grapevine in the historic Lent district, Maribor (Stajerska)

PTUJ

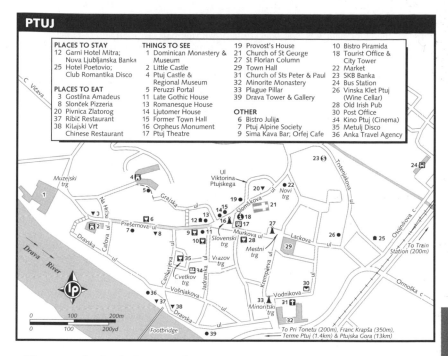

PLACES TO STAY
12 Garni Hotel Mitra;
   Nova Ljubljanska Banka
25 Hotel Poetovio;
   Club Romantika Disco

PLACES TO EAT
3 Gostilna Amadeus
8 Slonček Pizzeria
20 Pivnica Zlatorog
37 Ribič Restaurant
38 Kitajski Vrt
   Chinese Restaurant

THINGS TO SEE
1 Dominican Monastery &
   Museum
2 Little Castle
4 Ptuj Castle &
   Regional Museum
5 Peruzzi Portal
11 Late Gothic House
13 Romanesque House
14 Ljutomer House
15 Former Town Hall
16 Orpheus Monument
17 Ptuj Theatre

19 Provost's House
21 Church of St George
27 St Florian Column
29 Town Hall
31 Church of Sts Peter & Paul
32 Minorite Monastery
33 Plague Pillar
39 Drava Tower & Gallery

OTHER
6 Bistro Julija
7 Ptuj Alpine Society
9 Sima Kava Bar; Orfej Cafe

10 Bistro Piramida
18 Tourist Office &
   City Tower
22 Market
23 SKB Banka
24 Bus Station
26 Vinska Klet Ptuj
   (Wine Cellar)
28 Old Irish Pub
30 Post Office
34 Kino Ptuj (Cinema)
35 Metulj Disco
36 Anka Travel Agency

a Western style. Partly because of these paintings, Turkish dress became all the rage for a time in the 18th century.

The museum is open from 9 am to 5 pm daily in winter and to 6 pm in summer (8 pm at weekends in July and August). Entry for adults/children is 600/300 SIT (150/90 SIT extra with guide), and the ticket includes admission to the former Dominican monastery.

Walking Tour

Ptuj's Gothic centre, with its Renaissance and baroque additions, is a joy to explore on foot. It's unlikely that you'll get lost in this small place but if you do, explanatory signs in four languages (including English) will tell you where you are. The arched spans that look like little bridges above some of the narrow streets are to support the older buildings.

Start a walking tour of Ptuj in **Minoritski trg**, which has a 17th-century **plague pillar** of Mary and the Infant Jesus that was restored in 1994. This is the site of the **Minorite**

monastery that was built in the 13th century. Because the Minorites dedicated themselves to teaching, the order was not dissolved under the Habsburg edict of the late 18th century and it has continued to function in Ptuj for more than seven centuries.

The **Church of Sts Peter and Paul**, on the northern side of the monastery's inner courtyard, was one of the most beautiful examples of early Gothic architecture in Slovenia until it was reduced to rubble by Allied bombing in January 1945. Only the presbytery, with a medieval altar and striking modern stained-glass windows, has been restored.

The arcaded monastery, which dates from the second half of the 17th century, has two things worth seeing. The **summer refectory** on the 1st floor, which managed to escape wartime destruction and served as the chapel until recently, contains beautiful 17th-century stucco work and a dozen ceiling paintings of Sts Peter (north side) and Paul (south side). One panel depicts the martyrdom of poor St

Stephen, who was stoned to death by a group of pagans including Saul, who was later baptised as Paul. The monastery also contains a rich, 5000-volume **library** of important manuscripts including part of a 10th-century codex used to cover a prayer book around 1590 and an original copy of the New Testament (1561) translated by Primož Trubar. It is one of the most valuable documents of the Slovenian patrimony. The monastery doesn't have regular opening hours, but you can ring the bell to the right of the church entrance and ask one of the brothers in residence if you can visit.

If you walk northward on Krempljeva ulica, you'll soon reach Mestni trg, the rectangular square once called Florianplatz in honour of the **St Florian Column** (1745) in the centre. To the east at No 1 is the neo-Gothic **town hall** (1907), designed by an architect from Graz and the most beautiful 'new' building in Ptuj.

Murkova ulica, with some interesting old houses, leads westward to **Slovenski trg**, the heart of old Ptuj. This funnel-shaped square, which is higher than Mestni trg, contains the lion's share of Ptuj's most beautiful buildings.

The most obvious structure here is the **City Tower** (Mestni Stolp), built in the 16th century as a belfry and later turned into a watch tower. Roman tombstones and sacrificial altars from Poetovio were incorporated into the tower's exterior in 1830; you can still make out reliefs of Medusa's head, dolphins and a man on horseback.

In front of the City Tower stands the 5m **Orpheus Monument**, a Roman tombstone from the 2nd century with scenes from the Orpheus myth. It was used as a pillory in the Middle Ages; the guilty were shackled to iron rings attached to the holes at the base. The attractive building on the right (No 13) is the **Ptuj Theatre**, originally built in 1786. Until 1918 it staged plays only in German. The theatre was well known for its avant-garde productions in the late 1930s.

Behind the City Tower is the **Parish Church of St George**, which reveals a melange of styles from the Romanesque to neo-Gothic. The church contains some lovely 15th-century choir chairs decorated with animals, a carved relief of the Epiphany dating from 1515 and frescoes in the middle of the south aisle, a 15th-century stone pietà and, in the baptismal chapel at the start of the south aisle, the so-called **Konrad Laib altar**, a three-winged altar painting from 1460 (presently being restored). In the north aisle, under glass, is a carved 15th-century statue of St George slaying the dragon.

On the northern side of Slovenski trg are several interesting buildings including the 16th-century **Provost's House** at No 10, the baroque **former town hall** at No 6 and, next door at No 5, **Ljutomer House**, whose Mediterranean-style loge was built in 1565 by Italian workers who had come to Ptuj to fortify it against the Turks.

The shortest way to the castle from here is to follow narrow Grajska ulica, which leads to a covered wooden stairway and the Renaissance **Peruzzi Portal**. Alternatively, you could continue westward and explore pedestrian **Prešernova ulica**, the town's market in the Middle Ages.

The **Late-Gothic House**, dating from about 1400, at No 1 has an unusual projection held up by a black man's head. Opposite at No 4 is the sombre **Romanesque House**, the oldest building in Ptuj. The yellow pile at Prešernova ulica 35 is the **Little Castle** (Mali Grad), home to the Salzburg bishops and a number of aristocratic families over the centuries. The building to the west housed a **prison** from the 19th century. During WWII many Partisans, including the local hero Jože Lacko, were tortured and died here. From the western end of Prešernova ulica you can follow the gravel path eastward to the castle.

Just past the small park at Muzejski trg 1 is the former **Dominican monastery**, which now contains the Ptuj Regional Museum's **archaeological collection**. The monastery was built in 1226 but abandoned in the late 18th century when Habsburg Emperor Joseph II dissolved all religious orders. The beautiful eastern wing has a cross-ribbed Romanesque window and Gothic cloisters with 15th-century frescoes of Dominican monks in their black and white garb. There's also a refectory with 18th-century

Kurent: Carnival Time in Ptuj

Ptuj – and many towns on the surrounding plain and in the hills – mark Shrovetide by Kurentovanje, a rite of spring and fertility that may date back to the time of the early Slavs. Such celebrations are not unique to Slovenia; they still take place at Mohács in Hungary and in Serbia and Bulgaria. But the Kurentovanje is among the most extravagant of these celebrations.

The main character of the rite is Kurent, god of unrestrained pleasure and hedonism – a 'Slovenian Dionysus'. The Kurents (there are many groups of them) are dressed in sheepskins with cowbells dangling from their belts. On their heads they wear huge furry caps decorated with feathers, sticks or horns and coloured streamers. The leather face masks have eyeholes outlined in red, trunk-like noses and enormous red tongues that hang down to the chest.

The Kurents move from house to house in procession scaring off evil spirits with their bells and wooden clubs topped with hedgehog spines. A devil (hudič), covered in a net to catch souls, leads each group. Young girls present the Kurents with handkerchiefs (which they then fasten to their belts), and people smash little clay pots at their feet for luck and good health.

Kurent, the bane of evil spirits

stucco work, a chapter hall and a large Roman coin collection. But the main reason for coming is to see the Roman tombstones, altars and wonderful mosaics unearthed in Ptuj and at the **Mithraic shrines** at Zgornji Breg and Spodnja Hajdina, a couple of kilometres west of town. A guide will explain the significance of all the stones and help bring them to life. Apart from Mithra himself and the Sol deity that looks not unlike the American Statue of Liberty, there are the *nutrices,* the wet nurses who nourished the offspring of Roman aristocrats, and ancient Jewish tombstones. The Dominican monastery collection has the same opening hours and entry fees as the castle.

You can return to Minoritski trg by following Dravska ulica to the round **Drava Tower** (Dravski Stolp), a Renaissance water tower built by Italian workers for defence against the Turks in 1551. It now houses a gallery featuring the works of the graphic artist France Mihelič. It is open from 10 am to 1 pm and 4 to 7 pm Tuesday to Friday.

Activities

Terme Ptuj (☎ 782 78 21), a thermal spa about 2km west of town on the right (or south) bank of the Drava at Pot v Toplice 9, is primarily a recreational centre with two outdoor swimming pools, three indoor thermal ones (water temperature is 32° to 34°C) and eight tennis courts. A full-day entrance to the pools is 1300/900 SIT for adults/children on weekdays, or 1400/1000 SIT at weekends. You can also rent bicycles here.

Licences for river fishing are available from the Anka travel agency (☎ 780 65 00) at Dravska ulica 10 near the Ribič restaurant.

Special Events

Kurentovanje, a rite of spring celebrated for 10 days in February leading up to Shrove Tuesday, is the most popular and best-known folklore event in Slovenia (see the boxed text 'Kurent: Carnival Time in Ptuj'). Ask the tourist office for details about this year's festivities.

There is a September series of concerts in Ptuj called Glasbeni September. Venues include the Minorite monastery refectory, the Church of St George, the Knights' Hall in Ptuj Castle and Ptuj Theatre.

Three traditional fairs that take place in Novi trg in Ptuj are those dedicated to St George (Jurij) in late April, St Oswald (Ožbalt) in early August, and St Catherine (Katarina) in late November.

Places to Stay

The crowded **Terme Ptuj camping ground** (☎ 783 79 41) charges between 1250 and 1500 SIT per person and is open from May to September. Prices include use of the pools and other recreational facilities. Terme Ptuj also has **bungalows** available (6700 to 7200 SIT for singles, 10,900 to 11,900 SIT for doubles) as well as modern **apartments** in larger villas accommodating two people from 7500 SIT.

The tourist office can arrange **private rooms**, but they're not cheap (about 3000 SIT per person) and most are on the other side of the Drava from the centre, near Terme Ptuj. **Pri Tonetu** (☎ 783 55 01, Zadružni trg 13), on the way to the spa, and **Franc Krapša** (☎ 787 75 70, Maistrova 19) both charge about 3000 SIT per person.

The 29-room **Hotel Poetovio** (☎ 779 82 01, fax 779 82 41, Trstenjakova ulica 13) is the cheaper of Ptuj's two hotels: bright and airy singles/doubles/triples with shower and breakfast are 6000/8000/10,000 SIT. The Poetovio is not a bad place, but the Club Romantika disco below (open till 4 am Friday and Saturday nights) may make sleep just a tad difficult.

The 21-room **Garni Hotel Mitra** (☎/fax 774 21 01, ✉ fredi@zerak.com, Prešernova ulica 6) is one of provincial Slovenia's more interesting hotels. Though the guestrooms are fairly ordinary, they are certainly large. You can't beat the location but the prices are high: 7700 SIT for a single with shower and breakfast, and 10,000 SIT for a double.

Places to Eat

Slonček (Prešernova ulica 19), behind an interesting marble fountain, serves pizza and some meatless dishes from 9 am to 10 pm daily, except Sunday. The **Pivnica Zlatorog** (Slomškova ulica 20) also has pizza and is open from 9 am to 11 pm weekdays and from noon Sunday. **Grajska Kavarna** in the castle courtyard serves drinks and snacks from 9 am to 9 pm weekdays and till 11 pm weekends.

Gostilna Amadeus (☎ 771 70 51, Prešernova ulica 36), a pleasant pub near the foot of the road to the castle, serves štruklji (dumplings; 500 SIT), steak and pork dishes (1250 to 3100 SIT) and fish (1100 to 1350 SIT), and is open from 9 am to 11 pm daily (to midnight Friday and Saturday).

One of the best restaurants in Ptuj, with excellent food, service and location, is the **Ribič** (☎ 787 75 60, Dravska ulica 9), facing the river. The speciality here is fish – especially boiled or fried trout (1350 SIT) – and the mushroom and seafood soups (495 SIT) are exceptional. If the oil on the salad tastes odd (nutty, a little smoky) that's because it's pumpkin-seed oil (bučno olje), a speciality of the Drava Plain region and available in most shops. Ribič, which has a group playing Slovenian folk music some nights, is open from 10 am to 11 pm daily.

Ptuj's Chinese restaurant, the **Kitajski Vrt** (Chinese Garden; Dravska ulica 7), is almost opposite the Ribič. Starters are 300 to 550 SIT, main meat dishes like crispy duck cost 1420 SIT, and vegetable ones about 850 SIT.

There's a **market** selling fruit, vegetables and more on Novi trg. It's open from very early in the morning to about 3 pm daily.

Entertainment

The **Ptuj Theatre** (Slovenski trg 13) beside the City Tower stages a varied program year-round; check what's playing at www .gledalisce-ptuj.si. For cinema, try the **Kino Ptuj** (☎ 773 32 61) in Cvetkov trg, which has a couple of screenings a day, usually at 6 and 8 pm.

Prešernova ulica has several decent pubs and cafes, including **Sima Kava Bar** at No 3, **Orfej** at No 5, **Bistro Julija** at No 20 and, opposite the Little Castle, **Amadeus** at No 36. The popular **Old Irish Pub** on Murkova ulica is open from 8 am to 11 pm (till midnight Friday and Saturday, and from 4 pm

Sunday). Another popular watering hole is *Bistro Piramida* at the northern end of Jadranska ulica, open from 8 pm till 11 pm (from noon Sunday).

There's a disco called *Metulj* at Cvetkov trg, which can be reached by walking south along Cankarjeva ulica from Prešernova ulica. It's open from 5 pm to 4 am Friday and Saturday. The *Club Romantika* disco in the cellar of the Hotel Poetovio is open from 8 pm to 4 am Friday and Saturday.

Shopping

Vinska Klet Ptuj (☎ 787 98 10) at Trstenjakova ulica 10 is the place to go if you want to buy or taste wine – it's one of the largest cellars in Slovenia. If you can't make it to the wine-growing regions to the south or east, try some Haloze Chardonnay, Šipon or Laški Rizling here. The cellar also has stocks of Zlata Trta, the 'Golden Vine' sweet wine dating from 1917; it is the oldest vintage in Slovenia. The 'Wine Cellar' is open from 7 am to 7 pm weekdays and till noon Saturday.

Getting There & Away

Bus Buses are frequent from Ptuj to Kidričevo, Maribor, Majšperk, and Ormož, but count on only about a half-dozen on Saturday and far fewer (or none) on Sunday.

Other destinations and their daily frequencies include Celje (one via Maribor), Ljubljana (one via Maribor), Ljutomer (three), Rogaška Slatina via Majšperk (one), Slovenska Bistrica (one) and Radenci (four).

Two buses a week (at 5.30 pm Monday and Friday) head for Stuttgart in Germany. For destinations in Croatia, count on three buses a day to Varaždin and three to Zagreb (via Varaždin or Krapina).

Train You can reach Ptuj up to a dozen times a day by train from Ljubljana (three hours, 155km) via Zidani Most and Pragersko. Up to nine trains go to Maribor (one hour, 37km). Four trains a day head for Murska Sobota via Ormož.

Getting Around

Book a taxi on ☎ 780 01 40, mobile ☎ 041-645 876 or ☎ 041-414 925.

AROUND PTUJ
Ptujska Gora

☎ 02 • postcode 2323 • pop 1136

The pilgrimage **Church of the Virgin Mary** (Župnijska cerkev sv Marije) in this village some 13km south-west of Ptuj, contains one of the most treasured objects in Slovenia – a 15th-century carved **Misericordia** of the Virgin Mary and the Child Jesus sheltering both rich and poor under an enormous cloak held up by seven angels.

The carving, which is above the main altar, is as important an historic document as it is a work of art. Among the lifelike faces of the faithful are the Counts of Celje (Frederick II and the three Hermans). It rivals the altar carving (1489) by Wit Stwosz in Kraków's Church of Mary for its grace and beauty.

The church itself, built in the late 14th century, is the finest example of a three-nave Gothic church in Slovenia. Among some of the other treasures inside is a small wooden **statue of St James** on one of the pillars on the south aisle, 15th-century **frescoes** of Christ's Passion, under the porch and to the right as you enter, medieval paintings of saints, including St Nicholas and St Dorothy. The abstract stained-glass windows date from this century. Look behind the modern tabernacle in the chapel to the right of the main altar for frescoes of St Peter and St Michael the Archangel.

The church, open from 7 am to 7 pm daily in summer and to 3 pm in winter, perches atop Black Hill (Črna Gora), an easy 10-minute walk from where the bus headed for Majšperk will let you off. The Galerija Paleta, to the north of the church at house No 38, has some interesting artwork and souvenirs for sale, and there's a small eatery called *Gostišče Dragica* at No 37.

Štatenberg

☎ 02 • postcode 2322 • pop 173

About 9km south-west of Ptujska Gora in the Dravinja Valley is Štatenberg, site of an 18th-century baroque manor house. The manor (☎ 803 02 16) has impressive stucco work, frescoes and rooms full of antique (if moth-eaten) furniture and tapestries.

ŠTAJERSKA

Štatenberg was built in the first half of the 18th century not far from the site of another castle that had been occupied and razed by Slovenian and Croatian peasants under Matija Gubec in 1573. It was designed by an Italian architect for the Attems family.

The manor consists of a landscaped central courtyard enclosed by two side wings and the central building. On the ground floor of the latter is an arcaded hall with baroque stucco work; seven residential rooms and the lovely **Great Hall** are on the 1st floor. The Great Hall has a frescoed ceiling with mythological scenes as well as statues of Greek and Roman gods in the corners. The other rooms contain carved armoires, rugs, 19th-century portraits and a bed in which Empress Maria Theresa once slept. Štatenberg's rooms are open from 11 am till 6 pm daily except Monday. The entrance fee is 200/100 SIT for adults/children.

There's a small restaurant in the main building, open from 11 am to midnight daily except Monday. The surrounding park has four small fishing ponds, and there are a couple of other restaurants in the area. The one on the main road across from the entrance to the castle is called *Gostilna Marof*. The other, *Gostilna Lesjak Karel*, is at house No 36 in Makole, a village on the Dravinja River about 1.5km to the south-west.

Štatenberg can be reached on the Poljčane bus from Ptuj.

Wine Routes

Ptuj is within easy striking distance of two important wine-growing areas: the **Haloze** district and the **Jeruzalem-Ljutomer** district. They are accessible on foot, by car and, best of all, by bike.

The Haloze Hills extend for about 30km from Makole south-west of Ptuj to Goričak on the border with Croatia. The footpath taking in this land of gentle hills, vines, corn and sunflowers is called the Haloze Trail (Haloška Pot) and is accessible from near Štatenberg Manor. But it's much easier to pick up the trail near **Borl Castle**, 11km south-east of Ptuj.

Borl was originally built in the 13th century and fell to the Hungarians until the late 15th century. It changed ownership again and again and was used as a detention centre both by the Nazis and then the communists after the war. It was even a hotel and restaurant for a while. Today there's not much here but an old baroque altar in a disused church and a few Kurent masks scattered about, though concerts are sometimes held in the courtyard in summer. There's a small *restaurant* near the entrance where you can try the local Haložan wine, and the surrounding parkland (with an unofficial camping ground) is lovely.

A road called the **Wind Rattle Route** (after the unusual wind-powered noisemakers called *klopotci* which are used to scare the crows away from the vines) follows a 50km course from Ptujska Gora to Zavrč via Dolena, Gorca and the fine town of Cirkulane. Ask the tourist office in Ptuj for a map.

The Jeruzalem-Ljutomer wine road begins at Ormož and continues for 18km north to Ljutomer (population 3700), the main seat in the area, via the hill-top village of Jeruzalem. There are quite a few cellars and small restaurants along the way, especially around Ivanjkovci, where you can sample any of the region's local whites. They include the *Jože Kupljen cellar* (☎ 719 40 01) in Veličane (house No 63).

MARIBOR

☎ 02 • postcode 2000 • pop 103,000

Though it is the nation's second-largest city, Maribor counts less than half the population of Ljubljana and, frankly, feels more like a large provincial town than north-east Slovenia's economic, communications and cultural centre. It has the country's only university outside the capital and boasts an important museum, a number of galleries, a theatre built in 1786 and an attractive Old Town along the Drava River. Maribor is also the gateway to the Maribor Pohorje, a hilly recreational area to the south-west, and the Slovenske Gorice wine-growing region to the north and the east.

History

Maribor has been inhabited continuously since the Neolithic period, but it did not rise to prominence until the Middle Ages when a fortress called Marchburg was built on Piramida, a hill north of the present-day city, to protect the Drava Valley from the Magyar invasions. The settlement that later developed along the river was given town status in 1254. It grew wealthy through the timber and wine trade, financed to a large degree by the town's Jewish community, and the waterfront landing (Pristan) in the Lent district became one of the busiest ports in the country.

The town was fortified with walls in the 14th century to protect it first against the Hungarians and then the Turks; four defence towers still stand along the Drava. Though its fortunes declined somewhat in later centuries – the Jews were expelled from the town in the late 1400s and it competed in commerce with Ptuj – most of the town's important buildings were erected then.

The tide turned in 1846 when the railroad from Vienna reached here – the first town in Slovenia to have train connections with the imperial capital – and by 1861 three main routes linking Vienna, Budapest and Trieste intersected at Pragersko to the south. The town, by then known as Maribor, became the centre of Slovene-speaking Styria, a kind of counter-balance to German Graz in Austria, and began to industrialise. The bishopric was moved from Šent Andraž (now St Andrä near Wolfsberg in Austria) to Maribor in 1859, and two important Slovenian newspapers began publication.

Maribor remained Slovenian within the Kingdom of Serbs, Croats and Slovenes after WWI, due to the efforts of General Rudolf Maister, and it continued to develop in the 1920s and 1930s. But the air raids during WWII devastated the city and by 1945 two thirds of it lay in ruin. New areas were opened up on the south bank of the Drava, and in the 1950s Maribor was one of Slovenia's most 'proletarian' cities. Much of that is still evident from the factories and housing estates south of the Old Town.

Orientation

Maribor sits on both sides of the Drava River but the Lent waterfront area and other parts of the Old Town are on the north bank.

There are several main squares, with funnel-shaped Grajski trg the historical centre. The Maribor Pohorje lies to the south-west.

Maribor's enormous postmodern bus station – a 1980s urban 'prestige project' and now somewhat decayed – is east of Grajski trg on Mlinska ulica. The train station is about 400m north on Partizanska cesta. Maribor airport (☎ 629 17 90) at Skoke, about 8km south-east of the Old Town, is one of only three international ones in the country, but there are no scheduled flights.

Information

Tourist Offices The helpful Maribor Tourist Information Centre (Matic; ☎ 251 12 62, fax 251 52 71, ⓔ matic@maribor.si) is across the road from the train station at Partizanska cesta 47. It's open from 9 am to 6 pm weekdays and till 1 pm Saturday. Matic can arrange guided tours of the city – a two-hour tour for a group of up to six people costs 7000 SIT.

Money A Banka has a branch and ATM in the mall at the eastern end of Glavni trg. It is open from 8 am till 6 pm weekdays and to 11 am Saturday. There's a Nova KBM bank with ATM opposite Maribor Castle on Slovenska ulica. Down a small passageway to the right of McDonald's on Grajski trg is the Enka exchange counter (cash only – no travellers cheques), open from 8 am to 6 pm weekdays and till noon Saturday. If you arrive in town without local currency on a Sunday, go to the Slovenijaturist office at the train station. It's open from 8 am to 8 pm Monday to Saturday, and from 10 am to 5 pm Sunday.

Post & Communications The main post office, with cardphones only, is near the train station at Partizanska cesta 54 and is open 24 hours a day seven days a week (the exchange desk is open from 7 am to 7 pm weekdays, and 8 am to noon Saturday). There are more convenient branches at Partizanska cesta 1, open 7 am to 7 pm weekdays and 8 am to noon Saturday, and at Slomškov trg 10, open from 7 am to 8 pm weekdays and till 1 pm Saturday.

Travel Agencies Slovenijaturist (☎ 251 89 90) has an office at the train station; see Money. Kompas (☎ 251 67 51), on the east side of Maribor Castle at Trg Svobode 1, and Globtour (☎ 234 08 70) at the Hotel Slavija (entrance on Sodna ulica) both keep the same hours: from 8.30 am to 6.30 pm weekdays and till noon Saturday.

Bookshops Mladinska Knjiga at Gosposka ulica 28 sells regional and city maps and a few guides in English. It also has the 1:50,000-scale map *Pohorje* from GZS, which includes the Maribor Pohorje area. MK is open from 9 am to 6 pm weekdays and from 8 am till noon Saturday. There's a good selection of maps, guidebooks and English-language fiction at the Cankarjeva Založba bookshop beside the university library on Smetanova ulica.

Walking Tour

Start a walking tour of Maribor in **Grajski trg**, the centre of the Old Town and closed to traffic. In the middle of the square stands the 17th-century **St Florian Column**, dedicated to the patron of fire-fighting.

Maribor Castle, a successor to the Piramida fortress of medieval times, is on the north-east corner at Grajska ulica 2. The 15th-century castle contains a **Festival Hall** with a remarkably disproportionate ceiling painting, a **baroque chapel** and a magnificent **rococo staircase** near the exit. The staircase, with its pink walls, stucco work and figures arrayed on the bannisters, is worth a visit in itself. The castle also contains the exhibits of the **Maribor Regional Museum** (Pokrajinski Muzej Maribor).

The museum's collection, one of the richest in Slovenia, is arranged on two levels. On the ground floor there are archaeological, ethnographic and clothing exhibits with 19th-century beehive panels painted with Biblical scenes from the Mislinja and Drava Valleys, models of Štajerska-style hayracks, Kurent costumes and wax votives from the area around Ptuj, and heaps about the wine industry. Don't miss the mannequins displaying what the well-dressed Maribor woman wore in the 19th century or Marshal Tito's dress uniform as commander of the Yugoslav armed forces.

Upstairs you'll pass through a loggia with Greek and Roman statuary and 14th-century Jewish gravestones. Farther on there are rooms devoted to Maribor's history and its guilds and crafts (glassware, wrought ironwork, clockmaking), a complete 18th-century pharmacy and altar paintings and sculptures from the 15th to the 18th centuries. Taking pride of place among the sculptures are the exquisite **statues by Jožef Straub** (1712–56) taken from the Church of St Joseph in the south-western suburb of Studenci. The works depicting the Angel of Grapes and Zacharias are especially fine.

The regional museum is open from 9 am to 5 pm Tuesday to Saturday and from 10 am to 2 pm Sunday. The entrance fee for adults/children and students is 300/100 SIT.

A few steps to the east is **Trg Svobode**. This and the two leafy squares to the north – Maistrov trg and Rakušev trg – would be unremarkable except for the honeycomb of **wine cellars** below that cover an area of 20,000 sq metres and can store 7 million litres. The cellars, dating from the early 19th century, are managed by the Vinag wine export company at Trg Svobode 3 and are filled with old oak barrels, steel fermentation tanks and an 'archive' of vintage wine – all at a constant 15°C. There's a small cellar open to the public, but if you're serious about wine, ask at reception (☎ 220 81 11) for a tour of the cellars (500 SIT per person including wine tasting). The wine shop here has a large selection of local vintages, including Mariborčan, Laški Rizling, Chardonnay, Traminer and Gold Muscatel. It is open from 7.30 am to 7 pm weekdays and to 2 pm Saturday.

Two blocks north of the castle, at the corner of Ulica heroja Tomšiča and Maistrova ulica, is a 19th-century mansion housing the **National Liberation Museum**, whose collections document Slovenia's struggle for freedom throughout the 20th century. It's open from 8 am to 6 pm weekdays, and from 9 am till noon Saturday. Entry costs 200/100 SIT.

Still farther north is Maribor's **City Park** (Mestni Park), a lovely arboretum with three little ponds, swans and a bandstand. It also

MARIBOR

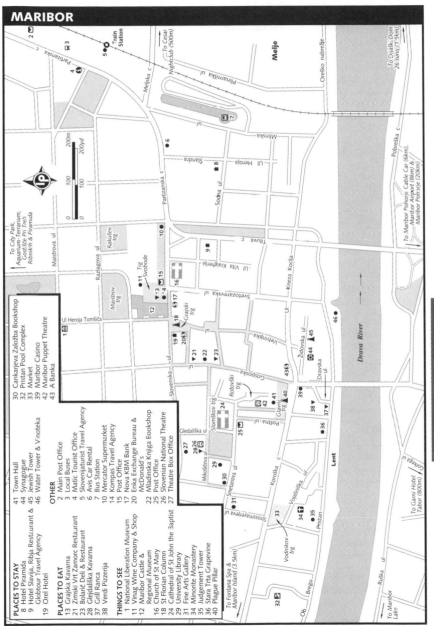

ŠTAJERSKA

PLACES TO STAY
8 Hotel Piramida
9 Hotel Slavija, Ribja Restaurant & Globtour Travel Agency
19 Orel Hotel

PLACES TO EAT
13 Grajska Kavarna
21 Zimski Vrt Zamorc Restaurant
23 Bolaič Deli & Restaurant
28 Gledališka Kavarna
37 Grill Ranca
38 Verdi Pizzerija

THINGS TO SEE
1 National Liberation Museum
11 Vinag Wine Company & Shop
12 Maribor Castle & Regional Museum
16 Church of St Mary
18 St Florian Column
24 Cathedral of St John the 3aptist
29 University Library
31 Fine Arts Gallery
34 Minorite Monastery
35 Judgement Tower
36 Stara Trta Grapevine
40 Plague Pillar

41 Town Hall
44 Synagogue
45 Jewish Tower
46 Water Tower & V noteka

OTHER
2 Main Post Office
3 Local Buses
4 Matic Tourist Office
5 Slovenijaturist Travel Agency
6 Avis Car Rental
7 Bus Station
10 Mercator Supermarket
14 Kompas Travel Agency
15 Post Office
17 Nova KBM Bank
20 Enka Exchange Bureau & McDonald's
22 Mladinska Knjiga Bookshop
25 Post Office
26 Slovenian National Theatre
27 Theatre Box Office

30 Cankarjeva Založba Bookshop
32 Pristan Pool Complex
33 Market
39 Maribor Casino
42 Maribor Puppet Theatre
43 A Banka

contains a rather sad **Aquarium-Terrarium** (Akvarij-Terarij) with about 40 small tanks filled with tropical fish and reptiles. It's open from 8 am to 7 pm weekdays. On Saturday and Sunday the hours are from 9 am till noon and from 2 to 7 pm. The entrance fee is 525/450 SIT for adults/children. To the north-east is **Piramida**, where the titans of Marchburg once held sway.

Return to the Old Town via Trubarjeva ulica and Gledališka ulica, with the latter leading into **Slomškov trg**. The square is named after Anton Martin Slomšek (1800–62), the Slovenian bishop and politician who was instrumental in having the episcopate moved to Maribor and is now a candidate for sainthood. That's him seated in front of the cathedral just south-west of the **light pillar**, a 16th-century lantern that once stood in the church graveyard.

The **Cathedral of St John the Baptist** dates from the 13th century and shows elements of virtually every architectural style from Romanesque to modern (including inept 19th-century attempts to 're-Gothicise' certain bits). Of special interest is the flamboyant Gothic presbytery and the choir stalls with reliefs showing scenes from the life of the patron saint. The grand building across the park to the west is the **University Library**. The **Slovenian National Theatre** is on the northern side.

Maribor's **Fine Arts Gallery** (Umetnostna Galerija) is south-west of Slomškov trg at Strossmayerjeva ulica 6. It is open from 9 am to 1 pm and from 4 to 7 pm Tuesday to Saturday. Sunday hours are from 9 am to 1 pm. Entry is 200/100 SIT.

If you walk south across Koroška cesta past the market and the dilapidated remains of the **Minorite monastery** to the waterfront, you'll come to the round **Judgement Tower** (Sodni Stolp), the first of four defence towers still standing. This is the start of Lent, Maribor's historical waterfront area.

A few steps east along the Pristan embankment at Vojašniška ulica 8 is Maribor's most celebrated possession, a grapevine called **Stara Trta** that is still producing some 35L of red wine each year after being planted more than four centuries ago. It is

tended by a city-appointed viticulturist and small bottles of the almost-black Žametna Črnina (Black Velvet) are distributed to visiting dignitaries as 'keys' to Maribor. Some people say it has a sourish taste.

Glavni trg, Maribor's market place in the Middle Ages, is north-east of here. In the centre of the square is perhaps the most extravagant **plague pillar** found anywhere in Central Europe. Designed by Jožef Straub and erected in 1743, it includes the Virgin Mary surrounded by a half-dozen saints. At No 14 of the square is the **town hall**, built in 1565 by Venetian craftsmen living in Štajerska. The **Maribor Puppet Theatre** is at No 2 of the lovely arcaded courtyard behind called Rotovški trg.

Running north from Glavni trg is **Gosposka ulica**, once the residential area of well-to-do burghers and now a fashionable shopping street for pedestrians.

To the east of Glavni trg is **Židovska ulica**, the centre of the Jewish district in the Middle Ages. The 15th-century **synagogue** at No 4 has been renovated while the square **Jewish Tower** (Židovski Stolp) nearby is now a photo gallery and the headquarters of the local photographers' club.

Nearby at Usnjarska ulica 10 is the five-sided **Water Tower** (Vodni Stolp), a 16th-century defence tower containing Slovenia's oldest vinoteka. You can taste up to 300 different Slovenian wines here daily between 2 and 10 pm. A tasting of three different wines, with bread and cheese, costs 600 SIT.

Activities

Many of the outdoor activities available in the Maribor area are centred on the Maribor Pohorje. See the following Around Maribor section for details.

Maribor has several outdoor swimming pools, but the most pleasant places to swim are on Maribor Island (Mariborski Otok), a sand bank at the end of a dammed-off portion of the Drava River called Maribor Lake (Mariborsko Jezero) about 4km west of the Old Town. Swimming in the river is allowed here and a sunbathing area has been reserved for nude bathing. It's open from 9 am to 7 pm from June to September only. Local bus No

15 from the train station will drop you off at the Kamnica stop, near the start of the footpath leading to the bridge and the island.

The latest arrival is the Fontana Terme Maribor (☎ 234 41 00), a huge spa complex west of the centre at Koroška cesta 172. It offers thermal pools and whirlpools with a water temperature of 33° to 37°C, sauna, solarium, fitness centre and massage. The Fontana complex is open from 9 am to 9 pm year-round and entry is 1500 SIT for four hours, 2000 SIT for a full day.

A much less flash bathing venue is the Pristan pool complex on the river west of Lent (entrance from Ob Bregu or Koroška cesta 33). It has a pool, sauna, gym and massage. The pool (700 SIT) is open from 7 am to 6 pm weekdays and from 8 am to 7.30 pm at weekends. The sauna (1900 SIT) is open from 8 am to 8 pm Wednesday to Saturday.

The Maribor Flying Centre (☎ 629 62 06) at the airport in Skoke, about 8km south-east of the Old Town, has several sightseeing flights available including one that takes in Maribor, Ptuj and Slovenska Bistrica for about €18 per person or €51 for a group of five.

Special Events

Maribor hosts a lot of events throughout the year, including the Slovenian and International Choir Competitions in June, the International Puppet Festival throughout most of the summer and the Slovenian Theatre Festival in the second half of October. But the biggest event on the city's calendar is the Lent Festival, a two-week celebration of folklore, culture and music in late June/ early July when stages are set up throughout the Old Town. Among the most colourful ceremonies is the 'baptism' of the rafts on the Drava and the International Jazz Festival is held here at the same time. Grapes are harvested from Stara Trta, the 'Old Vine' in Lent, in early October.

Places to Stay

Private Rooms Matic and Slovenijaturist can organise private rooms for about €25 per person in a single room, and €15 per person in a double.

Hostels The *Dijaški Dom 26 Junij* (☎ 471 27 99, Železnikova ulica 12) in the southeastern suburb of Pobrežje accepts travellers in July and August. From the train station take bus No 3 (which may have a Hostelling International symbol on the front of it) and get off at the cemetery stop. The price is 2000 SIT per person.

Hotels Maribor's three big hotels cater almost exclusively to business travellers from Austria and Germany and charge accordingly. The most central of the three, the rather gloomy 231-bed *Orel Hotel* (☎ 251 61 71, fax 251 84 97, ℮ orel@termemb.si, Grajski trg 3a), charges from 11,500 SIT for a single with shower and breakfast and 16,100 SIT for a double. The 120-room *Hotel Slavija Best Western* (☎ 251 36 61, fax 252 28 57, ℮ slavija@eunet.si, Ulica Vita Kraigherija 3), a modern 10-storey block facing a busy street, has singles for 10,500 SIT and doubles for 14,200 SIT. The *Hotel Piramida* (☎ 251 59 71, fax 251 59 84, ℮ piramida@termemb.si, Ulica heroja Šlandra 10), due east, is a former tourist hotel tarted up with a bit of paint and marble. Singles with shower and breakfast start at €62, doubles at €76.

For cheaper hotel accommodation you'll have to head for the hills of the Maribor Pohorje (see Around Maribor) or try the friendly *Garni Hotel Tabor* (☎ 421 64 10, fax 421 64 40, ℮ garni.tabor@amis.net, Ulica heroja Zidanška 18) in Studenci to the south-west across the Drava. Singles/doubles with shower are 7100/11,300 SIT.

Places to Eat

One of the cheapest places to eat is the *Bolarič* deli and self-service restaurant on Jurčičeva ulica, where snacks and sandwiches cost from 350 to 800 SIT. It is open from 7 am to 7 pm weekdays, till 1 pm Saturday. There's also a *McDonald's* (Grajski trg 1).

For pizza, head for *Verdi* (Dravska ulica 8) just off Pristan; look for the sign with the three rats! Verdi is open from 10 am to midnight daily. Nearby, facing the Drava, *Grill Ranca* (Vojašniška ulica 4) serves simple Balkan grills like pleskavica and čevapčiči for between 600 and 900 SIT and is open from 8 am to 11 pm daily.

The otherwise expensive **Ribja** (☎ 251 36 61) at the Hotel Slavija has good set lunches, including some vegetarian ones, for between 850 and 1150 SIT. The upmarket **Zimski Vrt Zamorc** (☎ 251 27 17, Gosposka ulica 30), a 'Winter Garden' restaurant with lots of marble, hanging vines and an atrium, is around the corner from the Orel Hotel. It's open from 8 am to 10 pm daily.

A great place for a meal if you want to get out of the city but don't feel like travelling is **Gostišče Pri Treh Ribnikih** (☎ 251 13 71, Ribniška ulica 3) near the three fish ponds in City Park. Oddly, its specialities are cheese štruklji (dumplings) and game dishes – not fish. The restaurant is open from 10 am to 10 pm daily.

Two lovely cafes in Maribor are the **Grajska Kavarna** (Trg Svobode 2) in the castle, open from 8 am to 10 pm Monday to Saturday, and the **Glejdališka Kavarna** next to the Slovenian National Theatre on Miklošičeva ulica, open from 8 am to midnight weekdays, from 10 am to 2 pm and 7 pm to 2 am Saturday, and from 7 pm to 1 am Sunday. The Glejdališka Kavarna attracts a gay crowd.

There's a **market** selling produce at Vodnikov trg, and a **Mercator supermarket** on the corner of Partizanska and Prešernova, open from 7 am to 8 pm Monday to Saturday and till 11 am Sunday.

Entertainment

The **Slovenian National Theatre** (Slovensko Narodno Gledališče; SNG) in Maribor has one of the best reputations in the country and its productions, including Faust directed by Tomaž Pandur, have received critical acclaim throughout Europe. The city's ballet and opera companies also perform here – tickets are around the 3000 SIT mark. The ticket office (☎ 250 11 13/14), on the theatre's north side at Slovenska ulica 27, is open from 10 am to 3 pm weekdays, to 1 pm Saturday and one or two hours before performances. Maribor's second famous theatre is the **Maribor Puppet Theatre** (Lutkovno Gledališče Maribor; Ratovški trg 2), with productions year-round.

Concerts are held in several locations, including the castle's Festival Hall and the cathedral. Ask the tourist office for a list. The **Jazz Club Satchmo** (Strossmayerjeva ulica 6) meets in the Fine Arts Gallery building from 9 pm to 1 am nightly.

The pubs and restaurants along the Drava in Lent are pretty lively on summer evenings. The beer in these parts is Gambrinus, brewed in Maribor for more than two centuries. If you're looking to bop, you can try **Cesar** (Ulica heroja Šaranoviča 27) in Melje, east of the train station, a district not unlike the Metlikova squat in Ljubljana. Cesar rages from 9 pm to 4 am Friday and Saturday, and there's a 1000 SIT cover charge.

Maribor Casino (☎ 252 11 55) at Glavni trg 1 is open from 6 pm to 2 am daily and offers slot machines, American and French roulette and blackjack. Admission is free.

Getting There & Away

Bus You can reach virtually any large town in Slovenia (and destinations in Austria, Hungary, Croatia and even Germany) from Maribor. The bus station is huge, with some 30 stands, shops, bars, cafes and a large left-luggage office open from 7 am to 9 pm.

Bus services are frequent to Celje, Dravograd, Gornja Radgona, Lenart, Lendava, Ljubljana, Ljutomer, Lovrenc, Murska Sobota, Ptuj, Radenci, Selnica and Slovenska Bistrica.

Other destinations and their daily frequencies include the Areh Hotel in the Maribor Pohorje (two, at 8 and 11.35 am weekdays), Gornji Grad (one), Koper (one), Majšperk (two), Moravske Toplice (two), Nova Gorica (one), Novo Mesto (one), Ormož (five), Podčetrtek (one), Postojna (two), Rogaška Slatina (seven), Slovenj Gradec (eight) and Velenje (three).

Four buses a day go to Varaždin and Zagreb in Croatia and there's a daily bus to Graz in Austria at 7.30 am. There are daily buses to Munich and Frankfurt in Germany (departing 6.50 pm) and one to Stuttgart (9.45 am). For Hungary there's a bus for Budapest at 20 minutes after midnight on Wednesday, Friday and Saturday.

Train Maribor is on the train line linking Zidani Most and Celje with the Austrian cities of Graz and Vienna. The information desk is open from 6 am to 8 pm Monday to Saturday and from 8 am Sunday.

From Ljubljana (156km), you can reach Maribor on the ICS express service (2050 SIT, 1¾ hours, eight trains a day), or any of 20 slower trains (1220 SIT, 2¾ hours). About a half-dozen trains a day, originating in Maribor, go east through Pragersko to Ormož (1¼ hours, 59km), from where you can make your way into Croatia. Connections can be made at Ormož for trains to Murska Sobota.

Four trains head west each day for Dravograd (1½ hours, 64km) and other stops in Koroška. Two of those trains cross the Austrian border at Holmec and carry on to Klagenfurt (Celovec). There are also services from Maribor to Zagreb (2852 SIT, 2½ hours), Vienna (6712 SIT, 3½ hours), Belgrade (8153 SIT, 8½ hours) and Venice (9729 SIT, eight hours).

Car Avis (☎ 228 79 10) has an office at Partizanska cesta 24, open from 8 am to 4 pm weekdays and till noon Saturday. There's a large underground car park just south of the Hotel Slavija (entrance on Ulica kneza Koclja); the cost is 200 SIT per hour.

Getting Around
Maribor and its surrounds are well served by local buses. They depart from the stands about 200m north of the train station's main entrance.

For a local taxi, ring (free call) ☎ 080-11 12 or ☎ 080-11 22.

AROUND MARIBOR
Maribor Pohorje
☎ 02 • postcode 2208

Maribor's green lung and its central playground, the eastern edge of the Pohorje Massif (Mariborsko Pohorje in Slovene) can be easily reached by car, bus or cable car from town. The area has any number of activities on offer – from skiing and hiking to horse riding and mountain biking – and is a welcome respite from the city, especially in summer.

Skiing The ski grounds of the Maribor Pohorje stretch from the Hotel Habakuk near the lower cable-car station to Žigartov Vrh (1347m) west of the Areh Hotel. With some 60km of slopes, 25km of cross-country runs and 16 ski lifts, this is Slovenia's largest ski area and long waits for tows, which can be a problem in Slovenia, are virtually nonexistent here.

The season generally lasts from December to March, but there are snow cannons along the 870m run where the annual Women's World Cup Slalom and Giant Slalom Competition – the Zlata Lisica (Golden Fox) trophy – takes place in January.

Ski equipment can be rented at the Bellevue Hotel (1050m) or from the small cabin between the Areh Hotel and the pretty little 17th-century pilgrimage church nearby. A daily ski pass costs around 4300 SIT (2200 SIT for children) and a weekly one is 18,800 SIT (10,200 SIT). There's also a ski school.

Hiking There are heaps of easy walks in every direction from the Areh Hotel, but following a stretch of the marked Slovenian Alpine Trail (which originates in Maribor) west and then south-west for 5km will take you to the two **Šumik waterfalls** and **Pragozd** – one of the few virgin forests left in Europe. Another 6km to the south-west is Black Lake (Črno Jezero), the source of the swift-running Lobnica River, and Osankarica, where the Pohorje battalion of Partisans was wiped out by the Germans in January 1943. This is a remarkably beautiful hike and the joy of it is that with all the streams around you don't have to carry as much water as you normally would while hiking in summer.

Other Activities You can rent horses from the Bellevue Hotel for about 500 SIT if you are content to sit in the paddock. It costs 1700 SIT per hour, or 7000 SIT for five hours, to take them outside. A trip in a horse-drawn coach costs 3000 SIT for an hour. Both the Areh and the Bellevue Hotels also have mountain bikes, an ideal way to explore the back roads and trails of the Maribor Pohorje. The rental charge is 500 SIT per hour or 2500 SIT for the day. The

ŠTAJERSKA

Poštarski Dom mountain lodge has tennis courts.

Places to Stay & Eat There are plenty of places to stay in the Maribor Pohorje, including more than a dozen *mountain lodges* and *holiday homes*, many of them run by the Športni Center Pohorje (☎ 220 88 41, fax 220 88 49, [e] info@pohorje.org). Its main office in Maribor at Mladinska ulica 29 will provide you with a list and basic map. Places close to main roads include *Ruška Koča pri Arehu* (☎ 603 27 41) and *Poštarski Dom* (☎ 603 61 00). Most have cooking facilities and are open all year; overnight prices range from 1500 to 3500 SIT per person.

The 84-bed *Areh Hotel* (☎ 603 26 01) is a very pleasant ski lodge with rustic, wood-panelled rooms, a pleasant restaurant and helpful staff. It is at the summit of Areh peak (1250m), about 6km south-west of the upper cable car station. Singles with shower and breakfast cost 5700 SIT, doubles 7700 SIT.

The 75-bed *Bellevue Hotel* (☎ 603 21 51), beside the upper cable-car station, is not as nice as the Areh but it has pleasant outside terraces for eating and drinking in warm weather. A double room costs 6100 SIT.

The huge, five-star *Hotel Habakuk* (☎ 300 81 00, fax 300 81 28, [e] habakuk@termemb .si), near the lower cable car station, offers luxurious accommodation along with health and beauty treatments. Singles cost from €89 to €99, doubles from €116 to €128, depending on season (high season is January to March).

Getting There & Away You can drive or, if ambitious, cycle the 20km from the Old Town in Maribor south past the Renaissance-style Betnava Castle, turning west at Spodnje Hoče before reaching a fork in the road at a small waterfall. Go left and you'll reach the Areh Hotel after about 5km. A right turn and less than 4km brings you to the Bellevue Hotel.

A much easier – and more exhilarating – way to get to the Bellevue and the heart of the Maribor Pohorje is to take the cable car (*vzpenjača;* ☎ 613 18 50 for information)

from the station on Pohorska ulica in Zgornje Radvanje 6km south-west of the Old Town. The ride above the chestnut trees lasts only 15 minutes but offers excellent views of the city and surrounding countryside. There are clamps on the outside of each cabin for mountain bikes.

From the train station in Maribor take local bus No 6, which leaves about every 20 minutes, and get off at the terminus. The cable car runs every hour from 8 am to 8 pm with one last trip again at 10 pm. A return ticket for adults/children is 1000/500 SIT.

The Hayrack: A National Icon

Nothing is as Slovenian as the *kozolec*, the hayrack seen almost everywhere in the country except in Prekmurje and parts of Primorska. Because the ground in Alpine and hilly areas can be damp, wheat and hay are hung from racks, allowing the wind to do the job faster and more thoroughly.

Until the late 19th century, the kozolec was looked upon as just another tool to make a farmer's work easier and the land more productive. Then the artist Ivan Grohar made it the centrepiece of many of his impressionist paintings, and the kozolec became as much a part of the cultural landscape as the physical one. Today it is virtually a national icon and a sure way to reduce *zamejci* (ethnic Slovenes living outside the national borders) to nostalgic tears is to send them a postcard or Christmas card of a kozolec on a distant slope covered in snow.

There are many different types of Slovenian hayracks: single ones standing alone or with sloped 'lean-to' roofs, parallel and stretched ones and double hayracks *(toplarji)*, often with roofs and storage areas on top. Simple hayracks are not unknown in other parts of Alpine Central Europe, but toplarji, decorated or plain, are unique to Slovenia.

Hayracks were made of hardwood (usually oak) from the early 17th century. Today, however, the hayrack's future is in concrete, and the new stretched ones can go on forever.

Regular buses make the run between the Bellevue and Areh Hotels.

CENTRAL POHORJE REGION
☎ 03 • postcode 3214

Travellers can easily sample Pohorje's recreational offerings along its eastern and western fringes from Maribor and Slovenj Gradec in Koroška. But the pear-shaped massif's highest and most beautiful area is in the centre.

While it's true that the Pohorje peaks can't hold a candle to those of the Julian and the Kamnik-Savinja Alps – most here barely clear the 1500m mark – this is the only part of the country where you can appreciate the sheer vastness of the mountains without feeling hemmed in or vertiginous. What's more, hiking and trekking in the winter here is as good as it is in the summer. Though the Pohorje was once covered in forests, lumberjacks and charcoal makers exploited the woods for the sawmills, forges and glassworks of Štajerska and Koroška in the 19th century. Many of the hillsides have been cleared and are now given over to brush, pasture and meadows. Others were replanted with oak trees.

Zreče (population 3575), about 40km south-west of Maribor, is the springboard for the central Pohorje region. Though certainly not Slovenia's most attractive town (the Unior tool-manufacturing company dominates the place), it has the modest Terme Zreče spa and is within easy striking distance of the ski and sport centre around Rogla (1517m), 16km to the north. The central Pohorje region is also very well developed for rural tourism, with dozens of local farmhouses offering accommodation.

Information

There is a tourist office (☎ 759 04 70, fax 759 04 71, ✉ obcina.zrecc@siol.net) in Tržnica Zreče, the shopping centre next to Zreče's small bus station. It's open from 9 am to 6 pm weekdays and till noon Saturday. Staff at the Dobrava Hotel, Cesta na Roglo 15, at Terme Zreče, which is owned by the Unior Turizem travel group (☎ 757 60 00, fax 576 24 46), can help with information.

There's a Banka Celje branch in the Tržnica Zreče shopping centre, about 150m from the spa's main entrance. It is open from 8 am to 1 pm and 1.30 to 5 pm weekdays and to 11.30 am Saturday. The bus station also has an exchange office. The post office, opposite the bank to the west, is open from 8 am to 6 pm weekdays and till noon Saturday.

Terme Zreče

The thermal spa at Zreče (☎ 757 60 00, fax 576 24 46) is a serious treatment centre for post-operative therapy and locomotor disorders (especially those involving sports injuries), but it is also a place where you can have fun. Along with an indoor thermal pool (water temperature is 32°C) and a couple of jacuzzis, there's a large covered recreational pool and two outdoor ones. A fee of 1600 SIT gets you use of the pool, saunas and steam room; it's 1200 SIT for the pool alone. The spa complex also has a very well-equipped gym (900 SIT entry). You won't soon forget a massage with aromatic oils or the medicinal mud treatment.

Rogla

Rogla is a true sports centre and many teams – including Slovenian and Croatian Olympic teams – come here to train. With all those spruce trees producing so much oxygen there's enough to go around for everyone. No matter where you look, it seems that someone is bouncing, lifting or pushing something, and the hiking and skiing are excellent.

Hiking The *Rogla Footpaths* hiking map produced by Unior Turizem and available everywhere in Zreče and Rogla outlines seven trails (most of them open to mountain bikes) from Rogla. They all follow well-marked circular paths and are as short as 2km (30 minutes) and as long as 32km (eight hours). The latter is hike No 5 and covers much of the hike described in the earlier Around Maribor section – Šumik waterfalls, Black Lake, Osankarica – but from the other side.

Another good one is the 12km hike No 3 (three hours) that leads north-west to the

Lovrenc Lakes (Lovrenska Jezera), a turf swamp with 19 lakes that are considered a natural phenomenon. This area is also known for its unique vegetation.

Skiing Rogla's 15km of slopes and 30km of cross-country trails are served by two chairlifts and 11 tows. The season is a relatively long one – from late November till April – and there are cannons for artificial snow. A daily ski pass in full season costs 4000/2800 SIT for adults/children and a seven-day one is 18,800/13,200 SIT. There's also a ski school (☎ 757 74 68), charging 4000 SIT for one-hour individual lessons, and you can rent equipment at the Planja Hotel. Rogla has become the main centre for snowboarding in Slovenia; lessons for individuals cost 4000 SIT per hour.

Horse Riding The Rogla Equine Centre (☎ 577 52 10 or ☎ 575 43 22) is about 3km north-east of Rogla at Koča na Pesku, a mountain hut with a small restaurant, and opens from 10 am to 5 pm daily. An hour's ride in the hills costs 1500 SIT, a lesson 2000 SIT. A 45-minute horse-drawn sleigh ride in winter is 2000 to 4000 SIT, depending on the destination, and it also has sleighs pulled by huskies.

Other Activities The sports centre (☎ 757 71 00) at Rogla has an indoor pool open from 9 am to 9 pm, a covered stadium for all kinds of team sports (including basketball and volleyball), jogging tracks, lawn bowls, squash and badminton courts, and indoor and outdoor tennis courts. The badminton courts cost 1900 SIT an hour to rent, and the squash courts are 1400 SIT for 45 minutes. Mountain bikes can be rented for 600 SIT an hour or 2000 SIT for four hours.

Places to Stay

The cheapest place to stay at the Rogla Holiday Centre (☎ 757 71 00, fax 576 60 10 – for all the accommodation options listed here) is the *Jelka Hostel*, open from June to mid-October and December to March. For €11 you get a bed in one of four dormitory rooms and breakfast.

The *Depandansa Brinje*, a poky annexe of the Planja Hotel, charges 5900 SIT for a double in summer and 6700 SIT through most of the winter, while the hotel *bungalows* for two people are 8200 to 9900 SIT. The most expensive accommodation at Rogla is at the *Planja Hotel*, which has a three-star wing with 176 beds and a four-star one with 75 beds. Frankly, the cheaper wing's rooms are brighter and more attractive but they aren't a bargain: expect to pay from 9500 to 10,900 SIT per person.

A much better deal is available at the many farmhouses in the region, particularly along Cesta Kmečnega near Resnik, about 7km south-west of Rogla. The *Pačnik Farmhouse* (☎ 576 22 02), for example, at No 21 is open in summer and winter and has five rooms, while *Kočnik-Kovše* (☎ 576 07 28) at No 33 has four rooms and is open all year. There are more farmhouses with accommodation in nearby Skomarje and Padeški Vrh and, closer to Zreče, in Stranice and Križevec. The usual farmhouse prices apply: from about €15 per person in a 2nd-category room with shared bath and breakfast in the low season to €23 per person for a 1st-category room with private bath and meals in the high season.

There's no particular reason for staying at Terme Zreče; all the fun is up in Rogla, anyway. But if you're a serious disciple of things thermal, the spa's 54-room *Dobrava Hotel* (☎ 757 60 00, fax 576 24 46), an unexceptional block near the entrance, has singles with shower and breakfast for 8900 to 10,400 SIT, depending on the season, and doubles for 13,800 to 17,200 SIT. Make sure you get one of the rooms with a balcony, though. More pleasant are the 10 *villas* with four apartments each in a small wooded area behind the main spa building. Each apartment has a kitchen, eating area, sitting room and one or two bedrooms. Prices are 11,400 to 13,600 SIT for an apartment for two.

Places to Eat

If you get tired of the restaurant at Terme Zreče and its *Zreška Klet* wine cellar, try the *Gostilna Jančič* (*Cesta na Roglo 4b*) opposite the shopping centre, or the *Kavarna*

ŠTAJERSKA

Težak with lighter fare next door at No 4c. Both are open to 10 or 11 pm daily. There's a big *Mercator supermarket (Cesta na Roglo 11)* in the shopping centre.

The pizza and pasta dishes at the *Macarena (Boharina cesta 2)*, en route to Rogla from Zreče, can be recommended. In Rogla there's a cheap *self-service restaurant* in the Planja Hotel and a *pizzerija* just north of the hotel near the ski lift. The *Stara Koča* is a rustic little bistro in one of Rogla's original wooden buildings.

Getting There & Away

There are regular connections from Zreče to Celje, Planina, Slovenske Konjice and Velenje. Two buses a day from Celje and at least three from Slovenske Konjice stop at Zreče and then carry on to Rogla. Local buses make the runs from Zreče bus station to Rogla and to Resnik. In winter there are special ski buses from both Zreče (five up and five down per day) as well as Celje and Slovenske Konjice. Terme Zreče runs four morning buses up to Rogla for its guests, with the same number returning in the afternoon.

CELJE

☎ 03 • postcode 3000 • pop 40,000

Celje (Cilli in German) is not Štajerska's largest city – Maribor, 60km to the north-east, has more than three times as many people – nor is it the province's most attractive centre. But it has played a pivotal role in Slovenian history on at least two occasions.

History

Celje was settled by the Illyrians and the Celtic tribes who were subdued by the Romans in about 15 BC. As Celeia, it was the administrative centre of the Roman province of Noricum between the 1st and 5th centuries, and roads linked it with other Roman settlements at Virunum (near Klagenfurt in Austria), Poetovio (Ptuj) and Emona (Ljubljana). Celeia was an affluent town, as is evident from the large baths, mosaics and temples unearthed in the area. In fact, it flourished to such a degree that it gained the nickname *Troia secunda,* the 'second Troy'. Celeia's glory days came to

an end when it was sacked by the Huns in 452 and overrun by subsequent tribes during the Great Migrations.

Celje's second Camelot came in the mid-14th century when members of the Žonek family took control of the area. The Counts – later the Dukes – of Celje, one of the richest and most powerful feudal dynasties in Central Europe, were the last on Slovenian soil to challenge absolute rule by the Habsburgs, and they united much of Slovenia for a time. Under their rule, which lasted for just a century, Celje acquired the status of a town, and they built the castles, town fortifications and most of the churches still standing today. The counts left Celje and the nation an invaluable legacy and a part of their emblem – three gold stars forming an inverted triangle – has been incorporated into the Slovenian state flag and seal.

Celje was never able to repeat those glory days and plagues, floods, invasions and revolts struck the town over the ensuing centuries. Celje was, in fact, more German than Slovene until the end of WWI when the town government passed into local hands for the first time.

Orientation

Celje's compact Old Town – encompassing just about everything of interest to travellers – is bordered by Levstikova ulica and Gregorčičeva ulica to the north and north-west, the area around the Lower Castle to the west, the train tracks to the east and the Savinja River to the south.

The town has two main squares: Glavni trg at the end of Stanetova ulica (a pedestrian street where most of the action is) and Krekov trg opposite the train station. The main bus station is 400m north of the train station opposite the Church of St Maximilian on Aškičeva ulica. Local and suburban buses stop south of the train station on Ulica XIV Divizije.

Information

Tourist Offices The tourist office (☎/fax 548 10 62) is at Prešernova ulica 17 in the same building as the Museum of Recent History. It has a lot of brochures and can

STAJERSKA

sell you a map and the useful *Celje Guide* (1460 SIT). The office is open from 10 am to 6 pm (5 pm in winter) Tuesday to Friday and from 9 am till noon Saturday.

Money Banka Celje is at Vodnikova ulica 2, open from 8 am to noon and 2 to 5 pm weekdays, to 11.30 am Saturday. A Banka, at Krekov trg 7 opposite the train station, is open from 8 am till noon and 2 to 5 pm weekdays and to 11 am Saturday.

Post & Communications The main post office is at Krekov trg 9 and is open from 7 am to 7 pm weekdays, to 5 pm Saturday and from 9 to 11 am Sunday.

Travel Agencies Kompas (☎ 544 33 00), in a lovely Renaissance house at Glavni trg 1, can arrange accommodation and rents cars. It is open from 8 am to 5 pm weekdays and till noon Saturday. Globtour (☎ 544 25 11) has an office at Razlagova ulica 1 next to the Hotel Evropa. It keeps the same hours as Kompas.

Bookshops Mladinska Knjiga at Stanetova ulica 3 sells regional maps and guides including the *Celje Guide*. Another good place for maps is Naša Knjiga across the same street at No 10. Both are open from 7.30 am to 7 pm weekdays and from 8 am till noon Saturday.

Walking Tour
You can begin an easy walking tour of Celje, which takes in virtually everything of importance and interest in the town, from the main bus station.

Opposite, on the western side of Aškičeva ulica, is the **Church of St Maximilian**, named after the bishop who was beheaded in Celje in the 3rd century. The church was built in the Gothic style in the 15th century (as was the small **chapel** to the south-west) but has undergone many changes and additions since then.

Continue southward along Stanetova ulica, past the **Banka Celje** building designed by Jože Plečnik in 1929 and the spot where the town gates stood in the Middle Ages. The

shop on the corner of the next intersection with Prešernova ulica was once the **Merkur coffee house**, the most important gathering spot for Celje intellectuals in the 19th century. Prešernova ulica leads eastward to Krekov trg, where you'll find the **Hotel Evropa**, Celje's oldest, and **Celje Hall** (Celjski Dom), the social centre for the city's German citizens at the end of the 19th century.

South along Razlagova ulica you'll pass a medieval **defence tower** on the right and, about 150m farther on, the **Water Tower**, part of the city wall and ramparts and built between 1451 and 1473. Many of the blocks used are of Roman origin.

From the Savinja embankment, at the point where the old Capuchin Bridge once stood, there's an excellent view of **Celje Castle** perched on an escarpment to the south-east. Directly opposite is **City Park** (Mestni Park), the **Capuchin Church of St Cecilia** in Breg and, high up on a hill, the **Church of St Nicholas**.

A walk up to the **castle**, Slovenia's largest, via a footpath from Cesta na Grad takes about half an hour from here. The castle was originally built in the early 13th century and went through several transformations, especially under the Counts of Celje in the 14th and 15th centuries.

When the castle lost its strategic importance it was left to deteriorate and subsequent owners used the stone blocks to build other structures, including parts of the Lower Castle and the Old County Palace. A surprisingly large portion remains intact, however, and has been restored, including the 35m **Frederick Tower**.

On your way back to the Old Town you can walk up to Nicholas Hill, topped by the Church of St Nicholas, for a wonderful view of the castle, the Old Town and the Savinja River. Or you can explore the Breg area. A stairway with 90 steps at Breg 2 leads to the **Church of St Cecilia**. The Germans used the nearby monastery (now apartments) as a prison during WWII. Between the church and the City Park off Maistrova ulica is the reconstructed Roman **Temple of Hercules** dating from the 2nd century. A birch-lined park along the Savinja's northern embankment

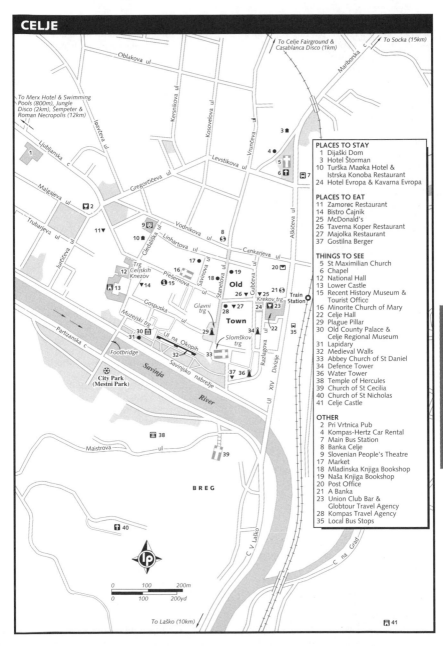

CELJE

To Celje Fairground & Casablanca Disco (1km)

To Socka (15km)

To Merx Hotel & Swimming Pools (800m), Jungle Disco (2km), Šempeter & Roman Necropolis (12km)

Train Station

Old Town

Footbridge

Savinja River

City Park (Mestni Park)

BREG

To Laško (10km)

PLACES TO STAY
1 Dijaški Dom
3 Hotel Štorman
10 Turška Mačka Hotel &
   Istrska Konoba Restaurant
24 Hotel Evropa & Kavarna Evropa

PLACES TO EAT
11 Zamorec Restaurant
14 Bistro Čajnik
25 McDonald's
26 Taverna Koper Restaurant
27 Majolka Restaurant
37 Gostilna Berger

THINGS TO SEE
5 St Maximilian Church
6 Chapel
12 National Hall
13 Lower Castle
15 Recent History Museum &
   Tourist Office
16 Minorite Church of Mary
22 Celje Hall
29 Plague Pillar
30 Old County Palace &
   Celje Regional Museum
31 Lapidary
32 Medieval Walls
33 Abbey Church of St Daniel
34 Defence Tower
36 Water Tower
38 Temple of Hercules
39 Church of St Cecilia
40 Church of St Nicholas
41 Celje Castle

OTHER
2 Pri Vrtnica Pub
4 Kompas-Hertz Car Rental
7 Main Bus Station
8 Banka Celje
9 Slovenian People's Theatre
17 Market
18 Mladinska Knjiga Bookshop
19 Naša Knjiga Bookshop
20 Post Office
21 A Banka
23 Union Club Bar &
   Globtour Travel Agency
28 Kompas Travel Agency
35 Local Bus Stops

ŠTAJERSKA

0   100   200m
0   100   200yd

has a **lapidary** of Roman remains unearthed in the Celje area. Overlooking it, at Muzejski trg 1, is the 16th-century **Old County Palace**, a Renaissance building with a two-level arcade around a courtyard. The palace now contains the **Celje Regional Museum** (Pokrajinski Muzej Celje).

Needless to say, the museum puts much emphasis on Celeia and the Counts of Celje, right down to exhibiting 18 of the nobles' skulls in glass cases. (They were taken from the Minorite church in 1956; the one belonging to Ulric is particularly gruesome.) The museum has 13 rooms, many of them done up in styles from different periods (eg, baroque, neoclassical, Biedemeier, Secessionist), painted with various scenes and filled with fine furniture. Don't miss the 18th-century cabinet with hunting scenes inlaid with ivory, the 20-drawer 'bank' desk with secret compartment and the neoclassical clock/music box that still works. But the museum's main attraction is the **Celje Ceiling**, an enormous trompe l'oeil painting in the main hall of columns, towers, frolicking angels, noblemen and ladies looking down at you looking up at them. Completed in about 1600 by a Polish artist, the mural was meant to lift the ceiling up to the sky and it does just that. Other panels represent the four seasons and show scenes from Roman and Greek mythology. The museum is open from 10 am to 6 pm Tuesday to Friday, from 9 am till noon Saturday, and from 2 to 6 pm Sunday. Entry is 600/400 SIT for adults/children.

Trg Celskih Knezov leads north from the western end of Muzejski trg. At the start of the square you'll find the **Lower Castle**, built in the 14th century as a residence for the Celje counts, and at No 9 the **National Hall** (Narodni Dom), the cultural and social centre for Celje's Slovenes at the end of the 19th century. Both buildings now contain art galleries, open from 10 am till 1 pm and from 4 to 6 pm Tuesday to Friday and on Saturday morning.

Walking eastward along Prešernova ulica, you'll pass the **Museum of Recent History** in the former town hall building (built in 1830) at No 17. The museum records the life of Celje from the late 19th century onwards,

and includes a re-creation of an early 20th-century street complete with tailor, hairdresser, clockmaker and goldsmith. It also contains **Herman's Den** (Hermanov Brlog), the first children's museum in Slovenia. The Museum of Recent History keeps the same hours as the Celje Regional Museum. The entry fee is 500/200 SIT.

Opposite the museum is the **Minorite Church of Mary**, where the bones of the Celje counts once rested. Until recently a relief depicting the Madonna and Child and the counts Herman I and Herman II hung above the doorway leading from the nave into the sacristy, but that too has disappeared. Nothing is forever, it seems, in the Church of Mary.

Prešernova ulica leads to **Glavni trg**, the heart of the Old Town. It is filled with lovely 17th- and 18th-century town houses and, in summer, outdoor cafes. In the centre of the square, where a pillory once stood, is the requisite **plague pillar** (1776) dedicated to Mary.

In Slomškov trg, a few steps to the southeast, you'll find the **Abbey Church of St Daniel** dating from the early 14th century. The church has some magnificent frescoes and tombstones, but its most important item is the 15th-century carved wooden **pietà** in the Chapel of the Sorrowful Mother. The walls are decorated here with carved stone and the vaults with frescoes are from the early 15th century.

Parts of Celje's **medieval walls and ramparts** can be seen along Ulica na Okopih, west of the Abbey Church of St Daniel.

Activities

There are a couple of open-air swimming pools behind the Merx Hotel on Ljubljanska cesta and an indoor one at the Celje Fairground at Dečkova cesta 1, north-east of the Old Town. If you're not satisfied with these, you might consider a day trip 10km south to the spa (☎ 573 13 12) at **Laško**, a town also celebrated for the beer which has been brewed here since 1825 and for a renovated castle called Tabor. Some Slovenes say the gourmet restaurant there, Na Taboru, (☎ 573 16 00) is the country's finest.

The Šeško Riding Centre (☎ 577 82 82) at Socka (house No 33), 15km north of Celje, has horses available for hire for experienced riders and offers lessons to beginners. The centre is in stunning countryside on the edge of the Pohorje Massif. It is open in summer from 8 to 11 am and 4 to 8 pm and in winter from 9 am to noon and from 2 to 6 pm.

The *Celje Guide* lists a number of walks and hikes into the surrounding countryside lasting between one and four hours. The longest one (28km) leads south-east to **Mt Tovst** (834m) and the picturesque village of Svetina via the Celjska Koča mountain hut. This can also be done by car or bicycle.

Places to Stay

The *Dijaški Dom* (☎ 548 44 20, Ljubljanska cesta 21), 600m west of the tourist office, accepts travellers in July and August and charges 2000 SIT per person.

The cheapest hotel in Celje is the evocatively named *Turška Mačka* (Turkish Cat; ☎ 548 46 11, fax 544 29 08, Gledališka ulica 7), a 26-room hotel hard by the Slovenian People's Theatre. It is also the nicest place to stay in Celje with small but comfortable rooms, a good seafood restaurant and friendly staff. Singles with shower, TV and breakfast are 6500 SIT, doubles are 10,300 SIT.

The *Hotel Evropa* (☎ 544 34 00, fax 544 34 34, e hotel.evropa@siol.net, Krekov trg 4) has a good location near the train station and pleasant, helpful staff. Attractive, renovated rooms with shower, minibar, TV and breakfast on the 1st and 2nd floors are 9400/13,400 SIT for a single/double; the older, gloomier rooms on the 3rd and 4th floors are 7200/10,400 SIT.

The newly renovated *Hotel Štorman* (☎ 426 04 26, fax 426 03 95, Mariborska cesta 3) is a bright yellow, nine-storey block just a little north of the bus station. Aimed at the business market, single/double/triple rooms with shower, TV and breakfast are 8250/12,650/14,850 SIT.

The far-flung *Merx Hotel* (☎ 545 22 18, fax 545 20 18, Ljubljanska cesta 39) has only 36 beds and is not very convenient for the Old Town, but it is as close as you'll get

to the Savinja River. There are also public swimming pools behind the hotel. Singles/doubles with shower and breakfast are 6340/10,680 SIT.

Places to Eat

Two pizza places at Prešernova ulica's eastern end can be recommended. The nothing-special *Majolka* at No 3 is open from 7 am to 8 pm weekdays, to 3 pm Saturday and from 11 am to 3 pm Sunday, with pizzas in the 520 to 650 SIT range The set lunch is 830 SIT. *Taverna Koper* at No 2, and about two centuries younger in style and atmosphere, has both pizza and pasta dishes. It is open from 9 am to 5 pm weekdays and from 10 am to 2 pm Saturday. Set lunches go for 700 to 850 SIT. The *Gostilna Berger* at the southern end of Razlagova ulica has set menus of hearty Slovenian food from 800 SIT.

The *Zamorec* (Ljubljanska cesta 5) is one of the oldest eateries in Celje, but its claim to fame – it was the meeting place of an important Slovenian cultural society in the late 19th century – does nothing for the food. If you want something a bit more up-to-date, you'll find a *McDonald's* on Krekov trg.

One of the most interesting places for a meal in Celje is the *Istrska Konoba* restaurant at the Turška Mačka Hotel, which specialises in Istrian fish dishes and wine and was designed by the Karst artist Lojze Spacal (check the lovely stained glass). It's open till 11 pm.

The renovated *Kavarna Evropa* in the Hotel Evropa – all dark wood panelling, gilt mouldings and chandeliers – is a good place for a cup of coffee. If tea is your drink, head for the *Bistro Cajnik* on Trg Celjskih Knezov; it's open from 6 am to 11 pm daily (from 7 am Sunday).

There's a daily outdoor *market* selling fresh fruit, vegetables and other foodstuffs on the corner of Savinova ulica and Linhartova ulica behind the Minorite church.

Entertainment

The *Slovenian People's Theatre* (Slovenski Ljudsko Gledališče or SLG; Gledališki trg 5) stages six plays a season, not always in Slovene. The box office (☎ 544 29 10 or

☎ 544 18 61) is open from 9 to 11 am and from 5 to 7 pm weekdays.

A couple of popular discos are *Jungle* in the north-western suburb of Lava (No 7), open most days till 3 am, and *Casablanca (Dečkova cesta 1)* at the Celje Fairground, open from 10 pm to 5 am Friday and Saturday. The *Pri Vrtnica* pub and cafe on Malgajeva ulica is a popular hang-out, as is the central *Union Club* bar in the Celje Hall on Krekov trg.

Getting There & Away

Bus For places like Šempeter (stand No 4; 220 SIT; departures at least hourly), Škofja Vas (stand No 1) and Šentjur (stand No 3), go to the bus stops south of the train station on Ulica XIV Divizije.

Intercity buses, which leave from the main station, run at least once an hour (less frequently at weekends) to Ljubljana, Maribor, Rimske Toplice, Rogaška Slatina, Slovenske Konjice and Velenje. Other destinations accessible by bus from Celje and their daily frequencies include Bled (one, departing at 5.45 am), Bistrica na Sotli (seven), Črna (two), Dravograd (three), Gornji Grad (six), Koper and Piran (two, departing at 4.50 and 8.20 am), Kranj (one), Krško (four), Lendava on the Hungarian border (four), Logarska Dolina (one), Murska Sobota (five), Mozirje (12), Nova Gorica (one), Podčetrtek (eight), Ptuj (one, departing at 5.20 am), Planinski Vrh (three) and Zreče (13). International destinations include Varaždin in Croatia (leaves at 8.20 am Saturday and Sunday).

Train Celje is one of the few rail hubs in all of Slovenia and for once you have a real choice between taking the train or the bus. Celje is on the main line between Ljubljana and Maribor, and the ICS express train (see the Getting There & Away section in the Ljubljana chapter) stops here. From Ljubljana (880 SIT, 1¼ hours, 89km) you can reach Celje up to 22 times a day on regular trains and eight times a day by ICS.

Celje is also on the line linking Zidani Most (connections to and from Ljubljana and Zagreb) with Maribor (1¼ hours,

67km) and the Austrian cities of Graz and Vienna.

A spur line links Celje with Velenje (50 minutes, 38km) via Šempeter up to 10 times a day in each direction. A third line connects Celje with Zabok in Croatia via Rogaška Slatina (50 minutes, 36km), Rogatec and Dobovec. Up to six trains arrive and depart each day.

Car Kompas-Hertz (☎ 544 27 80) has an office near the Hotel Štorman at Mariborska cesta 1b. Globtour (see Travel Agencies earlier in this section) also rents cars.

Getting Around

Parking can be difficult in Celje's Old Town and you will have to pay for the privilege – around 150 SIT per hour from 6 am to 4 pm weekdays, and until 1 pm Saturday. For a local taxi ring ☎ 544 22 00.

AROUND CELJE
Šempeter
☎ 03 • postcode 3311 • pop 3935

Some 12km west of Celje and accessible by bus and train, Šempeter is the site of a **Roman necropolis** reconstructed between 1952 and 1966. The burial ground contains four complete tombs and scores of columns, stelae and fragments carved with portraits, mythological creatures and scenes from daily life.

The marble stones, quarried in the Pohorje near Slovenska Bistrica between the 1st and 3rd centuries, were washed away and buried when the Savinja River flooded in AD 268. They have been divided into about two dozen groups linked by footpaths.

Tomb No I, the oldest of them all, was commissioned by Gallus Vindonius, a Celtic nobleman who lived on a nearby estate in the 1st century. The largest is the **Priscianus tomb** (No II), raised in honour of a Roman official and his son. (Notice the kidnapping scene on the side relief.) The most beautiful is the **Ennius tomb** (No III) with reliefs of animals and, on the front panel, the princess Europa riding a bull. If you compare these three with the more recent tomb erected in about 250 in honour of

Secundanius, it is obvious that Roman power and wealth in these parts was already very much on the decline in the middle of the 3rd century.

The necropolis is open from 9 am to 3 pm weekdays, to 5 pm Saturday and from 2 to 5 pm Sunday, and costs 500/300 SIT to visit. There's a small *bistro* near the entrance but if you want something more substantial the *Gostišče Štorman* (☎ 703 83 00, Šempeter 5a), one of the first private restaurants to open in Slovenia under the former regime, is about 2km east of the site on the road to Celje. It is open from 7 am till midnight, except on the first Sunday of every month.

UPPER SAVINJA VALLEY
☎ 03

The Upper Savinja Valley (Zgornja Savinjska Dolina) refers to the drainage areas and tributaries of the Savinja River from its source in the eastern Savinja Alps to a gorge at Letuš, some 12km north-west of Šempeter. Bounded by forests, ancient churches, traditional farmhouses and Alpine peaks of more than 2000m, the valley is a land of incomparable beauty. There are activities here to suit every taste – from hiking, mountain biking and rock climbing to fishing, kayaking and swimming in the Savinja.

The Savinja begins its rapid flow above Rinka, at 90m Slovenia's highest waterfall, then enters Logarska Dolina (Logar Valley) and continues past isolated hamlets and farmland. The region beyond the gorge at Ljubno is quite different, with a number of towns – really overgrown villages – of historical importance, including Radmirje, Gornji Grad, Nazarje and Mozirje.

Tools found in a cave at Mt Olševa, north-west of Solčava village, suggest that the Upper Savinja Valley was inhabited during the Stone Age. Remains of three Roman settlements have also been unearthed around Mozirje. The valley has been exploited for its timber since the Middle Ages, and until WWII the Savinja was used to power some 200 sawmills. Raftsmen transported the timber from Ljubno to Mozirje and Celje and some of the logs travelled as far as Romania. The trade

brought wealth and special rights to the valley, evident from the many fine buildings still standing here.

The small English-language brochure entitled *Zgornja Savinjska Dolina – The Short Guidebook* is helpful if you intend spending a fair bit of time in the area. It lists numerous trails, the best places for rock climbing, isolated farmhouses with accommodation etc. Serious hikers should pick up a copy of the 1:50,000 *Zgornja Savinjska Dolina* map by GZS.

The following itinerary follows the 45km valley road from Mozirje to Rinka Waterfall, with a side trip to Radmirje and Gornji Grad. It can be done by bus or car but it is tailor-made for a bicycle trip.

Mozirje

The administrative centre of the Upper Savinja Valley on the river's west bank, Mozirje (population 1900) is a town with a long history, yet with little to show for its past.

Information The Penzion Kozorog (☎ 583 10 22) at Na Trgu 32 can provide information. Nova Ljubljanska Banka has a branch in the centre of town at Na Trgu 9; it's open from 8 am to 1 pm and 2 to 6 pm weekdays and till noon Saturday. The post office is 200m to the south around the bend in the road at Savinjska cesta 3, and the bus station is on the main road opposite the Savinjski Gaj botanical garden.

Things to See & Do The much-rebuilt Gothic **Church of St George** is at the western end of Na Trgu just after you cross the small Trnava Stream. You might like to walk over to **Savinjski Gaj** (Savinja Grove), a botanic park with an **open-air ethnographic museum** south of town across the river (open April to October). In winter, continue 4km north-west to Žekovec where a cable car runs to the **ski centre** (☎ 583 11 11) at Golte. There are slopes of up to 1500m, and 12.5km of ski trails. Otherwise there's little to hold you in this one-horse town.

Places to Stay & Eat The *Penzion Kozorog* (☎ 583 10 22, Na Trgu 32) provides a dozen double rooms for 2500 SIT per person. The restaurant, open to 11 pm (10 pm Sunday), is a simple but inexpensive affair; for something better try the *Gaj* restaurant at the Savinjski Gaj botanic garden. The *Levec Farmhouse* (☎ *583 18 61*), 800m south-east of Savinjski Gaj in Loke (house No 19), has five rooms and is open all year.

Nazarje

The town of 'Nazareth' (population 1835) is 2km due south of Mozirje on the Savinja.

Information The Nazarje Tourist Association (☎ 583 23 23) is at Savinjska cesta 2. There's a Nova Ljubljanska Banka in the building next to Vrbovec Castle on Savinjska cesta, open from 8 to 11 am and 1.30 to 3.30 pm weekdays and from 7.30 to 11 am Saturday.

Things to See & Do At **Vrbovec Castle**, a 15th-century pile at the confluence of the Savinja and Dreta Rivers, there are a couple of large towers; today the castle houses a music school and offices of the Glin logging company, the industry that built Nazarje – there's a huge pulp processing plant just across the road.

Towering above the town on a hill called Gradišče is the **Franciscan monastery** and its **Church of the Virgin Mary**, which were all but flattened by Allied bombs during WWII but have since been rebuilt. The twin-spired church has a choir loft with fine grill work; the original chapel, built by Bishop Tomaž Hren of Ljubljana in the early 17th century, now serves as the presbytery. The monastery has a lovely garden surrounded by an arcaded courtyard. You can drive up to the monastery or climb to it up 200-odd steps.

You can hire **horses** at the Burger Horse Riding Centre (☎ 583 12 65) at Lačja Vas (house No 22), in a beautiful valley 3km south-west of Nazarje. Carriage rides are also available if there are enough people interested.

Places to Stay & Eat Some 3km west of Nazarje you'll find a couple of camping grounds on opposite sides of the river.

Menina (☎ *583 17 87*), which charges 1100 SIT per person, is in Varpolje on the north bank while *Savinja* (☎ *583 14 63*), which charges 750 to 900 SIT, is in Spodnje Pobrežje on the south bank. In Nazarje, the *Gostišče Grad Vrbovec* restaurant and guesthouse (☎ *583 20 00, Savinjska cesta 8*) is in the complex next to the castle. You'll also find the simple *Okrepčevalnica Izoles* and a pizzeria called *Panda* here.

Radmirje

The road to Radmirje (population 440), a village 9km to the west, is very picturesque with Štajerska-style hayracks, little white churches and stone farmhouses larger than the average in Slovenia.

Things to See & Do Radmirje is famous for two churches. The **Church of St Michael** in the centre of town dates from the late 14th century. The **Church of St Francis Xavier**, on Straža Hill to the south-west, has been rebuilt several times over the centuries; the present structure is only about 200 years old. It was established as a pilgrimage church by the bishop of Gornji Grad during a period of great fires and the plague. European monarchs paid homage at the site and the church's rich **treasury** contains Mass vestments donated by the kings of Poland and France and a gold chalice from Habsburg Empress Maria Theresa. There's an old wayside shrine *(znamenje)* with folk paintings in the little dale below the church.

About 500m before the turn-off to Radmirje and Kamnik, the Prodnik Sports Centre (☎ 584 13 17) on the main road at Juvanje 1 organises **kayak, canoe and raft trips** on the Savinja and also rents equipment.

Gornji Grad

The windy town of Gornji Grad (Oberburg in German), with a population of 1845, is in the Zadrečka Valley 6km south-west of Radmirje.

Information The little kiosk near the courtyard, west of the massive baroque church, houses a tourist information centre in summer. Buses stop in the main square –

Attemsov trg – in front of the church. The Nova Ljubljanska Banka on the square is open from 8 am till noon and from 3 to 4 pm weekdays. The post office is nearby at house No 79. It is open from 8 am to 6 pm weekdays with a couple of half-hour breaks, and till noon Saturday.

Things to See Gornji Grad was the site of a large **castle** until the last days of WWII when it was flattened. Today, all that is left is the entrance to the fortification and two defence towers. The town was associated for centuries with the Ljubljana diocese. The **former Benedictine monastery**, for example, was converted into a manor house for Ljubljana's bishops in the 15th century. Today, one of its towers (at Attemsov trg 2) contains a small **folk collection** with everyday objects relating to life on the Menina Planina, an area of mountain pastures and slopes south of town. It is open from 11 am to 4 pm weekdays.

In the same complex, the large baroque **Church of Sts Hermagoras and Fortunatus** was built in the mid-18th century and modelled after the cathedral in Ljubljana. Its enormous, 56m-high dome notwithstanding, the interior of the church is surprisingly light and airy. The side altar pictures by the 18th-century Austrian artist Martin Johann Kremser-Schmidt (1718–1801) are especially fine. Outside, near the entrance, are bits and pieces from an earlier church, including a 16th-century altar portraying the crucifixion of St Andrew. The fountain in the courtyard still appears to be a meeting place for local people. The church is open from 9 am to 7 pm daily.

Places to Stay & Eat In Gornji Grad, the 25-bed *Gostišče Trobej (☎ 584 30 06, Attemsov trg 12)* has double rooms with showers for €33. The *Pizzeria 902 (Attemsov trg 25)* is decent, but if you need something more substantial, try *Gostilna Pri Jošku (Attemsov trg 21)*, one of the oldest traditional eateries in Slovenia. Its specialities are boiled beef with horseradish and *žlikrofi* (Slovenian 'ravioli' made with cheese, bacon and chives). Pri Jošku is open from 6 am to 9 pm daily, except Wednesday.

Ljubno ob Savinji to Solčava

After the town of Ljubno ob Savinji, the Upper Savinja Valley begins to feel – and smell – truly Alpine, with the mountains so close you can almost touch them, the houses built entirely of wood and the heady scent of pine in the air. The road continues along the winding Savinja, past wooden bridges, more hayracks and, in a gorge 4km beyond **Luče** and visible from the main road, a curious rock tower called **Igla** (Needle).

Just before **Rogovilc**, the usual starting point for canoe and kayak trips on the Savinja, there's a turn south to **Robanov Kot**, a pristine valley and protected park with trails and farmhouse accommodation.

To the north-east of Robanov Kot and below Mt Raduha (2062m) there's an ice cave called **Snežna Jama** (actually Snow Cave; ☎ 572 32 11 for information) open to the public at the weekend in summer. It is accessible by car via a forest road.

Solčava, at 642m the highest town in the valley, has some lovely road markers with folk icons and painted barns. To the north is the Alpine village of **Podolševa**, where you can spend the night. The road from Solčava north to Podolševa, which continues west and down into Logarska Dolina, is one of the most panoramic in Slovenia.

Logarska Dolina

Most of the glacial 'Forester's Valley' – about 7.5km long and no more than 500m wide – has been a landscape park since 1987. This 'pearl of the Alpine region' is a wonderful place to explore for a few days with more than 30 natural attractions such as caves, springs, peaks and waterfalls.

Information The tourist office (☎ 584 71 11, fax 838 90 03, Ⓔ logarska@siol.net) is at the Plesnik Hotel at Logarska Dolina 9. Here you can organise all kinds of outdoor activities, and hire guides and equipment. You can also seek information from the staff at the entrance to the landscape park.

Things to See & Do The park is open year-round, but from April to September (and at weekends only in October) cars and

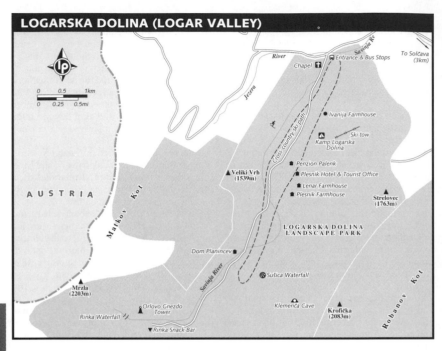

LOGARSKA DOLINA (LOGAR VALLEY)

motorcyclists entering the park must pay 800 SIT; cyclists and hikers get in free. A single road goes past a small chapel and through the woods to **Rinka Waterfall**, the main event here, but there are plenty of trails to explore and up to 20 additional waterfalls in the area.

The bottom of Rinka Waterfall is only about 10 minutes on foot from the car park at the end of the valley road, and you can climb to the top in about 20 minutes. It's not very difficult, but it can get slippery. From the top of the falls to the west you can see three peaks reaching higher than 2200m: Kranjska Rinka, Koroška Rinka and Štajerska Rinka. Until 1918 they formed the triple border of Carniola (Kranjska), Carinthia (Koroška) and Styria (Štajerska).

Opposite Dom Planincev is a trail leading to **Sušica Waterfall** and **Klemenča Cave**.

Another magnificent and much less explored valley, the 6km-long **Matkov Kot**, runs parallel to Logarska Dolina and the

border with Austria. You can reach here by road by turning west as you leave Logarska Dolina. Some think this valley was once a lake. There are several farmhouses with accommodation in the valley.

The tourist office at the Plesnik Hotel can organise any number of **activities** – from horse riding and coach rides for up to five people to paragliding, guided mountaineering and rock climbing up to grade IV. It also rents mountain bikes for 600 SIT per hour (2500 SIT for six hours). Nonresidents can use the swimming pool and sauna at the Plesnik Hotel for 1600 SIT a day. The valley also has some very basic ski facilities, including a tiny, 500m ski tow and 15km of cross-country ski trails.

Places to Stay & Eat The *Kamp Logarska Dolina* (☎ 584 70 16, Logarska Dolina 8) lies about 1.5km from the park entrance. The *Ivanija Farmhouse* (☎ 584 71 07) nearby also offers accommodation for €16 per person. A couple of kilometres farther south are two more farmhouses charging the same rate – *Lenar* (☎ *838 90 06, Logarska Dolina 11*) and *Plesnik* (☎ *838 90 09, Logarska Dolina 13*).

The nearby, 24-bed *Penzion Palenk* (same contact details as Plesnik Hotel) is a bit upmarket (€36/30 per person in a single/double) but nothing comes close to the 64-bed *Plesnik Hotel* (☎ *839 23 00, fax 839 23 12,* e *plesnik.doo@siol.net, Logarska Dolina 10*). It has a pool, sauna, a fine restaurant and lovely public area, but don't expect all that to come cheaply: single rates are €71 to €77, doubles are €92 to €102.

There's no shortage of places to eat here either. Along with the upmarket restaurants at the Plesnik Hotel and the Penzion Palenk is the *Dom Planincev*, 2.5km from Rinka, which has a relaxed, rustic feel to it. There's a simple snack bar called *Rinka* near the car

park close to the waterfall and another in a tall wooden tower called *Orlovo Gnezdo* (Eyrie) overlooking the falls.

Getting There & Away

From Mozirje, there is an hourly bus service to Celje. There are six buses a day to Gornji Grad, one to Kamnik, three to Solčava and six to Velenje. Up to three buses a day originating in Celje continue along the valley road to Logarska Dolina and the Rinka Waterfall car park.

From Gornji Grad, buses go to Ljubljana (three a day on weekdays, departing at 4.35 and 5.38 am and 12.36 pm; one on Saturday at 4.35 am; and one on Sunday at 12.01 pm), Celje (six a day), Kamnik (two to six), Ljubno (two), Maribor (one), Mozirje (10) and Velenje (two). There's an early morning bus on Sunday to Logarska Dolina from June to September only (departing at 7.51 am).

Koroška

Koroška (Carinthia in English, Kärnten in German) is Slovenia's smallest province – a mere shadow of what it once was. Until the end of WWI, Carinthia included a very large area as well as the cities of Klagenfurt (Celovec) and Villach (Beljak), both now in Austria.

Koroška, a region of dark forests, mountains and highland meadows, is essentially just three valleys bounded by the Pohorje Massif on the east, the last of the Karavanke peaks (Mt Peca, where good King Matjaž is said to be resting) on the west and the hills of Kobansko to the north. The Drava Valley runs east to west and includes the towns of Dravograd, Muta and Vuzenica. The Mežica and Mislinja Valleys fan out from the Drava; the former is an industrial area with towns like Ravne na Koroškem and Prevalje while the latter's main centre is Slovenj Gradec.

Koroška is an excellent area for outdoor activities, including skiing, flying, horse riding and especially hiking. The E6 European Hiking Trail running from the Baltic to the Adriatic enters Slovenia at Radlje ob Dravi and the Slovenian Alpine Trail from Maribor to Ankaran passes through the heart of Koroška. Parts of these trails can be easily covered from many towns in the area.

History

Koroška has a special place in the hearts and minds of most Slovenes. The Duchy of Carantania (Karantanija), the first Slovenian – and Slavic, for that matter – state dating back to the 7th century, was centred here, and the word 'Carinthia' is derived from that name. The region was heavily fortified with castles during the Middle Ages and, from the 12th century onward, was an important cultural and artistic centre. Development came to western Koroška in the early 19th century with the opening of iron mines at Prevalje and Ravne na Koroškem; in 1863 a railway linked Maribor with Klagenfurt via the mountain pass at Holmec.

Highlights

- View the paintings of Jože Tisnikar at the Gallery of Fine Arts in Slovenj Gradec
- Experience a sightseeing flight of the Mislinja Valley from the Koroški Aeroclub south of Slovenj Gradec
- Visit the Rotunda of St John the Baptist at Muta, one of the oldest churches in the country
- See the 15th-century frescoes of the Final Judgment in the Church of the Holy Spirit in Slovenj Gradec

AUSTRIA

• Slovenj Gradec p302

In the plebiscite ordered by the victorious Allies after WWI, Slovenes living on the northern side of the Karavanke, the 120km-long mountain ridge that separates much of north-west and north-central Slovenia from Austria, voted to put their economic future in the hands of Vienna, while the mining region of the Mežica Valley went to Slovenia. Understandably, the results of that vote have never sat very well with the Slovenes on the southern side of the mountains. In fact, under the communist regime, school children were taught a very different version of what actually took place in 1920.

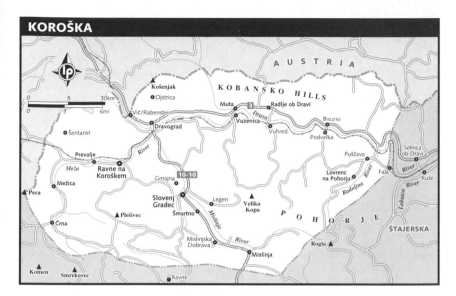

KOROŠKA

The fact remains that the Slovenian nation lost 90,000 of its nationals to Austria (along with 400,000 to Italy and 5000 to Hungary – some 37% of its total population of 1.3 million people at the time) and it still rankles. In one popular guide to Slovenian art and architecture published in Ljubljana, Slovenian Koroška is referred to as the 'Carinthian corner'.

SLOVENJ GRADEC
☎ 0602 • postcode 2380 • pop 8000
Slovenj Gradec is not the capital of Koroška – that distinction goes to the industrial centre of Ravne na Koroškem to the north-west – but it is certainly the province's cultural and recreational centre. A number of museums, galleries and historical churches line its main square, and the sporting opportunities in the Pohorje Massif to the east are endless. It is a wonderful place for a brief stopover en route to Štajerska or Austria.

History
The history of Slovenj Gradec is closely tied to Stari Trg, a suburb south-west of the Old Town where there was a Roman settlement called Colatio from the 1st to the 3rd

centuries. At that time an important Roman road from Celeia (Celje) to Virunum (near Klagenfurt in Austria) passed through Colatio. A castle called Grez to the west of the Old Town is first mentioned in the late 11th century though a fort had probably stood on the site as early as the late Iron Age.

Slovenj Gradec came into its own when the settlement shifted to an area between the Mislinja and Suhodolnica Rivers in the 12th century. It was an important trade centre in the Middle Ages and minted its own coins. Later it became an important cultural and artistic centre with many artisans and craft guilds. But the town did have its share of troubles: the Turks attacked several times from the 15th century; the Mislinja Valley was ravaged by locusts in 1477; and Slovenj Gradec was captured by the Hungarians under King Matthias Corvinus 11 years later.

Among the prominent Habsburg nobles based in Slovenj Gradec over the centuries were members of the Windisch-Grätz family, a variant of the German name for the town (Windisch Graz). *Windisch* (or *wendisch*) was the general German word for 'Slavic' until the 19th century. 'Gradec' is Slovene for 'Graz'.

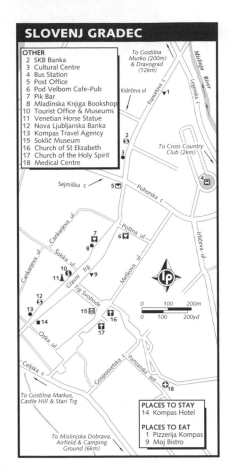

SLOVENJ GRADEC

OTHER
2 SKB Banka
3 Cultural Centre
4 Bus Station
5 Post Office
6 Pod Velbom Cafe-Pub
7 Pik Bar
8 Mladinska Knjiga Bookshop
10 Tourist Office & Museums
11 Venetian Horse Statue
12 Nova Ljubljanska Banka
13 Kompas Travel Agency
15 Soklič Museum
16 Church of St Elizabeth
17 Church of the Holy Spirit
18 Medical Centre

To Gostilna
Murko (200m)
& Dravograd
(12km)

Mislinja River

Kidričeva ul

Francetova c

Legenska c

To Cross Country
Club (2km)

Sejmiška c

Pohorska c

Cankarjeva ul

Šolska ul

Poštna ul

Iršičeva ul

Cankarjeva ul

Glavni Trg

Meškova ul

Trg Svobode

0   100   200m
0   100   200yd

Ozka ul

Celjska c

Gospovetska c

Partizanska pot

To Gostilna Markus,
Castle Hill & Stari Trg

To Mislinjska Dobrava,
Airfield & Camping
Ground (6km)

PLACES TO STAY
14 Kompas Hotel

PLACES TO EAT
1 Pizzerija Kompas
9 Moj Bistro

Orientation

Slovenj Gradec's main street is Glavni trg, a colourful 'square' of old town houses and shops. Castle Hill (Grajski Grič) and Stari Trg are to the west and south-west; the northern side of the Old Town is scarred by saw mills and paper factories.

The bus station is about 400m north-east of the tourist office at Pohorska cesta 15. Slovenj Gradec is not on a train line.

Information

The tourist office (☎ 881 21 16, fax 881 21 17, e tic@mesto-sg.si), on the ground floor of the former town hall at Glavni trg 24, can provide information and arrange accommodation. It sells guides to the region, including the useful (but expensive at 1500 SIT) *Guide to Mislinjska Valley* in English. The office is open from 8 am to 7 pm weekdays and 9 am to noon and 3 to 4 pm at weekends. Kompas (☎ 882 28 00), Glavni trg 38, will answer general questions and book private rooms. It is open from 8 am to 1 pm and 4 to 6 pm weekdays and till noon Saturday.

Nova Ljubljanska Banka at Glavni trg 30 is open from 8 am to 5 pm weekdays and till 11 am Saturday. SKB Banka has a branch at Francetova cesta 7, open from 8.30 am till noon and 2 to 5 pm weekdays only. The post office is at the northern end of Glavni trg on Francetova cesta. It is open from 8 am to 6 pm weekdays and till noon Saturday.

Mladinska Knjiga, the bookshop at Glavni trg 8, has regional maps if you've arrived in Koroška unprepared and want to do some hiking. It is open from 7.30 am to 6.30 pm weekdays and till noon Saturday.

Slovenj Gradec's medical centre (☎ 884 10 31) is south-east of Glavni trg at Partizanska pot 16.

Museums

The former town hall at Glavni trg 24, where the tourist office is located, contains two important museums. The **Koroška Regional Museum** (open 8 am to 6 pm Tuesday to Friday and 9 am till noon Saturday and Sunday; 300 SIT) has exhibits on the 2nd floor devoted to the history of Slovenj Gradec and the Koroška region – from local sport heroes' awards and farm implements to models of wartime hospital rooms and schools – and a very good archaeological collection on the ground floor.

Most of the latter deals with the Roman settlement of Colatio and includes jewellery and other effects taken from a Slavic burial ground at Puščava near Castle Hill. This part of the town hall served as a German prison during WWII.

The **Gallery of Fine Arts** on the 1st floor is open from 9 am to 6 Tuesday to Sunday (but closed from noon to 3 pm Saturday and Sunday); admission is 300 SIT. It has rotating exhibits but counts among its permanent collection African folk art, bronze sculptures by Franc Berneker (1874–1932) and naive paintings by Jože Tisnikar (1928–). Tisnikar is among the most interesting and original artists in Slovenia, and his obsession with corpses, distorted figures and oversized insects (perhaps inspired by that locust attack in the late 15th century) is at once disturbing and funny. Don't miss *Rojstva in Smrt* (Birth and Death) and *Stopala* (Feet). The paintings are all very black and blue.

The interesting **sculpture** in the courtyard is of the French poet Guillaume Apollinaire done by Ossip Zadkine in 1946. Outside the town hall is the odd, life-size **Venetian Horse** by contemporary sculptor Oskar Kogoj. It has become something of a symbol for the town.

The items on display at the **Soklič Museum** in the church rectory at Trg Svobode 5 were amassed by Jakob Soklič (1893–1972), a priest who began squirrelling away bits and bobs in the 1930s. Among the mediocre watercolours and oils of peasant idylls and the umpteen portraits of Hugo Wolf (a Slovenian composer who was born at Glavni trg 40 in 1860) are green goblets and beakers from nearby Glažuta (an important glass-manufacturing town in the 19th century), local embroidery and linen, religious artefacts and some 18th-century furniture. The statue of a saint holding a chalice, with a snake coming out of it, represents St John the Evangelist. (In quite a reversed role for a biblical reptile, a serpent once warned the apostle that he was about to quaff poisoned wine.) The museum is open on request; ask at the regional museum or the tourist office.

Churches

The sombre **Church of St Elizabeth** (1251), the town's oldest structure, is at the end of Trg Svobode. But aside from the Romanesque nave and a couple of windows, almost everything here is baroque, including the massive gold altar and the altar paintings done by local artist Franc Mihael Strauss (1647–1740) and his son Janez Andrej Strauss (1721–82). Far more interesting is

the 15th-century **Church of the Holy Spirit** next door with an interior covered with Gothic frescoes by Andrej of Otting. The 27 panels on the north wall represent the Passion of Christ; the scenes on the archway are of the Final Judgment. As always, the most disturbing scenes are those of the devil leading the damned down, down, down...

Stari Trg, where the Romans once frolicked, is nothing but an empty field now, but on Castle Hill (530m) there is the lovingly restored 13th-century **Parish Church of St Pancras**, the oldest hall church in the country, with a bell tower that is part of the 17th-century fortifications. The house to the left of the church holds the key. Castle Hill is about a 25-minute walk to the northwest from Stari Trg; just follow the **Calvary** and its baroque **Stations of the Cross** up the hill. If you continue along the path past the church you'll reach Puščava, site of an early Slavic burial ground.

Activities

There are plenty of opportunities for recreation near the airfield in Mislinjska Dobrava some 6km south-east of Slovenj Gradec; take the Velenje road (No 10-10) for 5km and then turn east for another 800m. The bus to Mislinja or Velenje will drop you off along the main road.

First you'll come to the Slovenj Gradec Riding Club (☎ 885 35 47), which has horses for rent both within the hippodrome and cross-country, and tennis courts. Next is the Koroški Aeroclub (☎ 885 36 30), which offers 10-minute sightseeing flights of the Mislinja Valley for 6500 SIT for up to three people.

The Cross Country Club (☎ 885 30 58), 2km south-east of Slovenj Gradec on Legenska cesta, also has horses for riding.

Three ski slopes are within striking distance of Slovenj Gradec, but the closest is Kope (☎ 884 23 91 for information), 1380m above the Mislinja Valley on the western edge of the Pohorje Massif. The ski grounds have 9km of runs and seven lifts on Mala Kopa and Velika Kopa peaks. To reach Kope, follow the Velenje road for 3km south and then turn east. The ski area is another

13km at the end of the road. Special ski buses make the run in winter, depending on the snowfall.

The *Guide to the Mislinjska Valley* outlines a number of hikes and bicycle trips in the area, including some along sections of the E6 European Hiking and Slovenian Alpine trails. Pohorje is unique in Slovenia in that there is no real 'off season' for hiking; the meadows and paths are generally as good in the winter as they are in summer.

The Slovenian Alpine Trail passes through Stari Trg and the centre of Slovenj Gradec before continuing up to Mala Kopa (1524m), where it meets the E6. There is a mountain hut at 1102m to the north-west – *Koča pod Kremžarjevim Vrhom* (☎ 884 48 83) – which is open daily June to October and weekends only the rest of the year. The E6 heads north through Vuhred and Radlje ob Dravi to Austria while the Slovenian Alpine Trail carries on eastward to Rogla and Maribor. There is more accommodation on Velika Kopa (1543m) at the *Grmovškov Dom* (☎ 885 38 55), which is open year-round. If you are going to do a fair amount of hiking in the western Pohorje, pick up a copy of the 1:50,000-scale *Pohorje* GZS map before setting out.

Special Events
The Slovenj Gradec Summer Festival of music and other activities takes place from June to September. There is a bonfire and celebrations on Midsummer Night (Kresna Noč) on 23 June.

Places to Stay
The *Medeni Raj camping ground* (☎ 885 34 83) is just beyond the airfield in Mislinjska Dobrava. 'Sweet Paradise' is a small, friendly place set among pine trees and costs about 1500 SIT per person. The camping ground also has bungalows (singles/doubles for 4500/6500 SIT including breakfast), and the small restaurant there is open till 10 pm.

The tourist office can arrange accommodation in *private rooms* both in and out of town for about 2500 SIT per person, but the list is very short.

The only hotel option in town is the 68-room *Kompas Hotel* (☎ 884 22 95, fax 884 31 79, Glavni trg 43). Single rooms with shower and breakfast are 5500 SIT, doubles 9800 SIT. The rooms are no great shakes and the dark corridors seem to go on forever, but there is a pleasant courtyard out the back.

Places to Eat
In the centre of town, *Moj Bistro* (*Glavni trg 25*) offers drinks, snacks and light meals from 7 am to 11 pm daily. *Pizzerija Kompas* (*Francetova cesta 14*) serves something round and doughy with tomato sauce on top that some people might call pizza. Still, it's cheap enough and the people are friendly. It's open till 9.30 pm. *Gostilna Murko* (*Francetova cesta 24*), about 400m north, is a rather chi-chi establishment popular with Austrian tourists on the go. It's open till 10 pm daily.

If you've got wheels, the *Restavracija Tina* at the Bošnik farmhouse, about 4km north-west of Slovenj Gradec in Gmajna (house No 30), is an excellent choice. Among the specialities of the house is *obara z ajdovimi žganci*, a rich stew with buckwheat groats. In Stari Trg at house No 251, *Gostilna Markus* has fish specialities and wine from its own vineyard.

Entertainment
Classical music concerts are sometimes held at the *Church of St Elizabeth* on Trg Svobode and the *Slovenj Gradec Cultural Centre* (☎ 884 11 93, Francetova cesta 5). If you're interested in chatting up Austrian businesspeople, head for the *nightclub* at the Kompas Hotel between 10 pm and 3 am. Otherwise, the best places for meeting people include the *Pod Velbom* cafe-pub (*Glavni trg 1*) at the start of Poštna ulica, open to 11 pm or midnight daily, and the *Pik Bar* (*Glavni trg 6*), next to Mladinska Knjiga.

Getting There & Away
There are frequent buses to Črna, Dravograd, Mislinja, Radlje ob Dravi, Ravne na Koroškem and Velenje. Other destinations

served by bus from Slovenj Gradec include Celje (three a day), Gornji Grad (one), Legen (eight), Ljubljana (four to five), Maribor (eight), Piran (one on weekdays) and Vuhred (four).

DRAVOGRAD

☎ 02 • postcode 2370 • pop 3500

Situated on the left (north) bank of the Drava, Slovenia's second-longest river (144km), 'Drava Castle' is much smaller than its sister city 12km to the south, but just as old, with a recorded history dating back to the 12th century. It was then that the castle, the ruins of which can be seen on the hill to the north of town, was built. Situated on a bend in the Drava at the point where the smaller Meža and Mislinja Rivers flow into it, the castle and the town were of great strategic importance for centuries.

Today, Dravograd is a sleepy place with few sights of its own. But it is a good springboard for exploring the Kobansko Hills to the north and the Drava Valley to the east. The Austrian border (crossing at Vič/Rabenstein) is just 3.5km north-west of Dravograd.

Orientation & Information

While Dravograd's historical centre and its main street, Trg 4 Julija, are on the north bank of the Drava, the bus and train stations are about 1km south-east on the south bank.

Dravograd's tourist office (☎ 878 30 11) is open three days a week only: from 8 am to 2 pm Monday, and 8 am to noon Wednesday and Friday. Nova Ljubljanska Banka, open from 8 am to 5 pm weekdays and till 11 am Saturday, is at Trg 4 Julija 42 two doors east of the Church of St Vitus.

The post office is at the eastern end of Trg Julija just before you cross the bridge over the Drava. It is open from 8 am to 6 pm weekdays and till noon Saturday.

Things to See & Do

The **Church of St Vitus** at the western end – ie, the top – of Trg 4 Julija is one of the most important Romanesque buildings extant in Slovenia. Built in the second half of the 12th century and only recently renovated, it

is a solid structure of light-brown stone with a high tower between the nave and the small circular presbytery. While the occupants in the house next door are more than happy to hand you the key, there's not much to see inside except for a beamed ceiling and a fresco of St Cyril and St Methodius. The church is used almost exclusively for wedding ceremonies; Mass is said only on the patron's feast day in June. The Gothic-style **Church of St John** on a bend in the Drava, a short distance to the west of St Vitus, has a fine baroque interior.

The basement of the **town hall** at Trg 4 Julija 7 was used as a Gestapo prison and torture chamber during WWII. The hydro-electric dam on the Drava nearest Dravograd was built by German soldiers during the war, and many of them were lodged in town. The remains of a bombed-out bridge run parallel to the new one over the Drava.

It's an easy hike north from Dravograd to the **castle ruins** (not much more than a wall); just turn up Pod Gradom, a lane just before the Apolon Bar at Trg 4 Julija 22. The more energetic may want to carry on farther into the **Kobansko Hills**, where you just might encounter some traditional charcoal burners. A circular section of the Kozjak Mountain Trail leads north past Goriški Vrh to Mt Košenjak (1522m) and returns to Dravograd via Ojstrica.

Places to Stay

The 16-room *Penzion Kudrnovsky* (☎ *878 43 70, Meža cesta 3*) is by the train and bus stations. The cost for singles/doubles here is 3200/5500 SIT, and there's a pleasant restaurant, with an outside cafe in summer, open to 10 pm daily.

A bit out of town – about 1.5km north-west of Trg 4 Julija in a shopping centre at Koroška cesta 48 – is the garish yellow *Traberg Hotel* (☎ *878 44 40, fax 878 00 33*) with 63 beds. Singles/doubles are 8420/11,380 SIT. Its Al Capone nightclub (open 10 pm to 4 am) with 'erotic shows' was clearly set up to entice Avstrijci from over the border.

If you don your hiking boots and set out for Mt Košenjak, there is accommodation

KOROŠKA

on weekends at the *Planinski Dom Košenjak* (☎ *878 35 44*).

If you have your own transport and would like to get away from it all, consider spending a night or two in one of the dozen or so farmhouses in the picturesque village of Šentanel in the Mežica Valley, 6km north-west of Prevalje. Prevalje is 12km south-west of Dravograd and easily accessible by bus and train. The *Ploder farmhouse* (☎ *823 11 04*) at No 3 in Šentanel has 15 rooms and is open in July and August, while the more isolated *Marin farmhouse* (☎ *823 14 09*) at No 8 in Šentanel and open year-round has 11. Both charge between 3500 and 5000 SIT per person, depending on the season and room category.

Places to Eat

Trg 4 Julija has a handful of bistros, cafes and small restaurants, including the *Taverna Pagat* (*Trg 4 Julija 34*) and the *Bistro Wolf* (*Trg 4 Julija 36*). More pleasant, though, is the *Na Klancu* (*Trg 4 Julija 27*), a restaurant with a back terrace facing the Drava.

Getting There & Away

If you're headed for Črna, Maribor via Radlje ob Dravi, Prevalje, Slovenj Gradec or Velenje, count on a bus about every half-hour or so. Three buses a day go to Celje, one to Gornji Grad, five to Ljubljana and two to Piran. There's also a daily bus to Klagenfurt (Celovec) in Austria.

Dravograd is on the rail line linking Maribor and Bleiburg (Pliberk) and Klagenfurt in Austria. Up to five trains a day depart for Maribor (1½ hours, 64km) via Vuzenica and Vuhred. The same number leave for Ravne na Koroškem and Prevalje (20 minutes, 12km), two of which cross the border into Austria.

AROUND DRAVOGRAD

An excellent bike trip follows the spectacular Drava Valley through the Pohorje and Kobansko Hills, 60km eastward to Maribor. The river, whose highest flow is reached at the start of the summer, is at its most scenic at Brezno and just above Fala, where it narrows into a gorge. Just before Maribor the Drava widens into a lake with the help of a major dam.

You don't have to go that far to see some great scenery, though. **Vuzenica** and **Muta**, two very attractive villages, are just 14km from Dravograd. The two towns can also be reached on the Maribor bus.

The **Church of St Nicholas** at Vuzenica (population 2916), on the Drava's right bank, was built in the 12th century and expanded later. Its outstanding features include a star-vaulted ceiling typical of Koroška, 15th-century frescoes in the porch and an original fortified wall surrounding the churchyard. The ruins of a 16th-century **castle** can be seen on Pisterjev Vrh north-east of town.

Muta (population 3727), a two-tier village across the Drava from Vuzenica, has churches on both levels, but you want the one in the lower town (Spodnja Muta) near the main road. The **Rotunda of St John the Baptist**, one of the oldest churches in Slovenia, is an austere round structure from the early 1200s. Its shape, wooden roof and steeple are typical of the province, and the tiny church appears quite content with itself sitting in a field with the hills far behind it. There are fragmented reliefs on the east side of the apse and near the west entrance; if you can manage to wrest the key from the farmhouse next door at Liverska ulica 12, you can see the 14th-century frescoes in the choir. The larger **Church of St Margaret** up in Zgornja Muta is 'new', dating from the 17th century.

Prekmurje

Prekmurje, Slovenia's 'forgotten' corner, is mostly a broad plain that extends for 20km to 30km – as its name suggests – 'beyond the Mura'. Its isolation is rooted in history – until 1924 not a single bridge spanned the sluggish Mura River and crossings were made by ferry. As a result, Prekmurje retains much of its traditional music, folklore and even architecture in its distinctive Pannonian-style farmhouses.

Until the end of WWI almost all of Prekmurje belonged to the Austro-Hungarian crown and a sizable Magyar minority still lives here, especially around the spa town of Lendava, Slovenia's easternmost city and its oil capital, and in Murska Sobota, which Hungarians call Muraszombat. In many ways Prekmurje looks and feels more like Hungary than Slovenia, emphasised by the abundance of white storks, large thatched farmhouses with attached barns and other farm buildings under a single roof (see the boxed text 'The Farmhouses of Prekmurje' later in this chapter), a substantial Roma (Gypsy) population – especially around the village of Pušča west of Murska Sobota – as well as the occasional Hungarian-style *čarda* (inn).

For most Slovenes, Prekmurje means a local version of *golaž* (goulash) cooked with paprika, a rich pastry called *gibanica* and a people who are generally more volatile and quick-tempered than most others in the nation. For travellers the province is a springboard into Austria or Hungary and a place to relax and enjoy one of the many thermal spas in the region. Winters can be very cold on the plain, though, and summers extremely hot.

MURSKA SOBOTA
☎ 02 • postcode 9000 • pop 14,000
The capital and administrative centre of Prekmurje, Murska Sobota is a scruffy industrial town with little to recommend it, except for an odd architectural mix of neoclassical, Secessionist and 'socialist

Highlights

- Visit Plečnik's masterful Church of the Ascension in the flower-bedecked village of Bogojina
- See the last of Prekmurje's celebrated floating mills on the Mura River near Veržej
- Admire the wonderful 14th-century frescoes at the Church of St Martin in Martjanci
- Watch for the arrival of the white storks in spring

baroque' buildings. But the surrounding countryside, potters villages and thermal spas make it a good starting point for travellers to the region.

History
Murska Sobota was little more than a market town – its name means 'Mura Saturday', indicating when the market took place – until two pivotal events last century.

The first was the opening of the railway in 1907, which linked Murska Sobota with Hungary proper via Šalovci to the south. The second event was ultimately even more

PREKMURJE

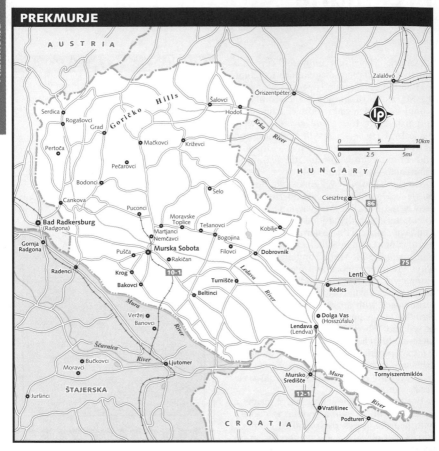

significant for the city. With the formation of the Kingdom of Serbs, Croats and Slovenes in 1918 and the transfer of territory, Murska Sobota found itself more or less in the centre of Prekmurje and development really began. The area was occupied by Hungary during WWII.

Orientation
The centre of Murska Sobota, Trg Zmage (Victory Square), lies south-east of large, shady Mestni Park (City Park). The bus station is some 400m due south of the square on Slomškova ulica next to the Diana Hotel.

The train station is about 600m south-east of Trg Zmage; follow Slovenska ulica, the main street lined with fruit stands and kiosks, southward and turn east on Ulica Arhitekta Novaka.

Information
There is no tourist office in Murska Sobota. If you need help or information, the staff at the tourist office in Moravske Toplice, 7km to the north-east, will help you out.

Pomurska Banka has a big branch at Trg Zmage 7 and is open from 8.30 am to noon and 2 to 5 pm weekdays, and to 11 am

Saturday. The SKB Banka at Kocljeva ulica 14 is open from 8.30 am till noon and 2 to 5 pm weekdays only.

The main post office, which is next door to Pomurska Banka on Trg Zmage, is open from 7 am to 7 pm weekdays, to 1 pm Saturday and from 9 to 11 am Sunday.

Dobra Knjiga, a bookshop at Slovenska ulica 11, has a decent selection of regional maps if you plan to do any hiking in the area. It is open from 7 am to 6 pm weekdays and till noon Saturday.

Sobota Castle

This late-15th-century manor house is in the centre of City Park at the end of Trubarjev drevored and houses the recently renovated **Murska Sobota Regional Museum** on the 2nd floor; enter from the north side. The largest collection of the museum is an ethnographic one devoted to the culture and traditional lifestyles of the Prekmurje region. Anyone who has visited such collections in southern Transdanubia, just across the border, will find the farm implements, painted jugs, costumes and woodcarvings in the vaulted rooms almost identical to their Hungarian counterparts. The museum was closed for renovation at the time of research, but is normally open from 10 am to 5 pm Tuesday to Friday and to 1 pm Saturday and Sunday.

The castle itself, with Renaissance and baroque elements, is interesting. Have a walk around the outside to spot the two Atlases supporting the balcony on the east side, the older chapel on the west and the lovely baroque gable with a clock on the north side.

Other Attractions

You may be surprised to see heavy artillery guns and statues of Yugoslav and Soviet soldiers at the eastern entrance of **City Park**. This is the **Liberation Monument**, which somehow managed to stay in place despite the 'house cleaning' that the rest of Slovenia did after independence.

Opposite the park entrance is the neo-Gothic **Evangelical Church**, the main Lutheran seat in Slovenia. Prekmurje has long been a Protestant stronghold, and the majority of Slovenian Protestants live in this province. The church dates only from 1910, but its ceilings painted with geometric shapes and muted shades of blue and green are a welcome relief from the overwrought baroque gold and marble decor found in most Catholic churches.

The **Parish Church of St Nicholas** near the train station is an early-20th-century structure built around a Gothic presbytery with 14th-century frescoes.

The **Murska Sobota Gallery** at Kocljeva ulica 7 has revolving exhibits and is arguably the best gallery in Prekmurje. It's open from 8 am to 6 pm weekdays (to 4 pm Monday), from 10 am till noon Saturday and 9 am till noon Sunday.

Places to Stay

The closest *camping ground* to Murska Sobota is at Moravske Toplice (see later in this chapter). The *Terme Banovci* (☎ 513 14 00) camping ground at a small spa near Veržej, about 13km south of Murska Sobota, is one of the few naturist camping grounds in Slovenia. It's open April to October (Indian summer providing) and costs 1250 SIT per person. Nearby on the Mura River is the last of the region's celebrated floating mills.

The *Dijaški Dom Murska Sobota* (☎ 521 10 43, Tomšičeva ulica 15), a student dormitory south-west of the centre, accepts travellers in summer only.

The only hotel in the town centre is the expensive *Diana Hotel* (☎ 514 12 00, fax 532 10 97, Slovenska ulica 52), a garishly painted concrete block with 96 rooms. Its singles with shower and breakfast are 7750 SIT, doubles are 12,800 SIT. At those rates, you should indeed get 'unlimited use' of the indoor swimming pool, sauna and fitness centre, as advertised.

The *Čarda Motel* (☎ 548 11 18), about 2.5km north of town in the village of Nemčavci (on the road to Moravske Toplice), charges about 3300 SIT per person.

Places to Eat

There's an inexpensive *bife* in the market south of Trg Zmage, open from 8 am to

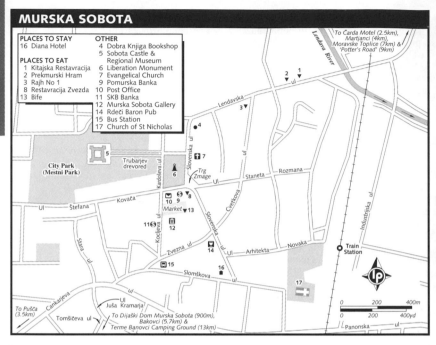

MURSKA SOBOTA

PLACES TO STAY
16 Diana Hotel

PLACES TO EAT
1 Kitajska Restavracija
2 Prekmurski Hram
3 Rajh No 1
8 Restavracija Zvezda
13 Bife

OTHER
4 Dobra Knjiga Bookshop
5 Sobota Castle &
  Regional Museum
6 Liberation Monument
7 Evangelical Church
9 Pomurska Banka
10 Post Office
11 SKB Banka
12 Murska Sobota Gallery
14 Rdeči Baron Pub
15 Bus Station
17 Church of St Nicholas

3 pm weekdays and till noon Saturday. The *Restavracija Zvezda (Trg Zmage 8)* is no great shakes, but in warmer months the outside terrace under the chestnut trees becomes the focal point of Murska Sobota. It is open from 7 am daily, closing at midnight through the week, 1 am Friday and Saturday, and 10 pm Sunday. *Grajski Hram* at Sobota Castle is open from 10 am to 5 pm weekdays only.

You'll find better restaurants along Lendavska ulica, a few minutes walk to the north-east from Trg Zmage. *Prekmurski Hram (Lendavska ulica 35a)* has regional specialities, and is a good place to try some of the local Laški Rizling wine from one of Prekmurje's wine-growing areas, while the *Rajh No 1* 'mini-restaurant' on the corner of Lendavska ulica and Cvetkova ulica is an upmarket *špagetarija* and *picerija*. Both are open from 8 am to 10 pm (closed Sunday). *Kitajska Restavracija (Lendavska ulica 39e)* is, as its name indicates, a Chinese restaurant with the usual range of Chinese dishes and is open from 11 am to 11 pm daily (closes 7 pm Sunday).

If you're under your own steam, head for the *Gostilna Rajh (Soboška ulica 32)* in Bakovci, a village 5km south-west of Murska Sobota. The Rajh specialises in local food and boasts a huge cellar of regional wines. Dishes to consider include the *bograč golaž* (Hungarian-style goulash 'soup'); roast suckling pig served with 'twice-cooked' noodles; and, of course, the gibanica pastry.

Entertainment

A couple of pleasant pubs can be found along Slovenska ulica, including *Rdeči Baron (Slovenska ulica 42)* and there are no prizes for guessing that *rdeč* means 'red' in Slovene. It's open to 11 pm Monday to Thursday and till midnight Friday and Saturday. The *disco* at the Diana Hotel rages till 4 am Friday and Saturday.

Getting There & Away

Bus Buses leave Murska Sobota at least 10 times a day for Dobrovnik, Gornja Radgona (via Radenci) on the Austrian border, Lendava near the Hungarian border, Ljutomer, Mačkovci, Maribor, Moravske Toplice, Rakičan and Turnišče (via Dobrovnik or Beltinci). Other destinations include Beltinci, Grad (six), Hodoš on the Hungarian border (eight), Ljubljana via Maribor or Ljutomer (four), Piran (one) and Ptuj (two). Sunday departures for Ljubljana are at 5.45 am, and 1.38 and 4.30 pm.

A bus headed for Lenti in Hungary leaves Murska Sobota at 9.10 am from Thursday to Saturday.

Train Murska Sobota is on a spur that connects it with the main line (to Ljubljana, Maribor, Vienna and Budapest) at Ormož (45 minutes, 39km). There are up to nine departures a day, and the train stops at Beltinci, Ljutomer and Veržej.

AROUND MURSKA SOBOTA
Martjanci

The **Parish Church of St Martin** in this village 4km north of Murska Sobota, on the road to Moravske Toplice, contains wonderful 14th-century frescoes painted on the sanctuary's vaulted ceiling and walls by Johannes Aquila of Radgona. They depict angels bearing inscriptions, the Apostles, scenes from the life of St Martin and even a self-portrait of Master Johannes himself. Not to be outdone by the artist, the church's benefactor had his likeness appear in several scenes on the north arch and west wall.

MORAVSKE TOPLICE
☎ 02 • postcode 9226 • pop 700

The thermal spa of Moravske Toplice, 7km north-east of Murska Sobota, boasts the hottest water in Slovenia – 72°C at source and cooled to 38°C for use in its many pools and basins. Though it's one of the newest spas in the country – the spring was discovered in 1960 during exploratory oil drilling – many young Slovenes consider the clientele too geriatric for their liking, preferring the small *au naturel* spa at Banovci. But

Moravske Toplice is every bit a health resort geared for recreation, with enough sporting facilities to cater to every taste.

Information

The tourist office (☎ 538 15 20, fax 538 15 02, e tic.moravci@siol.net) is on the left as you enter the village, at Kranjčeva ulica 3, a short distance north-west of the spa complex. It is open from 8 am to 8 pm Monday to Saturday (to 6 pm in winter) and to 2 pm Sunday.

There's a Pomurska Banka branch near the entrance to the spa open from 8 am to noon and 1 to 4 pm weekdays only. The post office, next to the tourist office on Kranjčeva ulica, is open from 8 am to 6 pm weekdays and till noon Saturday.

Thermal Spa

The resort, at Kranjčeva ulica 12, has nine indoor and outdoor pools filled with thermal water and two large outdoor ones with ordinary heated water. The thermal water is recommended for relief of rheumatism and certain minor skin problems, and there are enough therapies and beauty treatments available to keep you occupied for a week. Many visitors, though, simply come to sit in the warm water, cycle in the countryside or walk in the nearby vineyards. If you're staying at the resort, you get use of the pools for free; otherwise you'll have to pay 1500 SIT for the privilege. The spa resort also has several tennis courts, a fitness room/gym and saunas.

Places to Stay & Eat

The tourist office can organise *private rooms* for between 2400 SIT and 3500 SIT per person, depending on the season and the category. If you're going freelance, there are rooms available at Nos 5, 13, 16 and 32 Kranjčeva ulica. *Apartments* that are booked through the tourist office cost 2000 to 2500 SIT per person.

All the accommodation at the *Zdravilišče Moravske Toplice* (Moravske Toplice Thermal Spa; ☎ 512 22 00, fax 548 16 07, e info@zdrav-moravci.si, Kranjčeva ulica 12) shares the same contact numbers.

The five-hectare *camping ground* can accommodate 200 guests and is open year-round. Use of the swimming pool nearby is included in the daily charge of 2177 SIT per person (3277 SIT at weekends).

The resort's two hotels – big, modern structures of little interest – are expensive. Singles with shower and breakfast at the 274-bed *Hotel Ajda* are 11,700 to 12,600 SIT and doubles are 18,400 to 20,200 SIT, depending on the season. The 252-bed *Hotel Termal*, while cheaper, is still going to cost you a minimum of 9600 to 10,300 SIT for a single and 15,200 to 16,600 SIT for a double.

The only other option at the resort is to stay in one of the attractive *bungalows* done up to look like traditional Prekmurje peasant cottages, with thatched or tiled roofs and cool whitewashed walls. They cost 8100 SIT for one person and 12,200 SIT for two, and are open April to October only.

There's a basic *pizzeria* next to the Pomurska Banka at the entrance to the spa, open from 1 to 8 pm daily. A good place in which to sample Prekmurje's food specialities is at *Gostilna Kuhar (Kranjčeva 13)*.

Getting There & Around

Buses leave hourly from Kranjčeva ulica for Murska Sobota, and there are about a dozen a day to Dobrovnik. Other destinations include Kobilje (six buses a day), Lendava via Turnišče (six), Ljubljana (one via Maribor) and Maribor. The tourist office rents bicycles for 350 SIT an hour.

AROUND MORAVSKE TOPLICE

An excellent bike trip (also accessible on the Dobrovnik and Kobilje buses) is what could be called the **potters' road** which runs south-east from the spa. The road passes through the villages of Tešanovci, Bogojina and Filovci; to the north are the low Goričko Hills covered in vineyards. This is not Prekmurje's most important wine-growing region – that distinction goes to the areas around Lendava to the south-east and Gornja Radgona to the west – but it is just as lovely.

Tešanovci (population 1080), less than 2km from Moravske Toplice, is noted for its pottery *(lončarstvo)*, and you can visit workshops at house Nos 51 and 53 on the main road. Otherwise, Tešanovci is not an especially interesting place; carry on another 2.5km to **Bogojina** (population 1530), which should get an award for being the most attractive and tidy village in Prekmurje.

The main attraction here is the **Parish Church of the Ascension**, redesigned by Jože Plečnik between 1926 and 1927. The

The Farmhouses of Prekmurje

Along with gibanica cake and storks, Prekmurje is known for its traditional L-shaped farmhouses, among the most uniform regional dwellings in Slovenia. Anyone who has crossed the border into Hungary will recognise them; they are not dissimilar to the *kerített házak* (fenced-in houses) found in Transdanubia.

The thatched roof of a Prekmurje farmhouse extended into the central courtyard, and this sheltered 'portico' *(podsten)* allowed access from the outside to all the rooms when it rained. It was also used as a work area and a place to gossip with the family or neighbours on a warm summer afternoon.

The main living area consisted of a central entrance hall, which also served as the kitchen. The large open hearth was used to cook and also to heat the tile stoves in the rooms on either side: the 'first room' *(prva izba)*, with table and chairs, decorated trousseau chests and religious icons; and the 'back room' *(zadnja izba)*, used for sleeping. Connected to the house (though accessible only from the portico) were the work and storage shed, the barn and the stable.

Another distinctive feature of Prekmurje houses (though not uncommon in south-western Hungary) were the floral designs stencilled on the outside walls about a metre from the ground. They gave a little colour to the stark, whitewashed walls and varied from one house to another.

church is at the northern end of the village on a low hill; from the main road proceed past peasant houses bedecked with flowers and storks nesting on chimneys and telephone poles to No 147. To the original Romanesque and baroque structure, Plečnik added two asymmetrical aisles and a round tower reminiscent of the crow's nest on a ship. The interior is an odd mixture of black marble, brass and wood; the oak-beamed ceiling is fitted with ceramic plates and jugs collected from the area.

Filovci (population 522), another 2km beyond Bogojina, is famed throughout Slovenia for its *črna keramika* (black pottery), which can also be found in parts of southern and eastern Hungary. One of the best workshops to visit is at house No 29, where the Bojnec family works the wheels and fires its pots and pitchers in an old brick oven. The workshop is about 200m southwest of the main road, past the small church and over the bridge.

If you get hungry, there are a couple of decent gostilne in **Dobrovnik**, 3.5km beyond Filovci. *Pri Lujzi* is at house No 273a. *Lipot*, almost opposite at No 277a, has outside seating. Both are open till 10 pm.

RADENCI
☎ 02 • postcode 9252 • pop 5750
Strictly speaking, Radenci is not part of Prekmurje province because it is not 'beyond the Mura'. In fact, it lies about 1km from the river's south bank and is thus really 'on the Mura' (Pomurje). But let's not get technical... Radenci has always been closely tied historically and geographically with Prekmurje, and it is easily accessible from Murska Sobota, 13km to the east.

Radenci is best known for its health resort, parts of which still feel like a full-of-itself 19th-century spa town. Indeed, as one Slovenian wag put it, 'Radenci remains the preserve of highbrow intellectuals and rumble-tumble chamber music.' But when most Slovenes hear the name they think of Radenska Tri Srca – the Radenci Three Hearts mineral water that is bottled here and consumed in every restaurant and cafe in the land.

Orientation & Information
Radenci lies west and north of the Radgona-Kapel wine-growing area. To the north is a triangle of Austrian territory inhabited mostly by ethnic Slovenes. The border crossing is at Gornja Radgona/Bad Rakersburg, 6km north-west of Radenci.

For general information, go to reception in the Hotel Radin (☎ 520 10 00), where you can also change money.

Pomurska Banka has a branch at Panonska cesta 5–7, open from 7.30 am to 5 pm weekdays and to 11.30 am Saturday. The post office, open from 7 am to 7 pm weekdays and till noon Saturday, is on the same street opposite the Vikend restaurant.

Thermal Spa
The health resort has three claims to fame: water rich in carbon dioxide for drinking; mineral-laden thermal water for bathing that comes out at 41°C at source; and sulphurous Negova mud for smearing all over yourself. All three play a role in the therapeutic and beauty treatments so popular here.

Springs of mineral water were discovered in the early 19th century, and the bottling of Radenska water began in 1869. By the early 20th century, the water had become so popular that it was sent to the imperial court in Vienna and to the pope in Rome. The spa itself opened in 1882.

Today, three modern (and ugly) blocks overlook the older Victorian-style buildings and a large wooded park with paths, a chapel, pavilions and tame red squirrels. The complex has several pools, including an indoor recreational one, an outdoor thermal one with a temperature of about 34°C and an outdoor Olympic-size one. Guests can use the pools at will; outsiders pay 1000 SIT.

There's a small **museum** in the park devoted to the history and development of the spa and its famous mineral water. The museum is open from 10 am till noon daily (and from 3 to 4 pm Tuesday).

Activities
The tennis courts just south of the hotel complex can be rented for 1100 SIT per hour. Racquets (500 SIT) and balls are

PREKMURJE

available from the small kiosk there from 8 am to noon and 2 to 8 pm. Lessons cost 2000 SIT per hour. For badminton, table tennis and minigolf, go to the large outdoor pool. Mountain bikes are available for rent.

Excellent cycling excursions can be made into the surrounding wine country; head south-west along the 'wine road' *(vinska cesta)* for about 4km to Janžev Vrh and an old vineyard cottage called Janžev Hram or even farther south to Kapelski Vrh and Ivanjski Vrh. Almost all the wines produced here are whites; try the popular local one called Janževec or the Zlata Radgonska Penina sparkling wine.

Special Events

The spa puts on its famous chamber music concerts in summer.

Places to Stay

There are lots of *private rooms* available on Panonska cesta to the west and south of the spa's main entrance, including at house No 23. The price should be about 2500 SIT per person. The *Restavracija Vikend* (☎ 565 19 96, Panonska cesta 2) has rooms available for 2200 SIT per person.

The four *spa hotels* (☎ 520 10 00, fax 520 27 23) are much of a muchness and certainly no bargain. Singles at the cheapest of the four – the two-star *Hotel Terapija* –

range from 8300 to 9750 SIT, depending on the season, with doubles 14,700 to 17,600 SIT. Prices at the three-star *Hotel Miral* and the four-star *Hotel Izvir* and *Hotel Radin* are about 20% and 50% higher respectively.

Places to Eat

The *Restavracija Park* in the middle of the resort's large wooded park is a pleasant place for a meal in summer, but the mosquitoes may consume you first. It closes Monday. The *Restavracija Vikend* (see Places to Stay) is a big, raucous place that is open daily.

For something a little more colourful, head north-west for about 3km on the road to Austria to *Gostilna Klobasa* in Šratovci at house No 8 or to *Gostilna Adanič* in Mele at house No 27a. They're both open till about 10 pm.

Getting There & Away

There are frequent bus services to Maribor, Murska Sobota and Gornja Radgona. Other destinations include Celje (six a day), Koper (two), Lendava (up to 10), Ljubljana (up to eight), Ljutomer (six), Nova Gorica (one), Ormož (two), Piran (one) and Rogaška Slatina (one).

Passenger trains do not operate on the Ljutomer-Gornja Radgona line that passes through Radenci; it is used for freight only.

Language

Slovene *(slovenščina)* is a South Slavic language closely related to Croatian and Serbian and written in the Roman alphabet. Linguists have counted no fewer than 50 dialects and sub-dialects in little Slovenia, though the 'purest' form of the language is said to be spoken in north-west Dolenjska.

Slovene is a grammatically complex language with six cases for nouns and adjectives, three genders and four verb tenses. In addition to singular and plural, Slovene also has a separate 'dual' form to indicate 'two' of something: *miza*, 'one table', *mize*, 'three or more tables', but *mizi*, 'two tables'.

There are many irregularities in verb conjugations and noun declensions but adjectives precede the noun, as in English and there are no articles: 'a table' or 'the table' is just 'table', *miza*.

The Slovenian alphabet has 25 letters – the 'q', 'w', 'x' and 'y' of the English alphabet are not used but it contains the letters 'č', 'š' and 'ž' in both upper and lower case. (The little mark on top is called a *strešica*, or 'little roof', in Slovene.)

Pronunciation

Like English, Slovene is not a 'one letter-one value' language. The pronunciation of some vowels and consonants (eg, 'v' or 'l') can change from word to word even though the same letter is used in the spelling. Stress – where the emphasis falls on a word – is also irregular and, as in English, has to be learned for individual words. The following should be seen only as an approximate guide to Slovene pronunciation.

Consonants

Most Slovene consonants are pronounced more or less as they are in English. The following are the main exceptions:

c	as the 'ts' in 'hats'
č	as the 'ch' in 'church'
j	as the 'y' in 'yes'
l	as 'w' at the end of a syllable or before a vowel; elsewhere as the 'l' in 'lie'
lj	as the 'li' in 'million'
nj	as the 'ni' in 'onion'
r	a slightly trilled Spanish or Scottish 'r'
š	as the 'sh' in 'she'
šč	as the 'sh' and 'ch' in 'fresh chips'
v	as 'w' at the end of a syllable or before a vowel; elsewhere as the 'v' in 'via'
ž	as the 's' in 'pleasure'

Don't be fazed by vowel-less words like *trg*, 'square', or *vrt*, 'garden' (which are pronounced something like 'terg' and 'vert'), or by consonant clusters such as *ključ*, 'key' (which is pronounced 'klyooch').

Vowels

The five basic vowels in Slovene are 'a', 'e', 'i', 'o', 'u', but each can have several different pronunciations, depending on whether it's stressed, unstressed, long or short. The letter 'e', for example, can sound like the 'a' in 'gate', the 'e' in 'there' or the 'e' in 'bet'. Slovenian dictionaries often mark these differences with accents (é, ê, è), but they never appear elsewhere in the written language. Don't worry though, as you shouldn't have too much trouble being understood even if your pronunciation is slightly off.

The following is a very rough guide to the pronunciation of Slovenian vowels.

a	as in 'far' or as the 'u' in 'cut'
e	as in 'bet'
i	as in 'hit' or as the 'ee' in 'feet'
o	as in 'hot' or as in 'go'
u	as the 'oo' in 'soon' but shorter

For more words and phrases in Slovene, see the Glossary that follows this chapter. For a more in-depth look at the language get hold of Lonely Planet's *Eastern Europe* or *Central Europe phrasebook*.

Greetings & Civilities

Hello.	*Dober dan.* (polite)
Hi.	*Živijo/Zdravo.* (informal)
Goodbye.	*Na svidenje.*
Good morning.	*Dobro jutro.*
Good day./ Good afternoon.	*Dober dan.*
Good evening.	*Dober večer.*
Good night.	*Lahko noč.*
Please.	*Prosim.*
Thank you (very much).	*Hvala (lepa).*
You're welcome.	*Prosim/Ni za kaj.*
Yes.	*Ja.*
No.	*Ne.*
Maybe.	*Mogoče.*
I'm sorry. (forgive me)	*Oprostite.*
May I?	*Ali lahko?*
It's all right.	*Je v redu.*
No problem.	*Brez problema.*
How are you?	*Kako ste?* (polite) *Kako si?* (informal)
Fine, thanks.	*Dobro, hvala.*
What's your name?	*Kako vam je ime?* (polite) *Kako ti je ime?* (informal)
My name is ...	*Ime mi je ...*
Where are you from?	*Od kod ste?*
I'm from ...	*Sem iz ...*
How old are you?	*Koliko ste stari?*
I'm ... years old.	*Imam ... let.*
Are you married?	*Ali ste poročeni?*
Do you like ...?	*Ali imate radi ...?*
I like it very much.	*Imam zelo rad.*
I don't like ...	*Ne maram ...*
Just a minute.	*Samo trenutek.*

Language Difficulties

Do you speak English?	*Ali govorite angleško*
Does anyone here speak English?	*Ali kdo govori angleško*
I understand.	*Razumem.*
I don't understand.	*Ne razumem.*
I don't speak ...	*Ne govorim ...*
How do you say ... in Slovene?	*Kako se reče ... po slovensko?*
What does this mean?	*Kaj to pomeni?*
Please write it down.	*Prosim, zapišite si.*
Please show me (on the map).	*Prosim pokažite mi (na mapi)*

Paperwork

I have a visa/ permit.	*Imam vizum/ dovoljenje.*
surname	*priimek*
given name	*ime*
date/place of birth	*datum/kraj rojstva*
nationality	*državljanstvo*
male/female	*moški/ženska*
passport	*potni list*

Getting Around

I want to go to ...	*Rad bi šel v ...*
I want to book a seat for ...	*Rad bi rezerviral sedež za ...*
What time does the ... depart/arrive?	*Ob kateri uri je odhod/ prihod ...*
Where does the ... leave from?	*Od kje pelje ...*
boat	*ladje*
bus/tram	*avtobusa*
ferry	*trajekta*
hydrofoil	*gliserja*
plane	*letala*
train	*vlaka*
How long does the trip take?	*Koliko dolgo traja potovanje?*
The train is early/ delayed.	*Vlak ima je zgodnji/ zamudo.*
The train is on time.	*Vlak prihaja pravočasno.*
The train is cancelled.	*Vožnja je stornirana.*
Do I need to change?	*Ali moram presesti?*
You must change trains/platforms.	*Presesti morate vlak/peron.*
left-luggage office/ locker	*garderoba*
one-way ticket	*enosmerna vozovnica*
platform	*peron*

return ticket	*povratna vozovnica*
(bus/train) station	*(avtobusna/železniška) postaja*
ticket	*vozovnica*
ticket office	*blagajna*
timetable	*vozni red*

I'd like to hire a ...	*Rad bi najel ...*
bicycle	*kolo*
car	*avto*
guide	*vodiča*
horse	*konja*
motorcycle	*motorno kolo*

Directions

How do I get to ...?	*Kako pridem do ...?*
Where is ...?	*Kje je ...?*
Is it near/far?	*Ali je blizu/daleč?*
What street/road is this?	*Katera ulica/cesta je to?*
What town/what village is this?	*Katero mesto/katera vas je to?*

(Go) straight ahead.	*(Pojdite) naravnost naprej.*
(Turn) left/right at the ...	*(Zavijte) na levo/ desno pri ...*
traffic light	*semaforju*
next corner	*naslednjem ovinku*
second corner	*drugem ovinku*
third corner	*tretjem ovinku*

up	*zgoraj*
down	*spodaj*
behind	*za*
opposite	*nasproti*
north	*sever*
south	*jug*
east	*vzhod*
west	*zahod*
here	*tu*
there	*tam*
everywhere	*povsod*

Accommodation

I'm looking for a ...	*Iščem ...*
youth hostel	*počitniški dom*
camping ground	*kamping*
hotel	*hotel*
guesthouse	*gostišče/penzion*

Signs – Slovene

Vhod	**Entrance**
Izhod	**Exit**
Informacije	**Information**
Odprto	**Open**
Zaprto	**Closed**
Prepovedano	**Prohibited**
Stranišče	**Toilets**
Moški	**Men**
Ženske	**Women**

I'm looking for the manager/owner.	*Iščem direktorja/ lastnika.*
What's the address?	*Na katerem naslovu je?*

Do you have a ... available?	*Ali imate ... prosto?*
bed	*posteljo*
cheap room	*poceni sobo*
single room	*enoposteljno sobo*
double room	*dvoposteljno sobo*

for one night	*za eno noč*
for two nights	*za dve noči*

How much is it per night/per person?	*Koliko stane na noč/ na osebo?*
Is breakfast included?	*Ali je zajtrk vključen?*
Is service included?	*Ali je postrežba vključena?*
Can I see the room?	*Lahko vidim sobo?*
Where is the toilet?	*Kje je stranišče?*

It's very ...	*Je zelo ...*
dirty	*umazana*
noisy	*hrupna*
expensive	*draga*

I'm/We're leaving now.	*Danes odhajam/ odhajamo.*

Do you have (a) ...?	*Ali imate ...?*
clean sheet	*čisto rjuho*
hot water	*toplo vodo*
key	*ključ*
shower	*tuš*
towel	*brisača*

Around Town

Where is the/a ...?	*Kje je ...?*
bank	*banka*
city centre	*središče mesta/ center*
embassy	*ambasada*
exchange office	*menjalnica*
hospital	*bolnišnica*
market	*tržnica*
police	*policija*
post office	*pošta*
public toilet	*javno stranišče*
restaurant	*restavracija*
tourist office	*turistični informacijski center (TIC)*

I want to make a telephone call.	*Rad bi telefoniral.*

I want to change ...	*Rad bi zamenjal ...*
some money	*nekaj denarja*
travellers cheques	*potovalne čeke*

abbey	*opatija*
beach	*plaža*
bridge	*most*
castle	*grad*
cathedral	*stolnica*
church	*cerkev*
hospital	*bolnišnica*
island	*otok*
lake	*jezero*
main square	*glavni trg*
manor	*dvorec*
market	*tržnica*
old city	*staro mesto*
palace	*palača*
ruins	*ruševine*
sea	*morje*
square	*trg*
tower	*stolp*

Shopping

How much is it?	*Koliko stane?*
I'd like to buy it.	*Rad bi kupil.*
It's too expensive for me.	*Predrago je za mene.*
Can I look at it?	*Ali lahko pogledam?*
I'm just looking.	*Samo gledam.*

I'm looking for ...	*Iščem ...*
Do you have another colour/ size?	*Ali imate drugo barvo/velikost?*

chemist	*lekarno*
clothing	*oblačila*
souvenirs	*spominke*
more	*več*
less	*manj*
big/bigger	*velik/večji*
small/smaller	*majhen/manjši*
cheap/cheaper	*poceni/cenejši*

Time & Dates

When?	*Kdaj?*
today	*danes*
tonight	*danes zvečer*
tomorrow	*jutri*
the day after tomorrow	*pojutrišnjem*
yesterday	*včeraj*
all day	*ves dan*
every day	*vsak dan*

Monday	*ponedeljek*
Tuesday	*torek*
Wednesday	*sreda*
Thursday	*četrtek*
Friday	*petek*
Saturday	*sobota*
Sunday	*nedelja*

January	*januar*
February	*februar*
March	*marec*
April	*april*
May	*maj*
June	*junij*
July	*julij*
August	*avgust*
September	*september*
October	*oktober*
November	*november*
December	*december*

What time is it?	*Koliko je ura?*
It's ... o'clock	*Ura je ...*
in the morning	*zjutraj*
in the evening	*zvečer*

1.15	četrt na dve
(lit: one quarter of two)	
1.30	pol dveh
(lit: half of two)	
1.45	tri cetrt na dve
(lit: three quarters of two)	

Numbers

0	nič
1	ena
2	dve
3	tri
4	štiri
5	pet
6	šest
7	sedem
8	osem
9	devet
10	deset
11	enajst
12	dvanajst
13	trinajst
14	štirinajst
15	petnajst
16	šestnajst
17	sedemnajst
18	osemnajst
19	devetnajst
20	dvajset
21	enaindvajset
22	dvaindvajset
30	trideset
40	štirideset
50	petdeset
60	šestdeset
70	sedemdeset
80	osemdeset
90	devetdeset
100	sto
101	sto ena
110	sto deset
1000	tisoč

one million	milijon

Health

I'm ...	Sem ...
diabetic	diabetik
epileptic	epileptik
asthmatic	astmatik

Emergencies – Slovene

Help!	Na pomoč!
Call a doctor!	Pokličite zdravnika!
Call the police!	Pokličite policijo!
Go away!	Pojdite stran!
I've been robbed.	Bil sem oropan.
I want to contact my embassy/consulate.	Hočem govoriti z mojo ambasado/z mojim konzulatom.
I'm lost.	Izgubil/Izgubila sem se. (m/f)

I'm allergic to penicillin/ antibiotics.	Alergičen sem na penicilin/ antibiotike.
antiseptic	antiseptičen/razkužilo
aspirin	aspirin
condoms	kondomi
contraceptive	kontracepcijsko sredstvo
diarrhoea	driska
medicine	zdravilo
nausea	slabost
sunblock cream	zaščitna krema proti soncu
tampons	tamponi

FOOD

I'm hungry/thirsty.	Lačen/žejen sem.
breakfast	zajtrk
lunch	kosilo
dinner	večerja
set menu	meni
grocery store	samopostrežba
delicatessen	delikatesa
market	tržnica
restaurant	restavracija
waiter/waitress	natakar/natakarica

I'd like the set lunch, please.	Lahko dobim meni, prosim?
Is service included in the bill?	Ali je napitnina vključena?
I'm a vegetarian.	Vegetarijanec sem.
I'd like some ...	Rad bi nekaj ...
Another, please.	Še enkrat, prosim.
The bill, please.	Račun, prosim.
I don't eat ...	Ne jem ...

beef	govedina
bread	kruh
butter	maslo
cheese	sir
chicken	piščanec
eggs	jajca
fish	riba
food	hrana
fruit	sadje
meat	meso
pepper	poper
pork	svinjina
salt	sol
soup	juha
sugar	sladkor
vegetables	zelenjava
hot/cold	topel/hladen
with/without	z/brez

Menu Decoder

The following is a menu *(jedilni list)* sampler with dishes listed in the way most Slovenian restaurants would group them. It's not complete by any means, but it will give you a good idea of what to expect.

Cold Starters – *Hladne Začetne Jedi* or *Hladne Predjede*

domača salama – home-style salami
francoska solata – diced potatoes and vegetables with mayonnaise
gnjat/šunka s hrenom – smoked/boiled ham with horseradish
kraški pršut z olivami – karst ham (prosciutto) with salty black olives
narezek – assorted smoked meats/cold cuts
riba v marinadi – marinated fish

Soups – *Juhe*

dnevna juha – soup of the day
gobova kremna juha – creamed mushroom soup
goveja juha z rezanci – beef broth with little egg noodles
grahova juha – pea soup
paradižnikova juha – tomato soup
prežganka – toasted rye-flour soup thickened with cream
zelenjavna juha – vegetable soup

Warm Starters – *Tople Začetne Jedi* or *Tople Predjedi*

drobnjakovi štruklji – dumplings of cottage cheese and chives
ocvrti sir s tatarsko omako – deep-fried cheese with tartare sauce
omlet s sirom/šunko – omelette with cheese/ham
rižota z gobami – risotto with mushrooms
špageti po bolonjska – spaghetti bolognese
žlikrofi – ravioli of cheese, bacon and chives

Ready-Made Dishes – *Pripravljene Jedi* or *Gotova Jedilna*

bograč golaž – beef goulash served in a pot
jota – beans, sauerkraut and potatoes or barley cooked with salt pork in a pot
kuhana govedina s hrenom – boiled beef with horseradish
kurja obara z ajdovimi žganci – chicken stew or 'gumbo' with buckwheat groats
pečen piščanec – roast chicken
prekajena svinjska rebrca s kislim zeljem – smoked pork ribs with sauerkraut
ričet – barley stew with smoked pork ribs
svinjska pečenka – roast pork

Dishes Made to Order – *Jedi po Naročilu*

čebulna bržola – braised beef with onions
ciganska jetra – liver Gypsy-style
dunajski zrezek – Wiener schnitzel (breaded cutlet of veal or pork)
kmečka pojedina – 'farmer's feast', smoked meats and sauerkraut
kranjska klobasa z gočico – Carniolan sausage with mustard
ljubljanski zrezek – breaded cutlet with cheese
mešano meso na žaru – mixed grill
ocvrti piščanec – fried chicken
pariški zrezek – cutlet fried in egg batter
puranov zrezek s šampinjoni – turkey steak with white mushrooms

Fish – *Ribe*

brancin z maslom – sea bass in butter
kuhana/pečena postrv – boiled/grilled trout
lignji or *kalamari na žaru* – grilled squid
morski list v belem vinu – sole in white wine
ocvrti oslič – fried cod
orada na žaru – grilled sea bream

pečene sardele – grilled sardines
ribja plošča – seafood plate
škampi – scampi (prawns)
školjke – shellfish (clams, mussels etc)

Side Dishes – *Priloge* or *Prikuhe*
ajdovi/koruzni žganci – buckwheat/corn groats
bučke – squash or pumpkin
cvetača or *karfijola* – cauliflower
grah – sweet peas
korenje – carrots
kruhovi cmoki – bread dumplings
mlinci – small pancakes
ocvrti krompir or *pomfri* – chips (French fries)
pire krompir – mashed potatoes
pražen krompir – fried potatoes
riž – rice
špinača – spinach
stročji fižol – string beans
testenine – pasta
zelenjavne prikuhe – side vegetables

Salads – *Solate*
fižolova solata – bean salad
kisle kumarice – pickled cucumbers
kumarična solata – cucumber salad
paradižnikova solata – tomato salad
rdeča pesa – pickled beetroot (beets)
sezonska/mešana solata – seasonal/mixed salad
srbska solata – 'Serbian salad' of tomatoes and green peppers
zelena solata – lettuce salad
zelnjata solata – cabbage salad

Fruit – *Sadje*
ananas – pineapple
breskev – peach
češnje – cherries
češplja – plum
grozdje – grapes
hruška – pear
jabolko – apple
jagode – strawberries
kompot – stewed fruit (many types)
lešniki – hazelnuts
maline – raspberries
marelica – apricot

orehi – walnuts
pomaranča – orange
višnje – sour cherries (morellos)

Desserts/Cheese – *Sladice/Siri*
jabolčni zavitek – apple strudel
krofi – raised doughnuts
orehova potica – Slovenian nut roll
pulačinke z marmelado/orehi/čokolado – thin pancakes with marmelade, nuts or chocolate
prekmurska gibanica – layers of flaky pastry with fruit, nut, cheese and poppy-seed filling and topped with cream
sadna kupa – fruit salad with whipped cream
sirova polšča – cheese plate
sladoled – ice cream
torta – cake

Snack Food
burek – flaky pastry stuffed with meat, cheese or apple
čevapčiči – spicy meatballs of beef or pork
pica – another way to spell 'pizza'
pljeskavica – spicy, Serbian-style meat patties
pomfri – chips (French fries)
ražnjiči – shish kebab
vroča hrenovka – hot dog

DRINKS
water	*voda*
mineral water	*mineralna voda/ Radenska* (brand-name)
milk	*mleko*
fruit juice	*sadni sok*
apple juice	*jabolčni sok*
orange juice	*pomarančni sok*
soft drinks	*brezalkoholne pijače*
lemonade	*limonada*
tonic water with ice	*tonik z ledom*
with ice	*z ledom*
tea	*čaj*
mountain-flower tea	*planinski čaj*
herbal tea	*zeliščni čaj*
coffee	*kava*
cappuccino	*kapučino*
coffee with whipped cream	*kava s smetano*

Alcoholic Drinks
Na zdravje! – Cheers!

brinjevec – juniper-flavoured brandy
češnjevec – cherry brandy (kirsch)
jabolčnik – apple cider
sadjevec – apple brandy (apple jack)
slivovka – plum brandy
viljemovka – pear brandy
vinjak – wine brandy
žganje – brandy

Wine Glossary
arhivsko vino – vintage wine
belo vino – white wine
brizganec or *špricar* – spritzer (wine cooler)
buteljka – bottle
črno vino – red (literally 'black') wine
kakovostno vino – quality wine
kozarec – glass
kuhano vino – mulled wine
namizno vino – table wine

peneče vino – sparkling wine
polsladko – semisweet
polsuho – semidry/medium
rose – rosé wine
sladko or *desertno* – sweet wine
suho – dry
vino – wine
vinoteka – wine shop with tastings
vinska karta – wine list
vinska klet – wine cellar
vinski hram – wine bar/room
vrhunsko vino – premium wine

Beer Glossary
malo pivo – beer measuring 0.3L
pivnica – pub/beer hall
pivo – beer
svetlo pivo – lager
temno pivo – dark beer/stout
točeno pivo – draught beer
veliko pivo – beer measuring 0.5L
vrček – mug

Glossary

If you can't find the word you're looking for here, try the Language chapter.

AMZS – Avto-Moto Zveza Slovenije (Automobile Association of Slovenia)
avtocesta – motorway, highway

bife – snack and/or drinks bar
bivak – bivouac (basic mountain shelter)
breg – river bank
burja – bora (cold north-east wind)

čaj – tea
čakalnica – waiting room
cena – price
cenik – price list
cerkev – church
cesta – road (abbreviated **c**)

DDV – Value Added Tax (VAT)
delovni čas – opening/business hours
dijaški dom – student dormitory, hostel
dolina – valley
dom – house; mountain cottage or lodge
drevored – avenue
dvorana – hall
dvorišče – courtyard

fijaker – horse-drawn carriage

gaj – grove, park
garderoba – left-luggage office, coat check
gledališče – theatre
gora – mountain
gostilna – inn-style restaurant
gostišče – inn-style restaurant usually with accommodation
gozd – forest, grove
grad – castle
greben – ridge, crest
GRS – Gorska Reševalna Služba (Mountain Rescue Service)
GZS – Geodetski Zavod Slovenije (Geodesic Institute of Slovenia)

Hallstatt – early Iron Age Celtic culture (800–500 BC)

hiša – house
hrib – hill

izhod – exit
izvir – source (of a river, stream etc)

jama – cave
jedilni list – menu
jezero – lake
jug – south

kamnolom – quarry
kamp – camping ground
Karst – limestone region of underground rivers and caves in Primorska
kavarna – coffee shop, cafe
klet – cellar
knjigarna – bookshop
knjižnica – library
koča – mountain cottage or hut
kosilo – set lunch menu
kot – glacial valley, corner
kotlina – basin
kozolec – hayrack distinct to Slovenia
kras – karst
krčma – drinks bar (sometimes with food)

La Tène – late Iron Age culture (450–390 BC)
lekarna – pharmacy
LPP – Ljubljanski Potniški Promet (Ljubljana city bus network)

mal – little
malica – mid-morning snack
menjalnica – private currency exchange office
mesto – town
morje – sea
moški – men (toilet)
most – bridge
muzej – museum

na – on
nabrežje – embankment
narod – nation
naselje – colony, development
nasip – dike, embankment
nov – new

občina – administrative division; county or commune
obvoz – detour (road sign)
obvoznica – ring road, bypass
odhod – departure
odprto – open
okrepčevalnica – snack bar
otok – island

panjska končnica – beehive panel painted with Slovenian folk motifs
peron – train-station platform
pivnica – pub, beer hall
pivo – beer
planina – Alpine pasture
planota – plateau
pod – under, below
podhod – pedestrian underpass
polje – collapsed limestone area under cultivation
pot – trail
potok – stream
potovanje – travel
prehod – passage
prekop – canal
prenočišče – accommodation
prevoz – transport
pri – at, near, by
prihod – arrival
PZS – Planinska Zveza Slovenije (Alpine Association of Slovenia)

reka – river
restavracija – restaurant
rini – push (door)
rob – escarpment, edge

samopostrežna restavracija – self-service restaurant
samostan – monastery
Secessionism – art and architectural style similar to Art Nouveau
sedežnica – chairlift
sedlo – pass, saddle
sever – north
SIT – tolar (international currency code)
slaščičarna – shop selling ice cream, sweets
SNTO – Slovenska Nacionalna Turistična Organizacija (Slovenian Tourist Board)
sobe – rooms available (sign)

soteska – ravine, gorge
sprehajališče – walkway, promenade
star – old
stena – wall, cliff
steza – path
stolp – tower
Sv – Saint
SŽ – Slovenske Železnice (Slovenian Railways)

terme – Italian for 'spa'
TIC – Tourist Information Centre
TNP – Triglavski Narodni Park (Triglav National Park)
toplar – double-linked hayrack unique to Slovenia
toplice – spa
trg – square

ulica – street (abbreviated **ul**)

vas – village
velik – great, big
vhod – entrance
vila – villa
vinoteka – wine bar
vinska cesta – wine road
vinska klet – wine cellar
vleci – pull (door)
vozni red – timetable
vozovnica – ticket
vrata – gate
vrh – summit, peak
vrt – garden, park
vrtača – sinkhole
vzhod – east
vzpenjača – cable car, gondola

zahod – west
zaprto – closed
zavetišče – mountain 'refuge' with refreshments and sometimes accommodation
zdravilišče – health resort, spa
zdravstveni dom – medical centre, clinic
žegnanje – a patron's festival at a church or chapel
ženske – women (toilet)
žičnica – cable car
znamenje – religious road sign, wayside shrine

Alternative Place Names

ABBREVIATIONS

(C) Croatian
(Cz) Czech
(E) English
(G) German

(H) Hungarian
(I) Italian
(S) Slovene

Adriatic Sea (E) – Jadran, Jadransko
Morje (S)
Aquileia (I) – Oglej (S)
Austria (E) – Österreich (G), Avstrija (S)

Bad Radkersburg (G) – Radgona (S)
Bleiburg (G) – Pliberk (S)
Budapest (H) – Budimpešta (S)

Cividale (I) – Čedad (S)
Croatia (E) – Hrvatska (C), Hrvaška (S)

Dolenjska (S) – Lower Carniola (E)

Eisenkappel (G) – Železna Kapla (S)

Gorenjska (S) – Upper Carniola (E)
Gorizia (I) – Gorica (S)
Graz (G) – Gradec (S)
Gulf of Trieste (E) – Tržaški Zaliv (S),
Golfo di Trieste (I)

Hungary (E) – Magyarország (H),
Madžarska (S)

Istria (E) – Istra (S)
Italy (E) – Italia (I), Italija (S)
Izola (S) – Isola (I)

Karnburg (G) – Krnski Grad (S)
Karst (E) – Kras (S)
Klagenfurt (G) – Celovec (S)
Kobarid (S) – Caporetto (I)
Koper (S) – Capodistria (I)

Koroška (S) – Carinthia (E), Kärnten (G)
Kranjska (S) – Carniola (E), Krain (G)

Leibnitz (G) – Lipnica (S)
Lendava (S) – Lendva (H)
Ljubljana (S) – Laibach (G)

Mediterranean Sea (E) – Sredozemlje,
Sredozemsko Morje (S)
Monfalcone (I) – Tržič (S)
Montenegro (E) – Črna Gora (S)
Murska Sobota (S) – Muraszombat (H)

Notranjska (S) – Inner Carniola (E)

Piran (S) – Pirano (I)
Portorož (S) – Portorose (I)
Prague (E) – Praga (S), Praha (Cz)

Rijeka (C) – Reka (S), Fiume (I)
Rome (E) – Rim (S), Roma (I)

Serbia (E) – Srbija (S)
Soča (S) – Isonzo (I)
Štajerska (S) – Styria (E), Steiermark (G)

Tarvisio (I) – Trbiž (S)
Trieste (I) – Trst (S)

Udine (I) – Videm (S)

Venice (E) – Benetke (S), Venezia (I)
Vienna (E) – Dunaj (S), Wien (G)
Villach (G) – Beljak (S)

LONELY PLANET

Guides by Region

L onely Planet is known worldwide for publishing practical, reliable and no-nonsense travel information in our guides and on our Web site. The Lonely Planet list covers just about every accessible part of the world. Currently there are 16 series: Travel guides, Shoestring guides, Condensed guides, Phrasebooks, Read This First, Healthy Travel, Walking guides, Cycling guides, Watching Wildlife guides, Pisces Diving & Snorkeling guides, City Maps, Road Atlases, Out to Eat, World Food, Journeys travel literature and Pictorials.

AFRICA Africa on a shoestring • Cairo • Cairo City Map • Cape Town • Cape Town City Map • East Africa • Egypt • Egyptian Arabic phrasebook • Ethiopia, Eritrea & Djibouti • Ethiopian Amharic phrasebook • The Gambia & Senegal • Healthy Travel Africa • Kenya • Malawi • Morocco • Moroccan Arabic phrasebook • Mozambique • Read This First: Africa • South Africa, Lesotho & Swaziland • Southern Africa • Southern Africa Road Atlas • Swahili phrasebook • Tanzania, Zanzibar & Pemba • Trekking in East Africa • Tunisia • Watching Wildlife East Africa • Watching Wildlife Southern Africa • West Africa • World Food Morocco • Zimbabwe, Botswana & Namibia
Travel Literature: Mali Blues: Traveling to an African Beat • The Rainbird: A Central African Journey • Songs to an African Sunset: A Zimbabwean Story

AUSTRALIA & THE PACIFIC Auckland • Australia • Australian phrasebook • Australia Road Atlas • Cycling Australia • Cycling New Zealand • Fiji • Fijian phrasebook • Healthy Travel Australia, NZ & the Pacific • Islands of Australia's Great Barrier Reef • Melbourne • Melbourne City Map • Micronesia • New Caledonia • New South Wales • New Zealand • Northern Territory • Outback Australia • Out to Eat – Melbourne • Out to Eat – Sydney • Papua New Guinea • Pidgin phrasebook • Queensland • Rarotonga & the Cook Islands • Samoa • Solomon Islands • South Australia • South Pacific • South Pacific phrasebook • Sydney • Sydney City Map • Sydney Condensed • Tahiti & French Polynesia • Tasmania • Tonga • Tramping in New Zealand • Vanuatu • Victoria • Walking in Australia • Watching Wildlife Australia • Western Australia
Travel Literature: Islands in the Clouds: Travels in the Highlands of New Guinea • Kiwi Tracks: A New Zealand Journey • Sean & David's Long Drive

CENTRAL AMERICA & THE CARIBBEAN Bahamas, Turks & Caicos • Baja California • Belize, Guatemala & Yucatán • Bermuda • Central America on a shoestring • Costa Rica • Costa Rica Spanish phrasebook • Cuba • Dominican Republic & Haiti • Eastern Caribbean • Guatemala • Havana • Healthy Travel Central & South America • Jamaica • Mexico • Mexico City • Panama • Puerto Rico • Read This First: Central & South America • World Food Mexico • Yucatán
Travel Literature: Green Dreams: Travels in Central America

EUROPE Amsterdam • Amsterdam City Map • Amsterdam Condensed • Andalucía • Austria • Baltic States phrasebook • Barcelona • Barcelona City Map • Belgium & Luxembourg • Berlin • Berlin City Map • Britain • British phrasebook • Brussels, Bruges & Antwerp • Brussels City Map • Budapest • Budapest City Map • Canary Islands • Central Europe • Central Europe phrasebook • Copenhagen • Corfu & the Ionians • Corsica • Crete • Crete Condensed • Croatia • Cycling Britain • Cycling France • Cyprus • Czech & Slovak Republics • Denmark • Dublin • Dublin City Map • Eastern Europe • Eastern Europe phrasebook • Edinburgh • England • Estonia, Latvia & Lithuania • Europe on a shoestring • Europe phrasebook • Finland • Florence • France • Frankfurt Condensed • French phrasebook • Georgia, Armenia & Azerbaijan • Germany • German phrasebook • Greece • Greek Islands • Greek phrasebook • Hungary • Iceland, Greenland & the Faroe Islands • Ireland • Italian phrasebook • Italy • Krakow • Lisbon • The Loire • London • London City Map • London Condensed • Madrid • Malta • Mediterranean Europe • Mediterranean Europe phrasebook • Moscow • Munich • Netherlands • Normandy • Norway • Out to Eat – London • Out to Eat – Paris • Paris • Paris City Map • Paris Condensed • Poland • Polish phrasebook • Portugal • Portuguese phrasebook • Prague • Prague City Map • Provence & the Côte d'Azur • Read This First: Europe • Rhodes & the Dodecanese • Romania & Moldova • Rome • Rome City Map • Russia, Ukraine & Belarus • Russian phrasebook • Scandinavian & Baltic Europe • Scandinavian phrasebook • Scotland • Sicily • Slovenia • South-West France • Spain • Spanish phrasebook • St Petersburg • St Petersburg City Map • Sweden • Switzerland • Tuscany • Ukrainian phrasebook • Venice • Vienna • Walking in Britain • Walking in France • Walking in Ireland • Walking in Italy • Walking in Spain • Walking in Switzerland • Western Europe • World Food France • World Food Ireland • World Food Italy • World Food Spain
Travel Literature: After Yugoslavia • Love and War in the Apennines • The Olive Grove: Travels in Greece • On the Shores of the Mediterranean • Round Ireland in Low Gear • A Small Place in Italy

LONELY PLANET

Mail Order

Lonely Planet products are distributed worldwide.They are also available by mail order from Lonely Planet, so if you have difficulty finding a title please write to us. North and South American residents should write to 150 Linden St, Oakland, CA 94607, USA; European and African residents should write to 10a Spring Place, London NW5 3BH, UK; and residents of other countries to Locked Bag 1, Footscray, Victoria 3011, Australia.

INDIAN SUBCONTINENT & THE INDIAN OCEAN Bangladesh • Bengali phrasebook • Bhutan • Delhi • Goa • Healthy Travel Asia & India • Hindi & Urdu phrasebook • India • Indian Himalaya • Karakoram Highway • Kerala • Madagascar • Maldives • Mauritius, Réunion & Seychelles • Mumbai (Bombay) • Nepal • Nepali phrasebook • Pakistan • Rajasthan • Read This First: Asia & India • South India • Sri Lanka • Sri Lanka phrasebook • Tibet • Tibetan phrasebook • Trekking in the Indian Himalaya • Trekking in the Karakoram & Hindukush • Trekking in the Nepal Himalaya
Travel Literature: The Age of Kali: Indian Travels and Encounters • Hello Goodnight: A Life of Goa • In Rajasthan • Maverick in Madagascar • A Season in Heaven: True Tales from the Road to Kathmandu • Shopping for Buddhas • A Short Walk in the Hindu Kush • Slowly Down the Ganges

MIDDLE EAST & CENTRAL ASIA Bahrain, Kuwait & Qatar • Central Asia • Central Asia phrasebook • Dubai • Farsi (Persian) phrasebook • Hebrew phrasebook • Iran • Israel & the Palestinian Territories • Istanbul • Istanbul City Map • Istanbul to Cairo • Istanbul to Kathmandu • Jerusalem • Jerusalem City Map • Jordan • Lebanon • Middle East • Oman & the United Arab Emirates • Syria • Turkey • Turkish phrasebook • World Food Turkey • Yemen
Travel Literature: Black on Black: Iran Revisited • The Gates of Damascus • Kingdom of the Film Stars: Journey into Jordan

NORTH AMERICA Alaska • Boston • Boston City Map • Boston Condensed • British Columbia • California & Nevada • California Condensed • Canada • Chicago • Chicago City Map • Florida • Great Lakes • Hawaii • Hiking in Alaska • Hiking in the USA • Las Vegas • Los Angeles • Los Angeles City Map • Louisiana & the Deep South • Miami • Miami City Map • Montreal • New England • New Orleans • New York City • New York City City Map • New York City Condensed • New York, New Jersey & Pennsylvania • Oahu • Out to Eat – San Francisco • Pacific Northwest • Rocky Mountains • San Francisco • San Francisco City Map • Seattle • Southwest • Texas • Toronto • USA • USA phrasebook • Vancouver • Virginia & the Capital Region • Washington, DC • Washington, DC City Map • World Food New Orleans
Travel Literature: Caught Inside: A Surfer's Year on the California Coast • Drive Thru America

NORTH-EAST ASIA Beijing • Beijing City Map • Cantonese phrasebook • China • Hiking in Japan • Hong Kong • Hong Kong City Map • Hong Kong Condensed • Hong Kong, Macau & Guangzhou • Japan • Japanese phrasebook • Korea • Korean phrasebook • Kyoto • Mandarin phrasebook • Mongolia • Mongolian phrasebook • Seoul • Shanghai • South-West China • Taiwan • Tokyo • World Food Hong Kong
Travel Literature: In Xanadu: A Quest • Lost Japan

SOUTH AMERICA Argentina, Uruguay & Paraguay • Bolivia • Brazil • Brazilian phrasebook • Buenos Aires • Chile & Easter Island • Colombia • Ecuador & the Galapagos Islands • Healthy Travel Central & South America • Latin American Spanish phrasebook • Peru • Quechua phrasebook • Read This First: Central & South America • Rio de Janeiro • Rio de Janeiro City Map • Santiago de Chile • South America on a shoestring • Trekking in the Patagonian Andes • Venezuela
Travel Literature: Full Circle: A South American Journey

SOUTH-EAST ASIA Bali & Lombok • Bangkok • Bangkok City Map • Burmese phrasebook • Cambodia • Hanoi • Healthy Travel Asia & India • Hill Tribes phrasebook • Ho Chi Minh City • Indonesia • Indonesian phrasebook • Indonesia's Eastern Islands • Java • Lao phrasebook • Laos • Malay phrasebook • Malaysia, Singapore & Brunei • Myanmar (Burma) • Philippines • Pilipino (Tagalog) phrasebook • Read This First: Asia & India • Singapore • Singapore City Map • South-East Asia on a shoestring • South-East Asia phrasebook • Thailand • Thailand's Islands & Beaches • Thailand, Vietnam, Laos & Cambodia Road Atlas • Thai phrasebook • Vietnam • Vietnamese phrasebook • World Food Thailand • World Food Vietnam

ALSO AVAILABLE: Antarctica • The Arctic • The Blue Man: Tales of Travel, Love and Coffee • Brief Encounters: Stories of Love, Sex & Travel • Chasing Rickshaws • The Last Grain Race • Lonely Planet ... On the Edge: Adventurous Escapades from Around the World • Lonely Planet Unpacked • Not the Only Planet: Science Fiction Travel Stories • Sacred India • Travel Photography: A Guide to Taking Better Pictures • Travel with Children

LONELY PLANET

You already know that Lonely Planet produces more than this one guidebook, but you might not be aware of the other products we have on this region. Here is a selection of titles that you may want to check out as well:

Eastern Europe
ISBN 1 86450 149 9
US$24.99 • UK£14.99

Eastern Europe phrasebook
ISBN 1 86450 227 4
US$8.99 • UK£4.99

Read this First: Europe
ISBN 1 86450 136 7
US$14.99 • UK£8.99

Mediterranean Europe
ISBN 1 86450 154 5
US$27.99 • UK£15.99

Europe on a shoestring
ISBN 1 86450 150 2
US$24.99 • UK£14.99

After Yugoslavia
ISBN 1 86450 030 1
US$12.99 • UK£6.99

Central Europe
ISBN 1 86450 204 5
US$24.99 • UK£14.99

Central Europe phrasebook
ISBN 1 86450 226 6
US$7.99 • UK£4.50

Available wherever books are sold

Index

Abbreviations

Bel – Bela Krajina
Dol – Dolenjska
Gor – Gorenjska

Kor – Koroška
Lju – Ljubljana
Not – Notranjska

Pre – Prekmurje
Pri – Primorska
Sta – Štajerska

Text

A
accommodation 61-2
activities 55-60,
    see also individual entries
air travel
airports 68
    to/from Slovenia 68-70
    within Slovenia 74
Ajdovščina (Pri) 172
Alpine Association of Slovenia 57
animals 25
Ankaran (Pri) 193-5
architecture 29-30
arts 29-33

B
ballet 65
ballooning 60, 98, 265
Baza 20 (Dol) 236
beekeeping 128, 130-1
Beekeeping Museum (Gor) 128
beer 65
Begunje (Gor) 142
Bela Krajina 252-61, **253**
bicycle travel, see cycling
bird-watching 60, 198
Bistra Castle (Not) 210-11
Bizeljsko (Dol) 251
Black Cave (Not) 214
Bled (Gor) 132-42, **134**
Bled Castle (Gor) 135
Bled Island (Gor) 135-6
Blegoš (Gor) 120
boat travel 73
boating 59
Boč (Sta) 269
Bogenšperk Castle (Dol) 230-2
Bogojina (Pre) 312-13
Bohinj (Gor) 142-50, 156-7

Bold indicates maps.

Bohinjska Bistrica (Gor) 143-56
Boka Waterfall (Pri) 163-4
books 44-6,
    see also literature
border crossings 72-3
Bovec (Pri) 161-5, **163**
Brdo Castle (Gor) 127
Brežice (Dol) 248-50, **249**
bungee jumping 170
bus travel
    to/from Slovenia 70-1
    within Slovenia 74
business hours 52-3

C
camping 61
canoeing, see rafting & kayaking
canyoning 138, 146, 164, 168,
    170
car travel 72-3, 76-8
    car rental 78
    driving licence 36
    road distances 77
    road rules 78
castles 34
    Bled Castle (Gor) 135
    Bogenšperk Castle (Dol) 230-2
    Brdo Castle (Gor) 127
    Celje Castle (Sta) 290
    Kostanjevica Castle (Dol)
        245-6
    Ljubljana Castle 93
    Loka Castle (Gor) 119
    Maribor Castle (Sta) 280
    Mokrice Castle (Dol) 250-1
    Otočec Castle (Dol) 241-2
    Podčetrtek Castle (Sta) 264
    Podsreda Castle (Sta) 266-7
    Predjama Castle (Not) 216-17
    Ptuj Castle (Sta) 272-3
    Ribnica Castle (Dol) 225
    Snežnik Castle (Not) 221-2

Sobota Castle (Pre) 309
Štatenberg manor (Sta) 277-8
caves
    Black Cave (Not) 214
    Divača Cave (Pri) 183
    Island Cave (Not) 214
    Kostanjevica Cave (Dol) 246
    Križna Cave (Not) 221
    Krka Cave (Dol) 233
    Pivka Cave (Not) 214
    Planina Cave (Not) 214
    Postojna (Not) 211-14
    Ravne Cave (Pri) 179
    Škocjan Caves (Pri) 181-4, **182**
    Snežna Jame (Sta) 297
    Vilenica Cave (Pri) 183
caving 59
CD-ROMs 46
Celje (Sta) 289-94, **291**
Celje Castle (Sta) 290
Cerknica (Not) 217-21
Cerkno (Pri) 177-81
children, travel with 51-2
churches 34
    Chapter Church of St
        Nicholas (Dol) 238
    Church of St Cantianus
        (Gor) 124-5
    Church of St Francis Xavier
        (Sta) 296
    Church of St John the
        Baptist (Gor) 144-5
    Church of the Assumption
        (Gor) 136, (Dol) 227
    Church of the Holy Trinity
        (Pri) 187
    Church of the Virgin Mary
        (Sta) 277
    Three Parishes (Bel) 256
    Ursuline Church of the Holy
        Trinity (Lju) 94
cinema 66,
    see also film

Boxed Text

MAP LEGEND

CITY ROUTES

Freeway	Freeway	= = = = =	Unsealed Road
Highway	Primary Road		One Way Street
Road	Secondary Road		Pedestrian Street
Street	Street		Stepped Street
Lane	Lane	⇒ = = =	Tunnel
	On/Off Ramp		Footbridge

REGIONAL ROUTES

	Tollway, Freeway
	Primary Road
	Secondary Road
	Minor Road

BOUNDARIES

	International
	State
	Disputed
	Fortified Wall

HYDROGRAPHY

	River, Creek		Dry Lake; Salt Lake
	Canal		Spring; Rapids
	Lake		Waterfalls

TRANSPORT ROUTES & STATIONS

	Train		Ferry
	Underground Train		Walking Trail
	Metro		Walking Tour
	Tramway		Path
	Cable Car, Chairlift		Pier or Jetty

AREA FEATURES

	Building		Market		Beach		Campus
	Park, Gardens		Sports Ground	+ + + Cemetery		Plaza

POPULATION SYMBOLS

✿ CAPITAL	National Capital	● CITY	City
◉ CAPITAL	State Capital	● Town	Town
		● Village	Village
			Urban Area

MAP SYMBOLS

▪	Place to Stay	▼	Place to Eat	●	Point of Interest

✈	Airport	⊞	Cinema	℗	Parking	🏛	Stately Home
⊜	Bank	▢	Embassy	)(	Pass		Swimming Pool
⊕	Border Crossing	☂	Fountain		Police Station	☏	Telephone
▢▢	Bus Terminal, Stop	✚	Hospital		Pub or Bar	▢	Theatre
▲	Camping Area	▣	Internet Cafe		Ruins	◔	Toilet
▤	Castle	▮	Monument		Shopping Centre	▣	Tomb
⌂	Cave	▥	Museum	⚞	Ski Field	❶	Tourist Information

Note: not all symbols displayed above appear in this book

LONELY PLANET OFFICES

Australia
Locked Bag 1, Footscray, Victoria 3011
☎ 03 8379 8000 fax 03 8379 8111
email: talk2us@lonelyplanet.com.au

USA
150 Linden St, Oakland, CA 94607
☎ 510 893 8555 TOLL FREE: 800 275 8555
fax 510 893 8572
email: info@lonelyplanet.com

UK
10a Spring Place, London NW5 3BH
☎ 020 7428 4800 fax 020 7428 4828
email: go@lonelyplanet.co.uk

France
1 rue du Dahomey, 75011 Paris
☎ 01 55 25 33 00 fax 01 55 25 33 01
email: bip@lonelyplanet.fr
www.lonelyplanet.fr

World Wide Web: www.lonelyplanet.com *or* AOL keyword: lp
Lonely Planet Images: lpi@lonelyplanet.com.au